The Handbook of Sociolinguistics

B

Blackwell Handbooks in Linguistics

The Handbook of Sociolinguistics

Edited by

Florian Coulmas

Copyright © Blackwell Publishers Ltd 1997

First published 1997
First published in paperback 1998
Reprinted 2000

Blackwell Publishers Ltd
108 Cowley Road
Oxford OX4 1JF
UK

Blackwell Publishers Inc.
350 Main Street
Malden, Massachusetts 02148
USA

British Library Cataloguing in Publication Data
A CIP catalogue record for this book is available from the British Library.

Library of Congress Cataloging-in-Publication Data
The handbook of socioliguistics / edited by Florian Coulmas.
      p.   cm. — (Blackwell handbooks in linguistics: 4)
      Includes bibliographical references and index.
      ISBN 0–631–19339–1 (hardcover : alk.paper)
      ISBN 0–631–21193–4 (pbk : alk.paper)
      1. Sociolinguistics—Handbooks, manuals, etc. I. Coulmas, Florian.
      II. Series.
  P40.H3426 1996   95–47148
  306.4'4—dc20   CIP

Typeset in Palatino on 10/12pt
By Pure Tech India Ltd, Pondicherry
Printed in Great Britain by T.J. International Ltd, Padstow, Cornwall

This book is printed on acid-free paper

Contents

Figures

Tables

Contributors

Gertraud Benke
Universität Wien, Vienna

Matthias Brenzinger
Universität zu Köln, Cologne

William Bright
Boulder, Colorado

Michael Clyne
Monash University, Clayton, Victoria

Florian Coulmas
Chuo University, Tokyo

Colette Grinevald Craig
University of Oregon, Eugene

Denise Daoust
Université du Québec à Montréal

Norman Denison
Universität Graz

Penelope Eckert
Institute for Research on Learning, Palo Alto, and Stanford University

Edward Finegan
University of Southern California, Los Angeles

Joshua A. Fishman
Yeshiva University, New York, and Stanford University

Ofelia García
City College of New York

John Honey
Osaka International University

Gabriele Kasper
University of Hawai'i at Manoa

R. B. Le Page
University of York

Gerhard Leitner
Freie Universität Berlin

Grant D. McConnell
Université Laval, Québec

John McWhorter
University of California, Berkeley

James Milroy
University of Newcastle upon Tyne

Lesley Milroy
University of Newcastle upon Tyne

Carol Myers-Scotton
University of South Carolina, Columbia

Peter Hans Nelde
*Research Centre on
Multilingualism, Katholieke
Universiteit Brussel, Brussels*

John R. Rickford
Stanford University

Celia Roberts
Thames Valley University, London

Harold F. Schiffman
*University of Pennsylvania,
Philadelphia*

Brian Street
University of Sussex, Brighton

Michael Stubbs
Universität Trier

Andrée Tabouret-Keller
*Université Louis Pasteur,
Strasbourg*

Albert Verdoodt
*Université Catholique de Louvain,
Louvain-la-Neuve*

Ludo Verhoeven
Nijmegen University

Ruth Wodak
Universität Wien, Vienna

Walt Wolfram
*North Carolina State University,
Raleigh*

Introduction

FLORIAN COULMAS

During the past four and a half decades, studies of the relations between language and society have coalesced to form the field of academic research known as *sociolinguistics*. In 1952 the late Haver C. Currie published a paper, first drafted in 1949, entitled "Projection of sociolinguistics: the relationship of speech to social status" (reprinted in 1971). It took some time for the term "sociolinguistics," for which Currie claims priority, to take root, but by the early 1960s the first sociolinguistic conferences were being held and anthologies of articles dealing with properties of language calling for the inclusion of social factors in their analysis had started to appear. In the meantime, hundreds of research papers and books on the social organization of language behavior have been published, and sociolinguistics has become a recognized branch of the social sciences with its own scholarly journals, conferences, textbooks, and readers of seminal articles. The sociolinguistic enterprise has grown so much that it is difficult to keep up with developments in its various subfields. Written by leading researchers in the field, this *Handbook* offers an introduction to and an overview of the state of the art in key areas of sociolinguistic inquiry.

The Micro–Macro Distinction

The primary concern of sociolinguistic scholarship is to study correlations between language use and social structure. Its focus is different from other disciplines that take an interest in language, in particular from what are sometimes called "autonomous" or "theoretical linguistics," psycholinguistics, and neurolinguistics, which are interested respectively in the human mind, the individual's acquisition and use of language, and the cognitive and biological apparatus of language storage and processing. Sociolinguistics is concerned with describing language use as a social phenomenon and, where possible, it attempts to establish causal links between language and society, pursuing the complementary questions of what language contributes to making community possible and how communities shape their languages by using them. Since sociolinguistics is a meeting ground for linguists and social scientists, some of whom seek to understand the social aspects of language while others are primarily concerned with linguistic aspects of society, it is not surprising that there are as it were two centers of gravity, known as *micro-* and *macro-sociolinguistics* or alternatively *sociolinguistics in the narrow sense* and *sociology of language*. These represent different orientations and research agendas, micro-issues being more likely to be investigated by linguists, dialectologists, and others in language-centered fields, whereas macro-issues are more frequently taken up by sociologists and social psychologists. However, there is general agreement that both perspectives are indispensable for a full understanding of language as a social phenomenon.

Stated in very general terms, micro-sociolinguistics investigates how social structure influences the way people talk and how language varieties and patterns of use correlate with social attributes such as class, sex, and age. Macro-sociolinguistics, on the other hand, studies what societies do with their languages, that is, attitudes and attachments that account for the functional distribution of speech forms in society, language shift, maintenance, and replacement, the delimitation and interaction of speech communities. Along these lines, the organization of this book also reflects the micro–macro distinction: Part I addresses two fundamental issues, the historical evolution of sociolinguistic thought (Le Page) and the basics of language demography (Verdoodt). This is followed by Part II which deals with social dimensions of language, or micro-issues, and Part III which deals with linguistic dimensions of society, or macro-issues. A range of applications of sociolinguistic research is treated in Part IV. This partition offers some orientation, but the assignment of chapters to Parts II and III should not be regarded as more than it is, a matter of emphasis.

Many questions can be investigated with equal justification within micro- or macro-sociolinguistics. For instance, Uriel Weinreich's (1968) concern with language contact focused on the traces that can be detected in linguistic systems of the contact and interaction of neighboring speech communities through their bilingual members. However, the preconditions and consequences of language contact involve a range of interesting phenomena, social and linguistic, which have both micro- and macro-aspects. The following can all be viewed as consequences of language contact: Language generation, i.e., pidginization and creolization; language degeneration, i.e., language displacement; and novel patterns of language use, i.e., code-switching. Of these and some other matters, such as diglossia and the investigation of terms of address and kinship systems, it is impossible to say, without making arbitrary decisions, whether they should be treated properly in micro- or macro-sociolinguistics. Myers-Scotton's two books (1993a, b) dealing with micro- and macro-aspects of code-switching respectively, were originally conceived as one, but for technical reasons they were eventually published separately. Thus the divorce of sociolinguistics proper from the sociology of language is often one of appearance rather than substance. There is no sharp dividing line between the two, but a large area of common concern. Although sociolinguistic research centers about a number of different key issues, any rigid micro–macro compartmentalization seems quite contrived and unnecessary in the present state of knowledge about the complex interrelationships between social and linguistic structures. Contributions to a better understanding of language as a necessary condition and product of social life will continue to come from both quarters. Most articles in this *Handbook* draw in various proportions on insights from social sciences and language sciences.

Theories but No Theory

Some sociolinguists tend to be very defensive about their double reliance on social and language sciences because they consider this the major reason for what has been diagnosed as the theoretical deficit of sociolinguistics. Some expectations concerning the relationship between linguistics and other social sciences have not been borne out. In the heyday of structuralism, linguistics, particularly phonology, was envied for its systematic stringency and even celebrated as a model to be emulated by other social sciences (Lévi-Strauss, 1963). In the meantime, social scientists and linguists have parted company and the relationship between linguistics and the social sciences has been radically redefined. Social theory has gone its own system-theoretic way, maintaining at best a very esoteric interest in language and more commonly ignoring altogether the role of language in constructing society. At the same time, the advent of the powerful generative paradigm in linguistics led mainstream linguists to turn their back on society and sociology. The following quote is representative of the importance linguists attribute to the social functions of language.

> It is obvious that different communities exhibit variation in their speech: people in Paris speak French while those in Washington speak English and those in Montreal cope with both; it is equally clear that children don't speak the same way as their grandparents, that males and females are not necessarily identical in their linguistic abilities, and so on. In short, any social parameter whatsoever may be the locus of some linguistic difference. Unfortunately nothing of interest to linguistic theory follows from this. (Smith, 1989: 180)

If it is true that there is nothing of theoretical importance in variation, then it is obvious that linguistics fails to address a whole range of questions which would be asked by many who want to understand what language is and how it works. Some such questions are the following:

How is it that language can fulfill the function of communication despite variation?

What exactly does it mean that people in Washington and Montreal speak "English," even though it is clear for everyone with ears to listen that what is spoken in these two places differs in many significant ways?

What part of the speech of Anglo-Canadians in Montreal is baffling if only English is considered, but easily explained if we take notice of the fact that it coexists and, in the heads and conversations of bilinguals, interacts with French?

Is the range of language units that are judged to be the same and treated as such by linguists defined by physical parameters or social conventions?

Why do languages change, and what does it mean that they do; that is, what kind of an object is it that changes while in some sense preserving its identity?

By not admitting questions of this sort to its agenda; by refusing even to consider the possibility that the social factors of language should play a role in its analysis because language is essentially a socially constituted system; and by discounting variation as an imperfection rather than recognizing it as an inherent feature of human behavior and the working of the human mind, linguistics has constructed language as a highly abstract object about which statements can be made in the framework of a coherent theory. The question, however, is what this theory has to say about the nature of language.

Dismissing, as it does, variation as an accidental feature of language, linguistic theory does not even allow us to rely on empirical evidence, let alone make empirical evidence the basis of our understanding of what (a) language is. Since it is, as Smith says, evident that "different communities exhibit variation in their speech," it would seem equally evident that this is something to be accounted for by a theory of language.

Speech is what creates community and mediates between individuals and members of various subgroups who, as all experience tells us, are able to communicate with each other in spite of the fact that their codes are not completely congruous. If Occam's razor is applied, as a necessary abstraction for the sake of the theory, to variation and a homogeneous speech community is assumed, one might as well assume no community at all and conceive of *Homo loquens* as a solipsistic being which uses language as a means of organizing its thoughts, but has no need or ability to communicate these to others. Linguistic theory is hence a theory about language without human beings. It is a formal model of structural relationships of which it is basically unknown how they relate to actual speech. Whatever the merits of this model, it is hardly the theory that will help unravel the structural foundations of society which linguistics was once expected to provide.

On the other hand, as pointed out above, sociological theory generally pays minimal attention to language. Durkheim, Weber, and Parsons took little interest in language as a social fundamental. And even where language is assigned a role in the sociological enterprise of explaining social facts, as in Alfred Schütz's (1965) concept of "intersubjectivity," the foundation of ethnomethodology, or in Habermas's (1985) "universal pragmatics," it is at a highly abstract level probing the (universal) conditions that make social interaction possible. Only a few social scientists investigate actual speech or have anything to say about its variable nature. Sociological studies that are based on actual speech data, such as those by Bernstein (1971), Cicourel (1991), and Grimshaw (1980) are rare and not widely credited for contributing much to social theory. Thus, sociological dealings with language have not produced a theory of language use in social contexts any more than linguistics has.

To construct such a theory is seen by some as a vital task for putting sociolinguistics on more solid theoretical foundations (Figueroa, 1994). However, sociolinguists are divided among themselves as to the feasibility of such an endeavor. Fasold (1990: viiiff.) has expressed pessimism about a unified theory of sociolinguistics on a par with that of "linguistics proper," whereas Romaine (1994: 221ff.) thinks that such a theory is both desirable and feasible. It should, she argues, not only supplement linguistic theory with respect to phenomena which cannot be explained properly without reference to social factors, but should indeed form the core of a "socially constituted" theory of language, i.e., an alternative paradigm for studying all aspects of language.

On the sociological side, Williams (1992) has castigated sociolinguistics for failing to produce a theory of its own while at the same time uncritically relying on Parsonian structural functionalism and the individualistic consensualist view of society associated with it. He calls for a conflict model of society to be taken as the cornerstone of a sociolinguistic theory which takes into account social-class relations and power differentials within and across speech communities in analyzing the social forces governing speech behavior. The most promising approach to such a sociolinguistics, he argues, may be found in the work of French sociologists such as Bourdieu (1977) and Achard (1993). Many will grant Williams the proposal that a theory about language in society will not only be toothless but miss a crucial point if it fails to address power and social control. However, there is little agreement among sociologists about society's class stratification, and sociolinguists can hardly be expected to provide a definition that would turn *social class* into an unambiguous and operational concept. Thus, some of the difficulties that stand in the way of a convincing sociolinguistic theory stem from the fact that sociologists take language for granted rather than as an object of theorizing and at the same time they fail to furnish a social theory to which a theory of language use can be easily linked.

Another aspect of the theory question is that scientific fields differ considerably with respect to the importance that is accorded to theories. Sociology is a field that emphasizes abstract theories more than other social sciences, and sociologists have little patience with purely descriptive research. The same can be said of "linguistics proper." The major purpose of empirical studies in both sociology and linguistics is to test theories. By contrast, sociolinguistics is preoccupied with descriptive research. Methodological questions concerning the delimitation, collection, and processing of empirical data have therefore been much more in the foreground than theory construction. Survey sampling, participant observation, questionnaire design, interview and elicitation techniques, multivariate analyses and other methodological tools have been developed or adapted to fit language data. In contradistinction to the formal modelling along the lines of syntactic theory, logic, and computer science, sociolinguistic method is mostly empirical, dealing as it does with observable speech behavior. This is not to say, however, that sociolinguistic research is atheoretical. As documented in this *Handbook*, a number of viable theories have grown out of sociolinguistic research. The emphasis here is on the plural, because there can be no denying that a single all-embracing sociolinguistic theory does not exist. However, this is a result not of the empirical inclination of sociolinguistics and its emphasis on descriptive studies, but simply of the great diversity of phenomena that sociolinguists investigate. A brief overview of the major sociolinguistic phenomena requiring theoretical explanation by reference to general principles or laws must suffice here.

Major Topics

Language change An important current of sociolinguistic research focuses on language change, and some of the most influential scholars in the field consider that the proper task of a sociolinguistic theory should be to explain and predict language change. Although based on assumptions that differ considerably in detail, this is the common position underlying three major recent works (Milroy, 1992; Labov, 1994; Chambers, 1994). What are the causes and mechanisms of language change? Why are certain distinctions maintained while others are lost? What are the forces that resist language change? What are the underlying principles that make predictions of changes in select communities possible? Such are the questions dealt with in this area of sociolinguistic scholarship. In this *Handbook* they are addressed in the chapters by Bright (5) and Denison (4).

Variation Closely related to the pursuit of knowledge about language change is variation research. Indeed, both are often subsumed under the same heading, historical change being conceived as one kind of variation. Among the general questions addressed in this connection are the following: What is language variation and what does it imply for our conception of what (a) language is? What are the relevant social attributes that have a bearing on language variation? How do temporal, regional, and social variations interact? These and related issues are dealt with in the chapters by Honey (6) and Lesley and James Milroy (3). In addition, more specific issues concerning variation are the subject of three other chapters by Wolfram (7, dialect), Wodak and Benke (8, sex), and Eckert (9, age).

The medium of communication is yet another dimension of linguistic variation sociolinguistic research should direct more attention to than it has in the past. Two chapters specifically devoted to this general area have therefore been included in this *Handbook*: Roberts and Street (10) discuss the role of literacy in society and the differences between spoken and written language. They argue that literacy should not be conceptualized as a technology, but rather as a social practice which can be understood only if it is seen in interaction with other communication practices. Concentrating on a kind of communicative practice typical of modern society, Leitner (11) reviews research carried out over the past several years on communication styles and language varieties characteristic of mass media.

Boundary marker Another major theme in sociolinguistic research is the symbolic function of language as a means of group formation. In treating this theme, theories have been proposed about language in ethnic group relations (Giles, Bourhis, and Taylor, 1977; Landry and Allard, 1994); language alliance as acts of identity (Le Page and Tabouret-Keller, 1985); linguistic nationalism and language shift and loyalty (Fishman, 1978, 1993; Gal, 1979). The chapters by Fishman (20) and Tabouret-Keller (19) address major findings in this area. McConnell's chapter (21) puts the sociolinguistic universe of the language usage of human groups into a global perspective.

Multilingualism A great deal of effort by sociolinguists has been devoted to the investigation of social aggregates characterized by the use by some or all of its members of two or more languages. Once again, much work in this field is descriptive and taxonomic with an emphasis on identifying and differentiating different patterns of speech involving more than one language. Several explanations of coexisting or competing languages in the speech behavior of individuals and groups have been advanced which are theoretical in nature, constitute testable hypotheses, or models which can then be evaluated with regard to how large a proportion of such a corpus they can satisfactorily account for. Deserving of mention here is work about the functional distribution of languages in a society associated with the notion of "diglossia" (Ferguson, 1959); the dynamics of societal multilingualism involving language shift (Veltman, 1983) and language attrition (Dorian, 1977); and code-switching (Blom and Gumperz, 1972). These aspects of the sociolinguistic research agenda are reviewed in the chapters by Schiffman (12, diglossia), Clyne (18, multilingualism), Nelde (17, language conflict), and Myers-Scotton (13, code-switching).

The retreat or replacement of languages and the emergence of new ones must also be seen as effects of multilingualism and language contact. These phenomena, which have attracted much attention with research topics on both the level of language structure and patterns of usage, are treated in the chapters by Rickford and McWhorter (14), Craig (15), and Brenzinger (16).

Relativism The linguistic relativity hypothesis, which occupied an important position in the works of Sapir and Whorf, has also played a role in sociolinguistics. When Bernstein (1971) first introduced the notions of a "restricted" and "elaborated" code, these were rather hastily interpreted on the background of relativistic and deterministic assumptions. Differential cognitive abilities of the speakers of the codes Bernstein had identified seemed to be an inescapable consequence. A bigger problem than the fact that such a difference could not be substantiated was that it was politically unwelcome. Bernstein's approach to class-related differences in speech behavior was therefore quickly put aside and influenced the development of sociolinguistic discourse perhaps less than it should have done.

Whether or to what extent the structure of one's language (assuming it is only one) shapes one's view of the world remains an unresolved issue. Yet the idea that language exercises an influence on people's perception and concepts is still espoused by many (Lucy, 1992) and often forms the underlying paradigm for describing the relation between language and society (Chaika, 1989). The view that gender-related language variation corresponds to different views of the world and that misunderstandings between men and women arise because the male and female world views as encoded in language do not coincide is an instance of Whorfian relativism that has proved to be quite popular. Stubbs's chapter (22) gives an overview of research into linguistic relativism and examines the question of what kind of speech data can be used for raising work along these lines to a level of empirical testability.

Relativism is also an issue when it comes to the problem of comparing speech communities, their linguistic resources, and conventions of language use. In this connection many descriptions of politeness phenomena in various languages have been published in recent years and have stimulated theoretical discussions about such questions as whether politeness can be defined independently of a given language or speech community; whether it can be measured and how it can be compared across languages; and whether politeness should be construed as a notion belonging to the language system, language use, or both. On the basis of a review of an extensive body of literature, Kasper's chapter (23) assesses the findings and makes suggestions for viable approaches in the study of linguistic politeness.

Applications of Sociolinguistic Research

From its inception, sociolinguistics has been concerned in a very practical sense with the functions language fulfills in social institutions and the organization of society. Research into the relationship between dialect and social class grew out of a perception that, in many settings, language was used as a means of social control and discrimination. Much work reflects a desire to understand better the ways in which language is used to perpetuate social distinctions, power differentials, advantages, and stigmas. Thus sociolinguistics has always been and continues to be a field of scholarship in which potential applications of research findings are readily apparent. For example, school curricula have traditionally presupposed standard language, ignoring the fact that the standard is accorded preferred status for social reasons alone and is hence closer to the speech of some children than to that of others. That, by virtue of this class-related distinction and the higher prestige associated with standard language, the language that is spoken in the surroundings of children's primary socialization influences their life chances was recognized as one of the linguistic mechanisms of sustaining social systems, a mechanism that stood in the way of realizing equality of opportunity.

Many sociolinguistic projects were therefore designed not only to understand the properties and functions of class-specific speech and the differences between standard language and dialects, but also to enable both teachers and pupils to cope with these differences in a non-discriminatory way and thus help reduce language-related prejudice. Language in socialization and education are two areas of applied sociolinguistic scholarship that have been especially active and prolific. They are reviewed in this *Handbook* by Verhoeven (chapter 24).

In the wake of extensive migration across linguistic and national borders, education systems in many countries have been confronted with school populations of diverse linguistic backgrounds. The presence in many societies of linguistic minorities – both autochthonous and recent migrant communities – has put the issue of bilingual education on the agenda of municipal, regional, and national governments. More often than not, the public debate surrounding language and the rights of linguistic minorities is controversial and highly politicized. In some cases, the courts have become battlegrounds for issues having to do with community rights and claims by speakers of minority languages to have their children instructed in these languages (Cummins, 1984; Hakuta, 1986). Considerable pressure has been put on several countries – traditional immigrant countries such as the United States and Australia as well as former colonial powers, e.g., Britain and France, and target countries of modern labour migration, e.g., Germany – to redefine themselves as multilingual and multicultural and to adjust their school systems accordingly. This in turn has generated counter-pressure on the part of those who do not want to see the school charged with the responsibility to teach and thereby support community languages. In this unresolved dispute, bilingual education is regarded as socially beneficial or disruptive, as a social asset or a threat to national cohesion, largely dependent on political inclinations. As García's chapter (25) of this *Handbook* makes apparent, sociolinguists have an important role to play in this controversy, not just because they are called upon as expert witnesses by both sides, but also because their expertise is in demand when it comes to designing and evaluating bilingual education programs.

Sociolinguists are also actively engaged in language-related problems of professions outside education (Trudgill, 1984). Communication difficulties and breakdowns have been studied in the medical services delivery system (Mishler, 1984), control towers and cockpits (Cushing, 1994), business negotiations (Stalpers, 1993), the judicial system (Solan, 1994), and various other professional settings (Grimshaw et al., 1991). Recent years have seen the development of the role of language advisors in public administration and increased interest in language in industry and other areas of the economy (Coulmas, 1992). Limitations of space make it impossible to survey more than one of these fields of applied sociolinguistic scholarship. In view of the ever-growing importance of litigation in modern society, especially in the United States, the legal profession has been selected for this purpose. In his chapter (26), Finegan examines the contributions that sociolinguistic scholarship can make to resolving criminal cases and civil disputes.

To conclude the section on applied issues in sociolinguistics, Daoust provides a state-of-the-art report on language planning, an area of particular importance for a proper understanding of the intricate relationships between society and language, because it has to do with society's deliberate intervention in the course of a language's development. Other branches of the language sciences have very little to say about this, and theoretical linguistics in particular is both unable and disinclined to deal with it, since the very notion of planning a language interferes with its point of departure, the construct of "natural language." As a matter of fact, however, language planning is much more common than is usually thought. Language planning operates on the micro- and macro-levels of sociolinguistics dealing with such issues as graphization, standardization, lexical augmentation on one hand, and status, prestige, and the functional allocation of languages in a society on the other. While in most other fields of language-related inquiry language is taken as an object which has an existence of its own with which the speech community is confronted, language planning highlights a different aspect of the social nature of language, emphasizing as it does that, in some respects at least, speakers and writers are the creators and masters of their language, hence the importance of language planning for the sociolinguistic enterprise as a whole.

Apologies

Every collection is a selection. Given the size of this volume, it is evident that no claims can be made that it covers all the vast field of sociolinguistics. Critics will find it easy to point out domains of sociolinguistic research which are under-represented in this *Handbook*. For example, a whole range of studies in the general field of language in social psychology have been left out. Pragmatics and discourse analysis have no chapters of their own, although both are dealt with in several chapters, such as those by Wodak and Benke, Finegan, Kasper, and Stubbs. Sociolinguistic research techniques are discussed in several chapters, but their importance could have easily justified more extensive treatment had there been no limitations of space. The same is also true of the relationships of sociolinguistics with neighboring disciplines such as ethnography, psycholinguistics, and dialect geography. Yet the papers in this collection and its comprehensive bibliography should enable those interested in the major areas of sociolinguistic research to find informed answers to their questions, as well as directions about where to pursue them in greater depth.

Part I Foundations

1 The Evolution of a Sociolinguistic Theory of Language

R. B. LE PAGE

1 The language of stereotypes and the language of science

The Oxford scientist who recently claimed that most English people were scientifically illiterate because they still spoke of the sun going round the earth, revealed his own ignorance of the way stereotypes – as discussed, for example by Schaff (1984) or by Cameron (1990) – are embedded in language. It is a fair bet that he himself still speaks of the sun "rising" and "setting." In the following discussion of some of the work done on the relationship between individuals, linguistic systems, and groups, I emphasize the extent to which we all base much of the argument on stereotypes, which then do not serve us well enough as the basis of scientific models. Chief among them is the stereotype of "variation" in "a language." Stereotypes are, however, important parts of our data. We must try to understand the language of former generations when they spoke of languages "changing" or "dying," or being "genetically descended" from other languages, and so on. Anthropomorphic stereotypes are embedded in all these metaphors, and many more. In contradistinction to some sociological philosophy, I shall want to maintain that "languages don't do things: people do things: languages are abstractions from what people do." Of course, we are all making and using the abstractions.

2 An expanding universe

I have no space for an overview of the vast amount of work coming under the "sociolinguistics" or "sociology of language" umbrellas since the 1960s; most of the ground is covered in the other chapters of this book. Readers can also refer to the two encyclopedic volumes edited by Ammon, Dittmar, and Mattheier (1987, 1988) and to the earlier Dittmar (1976). The exponential increase has given rise to a number of new journals (see the bibliography). Verdoodt (1988) reports that the proliferation of papers accepted by the sociolinguistics section at successive World Congresses of Sociology was so great that after Mexico (1982) it was no longer possible to publish them. The biennial British Sociolinguistics Symposium was offered over 200 papers for its 1994 meeting. All are "studies of language in its social context" but otherwise the spread of subject matter is considerable. Many are relatively atheoretical. I shall confine myself to what is for me and for some others, such as Labov, DeCamp, Trudgill, the Milroys, and Romaine, a central concern: What should a linguistic system look like if we want it to take full and *explanatory* account of all the contextual factors which make it meaningful to the users? And even within this framework I must omit discussion of the "communicative competence" that Hymes deems necessary, and I shall follow Fishman in keeping "the sociology of language" separate.

3   *Some progenitors*

The complaint that early sociolinguistic work was sociologically uninformed is true; but then, we thought we were doing linguistics or, to be more precise, such long-practiced disciplines as historical and comparative philology, descriptive linguistics, dialect geography (Chambers and Trudgill, 1980, and Trudgill, 1992, contain useful accounts of the bridges between the latter and sociolinguistics, with a forward-looking plea for "geolinguistics"). The claims of these disciplines to be "scientific" reformulated more than once since the eighteenth century, are of some importance here, since they have influenced the more recent struggles of the "social sciences" both to be recognized as sciences and to absorb linguistic models to that end. Max Müller in his mid-nineteenth-century *Lectures on the Science of Language* made a strong claim that comparative philology had now been firmly established as a science. It had led to the establishment of "laws" and principles according to which languages were said to change and dialectal differences to reflect stages in the operation of those "laws." The constraints on change were stated in terms first of the *linguistic environment* and then where necessary in terms of the social context, for example, migration and social contact. In the 1940s A. S. C. Ross proposed various mathematical "proofs" for these processes of change, and of postulated relatedness (Ross, 1950). The claim to be "scientific" has been urged strongly by Chomsky (1966), tracing the ancestry of generative grammar from Descartes and the Port-Royal grammarians and relating it to universal grammar and to brain structure.

In the eighteenth and nineteenth centuries, there was also a movement to re-establish rural "folk values" in reaction to the squalid urbanization which accompanied the Industrial Revolution. We can juxtapose Samuel Johnson seeking to regularize English in his *Dictionary* (1755) (though finally confessing that "to enchain syllables, and to lash the wind, are equally the undertakings of pride") to dialect poets such as Barnes and Burns. The latter part of the nineteenth century saw the start of large-scale writing down of dialect forms, either in dictionaries (as in Joseph Wright's *English Dialect Dictionary* (1896–1905) or on maps. Mapping the geographical distribution of forms used led to the concept of the "isogloss," by analogy with isobars and isotherms: geographical boundaries between users of variant forms for "the same thing" in "the same language." Wenker, in Germany, collected his data between 1876 and 1887 by asking 50,000 village schoolteachers to write down their local dialect equivalent of each of 40 sentences, set out in a questionnaire in High German. (He was relying on the teachers for an accurate rendering of something of which they might in fact have only a partial knowledge.) Approximately the same method was used – though simply as a starting-point for a survey – by McIntosh in his *Survey of Scottish Dialects* (1952) and by myself in the *Linguistic Survey of the British Caribbean*, started with his help in 1952 (Le Page, 1952, 1957, 1958).

The French scholar Jules Gilliéron relied on the personal observations of a trained fieldworker, Edmond Edmont, visiting 639 locations in France and writing down the spoken forms for 1,500 items he elicited from the local informants he selected. Gilliéron's method, with some modifications, has since been used in dialect surveys of other European countries including England, and in the United States and Canada. Technical changes have influenced fieldwork practice and the analysis of data; in particular, methods of recording the responses of informants first on wax discs and then on magnetic tape. The increasing sophistication of electronic devices has led to recording longer stretches of spontaneous speech in place of single-word or sentence responses to questions about the names of things; tape-loop repeaters and sonographs have made possible minute discrimination in transcription.

4 Theoretical assumptions

Dialectology had already thrown into relief stereotypes and ideological presumptions which carried over into sociolinguistics. The older tendency had been to locate some "real old dialect" in rural areas in contradistinction to the "corrupt" speech of the towns. One of the major innovations of the 1950s, the move into urban dialectology, was partly a product of concern about the educational disadvantages of urban working-class children (see e.g., Bernstein, 1958; Dittmar, 1976) in Germany, in Britain, and the US. For rural surveys the typical informant was the nonmobile older rural male, the NORM. There was a pastoral implication of a static enduring landscape, so that one looked for *reasons for language change* rather than accepting (as one has to in urbanizing contexts) diversity as the base line and then searching for the way in which stereotypical concepts of homogeneous unchanging languages (with their connotations of social hierarchy and nationalism) come into existence. A static social structure was implicit in dialect geography; in order to compare like with like, the representative dialect speaker had to be relatively uncontaminated by education. The dialect areas outlined by isoglosses on the map were artifacts of the geographer; they had to be matched against such stereotypes as "southern dialect" or "Alemannic" or "langue d'oc," concepts which often related in the minds of outsiders to just one or two variables characterizing a complete, discrete system; whereas if one went on investigating features one found that isoglosses might converge and run parallel for part of the way and then diverge again, so that "dialects" were neither uniform nor discrete. The extent to which social variables other than regional ones could be built into mapping was limited, but some surveys, including my own, attempted to label variants as, for example, "old-fashioned" or "rare" or "common."

The assumptions commonly made about the social correlates of linguistic differences vary from culture to culture: whether they are primarily geographical or ethnic or economic or social class or caste (see e.g., Berntsten, 1978; Khubchandani, 1983) or sex- or age-related (see chapters 8 and 9); whether they relate to "solidarity" or "conflict" or "power" (cf. Brown and Gilman, 1960); whether a person's "dialect" is a constant for them or whether we are all (as my own hypothesis suggests) to some extent linguistic chameleons, depending on the identity we are trying to project in any particular context. We find important contrasts between societies in which caste and class are underscored by religion (compare older and younger Sikhs in Britain as studied by Agnihotri (1979)) or by skin-color, and so on. We tend to make observations of other cultures in terms of significant differences in our own; but in Le Page and Tabouret-Keller (1985: chapter 6) we document how the self-ascription of some Belizeans to ethnicity and skin-color differed significantly from the ascription we would have made ourselves. A good deal of the criticism of sociolinguistic work made by sociologists has picked on the simplistic nature of the social structures against which we have matched linguistic variation. We also tend to hear other languages in terms of salient structural features of our own, and perhaps therefore overlook linguistic features – prosodic features, for example – which are socially significant to other speakers of "the same language." This is particularly likely if we come to a community as outsiders, rather than as an insider like Labov in New York or Trudgill in Norwich. Being an insider carries its own dangers of seeking to confirm one's own stereotypes.

Salient problems and possibilities of dialect geography are explored by Chambers and Trudgill (1980), insofar as "dialects of one language" are concerned. In the West Indies, and in creole studies generally, however, we have been thrown hard against the questions "what constitutes a language?" and "what should a linguistic system look like if it is to take full account of the social and psychological realities?"

5 The development of contact linguistics in the 1950s

Romaine's 1989 study of *Bilingualism* begins by pointing out that it would be odd to encounter a book entitled *Monolingualism*; that is the state presupposed by most modern linguistic theory, and yet bi- (or multi-)lingualism is a far more common state, and was for Roman Jakobson (1953) "the fundamental problem of linguistics."

The *Oxford English Dictionary Supplement* (1986) records the term "sociolinguistic" as first used by Eugene Nida in the second edition of his standard work *Morphology* in 1949; as a discipline, "sociolinguistics" is first referred to in 1939 – in T. C. Hodson's paper, "Sociolinguistics in India" (in *Man in India*, XIX, 94). The term was used by Martinet in his preface to Weinreich's thesis *Languages in Contact* (1953), where he went on to say (p. vii):

> There was a time when the progress of research required that each community should be considered linguistically self-contained and homogeneous . . . Linguists will always have to revert at times to this pragmatic assumption. But we shall now have to stress the fact that a linguistic community is *never* homogeneous and hardly ever self-contained . . . linguistic diversity begins next door, nay, at home, and within one and the same man. It is not enough to point out that each individual is a battleground for conflicting types and habits . . . What we heedlessly and somewhat rashly call "a language" is the aggregate of millions of such microcosms many of which evince such aberrant linguistic comportment that the question arises whether they should not be grouped into other "languages." *What further complicates the picture, and may, at the same time, contribute to clarify it, is the feeling of linguistic allegiance which will largely determine the responses of every individual.* (my emphasis)

Chomsky's thesis, published four years later as *Syntactic Structures* (1957), was nevertheless predicated on the knowledge of that famous phantom, the idealized speaker-listener in a homogeneous speech community with complete knowledge of its language. Much of the story of "contact linguistics" in the early 1960s was of the search for a model which could accommodate both Martinet's very pertinent observations about data *and* Chomsky's concepts of a grammar whose adequacy could only be tested against that contradiction in terms, the intuition of the idealized native speaker.

Weinreich wrote in terms of a pair of discrete systems interfering with each other in the usage of individuals, citing Lotz (1950) to the effect that "every speech event belongs to a definite language" and Jakobson, Fant, and Halle (1952) on "code-switching." Weinreich supervised Beryl Bailey's thesis (1966), a grammar of "Jamaican Creole" (as she and I decided to call it, thus giving it discrete status as a language), written within the early transformational-generative model at his suggestion. In her introduction she acknowledged the difficulty of trying to draw lines of demarcation between the Creole and more standard varieties of English: "it is perhaps more accurate to think not of layers, but of *interwoven co-structures*" (my emphasis). "This very fluid linguistic situation could provide material for a fruitful and rewarding study on linguistic variation and the principles underlying it, but ... this is an attempt to describe *one* of the systems which lie at the core of this co-structure" (pp. 1–2). The difficulties in fact carry over into describing contact systems in terms of "pairs of discrete languages interacting," and into any situation where a speaker is "bi-dialectal" – as most of us are. (See in particular Gardner-Chloros, forthcoming.)

6   The 1960s

In both the US and Britain there had been a long tradition of anthropological linguistics allied to structuralist descriptions of exotic languages; in the US it was associated with such names as Boas and Sapir, in Britain (see, for example, Ardener, 1971), with Malinowski and J. R. Firth and his colleagues at the School of Oriental and African Studies in London. Each had given rise to distinctive theories of linguistic structure which helped to shape sociolinguistic research (see, for example, Hasan, 1992). But prior to Bernstein, comparatively little attention had been paid by *sociologists* to linguistics as an analytical tool.

Ferguson's notable paper on "diglossia," a functional analysis of different registers of "the same language," had appeared in 1959 (its application to Haiti, in particular, raised for creolists the critical question of what constituted a language – see Le Page, 1989). Labov's work on the social dynamics of Martha's Vineyard and then of New York City opened the eyes of some sociologists to the possibilities of such "scientific" analytical methods. In the summer of 1964, the Committee on Sociolinguistics of the US Social Science Research Council called a group of linguists and other "social scientists" together for an eight-week interdisciplinary seminar, reported on by Ferguson (1965). In Britain, my own department at York was set up in 1963/4 "for the study of language as a behavioural science," and the British SSRC began to take linguistic research under its wing. As Chomskyan theory appeared to sweep away all concern with variation in language by focusing exclusively on "competence" in "a language," Hymes and his anthropologist/ethnographer colleagues reacted by requiring linguistics to complete its scope by describing the "communicative competence" a speaker/listener needed to operate as a full member of a language community – a knowledge of all the appropriate ways of using the language. The first volume of Fishman's *Advances in the Sociology of Language* (1971) brought together three long retrospective and programmatic papers by Ervin-Tripp (1969), Grimshaw, and Labov on sociolinguistics, and – for half the book – Fishman himself, striving to keep "the sociology of language" distinct. Ervin-Tripp's paper is of particular interest for me; she is concerned to build a model of the *symbiotic relationship* between the formation and dynamics of human groups and the formation and dynamics of human language, as I was too. Towards the end of the 1960s Hymes and DeCamp came together to organize the 1968 Mona conference (see Hymes, 1971).

7 Models of inherently variable systems: implicational scales

F. G. Cassidy, David DeCamp, and Beryl Bailey were three American linguists who helped me with the Caribbean survey; British helpers included an Africanist (J. Berry), A. McIntosh, and A. S. C. Ross. Apart from his mathematical expertise, Ross had in fact published an early "sociolinguistic" study (1954) of differences between "Upper-class" ('U') and "non-Upper-class" ('Non-U') usage in England, a distinction made famous for a while by Nancy Mitford and Ross in *Noblesse Oblige* (1956), Mitford having furnished examples of each in *The Pursuit of Love* (1945) and in *Love in a Cold Climate* (1949).

At the end of his two-year stay in Jamaica DeCamp, who had earlier studied the English of San Francisco (1958/9), gave a paper to the first international conference on creole language studies (Le Page, 1961) on "Social factors in Jamaican dialects." On his return to the US he, like Bailey, was caught up in the Chomskyan revolution as he analyzed his large collection of Jamaican material and tried to systematize in social terms the variation inherent in it. While Bailey resolved the problem by idealizing the usage of "older people and members of the lower levels of the social code" (1966: 3) DeCamp treated his data as lying at different points on a linear continuum from broad Creole to more educated speech – what W. A. Stewart was to characterize as "basilect" to "acrolect." For the 1968 Mona conference (Hymes, 1971: 349–70) DeCamp presented a paper "Toward a generative analysis of a post-creole speech continuum," in which he recognized that the "system" he was evolving resembled that of the Guttman psychological implicational scalogram (1944), as he tried to preserve the Chomskyan concept of a grammar while showing how individuals might move across a continuum of lects. The overarching "grammar of the Jamaican language" was to contain a series of grammars each differing by a single rule-change from its neighbors on either side; the "implication" was that a person affected by, say, rule change 3 had also been affected by changes 2 and 1. Each "lect" was to be seen as socially marked.

Bickerton (1971, 1975), rejecting variable rules (see below), subsequently took up this same model for "the Guyanese language," and C.-J. N. Bailey used it (1973) as a base for his reformulation of nineteenth-century wave theory. These were brave attempts to build into generative theory both social and historical variation and to assess also (in terms of the degree of scalability of the data) the degree of relationship between the two ends of the continuum. But DeCamp was never able to fit more than 30 per cent of his data into such scales. Bickerton's use of the model seemed to imply that "the Guyanese language" and the people using it were on a historical escalator moving steadily from Creole towards the more standard English of the urban educated classes (cf. Romaine's (1982b) discussion of Labov, a model certainly not borne out by our own later work in Belize; it implied that all innovation came from the same direction, but much sociolinguistic work elsewhere has shown that this is rarely the case, and that one needs a multidimensional model. Moreover, it is frequently the case that change in a formal register is running counter to changes in more vernacular registers, which then ultimately either affect formal speech or lead to divergence and splitting.

The weaknesses of implicational scaling are discussed by Romaine (1982a), who nevertheless made use of it in her 1992 study of "Tok Pisin." She diagrams the trajectory of, for example, a sound-change through lexical diffusion and across communities in Papua-New Guinea, reflecting different degrees of the influence of substrate and superstrate languages on each member of the community. Variability of, for example, the pronunciation in "Tok Pisin" of initial p/f (as in /fo/~/po/*four* – pp. 181ff.) shows up the various social factors which may have to be taken into account to "explain" why some groups of adults or of children have adopted the [f] pronunciation throughout their vocabulary while others have it in only one or two items. Years of schooling, and urban vs. rural location, are the most significant non-linguistic correlates. On a global scale, urban society in Papua-New Guinea must be towards one extreme of the diffuse-focused spectrum, while the highly-focused languages of the remote mountain valleys are at the other.

8 The observer's paradox, and accommodation theory

One reason for the different solutions arrived at by Bailey and DeCamp may lie in what Labov has called "the observer's paradox" – in which sociolinguistics resembles quantum theory: It is not possible to observe the behavior either of very small particles or of an interlocutor without affecting that behavior. In Le Page, 1968, I demonstrated the effect my own presence had at the start of a girl's telling of an Anansi story compared with her delivery as soon as the traditional story-telling mode took charge. DeCamp was a white male American, Bailey a black female Jamaican-American. The selection of variants was to some extent at least a function of interlocutor and mode; interlocutors may incline to each other's usage, as the accommodation theory of Howard Giles (1984) suggests. There are, however, important caveats about this concept, which I discuss below.

9 Labov, "acts of identity," language variation and change, and variable rules

William Labov, after ten years as an industrial chemist, wrote his MA thesis as Weinreich's pupil at Columbia University; it was published in *Word* in 1963 as "The social motivation of a sound-change." It was based on data he collected in the summer resort of Martha's Vineyard, and demonstrated the linguistic acts of identity made by those who wished to be recognized as natives of the island as distinct from summer visitors and commuters. His doctoral thesis, *The Social Stratification of English in New York City* (again under Weinreich) was published in 1966. He had studied research methods at the Bureau of Social Research in New York; and while a graduate student had taken part in sociolinguistics meetings organized respectively by Gumperz, Ferguson, and Bright. In his thesis he approached sociolinguistic analysis primarily as a means of dealing with variation in a principled way – i.e., to account for it within the framework of categorical, invariant rules (Labov, 1971b: 461). In relating phonological variation and change to social class and social prestige in New York he had been preceded by studies of Black usage in Washington (Putnam and O'Hern, 1955) and by Ruth Reichstein's 1960 study (also in *Word*) of 570 girls at three socially differentiated Parisian schools. She quantified the incidence of the variants of three phonological variables and correlated them with the type of school, the *arrondissement*, the middle-class or lower-class occupation of the parents, and whether they came originally from Paris or from the provinces. She was able to show the direction of phonological change as affected by the usage of working-class districts near the center of Paris.

Labov's "stratified random sample" of New York speakers took account of their "ethnic origin" (New Yorkers, Italians, Jews, Blacks) and their assignation to a social class: Upper Middle, Lower Middle, Upper and Lower Working Class, on the basis of income, level of education, and occupation. (Trudgill's 1974 Norwich study followed Labov's schema fairly closely.) Labov introduced the variable of *style* into his analysis, recording formal and informal speech, reading aloud from a text, and reading a series of minimal word-pairs, to cover the range from least to most relaxed speech, a procedure we later followed in our Belize studies (Le Page and Tabouret-Keller, 1985). The "most relaxed" style was said to be marked by "channel cues" such as laughter, prosodic features, and speed. The assumption was made that the informants would be speaking "English."

Labov's most important innovation in the 1966 study was to quantify the incidence in different speech samples of variants of significant linguistic variables and then to write "variable rules." The quantities he plotted were not individual scores, but the mean scores for each social group in each style or mode. If we take as a simplified example his pilot study of the use of the variable "post-vocalic (r)," getting shop assistants in three different "classes" of New York stores to direct him first in a casual and then in an emphatic way to the "fourth floor," we can say that the group of shop assistants in each of the stores had an average incidence of some kind of rhoticity (r-coloring) which he calls (r-'), and an average complementary incidence of r-lessness (r-°), in the loci where (r-') might occur – that is, where (-r) is present in "the lexicon of the language." A "rule" might then emerge in the following "explanatory" way within the grammar of "New York English" (NYE):

1 The variable (r) can occur in NYE in the following position [statement here as to possible loci] either as (r-°) or (r-'), since a sound-change affecting it has not affected all speakers of NYE equally, for a variety of reasons.

2 Among a group of "working class New Yorkers" the mean incidence was observed to be in x percent of possible loci as (r-°) and in y percent of possible loci as (r-') when they were speaking in a relaxed way.

3 Among the same group speaking in a more formal and deliberate way there was a higher percentage of (r-'), lower (r-°).

4 The second score was in fact more like that of the mean relaxed usage of a middle-class group.

5 Therefore the motivation of the lower-class group when in a more formal context was to behave more like the middle-class group.

If we then divide the lower class into younger and older groups we may find that this tendency is more pronounced among the younger group. We might then form a hypothesis that a change is taking place in NYE towards a greater use of post-vocalic (r-') and seek a reason for the change – in this case, led by the middle class and possibly associated with the effects of literacy and an increase in spelling pronunciations (Labov did not advance this last possibility). An alternative hypothesis (again, not advanced by Labov) might be that within this society there is a mode of behavior appropriate to older people to which the younger group will switch as they age. Other hypotheses may be suggested if we divide the speakers by sex, or by ethnic group, or locality in which they live; and many of these have been tested in the work of Trudgill (1972, 1974, et seq.), Cheshire (1982), and other sociolinguists. Explanations may well be attitudinal, a feeling of social cohesion among a particular social group (see W. Edwards below) promoted by one or more of a number of factors (see, for example, both Labov's and Trudgill's 1972 concept of "covert prestige") in the light of which we may form and test more general explanatory hypotheses about correlations between linguistic behavior and social or idiosyncratic psychological motivation – for example, in the case of Labov's "lames" (1973a) and Milroy's "weak ties" (1992), people who did not keep to the linguistic or social rules of the group with which they might otherwise have been closely associated.

There has been a good deal of discussion of the problems raised by variable rules (see Fasold, 1970; Lavandera, 1978; Horvath, 1985; Romaine, 1985). In a 1970 paper ("The study of language in its social context") Labov set out his theoretical and methodological ideas and the discussion which had taken place around them. In a study of the statistical methods used, Cedergren and Sankoff (1974) proposed using a multiplicative rather than an additive probability model in order to retain the Chomskyan competence/performance distinction, to fit rule probabilities into competence and their frequencies into performance. But in spite of Labov's (1969) insistence that they are part of the speaker's knowledge of the group, part of a sociolectal grammar, they remain in fact statistical probability statements. Contrary to what Bickerton (1971) supposed in his objection to them and consequent support for implicational scales, they cannot be held to predict what a speaker will do on any particular occasion, however carefully the conditions are specified. The problems arise only if one forgets that sociolectal grammars are abstractions from a usually unspecifiable group of idiolects, however much they are buttressed from normative sources and stereotypically assigned autonomous status.

The question whether Black English, or any Creole, or indeed any one of very many vernaculars, should be treated as a discrete system or as a variety of some standard system can assume considerable ideological and political importance and has been tested in the US courts (see IGLSVL *Abstracts*, 1986, 1988 *passim*).

10 Non-standard English, Black English, Creole studies, and the 1968 Mona Conference

In the 1950s and early 1960s Basil Bernstein's "deficit hypothesis" – that work-ing-class children internalized a "restricted code" from their parents' limited syntax and so did badly at school where middle-class teachers judged them in terms of their own "elaborated code" – gained wide currency among educa-tionists in Europe (see Dittmar, 1976) and in the US (see Murray, 1983) where ambitious remedial programs such as Operation Headstart were conceived, particularly for Black children. Labov, who was opposed to the basic premises about the "deficient language" of these children, carried out for the US Office of Education and Welfare a study "of the structure of English used by Negro and Puerto Rican speakers in New York City" (see Labov, Cohen, and Robins, 1965). His well-known account of the variable rules he proposed for copula-less Black English constructions (Labov, 1969) derives from this study of Harlem street gangs. In his account, the Black English speaker's copula-less construc-tions (e.g., "The man sick") are derived from the standard grammar by a variable deletion rule which the speaker could apply wherever it was possible for prior contraction of the copula to take place. In fact, however, copula-less constructions are the norm in Caribbean Creole English, and it seems absurd to posit that the Black English speaker should start from a knowledge of the standard grammar and then apply a deletion rule to achieve the vernacular. It might be better to accept the use of such constructions alongside those of more standard English as examples of code-switching.

There were by this time a number of other educational, sociolinguistic, and sociological studies under way on Black English speakers by, for example, W. A. Stewart, J. L. Dillard, R. W. Shuy, R. Fasold, W. A. Wolfram (see bibliography). Work on pidgin and creole languages was expanding steadily; in the 1960s two volumes of my *Creole Language Studies*, B. L. Bailey's *Jamaican Creole Syntax*, Cassidy's *Jamaica Talk*, and the first edition of the *Dictionary of Jamaican English* (1967) were all published and came to the attention of the

Americans. In 1968 Dell Hymes and DeCamp organized the second international conference on pidgin and creole languages at Mona, Jamaica (Hymes, 1971) and Labov wound it up with an extended survey, "The notion of system in creole languages." Several speakers had approached the problem from different directions: DeCamp's "Analysis of a post-creole speech continuum," Gumperz and Wilson's study of "convergence and creolization" on the Indo-Aryan/Dravidian border in India, Samarin's "Salient and substantive pidginization," Tsuzaki's "Co-existent systems in Hawaiian English." The solutions included code-switching between coexistent systems, DeCamp's implicational scalograms, and the concept of mixed codes. Labov had concluded that creole/standard language and pidgin contact situations could not be fitted into the Chomskyan paradigm, and that DeCamp was mistaken in trying to do so; he felt that some of the pidgins discussed "may be less than languages ... the notion of syntax begins to give way." To make a leap forward in time, in Mülhäusler's (1986a, b) opinion (and my own) what has to give way is the stereotypical notion of "a language."

Studies of creoles and pidgins and of Black English have been important to theoretical linguistics, to the sociology of education, to social anthropology, and to sociolinguistics in both the US and Britain; see, for example, V. Edwards (1986), R. Hewitt (1986), S. Romaine (1988, 1992), M. Sebba (1993), and the work by W. Edwards cited below and by Bickerton, Fasold, Shuy, Stewart, Wolfram and others cited above. A number of writers (notably Thomason and Kaufman, 1988) have concluded (I think erroneously) that creole languages are a special case in language typology, standing outside the schema of "genetic relationship" regarded as the norm (see Le Page, 1994).

11 *The individual speaker and social networks*

L. Milroy's retention of the individual speaker at the center of her sociolinguistic study of three working-class districts of Belfast (1980, 1987a, b) took over an explicit concept of "social networks" as social structures which focus norms of behavior including language. She draws attention to the sense of belonging to a locality, in an urban context strongest in working-class districts (1987a: 15). She refers to the study by Blom and Gumperz (1972) of code-switching in Hemnes, Norway, between Standard Norwegian and varieties of the local dialect. They found the working-class networks more local and more tightly-knit than those of the elite, and the local dialect more focused. Both Blom and Gumperz, and Gal in her Oberwart study (1979), emphasize the role of close-knit networks in the maintenance of nonstandard language norms; they are also important in the maintenance of minority languages.

Milroy allowed her networks to define themselves as she was passed along them as "a friend of a friend." They were scored for density and multiplexity; "a network is said to be relatively dense if a large number of the persons to whom ego is linked are also linked to each other"; it is multiplex if, for example, "the same man may be connected to ego as co-employee, neighbor, kin and in many other capacities" (1987a: 50–1). The incidence of each variant of the chosen phonological variables was then correlated with these scores for each individual informant, the correlations plotted and then further examined for clusters significant for age or sex. Illustrated here is the strength or weakness of the ties within a community reflected in the degree of focusing or diffusion in the use of linguistic features within the group and the degree of attachment of individuals to the group, having either strong or weak ties.

According to Williams (1992) Milroy's assumption that the social group is an amalgam of individuals is "a rejection of the fundamental basis of sociological analysis" (p. 195). He had earlier (p. 13) cited Durkheim in support: "Collective representation, emotion, and tendencies are caused not by certain states of the consciousness of individuals but by the conditions in which the social group in its totality is placed" (Durkheim, 1938: 106). Williams is disparaging about all the sociolinguistic work he selects for discussion, finding implicit in it the sociological theories of the American J. Talcott Parsons, and no reflection of class solidarity and conflict. Labov's New York studies are among those condemned. In a 1992 paper, however, L. and J. Milroy attempt a careful integration of class distinctions and network relationships; they answer some of Labov's criticisms about the lack of explanatory power in the strength of network ties, and apply their ideas to the data about Black and White vernacular usage in Philadelphia published by Labov and Harris in 1986. They examine the role of strong network ties in resisting language change and of weak ties in bringing about change. In order to achieve this integration they adopt the analysis by the Danish Marxist anthropologist Thomas Højrup of social class as a "large-scale and ultimately economically-driven *process* that splits populations into sub-groups" characterized by what Højrup describes as "life models." In fact, a great deal of *Language and Social Networks* is about working-class solidarity in Belfast. The question of "sociolinguistic explanation" is discussed also by J. Milroy (1992a, b).

Social networks have since been used as exploratory tools by a number of sociolinguists – see, for example, Russell (1981), Bortoni-Ricardo (1985), Schmidt (1985), Lippi-Green (1989), Salami (1991), and W. Edwards (1992) in his study of "sociolinguistic behavior in a Detroit inner-city black neighborhood." Edwards illustrates the fact that the cultural significance of variation in the incidence of variants may itself be a variable, and emphasizes that "attitudinal characteristics are as important as objective social characteristics in influencing linguistic behavior" (p. 112).

12 *"Natural language," participant observation, and quantitative studies*

Methods of collecting data have been discussed in detail by L. Milroy in *Observing and Analysing Natural Language* (1987b), among others. The term "natural language" has two implications: on the one hand, that one is not working with the "unnatural" made-up sentences of grammar books; on the other, that one is bound to try to overcome Labov's "observer's paradox" as much as possible. (It is generally agreed that it is unethical to tape-record speakers without their knowledge.) Labov has tried to elicit a "natural" style by asking about exciting incidents in his informants' lives. In his Black English work in Harlem he made some use, as we did in Belize, of radio microphones worn by informants while playing together. In his Philadelphia project he combined what he felt to be the advantages of his earlier survey methods in obtaining "a representative sample of opinions and attitudes from an enum-erated population" with those of participant-observer procedures commonly used by social anthropologists and ethnographers, while reducing the distor-tions inherent in each: "by combining both methods, we can estimate the degree and direction of error in our final statement of the rules of the verna-cular" (1981: 4). In Belfast L. Milroy also made use of participant observation, for example, sitting in the kitchen with the "friend" she was visiting, with the tape recorder running, while friends and neighbors dropped in and chatted.

In our Belize study (Le Page and Tabouret-Keller, 1985) we made use of lengthy participant observation of families together with recorded structured interviews of the children. It is necessary, however, to question the stereotype of "most natural language." It is certainly true that in some contexts we monitor our speech more carefully than in others, sometimes to the point of hypercorrection (an important social indicator, as Labov (1972) pointed out). But we are always speaking to *somebody* even if it is only ourselves, and always (for the most part quite unconsciously) adopting a style, or trying to adopt a style, felt to be appropriate to our view of our relationship to our interlocutor. The whole process, and each style, are "natural," part of our "acts of identity." It is important not to equate this process with Giles's theory of "accommoda-tion": *we do not necessarily adapt to the style of our interlocutor, but rather to the image we have of ourselves in relation to our interlocutor.*

Labov's concept of stylistic variation was questioned by Cheshire (1982) in her investigation of variation within an English dialect. "Style-shifting," a concept paralleling "code-switching," was the framework for N. Coupland's (1980) investigation in a Cardiff workplace, and the subject of a number of other investigations, some linked with Giles's concept of "accommodation" (for example, in Giles and J. Coupland, 1991).

13   Acts of Identity

The hypothesis tested in our surveys of Cayo District, Belize, the northern part of St Lucia, and the Jamaican community in south-east London, derived from the problems of linguistic description which I had encountered during ten years' living and teaching in the West Indies (Le Page, 1968).

It states that individuals *create* (the use of this word does not imply consciousness or "rationality") their linguistic systems so as to resemble those of the group or groups they wish from time to time to be identified with, or so as to distinguish themselves from those they wish to distance themselves from. Their success in doing so is subject to constraints under four heads: their ability to identify the groups; the extent of their access to them and ability to analyze their linguistic systems; the strength of their motivation, which is likely to be multidimensional; and their ability to change their behavior – possibly mainly a function of age.

What we quantify here is the resultant of a multidimensional vector diagram. The hypothesis attempts to construct a general framework to connect individual motivation with the social and cultural organization with which it is in symbiotic relationship, and with the linguistic symptoms of that relationship. Statistical studies then provide the basis for an evaluation of the weighting to be given to various motives.

"Projection, focusing, diffusion." The model of speaking and listening which accompanies the hypothesis is of speakers projecting an image (in a cinematic sense) of themselves in relation to their universe, and getting feedback from others as to the extent to which their images coincide – and then either collectively focusing, or allowing these images to remain diffuse. A pair of speakers may agree on a common usage which contains two more or less discrete systems. It was common, for example, in parts of Cayo District for parents regularly to speak to their children in a kind of Spanish and be answered in a kind of Creole, each accepting the generational status of the other, each having a passive competence in both "languages."

Cayo District had recently had a road built through it from the Guatemalan frontier to the coast. "Spanish" speakers had moved into the newly-developing land from the west, "Creole" speakers from the east, "Maya" speakers from north and south, "Carib" or "Garifuna" speakers from the southeast. None of these labels represented a wholly well-focused system; our aim was to discover what was emerging from the linguistic and ethnic mélange. There were complex political implications in the changes taking place.

Without needing to make any prior assumptions about social groups of any kind we were able (using a cluster analysis program) to see what clusters or groups the children formed according to the similarity of their scores on up to 25 variables – five linguistic variables (phonological and morphological) in five modes of behavior, most formal to least formal, including oral storytelling. We were then able to test for each child the extent to which membership of a cluster correlated with any one of a number of nonlinguistic variables, and thus to rank those for their importance in motivating the child's language. We were able to trace the linguistic trajectory of each child as it moved from more formal to less formal behavior. In a follow-up study of 40 of our original 280 informants eight years later we were able to discuss and check the validity of our 1970 conclusions about the general move towards "Creole" as the lingua franca of a newly independent Belize, and the shift in the forms which were now understood by the term "Creole," away from the older Creole of the coast; also, conclusions about the political, economic, ethnic, and cultural forces at work. We worked always from the individual child towards the clusters of their trajectories, and from these to possible matches with social stereotypes and social facts. There were many problems with what was an ambitious program (see McEntegart and Le Page, 1982); nevertheless, the model proved to be a powerful one.

Romaine (1982) contains a number of valuable papers on "Sociolinguistic variation in speech communities," including her own "What is a speech community?" a critical survey of issues raised by work of the kind discussed above, as well as a critique (McEntegart and Le Page) by our statistician of the methods we used in Belize and St Lucia.

14 Code-switching and "interpretive sociolinguistics"

Clearly, sociolinguistic studies in multilingual communities must include "code-switching," "code mixing," and the use of "mixed codes." A puzzle here, in spite of Lotz's (1950) confident assertion referred to earlier, is, as Martinet says, to know to which code a unit belongs, other than to the idiolect of the speaker, whether to one or other of two or more discrete codes, or to an interlanguage. Gardner-Chloros (forthcoming) has argued cogently, and has exemplified from her wide range of code-switching data, the "mythological" nature of the concept of the discreteness of linguistic systems.

Some work has concentrated on trying to specify the syntactic constraints on switching (see, for example, Sankoff, Poplack, and Vanniarajan, 1991), other work on the social context, topic and domain (e.g., Gardner-Chloros, 1991); some combines both approaches. The Workshops of the European Science Foundation's Code-switching and Language Contact Network (ESF, 1990–1) heard no fewer than 51 papers. Attempts to develop universally valid theories are well represented among them, notably by Myers-Scotton, who has developed since 1983 "a model to explain the social motivations of code-switching" which she refers to as "the markedness model" (MM), underlying which is the premise that "speakers use making code choices to negotiate interpersonal relationships" (1990: 58). The "negotiation principle" she proposes directs the speaker to "choose the form of your conversational contribution such that it symbolizes the set of rights and obligations which you wish to be in force between speaker and addressee for the current exchange." This principle is said to rest on an innate theory of markedness and indexicality, and a "markedness metric" which "predisposes speakers to assign readings of markedness to codes in the community's linguistic repertoire for specific interactions in their community." The syntactic rules for the overlapping use of the languages involved are set out within a "Frame and process model." Another starting point not dissimilar from my own is that of Peter Auer, seeing bilingual individuals "using their verbal resources as social actors in everyday exchanges" (1991: 320), and building a theory of code alternation on the theory of contextualization developed by Gumperz (1982, 1992, etc.).

My heading here, "interpretive sociolinguistics," is borrowed from Auer and Di Luzio (1984); it seems an admirable term for work which starts from the observation of linguistic behavior and interprets it in terms of social meaning, rather than starting from social structure and looking for linguistic correlates. A good deal of work on code-switching is of this first kind, a model for which might be Blom and Gumperz's (1972) study of code-switching in Norway.

15 Conclusion

Cameron (1990) has harsh things to say about the "naive" and "crude" models of society that quantitative sociolinguistics uses; the way in which "the primacy of linguistic over social issues is vigorously asserted" by, for example, Trudgill (1978) and Hudson (1980), and in which the quest for "scientific status" has been part of the eschewing of sociological theory and acceptance of a vague claim that "language mirrors society." We need, she claims, a theory linking the "linguistic" to the "socio"; without it we are "stranded in an explanatory void." Ad hoc social theories are inadequate to make good the lack.

My own "acts of identity" hypothesis was an attempt to provide just such a linking theory. The multidimensional clusters of children are held to reflect the groups which they perceive in their society, this perception then having the function of gravity in their galaxies, within the constraints of the four riders. Our tests are to determine the extent to which the clusters they appear to form do match against the objective realities of their society. Both the groups and the linguistic properties they are endowed with are percepts of each individual and idiosyncratic, although clearly constrained by objective realities. The activities of "projection" and "focusing" provide the energy through which groups form. Nothing in this necessarily implies "consciousness" or "rationality" about the processes; we use these faculties to rationalize our acts of identity post hoc. This may well be dismissed as "ad hoc social theory"; it is rather a sociolinguistic hypothesis formed after many years of observing multilingual societies. "Explanation" lies in the complex psychological motivation of the individual, coerced by social forces. What is being "explained" is not linguistic variation – as both Dante (c. 1300) and Martinet have observed, what needs to be "explained" is the formation of the concept of a homogeneous "language." In *Acts of Identity* we set out how we saw such a concept evolving from observation of discourse, through the stereotypes denoted by such language-owning names as "English" or "French," to that of the most highly abstract and focused Chomskyan "grammar"; and how actual linguistic behavior was influenced by the stereotypes as progressively it was named, formalized, standardized, institutionalized, and totemized by a society.

Romaine (1984) challenges network studies on the grounds that they do not explain anything. But it is not true that networks are "theoretical constructs"; rather, they evaluate the ways in which people do relate to each other. They may not "explain" anything, but they give us insight into the way a society works. One weakness common to much sociolinguistic theorizing is a stereotypical view of cause and effect. Once both Fishman and I at a meeting in Quebec tried to point out that social ills there could not be cured by forcing everybody to use French, that language use was a symptom, not a cause, of their problems, and that at most language is in a symbiotic relationship with social factors. Nor is it true, as Cameron asserts, that speakers "inherit a system and can only choose from the options it makes available." Inherent within all linguistic systems are two fundamental characteristics which stereotypically are lost sight of: Their units and processes have values arrived at idiosyncratically and then negotiated collectively; and built into them is the capacity for analogical creativity, available to and made use of by every speaker-listener, and a source of language change. A language is best thought of as a game in which all the speakers can covertly propose and try out rules, and all the listeners are umpires.

NOTE

I am indebted to Dr Joan Russell for her help.

2 The Demography of Language

ALBERT F. VERDOODT

1 Demography

Demography is the science of populations. Like most sciences, it may be defined narrowly or broadly. "The narrowest sense is that of formal demography . . . concerned with size, distribution, structure, and change of populations. The components of change are births, deaths, and migrations" (Shryock et al., 1973: 2). In a broader sense, demography is concerned with gathering information of various kinds about population groups, including their mother tongues. It is in this broader sense that demography will be used here to stress the problems related to the collection of language data by censuses and surveys. We leave to specialized demographers the calculation of the degree as well as the mechanisms of the renewal and/or the disappearance of linguistic groups, which will be mentioned in section 5.

No language census exists for a great majority of countries. And where these censuses do exist, many are unreliable because of a lack of good enumeration techniques. Nevertheless, the European Union has recently constituted the Equipe Euromosaic to undertake a language usage survey in eight selected language groups. Moreover, the Eurobarometer number 28 included a question on conversational ability in the nine EU working languages, with a space for recording knowledge of other (e.g., regional, lesser used) tongues.

2 Language Characteristics

Public data on language characteristics usually take on three different forms:

Mother tongue, generally defined as the language learned in early childhood. Minor variations (which have profound implications for analysis) are found, such as "the language usually spoken in the individual's home in early childhood, although not necessarily spoken by him at present" (UN Department of Economic and Social Affairs, 1959: 2) or "the language first learned and still understood by an individual," as used today in the Canadian census

Main language, or equivalent stimuli. This measure takes several forms, such as "main language" (Finland), "language spoken most often at home" (Canadian censuses since 1971), language spoken fluently, language of inner thought. The wide range of possibilities makes it difficult to conduct meticulous comparative research on such data.

Ability to speak *designated languages*. Questions of this type usually refer to a short list of languages which are either national or official languages . . . (e.g., English and French in Canada) or regional languages in a well-defined political or administrative subdivision (e.g., Welsh in Wales, Gaelic in Scotland) (de Vries, 1988: 957).

Language-related questions in public surveys of the above kinds, which are also recommended by the UN, call for some comment.

Mother tongue claims by individuals may change from one census to another.

> A classical example (of mother tongue fluidity) is Muslims in India oscillating between the regional and religious. Muslims have much closer ties with Urdu than other religious groups. As Muslim population is mostly scattered throughout the country, so is Urdu. A large category of Muslims in many regions tend to have bilingual control over respective languages of the region (Telugu, Kannada, Marathi, etc.) and Urdu. From 1951 to 61, the Muslim population . . . increased by 25.6 percent, whereas the Urdu-speaking population shows an increase of 68.7 percent . . . Considering the socio-cultural situation of the Muslim pockets spread throughout the country, one does not find any evidence of genuine language displacement in daily life, i.e. abandoning any regional or minority language in favor of Urdu (as a mother tongue). (Khubchandani, 1974: 94)

All over the world, ideological biases play the role of the religious ones present in India (Nelde, 1979, 1992). This is true of groups where individuals clearly may not seek to communicate if they meet, and clearly do not agree to use the other's language – a fortiori to claim it – even when, in fact, they know it. But as a rule, most students of mother tongue

> have not even planned or conducted their own self-report studies but, instead, have depended on the data provided by governmental censuses. In this way, the general methodological and conceptual problem of agreement between self-reported and operative bilingualism is compounded by the political and social pressures which often affect censuses . . . Thus, the social science that should be

the most concerned with exploring and clarifying discrepancies between self-report and actual behavior, the most knowledgeable about the impact of social pressures on self-report . . . has depended almost exclusively on data with serious shortcomings in all of these matters. (Fishman 1971: 564)

Thus social categories (religion, social class) need to be validated by small-group interaction processes, if theory is to be strengthened by confirmation at a level unattainable when employing only higher-order categories.

Regarding the questions about ethnic origin, the United Nations points out: "Language, and particularly mother tongue, is probably a sensitive index. Common ancestral customs may be reflected in the mother tongue of individuals . . . not only among foreign born alone, but also among native born" (United Nations, *Demographic Yearbook*, 1963: 39). But caution should be observed: all the speakers of a language are not always members of the same ethnic group and vice versa (Isajiw, 1970: 1; Levy, 1960: 55). Moreover, ethnicity is not a salient notion for many.

Questions about the *"main" language*, without specification of domain, can be useful if the respondent can estimate some average across domains, which is difficult to assess for individuals who use different languages. Consequently, in plurilingual settings, specific reference should be made to one or more domains, for example, home (as in Canada), work, leisure, etc.

Questions about the ability to speak *designated languages* may cover a wide range of degrees of fluency. "The 1971 Canadian census involves . . . 'the person's ability to carry on a conversation on several topics'; but even this allows for considerable latitude in self-reporting" (de Vries, 1985: 358). Moreover, it taps the perceived capacity, not the current use.

Normally, language censuses which are based on self-report data are to be validated by more detailed surveys (cf. section 4), but also, as such. So "Canadian census reports . . . have included standard information about sampling variability and various components of measurement error. I am not aware of other countries giving comparable information about language statistics" (de Vries, 1988: 959). This is why Canadian language censuses are quite reliable, even for Quebec in its debate with Ottawa.

Because, as a rule, language censuses involve a complete count of the number of inhabitants by country or by region (Alsace, Catalonia, Wales, etc.), one of the most obvious sources of information about the quality of the data is the nonresponse rate. Other methods include "reenumeration of a sample of the population covered by the census, overall comparison of census results with data from independent sources . . . and demographic analysis, which includes the comparison of statistics from successive censuses . . . and the analysis of census data for internal consistency and reasonableness" (Shryock et al., 1973: 56).

Another way to validate language censuses is by more detailed surveys (cf. section 4). An alternative to censuses is a *population register* in which all vital events (births, deaths, marriages) are recorded. Of the countries or provinces which maintain such registers, only Finland and Quebec record mother tongue.

3 Deviations in Censuses

Deviations from accurate standards, according to demographers, can occur at every stage of censuses in planning, recording, compiling, validating, tabulating, and analyzing. "The degree of deviation in each attribute is likely to vary according to the nature of the consensus achieved among the members of a group or in the society at large in accounting for a particular trait" (Khubchandani, 1995: 110).

Since it is not possible to review the whole world here, we will restrict ourselves to two countries which constitute typical language laboratories: Belgium on the continent of Europe, and Canada, much larger, in the New World.

In the first language census of Belgium (in 1846) and in the second of Canada (1911) questions were restricted to asking what languages were usually spoken. But, soon after that, the questionnaires started stressing knowledge of the official tongues. In Belgium, where several regional unofficial autochthonous languages are in use, this narrowing of focus created a problem. A scientific committee of statisticians, sociologists, and linguists appointed by the Belgian government (Levy, 1960: 61) proposed to circumvent this difficulty by asking people if they understood and spoke the dialect of their region of residence or another one and, if so, which one. Moreover, the committee suggested not stressing only the official tongues, but also asking about the degree of knowledge of the languages of European institutions. For each of the Belgian official and the then working languages of the EC in 1960, questions would be asked about the four degrees of proficiency: understanding, speaking, reading, and writing.

Unlike Canada, Belgium never posed the delicate question of the mother tongue or the language spoken at home. In order to determine the affiliation of the bilinguals, the scientific committee preferred questions such as: "Of the languages you know, which one is more familiar to you?" And the Report of the Committee (1960: 14) mentions: "If some persons are really unable to estimate what language of the declared tongues is more familiar to them, they could leave this question unanswered." The French version of the questionnaire recommended by the scientific committee is reproduced at the end of this article (p. 43).

A final important difference from the Canadian bilingual (English–French) questionnaire is that the Belgian bilingual (French–Dutch) questionnaire had to be filled in by each person above 14 years of age and signed, while in Canada the census-taker alone notes down the answers.

Finally, the Belgian committee suggested that the possibility of obtaining reliable statistical returns should be safeguarded by parallel organizations of opinion polls or surveys which open the possibility of views being expressed outside the factual census. But unfortunately the committee failed to prescribe a systematic validation of the census as such. As a consequence, the Belgian language census did not hold out against the objections of a majority of parliamentarians, who decided in 1961 to suspend the language censuses and to create a legal linguistic border largely based on former censuses.

4 Surveys

Surveys, unlike censuses, are generally taken under private auspices. Dialect research methods

> were on the whole statistical, aimed at explaining early language states, but the end of the nineteenth century saw the preparation of . . . dialect atlases . . . By questioning speakers (fieldwork), it was possible to identify . . . areas in which certain grammatical rules applied or certain speech variants were used . . . Lines indicating . . . shifts were called *isoglosses*. Dialectologists have produced fundamental works on linguistic variation which teach us that speech communities are essentially heterogeneous . . . The speaker selection, however, was rarely effected according to strict sociological criteria . . . [Moreover] the problem of style selection in an interview situation has remained unsolved . . . It is agreed, however, that a speaker varies his style depending on whether the context is formal or informal, and that what matters is precisely to have speech samples of both extremes of the style continuum. (Dittmar, 1976: 115)

In addition to these general observations, in many dialect surveys dialectologists have generally preferred to investigate linguistically relatively homogeneous rural areas instead of sociolinguistically heterogeneous plurilingual urban settings.

Domain studies are more directly related to basic economic and social facts than individual speaker-type data and, in particular, than mother-tongue data. Sociolinguistic *domains* or spheres of life are sociological constructions, deduced from an analysis and a meticulous summing up of clearly opportune situations. All role relationships (i.e., sets of reciprocal rights and duties recognized and accepted by members of the same sociocultural system) require a suitable and typical place and a socially defined moment in order to come into play. When these three elements (role, place, and time) combine in the expected manner, according to the type of culture, they produce an opportune situation. Thus, when one observes that it is always by means of language A that contact is established between teachers and pupils in classrooms during lessons, one has an inkling that all these situations belong to the same domain (that of education). Moreover, if informants say that language A is suitable for all possible situations that can be either inferred or imagined within the domain of education and that it is not suitable for situations pertaining to a different domain (e.g., the family, the neighborhood, or manual labor), an evident correspondence has been established between a particular language and a particular sociolinguistic domain. The lasting existence of two or more complementary and non-conflicting languages (official or regional) for internal contacts within a particular group is called *diglossia*.

However successful the use of Fishman's (1972: 91–105) definition of diglossia may be, it does not explain why the language varieties or variants are functionally distributed as they are today in a given society. An analysis of the socioeconomic development, which includes a specification of the social classes and the geographical spaces to which the various speakers belong, is necessary.

One of the first analyses in relation to extralinguistic parameters was that carried out by Reichstein (1960) in Paris. Parisian schoolchildren from three socially different types of school were examined with regard to their use of three phonemic contrasts: 1 /a–a (e.g., in patte/pâte); 2 /ɛ–ɛ:/ (e.g., in belle/bêle) 3. /ɛ̄–õe/(e.g., in brin/brun). The analysis reveals that the contrasts disappear when the children become older, this development being more evident in working-class districts. This suggests an explanation of the change as a result of the pressure exerted by the lower social class, an extralinguistic parameter.

Another outstanding example of an in-depth survey, corresponding to some extent with Labov (1966c), is that of Fishman and others (1971). A variety of techniques, derived separately from the disciplines of sociology, linguistics, and psychology, were administered to the same respondents: 48 Spanish-English bilinguals who lived in a Puerto Rican neighborhood near New York.

> The techniques employed . . . comprise a "maxi-kit" from which the investigator can select the "mini-kit" he needs for work in the field . . . If his interests in questions are fairly unidimensional, and if language issues are not particularly sensitive, he can use direct questions of a census type. If, however, the investigation is dubious about the validity of answers to such questions, he should select a more indirect measure . . . such as the word frequency estimation technique. (Fishman et al., 1971: 500)

Using this technique, respondents are asked to rate, on an eight-point scale, the frequency with which they hear or use each of 150 different words of which half are in Spanish and half in English. The 75 words in each language were comprised of five sets of 15 words, the words for each set having been selected to represent a domain such as family, friendship, religion, education, and work. For example, some of the English words which represented the domain of education were teacher, blackboard, history, and science. Respondents rated all the words in one language before rating the words in the other. The items representing each domain were evenly distributed throughout the list of words in each language. If an investigater wishes to combine more instruments, he could also select the following items: (1) A task requiring the respondent to name, within a one-minute period, as many different words as possible that identify objects seen or found in a particular place, e.g., a church. In the case of Spanish-English bilinguals of New York, Spanish is indeed the language of religion. Consequently a positive relationship appears to exist between English religious productivity – if present – and English Repertoire Range; (2) A task requiring the respondent to listen to a brief, taped, bilingual conversation and comment on the appropriateness of language chosen for the particular purpose of that conversation.

If the investigator is concerned with more complex criteria, he or she may need to use a greater combination of techniques. Fishman and others (1971: 483–502) provide a description of these techniques, as well as of the factor analysis of the different types of tasks. Yet another exemplary survey, but on a larger scale, is that of Galician (Seminario de Sociolínguistica da Real Academia Galega, 1995).

On the macro-level, we refer to McConnell (chapter 21 in this book), and especially to the project, which has already produced five volumes, on "The written languages of the world: a survey of the degree and modes of use." The programming of the data base of this project resulted in the automatic calculation of vitality rates in eight domains (religion, schools, mass media, administration, courts, legislature, manufacturing industries, sales and services), and finally in the production of maps, histograms, and tables with the aim of visually representing the analyzed data (McConnell et al., 1993).

Restricted inquiries can verify or supplement language censuses. A report by the group "Mens en Ruimte" (1962), based on the sociological research tradition, constitutes a good case. The research was limited to four small Belgian sub-regions: (1) Sclimpré, a predominantly Walloon and French-speaking neighborhood of L'Ecluse with 71 inhabitants; (2) L'Ecluse village, a mixed language area with 220 inhabitants; (3) The transition area between L'Ecluse and the adjoining village of Meldert with 68 inhabitants; (4) Meldert village, a predominantly Brabantic and Dutch-speaking area with 300 inhabitants. The inquiry on the language situation comprised a preliminary phase on the socioeconomic situation and three more main phases: some identification data on each family; interviews with privileged witnesses; interviews with the families. The registration of language competence was simply based on questions about understanding, speaking, reading, and writing. The results showed that there exists an important gap between active and passive knowledge of the languages, especially for Dutch. The origin of this phenomenon may be found in the fact that at the municipal school of L'Ecluse teaching is in French. This school has a wide radius of attraction. Another conclusion of the survey is that it is possible to make an accurate and simple registration of language performance even in mixed language areas.

The population using *foreign languages* can be investigated from the perspective of language needs. It seems that Sweden and Great Britain, later Germany, the Netherlands, and Belgium pioneered in this field (Oud-de Glas,

1983: 19–34). In the Netherlands the final report of a large survey into the need for foreign languages in Dutch governmental departments and industry was published (Claessen et al., 1978). This study covered a random selection of 2,000 companies and 500 governmental departments. In addition, 400 foreign-language users, also selected at random from these companies and governmental departments, were questioned in order to find out which specific situations foreign languages were used in, in order to determine the sort of problems that arise. Three quarters of the private companies in which French was used and two thirds of the government departments experienced difficulties with this language. German and English gave rise to fewer problems; just over one third of the governmental departments and private firms experienced difficulties with these languages; they are after all Germanic languages, as is Dutch. A list of 24 language situations with questions concerning the frequency of the use of French, German, and English, and concerning the circumstances that gave rise to problems, were sent to persons who used these modern foreign languages. There were large differences between the categories of workers; in some the frequency of oral communication was much higher than in others. In French, oral communication plays a greater role than in other languages. The majority of problems arise in the use of French; in German and English problems are minimal.

The same type of research was conducted in academic education and research (Claessen et al., 1978a) as well as among secondary school students and ex-students (Claessen et al., 1978b). In Belgium, these three types of surveys (at work, in universities and secondary schools) were adapted and duplicated (Baetens-Beardsmore and Verdoodt, 1984).

5   Research Possibilities

There are numerous possibilities for research based on validated language censuses (as in Canadian statistics) or on scientific language surveys, or both. Such research should precede or accompany any language policy, as demonstrated by "Indicateurs de la situation linguistique au Québec" (1992), some data of which follow.

Regarding the language mostly spoken at home (as determined in the Canadian census since 1971), we find that the proportion of French-speaking households has grown by 1.8 percent, that of Anglophones by 0.8 percent between 1971 and 1986. The total fertility rate of French-speaking mothers was 1.66 children per woman in 1981 and 1.43 in 1986; the total fertility rate of English-speaking women was 1.29 in 1981 and 1.37 in 1981; for the allophone mothers (who do not use either English or French at home) this rate was 1.88 in 1981 and 1.66 in 1986.

Most important for the future of French is the fact that between 1980 and 1991, the proportion of allophone pupils going to a French school increased from 38.7 percent to 75.5 percent. However, the college graduation rate of Anglophones is still much higher than that of Francophones: 15 percent compared with 7 percent. When we consider total family incomes, the Anglophones are at an index of 115.9 in 1985 compared with the Francophones at 100. But the bilingual Anglophones, who were in the first place in 1970, are now being overtaken by the bilingual Francophones: index 159 compared with 161.

Regarding the consumption of newspapers, the allophones still read more English dailies than French ones. An important fraction of Francophones, 8.2 percent, watch television in English. The Anglophones devote only 5 percent of their television time to French. Finally, surveys show that French-speaking radio stations broadcast 78.7 percent of the listening hours; that is a little less than the proportion of Francophones, which is now 82.9 percent of the total population of the province of Quebec.

6 Sociolinguistics and Demography

Sociolinguists are all in some sense language demographers; they have to diagnose and describe speech differences. That is especially difficult in developing countries where the distinction between one language (often that of a minority) and another is not always as clearcut as in most industrialized states. There must normally be some linguistic distance between two languages in order to consider them as distinct. It is true, for example, that there is not much difference between Kirundi (spoken in Burundi) and Kirwanda (spoken in Ruanda). But the sociolinguist should find out whether a Kirwanda writer would accept his prose as being Kirundi, even if both languages are very similar.

Finally, it is socially worthwhile to identify and recognize all languages. Indeed, language is not simply a means of communicating messages. It is also very important as a symbol of identity and group membership. That is one of the reasons why the Council of Europe has composed a Charter for Regional or Minority Languages. This Charter is now submitted for the ratification of the member states. In its Article 7 we read that the parties shall base their policies, legislation, and practice on a number of objectives, among others the promotion of study and research on regional or minority languages at universities or equivalent institutions.

On its side, the European Union has created the European Bureau for Lesser-Used Languages. The United Kingdom Committee of this Bureau has organized, in association with the University of Hertfordshire, a colloquium on minority language population censuses and speech-community surveys. Let us conclude with some of the recommendations of this colloquium; they are addressed to the member-states of the European Union, but may be of real interest to all states or groups preoccupied with collecting language data:

Where states have (general) censuses, but no language question, a question on the autochthonous lesser-used language(s) of their state should be included.

Assistance should be provided for groups lacking both language censuses and surveys in order to provide the kinds of demographic data the language groups would wish for. Such assistance should be expected from state sources in the first instance.

Where good state language censuses exist, they form the basis for further social investigation of the demography of language groups. Here it is possible for surveys to elicit relationships between language-group demography and social and economic processes. Such surveys can be of great benefit in explaining language reproduction, and providing a basis for language planning.

Whether by means of censuses or surveys, a common core of basic demographic data should be sought in the case of all language groups. Whereas circumstances will differ between cases, a basic core of questions should feature numbers (of subjects) able to speak the language at a reasonable level of ability, together with such language abilities as understanding, reading, and writing the language. These abilities might ideally be associated with basic social and economic data such as age, gender, occupational and educational levels (see MacKinnon, 1995). These recommendations illustrate the fact that censuses are "more important not for actual (or absolute) numbers, but for relative numbers ... By stressing absolute numbers of the dominant language, the 1931 Scottish census listed only 7,000 non-English speakers, though the population included 136,000 Gaelic speakers ... The importance of demographic studies is in measuring the behaviour in one population (or its section) in comparison to another" (Khubchandani, 1995: 113).

Figure 2.1 The French version of the questionnaire recommended in Belgium in 1960.

ROYAUME DE BELGIQUE
MINISTERE DES AFFAIRES ECONOMIQUES
INSTITUT NATIONAL DE STATISTIQUE

RECENSEMENT DES LANGUES au.........

Le présent questionnaire ne peut porter aucune inscription manuscrite ni aucun cachet sur aucune de ses faces au moment de sa remise par l'agent recenseur. Il doit être rempli et signé par le recensé si celui-ci est âgé de 15 ans et plus, par le chef de ménage s'il est âgé de moins de 15 ans. Il doit être remis *sous enveloppe fermée* à l'agent recenseur, lors de la reprise du bulletin. L'Administration communale transmettra directement à L'Institut national de Statistique, toutes les enveloppes recueillies. Il est strictement interdit à l'agent recenseur ainsi qu'aux autorités communales d'ouvrir les enveloppes ou de s'informer des réponses.

I. *IDENTITE DU RECENSE*

Nom :_____ Prénoms :_____ Sexe : masculin - féminin (1)

Lieu de naissance : Commune :_____ Arrondissement :_____

Année de naissance :___ Etat-civil célibatair - marié - veuf - divorcé - séparé de corps et biens (1)

Adresse (rue n°, commune)_____

Nationalité :_____Profession principale :_____

II. *CONNAISSANCES LINGUISTIQUES DU RECENSE*

A. *Langues*: mette une croix dans le cases comportant une réponse affirmative.

FRANCAIS	
Le comprenez-vous?	
Savez-vous le parler?	
Savez-vous le lire?	
Savez-vous l'écrire?	

NEERLANDAIS (Flamand)	
Le comprenez-vous?	
Savez-vous l parler?	
Savez-vous le lire?	
Savez-vous l'écrire?	

ANGLAIS	
Le comprenez-vous?	
Savez-vous le parler?	
Savez-vous le lire?	
Savez-vous l'écrire?	

ALLEMAND	
Le comprenez-vous?	
Savez-vous le parler?	
Savez-vous le lire?	
Savez-vous l'écrire?	

ITALIEN	
Le comprenez-vous?	
Savez-vous le parler?	
Savez-vous le lire?	
Savez-vous l'écrire?	

Autres langues vivantes que vous comprenez :_____
Autres langues vivantes que vous savez parler :_____
Autres langues vivantes que vous savez lire :_____
Autres langues vivantes que vous savez écrire :_____

B. *Dialectes*

Comprenez-vous le dialecte de le région où vous résidez (2)____Savez-vous le parler (2)____
Comprenez-vous le dialecte d'une autre région du pays (2)_____
Si oui, de quelle région ?_____ Parlez-vous ce dialecte (2)_____

III. LANGUE PROPRE DU RECENSE (3)

Des diverses langues indiquées sous II A, laquelle vous est la plus familière ?_____

Signature du déclarant,

(1) Barrez ce qui ne convient pas.
(2) Répondez pas oui ou non.
(3) Pour les enfants n'ayant pas atteint l'âge de deux ans le jour de recensement, ne pas répondre à la question II mais indiquer à la question III la langue dans laquelle on leur apprend à s'exprimer dans les actes courants de la vie.

Part II Social Dimensions of Language

3 Varieties and Variation

JAMES MILROY and LESLEY MILROY

1 Introduction

As Edward Sapir remarked (1921: 147), "everyone knows that language is variable." Variability in language is within everyone's experience of using and listening to language, and most people show some degree of interest in it. Despite this, however, linguistic theory has until quite recently paid relatively little attention to variation, and in many branches of inquiry languages have been treated as if they were wholly or mainly invariant entities, or as if the variability that does exist within them were unimportant, accidental, or inessential. Variability within a language or dialect and variation across languages have not been central concerns in the dominant linguistic theories of this century – Saussurean theory, American and Prague School structuralism, and Chomskyan theory. One consequence of this, to which we return below, is that linguistic theorizing has been largely based on *standardized* forms of languages, rather than on the more variable forms of naturalistic speech.

Within descriptive linguistics, the main exception to this is what can be called the *variationist paradigm*, which is based on the research methods and analytic techniques developed by William Labov (see especially Labov 1966c, 1972), on the critique of current linguistics set out by Weinreich, Labov, and Herzog (1968), and on ideas developed in several papers by Labov himself. Many important principles are set out in this work, but the most relevant to the present discussion is the principle that *variability in language is, or may be shown to be, structured*. Weinreich, Labov, and Herzog (1968) observed that linguistic scholars generally had not only focused mainly on uniform states of language, but had also equated this uniformity with structuredness. That is, they had believed that only uniform states can be structured and had tended to dismiss variability in language as unstructured or random and therefore not worth studying. Many examples of this can be cited, and some are noticed in section 2 below. Because of this emphasis on invariance, however, linguists have often used as their subject matter "cleaned-up" or invented data, and not for the most part naturally occurring data (which is of course inclined to be variable). It should be noted that in contrast to this, the variationist paradigm is *empirical* in its methods, in that it depends on collecting naturalistic speech from real speakers and insisting on full *accountability* to the data so collected, no matter how messy some of the data may be.

A major reason for recent advances in variation studies is technological. Before tape recorders became easily available, students of spoken language had to rely on single-word citation forms and on memory. In the last 30 years, however, much attention has been devoted to collecting tape-recorded data in situations that are as "naturalistic" as possible. This advance has been of great importance in several branches of linguistic analysis, including work on inter-actional sociolinguistics, following the principles of John Gumperz and others, and work on conversational analysis by Sacks, Schegloff, and Jefferson, and others. The key difference between the variationist paradigm and other empirical approaches is that the former is focused on understanding variation and change in the structural parts of *language* rather than the behavior of *speakers* or the nature of speaker interaction. The activities of speakers in naturalistic settings are indeed studied, but not primarily for what they tell us about speakers or interaction between speakers; the interest is in what they tell us about varying structures of language and speakers' knowledge of these variable structures. The aim of the next section is to explore to some extent the range and depth of variation that exists in a language in terms of the different linguistic and extralinguistic dimensions in which variation is observed.

2 The Range and Depth of Variation: Some Examples

Language is inherently variable at a number of structural levels – in phonology, morphology, and syntax in particular. Phoneticians frequently point out that no two utterances of the same word by the same speaker are ever exactly alike, and it is also recognized that some variation in sound-patterns may be structured. One of these structured aspects of phonetic/phonological variation is labelled *assimilation*. For example, in a phrase such as *bacon and eggs* in British English, the final /n/ of "bacon" may be assimilated to the place of articulation of the preceding /k/ and realized as a velar rather than an alveolar nasal. This is likely to happen in relatively rapid or casual speech and is to that extent "stylistic": the same speaker may use either alternant (alveolar or velar) in a reasonably regular way according to situation and context. In morphology and syntax also, there are many alternative ways of saying the same thing, especially in nonstandard forms of languages – for example, variation between *you were* and *you was* in London English and between *can't* and *cannot* in Newcastle speech.

The quantitative paradigm explores the regularity in linguistic variation by examining certain dimensions that are external to language itself and relating variation in these to variation in language. These dimensions are normally social; however, strictly speaking, two of the dimensions that are involved in variation are perhaps better described as "natural" dimensions. These are the dimensions of *space* and *time*, which exist independently of human society and which have been studied extensively by linguists for some centuries. Language variation in space forms the subject matter of linguistic geography, which itself includes traditional dialectology of the kind exemplified by Orton and others (1963–9). Language variation in time forms the subject matter of historical linguistics. The main advances in recent years, however, have been in the more obviously "human" dimensions of variation, that is, in *social* variation in language, and it is important to notice here that this type of variation was the first to be studied *quantitatively*, i.e., by counting variants and comparing the incidence of variants in different speakers and groups of speakers. Quantification is an essential methodological tool of the variationist paradigm, and for this reason it is sometimes called *quantitative social dialectology*.

Investigators proceed by first selecting a *variable* (for example, a sound segment such as /a/, which is observed to vary in pronunciation) and quantifying occurrences of variants of this variable in the speech of different speakers and groups of speakers. The use of quantification represents an advance in descriptive techniques, as it enables investigators to make accurate statements about fine-grained differences between groups of speakers in a community. Formerly, such statements tended to be categorical: For example, a particular usage (such as /h/-dropping in British English, for example) might have been categorized as "working-class" and the "proper" use of /h/ middle class. In practice such usages are seldom categorical for any group of speakers. Table 3.1 shows variability in /h/ according to social class in Bradford and Norwich, England. It is clear from this that the use or non-use of initial /h/ is not categorical for any group in either city.

Table 3.1 Percentage of /h/-dropping in Bradford and Norwich (formal style) (after Chambers and Trudgill, 1980: 69, and Petyt, 1977).

	Bradford	*Norwich*
Middle middle class	12	6
Lower middle class	28	14
Upper working class	67	40
Middle working class	89	60
Lower working class	93	60

The use of quantification has led to speculation as to whether human linguistic competence is in fact probabilistic (see Cedergren and Sankoff, 1974; Fasold, 1990: 249–57) but the literal claim that speakers "know" the exact quantities in which different variants should be used by them in varying situations has not been generally accepted. The main advance brought about by using quantification is methodological, not theoretical. Quantitative methods of analysis have enabled us to propose socially based explanations for aspects of language variation in time, space, and social space. Generally, they have done this by relating variation in language to variation in society and situational contexts of speech. In order to demonstrate covariation between linguistic and social categories, it is normal to identify one or more *speaker variables*. The most widely used of these is *socioeconomic class*. Other variables that are commonly used include age of speaker, sex (gender) of speaker, ethnic group of speaker, and social network (we return below to the purpose of using speaker variables in this type of research). In addition, it is usual, where possible, to recognize *contextual style* as a variable, and this variable tends to cut across or interact with the speaker variables. It is not a speaker variable in quite the same sense as the others mentioned, as variation according to social context or occasion of use (i.e., "stylistic variation") is not a characteristic of the speaker as such, but of the speaker's relationship to the resources of the language and of the situational contexts in which the speaker finds himself at different times (see further below, section 5). All normal speakers of a language exhibit stylistic variation in speech, and patterns of stylistic variation exhibited by speakers, taken together with other variables, may reveal the direction of linguistic change in progress at some particular time. It is therefore desirable in fieldwork to obtain a range of styles from informants, and it should be noted that this has important implications for fieldwork methods. In particular, certain techniques have to be used in order to elicit casual or informal styles, which informants may tend to avoid in talking to an outsider such as the fieldworker. This problem is known as the *Observer's Paradox*. There is a considerable literature on fieldwork method relevant to the observer's paradox (see especially Labov, 1972a, and L. Milroy, 1987b).

3 Speaker Variables and the Speech Community

Whereas other branches of linguistics focus on "the language" or "the dialect," quantitative sociolinguistics focuses on the speech community. This is envisaged as a sociolinguistic entity rather than a purely linguistic one. It is not supposed that all speakers in the community speak in exactly the same way or that there is some "real" or "genuine" uniform language variety that characterizes the community. It is not even necessary that the members of such a community should all speak the same language, although the most influential quantitative work so far has focused on monolingual states of language. The speech community, according to Labov, is a locus in which speakers agree on the social meanings and evaluations of the variants used, and of course it incorporates variability in language use. In practice the speech communities studied by sociolinguists have been geographically very restricted, and this restrictedness is in itself important in the identification of the origins and diffusion of linguistic changes in progress. They are identified as happening, not in "the language" as a whole, but in some particular speech community, and the progress of these changes is then analyzed as they spread in the speech community, and possibly to other speech communities. Underlying all this is an assumption that access to speakers in present-day speech communities will bring us closer to understanding the origins of linguistic changes. It can also be argued on this basis that changes do not take place in the abstraction that we call "the language," but that they arise from the activities of speakers and then feed into the linguistic system. For this reason it has been proposed that a methodological distinction should be drawn between *innovation* and *change*. A linguistic innovation is an act of the speaker (or speakers). It may or may not become established in the linguistic system and become part of the language. If it does penetrate into the system, however, it becomes a linguistic change and will at that point display a regular structure of variation in terms of the social variables discussed above. This process is represented in figure 3.1.

Figure 3.1 Model of transition from speaker innovation to linguistic change.

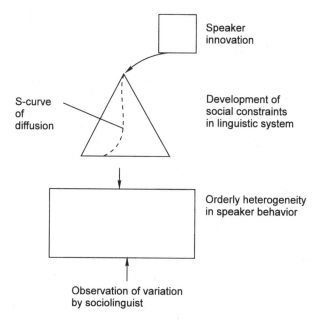

4 Language Maintenance, Standardization, and Change

A basic assumption of variation studies is that "at any time we care to look at a language . . . it is variable and in a state of change" (J. Milroy, 1992: 2). Sometimes change is rapid and sometimes it is slow, but there is no reason to believe that there can ever be a time when a spoken language is completely stable. It follows that the methods used for studying it should preferably recognize that languages are dynamic and not static phenomena. Traditionally, this has not been a central perception in the descriptive and comparative methodology, and language states at different times and places have often been studied as if these different states were like different physical objects that could be compared with each other as (largely invariant) wholes. It appears, however, that insofar as they are social or sociocultural phenomena, languages are subject to speaker-based processes that are initiated in social groups. When a language (such as French or English) is recognized by society as a single phenomenon, it can be assumed that it has been subject to a diachronic process of language *maintenance*. It seems to be necessary to invoke such a process in order to account for the existence of language states that are popularly perceived to be static (in reality they are not), and we give some attention to this process here.

In studies in the sociology of language the term *language maintenance* signifies the process of consciously maintaining – if necessary by government intervention – a particular form of a language in a population where there is linguistic diversity wide enough to make communication difficult; it is usually bilingual situations that are involved. In the histories of major languages, such as English and French, the process of maintenance has also been prominent – sometimes carried out by overt legislation, and sometimes in a less formal way by imposing the codified linguistic norms of elite social groups on society as a whole through education and literacy (for a discussion see Milroy and Milroy [1985], 1991; see also chapter 18). These processes of maintenance, which arise from the imposition of linguistic norms by powerful social groups, can be subsumed under the term *language standardization*. The chief linguistic consequence of standardization is a tendency to structural uniformity in a language, i.e., variability is resisted and suppressed by stigmatization of nonstandard variants. It should be noted, first, that standardization can be viewed as a diachronic process occupying an extended time-scale, and second, that it is continuously in progress, and not completed in any language except a dead one. Thus it is not correct to state (for example) that the standardization of English was completed at some particular time, such as the eighteenth century. Finally, it should further be noted that the speech communities in which quantitative sociolinguists have usually worked have been within nation states in which a standardized form of the language is considered to be a well established superordinate norm (as contrasted with pidgin situations, for example). As a consequence of this, an understanding of processes of change in such communities should ideally take account of this fact.

In the research projects carried out in Belfast by Milroy and Milroy (1975–82) the notion of language maintenance was extended to cover situations in which the pressure to maintain language states is noninstitutional. Individuals in small-scale communities do not systematically act as language planners or language maintainers, but in order to account for the survival of nonstandard or low-status varieties, noninstitutional norm enforcement of this kind must be assumed, and the effect of such norm enforcement is just as much a form of language maintenance as is overt standardization. If we wish to discriminate between the two types of maintenance – institutional and noninstitutional – we can call the latter kind *vernacular maintenance*. The hypothesis followed out in the Belfast research was that community norms of language are maintained by these informal pressures, and it was further suggested that relatively localized patterns of identity marking are involved.

In nation states in which there is consciousness of a standard language, vernacular maintenance can result in conflict between two opposing norms. This emphasis on societal conflict is one of the things that differentiates this research from that of Labov, and it has obvious consequences for the characterization of the idealized "speech community" in which every speaker agrees on the evaluation of the varying norms of language. If low-prestige varieties can persist and spread within urban societies, it may be that their speakers do not evaluate variants in the way that other sectors of the community do. Thus, for example, /h/-less, rather than /h/-pronouncing norms can be seen as favored rather than stigmatized in some small-scale communities. The pattern arising is of course one of conflict rather than consensus, and this conflict pattern can be at least partially understood as arising from the conflict between status-based ideologies and solidarity-based ideologies in the community. When the latter are dominant, localized noninstitutional norms of language will tend to be preserved (see further section 7 below on "social network").

5 Extra-linguistic Variables

The main speaker variables that have been used are noted above. Their use is methodological and exploratory, and not in itself explanatory. Thus it should not be assumed that to relate language variation to a social variable, such as social class, is to explain language variation as being *caused* by social class variation. There are several reasons for this caution, the chief of which is that there may be many aspects of social behavior that are not accounted for in a single social variable, and also underlying social factors that are subsumed under such a label as "social class" (such as educational level) which may sometimes yield more precise correlations than the main composite variable (in this case social class).

As the methodology is exploratory, it is also open-ended. It is not necessarily the case that all language variation can be accounted for by relating it to social variation, and no one has claimed to be able to do this. It is clearly likely that other factors are involved, including linguistic constraints (Weinreich, Labov, and Herzog, 1968), and a start has been made on investigating conversational or discoursal constraints on variation (Milroy, Milroy, and Docherty, 1994). Criticisms of sociolinguistic method (e.g., Cameron, 1990) on the grounds that it claims to account socially for all linguistic variation are therefore otiose. It is also likely in any study that there will be a residue of apparently random variation which is difficult to account for using the methods of quantitative sociolinguistics.

Of the social variables that are commonly used, two at least are composite (or complex) variables, in that they are calculated by reference to a number of indicators. These are socioeconomic (social) class and social network. Quantitative measurements of social class depend on such indicators as income, trade or profession, and educational level, while social network depends on indicators of density and multiplexity in a speaker's social relationships. Certain other social variables, such as age and sex of speaker, are mathematically simplex in that they do not depend on multiple indicators and do not need to be calculated in the form of numerical scores (this does not of course imply that correlations with age and sex are simple to interpret; see chapters 8 and 9). Whereas these simplex variables are verifiable from observation at the data collection stage, there can be and has been dispute about how the complex variables (especially social class) are to be conceptualized, calculated, and interpreted in specific investigations. The most controversial social variable is socioeconomic class.

Labov's (1966c) study in New York City proceeded by measuring covariation of language with variation in social class membership, and the social measurements used were imported from sociology. They depended, moreover, on a particular social theory associated with the work of Talcott Parsons (1952), which uses the concept of *stratificational* social class. This involves classifying individuals in a hierarchy of class groupings based on the idea of a continuum from highest to lowest, and is the most familiar way of treating social class in Western countries. However, there are other theories of social class, such as those associated with Marx, which are not stratificational, but which use a process model of class. Social class is seen as emanating from economic factors, such as the means of production and distribution, and resulting in two broad groupings in society – the proletariat and the bourgeoisie. Whereas the stratificational model results in a consensus view of society, in which there is general agreement within the hierarchy, the Marxist model plainly emphasizes conflict between the different interest groups. This difference in social models is reflected in the consensus-based and conflict-based models of the speech community that were mentioned above. In procedural terms, however, a stratificational model is much more readily adapted to quantitative use than is a process model (see further below).

Social class has been by far the most widely used social variable, and it appears that this emphasis on social class is not confined to modern sociolinguistics. It is quite prominent in work on the descriptive history of English, for example, and it is usual for lay people to assume that it is the most important social category. However, since Labov's New York study, it has become the central social variable in sociolinguistic research, in that results obtained from work on other variables (particularly gender) are interpreted in terms of social class or the closely associated notion of prestige. In the Labov methodology, the direction of style-shifting (toward "careful" style) corresponds to upward movement in the social hierarchy, and is interpreted in terms of it (this correspondence is further discussed and interpreted by Bell (1984)). It also affects the interpretation of gender difference in speech. Thus the fact that females tend to speak more "carefully" than males has been interpreted as arising from a desire on their part to acquire social prestige through their speech, as they could not traditionally acquire this through career success – as males could. This type of conclusion can be objected to on various grounds, but what is at issue here is the centrality of social class, not in the quantitative methodology itself, but in the *interpretation* of the results of that methodology. In what follows, the quantitative method is taken for granted as valid, and the emphasis is on the interpretation of sociolinguistic patterns arrived at in terms of speaker variables. We first consider gender.

6 Gender

Variation according to gender appears to be universal and, in terms of style, the tendency appears (in Western societies at least) to be always in the same direction. Females tend toward the careful end of the continuum and males toward the casual end. Similarly, it can be said that females favor "prestige" norms and males vernacular norms. This is something of a paradox because, although sociologists and anthropologists normally recognize that virtually all societies have accorded higher status and greater power to males than to females (for a useful survey see Giddens, 1989), it is females who tend to use higher status variants of language. There is also another factor involved, however, which may not have to do with prestige or "carefulness" of speech: This is that males appear to favor more localized variants, which carry some kind of identity-based social meaning in the local community, whereas females identify more with supra-local variants in speech. It should be noted that gender variation in speech is not necessarily evident to the casual observer. Normally, both sexes use the same variants, but in different quantities, and the differences are fine-grained; therefore, they can normally be demonstrated only by quantitative means.

Figure 3.2 Deletion of medial /ð/ in words of the type *mother, together*.

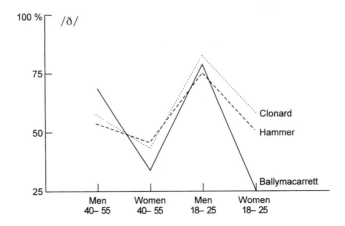

The inner-city Belfast study (Milroy and Milroy, 1978 etc.) dispensed with social class as a variable and concentrated first on variation according to age and sex differences. It demonstrated that, within the same social class or stratum, gender difference was always present and almost always moved in the same direction. Figure 3.2 demonstrates a clear gender difference in the variable [ð] (presence or absence of the medial consonant in words of the type: *mother, bother, together*) in two generations of speakers, with virtually no difference according to age.

Since then, clear patterns of gender differentiation have been demonstrated in a number of studies, so much so that it can be suggested that gender difference may be prior to class difference in driving linguistic variation and change. In an important study, Horvath (1985) has regraphed some of Labov's New York City data in terms of gender difference instead of social class. Figure 3.3 shows her results. In the graph the lower social classes are on the left (0–2) progressing upwards to the right to the upper middle class (9) at the extreme right of the diagram. It shows that, although there is certainly an effect of class, sex of speaker accounts for the distribution more satisfactorily than class. In the top half of the graph females are dominant, and in the bottom half males dominate. The one upper middle-class male, Nathan B., who appears in the bottom half of the graph has been discussed by Labov (1966) as anomalous. In a gender-based interpretation this individual is no longer anomalous: he is converging on the male norm rather than the class norm.

Other studies that suggest the priority of gender over class have been carried out in Newcastle upon Tyne under the direction of L. Milroy (for a summary see L. Milroy, 1992). Rigg (1987) studied glottalization of /p/, /t/, and /k/ in medial and word-final positions (as in *pepper, butter, flicker, what, top, lock*), and her findings are shown in figure 3.4 and table 3.2.

Figure 3.3 /ð/ in New York City (after Labov, 1966, and Horvath, 1985).

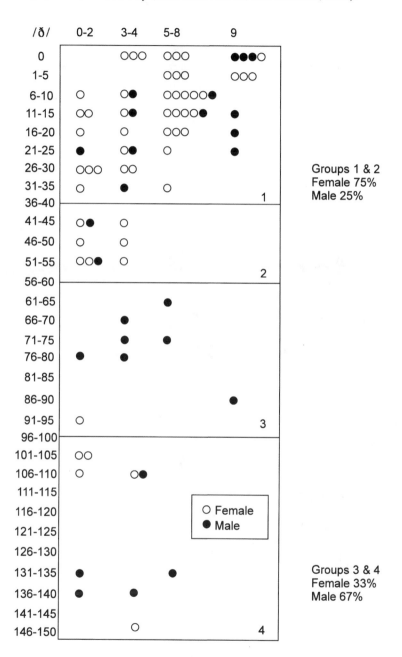

The most obvious finding here is that glottalization is sex-marked rather than class-marked (the effect of class is quite trivial). In the conversational style shown in table 3.2, the overall female scores do not overlap at all with the

Figure 3.4 Percentage of glottalized variants of /p/, /t/, and /k/ in word-medial position in two speech styles of 16 Tynesiders.

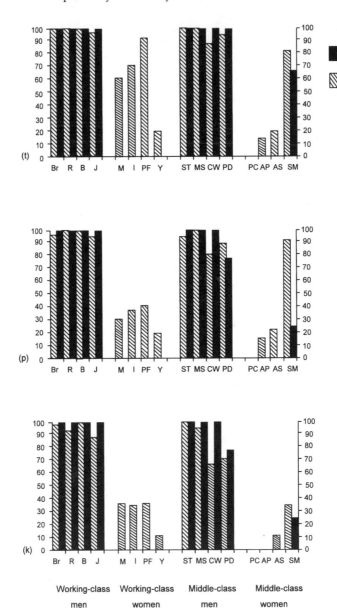

male scores. Hartley's (1992) study reported in Milroy, Milroy, and Hartley (1994) demonstrates further that, within the glottalization pattern, males lead in glottal reinforcement whereas, surprisingly, females lead in use of the glottal stop. Other studies of glottalization, such as Mees (1987) and

Table 3.2 Percentage of glottalized variants of three voiceless stops in spontaneous speech of 16 Tynesiders.

	Working class			Middle class		
	/p/	/t/	/k/	/p/	/t/	/k/
Male	99.5	97.0	94.5	96.5	91.0	80.5
Female	60.0	31.0	28.0	27.0	32.5	11.0

Kingsmore (1994), also associate the glottal stop with female usage. As it is hardly feasible to explain these findings in terms of prestige, it has been suggested that glottal reinforcement is favored by males as a traditional localized pattern, whereas the glottal stop is spreading at a supra-local level. Comments by Wells (1982) and others to the effect that the glottal stop is beginning to enter the prestige accent, Received Pronunciation, would seem to support an interpretation based on the idea of supra-local diffusion. Before leaving the subject of gender differentiation, we should further note that the priority of gender over class is also suggested by various studies in the Arab world (Alahdal, 1989; Jawad, 1987; Jabeur, 1987). Thus it is no longer clear that gender-marking in language should be interpreted in terms of class, status, or prestige as prior categories. It may be that female norms for some reason become the prestige norms in the course of time, and hence that gender differentiation is an important driving force in linguistic change, independently of class (for a different view see Labov, 1990).

7 Social Network

Social network was developed as a quantitative speaker variable by L. Milroy ([1980] 1987) as part of the Belfast inner-city study. The main methodological difference between network (as used here) and other variables that have been examined is that it is based, not on comparisons between groups of speakers, but on relationships contracted by individual speakers with other individuals. It is assumed that all individuals are embedded in networks of personal ties. Furthermore (following a considerable body of social anthropological research), it is argued that when these ties are strong, they can act as norm-enforcement mechanisms. The idea of social network was adopted from social science research as a means of accounting for patterns of vernacular maintenance over time. In the context of the Belfast research (and indeed more generally) this is an important issue, as stigmatized and low-status forms of language tend to persist despite strong pressure from "legitimized" norms.

This has always been difficult to explain. Social network analysis thus provides a methodology for studying the interaction between patterns of maintenance and patterns of change. A basic assumption is that, in order to understand how language changes are adopted by communities, we must also take account of patterns of resistance to change.

In his study of Harlem street-gangs and subsequently in Philadelphia, Labov (1972a; Labov and Harris, 1986) used typically ingenious methods to measure personal relationships, which are similar to (and indeed a precursor of) social network analysis. The main difference from social network analysis is that Labov's studies are of bounded groups, whereas social networks are in principle open-ended and anchored on the individual. Furthermore, Labov's research agenda does not specifically refer to a maintenance/change hypothesis and is not primarily concerned with accounting for language maintenance.

The Belfast research operationalized the network analysis by using a number of indicators of the network strength of individual speakers, which are based on the notions of *density* and *multiplexity*. A maximally dense network is one in which everyone knows everyone else, and a multiplex relationship is one in which A interacts with B in more than one capacity (for example, as workmate and friend). Statistical analysis suggested that the network variable was capable of accounting for certain patterns of linguistic variation, and further that the network variable interacted with the variables of gender and age. Extensive discussions of the use of statistical analysis in sociolinguistics are provided by Fasold (1984) and L. Milroy (1987b).

Quantitative social network analysis has been used in other urban monolingual situations, notably by Bortoni-Ricardo (1985) in Brazil. Here the method was successful in revealing patterns of adaptation to the urban dialect by rural migrants. Other examples of sociolinguistic applications of network analysis are Schmidt (1985: Australian Aboriginal adolescents), Lippi-Green (1989: an Alpine rural community in Austria), V. Edwards (1986: black adolescents in England), and W. Edwards (1990: black Detroit speakers). A network-based approach is also very suitable for analyzing situations of bilingualism, language contact, and language shift. The classic network-based study of language shift is Gal (1979: Hungarian/German-speaking peasant workers in Austria). More recently the method has been used to study language use and language shift in the Newcastle Chinese community (see Li, Milroy, and Pong, 1992; Li, 1994). Attempts have also been made to project the idea of social network on to past states of language (Van der Wurff, 1990). Whereas the maintenance/change model provides a framework in which past language changes may be discussed in an illuminating way, it is dubious whether the social networks of individuals who are no longer accessible to systematic observation can be adequately reconstructed.

Social network and social class

Social network and social class represent different orders of generalization about social organization. Class accounts for the hierarchical structure of society (arising from inequalities of wealth and power), whereas network deals with the dimension of solidarity at the level of the individual and his or her everyday contacts. An attempt has been made to link the two concepts together in a sociolinguistic model by using the notion of *weak* network ties (Milroy and Milroy, 1992).

It is evident that close-knit solidarity ties are characteristic of lower and higher social groups, and that, in the middle sectors of society, social network density and multiplexity tend to be weak. A process model of social class, such as Thomas Højrup's theory of *life-modes*, suggests that different kinds of social network structure do not occur accidentally, but "fall out" naturally from different life-modes, such as those of the self-employed, of wage-earners (both poor and relatively affluent), and of professionals. A high proportion of close-knit ties on the one hand, and of loose-knit ties on the other are consequent upon the life-modes which themselves are constitutive of distinct classes. In this way, different kinds of social network can be linked to the wider organization of society, and it is suggested that these links can be explicated by considering the properties of weak as well as strong ties (for details, see Milroy and Milroy, 1992).

8 The Sociolinguistic Variable

Critics of sociolinguistics have had much to say about the social variables discussed above, but much less about the idea of the linguistic variable. This is a relatively old concept in linguistics, most familiar in the idea of the *phoneme*, which typically manifests itself in the form of variants known as allophones. The sociolinguistic variable is also manifested in the form of variants. It differs from the phoneme, however, in that the focus is on social variation rather than exclusively on intra-linguistic variation. Thus the range of a sociolinguistic variable does not normally correspond to that of a phoneme, as different social values may be attached to different patterns within a given phoneme and may overlap with different phonemes. The nonidentity of the sociolinguistic variable with the phoneme is not always sufficiently emphasized by investigators.

In the foregoing it has been assumed, without comment, that sociolinguistic variables are usually phonological elements. In practice, this has often been so, but the principle underlying the method is more general than this. What is important is that variants of a variable should demonstrably be variants of the same underlying linguistic element. At higher levels of linguistic organization (particularly syntax) it is difficult to meet this condition, as it is often not clear that two syntactic variants (for example, active and passive sentence forms) have the same meaning and distribution in the language system. This difficulty is discussed by (among others) Romaine (1984), Lavandera (1978), L. Milroy (1987b). It is less often pointed out that comparable problems may also emerge at very particularistic levels of subphonemic organization. For example, in British English, the glottal stop (for /t/) occurs in different positions within words: medial, final, and in some dialects syllable-initially. However, not only does the likelihood of the glottal stop differ in these different positions; the variants that it alternates with may also differ in the different positions. Furthermore, the social meaning attached by the community to these variants may also vary according to where they occur in words or syllables. Therefore a correct quantitative statement depends on isolating environments in which we can be sure that we are dealing with variants of the same sociolinguistic phenomenon. If therefore we regard glottalization as a "variable," we must acknowledge that it is a complex variable that contains a number of subvariables within it, and it is possible that these subvariables will display different (even contrasting) patterns.

This problem of the correct input to the variable has not been widely discussed in the literature. It seems to be most prominent in what have been called "divergent dialect" studies, where the range of variation encountered is very large (for a discussion see J. Milroy, 1992: 68–75). It also happens in these studies that some salient variables do not occur frequently enough for quantification throughout the whole range (for treatment of such a variable see Milroy and Harris, 1980). It should also be noted that for reasons of time (and probably also in principle) investigators cannot quantify all the variation that exists in a speech community. Selection of representative variables depends on the skill of the investigators, and nonquantitative description is also necessary for a reasonably comprehensive account.

In the final section, we are concerned with the relevance of variation studies to our conception of what constitutes a language, a dialect, or a variety.

9 Languages and Dialects as Physical Entities

As we have noted, variation studies have led scholars to question the definition of "a language" and what kind of object a language is. Linguists have generally relied on a working assumption that there exists a structured and stable entity which we can call a language or a dialect of a language. This can be accessed or described in internal structural terms, e.g., as having a "phonology," "grammar," and "lexis," without reference to society – i.e., independently of the speakers who use it in their speech communities. As noted above (see section 1), it has also been usual to treat this entity as having an invariant underlying structure. Social dialectology has called into question the discreteness of these entities that we call languages, and seeks to contribute to a clearer understanding of what we actually mean when we say that we are describing a "language." In order to characterize a "language" or any quasi-discrete variety of a language, we need to invoke sociopolitical ·criteria in addition to structural linguistic criteria.

Sociolinguists (e.g., Downes, 1984; Chambers and Trudgill, 1980) commonly point out that boundaries between languages cannot be wholly determined in terms of structural difference or mutual (in)comprehensibility. Several Scandinavian languages, for example, are mutually comprehensible to a great extent and some dialects of English are not readily comprehensible to speakers of other dialects. There are many areas of the world in which variability within and between languages is very great, and some situations in which speakers may not be entirely certain as to which language they are speaking (see Grace, 1990, 1992, for comments on blurring of distinctions between certain Melanesian languages in speaker usage). Similarly, there are many situations in which two or more languages are mixed. Finally, there are rapidly changing situations, especially in the genesis and development of pidgin and creole languages, in which younger generations may use markedly different varieties of the language from those of older speakers.

From a variationist point of view, a language is a dynamic phenomenon. It is appropriate to liken languages to relatively fluid and variable physical states, and to use process models rather than product or static models in describing them.

It can be suggested that discreteness of individual *languages* is not inherent in the nature of *language* as a structural phenomenon: This apparent discreteness is socially or sociopolitically imposed. French is a "language" not merely because it has a linguistic structure that differentiates it from other languages and which is peculiarly "French," but also because its structures are recognized, prescribed, imposed, and agreed within a particular nation-state (and certain other areas formerly influenced by this nation-state). Separateness of languages is therefore largely the result of social and political processes, and among these processes language standardization is particularly important. Our tendency to think of languages as discrete phenomena is partly conditioned by the existence of standard languages, such as standard English and standard French.

This lack of discreteness in real language states is an important matter in the study of the histories of languages. In studies of language change, there are many examples of the tendency to regard a language as a physical entity. Yet it never seems to have been possible to specify *purely in terms of language structure* the precise point in history at which one language "became" another language. Therefore, just as it is difficult to specify discreteness of languages in space, so it is also difficult to differentiate them in time. The point in history at which one language becomes another may have more to do with political history than with linguistic differentiation.

A final point, which arises from the above discussion, is that variation studies have in many ways blurred the Saussurean distinction between synchronic and diachronic linguistics. Mesthrie (1992) has coined the useful term "panchronic" to describe such an orientation. As sociolinguists study speech communities at a single point in time, their analytic work is primarily synchronic, and their quantitative statements are synchronic statements. However, the paradigm has subtly altered the relationship between historical and other forms of linguistics, in that variation in time is grouped together with variation in space and social space as one aspect of linguistic variation. Similarly, as we have noted, process models of language in society have begun to have some impact. It is clear, however, that insofar as it is concerned with linguistic change, Labov (1994) considers the theoretical content of his work to be chiefly a contribution to historical linguistics. While this is certainly Labov's theoretical position, it is not necessarily a view shared by all sociolinguists. Equally important, as we have tried to show, is the development of an integrated account of variation encompassing not only dimensions of time and geographical space, but the various dimensions of social space, such as gender, generation, status, and network structure, discussed in earlier sections of this article.

4 Language Change in Progress: Variation as it Happens

NORMAN DENISON

Involvement with plurilingual and plurilectal communities, which may or may not be shorter or longer phases of language shift in progress, leads one to question an entire range of metaphors and seemingly self-evident concepts at the center of linguistics. Among these one might mention the very notion of "a language" as a self-contained and presumably homogeneous system of rules, a code "où tout se tient," the concept of a "native speaker" together with "native speaker competence" around which so much revolves in axiomatic models of linguistic description and explication. Dialectologists and those who work on the diachronic dimension of language have long been aware of the difficulties involved in trying to establish firm categories and boundaries in time and in synchronic structure to distinguish between one language (variety) and another or between adjacent diachronic "états de langue." Most boundaries of this kind turn out to be shifting and interpenetrable, and the same applies to the dividing lines between language (variety) internal structural categories.

A moment's reflection suffices to convince one that things could indeed not be different, otherwise languages would be unchanging and in principle unchangeable expressions of unchanging semantic content, incapable of adapting to shifting realities, communicational needs, and innovations. Nevertheless, the homogeneous rule-governed code metaphor seems to be not merely a theoretical fiction but an important psychological and social need, which contributes to the way in which speakers orient and define themselves, their community, their ethnicity, even their individual and group sense of identity, and it has a homogenizing, sharpening, and "focusing" (Le Page and

Tabouret-Keller, 1985) feedback effect on languages and their communicational efficiency. However, in order to account for the way language actually
functions (and changes) in plurilingual communities we need to set alongside
the code metaphor an equally relevant metaphor, which, together with its
initiator J. J. Gumperz (for a recent brief account of the term's implications see
Gumperz, 1990: 33–4) we call the *repertoire* view of language. This perspective
turns out to be no less relevant for variety identification, functioning, and
change in allegedly monolingual communities.

   We can begin by observing that no language is completely homogeneous or
monosystemic (as was already obvious to Schuchardt (1884: 1ff.)), and that
coexisting subsystems sometimes conflict with each other, imposing on
speakers the necessity to choose. If many speakers habitually make the
same choice in a particular instance and situation, this leads to the elimination
or marginalization of the unsuccessful alternative(s), that is, to change. The
degree of arbitrariness inevitable in such developments (if we compare one
instance with another) restores a modicum of heterogeneity to a balance
disturbed in the direction of homogeneity by each individual instance in
which *Systemzwang* (that is, the analogical force of one partial subsystem
upon another) prevails. Hence a minor process which at one time produced singular and plural pairs in English of the type wife:wives,
leaf:leaves, leads, under the "invariable singular stem" analogy of the type
dove:doves, price:prices, prize:prizes, to the heterogeneity introduced by
staff[1]:staves/staffs; staff[2]:staffs; stave:staves; roof:roofs/rooves and the like.
Once heterogeneity of this kind arises in a language there is no way of
predicting what its ultimate semantic fate may be. All kinds of unsatisfied
needs or emerging potential for distinctiveness in the content may be lurking
in the wings, waiting to latch on to any spare capacity which chance developments or reassessment of existing possibilities may throw up on the expression side of the linguistic repertoire. The following list is an attempt to illustrate
the kinds of distinctiveness to which perceptible differences in the expression
resources of a linguistic repertoire may in principle correspond. (It is important to remember that the "same" item of difference in linguistic substance
(e.g., in the phonetics) may have quite diverse functions from one language
community to another.)

No discernible semantic distinctiveness

1   No semantic distinctiveness of any kind is perceptible (an extreme case),
even where general structural considerations provide a framework, as in
English *either*, in which the stressed vowel shows free variation (/-iː-/ or
/-aɪ-/) at the lexical level, even though at the phonological level distinctiveness is present; likewise in *neither*. Note that the free variation applies even
within many idiolects (including the writer's), though caution suggests that in
the absence of pertinent statistics it might be wiser to speak of "apparent free
variation."

For reasons which will become apparent we will postpone discussion of categories 2 and 3 until after presentation of category 4, which follows.

Distinctiveness in basic semantics

4 The other extreme case is one in which a differentiation in *basic semantics* is triggered by distinctiveness on the expression side. This seems to be a much more frequent outcome of change in expression substance than the seemingly total absence of semantic consequences illustrated in 1. The semantics involved may be located in the lexis, the morphology, or elsewhere, as the following examples will illustrate. (a) The *lexical* opposition between "staff"[1] and "staff"[2] on the one hand and the new singular "stave," a back-formation from the form "staves", plural of "staff"[1]. (b) The semantic divergence between "staff"[1] and "staff"[2] henceforth marked by the availability of the form "staves" (with register distinction) alongside "staffs" as an alternative plural of "staff,"[1] but not for "staff"[2] (e.g., "military staff," "school staff"). (c) The (morphological) refunctioning of umlaut as the (sole) signal of plurality in, for example, English *foot/feet*, umlaut being in origin a chance consequence of vowel harmony. This is of course a classic case. Less well known, but perhaps more remarkable, is the reallocation of the diminutive suffixes (earlier: infixes) -*in* and -*it* in the Italian dialect of Ascona to the singular/plural distinction, after it had disappeared from most substantives as a result of the loss of final vowels, hence e.g. *üselin* – It. *uccell(in)o*, "(little) bird," *üselit* – It. *uccell(ett)i*, "(little) birds." To allow ourselves once more a thoroughly anthropomorphic comparison, our examples under (c) are powerfully suggestive of acts of piracy by a heavyweight linguistic substructure (number), faced with a loss of territory, to make good its losses at the expense of any lightweight phenomena (phonetic assimilation without a semantic function, near-synonymous diminutive formations) unfortunate enough to come its way. It is one of our aims to contribute, however modestly, to the demystification of such seemingly humanoid behavior on the part of language as a communication system most often described as code-like (hence prompting static images).

The remaining types of potentially distinctive differences in linguistic substance we may notionally situate between the two extremes illustrated by 1 (no discernible semantic distinctiveness) and 4 (distinctiveness in basic semantics): Category 2 involves a distinctive marking of one or more *speakers* or groups of speakers, category 3 affords sociosemantic distinctiveness of a *diatypic* ("stylistic") nature for the community as a whole.

Identificational distinctiveness between speakers and groups

2 Distinctiveness of this kind performs an *identificational* function in respect of (a) *single speakers* not constituting a communicational network (lisping, Churchillian sibilants in English, *idiolectal* selection (or an atypical frequency) of lexical items, for instance), (b) families, and (c) larger groups of speakers on

a primarily *territorial* basis (*dialects, regional accents*), or on a social or ethnic basis (*sociolects, social* or *ethnic accents*).

Sociosemantic distinctiveness

3 This category of distinctiveness shares the social aspect of differentiation with the sociolectal marking mentioned in 2 above, but it serves the community as a whole, not merely some part of it, to mark (and in part to define or constitute) situational categories of cultural relevance ("domains") through the selection of appropriate language varieties (*registers, diatypes*). These are conventional, but susceptible to gradual change by negotiation rather than static. Shifting conventions and individual or group nonconformism in the use of the *du/Sie* dichotomy in German provide an example of the principle involved. For a discussion of "diatypic" distinctiveness and the means by which it is typically realized see Denison, 1968.

The greatest advantage of the linguistic metaphors which give us the "deep/surface" dichotomy and the "expression/content" dichotomy is that they provide us with an insight into the dynamic (thus, ultimately, also diachronic) instability of the relationships between the two levels. This means that in any repertoire the function of linguistic substance and structure can slip, slide, jump, not only from item to item of the "content" within each of our four categories, but also from category to category. To some extent the ultimate explanations and detailed mechanisms of such processes are as yet lacking, but there can be little doubt that changing degrees of heterogeneity of linguistic substance have a triggering effect on both basic semantic and sociosemantic developments. In both types of change the destinies and changing needs of linguistic communities, involving different degrees of exposure to and contact with other communities (that is, speakers), are crucial. Therefore investigation of language change must remain incomplete so long as the study of system-internal forces is not supplemented by the consideration of speakers, that is, by sociolinguistic study in the widest sense (as Labov, for example, 1966, was perhaps the first fully to appreciate and embark upon).

For this writer too, a sociolinguistic approach to language and change in language involves constantly re-establishing in the mind the connection between language and speakers via language in use. This can be achieved by observations ranging from the global to the idiolectal. For practical purposes there are some obvious advantages in having available a relatively self-contained linguistic community of a size – say 500 speakers maximum – which makes individual acquaintance with a fair proportion of the total population feasible, given a generous observational time-scale (of decades rather than hours or days). A kind destiny provided the writer with just such an opportunity when he was introduced in 1962 to the village of Sauris, (then) a trilingual community, in the Carnian Alps of Friuli, northeast Italy. The visits and sojourns which ensued led to a series of papers published in various contexts, some to be drawn on in the following pages, but more important, they contributed to the views on language in general of this author to an extent not foreseeable at the outset, given the small size and apparent atypicality of the community. Now that (for various reasons) a stocktaking and codificational phase has been embarked upon (a dictionary of Sauris German is in preparation), it is perhaps appropriate to attempt to make these views more explicit.

First of all it will be necessary to sketch out briefly the relevant facts and assumptions concerning the Sauris linguistic community. From a combination of linguistic and (scant) documentary evidence (see Lessiak, 1959; Lorenzoni, 1938; Kranzmayer, 1956, 1960, 1981; Hornung, 1960, 1964, 1972, 1984; Denison, 1990) it is fairly certain that Sauris represents a late thirteenth-century migration of a small group of speakers of S Bavarian German dialect(s) from the area of the easternmost Tirolean and/or the westernmost Carinthian Lesach (roughly, the vicinity of Upper and Lower Tilliach, Kartitsch, Maria Luggau) to the uppermost basin – until then devoid of year-round human habitation – of the Lumiei, a northern tributary of the Tagliamento, which it enters after a precipitous descent through a narrow gorge, at Ampezzo Carnico. For almost seven centuries, from the establishment of the Sauris enclave until the completion of the road link with Ampezzo in the middle of the present century, contacts with the surrounding Friulian-speaking region and the wider (Veneto-speaking, then Italian-speaking) network remained extremely laborious and hazardous. The same held good, to an even greater degree, of traffic over the high mountain mule-track passes to the north with Carinthia and Tirol and the wider German-speaking world beyond. It was not until the end of the last century that men from Sauris joined the swelling seasonal migrations from Carnia northwards in pursuit of work opportunities.

Nevertheless, some trade and traffic with the nearest Romance vicinity was necessary from the earliest times. Sauris German has integrated Friulian loan material of all periods which reflects these contacts, and there is evidence in family names and vulgo names (traditional house names) of a relatively small but constant immigration into the community from the Carnian environs. Administrative records (of land and property ownership and transactions, for example), after the Latin of the earliest documents, were already in (Veneto-) Italian in the early eighteenth century (and probably much earlier, though a fire in the parish archives destroyed earlier records). By the early 1960s virtually all Sauris-born adults were orally trilingual (more precisely, triglossic) in Sauris German, Friulian, and Italian, and literate in Italian (see Denison, 1971, for details). Alongside Sauris German, the functions of which were restricted almost entirely to village-internal communication, Friulian and Italian had well-established community-internal functions in addition to their use in external transactions. Italian was and is the language of obligatory school education and of the more recently established kindergarten; it had replaced German (until relatively recently alongside Latin) in the church by the beginning of the present century, when a tradition of appointing priests from Sauris or from the related German linguistic island of Sappada (Pladen) came to an end. Friulian was in oral use in Sauris earlier than Italian, and showed signs of ousting Sauris German from some sections of the parish and the community (Denison, 1971: 168ff.) before it in turn began to lose ground rapidly to Italian.

Thirty years ago parents (and other adults) in Sauris were beginning to conform to a general, now global trend to acculturate their children from birth (to the best of their ability) to the mainstream culture via the mainstream language (variety). This took place at the expense of the non-mainstream elements in the linguistic (and, less obviously, cultural) heritage hitherto transmitted from generation to generation. In Sauris the present outcome is that active triglossia has become rare among those under thirty years of age, having been replaced (apart from some *passive* competence in Sauris German and/or – less commonly – Friulian) by Italian monoglossia for all practical purposes. Active triglossic competence is now best represented by those over 70, and a not inconsiderable amount of idiomatic, syntactical, and lexical structure characteristic of the Sauris German strand of the repertoire is best conserved by a surviving handful of octogenarians. It is not the universal phenomenon of linguistic change and renewal which is remarkable here, but the acceleration marking the approaching end of a process of language shift initiated more than seven centuries ago. The interest for linguistics and socio-linguistics of such processes has been documented by publications such as Dressler and Wodak-Leodolter, 1977; Denison, 1977, 1980, 1992a; Dorian, 1981, 1988; Denison and Tragut, 1990, involving the use of anthropomorphic metaphors like "language death" (see chapters 15 and 16).

From what has been said above it might be assumed that the S Bavarian linguistic repertoire the first settlers brought with them was rather homogeneous and lacking in evidence of (earlier) wider geographical contacts and social networks. The contrary is true. Comparison of Sauris German with historically closely related dialects, two of them represented by the "sister" linguistic islands of Sappada/Pladen (see Hornung, 1972) and Zarz-Deutsch Rut in Slovenia (see Lessiak, 1959; Kranzmayer and Lessiak, 1983), the latter extinct since World War II, and with the variety of SE German in use for wider communication at the time of migration in the thirteenth century, reveals a surprising amount of (already well-integrated) heterogeneity in the German of the earliest settlers, despite their point of departure, a rural Alpine area remote from the urban centers of the time. It does not suggest a static, uniform state of affairs with regard to language.

In the thirteenth century much of the spatial and historical diversification which characterized the local dialects and distinguished M(iddle) H(igh) G(erman) from E(arly) N(ew) H(igh) G(erman) forms was still in progress or had only recently been completed. There were S German, Bavarian, S Bavarian and local vowel changes, together with an adjustment to the S Bavarian velar plosive series, which left it (unlike more northerly German varieties) with a symmetrical plosive structure (voiced, voiceless, voiceless affricated: /g/,

/k/, /kx/) in the velar area as well as in the more forward articulation areas (/d/, /t/, /ts/; /b/, /p/, /pf/). Lexis, morphology, syntax, semantics, and idiom were of course also no less fluid at that period than at any other time. Linguistic influence from other varieties of German, Western Romance (Old French), the Romance south, and to a lesser extent from the Slavic east, made itself felt, and this can be most conveniently exemplified by lexical and morphological loans, since these are often phonetically marked as such (in a historical sense, for the linguist, though not for present-day speakers; for details see Denison, 1992a).

The following items were in all likelihood imported into pre-Saurian German from more prestigious varieties of wider currency, in particular from a S German trading and administrative variety based on urban speech, ultimately derived mainly from Vienna, but also from the language of the church and the military: ['tʃölʃɔft] – "Gesellschaft," "society, company"; ['untsöliç] – etym. "ungesellig" (etym. "asocial"), "lean, gaunt"; ['pfɛtərle] – "Pate," "godparent"; [ʃmɪərn] – "schlagen" (Vienn. "schmieren"), "to hit, to beat" (alongside "native" ['ʃmurbm] – "schmieren, einfetten," "to grease"); ['draksln] – "zu Boden werfen" (Ringkampf), "to throw in wrestling" (alongside "native" ['draʃln] – "drechseln, to use a lathe"); ['aufpasn] – "aufpassen," "watch out, listen, pay attention" (alongside "native" ['aufliːzn] – "listen, pay attention"); via the church ['haɪlıç] – "heilig," "holy"; [vlaɪʃ] – "Fleisch," "meat," "flesh"; [gaɪʃt] – (etym. "Geist") "courage"; (['gaɪʃtıç] – "tapfer," "courageous"); ['khaufmɔn] – "Kaufmann", "businessman, trader" (alongside "native" [khaːfn] – "kaufen," "to buy"). There are precise or close correspondences to these examples of "internal loans" from pre-Saurian times in related S Bavarian dialects, including the "sister" linguistic islands, and most are similarly phonetically marked (for the initiated).

The consequences in terms of the ultimate semantic distinctiveness or otherwise of linguistic substance thus imported from outside are to some degree a matter of chance. Hence the Sauris word [vlaɪʃ] – "meat, flesh," which owes its divergent historical phonetic shape to its being imported (together with its sacramental connotations) along with [gaɪʃt] and ['haɪlıç] (Kluge, s.v. Fleisch), having ousted without trace the secular "native" form *[vlaːʃ], has taken over the everyday register connotations which that form had, together with the sacramental connotations it would doubtless otherwise have marginally assumed, had it not been ousted. Net semantic difference: zero (our category 1). [gaɪʃtıç] underwent a basic semantic shift (our category 4) after importation, a shift which also gave it more mundane register connotations (sociosemantic shift, our category 3), but this seems to have had nothing to do with its imported status. ['haɪlıç] provided a near synonym for "native" ['baɪe] – "weih-," "sanctified," and its imported phonetics served to emphasize its basic semantic and sociosemantic distinctness from "native" [haːl] – "not/no longer injured; healthy" (our categories 3 and 4) in an additional way not available to standard German "heil" versus "heilig"; but whether this makes the bridge between the basic semantics (our category 4) of "heil" and "heilig" more available to standard German speakers than any connection between [haːl] and ['haɪlɪç] for speakers of Sauris German, is a moot point (compare English "whole," "hale," and "holy").

Wider network German was in MHG and ENHG times (as it is today) clearly a source not only of higher register linguistic imports, but also of slangy metaphorical usage for rural communities. Thus pre-Saurian German imported ['pfɪfɪç], which already had the meaning and connotation of modern German "pfiffig" – "cheeky, smart," [khaɪln] – "to punch, beat up," ['khɪtslɪç] – "oversensitive," ['khaɪçe] – "jail," ['ʃmɪərn] – "to hit" (see above), ['ʃpɪnən] – "spinnen," "to spin," also "to act in a crazy fashion." Loans from other outside sources also contributed to this sociosemantic reservoir of "slangy" terms (see e.g., [pʊkl] and [tʊʃn] below), but there are similar instances in which we have no formal grounds for deciding whether the metaphor is local, universal, or loaned: [drɛʃn] – "(Korn)dreschen, (einen Menschen) dreschen," "to thrash (corn, a person)," [mɪltsn] – "(lit. die Milz eines Menschen) drücken," "to squeeze (lit. someone's spleen)."

We may nevertheless point to the general effect of imported forms in Sauris German, which is that of a relatively high frequency of terms without direct motivation in the rest of the lexis. ['khɪtslɪç], for instance, ties up elsewhere in German with the verb *kitzeln* – "to tickle," but the Sauris verb is ['guːtsln], from which ['khɪtslɪç] is clearly not directly derived. Likewise, ['khaɪçe] – "jail" suggests the verb *keuchen, keichen* "to pant for lack of air in the lungs," which does not occur in Sauris German (the local verb being ['hoʊxatsn]); [khaɪln] – "to punch, beat up" is a metaphorical derivative of *Keil* – "wedge," which does not occur in Sauris German (where the corresponding substantive is ['beɪke] (<MHG *wegge*) – "wedge"), ['beɪbar] – "Weber," "weaver" lacks in Sauris German the etymologically corresponding verb ("weben" in standard German, "to weave"), this activity being expressed by the form ['bʊrkhn] (in Sauris di Sopra and Velt ['börkhn]), corresponding etymologically to standard German "wirken" (and similarly in Pladen/Sappada and elsewhere in S Bavarian). This lack of internal motivation thus applies to outside lexis from closely related (i.e., in this case, German) sources as well as to loan material from "foreign" varieties, though these latter cases are of course potentially much more marked in their linguistic substance.

Turning now to these pre-Saurian imports from "foreign" varieties, we note that Sauris German shares with Bavarian in general a small number of Slavonic lexical loans, mainly from contacts with early Slovene beginning as far back as the eighth century. Examples (see Kranzmayer, 1956, Hornung, 1964) are ['jauzn] – "midday meal," [deːtsn] – "pair of shafts for cart or sleigh," ['khoʊmat] – "collar for draught animal," ['kaɪʃe] – "shack," ['klɪtʃ] – "compartment, usually in cellar or stall, for potatoes or similar," ['ɛa-] in ['ɛabɪnt] – "warm wind in winter" – a later and more local loan from the same stem *jug – with its derivative *juzn – "south, southerly, midday" as ['jauzn] above, [baɪdn] – the Sauris German (and, in general, older German) name Weiden for Udine, capital of Friuli Province in NE Italy (<Slovene Viden); furthermore,

probably the verbs ['tʃuːdln] – "to drizzle" and ['tʃuːtrn] – "to go courting," together with ['tʃuːtrle] – "small boy" and ['tʃuːtrlɪəxtle] – "oil-lamp carried by young men at night en route to visit their girlfriends." Apart from the everyday rural and local semantics of this group, the only noteworthy feature it exhibits is the presence of two phonemes typical of loans: /k/ and /tʃ/.

Relatively little of the Western Romance (Old French) influence on medieval German worked its way through to the southeastern limits of the German-speaking area prior to the settlement of the linguistic islands (including Sauris). We have already mentioned ['pʊkl] – "Buckel," "hump" (deprecatingly) "back," and ['tʊʃn] – "slap," "strike, producing a bang, a noise." The first is from Old French *boucle* – "shield-boss" (see Kluge s.v. Buckel), the second also most likely from Old French, compare *toucher*, rather than by independent onomatopoeia (see Kluge s.v. Tusch). Further lexical loans from Old French are [praɪs] – "price, cost," [vaɪn] – "fine" (only adverbially, meaning "extremely"), [ɪn vaːl] – "*en faille*," with derivatives ['vaːln] – "to make a mistake," ['vaːlar] – "mistake," [vlöɪte] – etym. < *fleute* (OF), "accordion," [vlöɪtn] – "to play the accordion or any other musical instrument," [tɔnts] – "dance," [tɔntsn] – "to dance." All of these loans have a wider currency in the German-speaking area and most of them had fashionable connotations at the time of their entry into MHG round about 1200.

It is rather remarkable in the light of the relatively small number of lexical loans from Western Romance which reached the S Bavarian varieties of German, that at least three morphological loans in Sauris German are of Old French origin, namely the infinitive infix [-'ɪər-] borrowed from the Old French infinitive suffix, the double suffix [-a'raɪ] < Old French *-erie* and the Old French suffix *-ley* – originally the word *ley* < Latin *legem* (see Kluge s.v. -lei) "sort, kind" borrowed by Sauris German in the forms *-la, -las, -na, -nas*. Of these, the first two retained suffixal stress in German, thereby introducing a new prosodic stress scheme into the language for the first time, German having shifted the stress of earlier loans forward where necessary, to conform to the traditional Germanic stress pattern. Here again, it is strange that such a significant change was effected, even though the small number of lexical items involved with the suffixes and the rather low frequency of occurrence of the original items would not have led one to predict their potential for structural change.

To begin with the suffix which was of least consequence: The Sauris equivalent of standard German *-lei* was, in Sauris as elsewhere, relevant to only a very few lexical items, e.g. ['khaɪndrla] – "keinerlei," "no kind of," ['ɔldrla] "allerlei," "of every kind"; moreover it was unstressed, which was not only without consequence for the traditional stress structure of Sauris German (main stress on the stem syllable except in separable compound verbs and their derivatives), but also led to alternative assimilated and declined forms of ['ɔldrla]: ['ɔldrnan] (acc. sing. masc.), ['ɔldrlas/ɔldrnas] – "Allerlei-es."

However, the double suffix [-a'raɪ] – *-erei* < Old French *-erie*, and the verbal infinitive suffix (< German infix) [-'ɪər] – both represented new stress models and both became and remained productive in Sauris German. [-a'raɪ] added a basic semantic content, a sociosemantic (deprecatory) connotation and a new nuance to the resources for forming deverbal nouns with certain verb-like features (in this case, duration or extension) to the "native" means already used in nominalizations, e.g., [-at]/[-ɪkhat], [-ɪge], [-ax], plus those imported via lexical items from wider network German, e.g., [-haɪt], [-ʊŋkh], [-mas/-mʊs]. After the model of, e.g., [trɪŋkhaˈraɪ] – "boozing," [viˑlaˈraɪ] – "gluttony," [khrɪəgaˈraɪ] – "quarreling," [varvɪərəˈraɪ] – "enticement," we note newer formations like [vɔkhaˈraɪ] – "(the result of) swinish behavior" (< [vɔkhe] – "pig, swine"), [ʃkuːʃaˈraɪ] "(the result of) scaling off, flaking off" (<[ʃkuːʃa] – "shell, scale, flake" < Friul.).

Together with all the "foreign" loan material hitherto considered, the compound infinitive suffix [-ˈɪərn], composed of Old French *-ier* + German *-en*, might even more legitimately have been dealt with under the notion of "wider network German" influence, since it certainly reached the "Pre-Saurians" via intervening German-speaking territory. It is only in this way that we can understand that apparently not a single genuine French verb with its infinitive suffix directly reached the "Pre-Saurians" before their migration.

Of the *three* Sauris German verbs which can with relative certainty be said to have this French suffix, two have stems from Late Latin ([prʊˈbɪərn] – "to try," commoner form [proˈveːrn] < Friul./It.; and [prʊˈgɪərn] – "to purge, to squeeze out liquid from cheese," alternative form [prʊˈgeːrn] < Friul.). The third verb stem is without a doubt German, and is probably an old import from German hunting terminology, now part of general usage in both Sauris and standard German: [hɔlˈbɪərn] – "halbieren," originally perhaps "to split the spoils of the hunt two ways," now "to halve," "to share equally between two persons." In spite of the paucity of items in Sauris German with this Old French stressed form of the Romance infinitive suffix type, it seems to have represented the initial structural breakthrough which set the pattern for the South Romance infinitive suffixes in Sauris German which followed upon the settlement. Ever since, these have provided the chief morphological device for the easy access of speakers of this German dialect to Friulian and Italian verbs, whether for sporadic switching or for borrowing and integrating purposes. The suffixes are: [-ˈeːrn] for S Romance verbs whose infinitive suffixes derive from (Latin) forms in *-are, *-ere and *ēre; and [-iːrn] (n.b. *not* [-ɪərn]) for *-ire verbs. The use of [-ˈeːrn] for the *-are conjugation (elsewhere in linguistic island German one finds [-ˈaːrn] for *-are) has interesting implications for the historical phonology of certain Romance dialects in northern Italy and the geography of pre-Saurian contacts with them.

For the sake of completeness it should be mentioned that some verbal loans from S Romance do have the simple German infinitive suffix in *-(e)n*. For the most part they are of early date (pre-settlement or immediately post-settlement), e.g. [vɔntsn] – "to be left over" (compare It. *avanzare*, Friul. *vanzâ*), or of onomatopoeic origin, like [tsaˈʃklɔpfn] – "to explode" (compare Friul. *sclopâ*, It. *scoppiare*), or they are Sauris German verbal formations based on loaned substantives: [ˈtʃaɪnən] – "to have supper," based on [ˈtʃaɪne] – "supper" < *cena*, rather than directly < *cenare*; or, more recently, [varkhn] – "to run wildly (of cows)" based on the Friul. noun *varc* – "a stride, leap."

It should come as no surprise to discover that, in addition to the loans from Latin of common Germanic and Old High German age, which are part of the common heritage of any German dialect, Sauris German inherited an uninterrupted supply of specifically N Italian loans beginning with the arrival of Bavarian settlers at what was to become (and remain for many centuries) the linguistic frontier area between the German- and S Romance-speaking worlds, which ran from west to east along the mountain peaks to the south of the Pustertal and the Lesachtal. This very roughly valid observation should not, however, lead us to forget the side valleys, like Kals, which remained partly Ladin-speaking to the north of this line until well after the Pre-Saurians left the Lesachtal for the Lumiei valley, or the Gadertal, a side valley on the south side of the German-speaking Pustertal at Bruneck, which remains Ladin-speaking to the present day and is close to the old homeland of the Pre-Saurians. Nor should we forget German-speaking S Tirol to the south of the main watershed of the Alps, or the smaller German settlements like the 7 and 13 Communes in the Veneto (nor indeed the linguistic islands established only a short time later, like Sauris and Sappada).

The pre-settlement S Romance loans in Sauris German and in related Bavarian dialects were a natural consequence of this borderland situation. The breadth and depth of penetration of the loaned material varied, from the whole upper German area (including German Switzerland) to just one or two local S Bavarian dialects. Some idea of their scope can be gained from the flollowing brief selection (for a fuller account see Denison, 1992a: 147–9): [bʊ'teɪge] – "shop," [kɔfr] – "camphor," ['kɔntr] – "cupboard," ['koːpe] (compare It. *capo*) – "rich miser," ['oʊdar] – "notary," [pa'leɪnte] – "polenta," ['pfavln] (<< *favōnius* > German *Föhn*) – "to snow lightly," ['vötse] – "face" (pej.), ['vɪlge] (< *vigilia*) – "eve of feast," "festivity," ['vɪlgŋ] – "to give to collection during church service," ['tsiːgl] – (< *sitella*) – "pail"; only in Sauris, e.g. ['gə'ʃpeɪnst] – (< *dispensa*) – "church dispensation," [neɪŋkh] – "not even," ['miːge] – (< Veneto *amigo/-a*) – "friend," ['pfrɛaʒln] – "to crisp-fry (bacon)." There is good reason to consider all or most of these to be pre-settlement loans. Many of them are broadly datable on the basis of phonetic substitution regularities. Hence initial Latin and Romance /f-/ is represented in the oldest loans by present Sauris German /v-/, subsequently by /pf-/ and in later post-settlement loans by /f-/; Latin /w-/ (> Romance /v-/) in early loans by present Sauris German /b-/, in subsequent loans by /v-/.

When the founding fathers (and mothers) arrived in Sauris in the second half of the thirteenth century, they were hence no strangers to (doubtless direct) contacts with Romance-speaking neighbors. Given the (relative) ease of communication from their old home westwards towards Brixen via the Lesach and Pustertal valleys (for this there is evidence in Sauris children's lore; see Denison, 1990), the move to the upper reaches of the Lumiei must have seemed, before new contacts were built up with Forni di Sopra and Ampezzo Carnico, like an isolation more severe than ever before.

The idea here advanced is that the period immediately following migration was of necessity a phase of relative cultural and social self-reliance and separateness, exactly the kind of conditions under which linguistic consolidation and maximalization of code structures, homogenization of repertoire and rule reorganization can take place. Our thesis is that this was the period when Sauris German had its best chance of becoming a system linguist's language in its own right. In a sense it was similar to what some creolists have maintained happens when a pidgin becomes a creole. Settlers and their idiolects, though apparently all from the same area, seem not to have formed a single community before. As we shall see, some degree of idiolectal and dialectal diversity has indeed persisted up to the present. However, the most far-reaching consequences ensued, not because of the diversity which migrated, but because of the diversity which was left behind, as I tried to show in Denison, 1986, in respect of the phonology. After a general vowel shift which affected dialects (differentially) but left the prestige variety unchanged, plurilectal and pluriglossic speakers in Austria today, after some seven centuries of pretence by the community as a whole that the shift never took place, have psychosocially relocated the once phonemically distinct points of departure as mere register-conditioned variants.

So once again, as at the outset of the shift, in Austria [ʃaːdn] is more likely to be a prestigious realization of *schaden* – "to damage," than a dialectal realization of *scheiden* – "to part, diverge," and [ʃoːdn] is a dialectal or familiar realization of *schaden*. In Sauris, however, [ʃoːdn] is the only possible realization of /ʃoːdn/ – "to damage," [ʃaːdn] being the only possible realization of /ʃaːdn/ – "to part, diverge." In other words, after the separation from prestige variants there was no way back for Sauris German from phonemic distinctiveness to "sociophones." This is an illustration of the simple truth that "the same" is not the same in language, what makes it different being the different psychosocial situations of different communities and individuals.

At the same time as an independent phonology was consolidating itself (with basic semantic consequences) in Sauris, the community's new independence from embedding in the overall German linguistic environment was reflected in changes within the morphosyntactic structure, facilitated – even prompted – by seemingly chance convergences initially in the morphonology. The changes to be illustrated here had their origins in pre-migration times, as comparison with other Bavarian dialects shows, but they were able fully to unfold and achieve "legitimate norm status" only under linguistic island conditions, aided and abetted in due course by convergent influence from Romance.

In standard German, *auf(-)* and *an(-)* have, even in their manifold metaphorical extensions, relatively distinct semantics throughout their functions (adverb, verbal – and secondarily nominal – prefix, preposition). As prepositions, they indicate something like (a) "upon" versus (b) "at, by, in contact with the side of." In basilectal Bavarian, however, the semantics of (a) and part of the area of (b) – "in contact with the side of" – appear to be covered by allophones of the preposition *auf(-)* (the meanings "at, by" being covered by other prepositions like *bei, vor, neben*), while allophones of *an(-)* continue in the functions of adverb and prefix.

This situation is to some extent obscured, not only by intrusions from the standard language, but also by the presence of a dialectal allophone of *auf*, in combination with certain masculine and neuter forms of the definite article, which looks like the corresponding allophone of *an*. Hence Viennese *am Sessel* corresponds to standard German *auf (de)m Stuhl, an (de)m Stuhl* and (for some speakers) also to standard German *auf (de)n Stuhl, an (de)n Stuhl*. That the synchronically underlying morpheme is Viennese *auf* is demonstrated by substituting a feminine noun or the indefinite article. No Viennese speaker says **an der* . . . for standard *auf der* . . . or **[an a:n* . . .] for standard *auf einem* . . . or *auf einen* . . . The probability that *an* is not (or was not) a basilectal Bavarian preposition is further strengthened by correspondences like Bavarian *auf der Wand* = standard *an der Wand*.

Sauris German thus inherited, like the other Bavarian linguistic islands, a set of allophones in this area of preposition plus definite article which was susceptible of further movement, and proceeded to develop and then consolidate a subsystem unique to Sauris, in which the *feminine* definite article singular selects the prepositional allomorph [an-] for no directly obvious phonetic reason, as does the plural definite article (all genders) in the accusative. So in addition to [ame] (masc./neut. singl. dat.) alongside [afn] (masc. sing. acc.) and [af(s) – afs aɪs/af dɔx] (neut. acc.), we have ['ande] (fem. sing. acc.), ['andər] (fem. sing. dat.) and ['ande] (plur. acc. all genders), alongside [afn] (plur. dat. all genders). This integrated morphonological system, in which **[afde] and * [afdər] are impossible sequences, leaves the single uncombined basic form [af] unaffected: [af 'daɪndər 'bi:ze] – "auf deiner Wiese," [af 'daɪna 'bize] – "auf deine Wiese," [af 'daɪna 'bi:zn] – "auf deine Wiesen;" [af 'daɪnn'bi:zn] – "auf deinen Wiesen." Substitution of **[an] for [af] would make the last four sequences ungrammatical.

The single Romance morpheme (It., Friul. *su*) which covers a similar semantic space to the integrated single morpheme of Sauris German obviously constituted support for the unified semantics (though not for the allomorphic complexity) in the developing plurilingualism of the community. Romance influence probably played a decisive part later in the now frequent (though not mandatory) use of the definite article in Sauris German together with the possessive adjectives, though here an originally quite unrelated accident of Sauris phonetic development provided material for a contributory semantic reinterpretation.

In the form [af daɪndər bi:ze] quoted above, it is possible for a plurilingual to re-interpret the second word (actually: "thy + phonetic elision (d) + declensional suffix reflecting the feminine gender of [bi:ze] – "meadow" and its static relationship to the preposition af) as the appropriate dative form of the feminine definite article ([dər]). By an incredible coincidence, all the possessive stem forms end in -*n* or -*r*, both of which, before the common declensional suffix -*(e)r*, insert a transitional -*d*-; and by another coincidence possessive adjectival stem or declensional endings in -*n* and -*me* are homophonous with other bound allomorphs of the definite article paradigm. Therefore [mɪt daɪme hʊnte] is reinterpretable as "with thy (the) dog" (compare [mɪ(t)-me hʊnte] – "with the dog"), ['hɪntər inzərme 'haʊze] as "behind our (the) house" (compare ['hintərme 'haʊze] – "behind the house," ['hɪntər ɪnzərdər 'biːze] – "behind our (the) meadow" – and similarly with ['aɪrdər, 'aɪrme] – "your (the)," ['iːrme, 'iːrdər] – "their (the), her (the)." If we now remember that in MHG the use of the definite article *before* possessive adjectives (as in Italian and Friulian predominantly), though not common, was not unknown, it is not difficult to see how the above syntagmas might be seen as word-order alternatives of Romance-type sequences like ['mɪ(t)me 'daɪn 'hʊnte] – "with the (thy) dog", It. *con il tuo cane* (and Friul. correspondingly). In present-day Sauris German both types, ['mɪ(t)me 'daɪn 'hʊnte] and ['mɪt 'daɪme 'hʊnte] coexist. The general fieldwork ethic of refraining – so far as possible – from interfering with the object of study has prevented direct questioning of informants as to whether they perceive the presence of a definite article in the second variant or not.

Re-analysis in the opposite direction – the extraction and generalization of a nonexistent preposition from a declined (dative) form of the definite article – certainly took place (or was under way) in Bavarian before the Sauris migration and became a regular element of Sauris German nominal syntax. In Sauris and elsewhere in the area of Bavarian settlement (Carinthia, for instance) the MHG sequence *in(dë)me* ("in the" before masculine and neuter nouns) fell together with the prepositionless dative definite article (masculine and neuter) *dëme* in a single form (in Sauris: ['ɪme]); so that a re-analysis of [ar ɔts ɪme zuːne gəzoːt] – *er hat es dem Sohn gesagt* – "he said it to the son" as *er hat es im Sohn gesagt* – "he said it in the son" became possible, and this was generalized (by analogy) to the feminine: Alongside a) [s ɡɛlt ɔt-ar ɪndər khʊrçe geːbm] – "he gave the money in church" we now have b) [s ɡɛlt ɔt-ar ɪndər toʊxtər geːbm] – "he gave the money to the daughter." Here there is no directly *etymological* justification for the first syllable of [ɪndər] as 3rd pers. sing. def. art. fem., but the derivational ambiguity is again present in the plural – all genders – [ɪn], analyzable both as etym. *in* and etym. *in (dë)n* (>* [ɪnː] > [ɪn]). In view of the dialectal Bavarian evidence that this development had its origins in pre-Saurian Bavarian, it is possible to see postsettlement Romance influence in Sauris (in the shape of the prepositional dative with *a* + article in Italian and Friulian) only in the phase of total grammatical institutionalization in Sauris German – whatever the role of Romance may have been in the genesis of Bavarian (see E. and W. Mayerthaler, 1990). But note also the prepositional dative with *zu* in familiar South German *hat er zu mir gesagt* (not however with *geben*!) which, compared with *hat er mir gesagt*, also represents a step in the direction of an analytic case system.

In the period of linguistic consolidation we have been describing, early post-settlement lexical loans from the surrounding Romance area were integrated morphologically, especially in the formation of the plural: ['tsaːre] < Saura (a documented early form of "Sauris"), [pfu·rn] < Forn(i) (these are possibly pre-settlement forms), [aˈrantse(n)] "orange(s)," ['pleːre(n)] – "funnel(s)" (< Carnian Friul. *plera*), ['kaɪse(n)] – "black slug(s)" (< Carn. Friul. *caessa* – "snail slug," fem. of *cai* – "snail"), ['kleːve(n)] – "slope(s)" (< Carn. Friul. *cleva*), ['pa ʃkuˈʃoːdn/pa ʃkuˈʃoːrn] – a house name in Sauris di Sotto, etym. *bei des Kursoren* – "at the Cursor's [house]" (the *cursor(e)* being in former days the official messenger of the village administration), ['vouʃd/'veɪʃe] – "voice(s)" (< Carn. Friul. *vouš*, analogical umlaut in Sauris German plural, as already in "native" items) – and many more similarly integrated loans.

Nevertheless, homogenization tendencies in Sauris German did not by any means eliminate free variation or idiolectal and dialectal variation in the community. In particular, Sauris di Sopra (with Velt) shows dialectal diversity vis-à-vis the other parts of the community, most clearly in the phonology, e.g., S Sopra [-ö-] versus [-ʊ-] elsewhere, before [-r + cons.]: ['khörçe] vs ['khʊrçe] – "church", ['börʃt(le)] vs ['bʊrʃt(le)] – "(small) sausage," [vörbm] vs [vurbm] – "behavior" (but not where lengthening took place: S Sopra as elsewhere ['tu·rn] – "tower," ['pfu·rn] – "Forni"; and not where S Sopra [-ö-] < *[-e-] or *[-o-]: S Sopra and elsewhere ['hörte][1] < MHG *herte* – "hard" (but S Sopra ['hörte][2], elsewhere ['hʊrte] – "(cow-)herd, pastor"), S Sopra and elsewhere [vröʃ] – "frog," [göt] – "Gott," [mös] – "boggy ground." S Sopra [prɛt] – "board," pl. ['preɪtər], S Sotto pl. ['prɛtər], Lateis mostly ['preɪtər]. Territorially less well defined are variants such as ['khoːln/'khɔln] – "to bark," [dərˈziːdər/dərzaɪdər] – "since," ['aʊstiːvln/'aʊsteːvln] – "to panel," [ʃkarˈpöts/garˈʃpöts] – "light shoes of rubber and cloth," ['reɪʃlant/'leɪʃtrant] – "quick, agile," ['ʃleɪbeˈʃlɪrbl ʃlaɪbl (masc./fem.)] – "wooden disc (with holes) through the center of which a stirring stick is inserted into a butter-churn" (etym. = "Schlegelscheibe"), ['tɪʃtruːge/'trɪʃtruːge] – "drawer in a table for cutlery." Lexically: S Sopra ['kheɪmɪç] – "chimney," elsewhere ['liːe], ['ʃtoʊtn/ʃtoʊkhn] – "to congeal (of blood)," and many others, some adverbs having six or seven variants.

Not a few of the alternatives quoted are well documented (and in some cases coexist within small communities) in the old homeland of the Sauris settlers. There are also certain narrowly identificatory historical markers of the Sauris population as a whole (idioms of great age and in some cases of extremely restricted distribution in the old homeland, such as [z ɪst 'groːde 'khemən aˈkhɔtsnʃpoʊr] – "only a slight dusting of snow has fallen," lit. "just a cat- track has come" or [d ɪst net aˈlaːne] – "she is pregnant", lit. "not alone."

The above examples should suffice to show how, in natural languages without written codification or standardization, convergence and divergence follow hard on the heels of each other, go hand in hand, or – better – are often different facets of the same developments. All takes place inside the heads of speakers who are first and foremost responding to the changing circumstances and communicative requirements of their psychological and social environments. So long as the means available and sufficient to meet these requirements still stemmed in the main from the largely (though, as we have seen, by no means exclusively) German linguistic repertoire of the Sauris community, change took place broadly within the confines of that tradition. As soon as Friulian, as a whole additional code, and then Italian, as a huge further (powerfully standardized and codified) linguistic resource moved into the individual and group consciousness of the villagers for internal as well as external use, it was clear that something had to give, and there was no doubt that on all counts outside the (however important) sentimental aspect, it could only be the German dialect. This, unlike the wider network languages, was under no communicatively compelling necessity to reject "interference" in order to remain comprehensible to outsiders (for this had never been its function since the migration), whereas Friulian, and more especially Italian, were subject to precisely such a necessity.

Had "interference" assaulted Sauris German only in its substance, this could perhaps have contained the effects within a differentially affected spectrum of registers, absorbing large amounts of Romance structure and lexis in the "higher" registers and far less in the "lower," that is, the more locally focused registers (family, farming, etc.). English succeeded in this after 1066 in the face of intense Romance pressure and after a subsequently reversed bilingual transition period. Sauris German succeeded, improbably, for centuries, and Denison (1981, 1992a) quotes texts spontaneously recorded and transcribed which document the huge linguistic distance between the most and least familiar registers and the vast amounts of Romance substance and structure incorporated (plus code-switching) in the most affected variants. However, it seems that in Sauris the point of no return on the road to total language shift has been reached now, when, within the space of just three or four decades, Sauris German has all but surrendered the most crucial of its assets for survival: its function as the variety chiefly selected for the acculturation of preschool children (whose numbers have in any case become so reduced that the *biological* survival of the community is in doubt).

It is ironic that at precisely the time when *competence* in Sauris German (in the most rudimentary sense) is threatened, previous diatypic restrictions on its use (for reasons of prestige) no longer inhibit its remaining speakers. It has been introduced on a voluntary experimental basis into school, for instance. Gardner-Chloros, 1991, notes a similar readiness among Alsatian dialect speakers to set aside earlier domain inhibitions at a time when the language is ever less commonly being acquired by today's children. Sadly, the lifting of domain restrictions here too is almost certainly insufficient to offset the acquisition deficit. The resulting competence deficit leads to a drastically decreased awareness in younger speakers of the broad structural and lexical characteristics of the original "native" strand of their pluriglossic inheritance. If we wished to give a meaning to a term like "ethnolinguistic shift," this might be it.

5 Social Factors in Language Change

WILLIAM BRIGHT

Two fundamental facts of language are (a) that it is always changing, in all areas of structure (phonology, grammar, discourse style, semantics, and vocabulary) and (b) that it changes in different ways at diverse places and times. Some societies have made efforts to check the mutability of language; where literacy is present, special efforts have been made to stabilize written languages in particular. Such attempts typically involve *prescriptive grammars*, as well as codified *orthographies* made accessible through authoritative dictionaries; these identify conservative usages, linked with traditional literature and established social values, and they discourage departure from the established norms. In some countries, learned institutions like the Académie Française or the Academia Real de la Lengua Española have been given official responsibility for maintaining the linguistic status quo. In such a literate milieu, the written language is typically held up by educational institutions as a model for the spoken language; and innovative linguistic usages are discouraged in speech as well as writing – such as slang vocabulary (e.g., Eng. *booze* instead of *liquor*), analogical simplification in grammar (*he don't* instead of *he doesn't*), and departure from the orthographic norm in pronunciation (such as the merger of the vowel in *bad* and *bared* with that of *beard* [bɪəd] in some New York City speech). To the extent that such efforts to retard change are effective, they may be said to exemplify socially conditioned *nonchange* of language.

What is more typical, however, is that efforts to control language change have only limited success. Even in written English, which has been subjected to efforts at prescriptive control since the eighteenth century, changes of vocabulary, grammar, and spelling have taken place steadily; this is clear to anyone who now reads novels written in the eighteenth and nineteenth centuries.

In spoken language, prescriptivism is even less effective, and numerous changes can be observed within an individual lifetime. Speakers of English nowadays say and write *ice cream* with no awareness that, in 1900, this form was considered a vulgar error for *iced cream*; they also say, and sometimes write, *ice tea* for *iced tea*, as well as *can peaches* and *smoke fish* for *canned peaches* and *smoked fish*. Phonological changes by which American English *whine* [hwain] merges with *wine* [wain], or *caught* [kɔːt] with *cot* [kat], or *pin* [pɪn] with *pen* [pɛn] – or, indeed, *Mary* ['meiɹi] and *marry* ['mæɹi] with *merry* ['mɛɹi] – are common over broad geographical areas. In Great Britain, by contrast, the merger of *whine/wine* is standard, but the others are rare. Furthermore, such mergers are mostly below the level of awareness, and typically go uncensured by schoolteachers (who are likely to use the same pronunciations themselves).

The fact that language is universally changeable, and that it changes in different ways at different times and places, is of course the basic fact of historical linguistics. This is the reason behind the facts that Modern English is spoken in different ways in London, New York, Cape Town, and Sydney; that Modern English shows many differences from, as well as similarities to, the Old English of King Alfred the Great, with which it is mutually unintelligible; that French and Spanish are mutually unintelligible with each other and with Latin, although the modern languages show systematic correspondences with Latin; and that a more remote level of systematic correspondences involving Old English and Latin – as well as Ancient Greek, Sanskrit and other languages – enables us to relate those languages historically as "sisters" to each other, and as descendants of a prehistoric language that we call Proto-Indo-European.

Types of influence   In view of the above, it is understandable that linguists have wanted to understand the reasons why linguistic change occurs. Certain types of changes – involving a more or less simultaneous effect on large groups of people, up to entire societies – may be called *macrolinguistic*; these involve entire language structures, and often involve deliberate, conscious decisions, institutionally promulgated as part of *language planning* programs. One such process is that of *standardization*, in which a single dialect is put forward as the official norm for an entire multidialectal area. Again, when languages come into contact on a large scale, such as Spanish and English in the US, *bilingualism* may become common (sometimes with encouragement from governments and schools); this is likely to produce such typical *language contact* phenomena as *code-switching* between Spanish and English, the introduction of *loanwords* from one language into the other, and the assimilation of grammatical patterns toward those of the language to which social value is attached (in this case, English). A further result in some cases may be the limitation of Spanish language use to more restricted social contexts (e.g., the home), even to the point of the *obsolescence* of Spanish in some communities, and ultimate complete *language shift* in the direction of English. The ultimate stage of obsolescence is, of course, *language death*. Still other changes which may be called macrolinguistic, although they do not involve institutional actions, are *pidgini-zation* and *creolization*, in which contact between two or more languages – e.g., in the situation of a colonial plantation economy – results in a new language with vocabulary mainly derived from the socially dominant language, but with a drastically simplified grammar.

On a more *microlinguistic* level, linguistic changes may be initiated by a single individual, or by a small group, and subsequently imitated by others who attribute social value to them; in some cases, such innovations may spread through an entire society. In the case of new vocabulary items, the motivation may be *conscious*, in the form of a new concept or invention such as *radar*, for which the English term was coined in the twentieth century; in such cases, the person who initiated the item, and the circumstances of its spread, are often well known. However, such new vocabulary items are far from typical of linguistic changes in general. When *unconscious* changes occur in grammar, as when the older plural *kine* is replaced by *cows*, or in pronunci-ation, as in *which* [hwɪtʃ] > [wɪtʃ], we cannot pinpoint the initiating individuals or the paths of imitation. It is precisely the difficulty of discovering when and how such changes have occurred in the past, or of "catching them in the act" in the present, that has captured the imagination of many linguists and led them to study the mechanisms of language change.

Two types of misapprehension have often put obstacles in the way of this study. First, it used to be thought that it would never be possible to capture unconscious language change "in the act," simply because its operation re-quired too long a period of time. In this view, trying to observe language change is like trying to observe the motion of a clock's hands: One cannot see the change, but if we look again later, we perceive that change has occurred. Second, people have sometimes thought of language history in terms of abrupt changes from one literary period to another, such as the change of Middle English *soote* to Modern English *sweet*. However, as has been pointed out in particular by William Labov, whose research on language change and its causes has been especially important, we *can* observe language change operating in "apparent time" (1972: 275), simply by listening to the speech of three generations living in the same household. For example, in many Ameri-can families, members of the oldest generation never merge the vowels of *caught* and *cot*, but their children do so sometimes – most often when they are speaking informally – and their grandchildren do so always (see also Bailey et al., 1991). Furthermore, phonetic change does not take place abruptly between one historical period and another, but rather occurs in small gradations, with socially conditioned variation among alternative forms. Thus the locus of language change is not in large abstractions like "the English language," but rather in the variable daily use of individual speakers over time. If we study the speech of a single individual, the variation that we find may seem to contain a great deal of randomness; but as Labov has shown, if we undertake statistical and comparative study – involving multiple speakers, social con-texts, generations, and geographical locations – it is possible to discover coherent patterns of variation and change that characterize contemporary spoken English. Of course, confirmation of linguistic change in real-time studies remains desirable.

Language change as simplification   A traditional view of language change, sometimes expressed by prescriptive grammarians, is that unconscious change is in the direction of simplification, conceived as a universal tendency toward the use of minimum effort. Prescriptivists have even characterized the processes of change as resulting from laziness. In these terms, English *whale* merged with *wail* in many dialects because people found it "too effortful" to pronounce the *h*; *caught* merged with *cot* because some speakers found that the vocal calibration required to distinguish the vowels was just too much trouble. But since such changes have always been in operation, we would expect that they would have ultimately reduced all speech to the easiest possible sound, perhaps [ə::] – which has not happened. In fact, two other overriding motives are characteristic of language change: Speakers want to be able to understand each other, and they want to use language to express their social identity. All speakers frequently produce inadvertently simplified pro-nunciations of particular words; but in most cases, this low-level variability remains unimportant. The innovations are not repeated on later occasions by the original speakers, nor are they imitated by other speakers.

Again, in grammar, we can discern a tendency to simplify structure by *analogy*: Since English has *I don't, you don't, we don't, they don't*, we can save the trouble of mastering an irregularity if we replace *he doesn't* by *he don't*. But in fact *he don't* is stigmatized by most English speakers as rustic or uneducated, and there seems little chance of its becoming widely accepted. Furthermore, it is easy to find grammar changes which *increase* structural complexity. For instance, most English verbs have "weak" past tenses, formed by suffixation as in *walk/-ed*; but a minority are "strong," with vowel change, as in *sing/sang*. The tendency to simplify grammar by analogy should change verbs from the strong to the weak pattern, and it is a commonplace that children learning English often produce "incorrect" verb forms such as *swimmed*. But more complex types of analogical change, from weak to strong, also occur, as in the currently used *sneak/snuck* and *squeeze/squoze*. Complex irregularities remain a feature of English grammar.

Functional factors in language change   It has been proposed, especially by André Martinet (1955), that phonological change in particular is constrained and guided by the need to preserve communicative function in language. This view is associated in particular with arguments for patterns of internal change in language, involving *chain shifts*, in which one change is followed by others which serve to preserve contrasts that distinguish meaning; thus in Swedish, the fronting of *u* to high-mid [ʉ] was followed by the raising of *o* to [u], and this in turn by the raising of *å* (originally [ɔ]) to [o] (Hock, 1991: 156–7). Such patterns are discussed in detail by Labov (1994), in volume 1 of his *Principles of Language Change*. However, it is clear that, whatever the importance of language-internal factors may be, a major role in language change is played by sociolinguistic factors; these have formed a central area of Labov's research for many years, and are the topic of his forthcoming volume 2.

The role of imitation   A long-standing hypothesis in discussions of language change has been the idea that, once a change is initiated by a single individual (for whatever reason), its subsequent spread throughout a language community occurs when, and to the extent that, it is imitated by other speakers. This process indeed seems to operate in the area of new vocabulary, in cases where one person coins a new technical term (or creates a colorful new slang usage) and is then imitated by others. The way the process operates in the less conscious areas of phonology and grammar, however, is not so clear. There are anecdotes about how a change of [s] to [θ] in Castilian Spanish arose because a king of Spain had a lisp, or of how a French [r] changed to uvular [ʁ] because a French king had a speech defect – in each case the populace is supposed to have imitated the *prestige* of their monarch's speech – but these stories are hard to authenticate. In any case, such proposed explanations say, in effect, that the innovating pronunciation was *borrowed*; but linguistic borrowing is not always characterized by complete regularity across all vocabulary items, which is observable in the Castilian and French cases. In addition, the notion that imitation follows prestige models raises the question of how prestige itself is defined. It has sometimes been too easily assumed that prestige is any quality that people imitate! In fact, it is often observed that higher social classes adopt features of lower-class speech, as in many cases where middle-class White speakers have borrowed slang vocabulary from lower-class Black speakers; for some individuals, the borrowed features have connotations of masculinity or of natural authenticity – a kind of "inverse prestige." (Although many lower-class members assign low value to their own speech, they often feel that it would be "sissified" for them to imitate the upper classes.) Thus it is necessary to recognize both "change from above," where the language of higher social strata is dominant, and "change from below," where the model is the language of lower social strata. In short, although imitation must indeed be an important factor in language change, the concept is still not fully understood.

Grammatical change and phonological change   Two major factors in grammar change are often cited. First, phonological change often does away with distinctions among morphological elements, or may delete them entirely; then new syntactic constructions may be elaborated to take over the functions formerly served by morphology. Thus the noun case suffixes of Old English were phonologically reduced and lost (except for genitive *s*); in compensation, the language developed rules of word order to differentiate subject from object, which earlier had distinct suffixes, and increased the use of prepositions to specify other relationships involving nouns. A second factor in grammatical change is the operation of analogy, discussed above; although it may not be possible to predict exactly when or how analogical processes will operate, their role is clearly important. In addition, some recent research on syntactic change indicates that external social forces may be important (Kroch, 1989).

Sociolinguistic motivations for change   The research which opened the way for much subsequent work on social factors in phonological change was the study carried out by Labov (1963) on Martha's Vineyard, an island off the coast of Massachusetts. There he found that a centralization of [a] toward [ə], in the diphthongs [ai] and [au], was a social marker of loyalty to the Island community, as opposed to the outside world. In subsequent much more detailed work in New York City (Labov, 1966c), Labov showed that what had appeared as random phonetic variation, when studied in the speech of individual New Yorkers, was statistically patterned when correlated with, on the one hand, social class, and, on the other hand, the degree of formality in speech. The latter factor could be categorized on a scale which included five styles, in order of increasing formality: (A) casual style, (B) careful style, (C) reading aloud from text, (D) reading aloud from word-lists, and (D′) pronunciation of minimal word-pairs. Furthermore, he found that higher rank on the scale of social class was correlated with higher degrees on the scale of formality, both favoring conservative pronunciations; alternatively, if an innovation occurred more frequently in working-class speech, it would occur more frequently in the informal speech of all speakers. This kind of quantitative social dialectology, which has become almost synonymous with sociolinguistics for some people, is often discussed under the label *variation theory*.

One social class in particular was found to play a special role, namely the upward-aspiring lower middle class. This social group demonstrated *hypercorrect* behavior in the sense that, when speaking formally, they went *beyond* the highest-status group in adopting new prestige features (Labov, 1966b). Other behavior patterns typical of the lower middle class were a wide range of variation among styles in speech, a high degree of phonetic fluctuation within a given style, and a conscious striving for "correctness." Perhaps the most striking feature of what Labov has called the *linguistic insecurity* (1972: 117) of this group was demonstrated when they were asked to give subjective evaluations of their own speech: They were strongly negative about it. Yet, as was later shown clearly in Labov's Philadelphia research (see below), the lower middle class occupies a key role in the processes of language change in the urban eastern US.

The interaction of class stratification and style with the dimension of apparent time, as seen in change over generations, is shown with reference to syllable-final *r* in figure 5.1. In Style A (casual speech), for the two oldest age groups (50–75 and 40–49), there is little indication that the occurrence of *r* is significant. However, among speakers under 40 years old, *r* suddenly becomes a prestige marker for class 9 only (upper middle class). This sudden

Figure 5.1 Class stratification of syllable-final *r* for five speech styles. Style A is casual; B, careful; C, reading; D, word lists; D', minimal pairs. Within each style, the vertical scale shows index scores (maximum 100) for the occurrence of syllable-final *r*. The horizontal scale shows four age categories, and within each of those, socioeconomic class levels 0–8. Class level 9, the upper middle class, is indicated by the dotted line. The hatched areas represent the degree to which a given index score exceeds the level of the upper middle class. (Adapted from Labov, 1972, fig. 4.3, p. 116 and fig. 5.4, p. 137.)

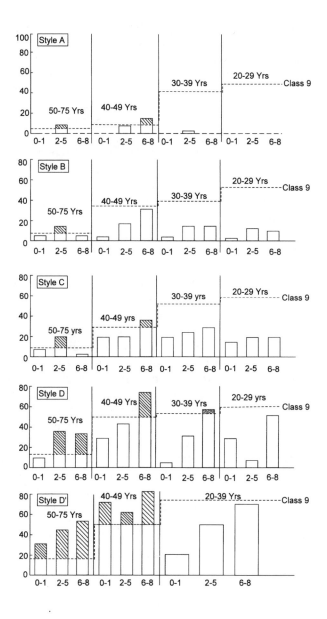

change in the status of *r* is apparently associated with the population changes accompanying World War II. Reading downward in the table, from more casual to more formal styles, we find a regular increase in the use of *r*. The larger left-to-right pattern shows the role of age group in two different ways: In class 9, younger speakers show more use of *r* than older speakers, but in the other classes, older speakers tend to use *r* more than younger ones. Reading from left to right, we see the familiar pattern of class behavior by which the lower middle class (levels 6–8) leads the working class and the lower class in the use of *r*.

The hatched areas in the figure point up the phenomenon of hypercorrection. Although all class and age groups tend to use more *r* as formality increases, it is lower middle-class speakers (class levels 6–8) of the middle-aged group (40–49 years) who show the greatest tendency to increase their use of *r* in formal styles – until, in the most formal styles D and D', they far surpass the level of the upper middle class (class 9). But there is a generational difference in the middle class: Younger speakers seem not to be fully aware of the prestige attached to the new *r* pronunciation, and have not acquired it to the same extent as their elders (Labov, 1972a: 59). The overall pattern shown by this figure reflects the relatively recent introduction, and subsequent spread through generations, of syllable-final *r* as a sociolinguistic prestige marker.

From such research by Labov and his colleagues, a new sociolinguistic approach to language change emerged in the 1960s, and was put forward in a classic essay by Weinreich, Labov, and Herzog (1968). The main features of this approach (conveniently summarized by Hock, 1991: 648–9) include the following: All speech involves low-level variation in pronunciation, with no consistent function. But sometimes, for linguistically arbitrary reasons, a feature of pronunciation may become associated with membership in a social group. At this point, the feature becomes important for speakers' knowledge of their language; they arrive at a generalization – a "rule" from the linguist's viewpoint – as to how the variable use conveys socially relevant information. This generalization may then be extended to new environments, new word classes, or related segments. At the same time, the social parameters for the generalization of the variable rule may be expanded to include additional individuals. If there are no opposing social pressures, the rule may expand throughout the entire lexicon and the entire speech community; if it achieves maximum expansion, it changes from variable to categorical status, so that a regular sound change can be recognized. Labov (1972a: 275) introduced the term *uniformitarian principle* for the hypothesis that this pattern of sound change implementation, generally observable in changes currently in progress, must have applied to all sound changes in past history.

In subsequent years, Labov and his students have concentrated on linguistic variation in the Philadelphia area, moving out from there to other parts of the US and the English-speaking world. Important collections of papers on the social and geographical dialectology of English, and on current changes in English phonology, have been published by Labov (1980b) and Eckert (1991).

The actuation problem The heart of Labov's system is the question of actuation: "Why do changes in a structural feature take place in a particular language at a given time, but not in other languages with the same feature, or in the same language at other times?" (Weinreich et al., 1968: 102). Labov has approached this question "by searching for the social location of the innovators: asking which speakers are in fact responsible for the continued innovation of sound changes, and how their influence spreads to affect the entire speech community" (Labov, 1980a: 252). Earlier linguists had suggested that innovation should originate more often among the lower social classes, because of their lesser exposure to the influence of the standard language – or alternatively, that innovation should originate among the upper classes, who would then provide a prestige model for lower classes to imitate. However, work in Philadelphia by Labov and his associates revealed that sound change could originate in any class *other* than the highest, and that the principal source of innovation was in fact located centrally in the social hierarchy (1980a: 253–4): namely, in that same lower middle class which had figured prominently in his New York research. But the riddle of actuation remained: What was the force that led to the continued renewal of sound change? It seemed evident that a key factor was the entrance of new ethnic and racial groups into the community; in Philadelphia this has been accompanied by strong emphasis on local ethnic identification, and by changes in both Black and White dialects which have the effect of making them increasingly divergent from each other (p. 263).

The influence of literacy Since written language generally changes more slowly than spoken language, it has been supposed that the presence of literacy in a community might act as a "drag" to retard change in the spoken language. However, the picture is complicated by the fact that in societies with limited literacy, as in India, literacy tends to exist mainly in the upper social classes; so, although we find that Brahmin speech is relatively conservative, it is not clear what the relative roles of social class and literacy are in producing this effect. Bright and Ramanujan (1964) attempted to study this question by examining the speech of Brahmin and non-Brahmin speakers of Kannada and Tulu, two neighboring and closely related Dravidian languages of South India. Kannada has a long-established writing system, in which most Brahmins (and many non-Brahmins) are literate. By contrast, Tulu has no commonly used script; when speakers of Tulu as a first language (L1) learn to read and write, they do so in a second language (L2) – Kannada, Sanskrit, or English. Studies revealed that, in Kannada, the Brahmin dialect was clearly more conservative than non-Brahmin speech; but in Tulu, the Brahmin dialect was as likely to innovate as that of non-Brahmins. This suggests that literacy in L1 does indeed exercise a conservative effect, independently of social class. For more recent work on the relationship between literacy and sociolinguistic change see Toon, 1991.

Men's and women's speech   It is well known that, within a speech community, differences may be found between men's and women's speech (see chapter 8) and the question arises: What is the role of sex/gender differentiation in language change? The topic has recently been discussed by Labov (1990). He notes that, in a situation of stable sociolinguistic stratification, women are more conservative linguistically; they tend to favor variants with overt social prestige, whereas men do the reverse. However, in a situation of ongoing change – in which overt social prestige comes from outside the group – women tend to use a higher frequency of new forms than men; among women, it is the "hypercorrect" behavior of the lower middle class (as described above) which is especially important. Labov believes that women play a crucial role in change from below, precisely because of the sexual asymmetry of the care-giving situation: Most of the early language input received by young children is from mothers and other female care-givers.

Lexical diffusion   It has been pointed out by William S.-Y. Wang and his associates (Wang, 1977) that phonological change sometimes seems to operate not in such a relatively rapid and sweeping manner as that envisioned by Labov, but rather through the slow borrowing or "diffusion" of individual lexical items between sister dialects. To the extent that sound change does proceed by lexical diffusion it is not gradual in the sense that it proceeds by phonetic gradations, but it spreads gradually through the lexicon and through social groups. When a large number of such borrowings occur, all involving the same phonological correspondence, we speak of a "sound change" as having taken place; however, numerous exceptions are typically found. Thus Early Modern English *oo* [uː] became modern [uw] in a large number of words, such as *loom* and *boot*; but in other words it becomes [uw] varying dialectally with [ʊ] in other words (e.g., *roof, root*), or [ʊ] alone (*wood, book*), or even [ʌ] (*flood, blood*; cf. Hock, 1991: 657). The linguistic and/or social factors that distinguish these two types of phonological change remain a matter of controversy.

Sociohistorical linguistics   An approach developed by Suzanne Romaine (1982) focuses on the sociolinguistic analysis of historical texts, as illuminated by our understanding of language variation occurring in present-day societies. In accordance with the uniformitarian principle, it is held that language variation in the past must have been similar to that observable today. From this it follows that we should be able to reconstruct some of the sociolinguistic mechanisms which underlie the variation observable in philological study. In other writing, Romaine (1984: 30–1) has noted that, instead of studying variation in terms of statistics-based "predictive" rules – which in fact cannot tell us what variant an individual will choose on a given occasion, or why – we might consider a hermeneutic approach, aimed at *understanding* rather than predicting.

Social class and social network Whereas Labov has operated with social class as a key factor in sociolinguistic change, an alternative view emphasizes the concept of *social network* (cf. Blom and Gumperz, 1972). This approach has recently received increased attention and quantification (J. Milroy, 1992; L. and J. Milroy, 1992). In this framework, an individual's social network is definable as the sum of relationships which he or she has contracted with others, and these may be spoken of in terms of relatively strong or weak ties. The Milroys' research suggests that strong ties within communities result in dialect maintenance and resistance to change; but individuals who have large numbers of weak ties outside the community tend to be innovators, and to serve as instigators of language change. This approach does not replace the concept of social class, but coexists with it in a two-level theory: Small-scale networks, in which individuals conduct their daily lives, coexist with larger-scale social classes, which determine relationships of power at the institutional level.

Conclusion The importance of sociolinguistic variation in the processes of unconscious language change, especially phonological change, has clearly been established beyond doubt; historical linguists of the future cannot escape being, to some degree, sociolinguists. Nevertheless, many questions remain to be answered. When a variant pronunciation first acquires social value, given that its linguistic character is arbitrary, can we identify the exact social factors which cause *that* precise variant to take on such significance, rather than some other? When a new phonological element approaches the crucial stage of actuation, can we pinpoint the social factors which cause *that* particular element to move from variable to categorical status, rather than some other element? Whether or not these problems can be definitively solved, sociolinguists have shed much light on the processes involved. Here as in other areas, progress must be made not by collecting linguistic facts and looking for social correlates, or by collecting social facts and looking for linguistic correlates – or even by collecting sets of correlations between linguistic and social facts – but by attempting to formulate a comprehensive viewpoint in which scholars can deal with linguistic and social aspects of communication simultaneously, as indeed we all do in our everyday lives.

NOTE

All thanks and no blame go to Florian Coulmas, Hans Hock, William Labov, Lise Menn, and Suzanne Romaine for helpful comments.

6 Sociophonology

JOHN HONEY

1.1 Introduction

While the sociolinguist studies all aspects of language variation, sociophonology is that aspect of the discipline which studies only those differences of *pronunciation* which are perceived as socially significant. These are differences which are unlikely to be part of the idiolect of only one speaker, but rather they are shared by groups of speakers, and may or may not coexist with other features of a regional or social dialect in its spoken form, such as distinctive grammatical forms, lexis, and idiom. "Pronunciation" is used here as a broad term which in this context includes other features such as intonation and "articulatory set."

It is a commonplace of linguistics that spoken language is more variable than written, and that variation in speech (aside from age and gender: see chapters 8 and 9) is a function of (a) region, (b) social group, and (c) situation. The speech forms of regional and social groups, in addition to the pronunciation of particular words in distinctive ways, are characterized by *generalized* sound features whose patterns are distinctive of each such group. To take the example of the dialects known respectively as British English and American English, most speakers of the former pronounce the two particular words *leisure* and *lever* as ['leʒə] and ['liːvə], but in American English the vowel values in the first syllable of each of the two words are reversed. In addition to such examples, the standard varieties of British and American English are distinguished by a whole pattern of regularized differences, including an important consonantal difference – the need in standard AmE to realize post-vocalic [r] – and many systematic vowel differences such as AmE [æ] for BrE [aː] in words like grass, path, plant; AmE [aː] for [ɒ] in words like hot, wash; and many more. It is the complex of these latter specific consonantal and vowel features which constitutes what we call *accent*, and which enables an individual speaker's accent to be identified as either standard British English or American English, or as being predominantly one or the other. In Britain and the USA, as in most countries, accent varieties are commonly described in terms of variation from or approximation to the sounds of a standard variety of accent (e.g., BrE, AmE, etc.).

1.2 Accent standardization: The case of RP

The emergence of standard varieties of language, which in Western Europe took place between the fifteenth and the nineteenth centuries, is referred to elsewhere in this book (chapter 13). The most substantial contributory factors were the rise first of a print culture and then of nation-states with mass education systems, bringing in their train vastly increased access to mass media of the written and later the spoken word. These changes were accompanied by the greatly accelerated geographical and social mobility associated with industrialization and urban agglomeration. Written forms of the language were the first to be standardized, with spoken standards usually following a considerable distance behind.

To take the case of England, the written standard developed from the use, in government records from the mid-fifteenth century onwards, of the East Midlands dialect associated with the region around Cambridge, London, and Oxford, and this variety was widely diffused by printing after 1476. The spoken version of this dialect soon acquired influence as a model, and by Shakespeare's time was being taught as such by schoolmasters. The eighteenth-century passion for linguistic prescription and codification – partly a function of greater social mobility – included a marked concern with the "correct" pronunciation of words.

The wider diffusion of this spoken standard, beyond the ranks of the upper social classes (and of the more educated members of the population) within a 60-mile radius of London, had to await the development from around 1870 onwards of an *interacting* system of boarding schools, known quaintly as "public schools" (i.e., exclusive private schools), attendance at one of which was normally preceded by attendance, from around age 7, at what in Britain is called a preparatory ("prep") school (Honey, 1977; Leinster-Mackay, 1984). Such attendance became after that date the expectation of all, and the actual experience of most, of the sons of the upper, upper-middle, and professional classes in England (and indeed Britain), and by 1900 of many of their daughters also, throughout ten very impressionable years of their lives. Moreover, thanks partly to the success of the products of these schools in dominating every area of British social life, and also because of an enormous popular literature based on this kind of schooling, the influence of this model of school life reached down into the humblest day school for the lower classes, so that the linguistic forms which the public schools promoted, and especially their standardized English accent, acquired general prestige throughout British society (Honey, 1988b). One consequence of all this was that, while upper-class families in the early part of the nineteenth century still spoke with accents strongly influenced by regional forms, after about 1870 it was rare for any member of the upper classes to speak with any traces of a regional accent. Another curious result was that, because the criteria for being a public school were fuzzy and no one knew exactly which schools counted, the mere fact of speaking with an RP accent came to imply that its speaker must be a "public school man," with all the social and occupational advantages which that status implied.

In the twentieth century the responsibility for the diffusion of the RP accent passed from the preparatory and public schools to the new medium of radio (established in 1922, in an organization where linguistic forms were closely controlled) and later to TV, which first reached a mass audience in the 1950s. This accent, originally labelled Public School Pronunciation by the phonetician Daniel Jones, has come to be known since 1926 as "Received Pronunciation" (RP), a term which uses the older sense of "received" as "generally accepted as authentic, especially among those qualified to know," as in "received opinion" (Honey, 1985).

1.3 Two forms of RP

The connotations of prestige which attach to British English RP must not, however, be allowed to obscure the fact that this blanket term itself embraces two forms of accent, which can conveniently be labelled as "marked" and "unmarked" RP, where markings are indicators of special social privilege or pretension. While neither form gives any clue as to the speaker's region of origin, unmarked RP is the mainstream variety, conventionally associated with BBC newsreaders and also with schoolteachers, doctors, and secretaries. Marked RP is associated with members (except nowadays the younger ones) of the royal family, with the aristocracy, and with an older generation of senior army and naval officers and university teachers at Cambridge and Oxford. Among many characteristic features, the pronunciation [ɔː] in words like *often*, *cross*, and *cloth* most readily identifies this variety of the RP accent to native speakers who hear it, as does the tendency to give words like *really* and *rarely* the same pronunciation, or to move (with Prince Charles) *abite* the *hice*. As with all accents, marked RP often involves a distinctive articulatory setting (see Honikman, 1964) which in turn gives its speakers a distinctive voice quality (see Laver, 1980). Originally part of a full British upper-class dialect or sociolect (since perhaps the sixteenth century) with other distinctive lexical and idiomatic features (Honey, 1989: 41), it used to confer special prestige on its speakers and opened many doors to jobs, to commissions in the armed forces, and in the marriage market. Until very recently its acquisition justified investment for one's children in especially expensive forms of education, at the most socially prestigious "public" schools like Eton and Harrow (and comparable schools for girls), followed by Cambridge or Oxford. It must further be noted that, beyond the groups of its own speakers, it could also arouse a degree of ridicule, and is now less common. Outside England (and especially the south of England), the unmarked form of RP may itself be regarded as hyperlectal (i.e., carrying overtones of social pretentiousness outside its own group of speakers), and this is also true for Scotland (and Scottish English has other hyperlectal forms of its own) and for former British possessions overseas like Australia, New Zealand, South Africa, Hong Kong, and Singapore, where a distinctive local accent has become established whose most educated variety is the effective model in the educational system and the preferred form for radio and TV newsreaders. (On the relative status of RP in Nigeria and in Hong Kong, compare Ufumata, 1990, with Bolton and Kwok, 1990.) In Australia, a vast country with remarkably little regional accent variation, it has been estimated that about a third of Australians speak with what is known as a *broad* Australian accent, just over half with a *general* Australian accent, and about one tenth use *cultivated* Australian, associated especially with education (McCrum et al., 1986: 294). In South Africa, accent features usually make it possible to distinguish among speakers of standard English as between mother-tongue English-speakers, Afrikaans-speakers, mother-tongue speakers of African languages, and "coloreds" (persons of mixed race), and often also South Africans of Indian descent.

These two forms of the standard accent of British English now coexist with a great variety of local accents which are the successors of the mass of local speech forms of medieval Britain. Readers of the classic novel *Wuthering Heights* (1847) are confronted by many baffling utterances such as "What is he abaht, girt eedle seeght!" (i.e., What has happened to him, the great idle spectacle!) in the mouth of the servant Joseph: They represent Emily Brontë's attempt to reproduce the dialect speech of a particular part of Yorkshire around that date. The extreme difficulty of understanding the lexis, grammar, and accent of such speakers faced visitors in all parts of Britain at that time, but the inexorable progress (already referred to) of standardization meant that by the middle of the present century it was difficult for researchers to find anyone who still spoke the old dialect forms with any convincing degree of "purity." Most speakers had by then adapted, in varying degrees, towards the standard, though their accents were still the strongest evidence of their local associations.

It is thus common in England for speakers, especially those who have experienced an extended education, to use a form of English which is entirely standard in respect of grammar, vocabulary, and idiom, but to do so with an accent which is not RP (i.e., the unmarked variety) but something between RP and the local accents in which the historic dialects were once spoken. And we also encounter many speakers, likewise from a background of extended education, who speak the same form of fully standard English but whose accents have moved *very close* to RP yet stopped fractionally short of it, retaining tiny traces of the accent features characteristic of their regional background. In the latter case these traces may relate to only one or two typical sounds, yet these are sufficient to cause the speaker to be identified as coming from that region. Well-known examples from British public life are the former political party leaders Neil Kinnock and Sir David Steel, and the broadcaster Brian Redhead, each of whom had in varying degrees small (even tiny) traces of a regional accent, yet each of whom was perceived as being "very" Welsh, or Scottish, or north-country (Honey, 1989: 81–2).

1.4 The accent continuum

The notion of a *continuum* or *spectrum* of linguistic variation, developed by Stewart (1964) and Bickerton (1971), employs a useful categorization of linguistic features as spread along a line which shows clustering around the *acrolect* (high prestige, standard variety), the *basilect* (the broadest form of popular speech, which for Australians, for example, involves a third of the population, but whose traditional form in Britain is now found only among "elderly people with little education" (Trudgill, 1983b: 187), and, in between them, the *mesolect*, the speech of the majority of the population. In using this to describe accent variety in British English, two considerations outlined above suggest refinements of this categorization to include the additional positions *hyperlect* (representing the socially privileged "marked RP" accent, i.e., the "posh" as opposed to the standard accent); and *paralect* to describe that variety which is very close to RP but retains a few tiny nonstandard features. In this typology, a speaker with barely perceptible nonstandard traces is described as having a close paralect of RP, one with more salient traces (but still very much closer to RP than to, say, the regional mesolect) a broad paralect; and, depending on *situation* and *register* (see section 1.9), might switch between these two paralects, or even between these and RP. We note that the speaker's level of education is the most obvious factor associated with a speaker's movement leftward along the continuum and in the direction of RP, though not always right up to it.

Figure 6.1 The accent continuum.

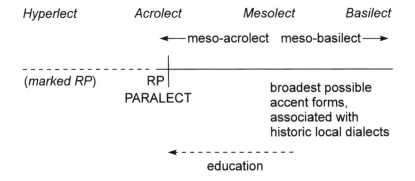

1.5 Implications of the concept of standard accent

It is often stated that RP speakers represent as few as 3 percent of the population of Britain, but this figure is a pure guess. Most crucially, it obscures the
significance of RP as a target, its influence as a model, and thus the considerable numbers who speak some kind of paralect of RP.

This latter point complicates all judgments of the precise phonological ingredients of "standard" accents. For example, there has been a spoken standard
for French since at least the second half of the twelfth century (based originally on that of the royal court in Paris) and even possibly much earlier (Lodge,
1993: 98, 102, 166)); and, as in Britain, monolingual nonstandard dialect speakers had disappeared in France by the 1970s (Hawkins, 1993: 60). This makes
it impossible to tell which part of France a speaker of standard French, with
this standard accent, comes from, whereas those who speak regional varieties
signal their regional origin as soon as they start speaking, largely as a result of
specifically regional features of their accent (Hawkins, 1993: 56). These include complicated sets of features, if one takes into account regional differences in the use of the vowel system, which thus becomes "a vehicle of a
multitude of connotations" (Sanders, 1993a: 45). For example, in standard
French the vowel sounds in words like *saule/sol* (willow/ground) and in the
second syllable of *couché* and *couchait* (slept/was sleeping) are held to distinguish between each word in these two pairs, but in many regional varieties of
French the distribution of vowel values in such pairs is quite different (Hawkins, 1993: 61). There may also be small consonantal differences, and class-
related differences in the use of optional liaisons between words (Durand,
1993: 259, 263).

But to pin down the distinctive features of the *standard* French accent
is much more difficult. A comparison of various linguistic authorities shows
"surprising divergences" as to what the standard accent is supposed
to consist of (Durand, 1993: 262). When Fouché (1956, 1959) claimed that
his description of the standard French accent was based on the "average" careful pronunciation of "cultivated" Parisians (quoted in Durand,
1993: 262), he did not define "average" nor who counts as cultivated, though
of course the perceptions of this informed observer are highly relevant.
A revealing study by Martinet and Walter (cited in Durand, 1993: 262)
showed considerable diversity and variability in the *formal* pronunciation of
17 highly educated Parisian adults, and this and his own specialist knowledge of the sociolinguistics of contemporary French have led Professor
Jacques Durand to question the empirical (as opposed to the normative or
pedagogical) nature of the concept of "standard" French pronunciation (Durand, 1993: 263), to the point of echoing the claim of Y.-C. Morin that the
notion of "standard" French is no more than a "linguistic Frankenstein"
(Morin, 1987).

Comparable claims have been made in respect of English. The British sociolinguist Michael Stubbs claimed (1976: 26) that "there is in fact no standard

English accent, and standard English can be spoken with any accent"; and W. R. O'Donnell and Loreto Todd claimed (1980: 143) that the notion of "standard" does not imply any particular pronunciation of English, and that "it is important to realize that RP is not a standard pronunciation; there is, in fact, no such standard." That this "standard," if it exists, accommodates a degree of variation is attested by, for example, a glance at John Wells's authoritative English *Pronunciation Dictionary* (1990), many of whose entries admit one or more variants. Moreover, RP is itself changing (Honey, 1989), even in the mouths of younger royals, with the absorption of one or two features from "popular London" (Cockney-influenced) speech such as word-final [t]-glottalling and, to a lesser extent, of vocalic [l], to the point where one observer has proposed the term "Estuary English" for this "broader" form of RP, found especially among speakers in suburban Greater London and adjacent counties around the Thames estuary (Rose-warne, 1994).

None of this, however, should blind us to the overwhelming influence as a model of RP (whatever its ingredients at any time), nor lead us into the trap of denying the existence of a "standard" version of anything simply because in its purest form it is difficult to define or measure. Philosophers such as Tarski and Karl Popper (see, for example, Magee, 1973) have demonstrated the nature of "regulative ideas," which do not correspond to precise measurement. Even the most exact measurement in millionths of a centimetre is likely to be inexact, and the fact that a millionth of a centimetre is unlikely to be met with in practical human experience does not invalidate the concept. In any case, one important reason why a standard accent may be difficult to describe is that listeners' *perceptions* of it may be more significant than its empirically observed phonological features. Furthermore, Professor Durand's despair about the concept of a "standard" French accent does not appear to take account of the notion of a paralect, which may account for much of the variation he observes, and the same may perhaps help to explain the judgments of Stubbs and of O'Donnell and Todd.

As a label for standard American English pronunciation, the term "General American" was proposed by Krapp (1919) and despite reservations among present-day linguists has some currency (along with terms which significantly refer to the media "networks" as models), partly because local variation in the USA is less marked than in Britain, though there are notable differences between General American and the stereotypical accents of, for example, New York, Boston, and Charleston, and the notion of regional standards is stronger. It is often said that in the USA a speaker's grammar is more likely to be the basis of positive or negative evaluations than her/his accent, but it is also widely reported that the accents of certain minority groups (African-Americans, Hispanics) can cause advertised accommodation to be declared "already let" to callers with such accents.

Modern standard German originated chiefly in the East Middle German dialect area, and the spoken standard is now termed *deutsche Hochlautung*

("DH"). Its characteristic phonetic elements, and the differences between these and those of some of the main regional dialects, are well described in Barbour and Stevenson (1990). The prestige accent is associated with education, but has fewer connotations of class superiority than RP is said to have in Britain. Despite what is often said to be a more marked resilience of local dialect than in Britain, and indeed a greater tolerance of accent features which express regional models of educatedness, there is an expectation that formal or scholarly registers should be expressed in formal standard German and with the DH accent, which demands considerable adjustments in the speech even of middle-class schoolchildren whose speech may be strongly influenced by regional dialect forms.

1.6 *The social significance of variation*

Much of the above, however, is merely descriptive of accent variation, and we must return to the fundamental point that the primary concern of sociophonology is rather to investigate the social significance of such variation. It is not possible to agree with J. E. Joseph (1987: 16) that "awareness of variants seems inevitably to be accompanied by value judgment," but all of the kinds of difference we have been noting carry the potential for positive or negative evaluations by listeners of the speakers concerned, and such evaluations are often general and systematic. Indeed, following Labov (1972b), a useful distinction can sometimes be made among *indicators*, which are variants to which little or no social significance is attached, and may indeed only be perceived by observers with linguistic training; *markers*, which are readily perceived and do have social significance; and *stereotypes*, which are popular and conscious but imprecise general characterizations of the speech forms of particular social groups. At their widest, such stereotypes are applied to whole languages: We all know of evaluations which describe particular languages (Italian is a favorite case) as "beautiful"; others (e.g., European languages which exploit velar/pharyngeal – "guttural" – sounds) are often described as "ugly" or "harsh." The language of the Kipsigis in East Africa was described by an experienced British colonial governor as the "most melodious" he'd ever heard in Africa (Allen, 1990: 109). Such judgments, however, do not always agree across cultures. An example of an apparently totally arbitrary phonaesthetic judgment is the widely observable fact that in many societies the lower ranges of generalized voice pitch (baritone, contralto) cause their speakers to be rated more highly for authority and personal attractiveness, and it is even claimed that the adult male speakers of certain languages (e.g., Germans) exploit such ranges more systematically than speakers of other languages.

A technique for examining the social evaluation of the different accents with which a language is spoken, in a given country, was developed first in Canada to explore the differential reactions to speakers of French and English respectively, and has produced interesting results in Britain and France in a series of experiments initiated by the British social psychologist Howard Giles and various associates (Honey, 1989: 60; Giles and Powesland, 1975; Hawkins, 1993). This is the "matched guise" method, by which various audiences hear stretches of speech spoken in different accents, and are asked to judge them, from sound alone, in terms of a list of qualities such as "intelligent," "hard-working," "friendly," etc. In the form in which it is usually administered, this method excludes or minimizes complicating factors like the speaker's gender and voice quality, though it must be a serious criticism that it does not appear to control systematically for "breadth" of accent, i.e., the extent to which its differences from standard are obvious to listeners. Despite this and other limitations, however, the fact remains that the general picture which it reveals, over a considerable number of tests with audiences taken from different samples of the population, shows a very high degree of consistency which is confirmed by other, more informal, experiments based on speakers who use their own natural accents.

For Britain, this general picture suggests a hierarchy of attitudes to accents, in which RP (in its unmarked form, though the experiments do not always make this important distinction) is at the top, followed by the most educated varieties of Scottish English and the corresponding accents of Wales and Ireland. "Marked" RP, where separately identified, ranks high. Below these there is a cluster of English provincial accents such as "northern" English, with Yorkshire generally high, and the West Country accent of the southwest of England. Five accents representing the British urban lower-class sociolects of Birmingham, Belfast, London ("Cockney"), Glasgow, and Liverpool ("Scouse," a variety which also involves a very distinctive articulatory setting; cf. Knowles, 1978) are regularly placed at the bottom of the scale, even by speakers of those varieties themselves. RP speakers are always held to rate more highly in terms of "status" and "competence" features like intelligence, leadership, self-confidence, wealth, and ambition; while nonstandard speakers often scored higher than RP on the "solidarity" qualities such as friendliness, kindheartedness, integrity, and humor, but many also attributed trustworthiness to RP speakers, as well as improbable features such as cleanliness and tallness. When a version of the same technique was applied to 244 native speakers of French, similar findings emerged (described in Paltridge and Giles, 1984, and usefully summarized in Hawkins, 1993), associating "status/competence" features with the prestige accent of French and "solidarity" qualities with regional varieties such as Provençal and Breton. In Britain, BBC listeners expect the news to be presented by RP speakers (perceived as educated and authoritative), whereas "practical" information on gardening or the weather is stereotypically given by speakers with broad paralects or even mesolectal accents; sports commentating reflects the social standing of the sport concerned, with mesolectal accents appropriate for reporting football, but RP accents for polo (Honey, 1989).

1.7 *Accounting for contemporary accent variation*

In the context of the widespread prevalence of such evaluations within countries like Britain, linguists ask the question why such varieties of accent persist. The remorseless processes of accent levelling, especially powerful in the twentieth century with the ever wider spread of education and the influence of radio and TV, appear to hit a barrier which prevents the total eradication of certain forms of accent (and indeed dialect) and ensures their survival in some degree, despite the obvious advantages – in terms of social prestige and judgments of one's own educatedness and competence – of adapting to the widely accessible standard. Why do large numbers of people cling to accents which receive so many kinds of negative evaluations, which these speakers themselves often share?

The starting point of our explanation must be the principle that different sounds (like other linguistic features, including grammar) encode value systems. For all speakers, the accent and dialect they use involves signals of the value system that they identify with. A classic paper by the American sociolinguist William Labov drew attention to systematic differences in the pronunciation of certain vowels, e.g., those in *right* and *house*, among the inhabitants of Martha's Vineyard, an island off the coast of Massachusetts which is used as a holiday resort by the citizens of the adjacent New England mainland. Labov demonstrates convincingly that the locals who use these sounds appear to do so unconsciously, but their function is to assert the fact that these speakers belong to the island, and it is to them, rather than the outsiders, that Martha's Vineyard really "belongs" (Labov, 1972b: 36). A comparable situation in the French resort of St Tropez has been described by Bouvier (1973: 232–3), quoted in Hawkins (1993).

We noted (in section 1.5) that many speakers of French use accent features to signal a *regional* identity, and in Britain Scottish, Welsh, and Northern Irish speakers also do this, indicating some kind of "nationalism" or *ethnicity*, though judging how far such use involves an element of choice must take into account the degree of access to a nonlocal standard in the local school systems. Thus, for example, the varieties of English accent in South Africa mentioned in section 1.3 result essentially from differential school experience; even so, some individuals in all these communities show a tendency to adapt to an educated South African English standard (Lanham and MacDonald, 1979). Other forms of motivation to maintain (or even adapt to) a nonstandard accent include support for the devolution of central government power to the regions and for environmental conservation (Barbour and Stevenson, 1990: 222, 237). The most commonly proposed motivation has to do with the equation linking standard accents (and dialects) with *status* as a function of power (political and economic; see especially St Clair, 1982: 165) and nonstandard ones with *solidarity* with a local community or with a low social class, and findings in the evaluation experiments discussed above strongly support this, insofar as they show friendliness, kindheartedness, etc. as stereotypical for nonstandard accent speakers. This account is vulnerable in making use of a fairly crude concept of power, whose *coercive* (as opposed to persuasive or authoritative) connotations are inappropriate to the way standard accents are used by many in the population without access to significant power, nor indeed enjoying significant economic privilege. The equation of a standard accent with "those at the highest socioeconomic level of a society" (cf. Giles and Powesland, 1975: 21) also fails to take account of the fact that many who are at that level in Britain, for example, speak with hyperlectal accents.

A more finely-tuned account of the notion of solidarity is provided by Lesley Milroy (1980; see also J. and L. Milroy, 1992). Her method of analysis of *social networks* examines "the informal social relationships contracted by an individual" as a way of explaining more precisely the patterns of nonstandard usage (including accent) of individuals in certain face-to-face communities. By tracing observable interactive links between people, the sociolinguist is able to explore, with greater accuracy than by the use of blunt sociological categories like social class, the way factors such as social cohesion in such communities operate to create, reinforce, and alter individuals' speech patterns. The result provides a persuasive explanation of why and how nonstandard speech forms persist in such environments, essentially because of the strength of individuals' identification with such communities, and the coerciveness of local public opinion which sees the use of nonlocal forms as some kind of disloyalty to the social group. We see here the strength of an alternative value-system, which has a higher estimation for the feeling of community supportiveness than for membership of the mainstream society.

1.8 *"Educatedness" and its alternatives*

Another explanation of the persistence of both nonstandard accents and dialects is provided (Honey, forthcoming) by an alternative description of the two sets of values which are involved in the choice of either form. By this analysis, standard forms are the expression of a complex of values associated with being in the mainstream of society, and with educatedness, which is in its turn associated with literacy. In contrast, nonstandard forms express local or regional particularism (with some of the functions of what in other contexts is called tribalism) and the rejection of (or dissociation from) a high regard for education. As Mattheier (1980; see also Barbour and Stevenson, 1990: 100–1) has shown, the process of modernization which involves urbanization and mass education also tends to promote the establishment of widely accepted or "mainstream" norms and values. Life in modernized societies puts an ever greater premium on qualities of occupational competence which are also increasingly tied to educatedness. Underlying a respect for educatedness is a set of attitudes towards literacy: As Barton (1994: 48) has put it, "every person, adult or child, has a view of literacy, about what it is and what it can do for them, about its importance and its limitations." Literacy as a historical phenomenon has been explored by many scholars, and though its implications have in particular respects been exaggerated, its general cognitive implications over time are so important as to mark it out as a catalyst which has helped to "transform human consciousness" and make it "essential for the realization of fuller, interior, human goals" (Ong, 1982: 78, 82; cf. also Honey, 1988a). Since literacy is embedded in language, standard forms of language (including accent) tend to be perceived as the only appropriate vehicles for education and literacy, while nonstandard forms thrive among those who have been disappointed in their own experience of formal education. Add to this a generational factor and the characteristic anti-authority phase of adolescence, and we are not surprised to find nonstandard accents and other forms adopted (indeed learned) as a badge among adolescents, including Black American gang members (Labov, 1972a: chapter 7), British teenagers in Reading (Cheshire, 1982) or young blacks in London and other parts of Britain (Sutcliffe, 1982; Sebba, 1993). Among some such peer groups, especially males, the value system which this nonstandard language encodes includes attitudes which, as well as rejecting or disparaging mainstream deference to "educatedness," are demeaning to women and glorify criminality, violence, and drug use. Though such varieties frequently celebrate macho values, many studies report that, in general, women have a stronger tendency than men to adapt their speech to the standard variety, and also to evaluate standard accents more highly (Cheshire, 1983: 44). Trudgill (see Chambers and Trudgill, 1980: 98–100) has proposed a useful distinction between *overt prestige*, which involves respect for mainstream norms, and *covert prestige*, which reflects the scale of values within a smaller social group, in which there is nevertheless a kind of respect for the mainstream forms (often perceived as "upper-class") as being in some sense "right" (see also Hudson, 1980: 201). Such conflicting motivations help explain the much greater *instability* of the phonological systems of nonstandard varieties (compared with the standard), the unreliability of such speakers in reporting on or judging their own use of particular features, and their blatant pretence (to researchers) that they themselves use the standard forms. Moreover, they help explain why such face-to-face communities may have to be more blatantly *coercive* than any school system in trying to maintain their own prescriptive norms, so that physical violence may be invoked to discipline deviations such as the use of a standard rather than the local nonstandard vowel in a particular word (J. and L. Milroy, 1991: 18–19, 58). Forms of local particularism or "tribalism" were expressed in a much earlier period in distinctive dress and social customs, but never more powerfully than by that most basic aspect of a group member's identity, spoken language.

The theme of George Bernard Shaw's *Pygmalion* (1912) (made into a musical (1956) and later filmed as *My Fair Lady*) was the transformation of a Cockney flower-girl into a potential duchess by changing her accent (i.e., in the direction of RP; Shaw did not make clear that the "marked" form was the more appropriate one). Modern sociolinguists tend to argue that accent and dialect stereotyping is inappropriate since any accent or dialect can be the vehicle of educated discourse (e.g., Trudgill, 1975: chapter 4; Trudgill, 1994: 2, 6). However, precisely because of the fact that different accents and dialects encode different value-systems, it is unreasonable to expect the linguistic expression of such differences to be disregarded while the underlying value-systems, which are the *raison d'être* for those accents and dialects, remain different. There are serious obstacles to the mixing of lexical, grammatical, as well as phonological features of varieties which are perceived as functionally appropriate to specific domains, and thus as not being *congruent* (for the concept of linguistic *congruence* see Honey (forthcoming). This concept of congruence/incongruence helps to explain why, although it is theoretically possible for standard English to be spoken with any accent (cf. Stubbs, 1976, quoted in section 1.5), in practice it is never heard spoken in the most basilectal accents.

   Since the concept of "educatedness" is fundamental in sociophonology, we need to emphasize that this is a changing concept. We saw that connection with royal courts and with the governing classes was originally the defining characteristic of standard accents, but that at an early stage there grew up alongside it a standard of educated speech, originally limited to the tiny fraction of the population who experienced extended education but later, with the advent of mass education systems, accessible to all. In the second half of the twentieth century, in countries like Britain, the category of educated people whose accents define RP is thus an ever widening one, and now speakers of ever broader paralects help to fashion it.

   "Educatedness" is closely associated with the notion of being "well-spoken," which seems to be common to all languages, and is especially associated with formal styles of speaking. Age is a factor both in the ingredients of any accent and in the evaluations it evokes (see especially Giles et al., 1990); next to childhood, adolescence seems a particularly formative period for accent adaptation, and many subjects report that their own accents were influenced by charismatic models among their secondary school teachers, including speakers of both the standard and paralects. Hockett (1958) considered that a person's range of accent flexibility is almost complete by age 17, but many individuals have shown the ability to adapt their accents at much later ages.

1.9 Sociosituational variation

Accent use is also a function of *register*, defined by Sanders (1993a: 27) as *sociosituational variation*, or variation dependent on the setting and the relationship between interlocutors. The complex of factors which determine the choice of register, as derived and elaborated by Sanders (1993: 38) from Offord (1990) in the context of French but obviously applicable to other languages, includes the age, sex, socioeconomic status, and regional background of both speaker and addressee, the degree of intimacy between the participants in the speech-event, and the formality of the situation (cf. Offord, 1990). Common observation shows that higher-status addressees are likely to call forth greater approximation to standard accents (and indeed hypercorrection (Labov, 1972b: 244) or "hyperadaptation" (Trudgill, 1994: 56, 67), while informal situations produce greater use of nonstandard accents and other spoken forms.

While sociolinguists like Labov and Trudgill attempt to correlate phonological variables with social class, and Milroy with social networks, *accommodation theory* explores the ways speakers adjust their speech in relation to the speech of their interlocutors (Giles and Smith, 1979), with *convergence* or *divergence* taking place as a function of some of the sociosituational factors that have been listed. An important contribution to situational sociophonology is Le Page and Tabouret-Keller's (1985) concept of "acts of identity," which offers an explanation of how and why speakers adjust, in any given situation, to the perceived norms of "imagined" communities (cf. Sebba, 1993: 126), given that they are strongly motivated to identify with those communities, and are able to modify their own behavior, including accent. Interlocutors' reactions, providing feedback, are also an important factor here, since it is well known that, for example, speakers of standard varieties who attempt to "accommodate" in the direction of nonstandard spoken forms are suspected of mockery, while accommodation in the other direction does not usually carry this implication.

The complexity of motivational and situational factors makes it difficult to apply in sociophonology the notion of implicational scales. According to this hypothesis, linguistic variables can be presented on an implicational scale that plots their relatedness, and enables predictions to be made, from the presence of one or more variables, about the likely presence of others. Though there may be some support for this in the field of syntax (for example), the greater instability of phonological compared with grammatical forms, the extent to which phonological features are controlled by their speakers and to which they are conscious of them, and the extent to which these features are salient in the social group concerned, make this whole notion much more problematical; see Chambers and Trudgill (1980: 152–61). Thus, for example, Barbour and Stevenson report (1990: 115) a study in which particular groups of speakers in parts of pre-unification Berlin were shown to use some specific sounds to give their speech a "Berlin tinge," but without otherwise adapting their pronunciation in a particular way.

1.10 Critical areas of influence

In English, a standard accent can be shown to enhance the credibility of a defendant or witness in a court case, and, as well as possibly being crucial to the outcome of a job interview, can even influence the kind of diagnosis a patient will receive from a doctor (Honey, 1989: 61, 190; on problems of sociolinguistic methodology in identifying the voices of speakers in legal proceedings, see J. Milroy, 1983). Indeed, sociophonology indicates that differences in accent – perhaps involving simply the differential use of post-vocalic [r'], or word-initial [h], or [t]-glottalling – have the potential to be more decisive than other dialect features such as grammar or lexis, because they may be salient in every social encounter in daily life. That teachers' expectations may be unduly influenced by pupils' accents is attested by a vast literature (see especially Robinson, 1979). Such differences may also be exploited by politicians in order to create a particular public image: On Margaret Thatcher, Bob Hawke, Harold Wilson, and Arthur Scargill, see Honey (1989); on the French communist leader Georges Marchais see Durand (1993: 263).

Despite criticisms (Robinson, 1979: 223–6) of specific aspects of methodology, the work of William Labov (especially 1972b) remains the most valuable introduction to the significance of particular phonological variables in the USA, the techniques of their investigation, and the nature of sociophonological change. For Britain the best introduction, though not always the best interpretation, is to be found in the work of Peter Trudgill and his collaborators (Trudgill 1974, 1978, 1983a, b; but see also Robinson, 1979, and Petyt, 1980: 158–9) and the publications of Howard Giles and associates.

7 Dialect in Society

WALT WOLFRAM

1 Introduction

For as long as observations about language have been recorded, the symbolic function of dialect in society has been recognized. Over three thousand years ago, the *sh* versus *s* pronunciation of *shibboleth* in the Hebrew word for "ear of corn" was used to detect impostors from true allies among the fleeing Ephraimites who attempted to disguise themselves as Gileadites. As indicated in the Biblical account, the social consequences of the dialect difference were quite severe:

> and whenever a survivor of Ephraim said, "Let me cross over," the men of Gilead asked him, "Are you an Ephraimite?" If he replied, "No," they said, "All right, say Shibboleth." If he said, "Sibboleth," because he could not pronounce the word correctly, they seized him and killed him at the fords of the Jordan. (Judges 12: 5–6)

The present-day social consequences of dialect differences may not be quite as gruesome as those described in the account given in the Old Testament, but the diagnostic differentiation of social groups on the basis of dialect remains symbolically just as significant.

The term *dialect* is used here to refer to any regional, social, or ethnic variety of a language. The language differences associated with dialect may occur on any level of language, thus including pronunciation, grammatical, semantic, and language use differences. At first glance, the distinction between "dialect" and "language" seems fairly straightforward – dialects are subdivisions of language. However, on closer inspection, the boundary between dialects and languages may become blurry as simple criteria such as structural affinity or mutual intelligibility break down. Thus, many of the so-called dialects of

Chinese such as Pekingese (Mandarin), Cantonese, and Wu (Shanghai), are mutually unintelligible in their spoken form. By the same token, Swedes and Norwegians are generally able to understand each other although their distinct cultures and literatures warrant their designation as different languages.

In a similar way, the notions of regional, social, and ethnic dialect are not nearly as obvious as we might assume at first glance. Speakers are at the same time affiliated with a number of different groups and their varying memberships may contribute to the variety of language they employ. Speakers located within the same geographical territory may be affiliated with quite different ethnic and/or social groups, and thus end up speaking quite disparate varieties even as they share a subset of regional language peculiarities. While it is certainly convenient to use the term dialect as we do here, to refer to the general notion of a language variety, more precise definition of the term relies on its correlation with the particular parameters of social structure that determine its existence in a given speech community.

Given the apparent inevitability of dialect differences and their widespread social recognition, it is somewhat surprising that the social patterning of these differences has not been accorded more systematic study in the examination of language and/or society. The methodical study of dialects per se did not begin until the latter part of the nineteenth century (Wenker, 1877; Gilliéron, 1902–10), and the serious study of dialects in their social context did not begin until the 1960s.

As it has developed over the past several decades, the systematic investigation of dialects in society has challenged some of the established perspectives of both linguistics and dialectology. Linguistics, as it progressed in the second half of the twentieth century, focused on the formal structure of language as an abstract cognitive system, with little attention given to the kinds of variants that were central to the examination of dialect variation. In accordance with more formal descriptive and explanatory goals, the primary data base became native speaker intuitions vis-à-vis actual language usage because of the insight these intuitions could provide to the cognitive processes underlying language. From this perspective, the social context of language was considered outside the purview of an abstract, cognitively based model of language description.

At the same time, dialectology in the twentieth century became more aligned with geography and history as it focused on the distribution of particular variants in geographical space and time. Accordingly, isolated sets of dialectally diagnostic lexical and phonological items collected through the direct elicitation of single instances of forms became primary data (e.g., Kurath and McDavid, 1961; Orton, Sanderson, and Widdowson, 1978; Carver, 1987). The social significance of dialect variants was examined to some extent through the correlation of dialect variants with the background of interview subjects, but it was secondary. For example, in the various surveys of the *Linguistic Atlas of the United States and Canada* (Kurath, 1939: 44), subjects were classified according to three different social types in terms of education and social contacts. However, the systematic examination of dialect in society lay beyond the goals of traditional dialectology.

The pioneering investigations of dialect in society by William Labov (1963, 1966, 1972a, b) clearly broke precedent with some of the reified traditions of both linguistics and dialectology in their assumptions, methodology, description, and explanation. For example, the investigation of language in its social context was seen by Labov (1966c) as central to the solution of fundamental problems in linguistic theory and description rather than as a specialized, interdisciplinary subfield combining distinct traditions of inquiry and description. Furthermore, the use of conversational speech data collected through the sociolinguistic interview was based on the assumption that naturally occurring speech reflected the most systematic data for the examination of language variation (Labov, 1972c) and on the assumption that the characterization of systematic variation should be integrated into the description of a language. And it was maintained that the description of language change and variation had to appeal to the role of language in its social context in order to achieve its ultimate goal of explanation.

The line of investigation that developed in social dialectology over the past several decades has altered in a significant way our fundamental understanding of the nature of dialect variation in society with respect to both the linguistic and social sides of the sociolinguistic equation. In the following sections, we consider the nature of dialect variation, the patterning of this variation within society, and the kinds of social consequences that obtain from the socially situated distribution of dialect.

2 The Nature of Dialect Variation

According to popular beliefs, dialect patterns are relatively straightforward and simple: All members of one group invariably use one particular dialect form while members of a different group categorically use another one. While this subjective impression is of sociolinguistic import, the objective reality of dialect distribution within society is far more complex and variable than this popular perception. On one level there is an intricate interaction between the systematic patterning of language and social structure; on another level, however, linguistic variation is inherent in the linguistic system, existing apart from the social meaning that may ultimately be assigned to it. In fact, one of the major shortcomings of traditional dialectology as it developed in North America and the United Kingdom over the past half century was its failure to come to grips with the underlying linguistic-systemic principles that guided the organization and direction of much linguistic variation subsumed under the rubric of dialect. The commonly adopted premise in dialectology that "each word has its own history" (Gilliéron, 1902–10) unfortunately often precluded the extended consideration of the internal linguistic-systemic principles that guide the orderly distribution of language variation. The following sections illustrate a couple of ways in which dialect variation is guided by the internal mechanisms of language systems. From that point, we proceed to show how such variation may distribute itself in society, and the kinds of social meaning that this variation is assigned.

2.1 The internal motivation of dialects

Following the "each word has its own history" edict of traditional dialectology, dialect differences have often been described as if they consisted of unrelated sets of items. Thus various phonetic productions of two different English vowels in assorted dialects of English, such as the /u/ of words such as *boot* and *tube* and the /ɔ:/ of words such as *bought* and *caught*, would be viewed as structurally independent entities because they involve different phonological units within the system. Similarly, the use of the socially diagnostic English reflexive *hisself* versus *himself* in *Kirk liked hisself* and the subject-verb concord pattern *We was down there yesterday* versus *We were down there yesterday* are viewed as socially diagnostic items quite independent of each other since there appears to be no inherent structural relationship between these forms. While the patterned co-occurrence of forms such as these may be noted as a part of an overall dialect profile, their coexistence within a given dialect is viewed as arbitrary from a descriptive-theoretical perspective.

Such a viewpoint seems far too limited in its assessment of the nature of language variation and change that serves as the foundation of dialect differentiation. Furthermore, there is empirical evidence that argues for a set of underlying principles that guide dialect variation, or at least the tendencies of variation, which exist independent of dialect contact and diffusion (Chambers, 1993). For example, vernacular dialects of English throughout the world (Wolfram and Fasold, 1974; Cheshire, 1982; Bailey and Görlach, 1983; Trudgill, 1990) with no apparent common diffusional source, share the feature of negative concord in sentences such as *They don't do nothing to nobody about nothing*. Such uniformity among vernacular dialects of English suggests that there are underlying, language-internal pressures that guide some types of dialect variation. In the case of negative concord, the predisposition of languages to generalize processes is a natural, internal mechanism that may account for the representation of this process among different, independent, vernacular varieties. A negative marking rule that specifies that the negative should be attached to a verb phrase element and all post-verbal indefinites is a more general rule than one that may select only one position for the placement of negation. The fact that other language adaptation situations manifest negative concord supports the contention that an underlying change and variation principle is at work in this case. For example, in both first language (Brown, 1973) and second language acquisition (Schumann, 1978), speakers go through a negative concord stage regardless of their normative target dialects.

In a similar vein, we may appeal to the process of *analogical levelling*, which exerts internally induced systemic pressure to align exceptional forms in conformity with dominant patterns, as the basis for explaining the wide-spread existence among unrelated vernacular varieties of English of the reflex-ive *hisself* within the paradigmatic set of *my-/your-/her-/our-self(ves)* or the extensive regularization of the past tense finite form of *be* in *I/you/she/we/you/they was* found. The underlying principles that govern dia-lect variation are essentially the same as those that govern language change in general (e.g., Kiparsky, 1989; Joseph and Janda, 1987; Kroch, 1989), but the ratification of variation and hence its identification as language change is derived from the social context in which the linguistic variation occurs. Although the social interpretation of language forms involved in vari-ation may appear somewhat capricious, it is not altogether whimsical. For example, the fact that standard dialects typically include more marked language forms – items or structures less natural in their linguistic composition – than their vernacular counterparts may be related to the fact that prescriptive norms often require speakers to recognize language forms on a conscious level. The practical dialect consequence of this socially as-cribed conscious attention to marked forms is the rejection of some natural linguistic changes that have resulted in unmarked forms (Kroch, 1978). For example, the persistence of the marked, irregular plural *oxen* instead of regu-larizing it to *oxes* can only be attributed to such socially ascribed, conscious attention.

Labov's delineation of vowel rotation alternatives in English (Labov, Yaeger, and Steiner, 1972; Labov, 1991, 1994) is a prototypical illustration of how dialects shift their vowel systems in orderly and predictable ways which are then assigned social meaning. Given the nature of vowel production, it is convenient to view different vowels as occupying "phonetic spaces" in a continuum of vowel positions. The notion of phonetic space is important because the shift of one vowel in phonetic space often has an effect on adjacent vowels. As one vowel moves (e.g., becomes higher or more backed in its phonetic position) phonetically closer to or further away from an adjacent vowel, the next vowel may shift its phonetic value to maintain adequate phonetic distance in relation to the vowel that has moved initially. A whole sequence of vowel rotation may thus be set in motion.

The pattern of phonetic rotation in vowels, known as *chain shifting* or the *push-pull chain*, is actively involved in differentiating the current charac-ter of long vowels. In the southern vowel shift, the vowel of *bed* takes on a glide, becoming more like *beyd* [bɛɪd]. Meanwhile, the front long vowels (the vowels of *beet* and *late*) are moving downward and somewhat backward, and the back vowels are moving forward. This scheme is represented in figure 7.2. Figures 7.1 and 7.2 show quite different rotational shifts in terms of direction-ality, but a unifying set of principles dictates the systematic movement of vowels in both shift patterns. In chain shifts, several primary descriptive principles are:

Figure 7.1 Vowel rotation in northern cities shift (adapted from Labov, 1991).

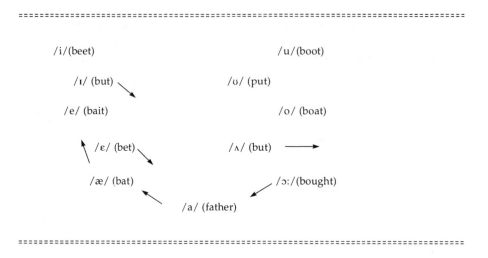

Figure 7.2 The southern vowel shift (adapted from Labov, 1991).

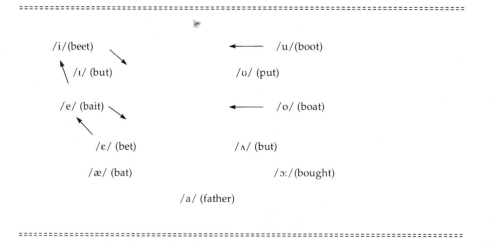

Principle I: Peripheral vowels (typically long and tense) rise.
Principle II: Non-Peripheral (typically short and lax) nuclei fall.
Principle III: Back vowels move to the front.

Various subsets of vowel rotations may be noted, as in the northern cities vowel shift and the southern vowel shift, and vowels may change their status with respect to peripherality so that systems may be altered rather drastically, but the underlying principles seem to be generalizable. While the operation of the underlying principles is more detailed than that presented here, and the underlying explanation of these descriptive shifts in terms of phonetic production and/or communicative strategy needs explication, principles that apply generally to vowel subsystems illustrate in an important way how dialect differences are sensitive to language-internal principles of organization and change. The search for underlying principles guiding dialect change and variation does not eliminate the need to view some aspects of dialect difference as isolated units (particularly with respect to lexical variation), but the appeal to internal-systemic principles of change and variation has taken the linguistic understanding of dialect description a giant step forward.

2.2 *Systematic variability*

Another dimension that needs to be admitted into the perspective on dialects in society is the systematic nature of variability. One of the important discoveries to emerge from the detailed study of dialects over the past several decades is the fact that dialects are sometimes differentiated not by the discrete or categorical use or nonuse of forms, but by the relative frequency with which different variants of a form occurred. For a number of phonological and grammatical dialect features, it can be shown that dialects are more typically differentiated by the extent to which these features are found rather than the mere absence or presence of particular variants. For example, studies of the alternation of -*in'* [ɪn] and -*ing* [ɪŋ] in words like *swimmin'* or *swimming* show that, while practically all dialects of English show this alternation, different dialects are distinguished by the relative frequency with which we find -*in'* and -*ing* in particular language varieties. Thus we found in a study of speaker representing different social classes in Detroit, Michigan, that the mean use of *in'* ranged from almost 20 percent use for speakers demographically defined as upper middle class to approximately 80 percent usage by speakers designated as lower working class (Shuy, Wolfram, and Riley, 1967). It is important to note that ALL of the individual speakers exhibit variability between -*ing* and -*in'*. In the study of variation, frequency levels are computed by first noting all those cases where a form like *in'* MIGHT HAVE occurred (namely, an unstressed syllable), followed by a tabulation of the number of cases in which -*in'* ACTUALLY occurred.

The fact that there is fluctuation between forms such as - *ing* and *in'* does not mean that the fluctuation is random or haphazard. Although we cannot predict which variant might be used in a given utterance, there are factors that can increase or decrease the likelihood that certain variants will occur. These factors are known technically as *constraints on variability*. The constraints are of two major types. First, there are various social or *external* factors which systematically increase or decrease the likelihood that a particular variant will occur. For example, the reference to social class above is an appeal to an external factor, since we can say that a speaker from the lower working class is more likely to use *-in'* for *-ing* than are speakers from other classes.

Not all of the systematic effects on variability, however, can be accounted for simply by appealing to various social factors. There are also aspects of the linguistic system itself, known as *internal factors*, that may affect the variability of particular forms apart from social constraints. Particular kinds of linguistic contexts, such as the kinds of surrounding forms or the type of construction in which the form occurs, may also influence the relative frequency with which these forms occur. The systematic effect of linguistic and social factors on the relative frequency of particular forms can best be understood by way of an actual case from phonology. Consider the example of word-final consonant cluster reduction as it affects sound sequences such as *st, nd, ld, kt*, and so forth in various English dialects. The rule of word-final consonant cluster reduction may reduce items such as *west, wind, cold*, and *act* to *wes', win', col'*, and *ac'* respectively. The incidence of reduction is quite variable, but certain linguistic factors systematically favor or inhibit the operation of the reduction process. The linguistic factors or constraints include whether the following word begins with a consonant as opposed to a vowel (more precisely, a nonconsonant), and the way in which the cluster is formed. With respect to the phonological environment that follows the cluster, the likelihood of reduction is increased when the cluster is followed by a word beginning with a consonant. This means that cluster reduction is more frequent in contexts such as *west coast* or *cold cuts* than in contexts like *west end* or *cold apple*. An individual speaker might, for example, reveal consonant cluster reduction in 75 percent of all cases where reduction could take place when the cluster is followed by a word beginning with a consonant (as in *west coast*) but in only 25 percent of all cases where the cluster is followed by a nonconsonant (as in *west end*). The important observation is that reduction may take place in both kinds of linguistic contexts, but it is consistently FAVORED in those contexts where the word following the cluster begins with a consonant.

As mentioned earlier, cluster reduction is also influenced by the way in which the cluster is formed. Clusters that are a part of an inherent word base, such as *wind* or *guest*, are more likely to undergo reduction than clusters that are formed through the addition of an *-ed* suffix, such as *guessed* (which ends in [st] phonetically – that is, [gɛst]) and *wined* (which ends in [nd] phonetically – that is, [waɪnd]). Again, reduction takes place in both types of clusters, but it applies more frequently when the cluster is an inherent part of a word rather than the result of the *-ed* suffix addition. When we compare the relative effects of different linguistic constraints on final consonant cluster reduction, we find that some linguistic factors have a greater influence on variability than others. Thus, in some dialects of English, the influence of the following segment (the consonant versus nonconsonant) is more important than the constraint based on cluster formation type (e.g., non *-ed* versus *-ed* clusters).

In many cases, linguistic constraints on variability can be ordered differently across varieties. Table 7.1 presents a comparison of word-final cluster reduction for different dialects of English, based upon a sample of speakers in each population. As seen in Table 7.1, all the varieties of English represented here show clusters to be systematically influenced by the following phonological context and the cluster formation type, although the proportional differences and the relationship between the linguistic constraints is not always the same. In some cases, such as Standard English and Appalachian vernacular English, the influence of the following consonant is more important than the cluster type, whereas in other cases, such as southern white working-class and southern African-American working-class speech, the influence of the cluster type is a more important constraint than the following phonological context.

The analysis of linguistic constraints on variability can get much more sophisticated than the simple kinds of "raw" frequency tabulations and comparisons introduced here (Guy, 1993), but this overview reveals the subtle and complex ways in which dialect differences are internally constrained, in terms of both their qualitative and quantitative linguistic dimensions.

Table 7.1 Comparison of Consonant cluster reduction in representative vernacular dialects of English (adapted from Wolfram, 1991).

LANGUAGE VARIETY	*Followed by consonant*		*Followed by vowel*	
	Not -ed % re-duction	-ed % re-duction	Not -ed % re-duction	-ed % re-duction
Standard English	66	36	12	3
Northern white working class	67	23	19	3
Southern white working class	56	16	25	10
Appalachian working class	74	67	17	5
Northern African-American working class	97	76	72	34
Southern African-American working class	88	50	72	36
Chicano working class	91	61	66	22
Puerto Rican working class	93	78	63	23
Italian working class	67	39	14	10
American Indian Puebloan English	98	92	88	81
Vietnamese English	98	93	75	60

3   The Social Distribution of Dialect

In many respects, describing the social distribution of language variation is dependent upon the kinds of group affiliations, interactional relations, and sociocultural ideologies operating within a society. The range of social factors and conditions that may be correlated with linguistic variation is quite wide-ranging (e.g., Preston, 1986a), but there is little agreement about a definitive set of social factors that vary with linguistic variation or an underlying, unitary, social or sociopsychological explanation of these parameters. Covari-ation between linguistic variation and social variation is multifarious and multidimensional, as the individual members of a society are at once affiliated with a range of overlapping groups with varying sociocultural ideologies, assume a variety of functional roles within and across groups, and participate in an assortment of interactional situations. In early studies of dialect in society (e.g., Labov, 1966c; Wolfram, 1969) it was common for linguists to appropriate a set of predetermined background demographic variables such as region, socioeconomic class, ethnicity, age, and sex, and to show the covari-ance of linguistic forms with these variables, either in isolation or, more commonly, in intersecting arrays. Later descriptions focused on the nature of communication networks (L. Milroy, 1980), the dynamics of situational con-text (Biber and Finegan, 1993), and the projection of social identity (LePage and Tabouret-Keller, 1986) in an effort to describe more authentically the social reality of dialect in society. (See chapters 8, 9, and 19 by Wodak and Benke, Eckert, and Tabouret-Keller for a discussion of some of these factors.) For our purposes here, it is sufficient but critical to recognize that many of the social variables typically appealed to in studies of covariance are abstractions extracted from an intricate, interactive, and multidimensional social reality. For example, McConnell-Ginet (1988) and Eckert (1989) point out that dialect differences correlated with gender differences assume a social construction based upon the biological category of sex. But the social construction of gender may be exceedingly complex, as it involves roles and ideologies crea-ting differential ways for men and women to experience life, culture, and society. As Eckert notes, "there is no apparent reason to believe that there is a simple, constant relation between gender and variation" (Eckert, 1989: 247). Similar provisos could be offered for virtually any of the traditional variables examined in the covariation of social and linguistic factors.

The perspective on dialect in society implied in the preceding discussion is an ethnographically informed one, since only such a vantage point can reveal the local kinds of affiliations, interactions, and ideologies that lead to the symbolic functions of dialect within a given community. Our recent studies of Ocracoke, a post-insular island community located 20 miles from the main-land state of North Carolina, reveal how an ethnographic perspective is needed to inform the role of dialect in a community setting (Schilling-Estes and Wolfram, 1994; Wolfram and Schilling-Estes, 1995). In this post-insular setting, some of the patterns of covariation between linguistic variables and traditional background demographic factors and/or social networks do not match the patterns of covariation that might be expected, based upon traditional sociolinguistic studies. For example, we do not find a unilateral regression pattern between age or socioeconomic class and the loss of traditional island dialect variants. Thus the use of a classic island variable, in which the *ay* diphthong of *high* and *tide* is backed and raised so that it is pronounced close to the *oy* vowel of *boy* or *Boyd*, is often found more frequently among a group of middle-aged, college-educated men who have a fairly wide range of contact outside the local networks than among their older and younger cohorts. Furthermore, the incidence of this island feature does not correlate neatly with the density and multiplicity of the social networks of these middle-aged men. For example, several of the men who use the highest incidence of this traditional island pronunciation are currently married to outsiders and have a fairly wide set of social networks extending well beyond local community members. At the same time, our ethnographic studies showed that these men are part of a highly symbolic, local "poker game network" which consists of a small, indigenous group of men who meet a couple of times a week to play poker. This group reflects strong, traditional island values, including the projection of island identity through the use of symbolic dialect choices that include the now stereotypical *oy* production in words such as *hoi toide* for "high tide." In fact, islanders are often referred to as *hoi toiders*, in reference to this production. While the descriptive details of the selective retention and enhancement of the *oy* production are much more intricate sociolinguistically than outlined here (see Wolfram and Schilling-Estes, 1995), the essential point is that our understanding of the local social meaning of varying dialect forms is dependent to a large extent on understanding the local social relations, ideology, and values of a community caught in the midst of a fairly dramatic transition from a self-contained, marine-based economy to a vibrant tourist industry. This uneasy but symbiotic relation between *dingbatters*, as outsiders are called by community members, and ancestral islanders, whose genealogy on the island can be traced for at least several generations, is obviously manifested in the curvilinear relationship shown in the distribution of dialect forms in apparent time. Group affiliation, communication networks, social identity, and social context all come into play in determining the role of this dialect variable in the Ocracoke community. But we can only ascribe social meaning to the patterns of covariance between dialect variables and social variables as we understand the sociohistorical background, the interactions, the ideologies, and the identities that define the local social context of dialect.

3.1 *Patterns of distribution*

Quite obviously, not all dialect structures are distributed in the same way within society. Given varying histories of dialect contact, dialect diffusion, and internal dialect change, and the varieties of social meaning ascribed to dialect forms, linguistic variables may align with given social groupings in a variety of ways. The pattern of dialect distribution which most closely matches the popular perception of dialect differences is referred to as *group-exclusive usage*, where one group of speakers uses a form but another group never does. In its ideal interpretation, group-exclusive usage means that ALL members of a particular community of speakers would use the dialect form whereas NO members of other groups would ever use it. This ideal pattern is rarely, if ever, manifested in dialects. The kinds of social grouping that take place in society are just too complex for this pattern to work out so neatly. In some cases, distinctions between groups exist on a continuum rather than in discrete sets. Furthermore, as we mentioned above, the definition of a social group usually involves a constellation of characteristics rather than a single dimension, thus making the simple correlation of a linguistic form with social structure intricate and multidimensional.

Notwithstanding the qualifications that have to be made when talking about group-exclusive dialect features, there certainly are items that are not shared across groups of speakers. The essential aspect of these dialect forms, however, seems to be the fact that speakers from other groups do NOT use these forms rather than the fact that all the members of a particular group use them. Group-exclusive usage is therefore easier to define negatively than positively. Viewed in this way, there are many dialect features on all levels of language organization that show group-exclusive social distribution.

According to Smith (1985), group-exclusive patterns of dialect distribution may be *saturated* or *unsaturated*. Saturated patterns refer to those that typify the vast majority of speakers within a particular social group or speech community and unsaturated patterns refer to those that are less pervasive, but still group-exclusive. For example, among younger working-class African-Americans, the "habitual *be*" form with *verb + ing* as in *They usually be going to the movies* might be considered a saturated form since the majority of speakers in this group use this form at one time or another. Note that the definition of the group in this case must include at least ethnicity, status, and age. By the same token, speakers of other varieties of English do not typically use this construction. In contrast, the use of the specialized future perfect construction *be done* as in *The chicken be done jumped out the pen* for the same population of working-class African-American speakers might be considered an unsaturated, group-exclusive form, since few, but only speakers of this variety, have been found to use this construction.

Descriptive qualifications such as "saturated" and "unsaturated" group-exclusive usage are useful approximate labels, but they have not yet been defined with any rigor. That is, the classification of a form as saturated or unsaturated is not determined on the basis of a specific proportion of speakers sampled within a given population (e.g., more than 75 percent of the speakers in a representative sample use the form in saturated usage and less than 20 percent of the speakers use the form in unsaturated usage). These designations are imprecise and limited, although admittedly convenient as informal characterizations of dialect patterns.

Group-exclusive dialect forms may be taken for granted in one dialect while, at the same time, they are quite obtrusive to speakers from other dialect areas. In American English, speakers from other regions may thus be quick to comment on how strange forms like *youns* "you pl.," *The house needs painted*, and *gumband* "rubber band" seem of them when visiting Pittsburgh, Pennsylvania, much to the surprise of the lifetime resident of Pittsburgh who has assumed that these were in common use. With increased interaction across dialect groups, however, speakers may become aware of some of their own group-exclusive usages. As the consciousness about these forms is raised, some of them may take on symbolic significance in identifying people from a given locale or social group. And from these features come the stereotypes of particular regional and ethnic dialects found in popular caricatures. However, it is important to remember that the stereotypical, symbolic caricatures by outsiders, and sometimes even by insiders, are often not linguistically faithful to the actual use of the form by speakers from the particular speech community.

In contrast to group-exclusive forms, *group-preferential* forms are distributed across different groups or communities of speakers, but members of one group simply are more likely to use the form than members of another group. For example, a fine-grained spectrum of color terms (e.g., *mauve, plum*, etc.) is often associated with females in the United States, but there are certainly males who make similar distinctions, and, of course, there are females who do not make such refined color designations. The association of a narrowly defined color spectrum with female speakers is thus statistically based, as more women make these distinctions than men. We refer to this narrowly defined color spectrum as a group-preferential pattern rather than a group-exclusive one. Group-preferential patterns may derive from the nature of the dialect variable or the nature of the social reality that underlies the social variable. For example, as we noted earlier, there are dimensions of group affiliation, interactional relationship, and ideological perspective that make the social construct of gender far more complex than a designation of group membership based solely on biological sex. We would not expect the symbolic effect of a group-preferential pattern to be as socially distinct as a group-exclusive marking, although popular stereotypes of group-preferential dialect patterns sometimes treat them symbolically as if they were group-exclusive. The popular characterization of vernacular dialects of English in their use of *dese, dem*, and *dose* for *these, them*, and *those* is such an instance, where the stereotype of group-exclusive behavior actually betrays a fairly complex pattern which is really group-preferential and also highly variable.

Variable use of socially diagnostic forms may also be distributed in different ways with respect to social variables. For example, given a continuous axis of age, a particular linguistic variable may show continuous unilateral regression between the incidence of a linguistic variant and age, that is, we find a regular slope between decreasing age and the incidence of the variant. For example, the increasing use of post-vocalic *r* for Anglos in the American South (e.g, *bear* for *bea'* or *car* for *ca'*) may show a linear progression in which increasing age is coterminous with the increasing incidence of post-vocalic *r*. This is sometimes referred to as *fine stratification*. Or the pattern may show *sharp* or *gradient stratification*, in which there is an abrupt change in the relative incidence of a feature at some point on a continuous social axis. For example, in the African-American community, there is a sharp decrease in the incidence of subject-verb concord as in *She go to the store* for *She goes to the store* at a midpoint in the social continuum that roughly divides the upper working and lower middle class (Wolfram, 1969). Finally, a *curvilinear* pattern might be revealed in the distribution of a socially diagnostic variable, in which the slope of the correlation line between linguistic variation and social variation reverses its direction at some point in the correlation. For example, on the island of Ocracoke, off the coast of North Carolina, the pattern of *ay* backing and raising of items such as *high tide* shows that middle-aged men in the poker game network have a higher incidence of backing and raising than their older and younger cohorts, thus showing a curvilinear pattern of distribution over age. The different kinds of covariation patterns between dialect features and social factors are shown in figure 7.3.

Stable linguistic variables defined primarily on the standard–nonstandard continuum of English tend to be sharply stratified, whereas linguistic features undergoing change often exhibit fine stratification. This is due in part to the role of social factors in language change within a community. Change tends to start in a given social class and spread from that point to other social classes in a diffuse manner. The kind of correlation that exists between social factors and linguistic variation may thus be a function of both social and linguistic considerations; there is no single pattern that can be applied to this covariation.

3.2   The social evaluation of linguistic features

Although there is no inherent social value associated with the variants of a linguistic variable, it is not surprising that the social values assigned to certain groups in society will be attached to the linguistic forms used by the members of these groups. While this general pattern of social evaluation holds, the correlation of particular linguistic variables with social stratification is not always so direct, as sociolinguistic history molds the diagnostic role of language structures in various ways.

The use of particular language variants may be evaluated as socially prestigious or socially stigmatized. *Socially prestigious* variants are those forms that are positively valued through their association with high status groups as linguistic markers of status, whereas *socially stigmatized* variants carry a stigma through their association with low-status groups. It is essential to understand that stigmatized and prestigious variants do not exist on a single axis in which the alternative to a socially stigmatized variant is a socially prestigious

Figure 7.3 Possible relations of linguistic and social variables.

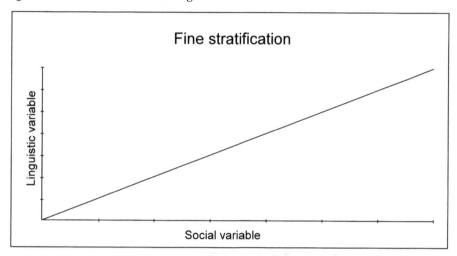

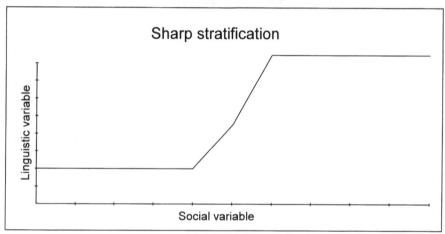

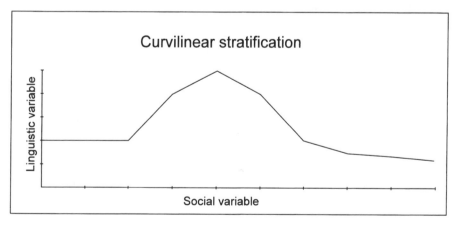

one, or vice versa. The absence of negative concord in sentences such as *She didn't do anything*, for example, in standard varieties of English is not particularly prestigious; it is simply NOT stigmatized. On the other hand, there may be particular patterns of negative formation that carry prestige in some varieties. For example, the choice of single negative marking on the post-verbal indefinite negatives (e.g., *He'll do nothing*) rather than on the auxiliary (e.g., *He won't do anything*) may be considered a prestigious option in some varieties of English, but the alternative marking in the auxiliary is not considered stigmatized.

The discussion of sociolinguistic evaluation up to this point has assumed a particular vantage point about norms of linguistic behavior, namely the perspective of widespread, institutional norms established by higher status groups. These norms are overtly perpetuated by the agents of standardization in society – language academies, teachers, the media, and other authorities responsible for setting the standards of behavior. Community-wide knowledge of these norms is usually acknowledged across a full range of social classes. Linguistic forms that are assigned their social evaluation on the basis of this widespread recognition of social significance are said to carry *overt prestige*. At the same time, however, there may exist another set of norms which relates primarily to solidarity with more locally defined social groups, irrespective of their social status position. When forms are positively valued apart from, or even in opposition to, their social significance for the wider society, they are said to have *covert prestige*. In the case of overt prestige, the social evaluation lies in a unified, widely accepted set of social norms, whereas in the case of covert prestige, the positive social significance lies in the local culture of social relations. Thus it is possible for a socially stigmatized variant in one setting to have covert prestige in another. A youth who adopts vernacular forms in order to maintain solidarity with a group of friends clearly indicates the covert prestige of these features on a local level, even if the same features stigmatize the speaker in a wider, mainstream context such as school. The notion of covert prestige is important in understanding why vernacular speakers do not rush to become standard dialect speakers, even when these speakers may evaluate the social significance of linguistic variation in a way which superficially matches that of their high-status counterparts. Thus widely recognized stigmatized features in English, such as negative concord, nonstandard subject verb agreement, and different irregular verb paradigms, may function at the same time in a positive, covertly prestigious way in terms of local norms.

There are several different ways in which speakers within the sociolinguistic community may react to socially diagnostic variables. Speakers may treat some features as *social stereotypes*, where they comment overtly on their use. In English, items such as *ain't*, "double negatives," and "*dese, dem,* and *dose*" are classic features of this type on a general level, but particular dialects may have stereotypes on a more local level. Thus the production of *hoi toiders* for *high tiders* has become a stereotype for the island community of Ocracoke, the plural *youns* a stereotype for the city of Pittsburgh, and the use of habitual *be* in *They be doing it* is rapidly becoming a stereotyped form for urban working-class African-American dialects in the United States. Sociolinguistic stereo-types tend to be overly categorical and are often linguistically naive, although they may derive from a basic sociolinguistic reality. For example, the stereo-type that working-class speakers ALWAYS use *dese, dem,* and *dose* forms and middle-class speakers NEVER do is not supported empirically, although there certainly is a correlation between the relative frequency of the nonstandard variant and social stratification. Furthermore, stereotypes tend to focus on single vocabulary items or selective subsets of items rather than more general phonological and grammatical patterns.

Another type of sociolinguistic role is assumed by the *social marker*. In the case of social markers, variants show clear-cut social stratification, but they do not show the level of conscious awareness found for the social stereotype. Various vowel shifts, such as the northern cities vowel shift discussed earlier, seem to function as social markers. There is clear-cut social stratification of the linguistic variants, and participants in the community may even recognize this distribution, but the structure does not evoke the kind of strongly evalu-ated overt commentary that the social stereotype does. Even if participants don't talk about these features in any direct manner, there are still indications that they are aware of their existence. This awareness is often indicated by shifts in the use of variants across different styles of speaking.

The third possible sociolinguistic role is called the *social indicator*. Social indicators are linguistic structures that correlate with social stratification without having an effect on listeners' judgment of social status. Whereas social stereotypes and social markers are sensitive to situational variation, social indicators do not show such sensitivity, as shown by the fact that levels of usage remain constant across formal and informal styles. This suggests that the correlation of socially diagnostic variables with social factors operates on a more unconscious level than it does for social markers or stereotypes.

The social recognition and evaluation of dialects does not relate just to particular dialect variables but to entire dialect communities. Research on *perceptual dialectology* (Preston, 1986b) shows that overall dialect perception is generated by linguistic differences, popular culture caricatures, and local identification strategies. For example, caricatures of New York City speech make this a highly recognized dialect area for virtually all American English speakers, regardless of their geographical locale. At the same time, the percep-tual location of other regional areas may be subjected to a "proximity factor," in which the more distant the dialect is geographically, the more likely it is to be classified globally.

4 Dialects and Social Commitment

The preceding discussion has viewed the role of dialects in society primarily on a micro-level, as we have examined the relations that exist between language variables and social variables. There are, however, issues related to the broadly based position of dialects in society. In this final section, we address some of these broader issues and consider the social role that sociolinguists can assume in addressing concerns relevant to dialects in society.

We have assumed in our discussion that dialects will continue to flourish in contemporary society, but many popular accounts of dialects question their enduring vitality. For example, in the United States it is often reported that dialects are levelling because of the widespread exposure to a standard, relatively homogenized dialect through the media, the increase in inter-regional travel and migration, and ready transportational access to virtually any dialect area of the country within a matter of hours.

Our preceding discussion indicates that the future of dialect diversity is assured on both a linguistic and social basis. For example, we have seen that the pressures of internally induced linguistic variation can take dialects in radically different directions once a particular linguistic shift has been initiated. The vowel changes taking place in the northern cities and southern vowel shifts in the United States are apparently making these varieties more dissimilar than ever, and some of the current rotational shifts may lead to changes in the English vowel system that are as dramatic as those witnessed during the great vowel shift that took place from 1300 through 1500 (Labov, 1994).

On a social level, the persistence of social dissonance of one type or another and the apparent inevitability of asymmetric social grouping underly the maintenance of socially and ethnically defined varieties, although some relic dialects preserved historically through their insularity have been levelled significantly as they emerged from their isolated status. The vertical social axis underlying the standard–nonstandard continuum remains operative, thus ensuring the continued vitality of vernacular dialects in most societies. External social conditions added to internal linguistic conditions assure the future of robust dialect differences.

The fact that so many dialect differences are defined on a vertical social axis naturally leads to a symbolic sociopolitical and socio-educational role for dialect. The socially constructed perception that vernacular dialects are deficient linguistic systems carries with it an attendant set of attitudes and behaviors that can impact significantly on the social and educational lives of underclass, vernacular speakers. The failure to recognize the legitimacy of dialect differences may lead to a kind of discrimination that is as onerous as other types based upon race, ethnicity, or class. Unfortunately, the existence of dialect discrimination is still not considered to be on the same plane as other types of prejudice. J. Milroy and L. Milroy (1985: 3) note: "Although public discrimination on the grounds of race, religion and social class is not now publicly acceptable, it appears that discrimination on linguistic grounds is publicly acceptable, even though linguistic differences may themselves be associated with ethnic, religious and class differences." Dialect discrimination cannot be taken more lightly than any other case of potential discrimination, and there is now a precedent for litigation based upon such discrimination. A society that assumes responsibility for combating discrimination on the basis of race, ethnicity, class, sex, and age should feel obligated to extend the same treatment to dialect differences.

The relatively short history of social dialectology has shown that it is quite possible to combine a commitment to the objective description of sociolinguistic data and a concern for social issues relating to dialect. At various junctures over the past three decades, sociolinguists have become involved in several important sociopolitical and socio-educational issues related to dialect diversity.

According to Labov (1982), there are two primary principles that may motivate linguists to take social action, namely the *principle of error correction* and the *principle of debt incurred*. These are articulated as follows:

> *Principle of error correction*
> A scientist who becomes aware of a widespread idea or social practice with important consequences that is invalidated by his own data is obligated to bring this error to the attention of the widest possible audience (Labov, 1982: 172).

> *Principle of debt incurred*
> An investigator who has obtained linguistic data from members of a speech community has an obligation to use the knowledge based on that data for the benefit of the community, when it has need of it (Labov, 1982: 173).

There are several outstanding instances in the history of social dialectology where these principles have been applied. In the 1960s, sociolinguists in the United States took a prominent pro-difference stance in the so-called *deficit–difference controversy* that was taking place within education and within speech and language pathology (Baratz, 1968; Labov, 1969). Consonant with the principle of error correction, sociolinguists took a united stand against the classification and treatment of normal, natural dialect differences as language deficits or disorders. There is little doubt that sociolinguists played a major role in pushing the definition of linguistic normalcy toward a dialectally sensitive one, although the practical consequences of this definition are still being worked out in many clinical and educational settings (Wolfram and Adger, 1993).

In keeping with the principle of debt incurred, social dialectologists also rose to the occasion in the celebrated Ann Arbor decision (1979). Linguistic testimony was critical to Judge Joiner's ruling in favor of the African-American plaintiff children who brought suit against the Board of Education for not taking their dialect into account in reading instruction. In effect, the judge ruled that the defendants had failed to take appropriate action to overcome language barriers, in violation of Title 20 of the US Code, Section 1703 (f). In compliance with the judge's ruling, a series of workshops was conducted to upgrade awareness and to apply sociolinguistic expertise in reading instruction.

There is another level of social commitment that sociolinguistic investigators might adopt toward the dialect communities in which they conduct their research. This level is more positive and proactive, in that it involves the active pursuit of ways in which linguistic favors can be returned to the community. Thus I propose an additional principle of social commitment which I call *the principle of linguistic gratuity*.

> *Principle of linguistic gratuity*
> Investigators who have obtained linguistic data from members of a speech community should actively pursue positive ways in which they can return linguistic favors to the community.

This principle seems to be a reasonable extension of social commitment on the part of linguists. However, this level of social responsibility is not restricted by a qualification based on recognized community needs, as is Labov's principle of indebtedness. Instead, it is committed to a creative search for a community-based collaborative model to return linguistic favors – favors that accurately reflect the role of dialect in society vis-à-vis popular stereotypes. This may be done through popular books and articles about community dialects, work with preservation societies in collecting and archiving dialect data, and the development of dialect awareness curricula for community schools (see Wolfram and Schilling-Estes, 1995). Language is, in many ways, the most sacred of all cultural traditions and is the rightful property of its users. Those who study dialect therefore need to be sensitive to the symbolic role of language and to preserve this unique artifact that has been shared with us by archiving for present and future generations of speakers the rich legacy of community dialects. While social dialectologists may not view themselves as agents of social change, they do have a responsibility to share the truth about dialects and to address the social consequences that derive from the failure to understand the fundamental nature of dialect in society.

8 Gender as a Sociolinguistic Variable: New Perspectives on Variation Studies

RUTH WODAK and GERTRAUD BENKE

1 Definitions of Terms: Aims of Sociolinguistic Gender Research

1.1 Introduction

Sociolinguistic research on gender and sex started in the early 1970s. Specifically, two domains of language behavior were investigated: speech behavior of men and women on the phonological level, and the interaction behavior (conversational styles) between women and men in discourse.[1] In this paper we will concentrate on studies in sociophonology (variation studies). Nevertheless we would like to combine both approaches to trace the theoretical development of gender studies in linguistics, combining both approaches and thus providing a general framework for our paper.

Studies of gender-specific variation are often contradictory, depending on the author's implicit assumptions about sex and gender, the methodology, the samples used, etc. Thus, as Eckert and McConnell-Ginet (1992: 90) state, "women's language has been said to reflect their [our] conservatism, prestige consciousness, upward mobility, insecurity, deference, nurture, emotional expressivity, connectedness, sensitivity to others, solidarity. And men's language is heard as evincing their toughness, lack of affect, competitiveness, independence, competence, hierarchy, control."

Studies published so far have also made a lot of different claims, some of which are contradictory. For example, on the one hand standard language and prestige variants are associated with the elites, i.e., middle-class males; on the other hand, standard language is related to women, and the vernacular to men. Thus it is necessary to develop a critical approach to this vast literature. All the claims made about women and men at different times, in different circumstances, and with totally different samples, on the basis of different implicit ideologies about gender, have to be analyzed carefully and viewed in relation to the development of gender studies in the social sciences.

In our view, many studies have neglected the context of language behavior and have often analyzed gender by merely looking at the speakers' biological sex (see the arguments in Nichols, 1983; Eckert, 1989; Coates, 1990). Instead, we would like to propose that a context-sensitive approach which regards gender as a social construct would lead to more fruitful results.

In our overview of the different paradigms of variation studies (section 2) and in our discussion of some specific alternative approaches (section 3), we will focus on the following questions, based on theoretical and taxonomical considerations:

1 How are sex and gender related to each other? How is gender investigated empirically? Is there a notion of gender at all?
2 How is the context of language behavior analyzed, and which other variables are relevant?
3 Which methodologies are used? What kind of samples are collected and analyzed?
4 What are the underlying theoretical assumptions? Which social theory, which gender theory, which linguistic theory are implicitly or explicitly drawn upon?

1.2 Definitions

Gender and sex

The British sociologist Anthony Giddens defines "sex" as "biological or anatomical differences between men and women," whereas "gender" "concerns the psychological, social and cultural differences between males and females" (1989: 158). On the basis of these definitions, it seems relatively easy to distinguish between the two categories, although Giddens does mention some syndromes of "abnormal" development: the testicular feminization syndrome, and the androgenital syndrome. In these cases infants, designated as "female" at birth, even if chromosomally male, tend to develop female gender identity, and vice versa.

The important question in studying language behavior and gender empirically at this point concerns the connection (correlation, relationship) of sex and gender. Thus we need more differentiated definitions. Several questions have to be addressed; for example: Do all biologically female persons develop female gender? How are differences between women to be explained? Which other social categories intervene? In a social construction perspective, however, both sex and gender are seen as socially developed statuses (Lorber and Farrell, 1991: 7). Sex is then understood more as a continuum made up of chromosomal sex, gonadal sex, and hormonal sex, all of which "work in the presence and under the influence of a set of environments" (Fausto-Sterling, 1985: 71). It makes no sense therefore to assume that there is just one set of traits that characterize men in general and thus define masculinity; or likewise, that there is one set of traits for women, which define femininity. Such a unitary model of sexual character is a familiar part of sexual ideology and serves to reify inequality between men and women in our society. It also paves the way for all kinds of sociobiological explanations relating neurological facts to linguistic behavior (Chambers, 1992; see 2.5 below).

Connell (1993: 170ff.) therefore proposes a non-unitary model of gender; both femininity and masculinity vary, and understanding their context-dependent variety is regarded as central to the psychology of gender. Furthermore, he argues that since masculinity and femininity coexist in the same person, they should not be seen as polar opposites, but as separate dimensions: "Femininity and masculinity are not essences: they are ways of living certain relationships. It follows that static typologies of sexual character have to be replaced by histories, analyses of the joint production of sets of psychological forms" (Connell, 1993: 179).

Moreover, Lewontin (1982: 142), whose definition we would like to follow, stresses the relevance of the socialization process: the development of gender identity "depends on what label was attached to him or her as a child . . . Thus biological differences became a signal for, rather than a cause of, differentiation in social roles." This definition connects in an excellent way the impact of societal norms and evaluations, power structures, and the role of socialization. Thus it makes much more sense to talk of genders in the plural, because what it means to be a woman or to be a man changes from one generation to the next and is different for different racial, ethnic, and religious groups, as well as for members of different social classes (see Gal, 1989: 178; Stolcke, 1993: 20; Lorber and Farrell, 1991: 1ff.). Gender categories are social constructs, they institutionalize cultural and social statuses, and they have served to make male dominance over women appear natural: "gender inequality in class society results from a historically specific tendency to ideologically 'naturalize' prevailing socio-economic inequalities" (Stolcke, 1993: 19).

A further aspect has to be included: the negotiation of gender in actual interaction. This leads us to the understanding of gender "as a routine, methodical, and recurring accomplishment . . . 'doing gender' [emphasis by the authors] is undertaken by men and women, doing gender involves a complex of socially guided perceptual, interactional, and micropolitical activities that cast particular pursuits as expressions of masculine and feminine natures" (West and Zimmerman, 1991: 13–14).

Such an understanding and definition of gender marks the importance of context-oriented research (Wodak, 1994; Duranti and Goodwin, 1992); language behavior is always situated in certain contexts and cannot be regarded as isolated from these contexts. But unfortunately, although sociolinguistics explicitly includes societal context in its fundamental and constitutive assumptions about language and meaning, many survey studies on variation have dealt very superficially (or not at all) with the context of the data investigated.

Sociolinguistic variables

Bearing traditional methodologies in sociolinguistics in mind, it does not surprise us that Wardhaugh's (1992: 139–40) definition (which is used widely in introductory courses) of a "linguistic variable" does not mention the importance of context orientation at all: "A linguistic variable is a linguistic item which has identifiable variants." He distinguishes between two kinds of linguistic variables, variants (features) which are distinct, like [Ø] and [ŋ] in *singin'* [Ø] and *singing* [ŋ], and quantitative variants, whose differences are measured on a continuum, like [ɛ] . . . [e].[2] Traditionally, such linguistic variables are then correlated with social categories, like sex (gender), age, social class, ethnicity, etc., taken out of their respective contexts and without problematizing the meaning of these social categories (see Dittmar et al., 1988: 115; Guy, 1991: 5ff.; 1988, 40ff.; Santa Ana, 1992: 278ff.; Rickford, 1991: 611ff.). We will discuss the notion of context more extensively in section 3.

1.3 Theories in linguistic gender research

Early studies on language and gender usually considered the language or speech behavior of women in terms of a deficiency model, that is, they considered the speech behavior of men as stronger, more prestigious, and more desirable (Lakoff, 1975). The female style, seen as a sign of subordination and self-denial, was to be rejected. Then, in a second phase, the strengths of the styles more commonly used by women were observed and sometimes overgeneralized. Concepts arose such as WOMEN'S STYLE (= good) and MEN'S STYLE (= bad) (Trömel-Plötz, 1984). For example, the "female" style was described as being cooperative, the male in contrast as being competitive. Differences within one gender were neglected, the sexes were equated with the respective gender, and a unitary model served as the basis for investigation (see above). Lakoff's intuitive hypotheses were adhered to in many studies. As a result, a variety of methodological approaches were pursued (see Cameron, 1985; Wodak et al., 1987; Henley and Kramerae, 1991; Coates and Cameron, 1990; Trudgill, 1972, for examples). Not all of the earlier claims could be universally proven; some had to be differentiated (Dubois and Crouch, 1975; Crosby and Nyquist, 1977; Holmes, 1986; Gräszel, 1991).

In the second decade of linguistic gender studies, research in linguistics, sociology, anthropology, and communication sciences investigated subtle differences in the speech behavior of men and women, resulting in a situational ranking of the sexes. The category of gender played an important role in conversation and was different in every situational context (Wodak and Andraschko, 1994; Ochs, 1992; Henley and Kramerae, 1991). But once again these context specificities were inadequately discussed in many studies. Issues of power and dominance were of great relevance. The deficit theory was thus replaced by the dominance theory. Although these studies were still based on a unitary model of gender, they were more context-sensitive and took the power structures of society into consideration.

In the next phase, emphasis was put on research on gender socialization. There is an extensive literature showing that boys and girls learn different verbal and nonverbal skills in their mainly same-sex children's and peer groups (summarized in Wodak and Schulz, 1986; Günther and Kotthoff, 1991; Eckert, 1989). These skills remain relevant for adults in many situations (Wodak 1984, 1986; Maltz and Borker, 1982; Tannen, 1991). The differences in subcultures and socialization processes were emphasized, yet the power aspect seems to have been neglected. These approaches were summarized as "difference theory." The debate within gender studies was more and more mistakenly reduced to rather simple questions: Do men interrupt women more often than vice versa? Do men dominate topics of conversation? Are women hypercorrect?[3] Do all women use more standard language than men? Since the contexts in which men more often distinctly interrupted women were hardly specified, for example (West and Zimmerman 1991), the debate was and is reduced to general pro or con questions, instead of being concerned with tracing context-specific power relations.

Most recently, social constructivist approaches (see pp. 128–30; Fenstermaker, West, and Zimmerman, 1991: 303) have been taken into account. In this approach, gender is understood as an indirectly developed identity category, integrated into the formation of other identity categories. This depiction implies a non-unitary approach to gender. In general, gender roles in institutions and the communicative behavior of men and women are not separated from one another. Gender roles are produced, reproduced, and actualized through context-specific gender- distinct activities in communication.

Finally, Uchida (1992: 564) argues very consistently for a compromise between the dominance and difference approaches through a social-constructivist concept which we would like to take up:

> The issue at hand is not whether we should take the dominance/power-based approach or the difference/cultural approach or both approaches to analyze sex differences in discourse. Rather, it is how we can come up with a framework that allows us to see gender as a holistic and dynamic concept regarding language use

– a framework that allows us to see how we, in the social context, are doing gender through the use of language.

Naturally, this also relates to the level of sociolinguistic variation.

2 The Main Paradigms

2.1 *History*

The investigation of gender-specific language variation started in the 1960s with the sociophonological surveys of William Labov, especially his study on Martha's Vineyard and his New York study (Labov, 1966b). In these studies Labov considered sex as one factor among many influencing the variation of language behavior. To explain sociophonological variation he used the socio-logical concept of "prestige," emphasizing language attitudes as a causal factor in choosing a certain lect right from the beginning.

In the following decades most work within sociophonology employed the Labovian framework; deviating and critical approaches remained unnoticed. One example of such an early critical approach is that of Nichols (1976), who anticipated both methodological (participant observation) and theoretical de-velopments. She opposed the unitary model of women (see p. 129) – "They [women] make choices in the contexts of particular social networks rather than as some generalized response to the universal conditions of women" (Nichols, 1983: 54) and criticized the presumption of classifying women's socioeconomic status (SES) according to their husbands'.

A qualitatively new approach was presented in 1980 by Lesley Milroy and in the works of Lesley and James Milroy (L. Milroy, 1980; J. Milroy, 1981; L. Milroy, 1992; L. and J. Milroy, 1992). Their orientation towards the microsocio-logy of language usage, concentrating on social networks, paralleled new developments in other branches of linguistic interest – in discourse analysis, the ethnography of speaking, etc. – and pointed to the importance of context sensitivity.

We begin with a review of the two most important strands of sociophono-logical research: the Labovian tradition, with a brief discussion of the works of Labov and Trudgill, and the network approach with a short discussion of the studies of the Milroys (2.2). This will be followed by a more general discussion of the impact of these traditions on today's sociophonological research (2.3) which will be contrasted with approaches deriving from other traditions (2.4). Finally we will present a synopsis of the most important propositions explaining language variation due to gender and a brief sum-mary of the feminist critique of research on gender and sociophonological variation.

2.2 The Labovian tradition

1937

Labov

Labov was the first to notice the important role of sex/gender as a sociolinguistic variable. As a method of collecting the reliable, authentic data needed for sociolinguistic research, Labov (1966b) introduced the sociolinguistic interview, carefully designed to elicit different speech styles within a single interview. His studies show a stratification of phonological variables according to sex/gender, age, socioeconomic status (SES), and situational context. In order to integrate the observed intrapersonal variation (in different contexts) and interpersonal variation into approved linguistic theories, Labov formulated "variable rules." Like phonological context variables (e.g., assimilation) situational and personal features work as varying factors in a rule-governed process of speech production resulting in a specifically realized sociophonological variable.

Focusing primarily on language change, Labov emphasized two features of human language behavior: (a) Women of all classes and ages use more standard variants than their equivalent men. As the standard is usually regarded as the language of the elite, for the rest of the population an approximation to this standard implies a deviation from the language of one's own group. (b) The lower middle class (LMC) "hypercorrects" its language; it copies features of the middle class (MC), whose language behavior is more standard, in order to gain social prestige. But the LMC extends this copied usage to other phonological contexts as well (over-generalization) and thus stimulates language change. Here again (following (a)) women in particular are in the lead. Through child-rearing they transmit their hypercorrect language behavior to their children, for whom it becomes the perceived language. (Nevertheless women do not always introduce and lead in language change, as Labov's study of Martha's Vineyard (1963) demonstrates.) Figure 8.1 (Labov, 1990: 224) demonstrates the role of class and gender in hypercorrection.

In his early studies (1963, 1966b) Labov was already trying to go beyond mere description and explain language variation between different classes. To that end he made use of sociological concepts. A particularly important concept is that of group identification (or projection) which, in conjunction with language attitudes (that is, the prestige of a certain language variety), has a major impact on choosing a certain language variety over another. The status of a group and its particular language is thus a central sociolinguistic question.

The LMC (especially women) imitates the prestigious language of the MC in order to gain a better social position, to become MC itself. The concept of linguistic insecurity, which is connected with the LMC, plays a significant role. "The index of linguistic insecurity involves the proportion of cases in which people distinguish between the way they speak and another way of speaking that is 'correct' " (Labov, 1990: 225–6).

Figure 8.1 Style shifting of (oh) by three socioeconomic groups in New York City (after Labov, 1990: 224).

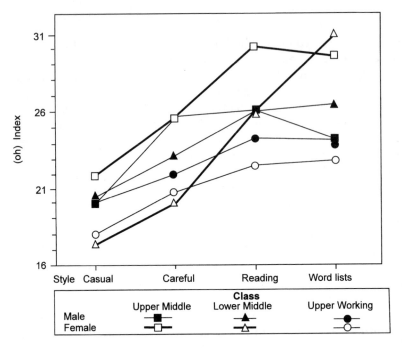

Regarding gender, Labov restricted himself in his early studies to determining the influence of gender/sex on language variation but did not try to solve the puzzle of the underlying causes of this influence: "Why do women do this? It cannot be only their sensitivity to prestige forms, since that explains only half of the pattern. We can say that they are more sensitive to prestige patterns, but why do they move forward faster in the first place? Our answers at the moment are no better than speculations" (Labov, 1991: 302). Furthermore Labov (1991: 181) claimed that the observed higher prestige-consciousness of women is dependent on their specific position within a certain society. In parts of India and Iran, for instance, where women do not participate in public discourse, they were less inclined to use (more) standard language (than men).

Labov (1990) tries to reconcile two slightly inconsistent questions: (1) Why is it that men use more non-standard varieties, and (2) why do women lead in language change? In a specific domain of conceived language norms, the deviation of women as opposed to that of men influences language change. As he did before, Labov (1990) stressed the child-rearing function of women, which leads to an imbalance in the enforcement of gender-specific language varieties. He specially emphasizes the observed correlation between "occupational roles" and sex/gender. While there might be no interaction at all at the beginning of a language change, in the course of time interaction evolves and

the relationship between the sociophonological variable and0gender differentiates the different classes. Thus Labov demonstrates that only a cross-tabula-
tion of sex/gender and class reveals interesting propositions about the nature
of the relation between sex/gender and a certain sociophonological variable
(see also Cravens and Gianelli, 1993).

So once again this study stresses the role of gender as an important factor in
sociophonological variation. But Labov does not explain why it is that women
use more standard forms. His literature survey gives us the following very
general reasons: "Women . . . are said to be more expressive than men or use
expressive symbols more than men or rely more on such symbols to assert
their position" and "Women are said to rely more on symbolic capital than
men because they possess less material power" (Labov, 1990: 214).

Trudgill

Peter Trudgill (1972, 1983b) works within a framework similar to that of
Labov, but he has a stronger emphasis on sociological reasons to account for
the observed gender-specific difference in language variation. His study of
Norwich (1972) includes first of all the already mentioned observation that
men use more nonstandard forms than women. The question is why working-
class (WC) men (and in this study young women as well) stick to their
low-prestige nonstandard variety. To explain this Trudgill has adopted
Labov's (1966b) notion of "covert prestige": for men nonstandard variants
fulfill the function of solidarity markers which highlight certain group values
like "masculinity." In other words, the notion of covert prestige captures the
hidden sociological function of vernaculars.

In explaining why, on the other hand, women in general use more standard
forms than men, Trudgill (1972: 91) states: "The social position of women in
our society is less secure than that of men . . . It may be . . . that it is more
necessary for women to secure and signal their social status linguistically."
Furthermore men are judged according to their work, yet women are assessed
according to their appearance, which includes language.

It is specifically this self-representation in a language that Trudgill examined
closely in his study. In self-evaluation tests he analyzes the gendered mis-
perception in self-perception. Women tend to exaggerate their actual usage
of standard forms; men on the contrary tend to underreport their standard
usage.

Network studies

The studies of James and Lesley Milroy (1980, 1981, 1987) represent a qualitatively new approach to language variation. As opposed to Labov, their research is more concerned with the internal variation within a certain group
(the working class (WC)) and not with the language community as a whole:
"Within working-class speech alone, this research has demonstrated that

there are considerable differences between individuals, between different speech-styles, between men and women, and between older and younger speakers" (J. Milroy, 1981: 89).

Like Trudgill (1972) they raise the question why members of the WC stick to their low-prestige vernacular. The Milroys' innovations are twofold: (a) On the methodological level, during data collection the researcher becomes part of the observed group, the social network under investigation. The researcher is introduced to the network as a friend or colleague of a member of it. (b) On the theoretical level, they employ the sociological concept of social networks: "networks generally have reference to a quantifiable set of relations individuals have to one another by reference to such facts as frequency of interaction, transactional (one-way) versus exchange (two-way) interactions, and so on" (Preston, 1987: 693).

These networks capture group structures, and the explanations of the observed sociophonological phenomena trace particular language behavior back to certain peculiarities of the obvious network structures, enabling a very fine-grained analysis, in complete contrast to the macrosociological approach of the former survey studies. Then networks themselves can be characterized by two parameters: density and multiplexity. Density signifies the number of people participating in a network and the number of relationships of a person to other members of this network. Multiplexity is an index for the polyfunctionality of network relations. For instance, a colleague from work can also be a friend. Within a single class the Milroys specially focus on age and sex/gender and the interrelationship of these two sociological variables.

The results of L. Milroy (1980) again confirm the tendencies mentioned above – women use more standard forms than men and men more nonstandard variables than women. But their ethnographic approach allows a more specific explanation of the language behavior observed; (young) men are subject to more rigid group pressure to speak in vernacular than women, and about women they state, "It would seem that female linguistic behavior is viewed more tolerantly by local peer-groups, so that women have, in a sense, more linguistic freedom than men" (J. Milroy, 1981: 37). The different language attitudes of men and women (J. Milroy, 1981; Trudgill, 1972; Smith, 1985) together with their different linguistic possibilities thus lead to antagonistic developments in language behavior.

J. Milroy (1992) connects the degree of differentiation of male and female language behavior while using stable variables (variables which show only a minor age gradation and which are therefore unlikely to be involved in an ongoing language change) with the stability of a social group. Social groups (or societies) which – as in Ballymacaert – have a very stable gender role differentiation show the greatest difference between male and female language behavior. Milroy analyzes these relations in a detailed study of language variation and its dependence on social networks. In general, dense and multiplex networks reinforce the linguistic norms of a certain group. But "agreement on norms . . . results not in uniformity of usage within a com-

Table 8.1 Contrasing patterns of distribution of two vowels involved in change, according to sex of speaker, relative frequency of innovatory variants and level of correlation with network strength (after L. Milroy, 1987a: 120).

	Change led by	*High correlation with network strength*
/a/	Males	Females
/ɛ/	Females	Males

munity, but in agreement on a pattern of stable differentiation" (J. Milroy, 1992: 90). The dense and multiplex network merely gives rise to the symbolic function of certain language variables, but it does not determine their actual use,[4] which is still dependent on the actual situation, on the specific interacting persons, and so on. The relationship between gender, social network, and language is still a very complex one. On the one hand, linguistic variables may function as network markers for women or for men (not necessarily for both). In this case a certain gender is highly correlated with a dense, multiplex network. On the other hand, linguistic variables may function as gender markers independent of any social network. Table 8.1 (J. Milroy, 1992: 120) makes a further proposition: If a linguistic variable functions as a network marker, this variable has to be a static one for this group. Language change has to be introduced by another group.

In sociophonology, the research design using social networks has one major drawback, as the Milroys themselves point out: Explanations using the inner structure of a social network need the network to be dense and multiplex. Therefore language change stemming from the MC or UC with their loose-knit networks cannot yet be investigated in this way.[5]

2.3 *Research deriving from Labov and the Milroys*

The work of Labov and the Milroys constitutes the overall framework for sociophonological studies concerned with gender until now. This implies a concentration on phonological variables; only a few studies deal with gender-specific differences in intonation (McConnell-Ginet, 1983), the biological but culturally transformed difference in ground frequency (Smith, 1985; Ohara, 1992; Romaine, 1994) or differences in the application of phonological rules (Leodolter, 1975).

The sociological variables usually included are mostly those already mentioned: age, sex/gender, an operationalization of class (mostly based on SES), and contextual styles. Network studies add some indexes for multiplexity and density or a single index for both.

There is no differentiation of "sex" and "gender", the classification usually employs an unproblematized notion of sex. Furthermore, most works do not dwell on the relationship between gender and other sociological variables; only a few studies beside Labov's are concerned with linguistic (*langue*-based) restrictions on the sociophonological variation of the linguistic variables under investigation. Generally no further sociological concepts and theories are used. The studies either aim at the description and explanation of mechanisms of language change as such, or they want to describe an observed language variation and find sociological reasons for it. Gender/sex is treated as one factor of a set, among which class (and sometimes age) are the most prominent.

Most of these studies concentrate on urban varieties of English (Swales, 1990). Lately, minority languages and their relationship to standard English have also received some attention, especially Black English (Edwards, 1990, 1992; Nichols, 1983) and the language behavior of Chicanos (Galindo and Gonzales, 1992; Santa Ana, 1992). In addition to sociophonological research in the US, Great Britain, Ireland, and Central America, we would like to mention the research of Australian sociolinguists, who developed interesting context-sensitive refinements of research methods (Horvath, 1985; Clyne, 1991) in response to the complex multilingualism of the country.

The majority of descriptive studies published so far confirms earlier results[6] – there is not a single known language which shows no gender difference on the sociophonological level at all (although not every variable has to have a gender differentiation). Nevertheless this difference is only a gradual one: If women have access to the standard variety, they will generally use more standard forms than men, who will tend to use more nonstandard forms. Women are more sensitive to deviation from the standard variety (in reception tests) and women are more likely to lead in language change. Despite these often reported tendencies, some sociolinguistic studies provide clearly contradictory results which are not consistent with these claims: Men use more standard language and men are the innovators in linguistic change.[7]

2.4 Other research traditions

New influences on the study of the relationship of language variation and gender stem from the European tradition of dialectology, bilingualism and multilingualism, and research on minorities and language contact (Zentella, 1987; Medicine, 1987; Hill, 1990). The multilingual situation enables a more detailed and focused approach to the study of social context and language choice. Results of multilingual studies show similar tendencies to those of monolingual studies: the standard variety of the latter can be equated with the prestigious, dominant language of the former. Women are usually initiators of the decreolization process (a critical analysis of the role of women in decreolization is provided by Escure, 1992).

Most of these research traditions, however, are still mainly interested in the study of language variation as such. Sex or sometimes gender as an empirically relevant social category is only seldom considered. (An exception is the more ethnographically oriented research on minorities.) Therefore some aspects influencing language variation have gained only minor attention and are mostly included in the overall framework of larger surveys. This is especially the case for research on gendered language attitudes.[8] Men and women judge standard and nonstandard language differently (Smith, 1985), they have different perception levels for linguistic variables (as shown in the self-evaluation tests of Trudgill, 1972) and they are judged differently when using the same language variety (Moosmüller, 1989, investigates this for Austrian German).

Parallel to these developments in sociophonology, the last two decades witnessed a growing interest in gender research in other linguistic areas, such as discourse analysis, conversation analysis, and the ethnography of speaking. Studies in these areas resulted in a variety of explanations for gender differences. In line with the growing importance of qualitative ethnographic approaches in sociophonology, these explanations are beginning to exercise an influence on sociophonology as well.

2.5 *Theoretical grounding and feminist critique*

At present we still find a discrepancy between sociophonological studies and the theoretical considerations and criticism inspired by feminist research regarding the studies and explanations provided so far. We would now like to present an overview of the most influential explanations and to list important criticisms.

The explanations put forth so far can be divided into three groups according to their concept of sex/gender: (a) biologically oriented explanations, (b) explanations which make use of the different social context of men and women without further questioning of these contexts (This approach can be subsumed under the two-culture approach presented below; (c) explanations which point directly to the unequal distribution of power between men and women (power and dominance approach).[9]

The biological approach

No contemporary explanation assumes total biological determination. Explanations of the difference in sound frequencies using the difference in physiology (men have a longer vocal tract) nevertheless stress the importance of the cultural transformation (Ohara, 1992; Smith, 1985). Only a few researchers think that there is a biological cause of the observed language variation (e.g., Chambers, 1992, who thinks that women have a better ability to learn languages and will therefore show more variation).

The two-culture approach

Language is used as a signifying code to maintain group identity. Male peer groups exert strong pressure on their members to use the vernacular (Milroy,

1981). Their use of the vernacular is due to their tendency to delimit themselves from women (Trudgill, 1972; Lippi-Green, 1989).

The dominant role of women in child-rearing leads to their more status-conscious language behavior, as they would like to enhance the future chances of their children by teaching them the standard variety (Labov, 1966, 1990). This is especially the case in language contact situations (Engel-Wodak and Rindler-Schjerve, 1985).

The status of men is derived from their occupation. Women who mostly work at home have to use symbolic systems including language to demonstrate their status (Eckert, 1989). The different occupations of men and women lead to a different exposure to other language varieties. Females' jobs are often further away from their own community and entail more contact with other people (e.g., salesperson, teacher) than do those of men, who share their workplace with members of the same speech community (factories, farming). This leads to the higher language proficiency of women, better control of more registers and styles, and an orientation to supra-regional language norms (Nichols, 1983).

The power and dominance approach

Female usage of the standard language is intended as a means of improving their own inferior position in a patriarchal society (Deuchar, 1990). The weaker a woman's position, the more she is forced to be polite. Standard language is only one of many ways to show this deference (Deuchar, 1990; Kotthoff, 1992).

Most of the approaches reviewed here imply that there is a "difference in culture" between male and female behavior (let us point out that the notion of "culture" in this context may be misleading). Moreover, one specific criticism of feminist science is that explanations in sociophonology fail to do justice to the power distribution within society and that they are not grounding their theories and results in theories of society (Kotthoff, 1992; Cameron, 1990; McConnell-Ginet, 1988). Additional criticism is directed at the quantitative methodology used. In general, critics stress the need to take context into account. As in the work of the Milroys, one has to look for the peculiarities of the society under investigation, the roles of women and men. Explanations should (at least at the present time) be more local (especially regarding the contradicting claims raised by different studies). The following list summarizes the most important points:

- There is a tendency for unwarranted generalizations of individual research findings from "some women" to "all women" (Eckert and McConnell-Ginet, 1992).
- Like all signs, a specific sociophonological variable can be polyfunctional. Hitherto most explanations seem to make use of a monofunctional concept of the social dimension of a linguistic variable.

- Language variation is a part of a more complex system of symbols. In explanations the signifying function of language variables has to be connected with the overall picture of societal structures.
- Using "sex" as a social variable reduces a complex social phenomenon in a misleading way. "Gender is always joined with real people's complex forms of participation in the communities to which they belong" (Eckert and McConnell-Ginet, 1992: 91).
- The methodology used is in itself sexist. On all the indexes, men usually have higher scores than women (Cameron, 1990). In quantitative studies, the factorial design is usually set up in such a way that men score higher than women on the observational measures taken.
- The male language is regarded as the language norm. Female language is treated as a deviation. Studies are often concerned with the particular deviating nature of women. Men's language behavior remains underreported (Cameron, 1990).
- Survey studies in the Labovian tradition neglect contextual influences.
- Network studies and similar approaches are often based on too small a sample and therefore do not allow for generalizations over the whole group under investigation, or for the language behavior of men and women as such.
- The distinction between gender and sex is often ignored.

In the following section some alternative studies, which try to avoid the shortcomings of traditional research, will be presented.

3 Some Alternative Approaches to Variation

3.1 The ethnographic approach

Variation of adolescents

Eckert and McConnell-Ginet (1992: 92ff.), starting from Labov's paradigm, propose to investigate "communities of practice" as the units of sociolinguistic research. Communities of practice are defined as "an aggregate of people who come together around mutual engagement in some common endeavor. Ways of doing things, ways of talking, beliefs, values, power relations – in short, practice – emerge in the course of their joint activity around that endeavor" (p. 95).

Gender is produced and reproduced in differential membership in such communities of practice. Gender itself is based, in the opinion of the two authors, on a non-unitary model: There is differentiation between the sexes, women define themselves with respect to other women, men to men; women and men differ in their routes of obtaining social status; and women are under constant pressure to display their persona (Eckert, 1989: 247ff.). Both Eckert and McConnell-Ginet argue very convincingly and provide many examples to support their view that survey studies in variation are too general and their level of abstractness too great. Many subtle and important intervening variables have been neglected, including the context, that is, the communities of practice.

Furthermore, Eckert argues (1989: 245ff.), the variables of age, sex, etc. are used in a very superficial way. As she points out, it would be more relevant to look at life stages instead of chunks in an age continuum. Thus many results on language change in "traditional" studies, such as those by Labov and Trudgill, may be biased. In her own study of a community of practice, a high school in a Detroit suburb, two years of participant observation allowed Eckert to understand the pressures and self-definitions of boys and girls in two different peer groups: the Jocks, middle-class youth, whose lives are centered around school; and the Burnouts, working-class youth, whose lives are centered around adult life in the city in rebellion against school.

Boys and girls undergo different socialization processes in each group, but in both groups the pressure is greater for girls if they want to be accepted and to be "popular":

> A star varsity athlete, for instance, regardless of his character or appearance, can enjoy considerable status. There is virtually nothing, however, that a girl lacking in social or physical gifts can do that will accord her social status. In other words, whereas it's enough for a boy to have accomplishments of the right sort, a girl must be a certain sort of person. (Eckert, 1989: 256)

The two groups differ in the kind of self-image they want to project: The Jocks are friendly and All-American, the Burnouts are tough and experienced. In both groups, the girls have to invest more energy to accommodate to such an image. Eckert investigated two sets of linguistic changes in relation to gender and the peer groups, an older and a new change: fronting of low vowels, backing and lowering of mid vowels (see figure 8.2).

Figure 8.2 The northern cities chain shift (after Eckert, 1989: 260).

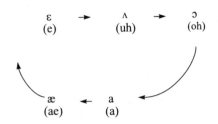

Table 8.2 Percentage of advanced tokens of the five vowels for each combination of social category and sex (numbers of tokens in parentheses) (after Eckert, 1989: 261)

| | Boys | | Girls | |
	Jocks	Burnouts	Jocks	Burnouts
(ae)	$39.7\left(\dfrac{211}{531}\right)$	$35.3\left(\dfrac{101}{286}\right)$	$62.2\left(\dfrac{244}{392}\right)$	$62\left(\dfrac{178}{287}\right)$
(a)	$21.4\left(\dfrac{117}{548}\right)$	$22\left(\dfrac{77}{350}\right)$	$33.8\left(\dfrac{152}{450}\right)$	$38.2\left(\dfrac{134}{350}\right)$
(oh)	$7.4\left(\dfrac{44}{598}\right)$	$10.2\left(\dfrac{34}{333}\right)$	$29.8\left(\dfrac{134}{450}\right)$	$38.7\left(\dfrac{131}{338}\right)$
(e)	$26.2\left(\dfrac{146}{557}\right)$	$33.2\left(\dfrac{113}{340}\right)$	$23.8\left(\dfrac{103}{433}\right)$	$30.9\left(\dfrac{103}{333}\right)$
(uh)	$24.6\left(\dfrac{122}{496}\right)$	$35.3\left(\dfrac{65}{184}\right)$	$25.8\left(\dfrac{94}{364}\right)$	$43\left(\dfrac{107}{249}\right)$

As table 8.2 shows, the girls lead the boys, and the Burnouts lead the Jocks in realizing these sound changes. In both sets of changes, the girls show more variation than the boys. In the case of the newer set of changes, the girls' patterns of variation show a greater difference between the Jocks and the Burnouts than do those of the boys. Obviously, the newer changes are perceived as indicators of counter-adult behavior and thus fit the image of the Burnouts. In both cases – the girls' differentiation of the newer changes and their greater use of older changes – the girls' phonological behavior is consonant with their greater need to use social symbols for self-presentation. These results, Eckert argues, are very much in accordance with her theory about gender, women, and men. Group membership seems to be more salient for one sex than for the other; girls assert their category identities through language more than boys; the impact of group ideology on language behavior is considerable and correlates with gender as well. The ethnographic study of the community of practice led to very different results than a survey would have done. Eckert concludes that many more "communities of practice" have to be investigated before any general claims on the role of gender and sex in sound change can be made.

Gender, minorities and code-switching

Ana Celia Zentella (1987), who comes from the bilingualism research paradigm, studied female identities in the Puerto Rican community of "El Barrio" in East Harlem, New York, between 1978 and 1981. The pressures on the Puerto Rican minority are high: As the most disadvantaged group in the United States, it has the highest poverty level. Moreover, Puerto Ricans are prone to several identity conflicts: "What am I? Puerto Rican or American? What color am I? White or Black? Which language should I speak, Spanish or English? Which Spanish should I speak, Puerto Rican's or Spain's? Which English should I speak, Black or White?" (Zentella, 1987: 169–71). Thus culture, race and language are issues of great conflict, with different values attached to them by different age groups and networks. Participant observation in this community revealed several different networks with different linguistic repertoires: older women who speak Spanish; younger mothers for whom English is the dominant language; "young dudes" for whom English is also dominant; and children who grow up bidialectal and bilingual. As Zentella notes, the young children "are always subject to the supervision of one of the networks. As a result, the children are intermittently addressed by monolingual standard or nonstandard Spanish speakers, monolingual standard and nonstandard English speakers, and by bilingual and bidialectal speakers of both languages" (p. 171). The standard Spanish of Puerto Rico varies with Puerto Rican English and/or Black English vernacular depending on the situational context and the interlocutors.

Children speak the language which is normally directed at them; female children specifically accommodate and are more polite (Deuchar, 1990).[10] The principal burden of maintaining the Spanish language lies on the shoulders of Puerto Rican women; a survey of language attitudes (Zentella, 1987) revealed that women do not regard English monolinguals as Puerto Rican anymore. On the one hand, women preserve older and more conservative forms, even if the language changes, yet on the other hand, women are also leading linguistic changes that correlate with the prestigious language variety. This aspect has not yet been studied thoroughly, and it is likely that this fact could also be dependent on networks or professions (Nichols, 1983).

Code-switching (see chapter 13) is an important strategy of communication in this community. In contrast to other opinions (Lakoff, 1975), which claim that code-switchers are not fluent in their codes, Zentella notes that the most prolific code-switchers are the most competent speakers of the language varieties and that these are mostly women:

> But contrary to prevalent stereotypes, the reality is that most Puerto Rican women do succeed in raising their children to be healthy people, despite the triple jeopardy of gender, race, and class, and despite the conflicts about national origin and linguistic and cultural differences. When we seek out the wellsprings

of the coping strength of these women, we find that bilingualism and code-switching are vital. (Zentella, 1987: 177)

Puerto Rican female survivors turn what others see as deficiencies or liabilities into strengths. These women are not only responsible for language education, they are also, as Zentella states, the leaders "for equity and excellence in education via the bilingual model" (p. 177). Thus the context-sensitive approach in combination with methodologies developed in research on bilingualism thus provides us with more detailed and subtle explanations of language change than survey studies.

3.2 Sociopsychological variation (SPV)

Language attitudes

The sociopsychological approach to variation has been pursued in Vienna since 1975. Some studies concentrate on actual language behavior (see below), while others, such as those by Moosmüller (1987–8, 1994), focus on regional and gender-specific language attitudes towards Austrian German. Moosmüller analyzed the language use and evaluation of opinion leaders: politicians, schoolteachers, university professors, and radio and TV anouncers. Negative attitudes towards dialect are greater when women use dialect in official contexts: "it is not surprising that being spoken to in dialect in certain contexts is perceived as a sign of disrespect" (Moosmüller, 1994: 273). In this study, the context-sensitive approach has allowed for a differentiation between regions, dialects, professions, and gender. The use of dialect is polyfunctional, both men and women use dialect for very specific occasions, for example, when responding aggressively to a politician in a parliamentary debate. Explanations stressing the notion of "covert prestige" (see p. 137) are barely scratching the surface in cases like these.

Situational parameters, social class and gender

In a study about the language of defendants in court (Leodolter, 1975 [= Wodak]) Ruth Wodak used audio recordings of a standardized setting (a courtroom) to study the sociophonological variation in Vienna, paying particular attention to social class, gender, topics, and certain situational factors. She developed a model (see also Wodak-Leodolter and Dressler, 1977; Dressler and Wodak, 1982; Moosmüller, 1989) which assumes a continuum of styles between the two poles of dialect and standard language in Viennese German. The linguistic model uses Stampe's natural phonology as a point of departure (Stampe, 1969).

In studying the interaction between one judge and 15 defendants (15 cases of examination, 2 women and 13 men), the style registers of each person and the frequencies of style-switching were uncovered, in connection with five

Figure 8.3 Interactions between a judge and defendants (after Leodolter, 1975: 260).

	Socio-psychological styles	Factors inherent in text	Psychological factors	Sociological factors	Interaction between judge and defendant
informal	1	dialect of judge	fears, emotions	no ambiguity, tolerance	threats of the judge
	2	side comments	irrelevant questions	no flexibility	questions too fast incomprehensible questions
	3	stories, narratives	neutral topics	experienced role	questions on everyday life
	4	facts learnt by heart	stereotypes	no role empathy, no role distance	question: what happened
formal	5	emphasis	insistence	no role empathy, no role distance	questions repeated

situational parameters which were defined according to psychological factors, sociological factors based on role theory, and on discursive characteristics of the interaction between judge and defendant (see figure 8.3; Leodolter, 1975: 260).

Wodak was interested in trials about car accidents, as this violation is not linked with a specific social class. The analysis of the repertoire of MC speakers revealed that they applied only a few variable rules and almost no input switches. Their language behavior contained very few style shifts due to the polite and kind questioning by the judge, and they showed almost no emotional involvement. In contrast, UMC-speakers and the working-class women covered the whole range of the linguistic repertoire including hypercorrect speech. Most of the WC men formed a different group of defendants, for they had already been convicted several times before (up to 20 times) and knew the situation. They spoke in pure dialect (accommodating to the dialect of the judge, who switched according to his interlocutor), applying all the dialect rules without shifting to the standard.

Moreover, the interaction between gender and social class could be detected: UMC men and the two women (WC, UMC) showed the largest linguistic repertoires. They also formed the group that was treated most harshly, even more than WC male defendants. Variation was thus shown to be dependent upon sociological, situational, and psychological factors. The fact that the specific interaction had to be taken into account corresponds to more recent claims about "doing gender" in context (see section 1.3) and about the role of gender in the whole set of attributes that form an individual's identity.

Mothers and daughters: Women and language change

The relationship between mothers and daughters is extremely complex and different from the relationship of mothers and sons. In this short summary,[11] we will focus on these variational aspects of Wodak's study, which provide insights into the processes of language change between generations of females, and supply assumptions about the formation of gender identity in the process of socialization of the daughter through the mother (Kotthoff, 1992: 132ff.). Again, an interaction between psychological and sociological factors determining the sociophonological variation was revealed.

In-depth interviews were conducted with 30 mother–daughter pairs from all social classes. Topics were family problems, education, negative and positive sanctions, self-images, problems with female identity, etc. All the women interviewed were asked about their relationships with their own mothers and daughters respectively. The interviews were transcribed and analyzed with respect to the significant linguistic variables in Viennese German.[12]

Wodak was specifically interested in determining whether the daughters used their linguistic styles to distinguish themselves from their mothers (Wodak, 1984). Was the variation therefore dependent on the relationship between mothers and daughters, on the family structure and the self-image and desired gender identity of the girls? Wodak (1985: 204) summarized the results in the following way: Family styles exist – "mother–daughter styles" – which sometimes contradict class-specific tendencies in variation. Professional women tended to speak more formally than nonprofessional mothers in all social classes. If the relationship between mother and daughter was ambivalent and in conflict, the daughter used a significantly different style from the mother, more formal or informal depending on the mother's style – thus there was no significant tendency towards language change between the generations. The differences between mother and daughter were bigger than between mother and son, even in stable and friendly relationships. Accommodation to peer groups is an important intervening variable. The same is true for social mobility – upwardly mobile daughters spoke hypercorrectly, in obvious demarcation from their mothers and their social class. One of the most significant results was the fact that some UMC daughters used even more dialect than WC daughters to distance themselves from their mothers; thus their style was triggered by a bad relationship to their mothers and not by the class factor. This study suggests that whole clusters of very different variables have to be taken into account. Variation is context-dependent and is influenced by psychological as well as sociological factors. No simple general claims can be made regarding language change.

4 Conclusions

At this point, we would like to return to the questions we posed at the beginning of our paper and sum up our observations regarding studies on gender and variation. Most of the sociolinguistic studies we have summarized throughout this article do not apply an explicit notion of "gender." Quite the contrary, they usually correlate phonological units (linguistic variables) with the sex of the participants; in other words, the linguistic behavior of men and women is investigated without trying to incorporate any theoretical implications of modern gender theories. Even in cases where such theories are considered, the empirical studies usually end up with a unitary model of gender (see p. 128) and with the simple division into the biological sexes (but see p. 129). Another important issue which becomes apparent in discussion of sociolinguistic research on gender and variation is the problematic nature of the integration of the context of the data. Except for studies using an ethnographic and/or interdisciplinary approach, context is reduced to the traditional sociological variables, such as age, social class, profession, and ethnicity, without any underlying sociological theory which would provide some explanatory power and justification. Other context phenomena are neglected. The interweaving of linguistic behavior with nonlinguistic behavior, the interdependence of language and context, the construction of context through language and the impact of context on language are not seriously considered in sociolinguistic theories on variation. We think that this is an aspect which should be discussed more thoroughly in future research, analogous to the developments in discourse studies (Duranti and Goodwin 1992).

Moreover, we would like to argue briefly that sociolinguistic studies would benefit from an inclusion of Pierre Bourdieu's habitus theory (see Dittmar and Schlobinski, 1988). We think that promising network approaches (see pp. 135–7) could easily be integrated into this theory. On the one hand, the differentiation of samples into groups with specific dispositions and characteristics allows for better interpretations and explanations than the use of traditionally defined social classes; on the other hand, it allows a step towards macrosociological conceptions without reductionism.

Bourdieu (1987: 279) defines linguistic behavior as the symbolic capital of the speakers and as part of her/his general habitus. According to Bourdieu, in a specific context the linguistic market creates a ranking of different linguistic registers, some having more prestige than others, due to the social values and norms of the elites. Thus the notion of power has to be included in sociolinguistic research on variation, as well as the dynamics of group ideologies (see Kotthoff, 1992: 137).

Turning to the evaluation of different methodologies applied in studies on gender and variation, we would like to underscore the manifold feminist critique of research procedures. Quantitative studies tend to simplify many phenomena; qualitative analyses, on the other hand, often rely on samples which are too small to draw general conclusions. Many categories are defined in a male-oriented way, male linguistic behavior is seen as unmarked, female linguistic behavior as deviating from the male norm. Most studies are undertaken in English-speaking countries, thus general explanations suffer from Anglo-European ethnocentrism. We would like to suggest a combination of methods, a multimethod approach (see Wodak, 1986), in which different aspects of the object under investigation are grasped by different quantitative and qualitative methods which complement and do not exclude each other.

Furthermore languages other than English (see Gal, 1992b) should be investigated more thoroughly. We would also like to point out that many American researchers neglect European literature, especially studies which are not published in English (this is true for sociolinguistics in general, for example, Swales, 1990).

Finally, if sociological theories of context and of conceptualizations of gender, etc. continue to be ignored, contradictory explanations will not disappear. Labov's statement (1991: 302) contains a more general truth: "Our answers at the moment are no better than speculations." Nevertheless, a closer look at variation studies is promising; alternative and innovative approaches are gaining more and more attention (Hall et al., 1992).

NOTES

1 See Tannen (1993a, b), Kotthoff and Wodak (1995), Hall et al. (1992), Chambers (1992), Coates and Cameron (1990), Klann-Delius (1987), Smith (1985), Holmes (1992), McConnell-Ginet (1988), Gal (1989, 1992), Uchida (1992) for recent overviews of these two domains.

2 Hudson (1990: 167) offers a much more extensive explanation and description of the "linguistic variable" and mentions context as an important factor for variation studies. But Hudson also restricts the context to the linguistic context and the speaker's group membership. Interaction itself and the embedding of interaction in situations which would allow us to use our concept of "doing gender" are neglected. The same is true for Holmes (1992: 151ff.).

3 See Cheshire and Gardner-Chloros (1994), Coates (1990) for a strong feminist critique of the traditional variation studies and their interpretations and explanations of the assumed female skills.

4 J. Milroy (1992) concludes that thus language variation does not necessarily lead to language change (as Labov would imply). Language differentiation may have a stable symbolic value.

5 Therefore L. and J. Milroy (1992) try to reconcile the network approach with theories of class.

6 For an overview see Cameron and Coates (1990), Labov (1990), Klann-Delius (1987), Chambers (1992), Trudgill (1972).

7 Examples are Thomas (1990), Salami (1991), Hughes (1992). Further references are to be found in Kotthoff (1992), Romaine (1994), Chambers (1992). Abu-Haider (1989) challenges the contradictory view of Arabic.

8 For a discussion of sex stereotypes and sex roles see Smith (1979), Smith (1985), D. N. and T. L. Ruble (1982), Rissel (1989).

9 See also Cheshire and Gardner-Chloros (1994), Deuchar (1990), Trudgill (1972), Cameron (1990).

10 For more information about accommodation theories see Burgoon (1990), Furnham (1990),

Kramerae (1990), Sachdev and Bourhis (1990).

11 Ruth Wodak studied these relationships on the discursive level (Wodak, 1984, 1986), in a cross-cultural comparison between a Viennese and a Los Angeles sample (Wodak and Schulz, 1986, 1991) and on the level of phonological variation, to supplement and validate the discourse studies (Wodak, 1983, 1984).

12 The mothers also underwent a psychoanalytic projective personality test (the Gieszentest) which led to a typology of their personalities: "mother types." These personality characteristics could also be correlated with the other variables.

9 Age as a Sociolinguistic Variable

PENELOPE ECKERT

1 Introduction

Aging is central to human experience. It is the achievement of physical and social capacities and skills, a continual unfolding of the individual's participation in the world, construction of personal history, and movement through the history of the community and of society. If *aging* is movement through time, *age* is a person's place at a given time in relation to the social order: a stage, a condition, a place in history. Age and aging are experienced both individually and as part of a cohort of people who share a life stage, and/or an experience of history.

The study of age in relation to language, particularly the study of sociolinguistic variation, lies at the intersection of life stage and history. The individual speaker or age cohort of speakers at any given moment represents simultaneously a place in history and a life stage. Age stratification of linguistic variables, then, can reflect change in the speech of the community as it moves through time (*historical change*), and change in the speech of the individual as he or she moves through life (*age grading*).

Much of the work that focuses on age in the field of variation concerns the disambiguation of age-stratified data, determining when change in apparent time, or time as reflected in age, is a reflection of historical change in real time and when it represents age grading. On the one hand, historical change will inevitably be reflected in age stratification. But for change in apparent time to regularly reflect change in real time, the speech of an age group would have to correspond in a predictable way to the state of the language at some fixed life stage. This means that the individual's linguistic system would have to remain relatively stable throughout life, or any changes in the linguistic system during the life course would have to be regular and predictable. Yet progress through the life course involves changes in family status, gender relations, employment status, social networks, place of residence, community participation, institutional participation, engagement in the marketplace – all of which have implications for patterns of variation. It is unlikely that speakers pass through all the identity changes of a lifetime without making any changes in their use of sociolinguistic variables.

Resolving the ambiguity between age grading and change in apparent time involves grappling with some fundamental linguistic issues: To what extent, and in what ways, can a speaker's language change over the life course? How are these changes embedded in life stages and life events? And to what extent does age interact with other social variables such as class, gender, and ethnicity? Answers to these questions require an understanding of the *linguistic life course*. Yet although age is one of a small number of social variables routinely included in community studies, there has been no concerted study of variation from a life-course perspective. Like gender, age correlates with variation by virtue of its social, not its biological status (although biology of course is part of the social construction of age and gender). The study of age as a sociolinguistic variable therefore requires that we focus on the nature and social status of age and aging. A life-course perspective raises some new issues in the study of variation, and points out blank spaces in our knowledge. The following discussion will begin with an examination of the reflection of linguistic change in age stratification, and move on to an examination of the social nature of age and its relation to variation.

2 Apparent and Real Time

Community studies of variation frequently show that increasing age correlates with increasing conservatism in speech. With just the evidence from apparent time, it is ambiguous whether the language patterns of the community are changing over the years or whether the speakers are becoming more conservative as they age – or both. Without evidence in real time, there is no way of establishing whether or not age-stratified patterns of variation actually reflect change in progress.

Several kinds of evidence have been called upon to provide real-time evidence: A number of studies have sought to approach real time by combining data on variation in apparent time with general sources on earlier stages of the language. Sources such as old recordings (Kemp and Yaeger-Dror, 1991), geographical evidence (Eckert, 1980), and historical accounts (Labov, 1972b, 1966) of the dialects under study have been used to contextualize contemporary data, and to establish the possibility that current age differences represent a continuation of an ongoing change process.

The validity and interpretability of evidence in real time depends on the
extent to which the samples representing different time periods are comparable: How close is the match between communities, and between the
speaker samples across and within communities? Replications of community
studies at some time distance are obviously the best source for evidence in real
time. Such studies are still relatively rare, but the lengthening history of the
study of variation, particularly since Labov's 1966 New York City study, is
beginning to produce replications. Two kinds of re-study of the same community are possible: studies of age cohorts as they pass through time, and
studies of life stages as they are occupied by successive age cohorts. Studies in
real time can also either follow the same individuals (panel study) or they can
collect samples of comparable but different individuals at successive points
in time (trend study). A trend study with an age-graded sample is the only
kind that can unequivocally show change in progress as it shows successive
cohorts at each life stage. A panel study is the only kind that can unequivocally show change in the individual lifetime, as it sees the same people at
different life stages. Trend studies, however, can yield convincing evidence of
both kinds of change.

Most community studies of change in real time have been trend studies,
such as Hermann (1929) in Charmey (Suisse Romande), Cedergren (1984) in
Panama, Fowler (1986) in New York, and Trudgill (1988) in Norwich. These
studies confirm that many, but not all, age-stratified variables represent
change in progress. Gauchat (1905) found apparent time evidence of five
changes in Charmey. Over 20 years later, Hermann (1929) revisited Charmey
and compared the speech of 40 speakers with Gauchat's evidence. From these
comparisons, Hermann found evidence of change for four of the five changes
in apparent time reported by Gauchat. Bailey and others (1991) compared
apparent time data from the Phonological Survey of Texas, gathered in the
late 1980s, with data from the *Linguistic Atlas of the Gulf States* (Pederson et al.,
1986), gathered in the mid-1970s. While this study covered a wider geographical area and hence cannot be considered a re-study of a community, it targeted
a fairly specific area and population. Indications of change in progress from
the apparent time data in the later sample were confirmed by differences
between the two samples. Trudgill (1988), revisiting Norwich at 20 years'
remove, found that variants occurring only in the speech of young people at
the earlier time had caught on as changes and were spreading through the
earlier age groups.

Other studies in apparent time have found evidence not only of historical
change, but of age grading. Cedergren (1984), in her trend study of Panama
City, compared two age-graded samples with a time depth of 20 years. In a
comparison of equivalent age-graded samples at two points in history, differences due to change in real time are reflected in differences between successive cohorts at the same age, while differences due to age grading are
reflected in differences within cohorts between the two times. Cedergren's
data (described in detail in Labov, 1994: 94–7) show a clear increase in the

lenition of /tʃ/ between successive cohorts at the same age, indicating a progress of change across the community. At the same time, in the middle-aged groups (roughly 30 to 70 years of age), the speakers increased their use of lenition over the 20 years between studies. Thus the same change that affected the community as a whole affected the speech of individuals in their lifetimes, showing that adult speakers can be active participants in sound change.

Paunonen (1994) separated men and women in a study that combined a trend study and a panel study, comparing three age cohorts, at two different points in time, of men and women who were young, middle-aged, and old in 1970 and 1990. One change examined in this study, the replacement of synthetic with analytic possessive constructions, showed change across cohorts but little change in the speech of individuals. The other, however, the reversal of a normative insertion of /d/, showed both community and individual change, both of which showed important gender effects. The trend study showed that women in general were becoming less normative through time. The panel study found older women mirroring this trend within their own lives: Those who were middle-aged in the 1970s were less normative in the 1990s, when they were old. (Paunonen's attribution of this development to change in the situation of women in Finland will be discussed in section 4.) On the other hand, men, and women who were young in the 1970s, became slightly more normative as they aged.

Paunonen's finding that gender interacts with age is most likely not unusual particularly, perhaps, in times of change in gender norms and practices. Labov (1994) has emphasized that uncovering patterns of change requires isolating segments of the community that participate differently in change. It has been established that women commonly lead in sound change, as do the upper working and lower middle classes. The progress of sound change can best be traced by separating these groups out in age stratifications. Studies that separate age stratification by class (Fowler, 1986 (n.b. discussed in Labov, 1994: 86–94); Labov, 1994: 53) and by gender (Labov, 1991), have shown that grossly combined age figures can mask specific group effects. If speakers are combined in age groups without attention to such effects, what might look like an overall age difference could actually be more specifically located. Studies like these are crucial to our understanding of variation over the life course. But our interpretation of complex results like those in Paunonen's study depends on an integrated view of variation over the life course.

3 Approaches to Age

Community studies of variation rely overwhelmingly on chronological age to group speakers; indeed to the Western social scientist, chronological age *is* age. However, inasmuch as social and biological development do not move in lock step with chronological age, or with each other, chronological age can only provide an approximate measure of the speaker's age-related place in society. To the extent that age stratification reflects historical change alone, the date of acquisition would be sufficient to group speakers in relation to time. And since individual differences in that age are relatively small in relation to the life span, chronological age would be an adequate measure. However, evidence that some kind of individual change takes place throughout life necessitates a longer view of development, and investigation of the social changes that underlie correlations with chronological age.

Because the span of ages is so great, it is difficult for community studies to achieve fine-grained age differentiations with any statistical significance. This necessitates the grouping of speakers, frequently in fairly broad age ranges or cohorts. Community studies have defined cohorts *etically* and *emically*. The etic approach groups speakers in arbitrarily determined but equal age spans such as decades (e.g., Trudgill, 1974; Labov, 1966), while the emic approach groups speakers according to some shared experience of time. This shared experience can be related to life stage or to history. Some studies (e.g., Wolfram, 1969; Horvath, 1985) have grouped speakers according to general life stage, particularly childhood, adolescence, young adulthood. As will be discussed in section 5, shared external events have also emerged as coherently defining linguistic cohorts.

While aging is universal, it is incorporated into social structure and invested with value in culturally specific ways. In all societies, age has significance because the individual's place in society, the community, and the family changes through time. The marking of maturation, whether by chronological age or by life event or stage, is regulatory, involving both authorization and control. The accomplishment of particular age-related landmarks authorizes the individual to assume particular roles, freedoms, and responsibilities. At the same time, it obligates the individual to give up old ones. Age systems, then, serve to mark not only an individual's progress in the life trajectory, but the individual's progress in relation to societal norms. Age systems often involve sanctions to enforce age-appropriate behavior; to enforce the normative timing of life events (such as the pressure on women to marry before a certain age), and life-stage or age-appropriate comportment. This can have a variety of linguistic instantiations, from pressure for linguistic conservatism in adulthood to pressure to use vernacular features in pre-adolescence.

In industrial society chronological age, measured as an accumulation of years since birth, serves as an official measure of the individual's place in the life course and in society, by reference to a societal dating system. But while chronological age lays out age as a homogeneous continuum based on calendar time, it is imbued with meaning by a variety of life landmarks, which are not necessarily evenly distributed over the life course. Certain birthdays are associated with transformations of personal (e.g., sweet sixteen) or institutional (e.g., legal majority) status. Simple decades can also have major social significance – unrelated to official landmarks, they serve more to mark a homogeneous passage of time as well as transformations in general life stage. Other aspects of the passage through life are less specifically tied to chronological age and more tied to life events, such as changes in religious status (bar and bat mitzvah, baptism), institutional status (first day of school, retirement), family status (marriage, first child), legal status (naturalization, first arrest), and physiological status (loss of the first tooth, onset of menses). These events in turn are associated with life stages: childhood, adolescence, young adulthood, middle age, old age. It is these general life stages that are most frequently invoked to explain behavior.

Although the relation of chronological age to biological and social age is approximate, it is given primacy in industrial society. The answer to an inquiry about an individual's age is invariably given in chronological years, not in terms of family or institutional status, or in terms of physical maturation. Indeed, family and institutional status and biological maturation are taken as indicators of chronological age, rather than vice versa. This can be reversed in societies that do not traditionally use chronological age. Fortes (1984: 110), for example, observed the Ashanti assigning a chronological age of 16 to females at the time of their nubility ceremonies, even though their actual birth dates were unknown. This was apparently a way to align their own assessment of these women's age with colonial law, under which women aged 16 and over were classified as adults.

Differences in age systems across cultures can have important sociolinguistic implications. Cross-cultural differences may show differences in life events, in the domains that are significant for the definition of those events, in the relative importance of generation and birth order, in the construction of cohorts, etc. An age-set society, for example, which groups people born within a period that can be as long as ten years, emphasizes solidarity within that set, frequently in opposition to other sets. In such a society, one might expect to see less continuous age stratification of variables than in an age-graded society in which the individual progresses according to personal developmental landmarks.

The relation between age and other social factors will also differ across cultures. Age systems do not affect people identically across the board. For example, the restriction of age sets in an age-set society to males, while women's age is treated more fluidly, no doubt could also have implications for interactions between gender and age in variation. Indeed, gender is quite explicitly constructed partially in its interaction with age. Certain landmarks, such as coming of age across societies, are gender-specific, and family, legal, and institutional status are commonly different for males and females. Guttmann (1975) even hypothesized a universal crossover between gender and age, claiming that while women become more autonomous, competitive, aggressive, and instrumental with aging, men become more dependent, passive, and expressive. Ethnic differences in industrial society may well juxtapose different age systems within a single community, so one cannot necessarily expect chronological age to correspond uniformly to social age even within a speech community. Class differences in industrial society also involve differences in age systems, since many aspects of the life trajectory are class-based. Entrance into young adulthood, for example, is earlier for work-ing-class than middle-class youth; and the relation between adult status and relation to the linguistic marketplace is also different for these groups.

It is important also to recognize that a middle-aged perspective pervades social research. Sociolinguistic studies overwhelmingly embody a middle-aged point of view, yielding a more static treatment of middle-aged speech than of the speech of other age groups. A number of researchers (e.g., Baltes and others (1980)) have pointed out the middle-aged bias in social science research. Studies of children focus on the process of socialization, studies of adolescents and young adults focus on learning adult roles, and studies of the elderly focus on the loss of adult abilities. (See Coupland and others (1991) for a critique of ageism within a sociolinguistic context.) Thus only the middle-aged life stage is treated outside of a developmental perspective: Only the middle-aged are seen as engaging in mature use, as "doing" language rather than learning or losing it. And the emphasis in research on language use in the early and the late years is on age-related cognitive and physical abilities, while the emphasis in research on the intervening years is on age-related forms of social participation.

The emphasis on adult socioeconomic class and on the standard language marketplace as tying class to language puts an adult focus on variation studies. Researchers tend to see adult patterns as defining variation, hence as constituting the sole target of development. Thus the development of patterns of variation is viewed as subsequent to early language development, and dependent on the development of adult-like social awareness. In other areas of language development, however, researchers (e.g., Ochs, 1988; Schieffelin and Ochs, 1986) have taken the integration of language development and socialization as fundamental. And inasmuch as the input for language development is itself variable (Labov, 1989), it would be ludicrous to believe that children ignore variability only to "acquire" it later on. The focus on adult social practice in the study of variation may well obscure age-specific use and interpretation among children. For this reason, a balanced view of sociolinguistic aging must merge a *developmental* perspective with a *mature-use* perspective for all age groups.

The developmental perspective recognizes that development is lifelong: Indeed, life is about change. Throughout the life course, speakers have a sense of moving forward in years and in maturity, anticipating the next developments in their lives and assuming new ways of being – and perhaps new ways of talking – as they go.

A mature-use perspective recognizes that sociolinguistic competence is age-specific, and that the speech of members of an age group is fully appropriate to that life stage. Taking middle-aged language as a universal norm and developmental target obscures the fact that ways of speaking at any life stage are part of the community structuring of language use, and that the linguistic resources employed at any stage in life have social meaning for and within that life stage. Thus small children are not simply striving to be older children; this striving is fully integrated into their competence at being small children, and strategically exercised.

An important factor in children's lives is a developmental imperative (Eckert, 1994): an emphasis on growing up, on being age-appropriate, or not being a "baby." This imperative continues in other forms throughout life, but is particularly intense and foregrounded in the earlier years. Emotional issues associated with maturation, and the relation between age-appropriateness and social status at all early ages is likely to be the ground on which children begin to develop a sense of the relation between linguistic features and social identity and status. The use of baby talk marks a developmental stage, but it also constitutes an important register (Andersen, 1990; Ferguson, 1977; Gleason, 1973) for a wider age group. Baby talk is clearly linked with small children's social identities, and it is only reasonable that the transition from baby talk as one's sole competence to baby talk as a stylistic device for children who are no longer limited to that way of speaking would be seamless. Baby talk is also not childbound. It serves not only as a register to use when speaking with small children, but features of baby talk are used among speakers of all ages, including mature adults. In this sense, certain aspects of child identity and social relations endure in the linguistic strategies of older people, making children's linguistic resources a community-wide resource. A life-course perspective, therefore, would begin with children's linguistic resources, social identities, and strategies, rather than with those of adults, and speculations about the age at which children have "complete" control over patterns of variation (e.g., Romaine, 1984: 102) would give way to speculations about how children's patterns are transformed into adult patterns. An adult bias leads the variationist to search children's speech only for variables that have been studied in the adult population, but it is possible that the beginnings of social awareness in language variability lie in other, childhood-specific, linguistic material.

While we are used to thinking of social maturation as age-related in the early and the late years, we are less likely to think of similar changes in mid-life as age-related. But it is difficult to find a difference between anticipating a promotion from elementary school to junior high, and anticipating a promotion from manager to vice president. In both cases, the individual anticipates and is concerned about the challenge of new experiences and expectations, and with honing new skills as he or she moves into a new life stage. A study of age as a sociolinguistic variable has to include perspectives based in a broader range of life stages.

4 The Linguistic Life Course

Some areas of language and variation development are better documented than others. Much more is known about fine age differences in the early years than in the later years, and in fact, less is known about age-related patterns of variation the farther we move along in the life course. Thought about the relation between variation and age centers around a set of life stages that are "native categories" in US culture, and commonly used as explanations for people's behavior: childhood (which includes pre-adolescence), adolescence (more finely divided into early adolescence and adolescence), adulthood (which is more finely divided into early adulthood and middle age), and old age, which is interestingly enough viewed separately from adulthood. Only adulthood is seen as a life stage that is independent of the care and support of adults, and it is not surprising that independence is an important issue for both adolescents and the elderly.

The emphasis in the field of variation on the vernacular and standard language as poles of social stratification and of stylistic ranges has led to a view of language development that involves a developing awareness of the standard language (Labov, 1964). Awareness of standard language involves awareness of the standard language market (Sankoff and Laberge, 1978), which is defined primarily in terms of participation in institutions – particularly educational and commercial – and in the social networks that support those institutions. Institutional age limits and landmarks, therefore, can have an important effect on many aspects of people's lives. It may determine their social networks as well as their need for language varieties. Children's and adolescents' lives are dominated by the institution of school and schooling, adult lives are dominated by the workplace, and many elderly lives by the retirement or nursing home. While the former two are bastions of standard language norms, the linguistic norms embodied in institutions for the elderly are more complicated.

Meanwhile, the local community, as the home of the vernacular, is another site for the development of resources for variation. While in the larger scheme of things the local vernacular marketplace exists in opposition to the global, standard marketplace, there is more going on in either marketplace than simple opposition to each other. The vernacular of one local community may live not only in opposition to the standard, but to surrounding vernaculars. And within communities, gender dynamics and age dynamics involve many things other than standard language concern. While standard language as embodied in an economic marketplace is of central importance to the understanding of variation, once again it is not what dominates the language development of children; rather, central concerns of children come to accommodate the socioeconomic sphere over time. An important focus on children is what aspects of identity are tied up with variation as it develops, and how socioeconomic concerns come to play a role.

4.1 Childhood

Quantitative research on variation in the early years of childhood is quite recent. Roberts's work with 3-year-olds in Philadelphia (Roberts, 1993; Roberts and Labov, 1992) has shown that children's language at this early age is inherently variable, much the same as the speech of the older people that serve as their models. This work has shown that 3-year-olds show variation in their use of both stable sociolinguistic variables (such as -*ing*, and t/d deletion) and in their use of patterns of local variation representing change in progress (such as the raising of short /a/ in Philadelphia). Labov (1989) found adult-like linguistic constraints in t/d deletion and -*ing* in the speech of three children aged 4, 6, and 7. The details of these patterns are dialect-specific, and closely approach those in the speech of adults in the same community.

There is also a good deal of evidence indicating that certain patterns cannot be learned after a fairly young age. Arvilla Payne's work (1980) in the Philadelphia suburb King of Prussia, showed that children moving in from a different dialect area before the age of 8 or 9 picked up simple local vowel shifts. They did not have the same success, however, at developing the Philadelphia short /a/ pattern, which required a knowledge of word-class assignment. Rather, it appeared that only children whose parents were from Philadelphia developed this pattern completely. Payne's conclusion was that while children may be able to add lower-level rules until adolescence, they cannot restructure their grammars as readily. Chambers's study (1992) of six Canadian children moving to Britain also provided evidence of a cutoff. In this case, Chambers found a close to perfect development of the opposition between long and short /o/ for a 9-year-old, and a sharp decrease in success for speakers over the age of 13.

If it is clear that patterns of inherent variation are acquired along with the rest of the phonological system, it is less clear what kind of social meaning these variables have for the child. It is well established that children develop sociolinguistic competence from the earliest stages of speech. Andersen (1990) provides ample evidence that children from a very early age engage in complex register variation and are acutely aware of the relation between social roles and language variability. Gender differences have been shown repeatedly in many aspects of linguistic behavior by the age of 4 (e.g., Staley, 1982), and children in early elementary school are already responsive to gender stereotypes in language (Edelsky, 1977). This is no doubt related to the fact that gender is probably the earliest and most intense category membership imposed on very small children. But early gender differences revolve around discursive strategies, and are clearly related to behavioral judgments such as whether one is "a nice girl." No doubt similar dynamics are at work when African-American children show early on in elementary school an awareness of the relation between Standard English and the school institution (Houston, 1969). Where there is a foregrounded relation between kinds of linguistic behavior and aspects of social identity, one may reasonably expect children to develop linguistic skills to reflect that relation. The relation between gender and variation, however, is far less straightforward than the relation between gender and the kinds of gender-differentiated language features that have been found among young children, for example, the amount of speech and the use of obscenities.

Researchers have sought evidence of the social use of variation in adult-like correlations, particularly with gender and class, and in patterns of stylistic variation. Stylistic variation quite obviously requires some kind of awareness of the significance of variables. But the younger the age group, the greater the chances that socioeconomic, and in some cases ethnic differentiation in language is not a matter of attending to sociolinguistic differentiation but of selective exposure. Since small children (particularly preschool children) are more isolated by socioeconomic class and ethnicity than by gender, gender differentiation could provide more convincing evidence that children are attending to social differentiation in their use of variables.

There are no robust correlations of variables with class or gender among very small children. This does not so much reflect negative results as lack of data. However, both differentiation and stylistic use appear among young elementary school children, and intensify through childhood to become quite full-blown in pre-adolescence. Romaine (1984) provided nonquantitative evidence of stylistic variation in the use of (aʊ) ([aw]~[u]) in the speech of 6-year-olds in Edinburgh, and Biondi (1975) found stylistic use of despirantized /θ/ and /ð/ among 6-year-old Italian-American children between speech and reading style.[1] Labov (1989) found stylistic variation in the use of t/d deletion and -*ing* by 6-, 7-, 9-year-olds. The most robust data on stylistic variation in children, however, begins with the speech of pre-adolescents, around age 10. Reid (1978) showed variation in two speech styles among 11-year-old boys, in the use of -*ing* and in the use of the glottal stop. Romaine's data from Edinburgh show variation in the use of the same two variables among 10-year-olds, between speech and reading style. The most robust findings on gender differences in variation are also among older children, beginning at age 10. Macaulay (1977) found gender differences in 10- and 15-year-olds, with a considerably greater difference among the 15-year-olds. Biondi (1975), as well, found gender differences among Italian-American children in Boston. In all these cases, boys were using more nonstandard forms than girls. Socioeconomic stratification also shows up regularly in the speech of pre-adolescents (Wolfram, 1969; Macaulay, 1977; Romaine, 1984).

It is possible that children learn some of the social functions of certain variables before they have developed the linguistic constraints, and that they use these variables on occasion – perhaps as conscious markers in particular lexical items. It is also possible that they develop fine linguistic conditioning for some variables before they put them to social use. It is inadvisable to take evidence from one variable as indicative of the entire system, since, inasmuch as different variables within a dialect may have quite different social functions, children may well develop awareness of some earlier than others. It is possible, for example, that children develop use of stable variables that are clearly related to formality (such as -*ing*) before sound changes in progress that are likely to have more complex social connotations. At any rate, to the extent that children develop patterns of sociolinguistic variation, one can expect the motivations to be age-specific and more local than those of adults. Fischer's (1958) work with New England school children is unusual in its attention to age-specific categories. In his short study showing stylistic variation in the use of -*ing*, he found a greater use of the full form in the speech of a "model" boy than in the speech of a "typical" boy. While this was a brief study, its considerable interest lies in the attention to social distinctions that are significant to school-age children: status as a troublemaker or teacher's pet can have greater significance than socioeconomic status. The relation between school orientation and class, which will be discussed in the next section, may in fact be an important factor in the continuity of linguistic patterns.

It has been recognized for some time (Hockett, 1950) that from a very early age, adults are not children's primary linguistic models. Interaction with siblings, neighbors, and friends exposes younger children to changes in progress as manifested in the speech of their older peers, and affords them the kind of social participation needed to understand the social meanings of those changes. Differences between children's patterns and the more conservative adults' patterns exist in a setting of foregrounded child–adult relations, and the developmental imperative imbues slightly older children with status that may serve as motivation for younger children to emulate them. Class differences in childhood friendship networks and neighborhood patterns can expose children differentially to the influence of older children. The working-class neighborhood orientation, for example, puts children beyond parental watch and into networks that include older children, particularly under the care of older siblings and their friends (Eckert, 1989). Thus there is plenty of opportunity for variation to develop social meaning among children that is quite specific to their own social practices, and it is in these practices that we must seek explanations. Meanwhile, the nature of children's linguistic input (i.e., how much time is spent with peers, and in what activities) may well differ dramatically across certain social boundaries such as class, gender, and ethnicity.

4.2 Adolescence

Adolescence as a life stage is specific to industrial society and the modern era. Of particular significance for sociolinguistics is that during adolescence, people who are in fact becoming adult are normatively denied adult roles, and isolated from the adult sphere in institutions of secondary education. In the US, children anticipate entrance into secondary school with a mixture of eagerness and trepidation. They see this new life stage as bringing greater freedom and new opportunities on the one hand, and making new social demands on the other. Kids do not all feel equally well prepared for this new environment, and status differences begin already in elementary school around this preparedness (Eckert, 1994). "Popular" groups take form, providing their members with a vaster network and hence information, protection, and support in a new environment, and fast change and construction of style – including linguistic style – becomes a crucial part of activity.

Part of what makes secondary school frightening and titillating to younger children is the fact that it is officially a time for children to move away from the family sphere and become officially their own people. In the US particularly, adolescents are expected to involve themselves in age-segregated networks. Eckert (1989) has speculated that the US public high school, by isolating students in a comprehensive institution, serves as a hothouse for the construction of identities. The tremendous symbolic activity that goes on in this context involves a good deal of linguistic innovation. It can be supposed that this is a product of an age cohort constructing itself by constructing difference within, on the one hand, and opposing itself to the adult and child age group on the other: a modification and acceleration of a process that no doubt begins in childhood.

Adolescence is the focus of development of the social use of the vernacular, and in general is seen as the time when linguistic change from below is advanced. Adolescents lead the entire age spectrum in sound change and in the general use of vernacular variables, and this lead is attributed to adolescents' engagement in constructing identities in opposition to – or at least independently of – their elders.

As the official transition from childhood to adolescence, adolescence is a time when children are expected to become serious about their adult occupations. It is therefore a time of transition from their parents' social sphere to one that they construct for themselves. Adolescent social structure and social practice is part of this process of construction. While patterns of variation in many community studies show children and adolescents participating in socioeconomic stratification according to their parents' socioeconomic class, this does not mean that adolescents are simply their parents' children. Rather, socioeconomic mobility appears to be sufficiently low at this stage for many adolescents' own identities to conform with those of their parents.

There is some evidence that a break does happen at this point. Wolfram's data (1969) on African-American English in Detroit show perfect correlations with class for children and adults, but less perfect correlations for adolescents. Macaulay (1977) also found better correlations for adolescents than for preadolescents. Eckert (1988), in a Detroit suburban study that included only adolescents, found parents' socioeconomic class disappearing as a correlate with variation in favor of the age-specific social categories that mediate social class for the adolescent age group. Habick (1991) found similar categories correlating with variation in a high school in southern Illinois. In these high schools, vernacular style is associated with a purely adolescent "burnout" style, which embodies class but which also brings class together with forms of school participation and class-based adolescent social values (Eckert, 1989).

One can see the connection between these adolescent developments and the early use of *-ing* by "typical" and "model" boys in Fischer's study. Studies of smaller networks in adolescence have also established direct connections between peer-group participation, orientation to vernacular culture, and patterns of variation. Cheshire's (1982) study of an adolescent social network, as defined by the use of a playground in Reading, could be seen as providing an analogous view of adolescents. Cheshire found correlations between linguistic variables and participation in "vernacular" culture, which she defined primarily in terms of "toughness" (carrying weapons, criminal activity, skill at fighting, swearing). Labov's work (1972a) with African-American early adolescents showed correlations of linguistic variables with places in social networks as defined by peer groups that defined themselves in relation to Harlem's vernacular culture and in opposition to legitimized institutional culture.

4.3　*Adulthood*

If adolescence is the life stage in which speakers push the envelope of variation, conservatism is said to set in during adulthood. Adults have regularly been shown (Labov, 1966; Wolfram, 1969; Trudgill, 1974; Macaulay, 1977; Horvath, 1985) to be more conservative in their use of variables than younger age groups. This conservatism has been attributed to the pressure for use of standard language in the workplace. Sankoff and Laberge (1978) showed a correlation between the use of standard variables in Montreal French and participation in the standard language marketplace as defined by normative institutions and the social networks that support them. These correlations were found among speakers who, by normal socioeconomic measures, would be grouped together, thus providing some evidence of a direct relation between institutional participation and the use of standard language. Nichols (1983) in her study of African-American women in the south, also showed the linguistic demands of the workplace as a key factor in patterns of variation.

In the same way, studies of social networks (Milroy, 1980; Edwards, 1992) have shown a relation between the use of vernacular variables and engagement in locally based networks. It is quite possible that the crossover pattern (Labov, 1966), whereby both stylistic extremes of the speech of the lower middle class cross over the values of the socioeconomic groups on either side (working class and upper middle class), is a function of that transitional group's simultaneous engagement in locally based networks and in standard language institutions.

While increased conservatism has been the main linguistic change attributed to adults, there is evidence from studies in real time that this is certainly not universal. Paunonen's findings (1994) in Finland, for example, showed women becoming more normative in their use of /d/ as they moved from early adulthood to middle age, but other women becoming less normative as they moved from middle to old age. He attributed this to changes in women's position in society, presumably associating a greater sense of choice and power with flouting of standard norms. However, one would expect this to be more true of the younger women than the older. It is possible, on the other hand, that older women are finding greater freedom with the release, for example, from family responsibilities – and perhaps they always have. Many women shed a variety of normative concerns along with their childrearing responsibilities, and it may well be that a relaxation of their language use is one aspect of this. Labov (1991) has pointed out mothers' roles in instilling standard language norms in children. If this is indeed so, one might consider child-rearing to constitute a standard language marketplace for women analogous to the workplace outside the home.

In general, though, adulthood has emerged as a vast wasteland in the study of variation. In sharp contrast to the year-by-year studies of children and adolescents, adults have been treated as a more or less homogeneous age mass. There have been no studies that attempted to substitute etic age categories, such as decades, with major life transitions such as family status, job status, or retirement. Indeed, although it has been claimed that people relax their conservatism somewhat after retirement, this has not been explicitly examined.

The retiring and retired age group is the least studied of all. The elderly constitute a heterogeneous group, but also a group whose numbers progressively diminish. Labov (1972), based on some evidence that older men's speech is less conservative than the immediately younger age group, suggested that older men's linguistic behavior seems to relax as they lose concern with power relationships. Disengagement from the marketplace could bring a loss of concern with standard language norms in general, and this loss of concern could be a matter of choice, in which one simply enjoyed greater egalitarianism. On the other hand, many of the aged suffer an unwelcome loss of power: they become physically vulnerable, many become economically vulnerable, and disengagement from the marketplace deprives many of influence. In addition, as the cohort ages, its numbers decrease, bringing a loss of age-group power. Keith (1980) observes that residents of retirement housing create communities with strong egalitarian norms, and suggests that this is held in common with other groups that are excluded from arenas of power.

Edwards (1992) uncovered two important differences between those on either side of the age of 60 in an inner-city neighborhood in Detroit. Gender was a significant variable only among those aged 60 and older, and the same older age group used a considerably higher proportion of AAVE variants than the younger age groups. An important social difference dividing these two large age groups is in network structure: The older speakers had the most locally based social networks. Bott (1957) observed that working-class people in enduring locally based networks show greater gender segregation, with men and women retaining their separate gender-segregated friendship networks into adulthood. Thus the network differences between the two age groups could explain both of the linguistic differences. If this is so, the differences must be differences in social change in the neighborhood, whereby the older people have been less geographically mobile, while the younger people's linguistic patterns are reflecting greater mobility. This case points to the importance of social change to age differences in variation.

5 Cohorts, Generations, Eras

To the extent that social and political events can affect the way people speak, age differences in variation can reflect social and political change. This gives a new meaning to the age cohort, and a new way of viewing the grouping of speakers into cohorts. Baby boomers and depression babies constitute emic cohorts in American society. Just as life stage is invoked to explain behavior, so is cohort membership – and indeed the two can overlap. When Americans whose childhoods coincided with the Depression reached middle age, both their cohort membership and their life stage were invoked to explain individuals' fiscal conservatism. The same puzzle of balancing historical insertion with life stage arises in the explanation of patterns of linguistic variation as well.

Several authors have examined the relation between age-based patterns of variation and speakers' experience of major historical events that happened during the age span of the population. Work on Quebec French (Clermont and Cedergren, 1979; Kemp, 1979; Kemp and Yaeger-Dror, 1991) has shown a variety of abrupt patterns of change in the speech of those born before and after the years of the Depression and World War II. This has been attributed to changes in linguistic norms accompanying political, social, and economic transformations in Canadian society during this period.

In addition to remarkable events or eras, fairly specific kinds of social change can bring about different relations to linguistic markets, and these changes commonly affect specific groups differently. Laferriere (1979) pointed out that differences in the educational and social mobility trajectories of three immigrant groups in Boston (Irish, Italian, and Jewish) could account for their differential use, as a group, of particular Boston phonological features. Speakers of the same age but from the different ethnic groups therefore represent quite different phases in the social history of their ethnic group.

Rickford (MS pp. 105–7) points out that changes in Guyanese attitudes about the education of girls yielded a major education differential between females under and over the age of 15. This differential could be expected to cause women overall to use fewer standard forms than men, and young people overall to use more standard forms than older people. Thus what looks like an overall effect is quite specifically located in society and in history. Indeed, the significance of age and the very stages of life do not stand still. Hence those at a particular life stage now may have a different experience of that stage than those who passed through it a generation ago.

6 Directions to Take

Aging has not yet been explicitly studied as a sociolinguistic variable; rather, we have had to rely so far on patchy knowledge of particular life stages. Filling in the picture will require attention to events in age spans that we have thought of as uninterrupted (e.g., middle age), and to the experience of life stages that are remote from our own (e.g., childhood and old age). In both cases, some of our assumptions may be part of the social construction of aging, and as social scientists we need to question those assumptions at the outset.

Just as each life stage needs to be examined in terms of its own practices, meanings, and experiences, those very life stages themselves may well be group-specific. Age groups are not necessarily uniform across or between communities, as different cultural and material conditions make different life trajectories. The normative nature of white middle-class age groups in itself is part of the experience of other groups. Adolescence, for example, is normatively a life stage in which people are free from economic and family responsibilities, rendering deviant a large proportion of people who fall in that age range. At certain times in history, there may be vast differences between age norms and actual practice for some, as social change affects the life trajectories of certain groups. Particularly in developmental studies, the overstudied English-speaking white middle-class child dominates our understanding of development. This leaves us with a very partial view of early linguistic development. Generalizations about development, whether social or linguistic, need to be examined and perhaps challenged in the light of evidence from a broader range of communities.

Because of the complexity of the social factors to which it corresponds, chronological age, like other major social variables such as social class and gender, is only a rough indicator of a composite of heterogeneous factors. The challenge for sociolinguistics, particularly for the study of variation, is to tease apart these various – and sometimes conflicting – factors. This requires directing our focus away from chronological age and towards the life experiences that give age meaning.

NOTE

1 Style difference are commonly elicited with the use of reading tasks. With children, particularly small ones, the interpretation of differences in reading style is particularly problematic.

10 Spoken and Written Language

CELIA ROBERTS and BRIAN STREET

1 Introduction

Until the middle of the twentieth century, linguists and anthropologists paid little attention to the relationship between and differences in spoken and written language. Since then, there has been a considerable literature attempting to define the differences between them (Goody and Watt, 1968; Ong, 1982; Olson, 1988). More recently, anthropologists and sociolinguists have challenged this literature, arguing that it treats literacy and oracy in purely technical terms, rather than as social practices embedded in power structures (Scribner and Cole, 1981; Heath, 1983; Street, 1984; Graff, 1987; Barton, 1994).

Attempts to define the differences between oral and written language have tended to be consistent in terms of the categories used to differentiate between them. Chafe (1982) contrasts the explicitness and context-free character of written language with the implicit and context-dependent nature of oral language. Biber (1988) and Biber and Finegan (1993) compare written versus spoken as: informational versus involved production, elaborated versus situation-dependent reference, and abstract versus nonabstract style. From a functional grammar perspective, Halliday (1985) contrasts the prosodic features and grammatical intricacy of speech with the high lexical density and grammatical metaphor of writing. However, the "great divide" between writing and speech is increasingly less convincing once context and actual social uses of the channels are taken more fully into account (Besnier, 1988).

An alternative position draws on a different theoretical perspective in which meanings are taken to reside in social practices and discourses rather than in formal properties of language (see Gee, 1990, for a current discussion in relation to literacies). Applying this perspective to oral and literacy practices shifts the focus away from traditional concern with differences between the channels and onto the ways in which meanings are constructed locally within particular contexts. It also signals that meanings in oral and literate discourse are structuring processes feeding in to wider social formations. Such a perspective draws on notions of the speech and literacy event (Hymes, 1964; Heath, 1983), on discourses and practices (Foucault, 1984; Bourdieu, 1991), on the concept of the dialogic in writing and oral practice (Bakhtin, 1981), on theories of context and contextualization (Malinowski, 1923; Gumperz, 1982a, b; Auer and Di Luzio, 1992), on theories of language socialization (Vygotsky, 1978; Schieffelin and Ochs, 1986) and the ethnography of education Collins, 1986; Bloome et al., 1989).

So the study of literacy and oracy is about particular types of discourses, certain "ways of being in the world" which draw on and draw in wider issues related to the construction of social knowledge, power relations, and identities. The study of meaning and language is concerned not with individual members of a group but with the identities inscribed in discourses and how they operate (Gee, 1992). The relationship of oral and written practices differs from one context to another and so also does the relationship between sociohistorical resources brought in and the use of these resources in local contexts (Bakhtin, 1981); in some settings, certain of these resources are fixed – as in most teacher–student classroom interactions – whereas in other settings there are fewer conventionalized practices and so the interactions are more genuinely dialogic – it is less of a struggle to improvise, make changes. Volosinov's (1973) conception of language as moving between the centrifugal and the centripetal is helpful in understanding this potential: Institutional pressures frequently work to make language use standardized and conventional (usually according to the conventions of dominant groups) while in other contexts language use pulls away from this central force and responds more immediately to constructions in situation. Whereas it used to be thought that written language tended more towards the former – towards centripetal force – while spoken tended more to the latter – to centrifugal and improvisatory features – recent research suggests that it is not the medium that determines these tendencies but the context. Oral language may operate in either centripetal or centrifugal ways, being dialogic or unidirectional depending on context.

2 Dominant Paradigms and their Critics

Much linguistic writing about literacy has been dominated by a somewhat reified debate about the relationship between written language and speech. Halliday (1985) uses evolutionary and functional arguments to support the view that spoken and written language differ in fundamental ways. Writing, he argues, has evolved differently from spoken language because it fulfills different functions. While agreeing with Halliday in his concern to trace developments and changes in written and oral language (cf. Clanchy, 1979; Graff, 1987; Halliday and Martin, 1993), recent scholars, particularly in anthropology and in critical linguistics, have been suspicious of his focus on evolution and on function (Street, 1984; Besnier, 1988). Evolutionary theory, for instance, has been criticized for being speculative and removed from real historical time into a distant past about which we can know little – especially about the uses of written and spoken language. The idea of evolution has a universalizing tendency: It does not help us explain why and how specific differences between written and spoken language have emerged and have been reproduced in given contexts. Similarly, the idea that writing emerged to fulfill different "functions" from speech has been criticized as essentialist: It does not fit well with the growing empirical evidence of variation between cultures and historical periods (Heath, 1983; Graff, 1987; Barton, 1994).

Tannen (1982) has attempted to develop a more sophisticated view of the social differences between written and spoken language than that offered by a functional approach. She claims that a greater degree of "involvement" is to be found in oral language as opposed to the "detachment" found in the written medium. Since writing lacks the paralinguistic channels available in face-to-face speech interactions, it is obliged to encode meaning only lexically and syntactically. In that sense, then, written language that is characterized by "involvement" is "oral-like" while oral language characterized by detachment is "written-like" (Chafe, 1982). Ethnographers such as Shuman (1986) and Besnier (1988) point out, to the contrary, that writing does involve many paralinguistic features, equivalent in some ways to the gesture, facial expression, intonation of spoken language – the choice of type or script, ink color, publishing signs such as hard covers, etc. all signify meaning beyond lexical and syntactic means. Macaulay (1990) similarly provides a critique of the arguments about cohesion and coherence evident in Tannen's account. She makes the point that writing is not necessarily more explicit than speech, arguing that cohesion is not about lexico-grammatical linkage but about frames of reference and experience. This could also be linked to Fairclough's notion of "coherence" as dependent on "discoursal common sense." For him this means that terms like cohesion and coherence, used so frequently in the pedagogic application of linguistics, are "ideological," since common sense is located within political and power relationships.

Besnier (1988), in a comprehensive survey of the differences that have been claimed between writing and speech, concludes that, once close ethnographic accounts are analyzed, few general differences remain. Not only is the idea of a "great divide" between writing and speech untenable, but he suggests, citing Biber's (1988) large corpus study of variation across speech and writing, even the notion of a "uni-dimensional continuum is inadequate to accommodate the variations in linguistic behaviour across contexts of oral and written communication" and "the structural characteristics of each register do not depend on whether it is produced in the spoken or written mode . . . spoken language is not necessarily more involved, more interactive, and less complex than written language" (1988: 710). These characteristics are instead viewed as dependent upon the communicative practices in specific contexts. The structured relationships of spoken and written language must be explained in terms of the social context of orality and literacy in different literacy traditions, rather than the cognitive demands of language production or isolated (universal) structural features of the spoken and written modes. If there are universal differences in channel, despite the growing evidence, they will be difficult to identify if we already presume such difference in the model of language we use in the first place, that is, if we assume features of "writing" and then, when we find these features in speech call them "writing-like" then the argument is circular and cannot be tested. The research models that Besnier critiques have themselves served to create and reproduce the differences between reading and writing that are currently treated as "natural" in both academic and popular discourses.

Alternative research challenges the dominant emphasis on a single, "neutral" Literacy with a big "L" and a single "y" and describes instead the specificity of literacies in particular places and times. Street has attempted to summarize the above debates with reference to the now classic distinction between "autonomous" and "ideological" models of literacy (Street, 1984). The exponents of an autonomous model of literacy, he argues, conceptualize literacy in technical terms, treating it as independent of social context, an autonomous variable whose consequences for society and cognition can be derived from its intrinsic character. Goody and Watt, for instance, in their seminal article to which much subsequent literature refers, maintain that writing is distinctive because it is, at least potentially, "an autonomous mode of communication" (Goody, 1968: 40). Walter Ong, probably the most influential writer on literacy in the USA, develops this idea more fully: "By isolating thought on a written surface, detached from any interlocutor, making utterance in this sense autonomous and indifferent to attack, writing presents utterance and thought as uninvolved in all else, somehow self-contained, complete" (1982: 132). David Olson has perhaps been the most explicit exponent of the "autonomous" model, arguing that "there is a transition from utterance to text both culturally and developmentally and that this transition can be described as one of increasing explicitness with language increasingly able to stand as an unambiguous and autonomous representation of meaning" (1977: 258). Where Goody has recently denied that his argument involves technological determinism or "autonomy" (cf. Goody, 1986 and 1987, especially the preface), Olson holds enthusiastically to the strong version of the autonomous model, repeating in a recent article the claim that "the media of communication, including writing, do not simply extend the existing structures of knowledge; they alter it" (Olson, 1988: 28; cf. also Olson, 1994). For him it is writing itself that has these major consequences: "writing did not simply extend the structure and uses of oral language and oral memory but altered the content and form in important ways." He represents the consequences of literacy not only in terms of social development and progress but also in terms of individual cognitive processes: "when writing began to serve the memory function, the mind could be redeployed to carry out more analytic activities such as examining contradictions and deriving logical implications. It is the availability of an explicit written record and its use for representing thought that impart to literacy its distinctive properties" (Olson, 1988: 28).

Researchers dissatisfied with the assumptions outlined above, and with the autonomous model of literacy, have come to view literacy practices as instead inextricably linked to cultural and power structures in society. Avoiding the reification of the autonomous model, they study these social practices rather than literacy in itself for their relationship to other aspects of social life. Scribner and Cole (1981), Finnegan (1988), and Lave (1988) argue, on the basis of detailed ethnographic and experimental research in different cultural contexts, that literacy does not develop specific powers of decontextualized thinking. Finnegan (1988), for example, in her study of the Limba in Sierra Leone, found that they used oral practices in complex, reflective ways requiring cognitive skills which were thought to be developed only by so-called literate communities. The contextual approach to literacy has been variously characterized by recent researchers. Whereas Baker (1994) refers to it as "cultural," Finnegan as "ethnographic," and Hill and Parry, (1994) as "pragmatic," Street (1984) has developed an "ideological" model, because it signals explicitly that literacy practices are aspects not only of "culture" but also of power structures. The very emphasis on the "neutrality" and "autonomy" of literacy by writers such as Goody, Olson, and Ong is itself, he claims, "ideological" in the sense of disguising this power dimension (Street, 1993). The term "ideological" is not being used here in its old-fashioned Marxist (and current anti-Marxist) sense of "false consciousness" and simple-minded dogma, but rather in the sense employed within contemporary anthropology, sociolinguistics, and cultural studies, where ideology is the site of tension between authority and power on the one hand and resistance and creativity on the other (Bourdieu, 1977; Mace, 1979; Centre for Contemporary Cultural Studies, 1980; Asad, 1980; Thompson, 1985; Grillo, 1989a, b; Fairclough, 1989; Eagleton, 1990). This tension operates through the medium of a variety of cultural practices, including particularly language and, of course, literacy. Similarly, a number of authors (Lankshear, 1987; McLaren, 1988; Gee, 1990; Freebody and Welsh, 1993; Luke, 1994) particularly in Australia and America, and in the development context, building on the work of Paulo Freire (1985), have represented analysis of the power dimension of literacy practices in terms of a "critical literacy," borrowing from broader sociological literature on social change and social institutions.

To operationalize these theoretical perspectives for research purposes a number of scholars have come to employ the concepts of "literacy practices" and "literacy events." "Literacy events" for Heath refer to "any occasion in which a piece of writing is integral to the nature of the participants' interactions and their interpretative processes" (Heath, 1982). The concept of "literacy practices" is pitched at a higher level of abstraction and refers to both behaviour and the social and cultural conceptualizations that give meaning to the uses of reading and/or writing. Literacy practices incorporate not only "literacy events," as empirical occasions to which literacy is integral, but also folk models of those events and the ideological preconceptions that underpin them (Street, 1993; Barton, 1994) Scribner and Cole (1981), from a psychological perspective, similarly developed a "practice account" of "literacy." Barton as a social linguist argues for some combination of these meanings and for continued use of both concepts: "Literacy *events* are the particular activities in which literacy has a role: they may be regular repeated activities. Literacy *practices* are the general cultural ways of utilising literacy that people draw upon in a literacy event" (Barton, 1991: 5). Grillo argues that "literacy is seen as one type of communicative practice" (Grillo, 1989a: 8). He locates the study of literacy in the broader context of the ethnographic study of communicative practices in different social contexts (cf. Hymes, 1974).

3 Literacy in Practice: The Oral Dimension of Literacy Events

Heath's classic account of literacy in three different communities in the Piedmont Carolinas likewise avoids the simple dichotomy between oral and literate that was standard in the literature until recently. She starts from the principle that literacy events are always embedded in oral events and that much of the linguistic practice is better understood in terms of the particular "mix" of channels than through analysis of each one separately. For instance, she describes the receipt of a letter by a woman in Trackton (a black, working-class community in the Piedmont Carolinas) as a communal activity in which friends and relatives cluster around her on a veranda and discuss its meaning. They interact with the written text, make oral commentaries, suggest interpretations and begin to develop the basis for a written reply: The whole is, in a sense, greater than the sum of its parts and, in order to describe this, linguists and ethnographers needed new concepts and analytic tools that avoided the reductionism of the oral/literate dichotomy. Baynham (1993) adopts a similar perspective in studying aspects of the linguistic repertoire among the Moroccan community in London. He focuses on the notion "mediators of literacy" as a communicative practice and compares it to the involvement of interpreters, formal and informal. He suggests that there are interesting comparisons and overlaps between mediated literacy events and communicative events in which interpreters are involved. Both communicative events, mediated literacy events and events involving interpreting, are common in the setting from which the data are drawn – the Moroccan community settled in West London. Community members who regularly function as mediators of literacy on a semiformal basis, such as volunteers in a community organization, are often drawn into interpreting as well. The two event types contrast in that mediated literacy events are typically a mix of oral and literate modes around some kind of "work on text" – what he terms "mode-switching" in an analogy with the sociolinguist's "code-switching" – while the interpreting event favors the oral mode, though not of course excluding the literate. His approach also extends the work on emergent sociolinguistic repertoires of second-generation community members with specific reference to literacy practices (Weinstein-Shr, 1993; TESOL Quarterly, 1993).

Literacy events are, then, oracy events as well, nicely summed up in Baynham's description "making texts talk" (Maybin and Moss, 1993). Such multilingual literacy events are the "barium meal" for the more general system of language practices, that is, the complexity of mode-switching and code-switching in linguistically and culturally complex societies throws into relief the complex shifts and switches which occur in all literacy events, in some ways analogous to the shifts in frame and footing in face-to-face interaction (Goffman, 1974).

4 Literacy in Practice: The Stigma of 'Illiteracy'

Following from the theoretical developments outlined above, this section describes four key aspects of literacy in practice: the stigma of "illiteracy"; schooled literacy; second language literacy; and literacy and nationalism. In each case the oral dimension of literacy practices is prominent in the recent research. Many literacy campaigns, in both the developed and developing worlds (cf. Giere and Hautcoeur, 1990) have presented "illiteracy" in such a negative way that a "stigma" has been created where many people had operated in the oral domain without feeling that it was a problem. Where this has happened, the concept of "illiteracy" has itself become one of the major problems in people's ability to see themselves as communicators. The rhetoric of public campaigns frequently reinforces rather than challenges these images. The literacy campaign in the UK, for instance, during the 1970s attempted to elicit funds from government by claiming that one million people in the UK were "illiterate" and further millions were functionally unable to manage the reading and writing requirements of the society. A major conference in 1973 to present the case to government and funding bodies was entitled: "Status Illiterate – Prospects Zero" (Mace, 1979). As practitioners and researchers became more closely involved with those who came forward for tuition it became apparent that their "problems" were more complex and less easily described in terms of a dichotomy between literacy and "illiteracy" (Mace, 1979; Hargreaves, 1980; Street, 1994). A National Institute for Adult Education research project notes that the major issue raised by students was of "confidence" rather than of literacy skills in themselves: Many had found

difficulty at school for a variety of reasons (health, moving schools, stigmatization by teachers, etc.) and had a poor self-image educationally. Many held
folk theories of literacy that meant they shared the common demeaning view
of those who could not spell, or had problems with particular genres, with
form-filling or official letters, etc. "Illiteracy" in common terminology is often
synonymous with ignorance, stupidity, cognitive deficit, etc. where current
research suggests the reality of people with literacy difficulties is varied and
more complex, both socially and in terms of literacy skills. A similar pattern
can be found in much development activity around literacy: King (1995)
describes how the Mexican literacy campaign in the 1970s, for instance, generated "stigma" among mestizos in urban areas while Indians living in rural
areas, where literacy played little part in everyday life, had not yet internalized the stigma and so saw little need to come forward to classes. Those
running the campaign had a vested interest in creating and publicizing the
stigma. UNESCO and other agencies concerned with literacy work in the
Third World frequently represent the state of "illiteracy" as "living in dark-
ness" (cf. Verhoeven, 1994) and lacking the mental understanding needed for
life in the "modern" world (cf. Oxenham, 1980) and early academic research,
based on misconceptions about the relationship between channels of communication and cognitive skills (Clammer, 1976) helped to reinforce these folk
theories.

The stigmatization of "illiteracy" is part of a wider ideological discourse
which devalues vernacular literacies and nonstandard varieties of oral practices. Notions of the "standard" (Haugen, 1972; Leith, 1983) invoke such
attitudes since they are about not tolerating variability. A standard is imposed
(Giles et al., 1975; Leith, 1983) and then maintained by the "guardians of
language" (J. and L. Milroy, 1985) who control and prescribe the rules of the
game within the political economy (Bourdieu, 1977, 1991; Gal, 1989). Despite
sociolinguists' best attempts to describe the variety, folk notions about the
standard and confusions about the relationships between grammar and writing, standard grammar and standard phonology, and about writing and
speaking more generally still persist (see Trudgill, 1983a) The social psychological literature has invariably attested the stigmatization of nonstandard
varieties. Studies on language attitudes, speech evaluation, and social markers
of speech have repeatedly shown that standard variety speakers are judged as
more competent and cleverer than the same speakers using a nonstandard
variety (e.g., Lambert, 1972; Giles et al., 1975; Giles and St Clair, 1979).

Similarly in the interactional sociolinguistic literature on intercultural communication, nonstandard varieties of language, it is argued, are a dimension
of racial discrimination, and in ethnographic studies of code-switching and
linguistic variation as resource (Hewitt, 1986; Rampton, 1995), Creoles, patois,
and other varieties are frequently represented by their speakers as "broken"
languages as well as a resource for identity maintenance and resistance to
hegemonic practices. Since identity is communicatively produced, communicative resources can be used to charge a particular setting with identity-

related meanings. Hewitt (1986) discusses how among young black people in South London two modalities of ethnicity are generated: One is stressed, political, and contesting, the other unstressed and realized through the local multi-ethnic vernacular. Heller (1992b) discusses the use of code-switching as part of the linguistic economy in Quebec and Ontario, where bilingual resources are used as a strategy in ethnic mobilization. Similarly Shuman and Camitta (see below) contrast the resistance to school literacy with the vernacular literacies practiced at home. All these studies contribute to an understanding of how the standard, the "literate," and the "schooled" come to be valued, and of the stigmatization and resistance to this hegemony through the use of vernacular and community resources.

Notions of oracy and so-called oral societies as operating in less cognitively complex ways fed into this stigmatization. Among others, Halliday (1985), Scribner and Cole (1981), Finnegan (1988), and Lave (1988) have argued that oral practices are as complex as written ones. From a functional grammar perspective, Halliday has suggested: "Contrary to what many people think, spoken language is on the whole, more complex than written language in its grammar and informal, spontaneous conversation is the most grammatically complex of all" (1985: 47).

5 Literacy in Practice: Schooled Literacy

Many of the theoretical perspectives regarding oral and written language outlined here have been applied in educational contexts and used to underpin pedagogy and curriculum design. One area in which the "autonomous" model of literacy has been challenged recently has been from the perspective of the ethnography of education. Ethnographic approaches to the study of language in education have been popular for some time, especially in the US: Villegas provides a useful overview of that literature which attempts to help teachers "understand what tools they need to be effective teachers in culturally diverse classrooms" (1991: 4). She cites the classic study by Susan Phillips (1983) of Warm Springs Indian reservation, which attempted to answer the question of why the children were silent during classroom lessons. Phillips, using ethnographic methods, compared their school participation patterns to how learning occurred in the community. She discovered that in their own community these children were used to a high degree of self-determination, that they learned by watching adults, and they were often taken care of by siblings whom they turned to for help. These ways of learning placed them at a disadvantage where the teacher kept close control of the interactions in the class, where verbal instruction was the main method of teaching, and where students had to display their knowledge in front of other students. This "cultural" explanation for differential learning performance has become a standard basis for analyzing "minority failure" in US schools and generated a wealth of comparable ethnographies (Gumperz and Hymes, 1972; Cazden, 1988). Interestingly for present purposes, the emphasis tended to be on oral language patterns, at least until Heath's (1983) account of the literacy practices of three communities in the Piedmont Carolinas. More recently, and drawing on the theoretical and methodological perspectives outlined above, to which Heath herself made a major contribution, researchers have focused more closely on the written dimension of schooled performance and on the relation of oral and written language.

Camitta (1993), for instance, spent three years with adolescents at a Community High School in Philadelphia, talking about their writing and sharing the intimacies this involved. The experience forced her to revise assumptions and beliefs about writing that she had held as a teacher at the school and which she suggests are dominant in educational circles in the USA. She gradually became aware of the texts and contexts for unofficial or self-sponsored writing practiced by adolescents: Writing, she discovered, was an important and varied activity and identified major areas that "organized" adolescent culture. She draws a contrast between this kind of writing and schooled texts: "The kinds of written texts I wish to study are not essays, the officially designated discourse genre of academia, but rather those that adolescents choose to write within the framework of adolescent culture and social organization." These texts she called "vernacular," "in the sense that they are most closely associated with culture which is neither elite nor institutional. By vernacular writing I mean writing which is traditional and indigenous to the diverse cultural processes of communities as distinguished from the uniform, inflexible standards of institutions" (Camitta, 1993: 228–9). She refers to a variety of disciplines for support, citing work in linguistics, cultural studies, literary criticism etc. in which the common feature of vernacular discourse is its derivation from folk or popular traditions and a lack of conformity to the standard. In the school context, however, such discourses have been treated mainly in moral and disciplinary terms, as rebellious, as inadequate attempts at proper literacy, along with graffiti and other literate forms that differ from the essay text model.

Amy Shuman (1986) similarly worked with adolescents at an inner-city Junior High School in the eastern USA. While her interest, like Camitta's, was in oral and written narratives, her particular focus was on storytelling rights: In standard written form these involve questions of legal copyright; in the context of vernacular literacies rights are embedded in everyday social relationships and interactions. These Shuman investigated through a variety of methods. She lived among groups of adolescents at the school for three years, tape-recorded many conversations, especially naturally occurring narrative performance, conducted interviews, designed a questionnaire with the help of the students themselves, and also obtained copies of written material from them, such as diaries, rap songs, and fight stories.

Shuman does not evaluate these students' texts by standard school criteria of competence, but rather as part of a single community's repertoire: From this perspective they represent choices among channels and genres of communication, rather than examples of greater or lesser deficiency, as the popular debate in many societies about "standards" would appear to require. The practices described by Shuman do not represent anomalies, rather they demonstrate "a need to re-evaluate the current models used for categorizing writing and speaking." Communicative competence, then, is relative to the speech community and its norms. Labov and others have demonstrated that there is much more of interest in the language practices of the inner city than is elicited by the standard tests and popular judgments. The work of Shuman, Camitta, Baynham and others is now revealing the rich repertoire of written as well as oral practices to be found there.

Addressing the question of why one particular variety of literacy among many comes to be seen and reproduced as the standard, given the growing evidence of variation in "vernacular" writing, a number of researchers have emphasized the privileging of schooled literacy as the model for all literacy (Cook-Gumperz, 1986; Street and Street, 1992; Gee, 1992). Micro-ethnographic accounts of schooled literacy practices have suggested that they are as much concerned with procedures and with establishing the authority of the educational institution – what Bloome and others (1989) refer to as "procedural display" – as with their claimed cognitive aims. Studies of literacy in the community demonstrate the variety and complexity of nonschooled practices and underline the ideological and historically recent emphasis on the schooled variety (Barton and Ivanic, 1992). Further empirical work along these lines might help link the new literacy theories with particular practices in both home and school. Until then, we have to be wary of generalization, although some account of the link between literacy and pedagogy is emerging.

New research on the written and oral aspects of educational language use has recently also been extended to higher education. There is a growing literature, for instance (cf. Taylor, 1988; Lea, 1994; Ivanic, forthcoming) on the gap between faculty expectations and student interpretations of what is expected in student writing. Mary Lea (1994) notes that faculty frequently assume that academic literacy – the formal, often detached and impersonal register of much writing in universities – will be learned over the years through constant interactions between tutors and students so that they can make these comments without having to make explicit the underlying assumptions. Recent research on students' own perspectives (Cohen, 1991; Ivanic, forthcoming) has brought it home that this is not necessarily the case; students and faculty are often at cross purposes regarding the notion of "making generalizations," "making themes more explicit," etc. which rest on hidden assumptions about the model of literacy – in this case of "academic literacy" – being held by the various participants. As Lea (1994) points out from her study of mature students, many were already skilled in writing before they came to university, but the demands of "academic literacy" seem to deskill them – "I thought I could write until I came here." Many students see the requirements of academic literacy – explicitness, formality, lack of the first person, etc. – as a "game" in which they are being asked to take on an identity that is "not me," that is not true to their image of their "true" self (Ivanic, forthcoming). It is at this level – identity, self-hood, personality – rather than simply at the level of writing technique, skills, grammar, etc. that the conflict and miscommunication around academic writing often occurs between students and tutors (Street, 1994). This represents a new research perspective on written language in the academy, with applications in researchers' own places of work.

6 Literacy in Practice: Second Language Literacy

In the literature on second and foreign language learning we find the same autonomous models as are dominant in the studies of education more generally. Hall (1993) uses Street's model to argue that there is an autonomous model of oral language in the language learning literature. A single path from listening through speaking to reading and finally writing is assumed (see, for example, Cummins, 1984).

This dominant paradigm is also in place in the use by language educationists of the notions of discourse analysis and communicative competence. Dubin (1989) argues that the latter concept developed by Hymes (1964) out of the investigation of how languages come to be used in specific communities has been turned into programmatic statements about the idealized language curriculum for second language learners. Whereas Hymes saw "competence" as about what people do with language, posing a research agenda that challenged a Chomskyan focus on idealized norms of grammar, the language learning literature, according to Dubin, has tended to take "competence" to mean "competencies" – a specific set of skills and technical uses of language that can be inculcated into learners and then measured at different levels of achievement. To put these shifts and confusions into perspective, she suggests that looking at ways in which recent scholars have characterized literacy as a field offers a window for viewing similar strands in applied linguistics.

The dominant strand in applied linguistics, the great majority of which refers to English language education, has constructed definitions of discourse and discourse analysis around a relatively narrow view of the relationship between language and its immediate context. Recent debates within second language learning have begun to contest this dominant view and argue for a more critical or ideological perspective (Phillipson, 1992; Santos, 1992; Pennycook, 1994). Pennycook argues for the need to look at discourse practices and consider under what conditions speech and writing come to be produced in the language classroom, rather than dealing with them in a technical way and focusing on their differences.

In the particular field of writing English as a second language, Santos (1992) points out the absence of discussion of ideological and political dimensions of the kind now evident in the literacy field. Pennycook (1994), in an important article on discourse in applied linguistics, asserts the need for alternative strands. Despite the work of critical linguists (Fowler et al., 1979; Fairclough, 1985, 1989; Kress, 1985) and a critical appraisal of language policy and planning (Phillipson, 1992; Pennycook, 1994), a critical or ideological perspective has not permeated the literature on second language speaking and writing. Pennycook argues for the need to look at discourse practices and to consider under what conditions language comes to be produced in the language classroom. This critical perspective would move language education away from a modularized view of language pedagogy based on the four skills of listening, speaking, reading, and writing and encourage instead a more contested notion of the work that second and foreign language teaching does in positioning learners and establishing the norms for linguistic power.

7 Literacy in Practice: Literacy and Nationalism

A number of recent studies of the emergence and persistence of nationalism have attributed a significant role in these processes to literacy. Those who argue that nationalism is a relatively modern phenomenon (Smith, 1986) ground a great deal of their case on the supposed nature of literacy. Gellner (1983), for instance, sees the homogeneity required by the modern State as being made possible only through a common national literacy, unavailable in previous "agro-literate" stages of social development. The literacy of these agro-literate societies was of what Goody (1977) calls the "restricted" kind. In the modern State, on the other hand, literacy has to be available to the mass of the population and not simply to an elite: indeed, it is the development of such mass literacy that explains the rise of the modern nation-state itself. "Modern industry requires a mobile, literate, technologically equipped population and the nation-state is the only agency capable of providing such a work force, through its support for a mass, public, compulsory and standardised education system" (Gellner, 1985: 29).

The literacy being referred to here appears to be that of the "autonomous" model. A single, nationally sanctioned literacy supposedly rises above the claims of the different ethnic communities that may constitute the State and creates the basis instead for a single "nation"-state that is culturally homogeneous and politically unified. The education system, according to Gellner, is at the heart of this process: It provides a neutral means of authenticating knowledge through reasonably impartial centers of learning, which issue certificates "on the basis of honest, impartially administered examination" (p. 29). Scholars who have focused on the concept of a plurality of literacies, rather than a single autonomous literacy, have been less inclined to take these claims at face value. While they are evidently part of the rhetoric of nationalism, they do not necessarily correspond to the social reality, in which it is much more usual to find a variety of different literacy practices. Accounts of the uses of literacy to express identity among youth groups in urban situations (Shuman, 1986; Weinstein-Shr, 1993; Camitta, 1993), of mode-switching as well as code-switching in the Moroccan community in London (Baynham, 1993), of mother-tongue literacy among Latin American migrants in Toronto (Klassen, 1991) and of "community" literacy in Lancaster, England (Barton and Ivanic, 1991), challenge the view of the modern world as consisting of homogeneous nations each with a single, homogenizing literacy. Likewise, scholars who stress the symbolic and cultural dimensions of ethnic ties and nations focus upon the variety of routes to nationalism and put less weight on the claims made for literacy in its emergence (Smith, 1986). The account of the growth and persistence of modern nationalism, they suggest, requires analysis not only of the exigencies of modern technology and economy but also of the ideological and cultural aspects of literacy practices. The issues of language and literacy and their role in the historical and contemporary development of nationalism have opened up to new historical and ethnographic accounts that challenge and will ultimately contribute to the development of the methods and insights traditionally employed by sociolinguists. One such area in which that expertise is already being allied to immediate policy debates and issues is within specific institutional settings, such as the workplace, the courts, etc., areas that are dealt with in the next section.

8 Literacy Events in Institutional Settings

Although speaking and writing relationships have been focused on educational contexts (see above) the dynamics and interrelationships of speaking and writing constitute the discourses which more generally hold all institutions together. The uses of oral and written language in institutional settings illustrate again the challenge to literacy as a neutral, technical achievement. Oral/literacy practices are part of much wider sets of knowledge and skills, which like communicative power are distributed differentially. Rockhill (1987), for example, discusses how managing bureaucratic forms means understanding all the complex regulations which underpin these forms, not just the technical skill of knowing which box to fill in. The managing of such forms is part of the "gatekeeping" process (Erickson and Shultz, 1982; Gumperz, 1982a), locating literacy in the structures of power and mixing and switching between spoken and written language to meet specific institutional demands, constructing and reproducing "how institutions think" (Douglas, 1986). Institutional ways of speaking and writing, central to the relationship between language and the political economy (Gal, 1989) are the sites of social legitimation and devaluation. The gatekeeping encounters represent those heightened moments of judgment and record-keeping when clients and applicants are evaluated as adequate, competent, and morally acceptable

(Silverman and Jones, 1976; Flett, 1979; Gumperz, 1982a, 1992; Erickson and Shultz, 1986).

Micro-ethnographic and sociolinguistic studies of gatekeeping encounters chart the means by which gatekeepers use their own communicative norms and conventions to judge the quality and adequacy of interviewees. These include the social and sociological presuppositions or schema of the particular institution, for example, symptom elicitation in medical interviews (Fisher and Todd, 1983), attempts to fit workers' experiences into bureaucratic categories to do with skills and qualifications in employment advice interviews (Roberts et al., 1992; Bremer et al., 1996), or the structuring of one's autobiography along ideological principles of personhood in Alcoholics Anonymous meetings (Erchak, 1992). They also include the verbal and nonverbal resources of the gatekeeping communicative style (R. and S. Scollon, 1981; Gumperz, 1982b; Phillips, 1992). Control of the particular mix of oral and written language in interviews is often a source of power. Heath (1983), for instance, describes the way in which a bank manager, through not showing forms to a client, forces her to second-guess what is written there in her oral responses in order to achieve a favorable outcome.

Since such encounters are joint accomplishments (Sacks, 1972; Sacks, Schegloff, and Jefferson, 1974; Atkinson and Heritage, 1984) the gatekeepers' records are constructed by their line of questioning and inferencing in the interaction as much as by their post-interview record-keeping and fitting of information into bureaucratic forms and categories. These records, such as medical notes, counselling files, or employment interview reports, fix a particular local encounter as a general statement about dispositions, competence, attitude, etc. Cicourel (1968) discusses how records are assembled to construct young people as juvenile delinquents, and Gubrium and Buckholdt's (1982) study of a US rehabilitation hospital shows how reports are "worked up" with reference to a particular audience. In all these contexts, the gatekeepers create the conditions for accountability of their actions with reference to the wider social practices of their institutions as part of the sociohistorical ordering and controlling of society through varied uses of oral and written language.

Three specific examples, all taken from multilingual settings, will further illustrate the oracy/literacy event as it is played out in institutional settings. Studies of the courtroom (Atkinson and Drew, 1979; Phillips, 1982; Shuy, 1986; Gibbons, 1994) detail the routinized practices which frame the event as a legal and adversarial one and which serve to constitute the legal profession, just as the texts of other professions show how they constitute themselves in writing (cf. Newman, 1989). Typically, the proceedings are taken down verbatim as a record. But in the American bilingual courtroom, where the language of the court is English but the language of the defendant is Spanish, such a record is mediated by the Spanish interpreter. Only what is said in English counts in the sense that only the English is recorded in writing (Berk-Seligson, 1990).

The Spanish interpreter can use a number of strategies to present the defendant/witness in a positive light. For example, he or she can alter the pragmatic force of the Spanish so that the defendant's blame or responsibility can be pushed into the background or their responses can be presented as more powerless. Similarly, the interpreter can lengthen the testimony in the English translation or convert fragmented speech style into flowing narrative. Overall, the interpreters can exercise a controlling influence over the impression the defendant/witness makes on the jury, since it is their version which is enforced as the accurate record of proceedings (cf. the reference to Baynham above).

Verbatim records of police proceedings, customs and excise and immigration interviews are of course also kept. These reports have been increasingly contested and are the subject of analysis by forensic linguists (Gibbons, 1994). The precarious nature of such reports is highlighted in instances where bilingual speakers produce nonstandard oral narratives which, in turn, are then reproduced in a standard written form by the note-taker. This record is subsequently used to argue for the linguistic competence of the accused when his or her responses under interrogation appear to implicate them as guilty. Issues of transcription have also been discussed in the ethnographic research literature (Clifford, 1990; Atkinson, 1992). Clifford suggests the inevitable tension, in representing an informant's own words, between authenticity and readability. Informants' words cannot be simply reproduced on the page; they have to be represented through writing conventions which are themselves matters of interpretation. Informants' speech is therefore written up in such a way as to represent them through the eyes of the writer: "the representation of speech can be used to convey the status and character of the speaker. The choice of conventions is thus a choice about the representation of persons as social and moral actors in the text" (Atkinson, 1992: 24). Although these issues of representation have been discussed in the literature on research methods, they are rarely the subject of open debate in the public domain.

Finally, contrastive studies of South Asian and white British counselling interviews (Gumperz and Roberts, 1991) detail the local, situated way in which documents are used to set contexts. In the data collected, South Asian clients routinely presented themselves nonverbally by presenting a document, letter, rent-book, or calendar and waited for the South Asian counsellor to infer their problems and their request from the document, whereas white British clients introduced themselves and their problems with a narrative account which blended fact and evaluative comment. This again illustrates the way in which oral and written resources are not only distributed differentially across events but are also sensitive to ethnic and cultural difference.

9 Discourse and Context: Connections to Wider Issues

The research on literacy events and practices and their relationship to institutional and national identities and institutions raises wider theoretical and methodological issues around the notions of discourse and context and their relationship. The "discoursing" of the social science disciplines has made the discussion of such a widely used term difficult to define. But despite the saturation of (and by) the academic community with this term, there has been little explicit work which focuses on the oral/literate mix in specific settings. Discourse in Foucaultian perspective as the complex of signs and practices structured through power relations to control our lives, or discourse as cultural capital within a market economy (Bourdieu, 1977, 1991), is represented at a level of abstraction which ignores the oral/written debate. Although Foucault and Bourdieu are concerned with the relationship between everyday practices and sociohistorical and economic conditions which shape them, there is no accounting for how these day-to-day practices come about.

At the other end of the spectrum, concern with the linguistic forms of discourse (Sinclair and Coulthard, 1975; Stubbs, 1983) or with the mechanisms of conversation which instantiate the practical reasoning ability of social actors (as in conversational analysis) limits analysis of social events to observed phenomena, focuses on talk rather than literacy/oracy events, and is not connected to the wider sociopolitical process. An interim position is taken by the critical linguists (Fowler, Hodge, and Kress, 1979; Fairclough, 1989) who relate linguistic processes to wider discourse formations, but still tend to read from specific texts to these wider discourses, rather than situating more ethnographic contextually sensitive accounts within the wider frame of knowledge/power relations which Foucault's definition of discourse argues for.

In this perspective, issues of what counts as literacy, for example, the free expression of the seventies classroom or the formal grammar of the nineties in western schooling, and what counts as oracy, again the storytelling, autobiographical accounts of 20 years ago or the specific schooled competences of the eighties and nineties, are the product of the dominant discourses of these times rather than any enlightened, liberated or realistic assessment of students' educational priorities. Changes in information technology and how they affect what we think of as oral/written discourse are also currently being researched, with reference, for instance, to dialogue processes in computer-mediated communication (Eklundh, 1986), to the uses of e-mail (Cole, 1985), and the relationship between text and talk in televisual forms, all of which may be treated as an issue of power/knowledge and identity, rather than just of technical progress (Gill, 1986).

Speaking and writing and their interrelationships are located within this wider conceptualization of discourse but are also experienced and acted out in specific local contexts. Recent work on contextualization (Gumperz, 1982a, b; Duranti and Goodwin, 1991; Auer and di Luzio, 1992) focuses on the connection between what is "brought about" and what is "brought along" in an event (Giddens, 1976; Hinnenkamp, 1989). In other words there is the contextual work done by participants in an event which actively creates context (McDermott, 1974; Erickson, 1975), the "brought about." There are contextual parameters which cannot be changed but which can be brought into focus or not (the brought along) and there are contextual schema which are brought along but subject to negotiation (Auer, 1992). More specifically, Gumperz's notion of "contextualization cues" channels semantic information into a message which in turn indexes sets of discourses and interactional experiences, which in Silverstein's (1992) term become part of "contextual reality." How this contextualization works and is differentially used and evaluated in settings where power relations are in focus is the subject of much of Gumperz's work and allies his approach to Bourdieu's concept of the linguistic marketplace, where linguistic and so symbolic resources are differentially distributed. What seems to be lacking still is sufficient ethnographic research which draws on this approach to context, sets the situated processes of writers and speakers within a wider critical perspective, and asks how these practices come to be produced and given value (or not).

10 Conclusion

Great claims have been made for "literacy" in its autonomous form. The term "literacy" itself set up and served to perpetuate the assumed differences between spoken and written language. Once essential differences between oracy and literacy were staked out, they could be unpacked from their communicative contexts and presented, paradoxically, both as a neutral set of skills to be acquired, and in the case of literacy and standard oral varieties, a value-laden and undifferentiated force for development and/or national integration.

Recent ethnographic research on oral and written language and on literacies has consistently argued that these social practices are complex, dynamic, and contextually specific. Oracies and literacies do not function independently of each other, or of wider sets of knowledge, or of profound issues of identity and social legitimation. Nor does literacy function in any simple way to create and maintain institutions and nation-states. Such functionalism ignores both the variety of routes through which groups come to be structured and controlled and the issues of power and authority.

Ideological and critical models of spoken and written language challenge this functionalism by raising questions about how the role and uses of literacy came to be defined in the way they are traditionally accepted. Such a challenge is particularly evident and significant within education where cultural capital is differentially distributed.

Illiteracy as stigma or literacy as development are not, as recent research has shown, claims that can be substantiated. But ethnographic studies in school and community, the charting of resistance to imposed literacy norms, and the devaluation of speaking practices, all illustrate the claims that can be made for the complex communicative practices which draw on written and spoken resources. These practices, studied within an ethnographic and historical tradition, both prescribe what counts as worthwhile within the dominant discourse and express the creativity of communities in resisting it. As such they are central to our understanding of the relationship between language and society.

11 The Sociolinguistics of Communication Media

GERHARD LEITNER

Introduction

Events would not happen the way they do and with the same impact without mass media. They inform and interpret, they entertain and educate with what is "out there." They are mirrors of "reality", as some critics believe, or, according to others, part of events themselves, a powerful "Fourth Estate" (Curran and Seaton, 1991). Whatever one thinks of this, media communication relies on and further develops language and other semiotic codes of society.

This paper is on the *sociolinguistics* of *communication media*.[1] Assisted by the sister disciplines of linguistics and mass communications, sociolinguistics will address media discourse in the context of the communication domain and will reveal what it is as performance, what the parameters are that determine its norm(s), what the public thinks of it, and what functions it aims to fulfill. This paper will concern itself with those forces in the wider sociolinguistic texture of a country and, finally, it will take up the role of the media as a public forum for language debates.

Two areas will be ignored: first, several types of mass media, that is, films, drama, and books. They can be mass media in their own right but also constituents of the program output of the press, radio, and television; they can be fictional or documentary. They deserve special treatment. The second omission is sound and visual codes and the interaction of different codes.

The first section will locate media discourse in the broader context of mass media research. The next one will look at media discourse, including the role of the media as public forums for linguistic debate. And the final section concludes with limitations of this account and the challenges of new technologies.

1 Communication Media and the Place of Media Discourse

Mass communications and macro-sociolinguistics consider mass media as social institutions (Schramm, 1975; Curran and Seaton, 1991) or domains (Fishman, 1974). Somewhat less consensual is a *functional* definition of media as communication domains.[2] But it is precisely that function that highlights media discourse and the factors behind it. A deeper understanding of the ways media perform that function calls for an outline of the communication process.

To begin with the communication flow: Content moves from a source, the medium, to a target, the recipients, and communication is unidirectional. Unidirectionality results from technical constraints but, as a definitional criterion, sets mass media off from telecommunication (Noelle-Neumann et al., 1994: 142). These constraints restrict recipient participation systematically and severely. But media types differ in the extent to which they inhibit access technically. The press, with its production delay between events and publication, imposes the severest constraints while electronic media are more accessible to direct or mediated participation of selected or self-selecting audiences. Either way, the communicative imbalance provides the media with power and control over the discourse.

Connected with technical matters is the second point, that is, the fact that communication may take place on a single or on several layers or axes. One intrinsic axis is the unidirectional movement of content from medium to recipients. TV commentators speaking directly to an audience are cases in point. But other axes show up in interviews, talk, or game shows. Interviews combine at least two speakers in a speech encounter, which defines a second axis. Live talkback shows, music shows, or game shows may be even more complex when they take place in front of an involved (participating) or uninvolved (watching) audience. Shifts from one axis to another are indicated by discourse signals which are largely under the control of media professionals. But the case may and indeed does arise of participants arguing about who has the right to structure discourse (Leitner, 1983).

The third aspect concerns the source of communicational content. While messages are about the "external" world, the nature of the relationship of media with "reality" is controversial.[3] Some researchers believe that media reflect "reality," others that they "co-orchestrate" dominant beliefs, etc. which are around anyway, others still that media create "reality." Gatekeepers, co-orchestrators, and manipulators encapsulate well-known notions. Without taking sides, it seems commonsensical to say that it is rare for media to be direct witnesses of some event, such as disasters. The routine case is that they get information in already mediated form from an outside agency. They depend on sources, for example, information departments, experts, stringers, "witnesses," press releases. Media staff also glean information themselves. The processing of incoming information is best described along a cline of mediation. One extreme case is the use of outside information without (much) mediation, the other its reduction to "mere" content, its incorporation into a message without attribution. To exemplify these extremes, when an expert presents the weather forecast, a witness talks about some disaster, a radio play or a concert is broadcast, there is relatively little mediation. Alternatively, information can be reduced to a summary, to excerpts. As processing necessitates acts of selection, categorization, and its transformation into *media discourse*, a degree of mediation is always involved (Clayman, 1990; Bell, 1991).

Fourth, the production of messages is controlled by factors that are internal to the domain or bear upon its work from the outside. Ownership, technology, media context, programming philosophy, but also media legislation can shape the production of messages. The media structure allocates responsibilities to several layers so that incoming content is taken through a hierarchy of levels and responsibilities until it becomes output and is couched in media discourse. The final production steps can be subject to control by style and editorial guidelines, language committees, or the professional routines. The *ultimate* encoder, the journalist, announcer, or presenter, is normally held responsible for the final shape of a message. While they represent the "voice of the medium" that recipients are most obviously confronted with, they are not the originators of the discourse. These steps are described by Schlesinger (1978) from a media sociological and Bell (1991) from a linguistic perspective.

Fifth, the fact that recipients are restricted in access and participation has been the source of much controversy. However, older theories that saw them primarily as the passive targets of message flows have been replaced by those that assign them a crucial role in determining uptake and wider effects. It is recipients that expose themselves to or withdraw from media output, they decode adequately or misconstrue content, they reinforce messages or alternatively nullify their effect. Media are therefore bound to incorporate into their messages a prototypical image of recipients and of the audience's desired or likely reactions. They "design" messages for an audience, a fact that differentiates *public* discourse from that of other domains, such as the law.

To sum up: Media are communication domains with specific communicative structures which are the cause of, broadly speaking, content becoming *public*, in other words, becoming accessible as public knowledge and for public debate. The discourse in which content is couched has been defined as a *public idiom* (Hall, 1978). It is not and cannot be homogeneous. What is more, each medium creates its own version. To emphasize a quotation from Hall: "The language employed will thus be the newspaper's own version of the language of the public to whom it is principally addressed" (1978: 48). Having located media discourse formally and functionally, we can turn to the media's part in processing content into media messages.

2 Media Discourse and Media Messages

The term "media discourse" refers to the forms, structures, and uses of language and other semiotic codes that are specific to the media. It also applies to the underlying cognitive systems (e.g., ideologies). Media discourse needs to be distinguished from the messages that it transports, a notion that describes the content and form of the "packages," such as articles or programs.[4]

Media messages and discourse are related to one another in three dimensions. That relationship will be outlined presently. A discussion of the impact and linguistic realization of references to sources, "reported" domains, and recipients will follow, and a survey of linguistic characteristics will conclude this section.

2.1 The dimensions of messages and media discourse

To begin with the messages–discourse relationship: From the production point of view, the processing of content occurs at several layers of an institutional hierarchy until it is transmitted as a media message. From the output perspective, messages are sequenced spatiotemporally. Cutting across these dimensions are particular formal constituents and themes, which are of concern to different layers of the institutional hierarchy and show up in various spatiotemporal slots.

Low-level output and the link-ups between parts of such output are the most obvious message types to which recipients are exposed, provoking their reaction. They can be illustrated by a commentary on the resignation of Haiti's military government, an interview with President Mandela, a talk show with a leading politician, or a soccer report on a match between Germany and Hungary. Such messages are at the interface of two dimensions. One points to the hierarchical structures of media domains, the other to spatiotemporal programming or layout sequences.

To begin with the former, the hierarchical dimension, low-level output is an instantiation of the program *format*, such as news, editorials, sports reports, game shows. Formats allow for variations which are broadcast at different times or appear in different locations in print. Spot news, evening bulletins, event and summary reports are cases in point. They can be grouped into broader higher-order categories such as news and current affairs, sport, local news, etc. on the grounds of similarity in orientation. *Orientation* is not a given category but derives from the classifications imposed by the media (or media outlets) on "reality," on the "reported domains" (see below). There follows *output in general*, for example, the business paper, the information or music channel. More abstract still is the media's definition of their *approach* to specific areas, such as classical or pop music, or the entire output. RTL does things one way, the BBC another. And finally, there are features that emanate from the technical *constraints on media* (both print and electronic).

Low-level messages occur in spatiotemporal sequences. Again two dimensions can be distinguished. One is the preplanning of sequences by the media, the program schemata, the other is the actual occurrence of some sequence which is determined by whatever content is available at a given time. As to the former, there are the days of the week, the hours, the sections and pages. Thus one can identify the weekend edition or program, the Sunday edition, the business or home news section, the "Friday Night." For the latter, one may observe that related or relatable items, for example, disasters in various locations, reports and commentaries on some event, may occur close by in space and/or time. Sequencing requires connections and conversely delimitation of one part from another. Such *messages* are frames and are, in their turn, peculiar to media types and organizations. In the press this is primarily a matter of layout, in electronic media of presentation.

The third dimension describes the fact that, irrespective of the media categorization of "reality," the orientation, some theme, text type, and/or some type of structure, e.g., interviews, may be components of various program formats. Themes such as women, racism, or violence may come as separate topics at low-level output, they may occur inside the political, the sport, or the business section, or be linguistic elements of media discourse.

Semiotic codes – language, sounds, visuals, and film – and elements of cognition, such as scripts, schemata, etc., are used in different ways along these dimensions. Language is the central carrier of low-level messages and of message sequences. It can be supported or sometimes replaced by acoustic or visual codes. But as one moves beyond the level of program formats or covers wider stretches of sequences, its role diminishes. Belief systems, derived from the interpretation of a media organization's role in the overall context, come to dominate. As a consequence, the dimensions per se and specifically the higher levels are the concern of mass communications (Curran and Seaton, 1991; Noelle-Neumann et al., 1994), rather than of linguistics and sociolinguistics.

As for language-oriented analyses, a few studies have been done on the evolution of some notion of orientation and theme (a third dimension). Thus Cardiff (1980) has revealed the development of the distinction between the serious and the popular as programming concepts and their manifestation in program types in the BBC. The history of sports reporting has been studied by Hargreaves (1986) and McChesney (1989). Racism, sexism, and violence as themes (in the third dimension) or as constituents of media discourse have also been studied (see below).

The majority of linguistic studies is of lower-level messages and sequences of messages with the goal of correlating findings with domain-specific factors that can serve as (partial) explanations. To begin with low-level output: Case studies of single examples of low-level output cannot distinguish the "normal/routine" from the "special," so they can be ignored. Collections or corpora of low-level output will be taken up below, but one should mention corpus linguistic analyses of particular lexical or grammatical features. Thus Virtanen

(1992) has looked at the placement of adverbial phrases.[5] Mention should also be made of studies of specific structural constituents such as headlines (e.g., Bell, 1991).

Higher-level message analyses have addressed a variety of concepts. To begin with program formats, GUMG (1980) highlights the role of professional routines in the production of British TV news programs, the interaction of different semiotic codes, and the patterning and meaning of types of news components. Bentele (1985) has suggested a "grammar" of news programs based on German data. Discourse structures of interviews (as programs of their own and/or as components of other programs), phone-ins, host programs, and debates, that is, multi-axis messages, have been identified in Scannel (1991), Leitner (1983), Heritage (1985), and Trösser (1983). Van Dijk (1988b) has suggested a model of the macro-text for international press reports. On the basis of German press soccer reports in print media, Simmler (1993) argues that text types can be predicted on the basis of layout characteristics. Linguistic properties of media texts have also been studied by Graustein and Thiele (1987) and Werlich (1976).

The analysis of some (third-dimension) theme in program formats over a period is a second and recurrent type of study, akin to content analysis. Fowler's (1991) analyses of health care, law and order, and gender, Walton and Davis's (1983) study of the assassination of an Italian president, and van Dijk's (1988) analysis of the assassination of President Gemayal reveal stable journalistic practices, the patterns of the transformation of "outside" content, and the role of cognitive frameworks in en- and decoding. Ferguson (1983) has studied syntactic features of style in live American sports reporting.

A third type of analysis is of language policies and attitudes. They manifest themselves typically across a variable range of program formats, defined by similarity of orientation, such as news reading, announcing, children's programs, editorials, or front-page reporting. The social and institutional forces behind their formulation and ways of implementing them have been revealed, for instance, by Leitner (1980, 1984).

Levels high up in the hierarchy, such as "full page," "full issue," and "full week" analyses, "running stories," have been suggested as objects of research by Fowler (1991) but have not yet been done (but see section 3 below).

2.2 Reported domains: The impact of sources

Having clarified the message hierarchy, one can turn back to the media's dependence on sources. Leitner has proposed an extension of the notion of domain since:

> unlike other domains, e.g. like economy or science . . . they [mass media, government and law] are totally unspecified with regard to the range of areas they deal with . . . It seems that they could be treated as higher domains than all others, or,

alternatively, as hyperdomains, which are unspecific with regard to topics etc. This option necessitates the distinction between domains and reported domains. (1992: 56)

Examples of reported domains are politics, science, sport, music, or the "social domain." Each has a number of subdomains. The social domain, for instance, may include accidents, murders, disasters, biographies, etc. The precise specification of what is in or outside some domain varies between media outlets. As media select content from reported domains they make it publicly available and in doing that they have to process the cognitive frameworks, linguistic norms, professional practices, and registers of the originating domains. Processing can mean integration, deletion, or modification. The following areas have attracted some interest.

The first concerns the accessing, processing, and linguistic identification of sources. GUMG (1980), Fowler (1991) and others have argued that there is a hierarchy of sources and a distinction between authoritative and nonauthoritative sources in news media, which shows in frequency of citation. It also affects practices of linguistic processing. The former type is less mediated than the latter. Bell (1991) outlines the processing steps of newsmakers' input, of agencies' material, and how integration may fail and lead to imperfect communication. Semantic processes of selection, deletion, summarization, and generalization have been described by van Dijk (1988a).

The second area concerns matters of representation and presentation (see section 2.4), in particular the effects of making publicly available expressions from reported domains. Suffice it to refer to the adaptation, that is, broadening or narrowing down, of the ideological "consensus" which media rely on (Hartley, 1982; Fowler, 1991). Based on Gulf War reports, Staczek (1993) showed how lexemes, idioms, and metaphors from the military domain have been incorporated. Siehr (1993) describes lexico-semantic conflicts in the process of German unification that derive from the use of legal terminology in the public domain. It is not always appreciated that such studies deal with media discourse, rather than with the language proper of the reported domain. Only a few have consciously addressed this issue. Simmler's analyses of the relationship of the sports domain with press sports reports (1991, 1993) and Hess-Lüttich's of German print media for adolescents (1983) are worth mentioning. Closely related is register research, such as Hoffmann's study of technical registers (1988).

2.3 Audience design: The impact of recipients

The active role of recipients in the communication process has already been referred to. While they are necessarily exposed to low-level output and normally perceive it as a member of some program format (soap opera, series, etc.), they need not notice higher-level planning and are certainly not bound to follow the media's agenda. In other words, the message dimensions bind the media but not the recipients.

In order to gain and maintain a stable audience, communication media must therefore include recipients' needs and expectations early on in message production. Bell (1991) suggests the notion of "audience design" for that, which he, however, studies only in low-level output. The question of how media gain knowledge on recipients is a matter of audience research (Noelle-Neumann et al., 1994). One frequently mentioned source is feedback through letters, phone calls, etc. from self-selecting recipients. Empirical investigations of recipients' reactions (e.g., comprehension studies) provide more objective input that may change media discourse to narrow down the gap with the "real" language of recipients.

Explicit decisions on audience design in low-level and framing messages deal with the selection and codification of linguistic expressions, e.g., the consideration of correctness norms, of "good usage," the use or disuse of taboo expressions, the avoidance of bias against gender or race. There is also a less conscious level of audience design that derives from professionalism and the overall media context. Bell (1984, 1990) has shown how it correlates with the social parameters of the audience.

Public service institutions have been found to be more amenable to explicit language debates than private companies. Thus the BBC commissioned a report on its language use after "a cultural shift . . . the levelling down to the speech and prose patterns of the largest common denominator rather than that of an élite" had been diagnosed (BBC, 1979). Similar measures were taken in Australia. Officially appointed media "watch-dogs" exist in many public service systems.

Audience design conflicts with other norms. The goal of objective reporting may conflict with a high level of audience empathy, the need to avoid obscene language with the colorful sociolects of recipients, the awareness of the role of language in forming prejudices against gender, race, or the disabled with recipients' expectations. The design and implementation of "acceptable" discourse require the ability to integrate diverging norms in the same way as with reported domains. Only a few studies mention these themes, but they form regular content in media style and editorial guidelines (see the next section).

2.4 *Presentation and representation: The creation of the message*

It has become clear by now that media discourse is not only a public idiom but also a *public discourse*, being source- and target-oriented. What then is the specific media contribution in the production of that discourse? Broadly speaking, it resides in the ability to provide a consensual frame of reference that integrates divergent demands and is sensitive to needs of the message dimensions, as well as to the stylistic requirements of themes. Two well-established categories can serve as an organizing framework for the discussion: presentation (style) and representation (content).

The former can be expressed in a variety of ways, ranging from layout and announcing to program and topic sequencing; from the choice of words to that of syntactic constructions and text types. It expresses media values such as immediacy and distance, involvement and objectivity, factuality and dramatization. It converts the media's "approach" into consistent patterns of semiotic codes and creates "product" identity. Representation is similarly broad and includes the scope of content and its institution-specific transformation (imprint), the approach to content, the definition of recipients' segments, and programming strategies. It embodies the media's ideological stance.

The distinction between presentation and representation is akin to linguistic theories that see language as a vehicle for the *how* and the *what* that is expressed. Drawing on Halliday's interpersonal and ideational functions, Kress suggests that the processing of events at the social level "has its analog on the linguistic level, in the *interpersonal function* of language" (1983: 44). Fowler argues strongly that "imbalances of access" to the media result "in partiality, not only in *what* assertions and attitudes are reported – a matter of content – but also in *how* they are reported – a matter of form or style" (1991: 23). And Leitner (1983) suggests they account for numerous aspects of media language and are related to sentence-based text and discourse theories. Moreover, professionals are more likely to discuss language topics in terms of style and approach than of content.

Theoretical and practical considerations suggest that the two notions are related rather than strictly separate from each other. The former has to do with the connection between language and cognition, the latter with the need to assign a function to linguistic (or other semiotic) expressions, while encoders may have intended, and decoders understood them, in different ways (cf. pp. 190–2). Practical problems will be ignored[6] but on theoretical issues Kress has this to say:

> in analyzing the mediating function of the media these two aspects must be considered: the primary classification of reality . . . and the modes in which these are presented to the audiences . . . Language enters into both . . . not only because of the parallel or analogical nature of processes on the social and the linguistic plane, but because ideological systems exist in and are articulated by the categories and processes of a given language . . . linguistic and ideological processes do not exist as distinct phenomena, they are indistinguishable, they are one and the same in substantial terms. (1983: 45)

In other words, both express and rely on ideological positions. But a conflict between the underlying ideologies of presentation and representation may arise. Once again, media must create a compromise in their discourse.

Presentation

Presentation deals with standardization, that is, processes of selection, codification, expansion, and acceptance of some variety of linguistic expression.[7]

The question of language choice (mainly in connection with codification) arises in these situations: multilingual countries; media for minority language groups; media for international and/or extranational distribution. Language choice in competitive situations and the propagation of minority languages have been looked at by Fox (1991). This volume contains studies on Irish, Icelandic, Gaelic, Occitan, and Czech and shows that policies are more successful if they are supported by benefits, such as adequate output and technology. In densely populated multilingual regions, as in parts of Asia, some languages, such as Hindi, Kannada, Mandarin Chinese, or Bahasa Malay are disadvantaged in the sense that they are not (fully established) official languages and/or are complemented by former colonial ones. But they may well be successful competitors with those dominant languages. As their reach is limited to small, if elite numbers, the commercial value of large languages can be a winning factor. There are no studies of such situations as yet. A particular self-image of a country may help create a language ecology that permits media to use both large and small languages. Australia's multiculturalism, to give one example, led to the spread of "ethnic" media and ethnic or community languages. In other words, media can be potent factors in language maintenance and revival. But they are, generally speaking, the object of decision-making processes at political levels rather than initiators (cf. section 2.5).

The more frequent case of selection concerns the choice of a variety from within a language, a situation again closely related to codification. Fishman (1974: 1644) maintained that

> the standard language *per se*, without further differentiation or accompaniment, is most fitted for communication across large but referential (or non-interacting) networks, such as those involving mass media, governmental pronouncements, legal codes and text books. The standard variety is the "safest" for those communications in which the speaker cannot know his diversified and numerous listeners.

Leitner (1980) found correlations between the social function of varieties, sociopolitical attitudes, the definition of the media's task, and overall media context in his comparison of German and British radio language policies. Crucial differences between Germany and Britain cast doubt on the general validity of Fishman's claim. For one, the standard variety was undisputed only in Britain and only for as long as the southeast dominated. Germany, in contrast, had always been organized around regions and educated regional varieties were preferred. Only during one short period when radio was indeed national was a national standard selected. It was soon replaced again by regional varieties. Studies on New Zealand (Bell, 1983) and Australia (Leitner, 1984) confirmed the correlation with media-internal parameters and attitudes on functions of varieties. But while Britain and Germany were discussed in terms of choosing from within the national speech repertoire (endo-normativity), Australia and New Zealand showed a conflict between national and foreign variety choice, in other words, between endo- and exo-normativity. With the help of ABC Australia moved to endo-normativity, whereas New Zealand still lags behind. By way of a generalization, one can conclude that former political status and language transplantation affect the media's role in fostering sociolinguistic identity. Choice has also been discussed in relation to English language media in Nigeria, where a shift from one exo-normative situation to another is noticeable. American English is gradually impinging on British English, while educated Nigerian English is still not recognized. Particularly in multilingual and Third World countries, the question of language choice may imply the question of translation. Content from some part of the country may be transmitted in one language that is not understood elsewhere in that country, news agencies favor English, and translation is a prerequisite for further processing and output. Simpson (1985) has looked at that issue in Nigeria.

Questions of choice are restricted to "significant" output and shade off into codification. In terms of the message hierarchy they are located at the level of clusters of program formats (scope), such as news, talks, announcing, and editorials. In Germany, for instance, radio debates had wide scope, including talks, quite apart from news, children's programs, announcing, and general presentation. In Britain, in contrast, talks were excluded.

Turning to a more frequently discussed theme in the media, codification, two situations must be distinguished. One is explicit codification, sanctioned or promoted through advisory bodies, and media-internal or official judges. The other is implicit codification through professional practices and/or the professional interpretation of media's roles. There is a domain-specific conflict between them for two reasons. One, explicit codification, while ideally more powerful and prestigious, is difficult to implement and control, in contrast to implicit codification, which is acquired and perpetuated through daily routine. A tension between norm and performance results. The BBC's inquiry (1979) was made in such a context. The BBC tried to rid itself of linguistic conservatism and close up the gap between its language and that of its audience (Leitner, 1980; Quirk, 1982). But significant sections of its audience perceived the new policies as jargon.

Again, media and countries differ and attitudes change over time. In the 1920s and 1930s the pronunciation of common words was a controversial matter in the BBC, along with the noncontroversial area of proper names. Today the focus is on good spoken style, as in other countries. In Germany, for instance, codification always emphasized style and the relationship with the recipients. The use of foreign words has been a continuous theme in Germany; in Britain and Australia Americanisms are foregrounded. An interesting contrast emerges if one compares English mother-tongue and second-language countries, since codification in the latter mainly focuses on correctness, intelligibility, and proximity to international English (Nihalani et al., 1979; Bansal and Harrison, 1983). Hussein and Zughoul (1993) have looked at the closely related question of lexical interference from English in journalistic Arabic.

Implicit codification, the result of professionalism, shows up, for instance, in noun-name phrase construction, as in examples 1 and 2:

> 1 Prime Minister Major has said . . .
> 2 England manager Graham Taylor . . .

Use of this pattern correlates with media outlets, speech community, time, audience type, and reported domains (Bell, 1991: 130 ff.; Jucker, 1992). It has reached the level of sociolinguistic marker in Britain as it is sanctioned by the BBC whose judgments are couched in terms of style, rather than of good usage:

> The dropping of the word *"The"* before titles probably began in the American magazine TIME, with the idea of creating a brisk and pacy style. It has now become a commonplace in British newspapers, and occasionally with broadcasters . . . This is not how people speak . . . We should write as we would speak. (BBC, n.d.)

De facto codification is visible also at higher message levels. Van Dijk (1988b) has suggested that topics are developed in cycles of decreasing importance. The typical macro-structure is that of the inverted pyramid, which suggests that full text consumption is not required. Simmler (1993), in contrast, argues that this model cannot be a general pattern. Soccer reports, which he studied in detail, are written for full consumption. It appears that reports may differ as a result of spatiotemporal properties of "reality." But despite disagreements one point seems uncontroversial: There is only a small number of basic text structures (Werlich, 1976).

In multi-axis messages, correlations between discourse structures, presentational norms, and broader media goals have also been revealed (cf. section 2.1 above; Burger, 1990; Scannel, 1991). Broader issues still, for instance, language modernization for Indian news media, are dealt with by Krishnamurti and Mukherjee (1984).

Representation

Representation must be seen in the light of the Whorfian hypothesis. Of two possible versions the weak one, which is commonly accepted, says that language influences cognition and interpretation but does not pre-empt alternative ways of making sense of "reality." Some event might be referred to as an "accident," a "mishap," or a "disaster" despite obvious semantic differences between these words. But the use of one expression rather than another implies a deliberate act of categorization. As language unavoidably involves such acts, none of this is controversial. What is controversial in media studies is whether media discourse adds another dimension of willful ideological bias. With regard to news media, criteria that predict to some extent what might be selected (and transformed) as news have been suggested by Galtung and Ruge (cf. Bell, 1991: 155–60). Fowler rightly argues that they "are rather to be seen as qualities of (potential) reports" (1991: 19) and adds, "they are not simply features of selection but, more importantly, features of representation; and so the distinction between 'selection' and 'transformation' ceases to be absolute."

Thus the selection and representation of some content, for instance, as "gossip" (in music shows), as "background" (in classical music, sports reporting), or as "hot news" (in news broadcasts) involve creative acts of categorization. Many studies have confirmed this (Fowler et al., 1979; GUMG, 1980; Fowler, 1991). Claims of deliberate acts of ideological distortion (GUMG, 1980) have been softened and, instead of "bias," the term *mediation* has come into use: " 'Mediation' and 'representation' will less provocatively cover the processes which lead to 'skewing' and 'judgement',"says Fowler (1991: 12). A related term is "transformation."

The manifestation of mediation in lexis, grammar, text or discourse type and mode, style, and scripts or schemata, has been addressed most extensively with news media and news reporting (Fowler et al., 1979; GUMG, 1980). It has been argued that media discourse, rather than being media-specific, reflects the dominant view of a society, the perspectives of the powerful. It relies on and creates a consensual aura that transcends program format and emanates from the approach to content. And as consensus has an integrative and a delimitative function, it aggrandizes what is inside and marginalizes what is outside (Davis and Walton, 1983). But the concept of "news" is often ill-defined or not defined at all. While GUMG (1980) and Schlesinger (1978), for instance, are clear in looking at news as a program (a program format), Fowler (1991) is extremely diffuse.

Van Dijk's study of international media discourse (1988a, b) should also be seen as providing insight into media representation. He points to cognitively grounded discourse categories (schemata, scripts, etc.) for both the categorization and organization of content. Structural-semantic notions such as evaluation, background, event (narration) have been proposed for the macro-structure of texts. In the area of style, informality and conversation are said to project images of familiarity, cooperativeness, and friendliness. On a deeper plane, they have a "reality-maintaining," i.e., a representational, function (Fowler, 1991: 57) that invites agreement and the sharing of media's consensus by recipients. Such multi-plane functions have also been revealed in multi-axis messages, such as topic structures and shifts, turn-taking, etc. in interviews (Harris, 1991).

Functional duality: Presentation and representation

It has become clear that presentation and representation address different issues of media discourse but are nonetheless related. Van Dijk's macro-structural model points to both functions. Leitner's analyses of variety choices in Britain, Australia, and Germany (1980, 1984) highlighted presentational factors, but Fowler (1991) correctly points out that the status of standard varieties confers an aura of officialdom on the discourse that carries repre-sentational overtones. I will now turn to cases where the multi-functionality of language expressions is at issue. First, there may be a shift at the encoding end from presentation to representation, and second, encoders' intentions may legitimately be read differently by recipients.

Designations for ethnic and other minorities are cases in point for the first situation. The list of names for people with "black" complexions (which already is a classification) in English includes *nigger, black man, blackfellow, coon, black, Afro-American, aborigine, aboriginals*. Debate about appropriate choices and the refutations of inappropriate terms has progressed from argu-ments in terms of mainly appropriate use and politeness (presentation) to ones in terms of the avoidance of racism (representation) (ABC, 1989).[8] To quote the ABC's recent position:

> The right of indigenous peoples to identify themselves is recognized in a num-ber of United Nations resolutions. When referring to Aborigines and Torres Strait Islanders, the terms preferred by these people should be used wherever possible. Failure to recognize this right results in language which is centred on white Anglo-Celtic values and preferences. (ABC, 1989: 25)

Designations for gender, disabled people, migrants, and ethnic communities provide ample evidence for similar developments inside the ABC, the BBC (1993), and elsewhere.

The second case is exemplified by the possibility of a clash between media's policies, practices, and the public's perception (attitudes). Reactions to the ABC's rulings on the avoidance of gender-specific language (1984) provide an example. *The Sun* headlined an article with "*ABC* plans attack on manhood!" and conti-nued: "Aunty is killing off men . . . sportsmen, gentlemen, aldermen, the whole lot" (May 7, 1984). Similar reactions appeared elsewhere but, despite the outrage and the discourse gap with the audience, the ABC adhered to its policy rulings.

Such shifts emphasize the fact that media discourse is sensitive to social changes, that it is not only a compromise but also dynamic, and that norms and practices may compete with one another. A medium may well want to go for a particular style, e.g., informality, but if it does, it is faced with beliefs and values associated with that style. To return to an example mentioned earlier. The BBC's rejection of noun-name collocations in examples 1 and 2 (p. 198) as outside natural conversation defines informality in a particular way, while American and Australian media take a different stance.

2.5 Media as a public forum and public use of media discourse

Relating the discourse of communication media to the media's functions is undoubtedly a crucial theme in sociolinguistics. But as the *public idiom* per se media discourse has a wider relevance that is well recognized by the public. The controversies that arise here take us back to the argument that media are a part of social life at large and represent a Fourth Estate (Curran and Seaton, 1991). From such a broad vision two lines of argument can be distinguished.

One is substantially sociopolitical and asks questions about how well or how poorly media discourse does the work it is expected to do: Does it adequately meet the sociopolitical demands made on it in a democratic society? What is its relation to other public discourse, such as the language of politics? Such issues tend to be discussed in broad terms, unrelated to specific discourse characteristics. They widen problems raised in connection with representation and provide the motivation for Fowler (1991), GUMG (1980), Bucher and Strassner (1991), and others to relate them to language and discourse. But presentational questions have also been addressed. The role of standards in the BBC (BBC, 1979) was couched in terms of sociopolitical demands. And empirical tests of comprehension have suggested that media discourse may fail to give equal access to all sections of the public because it is inherently difficult to understand. Such difficulties have been related to formal characteristics of media discourse, to the selection of varieties but also to the interaction of different semiotic codes. Media fail, it is concluded, in their mediating function (Burger, 1990: chapter 8).

The second theme is more narrowly linguistic and embeds media discourse into the framework of the language repertoire of society at large. If discussed under the heading of "authority" in language (J. and L. Milroy, 1985), public attitudes towards it within the broader context of correctness and norms are highlighted. As a corollary, media discourse can be seen as a useful tool in educational contexts.

The feedback function of recipients' reactions to and expert opinions on media discourse has been mentioned in section 2.3. Such reactions may initiate changes in audience design but they may have a wider role in representing content from the social domain. From this angle media constitute a public forum for debate about language. Several subthemes should be mentioned. First, some studies suggest that content on language issues indicates a speech community's sense of linguistic identity and propriety. That point was made with regard to Australia by Leitner (1984) and New Zealand by Bell (1990). Along the same lines, Reeve (1989) suggests that they can be used to reconstruct the history of Australian language attitudes. In Germany's "new Länder" (East Germany) letters to the editors and expert opinions often express great reservations against the use of *Anglicisms*, such as *insider*. Anglicisms are perceived as "West German" German, whereas "East German" German has remained "pure" despite the presence of Russian. Official French efforts to eliminate Anglicisms from public language must be understood in this light, just as the fact that usage guides to language often make extensive use of media data to illustrate bad language or style.[9]

Another subtheme has to do with the belief that media discourse may change, or inhibit desirable change in the language repertoire of some society. In many countries media language is perceived as something special, somewhat different from everyday speech. And special terms for the media language have come into use, such as *BBC English* in Britain, *network English* in the USA, or *Rundfunkaussprache* in Germany. Looking closely, two contradictory attitudes can be identified. On one hand, it is considered as something to emulate, to adopt in public discourse. Alternatively, it has been seen as something to avoid. Such criticisms have been mentioned above but, on a wider scale, media language has been charged with killing dialects and influencing language shift in multilingual societies (Andrzejewski, 1971).

And finally, some specific applied linguistic research starts from the premise that media language comes close to being "real," i.e., nonmonitored language performance. In light of the preceding sections that demonstrated that it is the object of substantial planning, this is clearly wrong. But the sheer quantity of media discourse output, its significance as a public idiom, still makes it a good tool in language teaching. Applications have been seen in both native and foreign language teaching. For instance, Baumgardner (1987) argues that Pakistani English should be used not only as a way of teaching English but of teaching it in its localized Pakistani format. In localized forms, English no longer carries the ideological overtones of the West. In contrast, many courses from the *BBC English* company incorporate "live," unmonitored media language, with the aim of familiarizing learners with varieties of English. Such efforts were initially based on a native Anglo-American model but increasingly accept the argument that English must be taught as an international language with widely differing manifestations (Leitner, 1989). The claim that it would necessarily carry a Western ideology is not accepted. Within that framework one must mention also Hosali and Tongue's dictionary for Indian users of English (1989), largely based on print media. Similarly, the (East) German dictionary of pronunciation, based on newsreaders' use of German, was used as a teaching tool for native and foreign language teaching.

3 Conclusions and New Challenges

In this paper I have provided a framework for media and messages in general. Media have been defined as communication domains, mass communication as essentially linking domains, the "outside" as reported domains, and recipients as embedded in their own social networks as individuals and members of groups. Media discourse was considered a public idiom located at the center of conflicting forces whose resolution leads to a temporary, dynamic, and variable compromise, and that is true with underlying norms, practices, and perceptions. But media discourse also represents one of the large communicative concerns of society.

The premises allowed an emphasis on methodological background and a survey of past research. There were some omissions, the most serious being the impact of wider international media context and the consideration of new user needs. Let me briefly turn to these.

There is a conflict between global and local media and production practices that calls for a redefinition of the notion of domain. Domains exist in particular societies, implying a language community, its norms, practices, and language ecology. But today's media increasingly transcend such boundaries. CNN, the BBC's World Service, the Australian ABC's Asian TV, *Sports Channel*, *Sky Channel*, the *Voice of America*, *The European* (newspaper), or *The Herald Tribune* are international media, consumed outside the country of origin. Like currency markets, media operate globally, ownership may be international, and large parts of media discourse develop in a global context. While talk of media imperialism and an imperialistic public domain may not be inappropriate, media will narrow down the inevitably growing gap in discourse expectations of national and international audiences.

The second point, new media uses, is related to the observation made above that the impact of small and/or socially disadvantaged languages is on the increase in media. Traditional text linguistics models the consumption of some *specific* output, a program, an article, and hence its discourse. Consumption is seen as occurring after, or at best simultaneously, with the transmission of the message. All media are trying to move away from this prototypical situation and to increase "audience design" features.

Print media, increasingly available electronically, anticipate a demand for *user-defined* stretches of text, not for single media texts. As that demand is growing with business companies, political parties, or diplomatic services, software is being developed in artificial intelligence and corpus linguistics that allows the scanning of user-defined, unlimited text (a whole page, a whole issue, a whole week's or year's output). As for electronic media, they are increasing output such as shows or newscasts in front of audiences that permit participation; they overcome the limits of the single locus of reporting, and even aim for interactive TV. As these developments become more relevant, media discourse as a public idiom will consider recipient-orientation in a new light. Novel connections between en- and decoders may lead not only to greater audience design but also to greater media standardization.

NOTES

1 See Bell (1991) and Burger (1990) for general introductions.

2 Some media are mainly carriers of advertisements, others have party

political functions or develop a corporate image. But, as all contain journalistic content as well, that definition can still be applied.

3 No term covers the entire spectrum of the media-external world. For news, etc. reality is used (Schlesinger, 1978; Fowler, 1991; Bell, 1991). I will suggest the term "reported domain" below.

4 As for the problem of differentiating discourse from the content it transports, see sections 2.4 and 1.3.

5 Cf. the bibliographies published by ICAME, Computer Centre of the Humanities, University of Bergen, Norway.

6 They refer to the well-known empirical problem of finding an intersubjectively verifiable classification. Van Dijk's application of his model to specific data, for instance, presents problems in this respect.

7 See section 2.5 for an expansion of this explanation.

8 The ABC accepted in 1973 that *Aboriginal* is a count noun and said *Aborigine* "remains . . . acceptable English" although it is "etymologically unsound" (95th meeting, 1973). Later, an Aboriginal member of the Senate said he "strongly favoured the use of the word *ABORIGINE* as a noun" (124th meeting, 1978). In 1989 the ABC reinterpreted the debate in terms of bias (representation).

9 Cf. also the studies on translation needs in Nigeria and lexical interference in Arabic by Simpson (1985) and Hussein and Zughoul (1993) respectively. Mention should also be made again of Krishnamurti and Mukherjee's collection of papers on language modernization (1984), and Shastri's study of code-mixing in India (n.d.).

12 Diglossia as a Sociolinguistic Situation

HAROLD F. SCHIFFMAN

1 Introduction

The sociolinguistic condition known as diglossia has attracted wide attention since the publication of Ferguson's seminal article (1959).[1] Despite its occurrence in many non-Western contexts, it is not simply a phenomenon of exotic Third-World cultures, but characterizes a number of languages found in various parts of the world, including Western Europe.[2]

1.1 Power and Prestige

Diglossic languages (and diglossic language situations) are usually described as consisting of two (or more) varieties that coexist in a speech community; the domains of linguistic behavior are parceled out in a kind of complementary distribution. These domains are usually ranked in a kind of hierarchy, from highly valued (H) to less valued (L); when the two varieties are recognized (or tacitly accepted) as genetically related, the H domains are usually the reserve of the more conservative form of the language, which is usually the literary dialect if there is a written form. "Formal" domains such as public speaking, religious texts and practice, education, and other prestigious kinds of usage are dominated by the H norm; the L norm is used for informal conversation, jokes, the street and the market, the telephone, and any other domains (e.g., letter writing, cinema, television) not reserved for the H norm. For diglossic situations involving two different (genetically unrelated) linguistic codes (sometimes referred to as "extended" diglossia) the one dominating the H domains has the greater international prestige or is the language of the local power elite or the dominant religious community and/or its priesthood. In

such cases the H-variety language is clearly the language of the more powerful section of the society, however power is defined.

Thus in French Canada, English occupies the H-variety niche because it has
the greatest prestige in North America (and perhaps internationally as well);
its population even within Canada is numerically greater than the community
of French speakers, and its speech community is economically dominant, both
in English Canada and in French Canada. Conversely, in France, French is the
H-variety in diglossic situations involving other languages or dialects, such as
Breton or Alsatian, where these varieties are only used as L-variety spoken
vehicles in the home, on the street, in the construction trades, etc.

It remains to be seen whether the same kind of imbalance of power exhibited
in nongenetic diglossia can be said to exist with regard to classical or genetic
diglossia. In many diglossic situations, only a minority or elite control the H
domain successfully, so those who know only L are at a disadvantage.

1.2 Ferguson's original formulation

Ferguson originally summarized diglossia (1959: 435) as follows:

> DIGLOSSIA is a relatively stable language situation in which, in addition to the
> primary dialects of the language (which may include a standard or regional stand-
> ards), there is a very divergent, highly codified (often grammatically more complex)
> superposed variety, the vehicle of a large and respected body of written literature,
> either of an earlier period or in another speech community, which is learned largely
> by formal education and is used for most written and formal spoken purposes but is
> not used by any section of the community for ordinary conversation.

The notion that diglossia could also be used to characterize other multilingual
situations where the H and L varieties were not genetically related, such as
Sanskrit (as H) and Kannada (as L) in India, was developed by Fishman (1967)
and research on diglossias since has focused to a great extent, though not
entirely, on characterizing various kinds of *extended* diglossias.

Post-1959 research on diglossia has concentrated on a number of variables
and important questions: function, prestige, literary heritage, acquisition,
standardization, stability, grammar, lexicon, phonology, the difference between diglossia and standard with dialects, the extent of distribution in space,
time, and in various language families, and finally what engenders diglossia
and what conditions favor its development.

1 Function: The functional differentiation of discrepant varieties in a
  diglossia is fundamental, thus distinguishing it from bilingualism. H
  and L are used for different purposes, and native speakers of the
  community would find it odd (even ludicrous, outrageous) if anyone
  used H in an L domain, or L in an H domain.

2 Prestige: In most diglossias examined, H was more highly valued (had greater prestige) than was L. The H variety is that of "great" literature, canonical religious texts, ancient poetry, of public speaking, pomp and circumstance. The L variety is felt to be less worthy, corrupt, "broken," vulgar, undignified, etc.

3 Literary heritage: In most diglossic languages, the literature is all in H variety; no written uses of L exist, except for "dialect" poetry, advertising, or "low" restricted genres.[3] In most diglossic languages, the H variety is thought to be *the* language; the existence of L variety is sometimes denied or it is claimed to be spoken only by lesser mortals (servants, women, children). In some traditions (e.g., Shakespeare's plays), L variety would be used to show certain characters as rustic, comical, uneducated, etc.

4 Acquisition: L variety is the variety learned first; it is the mother tongue, the language of the home. H variety is zacquired through schooling. Where linguists would therefore insist that the L variety is primary, native scholars see only the H variety as *the* language.

5 Standardization: H is strictly standardized; grammars, dictionaries, canonical texts, etc. exist for it, written by native grammarians. L is rarely standardized in the traditional sense, or if grammars exist, they are written by outsiders.

6 Stability: Diglossias are generally stable, persisting for centuries or even millennia. Occasionally L varieties gain domains and displace the H variety, but H only displaces L if H is the mother tongue of an elite, usually in a neighboring polity.

7 Grammar: The grammars of H are more complex than the grammars of the L variety. They have more complex tense systems, gender systems, agreement, syntax than the L variety.

8 Lexicon: Lexicon is often somewhat shared, but generally there is differentiation; H has vocabulary that L lacks, and vice versa.

9 Phonology: Two kinds of systems are discerned. One is where H and L share the same phonological elements, but H may have more complicated morphophonemics. Or H is a special subset of the L-variety inventory. (But speakers often fail to keep the two systems separate.) A second type is one where H has contrasts that L lacks, systematically substituting some other phoneme for the missing contrast; but L may "borrow" elements as *tatsamas*,[4] using the H-variety contrast in that particular item.

10 Difference between diglossia and standard with dialects. In diglossia, *no one* speaks the H variety as a mother tongue, only the L variety. In the standard with dialects situation, some speakers speak H as a mother tongue, while others speak L varieties as a mother tongue and acquire H as a second system.

11 Distribution of diglossia in language families, space, and time. Diglossia is not limited to any geographical area or language family,

and diglossias have existed for centuries or millennia (Arabic, South Asia). Most diglossias involve literacy, but oral diglossias are conceivable.[5]

12 What engenders diglossia and under what conditions?

(a) The existence of an ancient or prestigious literature, composed in the H variety, which the linguistic culture wishes to preserve as such.

(b) Literacy is usually a condition, but is usually restricted to a small elite. When conditions require universal literacy in H, pedagogical problems ensure.

(c) Diglossias do not spring up overnight; they take time to develop

These three factors, perhaps linked with religion, make diglossia extremely stable in Arabic and other linguistic cultures such as those of South Asia.

1.3 Extended diglossia (Fishman, 1967)

Given the extensive research on diglossia and many recent attempts to both refine and extend it, a review of some of these studies, especially those pertaining to the socioeconomic conditions in which diglossic languages are usually embedded, seems to be warranted. It should be noted, however, that diglossia is a *gradient, variable* phenomenon, which cannot easily be boxed into an either–or binary system of categorization. And as Ferguson himself recently pointed out (1991, in Hudson, 1991a), his original formulation of diglossia was not meant to encompass *all* instances of multilingualism or functional differentiation of languages. Thus many attempts to "refine" or "extend" diglossia, or to discern whether such and such is or is not a case of diglossia, may be barking up the wrong tree.

Fishman (1967) introduced the notion that diglossia could be extended to situations found in many societies where forms of two *genetically unrelated* (or at least historically distant) languages[6] occupy the H and L niches, such that one of the languages (e.g., Latin in medieval Europe) is used for religion, education, literacy, and other such prestigious domains, while another language (in the case of medieval Europe, the vernacular languages of that era) is rarely used for such purposes, being employed only for more informal, primarily spoken domains.

1.4 Diglossia and language shift

Diglossia has often been noted as a factor in language shift, especially in speech communities where a minority language is in a diglossic relationship with a majority language. Fishman (1967: 36) had previously noted that

[B]ilingualism without diglossia tends to be transitional both in terms of the linguistic repertoires of speech communities as well as in terms of the speech varieties involved per se. Without separate though complementary norms and values to establish and maintain functional separatism of the speech varieties, that language or variety which is fortunate enough to be associated with the predominant drift of social forces tends to displace the other(s).

1.5 Classical and extended diglossia

Various scholars have proposed terminologies for a taxonomy of diglossias. For what here is referred to as "classical" (Ferguson, 1959) and "extended" (Fishman, 1967) diglossia, Kloss has proposed the terms "in-diglossia" (for the kind where the two varieties are closely related) and "out-diglossia" (for situations where the two languages are unrelated or at best distantly related) (Kloss, 1966: 138). A classicist might prefer something like "endo-diglossia" and "exo-diglossia," i.e., prefixes that fit better with the original Greek roots of the terms. But it is clear to some researchers that there are important differences in the dynamics of societies characterized by these (at least) two basic kinds of diglossia. Fishman has also proposed a useful distinction between "consensually different languages" and "consensual dialects," since there is an unresolved debate as to whether Caribbean English (for example, but any Creole language/dialect could be used) is in fact genetically descended from English, i.e., is consensually a dialect of English, or is consensually (agreed to be classified as) a separate language. This would also be useful in situations found in South Asia, where some L varieties are associated with H varieties that are not in fact their closest genetic ancestor; for example, eastern varieties of Hindi (Bihari dialects, etc.) that have long been noted to have descended from eastern *apabhramsas* but are treated by their speakers as being dialects of standard Hindi; one could make the case that Sri Lankan Tamil may also be more closely related to Malayalam than it is to Tamil, but not in the minds of its speakers. And it seems to be the case that Swiss German was once consensually agreed to be in a diglossic hierarchy with Standard German, but that this consensus is now breaking down.

Scotton (1986) proposes the terms "narrow" for Ferguson's 1959 version of diglossia, and "broad" (or "diglossia extended") to refer to Fishman's expansion of the discussion. According to Scotton, few truly diglossic (in the 1959 sense) communities actually exist, because to meet the criteria, two conditions must hold: "(1) Everyone . . . speaks the Low variety as a mother tongue" and "(2) The High variety is never used . . . in informal conversations." Unambiguous examples of these are Tamil, *Letzebuergesch*, and Swiss German. Britto (1986) proposes the terms "Use-oriented" (or diatypical) and "User-oriented" (or dialectal) diglossia to refer roughly to the same dichotomy others have also attempted to define.[7]

Fishman's 1980 taxonomy of "kinds of linguistic relationships between H's and L's" is worth stating in full:

(a) *H as classical, L as vernacular, the two being genetically related,* e.g. classical and vernacular Arabic, classical or classicized Greek (Katarevusa) and demotiki, Latin and French among francophone scholars and clergy in earlier centuries, classical and vernacular Tamil, classical and vernacular Sinhalese, Sanskrit and Hindi, classical Mandarin and modern Pekinese, etc.[8]

(b) *H as classical, L as vernacular, the two **not** being genetically related,* e.g. Loshn koydesh (textual Hebrew / Aramaic) and Yiddish (Fishman, 1976) (or any one of the several dozen other non-semitic Jewish L's, as long as the latter operate in vernacular functions rather than in traditional literacy-related ones (Weinreich, 1980).

(c) *H as written/formal-spoken and L as vernacular, the two being genetically unrelated to each other;* e.g. Spanish and Guarani in Paraguay (Rubin, 1972), English (or French) and various vernaculars in post-colonial areas throughout the world . . .

(d) *H as written/formal-spoken and L as vernacular, the two being genetically related to each other.* Here only significantly discrepant written/formal-spoken and informal-spoken varieties will be admitted, such that without schooling the written/formal-spoken cannot even be understood (otherwise every dialect-standard situation in the world would qualify within this rubric), e.g. High German and Swiss German, standard spoken Pekinese [Putonghua] and Cantonese, Standard English and Caribbean Creole. (Fishman, 1980: 4)[9]

These differences range beyond the obvious ones of genetic vs nongenetic relationship, and in fact have to do primarily with power relationships in the societies characterized by them. Various scholars have proposed that extended diglossia is usually unstable, unless certain conditions having to do with power are not met. Classical diglossia, usually thought to be more stable than extended diglossia, can also be shown to be unstable under certain conditions. It may also be the case that the type of diglossia in question may also itself change, i.e., a narrow kind of diglossia may be replaced by a broad form without much overt awareness on the part of the speech community.

1.6 Diglossia as a continuum

Classical Fergusonian genetic endo-diglossia (Fishman's (a) and (d) types) characterizes a number of linguistic situations that have already received much attention in the literature. Fishman distinguishes usefully between classical and related and written/formal-spoken; he places Tamil in the former situation, whereas one could just as easily put it in the latter; one might say that Tamil actually has three norms (a classical, i.e., *Sangam* or Pandit style, modern literary/formal-spoken, and educated colloquial, not to mention local dialects). Between these styles there are shadings from one style into another, i.e., it is possible to write modern literary Tamil with an archaic lexicon but with nonarchaic grammar; it is also possible to swing in the other direction and make modern LT more spoken, or to make educated colloquial more literary in flavor, or more nonstandardly colloquial. In any event, though linguistic cultures think of diglossia as either–or, it is often a gradient cline, with one variant shading into another.

1.7 Diglossia and the linguistic culture that maintains it

Speech communities have belief systems about their language – origin myths, beliefs about "good" and "bad" language, taboos, shibboleths, and so on. These beliefs are part of the social conditions that affect the maintenance and transmission of that language. Thus the fact that a language is diglossic is actually a feature of the linguistic culture[10] of the area where that language is used, rather than of the language per se. To speak of a particular language as diglossic or not is at best imprecise, since a language (e.g., English) as spoken in one part of the world may exhibit little or no diglossia, while the same language (again using English as an example) as used in a Caribbean creole community would have to be considered diglossic. *Speakers* of a particular language can not be characterized as diglossic; only their behavior, or the behavior of the speech community can be considered diglossic. Thus beliefs and attitudes about the language condition the maintenance of diglossia as a fact of linguistic culture. In the case of the Tamils, for example, it is the set of beliefs about the antiquity and purity of Tamil that unites all members of the linguistic culture in its resistance to any change in the corpus or status of Tamil, by which of course is meant H-variety Tamil. (Schiffman, 1974: 127).

Diglossia and literacy

In a society where literacy is not universal, not all speakers control the use of the school-imparted H variety. This does not mean that illiterates have the option of using the L variety in H-variety domains; rather, the expectation is that they will remain silent[11] rather than exhibit inappropriate linguistic norms. Their linguistic behavior is in fact restricted to the L domains, and use of H domains is de facto the monopoly of the educated few.

Shifting domains and diglossia

While diglossia as a fact of linguistic culture may be stable, the distribution of *domains* reserved for one variety or other can vary; the dominance of a particular domain by a particular variety can shift, with one variety encroaching on domains previously restricted to another. In Tamil, for example, the political speech was once restricted to the domain of the H variety, but nowadays political speeches only begin and end in H; in between, L variety predominates (probably as a mark of solidarity). In journalism, especially in political cartoons, etc. one also sees a shift from H to L in many linguistic cultures. In Alemannic Switzerland and some other linguistic cultures, the development of television has opened up a domain that has become almost exclusively that of the L variety, especially in "live" interviews, talk shows, game shows, sports reporting, etc. where use of H would seem stilted and unnatural.[12, 13]

On the other hand, social forces within a particular linguistic culture can move to eliminate diglossia, as was the case when medieval Latin was displaced during the Renaissance by various European vernacular languages; diglossia is giving way in present-day Greece, where it had held sway until a government decree ordained the shift from H (*katharevousa*) to L (*demotiki*) in many domains.[14] Diglossia was more extreme in premodern Bengali and Telugu than it is today, as a result of movements led by prestigious writers (Tagore for Bengali) to democratize access to literacy and education, and modernize their languages. Latin held on in German linguistic culture until the early eighteenth century in a number of restricted domains (scholarly writing, university lectures). When and if diglossia is more or less eliminated, or made less extreme, by the choice of a more modern colloquial norm,[15] by rights we would have to speak of a kind of language shift. To ignore shift when it takes place within a diglossic continuum would be to perpetuate the notion that diglossia is in effect irrelevant.

Diglossia and linguistic areas

If diglossia is an aspect of linguistic culture, it may result from and be maintained by the existence of a linguistic area (Emeneau, 1956) in which diglossia is an areal feature as well as a feature of a particular linguistic culture within the area. In South Asia, and in those Southeast Asian linguistic cultures that use Indic writing systems, diglossia seems to be a well nigh inherent characteristic of the linguistic cultures,[16] since there is a tendency to develop diglossia even in languages that originally may not have exhibited a great degree of it. When Hindustani was chosen as the national language of independent India, supposedly because of its wide use as a lingua franca in the area, steps were immediately taken to develop an H variety, highly Sanskritized in vocabulary, since the vernaculars of Hindi then in existence seemed to be too "Low" for many citizens of the country. Of course diglossicization as a value may vary from subculture to subculture in the region, but it cannot be denied that the overall view in South Asia and peninsular Southeast Asia is pro-diglossic.

Partial vs total diglossia

Researchers have noted the situation where some speakers control H but others have L as a mother tongue, and learn H as a second system. Thus in some linguistic cultures, *all* speakers exhibit diglossic behavior (i.e., use both H and L varieties in complementary distribution), while in others, only some members of the society do.[17] This could be illustrated either by a society where everyone controls L, but only some actively control H, or the opposite case where everyone speaks and writes H, but some also control an L variety. We can refer to this dichotomy as *total* diglossia vs *partial* diglossia. This factor is distinct from the issue of whether diglossia is homogeneous or heterogeneous in the area (see below).

Homogeneous and heterogeneous diglossia

Even if diglossia is total and universal, we must determine whether the L norm is in fact one variety or more than one, i.e., is it *homogeneous* or *heterogeneous*. Is there an L variety that can be used for communication throughout the linguistic culture and with all segments of the speech community, such that no one is forced to resort to the H variety (written formal/spoken) or some other language, as a lingua franca?[18] In Switzerland, no one L variety is recognized as standard; speakers must learn to accommodate their variety to those of others, since the use of H *Schriftdeutsch* is not considered appropriate between Swiss citizens (Schiffman, 1991).

1.8 Diglossia and power and solidarity

Brown and Gilman (1960) introduced the notion that the use of certain pronouns (epitomized as T and V) can be an expression of power and/or solidarity. Rubin (1972) extended the analogy of T and V pronouns to the use of L and H varieties in Paraguay, a supposedly "bilingual" linguistic culture in which the two languages, Spanish and Guaraní, are in an extended diglossic relationship. In many of the linguistic cultures discussed here, the use (or misuse) of L and H varieties also can raise some of these same issues. Certainly the use of L where H is expected (or vice versa) constitutes a violation of communicative competence rules. If an outsider speaks *Hochdeutsch* in Alemannic Switzerland, addresses a hotel clerk in Hindi in Madras, or begins a conversation with a well-dressed stranger in Asunción in Guaraní, these are violations of social norms that stem from an inadequate understanding of the linguistic culture. Brown and Gilman (1960) established the notion that use of T pronouns (the familiar, nonrespect form) can have several social meanings. Reciprocal use of T by equals expresses solidarity, but between nonequals the giver of T is putting him- or herself in a position of power, and the receiver is expected to respond with V. Similarly, reciprocal V usage implies mutual respect and social distance; any nonreciprocal use of these pronouns is an expression of a differential of power.

   As Rubin demonstrated, in diglossic situations the use of H or L varieties in a given social exchange (as distinguished from societal patterned usage as a whole) may be seen as the same kind of T/V situation. The use of L may be an expression of solidarity and may not be offered to speakers whose social position is superior or distant. Similarly H may be the only variety appropriate in a given situation because the use of L would imply a solidarity that is reserved only for members of a particular in-group. The use of Black English by white speakers of American English in conversations with African-Americans would probably be considered insulting unless individual allowances had already been negotiated. The use of L-variety Tamil by non-Indians is considered inappropriate by many educated Tamilians, who may respond in H-variety Tamil or in English unless the use of L variety has already been negotiated (with explanations about the goals of the speaker and disclaimers about intended slurs and put-downs). The use of H-variety German in Alemannic Switzerland conversely may be seen as a power-trip designed to put the Swiss speaker at a disadvantage. The fact that the *Hochdeutsch* speaker may have no alternative L to use may be irrelevant; it certainly explains the desire to switch to "neutral" English or French. In Luxembourg, however, L variety and its use are expressions of *Letzebuergesch* nationality and ethnic solidarity, so while Luxembourg nationals expect L from all Luxembourgers, they switch readily to French or *Hochdeutsch* or English with foreigners, with no expectation that they will or should be able to speak L.

NOTES

1 The phenomenon was mentioned earlier, as *diglossie*, in the work of Marcais (1932–3).
2 There is neither time nor space here to review the literature; the reader is referred to Ferguson's pioneering article (Ferguson, 1959), Fishman's extension of diglossia to non-genetic situations (Fishman, 1967), and some of the more recent literature (and controversy) on the problems of typologizing diglossia (such as Britto, 1986). Recent state-of-the-art studies are Hudson (1991a) and the bibliographies in Hudson, 1992, and Fernandez, 1993.
3 In Tamil, the conversational portions of novels and short stories are in L variety, but not the narrative or descriptive portions.
4 Sanskrit for words borrowed "as is," without phonological adaptation in the host language.
5 In South Asia, there is evidence that a highly structured oral system for the transmission of sacred texts was, and

to some extent still is, in place. The reliance on orality was motivated in part by the power of spoken words to invoke the intervention of the gods. In the Indic tradition, if the text has been learned in the proper way and by the proper person (only male members of the priestly caste may receive the long training involved in the learning by rote of the texts) then the power of the word, when spoken, is irrevocable – the gods *must* act and will act. Writing the word on paper (stone, copper, whatever) is not a substitute for pronouncing it. The utterance of an invocation is thus automatically what modern speech-act theorists would call a *performative* speech act. In the saying of the word something is also *done*, and it cannot be undone. The mode of transmission, orality, involved memorization beginning at a young age, and the willingness to devote great amounts of the society's labor and resources to achieve the goal of maintenance and transmission of this textual tradition. Having set this in motion, it also became a cultural value to preserve the infrastructure needed to propel the system – a system of gurus, pandits, disciples, and in some cases monasticism; and of course the caste system, with a special niche and privileges for the hereditary priesthood.

Though diglossia in most Indian languages now involves literacy, there are still preliterate (or only orally literate) groups like the Todas of the Nilgiri Hills, for whom we can discern three distinct varieties of speech: spoken Toda, sung Toda (not automatically comprehensible to someone knowing spoken Toda), and trance-language Toda (probably a pidginized kind of Malayalam, but as yet unresearched) which can only be spoken by people in a trance, but can be understood by initiates who are in an unaltered state of consciousness. The central position of Toda songs in Toda culture has been documented thoroughly by Emeneau (1964, 1974); the body of songs is their only form of literature, and can be seen to be in a kind of diglossic relationship to spoken Toda.

6   Fishman later elaborated on his 1967 departure from the original presentation of Ferguson, who limited diglossia to "speech communities [where] two or more varieties of the same language are used by speakers under different conditions" with "no attempt . . . made . . . to examine the analogous situation where two distinct [related or unrelated] languages are used side by side throughout a speech community, each with a clearly defined role" (Ferguson, 1959: 325). For Fishman's 1980 taxonomy, see below. He notes at least four

different kinds of diglossia, but indicates that there are of course "various more complex cases within each of the . . . major clusters" including cases with more than one H variety, or more than one L variety (Fishman, 1980: 4).

7   Britto also provides a useful annotated glossary of linguistic terms (1986: 295–333), as well as a review of some of the controversy, if that is not too strong a word for it, surrounding Fishman's extension of Ferguson (1959).

8   Modern sinological linguistic usage for these terms are Classical Chinese and Putonghua or Beijing dialect of standard Chinese.

9   To distinguish the different kinds of genetic relationships in (a) and (d), let us use the analogy of *consanguineal descent* for (a), that is, L is *descended from* H, is a *daughter* of H, whereas in (d), the two are descended from a common ancestor, but laterally, as distant *cousins*.

10   By this is meant the set of behaviors, beliefs, myths, attitudes, and historical circumstances associated with a particular language.

11   Especially if it is a case of Fishman's type (d), where there is a written/formal-spoken norm.

12   Even in America one sees a style shift in these same genres of broadcasting, for example, when an anchorperson finishes reading a prepared news story and turns to someone in the field for an on-the-spot report, or at least a more relaxed discussion of something: "We *gonna* go now to Tom Brokaw, who's on the floor of the Convention."

13   But this does not mean that diglossia in Alemannic Switzerland is on its way out; many Swiss, while welcoming the expansion of L-variety domains, see a need to

retain domains for *Hochdeutsch* for a number of reasons. In Singapore, Chinese dialects have lost many domains to Mandarin, but have gained a new one – the religious domain. As many dialect speakers have converted to Christianity, religious services in Hokkien, Hakka, Teochew, and Cantonese now serve as the only important public domain for Chinese dialect use.

14 This shift was not a slow and "natural" one but was ordered by the government in response to pressures from "democratic" sectors of the society; the church continues to resist, which will probably result in some residual diglossia as long as the church has any influence.

15 Some scholars would claim that *all* languages are diglossic to some extent, so that diglossia would in effect never be eliminated; perhaps at best we can speak of the *perception* (or to use Fishman's term, the *consensus*) that diglossia does not exist.

16 This could also be said for any culture to which Buddhism was exported.

17 Another way to define this might be to use the term language *reach*, a term Pool (1991) uses in discussing the question of the proportion of a population sharing languages, that is, the *reach* of a language would be the degree of sharedness. One might also refer to the differences between partial and total diglossia as differences in *reach*.

18 In the complex Tamil linguistic culture already alluded to, there is an educated colloquial style that has become widely disseminated by the medium of the film, and this style is understood and probably actively controlled by all Tamils resident in Tamil Nadu, as well as by Malaysian and Singaporean Tamils, and Indian Tamils in Sri Lanka; it is passively understood by Sri Lanka Tamils and other Tamils domiciled in other parts of India, but not actively controlled by these latter. Sri Lankan Tamils must thus resort to written/formal-spoken to communicate with mainland Tamils, or must switch to English.

13 Code-switching

CAROL MYERS-SCOTTON

1 Introduction

In many of the world's bilingual communities, fluent bilinguals sometimes engage in code-switching by producing discourses which, in the same conversational turn or in consecutive turns, include morphemes from two or more of the varieties in their linguistic repertoire.[1] Thanks to a plethora of publications and conference presentations on code-switching since the late 1970s, an overview of CS in the middle 1990s can offer a rich characterization of CS itself, as well as comparing it more precisely with other language contact phenomena involving two or more languages.

Such an overview is necessary because, outside the community of CS researchers itself, some still assume that the main reason for CS is lack of sufficient proficiency to go on in the opening language, or that the selection of words in CS from one language rather than another is more or less random. It will become clear below that almost all researchers who study structural constraints on CS would deny that choice of language for all words is free, even if they disagree as to how choice is constrained.

It will also become apparent that the grammatical structure of CS and other language contact phenomena, such as first language attrition, follow the same principles. Another point to be discussed is the relationship of CS to borrowing. How borrowing and CS are similar or different as processes is discussed in section 4.

2 Goals

The first goal for this overview is to provide a more plausible characterization of CS, concerning both how it is grammatically structured and its nature as a sociolinguistic and psycholinguistic phenomenon. This will involve situating

CS within the set of linguistic varieties which show either morphemes from two or more languages or effects of one language on another. The second goal is to survey CS research today. Research trends which are apparent in current literature are introduced below; in subsequent sections they are discussed further. Only CS between languages is considered here; however, switching between dialects, and even more so, between styles or registers is also frequent (Bell, 1984; Coupland, 1984; Scotton, 1988c).

Early CS studies considered the social functions of switching (e.g., Blom and Gumperz, 1972; Scotton and Ury, 1977). The research question addressed, "why is it that speakers engage in CS?" largely received the answer that CS is a strategy to influence interpersonal relations. Throughout the 1980s and into the 1990s, CS researchers continued to find reasons to refine this answer. For example, first Gumperz (1982) and then Auer (1984) began to speak of CS as a "contextualization cue," one of a number of discourse devices (both verbal and nonverbal) which are used in signalling and interpreting speaker intentions. Most researchers studied the social functions of CS on a micro-level, but argued that interpersonal usage patterns in CS reflect group values and norms associated with the varieties in a community's repertoire (cf. Heller, 1988a; McConvell, 1988; Heller, 1988b; Bhatia and Ritchie, 1989; Jacobson, 1990; Eastman, 1992). For example, in various publications Myers-Scotton developed the theme of CS as a tool for the speaker and an index for the addressee of the negotiation of interpersonal relationships, with participants cast within a "rational actor" framework, weighing costs and rewards of choices made against a backdrop of awareness for all interaction types of "unmarked vs marked" choices (e.g., 1993b, 1995a). Earlier (Myers-)Scotton (1976) introduced the notion of CS as a strategy of neutrality in interpersonal interactions, a notion developed by Heller (1988b, 1992a) in reference to intergroup relations. Heller and others are not so concerned with CS as emblematic in interpersonal relations as they are with CS as one of the linguistic choices reflecting the dynamics of competition between ethnic groups in a larger political context (e.g., Woolard, 1991; Gal, 1979, 1992a).

Yet only a few researchers have provided macro-level studies associating the use of CS with the group identities of the speakers involved. One of the reasons for this may be perceived difficulties in quantifying the use of CS in any meaningful way, plus a distrust of self-reports on CS use. A more important reason for avoiding macro-level studies may be that those CS researchers interested in social motivations for CS on an interpersonal level do not see the quantified study of the social identity features of "who uses what linguistic varieties where and when and to whom" as explaining the motives for employing CS interpersonally. True, whether a person has the ability to participate in a conversation involving CS depends on that person's linguistic repertoire, and repertoire may correlate positively with certain demographic features (e.g., without education to a certain level, it is unlikely a person will be able to speak the linguistic variety associated with political and socioeconomic power in the community). But the study of factors associated with the linguistic repertoires of different individuals in a community is not the same thing as the study of the personal motivations for CS.

One macro-level aspect of CS, the association of degrees of CS usage with demographic variables, has been studied by Poplack and her associates (Poplack, Sankoff, and Miller, 1988; Poplack, 1988a, b). Specifically they considered which speakers in French-Canadian communities with different sociopolitical profiles are the most frequent users of either borrowed English lexemes or CS involving English. In addition to such factors as social class, they considered proficiency and community attitudes. They concluded that "the norms of the community override individual abilities" as the best predictor of an individual's use of CS (Poplack et al., 1988: 97–8). That is, the major insight this study offers is that what one's community peers do, not so much demographic variables or even one's own linguistic proficiency, is paramount.

The major interest among CS researchers shifted in the 1980s to characterizing the morphosyntactic constraints on intrasentential switching. This new focus attracted many entries to the field in the 1980s (e.g., Pfaff, 1979; Poplack, 1980, 1981; Sridhar and Sridhar, 1980; Bentahila and Davies, 1983; Joshi, 1985; Gardner-Chloros, 1987; Nishimura, 1989). These researchers focused on intrasentential CS and their research question became, "where in a sentence can a speaker change languages?" In the 1990s, the publication record already in place implies that structural constraints will be the major focus of CS research. Little research on the phonology of CS has been reported, but a new study supports the notion of surface level changeover from one language to another. Based on experimental evidence, Grosjean and Miller conclude, "When bilingual speakers insert a word or phrase from the guest language into the base language, the switch usually involves a total change, not only at the lexical but also at the phonetic level" (1994: 205).

Morphosyntactically based CS research has at least two major branches. Some consider CS patterns as an "empirical window" on the nature of lexical entries and/or of language production as well as competence (e.g., Azuma, 1993; de Bot and Schreuder, 1993; Myers-Scotton, 1993a, 1994, 1995a; Myers-Scotton and Jake, 1995). Others use CS as a test for the efficacy of various claims in current syntactic theories (e.g., Woolford, 1983; Ewing, 1984; DiSciullo, Muysken, and Singh, 1986; Stenson, 1990; Muysken, 1991; Halmari, 1993; Belazi, Rubin, and Toribio, 1994; Jake, 1994; Santorini and Mahootian, 1995).

At the same time, the social and discourse motivations for CS continue to attract many researchers in the 1990s. What is new is that some of them relate differences in the structural characteristics of CS to social or psycholinguistic characteristics of different groups in the community. This is especially evident in work which stresses CS as a reflection of macro-level phenomena, such as the dynamics of intergroup relations in the community (e.g., Treffers-Daller, 1992, on CS patterns as reflecting interethnic tensions in Brussels; Wei, 1994, on CS patterns in different generations of Cantonese-speaking Chinese immigrants in Tyneside in Britain) or the interaction between bilingual proficiency and attitudes toward group affiliations in the switching group (Bentahila and Davies, 1992, on Arabic/French bilinguals in Morocco; Backus, 1994, on Turkish/Dutch CS among Turkish immigrants in Tilburg, the Netherlands).

Others consider specific types of CS structures as organizing devices in discourse or study CS from the standpoint of its role in organizing discourse sequences (e.g., McConvell, 1988; Wei, 1994). For example, Auer (1995) argues that, in arriving at the intended social messages, an adequate analysis of CS pays prime attention to the conversational turn. He stresses "the criterion of juxtaposition," or that "the meaning of code-alternation depends in essential ways on its *sequential environment.*"

Finally, another new research direction is to view CS within the larger context of other types of bilingual speech production, and some second-language acquisition researchers are considering models of constraints on CS in proposing models to explain features of second-language production (Poulisse and Bongaerts, 1994).

3 The Structural Description of Code-switching

There still is no agreement among CS researchers themselves as to what constitutes CS. For example, Pandharipande (1992) labels as convergence between Hindi and Marathi what many would call CS. In contrast, de Bot and Schreuder (1993) discuss as CS the product of an interview request to speak Dutch, made to a Dutch immigrant long resident in Australia and unaccustomed to speaking Dutch. Many would rather call the result (Dutch with much English interference) an example of the late stages of first language attrition. Because of such mismatches in analysis, this discussion begins by establishing some boundaries.

To facilitate reference to the analysis of CS, uniformity in terminology is helpful. What follows comes from the Matrix Language Frame Model (Myers-Scotton, 1993a, 1995a), but others use the same or similar terms. The language which sets the grammatical frame in mixed constituents is the Matrix Language (ML). The grammatical frame is defined as morpheme order and system morphemes. System morphemes include inflections and most function words; they are defined by the features [– thematic role receiver/assigner] and often [+ quantification].[2] As such, they contrast with content morphemes, which either receive thematic roles (most nouns and adjectives) or assign them (most verbs, some prepositions) thematic roles. The other language(s) participating in CS is the Embedded Language(s) (EL).

The ML frames the projection of the complementizer (CP) which constitutes intrasentential CS. (A CP is synonymous with a clause with a complementizer (COMP) e.g., *because he came late*, with *because* as COMP). Note that COMP is often null (e.g., in a main clause) and a CP may contain many null elements.

Under the Matrix Language Frame model (MLF model), within the CP frame there can be three types of constituents, all of which are maximal projections within X-bar theory (e.g., N', NP, PP): (1) Mixed constituents (ML + EL constituents) contain content morphemes from both the ML and the EL, but have a grammatical frame from the ML. This means that all syntactically active system morphemes come only from the ML. (2) Similarly, ML islands have an ML grammatical frame, but differ in that all morphemes come from the ML. (3) In a parallel fashion, EL islands consist of only morphemes from the EL which are framed by the EL grammar.[3]

Example [1] illustrates the three types of constituents in a CP framed by the ML. In this case, the ML is Swahili, and English is the EL, and the discussion concerns a Nairobi, Kenya, supermarket and a temporary shortage of a certain laundry detergent. An example of a mixed constituent (ML + EL) is *ni-ko SURE* "I am sure"; the pronominal clitic for first person (*ni-*) and the copula form (*-ko*) are both system morphemes and come from Swahili, the ML. The English adjective *sure*, a content morpheme, may be inserted into the grammatical frame provided by the ML. The temporal PP *after two days* is an EL island; like many EL islands, this PP is an adjunct, not an argument of the verb. Finally, *u-ta-i-pata kwa wingi* "you will find it in abundance" is an ML island. In the second speaker's turn, the verb form *ni-me-DECIDE* "I have decided" is also a mixed constituent; the other constituents are ML islands. *Uchumi supermarket* is a cultural borrowing (compound noun).

[1] 1st speaker: Lakini ni-ko   **SURE** u-ki-end-a
           but   1S-COP sure   2S-CONDIT-go-FV

    AFTER TWO DAYS u-ta-i-pat-a   **UCHUMI SUPERMARKET**
                        2S-FUT-DO-get-FV

    kwa wingi
    in abundance
    "But I am sure if you go after two days you will find it [at] Uchumi Supermarket in abundance [Omo detergent mentioned earlier]."
    2nd speaker: Hata   siku   hizi ni-me-**DECIDE**
                even   days these 1S-PERFECT-decide
    kwanza ku-tumia   sabuni y-a mi-ti
    first   INFIN-use soap   of sticks
    "Even these days I have decided first to use bar soap."
Note: FV = final vowel
(Swahili/English, Myers-Scotton, 1993a: 4–5)

Central to the MLF model and some other models of intrasentential CS is the claim that although both languages are "on" during CS production, they do not participate equally. As noted above, the ML sets the relevant grammatical frame, a generalization which explains the structure of mixed constituents parsimoniously. The consequences of viewing mixed constituents in terms of the ML vs EL distinction are detailed in Myers-Scotton (1993a); however, Joshi (1985) used this distinction first. Further, the observations of some earlier researchers indicate they were aware of the differential participation of the languages in CS (e.g., Forson, 1979; Gibbons, 1987; Petersen, 1988). Sridhar and Sridhar (1980) and Grosjean and his associates (e.g., 1988) recognized that the participating languages had different roles by referring to them as the host language vs the guest language. Kamwangamalu (e.g., 1989) and Azuma (e.g., 1993) also incorporated the ML vs EL distinction into their models early on. Today, many studies recognize the distinction (e.g., Jake, 1994; Walters, 1994).

Prior to models distinguishing the role of the ML and the EL, researchers suggested constraints on CS in terms of surface-based interdictions: linear ordering (the Equivalence Constraint and variations on it; e.g., Pfaff, 1979; Poplack, 1980, 1981), grammatical categories (e.g., switches between pronouns and finite verbs; Timm, 1975), or word composition (e.g., Poplack's Free Morpheme Constraint). Numerous counter-examples to such claims followed soon (e.g., Nartey, 1982; Bentahila and Davies, 1983; Bokamba, 1988; Scotton, 1988b).

Taking a different tack, researchers using a Government and Binding (GB) framework attempt to constrain CS without considering the ML vs EL distinction (e.g., Woolford, 1983; DiSciullo, Muysken, and Singh, 1986). Counter-examples to these attempts, as well as to the earlier surface-based constraints, are found in many responses (e.g., Clyne, 1987; Bokamba, 1988; Romaine, 1989; Pandit, 1990; Myers-Scotton, 1993a). The claims of a more recent GB-based entry (Belazi et al., 1994) are also being challenged. Mahootian (1993) uses another theory based on X-bar theory, Lexicalized Tree-Adjoining Grammar. Models couched in terms of such syntactic theories make correct predictions only in some cases. At the same time, these models are too powerful, allowing for maximal projections with combinations of content and system morphemes which do not occur. These would include syntactically active system morphemes from the EL, combinations prohibited under the MLF model. Further, if the unit of analysis is the maximal projection rather than the ML, switching of the grammatical frame theoretically could occur with every new maximal projection. The unwelcome result is obviously limited generalizability in predicting structure beyond each new projection. At this level of abstraction, the generalization which the ML vs EL distinction captures is not evident.

From the structural point of view, past researchers identified two main types of CS, intrasentential and intersentential, basing the distinction on whether switching took place within the boundaries of a sentence. However, most current structural theories of CS argue that the relevant unit for analysis is not the sentence but rather the CP (complement phrase) or the maximal projection. What qualifies as a sentence in discourse may contain one or more CPs.

Based on the CP, a definition of intrasentential CS becomes this: A CP shows intrasentential CS if it contains at least one constituent with morphemes from Language X and Language Y (a mixed constituent). This CP may also contain other constituents which are monolingual (i.e., ML or EL islands). Also, intersentential CS is now best defined as switching between monolingual CPs which are in different languages.

While the same constituent level, the CP, is the basis for analysis in both types of CS, discussing the languages involved as the ML and EL only makes sense for intrasentential CS (switching within a CP). In intersentential CS (switching between CPs), there is no structural opposition between the ML and EL in terms of what they contribute to a constituent since all morphemes and structures are from one language in any single CP.

Any CP may be completely specified or it may include null elements whose content is clear from the discourse. Thus, in [2], which illustrates switching between CPs (intersentential CS), the English CP has a null subject. This clause *enjoyed the ice cream* cannot be considered as a conjoined clause under Marathi control, because Marathi requires that the identical subject be retained in a conjoined clause.

[2] to ghari ālā ani ø **enjoyed the ice cream**
    he home came and
"He came home and enjoyed the ice cream."
(Marathi/English, Pandharipande, 1990: 21)

While the ML is a structural construct, with clear structural consequences, its definition is based on social and psycholinguistic as well as structural factors. Yet, the ML is not the same construct as "the unmarked choice" of an interaction type. The two operate as analytic tools at two different levels for two different purposes. The unmarked choice is a construct at the discourse level to explain choosing one linguistic variety or one structural variant over others. Choosing the unmarked choice indexes choosing the rights and obligations set which the participants perceive as expected, given the social dimensions of the interaction.

In contrast, the ML is a construct at the level of the CP to explain morphosyntactic and lexical choices. The ML is defined in the following ways. As indicated above, the ML is the language projecting the morphosyntactic frame for the entire CP which shows intrasentential CS. Two other parts of the definition have to do with morpheme frequency: (a) Generally, the ML is the language contributing more morphemes in a sample of discourse-relevant intrasentential CS (minimally two contiguous CPs, either from a single speaker or from an adjacency pair produced by two speakers); (b) It is also generally the language of more morphemes in the discourse as a whole, including monolingual stretches. That speakers perceive the ML as "the language we are speaking" is related to the greater quantitative role of the ML as well as to its role in setting the grammatical frame of the CPs of intrasentential CS.

Yet while ML designation determines structure, its underpinnings are sociopsycholinguistic factors. For this reason, it is a dynamic construct, that is, the ML can change, even within the same discourse, if various situational factors change (e.g., topic, expressions of attitude, participants). Such changes of the

ML may be unusual in some communities; yet they may be frequent for some types of speakers, such as among the young Turks in the Netherlands mentioned below (Backus, 1994). Also, the ML can change over time for a community as the sociopsycholinguistic factors involved in its basis change within the community.

In those models making use of the ML as a construct, how surface level CS will be structured depends on decisions made at the conceptual level, the initial stage of language production. This is so because the ML is selected at this level. Based on such sociolinguistic and psycholinguistic considerations as community attitudes and proficiency, speakers select their discourse mode as well as the semantic/pragmatic messages they wish to convey. If these generally unconscious decisions result in intrasentential CS, selection of the ML is simultaneous and takes the same factors into account (Myers-Scotton and Jake, 1995).

4 Code-switching Compared with Other Bilingual Speech

Relevant to making any comparisons is a basic premise in CS research: Speakers engaged in CS are proficient bilinguals. They are so considered if they have the ability to produce well-formed constituents in their dialects of either language involved in their discourse; that is, they can consistently project grammatical frames according to the norms of their dialects. These are not necessarily those of the standard dialects. Further, showing more ability in one language than the other is usual.

There is a continuum of well-formedness in bilingual or "mixed" speech, with CS as one of the poles. This continuum takes account of two factors: the extent to which grammatical structures produced are predictable (i.e., there are demonstrable criteria for well-formedness) and speaker motivations (i.e., is the goal monolingual speech and/or does bilingual speech have social functions?).

These factors differentiate CS from its neighbors on the continuum. First, CS is structurally coherent (i.e., constituents are assembled in predictable ways). Specifically, this means that the grammatical frame for a CS constituent can always be characterized such that the source of that frame and the distribution of morphemes within it is predictable. This is the case for the recent structural models discussed in section 3.

No matter which grammatical model is followed, the argument can be made that CS shows predictable structures. For example, example [1] supports the prediction that in mixed constituents the grammatical frame (morpheme order and system morphemes – most function words and grammatical inflections) consistently comes from the ML while context morphemes may come from either language. In specific data sets, more specific predictions can be supported (e.g., frequent structural types of EL islands, the use of "do" constructions as a device for incorporating EL verbs, etc.).

The major motivations of CS also distinguish it from other language contact phenomena. In general, motivations can be conflated as any of the following or their combination: (a) to add a dimension to the socio-pragmatic force of one's "discourse persona" either through the individual lexical choices made or through the way in which CS is patterned; (b) to function as a discourse marker (e.g., signalling a change in topic, providing emphasis), or (c) to lexicalize semantic/pragmatic feature bundles from the EL which better convey the speaker's intentions than related lexemes from the ML (that is, existing ML and EL lexemes show a pragmatic mismatch), or (d) to lexicalize semantic/pragmatic feature bundles found only in the EL (there is a lexical gap in the ML). Variations on these motivations are discussed elsewhere in this overview; the relevant point here is that speakers *select* a bilingual mode because it suits their intentions. That selection is often below the level of consciousness is illustrated by the following example: A Senegalese politician who very effectively uses Wolof/French CS in his public speeches in Dakar still firmly stated in an interview that he did not mix Wolof and French (Swigart, 1994: 185).

In regard to their structuring, cases of language attrition (see chapter 15) border CS on the bilingual continuum. In fact, the same discourse may include CS while showing the effects of attrition. Attrition is a phenomenon found in the speech of some bilinguals and is characterized by waning ability in one language. Speakers lose either consistency in producing grammatical frames or lexemes in this language, or both.

Bilingual speech showing attrition coincides with CS in several ways, but with the resemblances fading over time: (1) Initially, the waning language still sets the grammatical frame, even though content morphemes from the waxing language are introduced; (2) Also initially, speakers are proficient enough in both languages to produce well-formed utterances in either language so that their bilingual speech may consist of both mixed constituents and islands which show the same predictable structure as does CS.

However, there are differences, too: (1) Over time, there is a gradual turnover in ML from the waning language to the speaker's waxing language, although this turnover may not be complete (see Myers-Scotton, forthcoming). Thus, as attrition advances, parts of the grammatical frame may come from one language and parts from the other. (2) To produce bilingual speech during attrition may not be the speaker's goal but only the product of necessity.

First-language attrition among adults often happens among immigrants when they join a community where another language is sociolinguistically dominant and the speakers become bilingual in this language. Of course, under such circumstances, language shift by the second generation often occurs.

Still, an alternative to shift is CS motivated by need, as noted above. If among immigrants a first language falls into disuse, and speakers can no longer speak it well enough to use it to construct grammatical frames to convey all of their intentions, CS may become a discourse strategy out of necessity, or because expressing certain ideas becomes associated with phrases in the second language. Such CS may show many EL islands from the L2, the more sociolinguistically dominant language in the new community. For example, EL islands are reported to be frequent among German immigrants to Australia whom Clyne studied, especially locative prepositional phrases (Clyne, 1987: 757).

As already suggested, over time any CS by speakers showing attrition/acquisition typically will show a change in the language setting the grammatical frame, the ML. Two studies of language attrition in children illustrate this (Kaufman and Aronoff, 1991; Kuhberg, 1992). Example [3] shows the types of sentences produced as a Hebrew-speaking child's acquisition of English progressed. She began this process upon coming to the United States at age $2\frac{1}{2}$. While Kaufman and Aronhoff (1991) focus on the idiosyncratic nature of the verb stem formation rules which the child creates for Hebrew verbs, we suggest instead that attention be paid to the systematicity of her grammatical frame, which is always from English from about age 3 onwards, that is, her speech can be called CS, but with a change in the ML.

> [3a] 3;7 my room is **isader**-ed
>   arrange-PAST
> [3b] 4;4 when it **icalcel**-z I will turn it off
>   ring-PRES
> (Kaufman and Aronoff, 1991: 186–7)

The same conclusion applies to the Turkish girls whom Kuhberg (1992) studied; over the time of the study (12 to 15 months) after they returned to Turkey from Germany, their production of German went through several stages, from monolingual German to German/Turkish CS and finally to CS with Turkish, not German, as the ML.

Second language acquisition (SLA) also belongs on the continuum with CS. Even though learner varieties (interlanguage) show little actual bilingual speech, learners frequently structure their utterances in terms of more than one language, that is, the grammatical frames which speakers are attempting to project are a composite, including many morphological realization patterns from the speakers' first language. In fact, if the definition of CS is extended to include not just morphemes from two or more languages, but also grammatical patterns, then both SLA and pidgin/creole formation are more obviously akin to CS (Myers-Scotton, 1995b). In these cases, however, the structures of the ML do not come from any single language and both the L1 and the L2 can function as embedded languages in that both can be sources of content morphemes or EL islands.

At the outset, (informal) SLA seems to be at its most bilingual and its least predictable stage, although one can predict generally it will consist only of content morphemes (Klein and Dietrich, 1994). Example [4] does show CS in SLA data from a Spanish worker in Germany. This utterance from the early stages of German acquisition shows an EL island from Spanish (*mucho trabajo*) as well as target language structures.

> [4] (In response to the question (in German) "What did you do? What kind of job?")
>
> Ja, ja bisəl arbaitə (. . .) **MUCHO TRABAJO,**   fi:1   arbai (. . .)
> yes, yes a little work   much work   much   work
> (Klein and Dittmar, 1979: 108)

Except as part of EL islands, system morphemes from the L1 rarely appear in SLA structures. For example, Poulisse and Bongaerts (1994) report that Dutch students who were advanced learners of English used some Dutch content morphemes, but no Dutch inflections at all. There were, however, some Dutch determiners (system/functional morphemes). Thus there is good evidence for an argument that when learner varieties/interlanguages contain morphemes from both the source and target language, they generally show predictability in line with that of the MLF model for CS about the source of content vs system morphemes (the L1 is like the EL as far as system morphemes are concerned and does not contribute system morphemes to mixed constituents).

Another form of bilingual speech closely related to both SLA and CS is pidgin/creole formation (see chapter 14). Pidginization and/or "immediate" creolization (i.e., pidginization is circumvented) resemble learner varieties of SLA because in both processes learners are attempting to structure utterances following the grammatical frame of which they do not yet have full command. Thus it is no surprise that utterances in both initial SLA varieties and pidgins are similar: They consist mainly, if not exclusively, of content morphemes. The difference is that the details of the target language frame are much more available to SLA speakers, so that SLA soon shows progression beyond the content morpheme stage to a more fully developed target-based frame. In the formative stages of pidgin/creole development, language switching/mixing is a likely strategy for the same reasons that it occurs during language attrition: inability to express or communicate all intentions in one language. However, such switching would differ from CS, as it is described here, because speakers would find it difficult to form a consensus on an ML frame; thus, switching in fully predictable ways is not possible (although see Myers-Scotton, 1995b).

As indicated at the outset of this overview, CS is not the same phenomenon as lexical borrowing. Yet the morphosyntactic treatment of both singly occurring CS lexemes and borrowed lexemes in the recipient language is very similar, and often identical. For this reason and because the process producing core borrowings (defined below) is related to that producing CS, the comparison between CS and borrowing deserves some detail. Finally, lexical borrowing requires discussion in relation to the bilingual continuum containing CS.

CS and borrowing are clearly related in their motivations; in both, elements from one language are inserted into the grammatical frame of another language because these elements meet speakers' expressive needs. However, CS and lexical borrowing are different: (1) Monolingual speakers of Language X can and do use borrowed lexemes from Language Y, while only persons actually bilingual in both Languages X and Y engage in CS. (2) A second difference has to do with the psycholinguistic status of borrowed vs CS lexemes. When a Language Y lexeme is an established borrowing in Language X, this means it has an entry in the mental lexicon of Language X (as well as presumably retaining an entry in Language Y). This is why it is readily accessible for use in monolingual speech in either Language X or Language Y. Both this established borrowing and a second type of Embedded Language lexeme, a CS form, may appear in X/Y CS. The difference is that a CS form only has an entry in the mental lexicon of Language Y, meaning its only monolingual appearance is in Language Y. (3) A third difference has to do with the relation between the structural and sociopolitical profiles of the two languages concerned. In lexical borrowing, lexemes from a more sociopolitical dominant language are normally incorporated into a less commanding language. In contrast, the structurally more activated language in CS may well be the sociolinguistically less commanding member of the language pair, as will become clear.

We now consider the different processes which bring about the two types of borrowed lexemes and the relation of only one of them to CS as a process. While both types of borrowings are often present when there is CS, only one type is part of a continuum involving singly occurring lexemes in CS. These are core borrowings; they stand for concepts or objects already covered by the recipient language (Scotton and Okeju, 1973; Mougeon and Beniak, 1991). Since core borrowed lexemes do not fill lexical gaps, there is no motivation to adopt them overnight, but rather over time. This reasoning motivates the hypothesis that the life of a core borrowing into Language X begins as a form which occurs in CS between Language X and Y. As CS forms, these lexemes occur either as a singly occurring form in a mixed constituent or as part of what is referred to as an EL island above, a constituent entirely in the EL. When their frequency reaches an unknown threshold level, these EL lexemes move from being CS forms to becoming borrowed forms and therefore now part of the lexicon of the recipient language as well as the donor language (cf. Myers-Scotton, 1993a: 201–3).

The type of borrowed form whose introduction need have nothing to do with CS is the cultural borrowed lexeme, which, almost necessarily enters the recipient language abruptly. Such lexemes fill lexical gaps which need immediate attention (e.g., borrowings of renditions of English *television* or *telephone*).

Once EL lexemes are borrowed forms, they may be used in monolingual speech as noted above. Thus, while they may also be used in CS, their presence is *not* diagnostic of CS.

There are, however, important similarities between how borrowed lexemes and singly occurring CS lexemes are treated in the grammatical frames in which they appear. This is the reason for an extended discussion of borrowings in an overview on CS. When either a borrowed or a CS lexeme from an EL appears in a constituent grammatically framed by the ML, the treatment of the EL lexemes is the same. Typically they are morphosyntactically integrated into the ML; they appear with ML system morphemes (i.e., they receive inflections from the ML and can be modified by ML function words) and in syntactic patterns dictated by the ML.[4] Example [5] shows how, in the same utterance, the speaker uses both a borrowed word (French *prison*) and its Wolof counterpart (*kaso*). What is of interest for this discussion is that they appear in very similar morphosyntactic frames (from Wolof).

[5] ... ENQUETE la, JE NE SAIS PAS, *ci PRISON* i Senegal ... Dangay wax ne JAMAIS, JAMAIS duma def loo xamene di nanu ma japp, yobu ma *ci kaso* bi. "It was an enquiry, I don't know, on Senegalese prisons ... You would say that never, never, will I do something that they will get me for and take me to prison."
(Wolof/French, Swigart, 1992a: 89)

We can summarize this section on borrowing with the following generalizations. There are real reasons *not* to group singly occurring CS lexemes with borrowed lexemes *if* one is characterizing the direction of borrowing, the types of words which are borrowed, or the types of speakers who use borrowed lexemes. However, it should be just as clear that there is no reason *not* to group borrowed lexemes with singly occurring CS lexemes when the issue is their morphosyntactic framing in mixed constituents in CS. And this generally is the issue when structural constraints on CS are the topic. Since both types of lexemes show substantially the same patterning of morphosyntactic integration, the model which explains the patterning for CS lexemes also explains that for borrowed lexemes. Thus, when delimiting the corpus to be explained by a model for CS, there is no need to exclude singly occurring EL lexemes on the grounds that they cannot be distinguished from borrowed lexemes (for an opposing view see Sankoff, Poplack, and Vanniarajan, 1990).

5 CS and Other Contact Phenomena

Convergence is another contact phenomenon on the bilingual continuum even though under convergence all morphemes in utterances come from a single language.

While convergence is similar to attrition, it also shows contrasts. Under convergence, there is a "rearrangement" of how grammatical frames are projected in one language under the influence of another language. While structural simplification may also accompany rearrangement in convergence, such simplification is much more the hallmark of attrition. This is because the speaker's ability to project any grammatical frames at all in the language showing attrition is waning. For this reason, attrition is often necessarily accompanied by CS to a waxing language. While CS does co-occur with convergence, there is not the same structural imperative for its presence.

Most cases of convergence come from communities where there is especially high sentiment to maintain a language, or speakers are very numerous, even in the face of another language as more sociolinguistically dominant. Thus, many examples of maintained languages in spite of convergence come from German-speaking communities in the United States which have a religious basis. In these communities, the grammatical frame of German is changing to incorporate aspects of English. For example, Huffines (1991) comments on the use of *du* "do" as a pro-form and the increasing use of past participles in nonsentence final position. Also, Spanish in the bilingual Puerto Rican New York community shows the effects of convergence to English. While example [6] is entirely in Spanish, the placement of the time phrase is unmarked for English not Spanish (in Spanish, its unmarked position would be sentence initial). Also, *cuatro años atras* "four years ago," a calque of the English time expression is used, instead of the Spanish equivalent, *hace quatro años*.

[6] Mucho cubanoh, cuatro años atras se mudaron pa'ca
"Many Cubans, four years ago, moved over here."
(Torres, 1989: 428–9)

Example [7], from the speech of a German immigrant to Australia, also illustrates restructuring of an L1. Convergence to English is apparent in word order; the German verb-second rule in main clauses is not followed (*werden*). In addition, it appears that the regular German conjugation pattern is being overgeneralized to the verb for "shear." The fact that *schert* approximates English *sheared* may also be a consideration.

[7] Jed-es Jahr die Schaf-e werd-en ge-scher-t
every/NEUTR year DET/PL sheep-PL become-3PL PPART-shear-PPART
"Every year the sheep are 'sheared'."
Note: St German: Jedes Jahr werden die Schafe geschoren
(German, Clyne, 1987: 750)

In convergence, while models for structural constraints on CS may predict correctly some ways in which such varieties are structured, they do not predict all. The reason is that convergence shows modification of one grammatical frame under the influence of another frame, but not a turnover to the second frame. Certainly, initial study of convergence indicates that not all aspects of the grammatical frame are modified at the same time, but morpheme order seems to change early on.

In those relatively rare instances when there is a turnover to a second grammatical frame, while maintaining many first language content morphemes, what has been called a "mixed language" results. Mixed languages result when there is a language shift which begins with a turnover in the ML, *but* a shift which does not go to completion. On this view, many language shifts which are complete should also begin in CS.

A suggested scenario is this: CS is a dominant discourse pattern in the community, but because of changes in the community's sociopolitical profile, there is a "turnover" in the ML for CS. The next step is that this CS-structured discourse is "reanalyzed" as "the community language" (i.e., a substantial part of the lexicon comes from the community's first language – the "new" Embedded Language in CS – but the grammatical frame comes from the "new" Matrix Language, the outside, more sociolinguistically dominant language which became the Matrix Language in CS). (See Myers-Scotton, 1993a: chapter 7.)

Ma'a may be such a mixed language (a Bantu grammar with a substantial Cushitic lexicon, discussed by Thomason and Kaufman (1988) and a subject of recent field work by Mous 1994). In other varieties cited, different grammatical subsystems come from different sources (Bakker, 1992, describes Michif as showing a French nominal system with Cree verbal morphology).

6 The Sociolinguistics of CS

6.1 CS patterning

While CS is a unified phenomenon from the structural point of view, different options in CS patterning are taken up in different communities, that is, "preference" is a production phenomenon subject to variation and is associated with cross-community differences in the saliency of relevant socio- and psycholinguistic factors.

A way to begin this discussion of patterning options is to recognize that one language is typically more prominent in either intersentential or intrasentential CS in at least three ways.

First, the Markedness Model (Scotton, 1983, 1988a; Myers-Scotton, 1993a, 1993c) claims that, for any interaction type and the participants involved, and among available linguistic varieties, there is an "unmarked choice." While there is a continuum of markedness between choices for any given interaction type in a community, one (or more) choice(s) is more unmarked than others, its status demonstrable by frequency. Discourses including CS are no different; that is, they also show an "unmarked choice."

Frequently, the unmarked choice in CS is comparatively more associated with in-group membership, an index of solidarity. In these cases, the unmarked choice is often *not* the language of greater sociopolitical prestige in the larger community. That such a variety should hold sway in CS is not surprising, given that CS is more typically an in-group mode of communication than one used with strangers or even acquaintances in many communities. For example, while Alsatian-speaking families in the Alsace area of France often also speak French, Alsatian is the main language of CS discourse (Gardner-Chloros, 1991). In other types of communities, where one of the potential partners in CS is hardly used in informal settings, the main venue for CS will not be in-group interactions, but formal encounters where relationships are being negotiated. For example, in the Arabic-speaking world, it is in interviews between educated strangers where much CS takes place. The interviewees wish to express their education and therefore mainly speak a variety which might be called "oral educated Arabic." Since they also wish to express their roots/sincerity/nationality, they switch to some features of the local colloquial variety of Arabic (Walters, 1994).

One can see how the unmarked choice for the interaction plays a role in setting certain quantitative dimensions of CS. First, one language usually quite obviously contributes more material (i.e., more CPs come from this language), especially if the discourse is more than a few turns long.

Second, the same social conditions promote CS patterning such that switching is most often from one language to the other and not in the other direction. For example, Irish is the language from which switches are made to English in Gaelic-speaking Ireland, not the other way around (Stenson, 1990); switches in Bukavu Swahili/French CS in Bukavu, Zaire (Goyvaerts and Zembele, 1992) are from Swahili to French. This was also the case among the Moroccan immigrants studied in Utrecht, the Netherlands (Nortier, 1990), who switched more often from Arabic to Dutch than vice versa.

Third, although this aspect of prominence has not been studied systematically, it seems that the unmarked choice is the language setting various aspects of the discourse frame, e.g., how narratives or arguments are organized.

In communities where CS *itself* is the main medium of in-group conversation, CS itself – rather than either language alone – is the unmarked choice. Multilingual urban communities in Africa and India often show CS as their unmarked informal medium, as do some immigrant communities or families in Europe and North America. Yet, even if CS itself is the unmarked choice, one language still dominates in setting the dimensions of CS.

6.2 CS and community norms

CS patterns may be indicative of how speakers view themselves in relation to the sociopolitical or cultural values attached to the linguistic varieties used in CS. For example, when CS itself is the main in-group medium, its use is evidence that speakers see both codes as salient indices of the values they incorporate in their identities, at least in the social context where it occurs.

This is often the case in the Third World, where an indigenous variety is used in a CS pattern with the language of the former colonial power (e.g., Baba Malay/English in Singapore (Pakir, 1989); SeSotho/English in South Africa (Khati, 1992).

In contrast, if much CS indexes positive associations with more than one language and the groups closely associated with these languages, little CS should index polarization between groups. That is, one would predict little CS at all in communities marked by intergroup tensions.[5] This prediction seems to hold for Brussels today (Treffers-Daller, 1992).

One would also expect little CS at all in communities where prescriptive attitudes about maintaining the "purity" of the language are part of the culture. Thus it is no surprise that in Basel, Switzerland, while immigrants from French-speaking areas and their children become fluent speakers of Swiss German, they do relatively little switching between their languages, compared to other second-generation immigrant groups in Europe. A striking comparison is the heavy incidence of CS among second-generation Italians in Basel or Zurich. Any switching among Francophone Swiss tends to be between turns rather than even between CPs and more rarely within a single CP (Jake and Myers-Scotton, 1994).

6.3 CS and language proficiency

Bentahila and Davies (1992) studied two groups of Moroccan Arabic/French bilinguals, with age and its interrelation to French proficiency as the main independent variable. The older group received its education while Morocco was still a French protectorate or soon afterward and show a very high proficiency in French along with their native Arabic variety. In contrast, the younger group was educated after the policy of Arabization was well underway. These speakers received the bulk of their schooling in Arabic, but studied French and scientific subjects in French.

While both groups engage in CS, their main patterns are different. The older group uses much more French, often producing full CPs in French. When these speakers engage in intrasentential CS, it often is marked by a switching to French NPs which are embedded in a larger Arabic frame (Bentahila and Davies, 1992: 449):

> [8] hda **LE DIX-SEPTIEME ETAGE** f dak **LE FEU ROUGE**
> near the seventeenth story at the fire red
> "near the seventeen-story [building] at the red light"

In contrast, the younger, Arabic-dominant group shows fewer full constituents in French in their CS discourse and more French content morphemes in mixed constituents. For example, these younger speakers inflect French verb stems with Arabic suffixes.

A similar division in CS patterns among Turks engaging in Turkish/Dutch CS in Tilburg, the Netherlands, can also be associated with linguistic proficiency. Backus (1994) explains a change from mainly intrasentential CS in the 1980s to intersentential CS in the 1990s as related to the newer CS speakers' high proficiency in both languages, brought about by extensive contact with both monolingual Turkish and Dutch. Examples [9a] and [9b] illustrate the contrast between the CS patterns of two different groups of young Turks. [9a] comes from speakers who came to the Netherlands when they were already of school age; they are Turkish-dominant bilinguals. Their speech shows much intrasentential CS (mixed constituents such as *O blond-e-dan* "that blonde [girl]" in which the Dutch NP is framed by Turkish system morphemes), as well as the "do" construction with a Dutch infinitive (*afstuder-en yap-tı* "do graduate"). In contrast, [9b] comes from speakers who had all of their schooling in the Netherlands. Their speech shows more instances of complete CPs in either Turkish or Dutch (intrasentential CS):

[9a] A: **O BLOND-E**-dan   al-ıyor-dum   **BURGEMEESTER**
DET blonde-DEF-ABL   take-PROG-PAST-1SG Burgemeester
VAN DAMSTREET da-ydi
van Damstreet   LOC-PRET
"I was taking [lessons] from that blonde girl, in the Burgemeester van Damstraat it was."

B: Şimdi o **AFSTUDER-EN**   yap-tı
now she graduate-INFIN   do-PAST-3S
"Now she's graduated."
(Turkish/Dutch, Backus, 1993: 74)

[9b] A: Türkiye-ye gid-inci   **BENT GEENTURK, HIER BEN JE OOK**
turkey-LOC go-SUBORD COP   ART/NEG   turk here be you also
GEEN NEDERLANDER yani, **JE BENT GEWOON** karısık
ART/NEG Dutch   I mean you be   just   mixed
"When you go to Turkey, you are not (considered) a Turk and here you are not a Dutch person either, you are just mixed up."

B: çok   yap-ınca   **DAN IS HET NIET MEER ERG** . . .
many   do-SUBORD then is it   not   more   bad . . .
"When many do it, then it's all right . . ."
(Turkish/Dutch, Backus, 1996: forthcoming)

Note that the CS pattern characterizing both the Moroccan Arabs and the Turks who were more balanced is the pattern with more instances of full constituents (or even full CPs) produced in one language. This finding is at odds with earlier claims (Poplack, 1980; Nortier, 1990) that the "more difficult" pattern of CS is one in which single nouns or verb stems are inserted into a frame from the other language. Myers-Scotton (1993a) arrives at a similar conclusion, based not so much on proficiency as on structure: No matter what the level of speaker proficiency, it should be easier to insert a verb stem in a frame of affixes from another language or to insert a noun in an otherwise fully specified NP in another language than it is to produce an entire constituent up to the level of CP as a monolingual segment.

Why should highly proficient bilinguals bother to engage in CS at all, which in both the Morocco and Tilburg case goes well beyond filling lexical gaps? The answer is that speakers wish to signal their memberships in the communities of speakers of both languages, not just one. CS is emblematic of dual membership, which is also the conclusion of Lüdi (1992), who discusses in-country Francophone immigrants to German-speaking areas in Switzerland.

7 Variation in Structural Patterns across Communities

A comparison of the two Moroccan groups has already demonstrated that there can be qualitative and quantitative differences in the role of the EL in CS. There, we saw that while the younger group inflected French verbs with Arabic affixes, the older group did not.

To date, there has been little emphasis on differences in the role of the EL across language pairs. The following examples are not exhaustive, but they give an idea of the types of phenomena whose study could be enlightening. First, data sets can be compared in terms of how EL verbs are treated. In some data sets, EL verbs inflected with ML suffixes are common, but they are not found at all in others. They are especially frequent when the ML is an agglutinative language (e.g., Finnish in Finnish/English CS in Halmari, 1993; Swahili and Shona in CS with English in Myers-Scotton, 1993a), but not necessarily so (e.g., they are not attested in Turkish/Dutch CS by Boeschoten, 1991, or Backus, 1993, 1994). And there are at least some cases in which the ML is not agglutinative, yet such verb forms appear (e.g., English verb stems inflected for Irish in Stenson, 1990). An alternative strategy for handling EL verbs is the "do construction." In diverse language pairs (from Japanese/English to Tamil/English to Chewa/English), an ML verb for "do" receives all relevant verbal inflections and is used in conjunction with a nonfinite EL verb form, typically the infinitive. See [10] for an example:

> [10] Avan enne **CONFUSE**-paNNiTTAan
>   3S/M 1S/OBJ confuse do/PAST
>   "He confused me."
>   (Tamil/English, Annamalai, 1989: 51)

A second way to look at EL material in CS is to classify it according to the lexical categories represented by singly occurring EL lexemes (e.g., Nortier, 1990, on Moroccan Arabic/Dutch CS in Utrecht, the Netherlands). Singly occurring forms were the largest class by far in her corpus.

A third way in which EL participation in CS can be studied is to consider the frequency of EL islands and their structural roles. (See Treffers-Daller, 1994; Jake and Myers-Scotton, 1996.)

A fourth aspect of EL participation in CS amenable to study is the occurrence of internal EL islands, well-formed EL intermediate constituents embedded in maximal projections which are framed by the ML. For example, such islands are very frequent when French is the EL (e.g., Arabic/French CS). In French, these internal islands involve a noun and generally consist of DET + N, but DET + N + ADJ also occurs (see example [8]). Although little studied as yet, these islands occur widely; examples are cited in Myers-Scotton (1993a: 152) from Shona/English and from an Asante/English corpus (Forson, 1979).

8 Conclusion

In this overview, we have attempted to outline the state of research in CS in two ways. First, we have surveyed recent and current directions in CS research itself. It is clear that two different strands of research have developed, one of longer standing and much more within the sociolinguistic mold than the other. In general, the social or discourse-organizing messages of CS are the subject of the former and older strand. A current new direction here is how differences in group patterns of CS reflect the group's attitudes regarding itself in relation to the larger community or reflect proficiency levels. The latter strand focuses on the morphosyntax of CS. In fact, some researchers here are interested exclusively in relating the constraints on CS to current syntactic theories. Others have broader concerns, such as what CS tells us about bilingual speech production and thus about the nature of linguistic competence (i.e., the mental organization of language). Exploring connections between these two strands is an appropriate goal for future studies.

This brings us to the second pole around which this overview has been organized. CS has been discussed, not in isolation, but in relation to other language contact phenomena, especially those in which morphemes from two or more languages appear (e.g., borrowing, language attrition, and second language acquisition). A major theme here has been that, while the structural results are different in each phenomenon, the argument can be made that the same linguistic principles are at work in structuring all types of such phenomena. What is worth emphasizing is that the reason there is a difference in structural outcomes in these phenomena may be mainly a function of differences in the sociolinguistic conditions under which the varieties develop and the related proficiency levels of speakers.

NOTES

1 I gratefully acknowledge support for this work under NSF grant no. SBR–9319780. I also thank the following for their comments on earlier drafts: Ad Backus, Janet Fuller, Janice Jake, Georges Lüdi, Carol Pfaff, S. R. Simango, and Longxing Wei.

2 For a fuller discussion of the content vs system morpheme distinction, see Myers-Scotton (1993a or 1995a). Of course, the designation of only those forms which assign or receive thematic roles as content morphemes does not imply that system morphemes have no content. The point is that the main distinguishing feature of system morphemes is their [+ quantification] designation, meaning that system morphemes are members of sets (generally closed sets) such that a specific system morpheme "quantifies" or "selects" a quality to be associated with the content morpheme which governs it. For example, English *this* "quantifies" its head noun in contrast to the way in which *that* performs its quantifying function.

3 Even though EL islands are well-formed according to EL specifications, their production is under ML "control" in various ways. For example, there is evidence that the ML controls which EL specifications (from a set of possible well-formed specifications) apply (Myers-Scotton, 1995a; Myers-Scotton and Jake, 1995). Of course the production of EL islands means that ML morphosyntactic procedures must be inhibited (but not "turned off") so that EL procedures may apply.

4 In some cases, neither borrowed lexemes nor CS lexemes receive full ML inflections; that is, they are either base forms or receive only some of the inflections which make ML lexemes well-formed.

5 In such communities, marked CS, to negotiate interpersonal social distance or for pragmatic "color," may well occur. Many of the examples in French/English CS in Francophone Canada reported in Poplack (1988a, b) seem to be marked switching for such "color" (i.e., English provides *le mot juste*).

14 Language Contact and Language Generation: Pidgins and Creoles

JOHN R. RICKFORD and JOHN McWHORTER

1 Introduction

Pidgins and creoles are new varieties of language generated in situations of language contact.[1] A *pidgin* is sharply restricted in social role, used for limited communication between speakers of two or more languages who have repeated or extended contacts with each other, for instance, through trade, enslavement, or migration. A pidgin usually combines elements of the native languages of its users and is typically simpler than those native languages insofar as it has fewer words, less morphology, and a more restricted range of phonological and syntactic options (Rickford, 1992: 224). A *creole*, in the classical sense of Hall (1966), is a pidgin that has acquired native speakers, usually, the descendants of pidgin speakers who grow up using the pidgin as their first language. In keeping with their extended social role, creoles typically have a larger vocabulary and more complicated grammatical resources than pidgins. However, some extended pidgins which serve as the primary language of their speakers (e.g., Tok Pisin in New Guinea, Sango in the Central African Republic) are already quite complex, and seem relatively unaffected by the acquisition of native speakers (Sankoff, 1979; Samarin, 1995).

We will expand and elaborate on these definitions in sections 2 and 3 below, but we should ask first why pidgins and creoles should be of interest to sociolinguistics. One answer is that these languages compel attention to their *social histories* and to the embedding of languages in their social contexts, even more so than ordinary languages do (Rickford, 1987: 52). As Hymes (1971: 5) puts it, "the processes of pidginization and creolization . . . seem to represent the extreme to which social factors can go in shaping the transmission and use of language." The pages of the *Journal of Pidgin and Creole Languages* are filled with argumentation about the sociohistorical matrices of pidginization and creolization (see, for instance, Baker, 1991a; Singler, 1986, 1992; Bickerton, 1992, 1994; Bruyn and Veenstra, 1993; McWhorter, 1994). There is simply no other area of sociolinguistics in which sociohistorical issues are raised so repeatedly and with such vigor.

A second, related answer is that these languages have served and continue to serve as data sources and testing grounds for models of *sociolinguistic variation and change*, for instance, the concept of diglossia (Ferguson, 1959; Winford, 1985; Valdman 1988), the quantitative and implicational paradigms (Bickerton, 1971; DeCamp, 1971a; Labov, 1971; Rickford, 1979; Winford, 1980), the sociopsychological "acts of identity" model (Edwards, 1983; Le Page and Tabouret-Keller, 1985), and sociolinguistic theories of language change (Romaine, 1988a). As De Rooij (1995: 53) observes, "For the student of pidgin and creole languages, there is no escape from the problem of variation." Far from wanting to escape it, researchers interested in the study of socio-linguistic variation, multilingualism, and code-switching are often at-tracted to pidgin- and creole-speaking communities for the opportunities they offer to study these topics and related ones, such as the relation of language to social class, power, and identity (Rickford, 1986; Morgan, 1994).

A third answer is that these languages exemplify in acute form many of the issues with which *applied sociolinguistics and language planning* are concerned, including the question of whether local vernaculars can be used as instru-ments of social integration and political liberation (Searle, 1984; Devonish, 1986), and the challenges of orthography, corpus development, and status planning required to make them into official or national languages (Baker, 1991b; Carrington, 1993; Romaine, 1994a; Alleyne, 1994; Winford, 1994). Less ambitiously but no less importantly, pidgins and creoles offer us oppor-tunities to draw on as well as contribute to macro-sociolinguistics via such topics as the emergence of vernacular literatures (Voorhoeve and Lichtveld, 1975; Barbag-Stoll, 1983; Braithwaite, 1984; Roberts, 1988; Adamson and van Rossem, 1995), the nature and effects of language attitudes (Rickford and Traugott, 1985), and the question of whether these varieties can be taken into account in improved methods of teaching children to read and write in school or in combating adult illiteracy (Cassidy, 1970; Craig, 1971, 1980; Sato, 1985; Romaine, 1992; Watson-Gegeo, 1994).

Finally, pidgin creole studies has what may be described as a "fractious energy" which contemporary sociolinguistics seems to lack. Creolists are constantly arguing about theories and subtheories – sometimes too snidely to be sure, but in a way that makes every conference and every issue of the *Journal of Pidgin and Creole Languages* exciting, and that constantly spawns new research. Readers will notice that even the co-authors of this paper disagree on some issues. Sociolinguistics could do with more of this energy.

2 Pidgins

2.1 Description

Pidgins have most commonly arisen as vehicles of trade between ethnic groups (e.g., Pidgin Yimas and other pidgins of Papua New Guinea); as linguae francae on plantations and in other multi-ethnic work situations (e.g., Fanakalo between the British and Zulus in the mines of Natal in South Africa); as linguae francae for multi-ethnic ship crews (e.g., Melanesian Pidgin English in Pacific trade of the early nineteenth century); and as languages of service (e.g., Tây Bôi between the French and their Vietnamese servants).

Structurally, pidgins are, as noted above, simpler than their source languages, particularly the language which provides the bulk of their lexicon. This is well exemplified by Russenorsk, a trade pidgin used by Norwegians and Russians in the nineteenth century.[2]

1 Russenorsk had a core lexical stock of 150 to 200 words (Broch and Jahr 1984: 30), unmarked for case, number, gender, or inflection: *moja snai* "I know," *Kristus snai* "Jesus knows."
2 There was a single preposition *på* used to encode a wide array of concepts: *på moja stova* "at my house," *på Arkangel* "to Archangel," *sprek på moja* "say to me," etc. (Fox, 1983: 56–7).
3 There was no expressed equative copula: *eta ø samme slag* "this is the same type" (p. 56).[3]
4 Subordination was expressed via juxtaposition: *Kristus grot vrei, tvoja ljugom* "Christ will be very angry if you lie" (Broch and Jahr, 1984: 31).
5 Limited lexical stock conditioned semantic extensions, such as the extension of *anner* "second" to the meaning of "next" as in *på anner ar* "next year" (Fox, 1983: 63), and reduplication, such as *morra-morradag* "the day after tomorrow" (Broch and Jahr, 1984: 37).

It must be noted, however, that relative simplicity cannot in itself be seen as diagnostic of pidginization. For example, we find limited morphology in Chinese as well as pidgins. One response to this conundrum has been to distinguish between simplification of *outer form* (i.e., morphosyntactic complexity) and simplification of *inner form* (i.e., lexical resources, semantic distinctions, pragmatic machinery). While languages like Chinese display simplification of outer form (lack of morphology), pidgins display this as well as simplification of inner form (constrained lexicon, limited semantic and pragmatic resources; see Hymes, 1971: 70). Pidgins can be further distinguished as being the only languages which combine simplification of inner form with two other factors: the combination of elements from different languages, and use by speakers of different native languages (Hymes, 1971).

Other types of simplified registers, such as foreigner talk (Ferguson, 1971) and argots, lack one of these traits.

Finally, pidgins have traditionally been defined as being conventionalized or having relatively established norms of usage, in contrast to jargons (or *pre-pidgin continua*) which are more variable, and strongly affected by the native language of their users. *Gastarbeiterdeutsch* (guest-worker's German) is jargon-like insofar as it varies according to whether its speaker is Turkish or Greek (HFP, 1975: 167), but speakers of Chinook Jargon (a pidgin in the American Northwest) regularly negated sentences with a clause-initial marker even when their native language provided no model (Thomason, 1983: 853–5).

While Russenorsk is an example of a pidgin established between groups of relatively equal status, pidgins often emerge within contexts of asymmetrical social status. Social dominance can result from various factors, such as power, as in the case of the British plantation trade in Melanesia establishing Melanesian Pidgin English, or prestige within a trade context, as in the case of Pidgin Yimas, developed between the Yimas who supply fish and the Arafundi who supply the lesser-valued sago (Foley, 1988: 168). In some cases, social dominance falls to those who were the original inhabitants of the area the pidgin emerges in, as in the case of the pidgin Fijian used by the British in Fiji (Siegel, 1987: 69–73) at the same time that Melanesian Pidgin English was emerging in other contexts.

In such cases, most of the pidgin's lexical stock is derived from the language of the socially dominant (the *superstrate* language) while the language or languages of the socially subordinate (the *substrate* language(s)) have most of their effect upon its phonology, syntax, and semantics (although the substrate indeed makes lexical contributions and the superstrate has significant influence upon structure). Note, for example, the following passage in the dialect of Melanesian Pidgin English spoken in Papua New Guinea, Tok Pisin (Hall, 1966: 149):

[1] Nau wanfela master em i-kisim mi . . . nau ol master i-kik, i-kikim em.
then one white-man he PM-get me then PL white-man PM-kick, PM-kick him
"Then a white man took me . . . then the white men were kicking, they were kicking it."

Note that the lexicon is drawn from English, even though in many cases the function of an item in English has been re-analyzed or extended. However, much of the structure is drawn from the Eastern Oceanic languages spoken by the originators of Tok Pisin. For example, the *i* predicate marker [PM], the *-im* (<*him*) transitive marker, and *ol* (<*all*) a plural marker [PL] all reflect Eastern Oceanic rather than English structure (Keesing, 1988: 105–32).

2.2 Genesis

Pidgins owe their structure to the interaction of various phenomena related to language contact. The preliminary input for them may, in some cases, derive from foreigner talk registers. As Ferguson and DeBose (1977: 104) show, people attempting to communicate in their language with foreigners use common if not universal simplification tendencies such as slow, exaggerated enunciation, uninflected forms, and the omission of articles, prepositions, and other function words. This practice has often passed from the individual domain into development as an established register regularly acquired and utilized by members of a community when communicating with outsiders. Such registers were pivotal in the emergence of pidgins such as Pidgin Fijian (Siegel, 1987) and Chinook Jargon (Thomason, 1983). Fijians established a register of their language with established norms of its own for use with outsiders, and it was this register that the British were expected to learn upon arrival in Fiji. Often, the establishment of such registers reflects a desire on the part of the speakers to reserve the use of the full language for themselves, as a reflection of elevated status or distinctness from foreigners (Foley, 1988: 163–4). For example, the Chinook Amerindians were explicitly opposed to non-native speakers acquiring their language, which led to the establishment of Chinook Jargon for use in trade (Hymes, 1980). There is no a priori reason to rule out the possibility that pidgins can arise without an established foreigner talk model, and indeed, such established registers are only occasionally explicitly attested. However, the observed sociolinguistic tendency for such registers to arise on both the idiolectal and community levels demonstrates the viability of incorporating foreigner talk within an account of pidgin genesis.

Furthermore, as we have seen above in Tok Pisin, substrate features are salient determiners of pidgin structure. One example beyond Tok Pisin is the serial verb constructions in Tây Bôi Pidgin French, derived from the Vietnamese substrate (Phillips, 1975: 164–71). Thomason and Kaufman (1988: 181–94) provide additional examples of such transfer from Chinook Jargon, Kituba, Hiri Motu, Bislama, and Chinese Pidgin Russian, among other languages, arguing that the diverse marked features which these languages illustrate are only explicable by reference to their different substrates. An oversimplified but heuristically useful characterization of pidgins would be that they result from the interaction between superstrate-based foreigner talk and structural features derived from the substrate languages. Note, however, that the substrate speakers can be thought to contribute a foreigner talk register of their own grammars to the emerging pidgin, as documented in the Melanesian Pidgin English case by Keesing (1988: 89–104).

2.3 *Pidginization and simplification as a cline*

Our reference to prototypical pidgins like Russenorsk and Tok Pisin (themselves quite different in terms of the size of their lexicon, the complexity of their structure, and their historical trajectories) should not be taken to indicate that the distinction between full languages and pidgins is binary. Pidginization manifests itself in degrees, as do most language contact phenomena, such that pidginization can be seen as one end of a cline which begins with full acquisition, proceeds through cases of language shift such as Irish English and Yiddish, and culminates in pidgins like Russenorsk and Tok Pisin. Various pidgins, however, fall between Russenorsk and Yiddish along this cline, therefore displaying more vigorous reflections of structural complexity, and a vaster lexical stock. Such cases typically stem from either richer contact between superstrate and substrate speakers than was the case between the originators of deeper pidgins, or from close genetic relationship between superstrate and substrate languages.[4]

For example, the pidginized Assamese called Naga Pidgin displays more inflection than most pidgins; this feature is due in part to the fact that the Nagas encountered Assamese not only as a trade language but as a language of instruction (Bhattachariya, 1994). Similarly, Kituba, a pidgin resulting from interaction between various dialects of Kikongo, also displays greater than average morphology – in this case because its speakers shared a core of grammatical structure which they could readily incorporate into a pidgin regardless of its complexity to non-Kikongos (Mufwene, 1986). We see how genetic relatedness acts as a brake upon pidginization particularly clearly in the case of Hiri Motu, the pidginized register of the Austronesian language Motu. Hiri Motu exists in two dialects. That spoken by speakers of Papuan languages is prototypically reduced along the lines of Tok Pisin, while that spoken by Austronesian speakers displays more Motu structure (Dutton, 1985).

2.4 Life-cycle issues

Pidgins figured in the classic formulation of the contact language life cycle offered by Hall (1966), in which they were couched as the initial stage in a process which proceeded through creolization and ended in eventual decreolization towards a lexifier. The elegance and renown of this formulation have had the effect, however, of obscuring the various alternative fates which a pidgin in fact may experience. Creolization is indeed one of the alternatives; however, just as commonly encountered are stasis and death.

Creolization is associated with expansion of structural form, the result being the transformation of an erstwhile pidgin into a full language. Under Hall's definition, as well as that of many scholars of contact languages today, creolization is equated with nativization (adoption as a first language by children). However, research demonstrates that the transformation of a pidgin into a creole is sometimes achieved via general expansion of social domain, such that the language develops via heavy usage in a wide variety of contexts, accomplished by adults as well as by children. As such, it is perhaps more appropriate to equate the transformation of a pidgin into a creole not with nativization, but with expansion through extension in social role (Hymes, 1971: 79).

For example, Keesing (1988) demonstrates that Melanesian Pidgin English emerged as a jargon used by multi-ethnic ship crews on whaling ships in the Pacific in the early nineteenth century and then was transformed into the lingua franca among multi-ethnic plantation workers in the sandalwood and sea cucumber trades; he ascribes a relatively negligible presence to children at this stage. While one of the dialects of this language, Tok Pisin, has been adopted as a first language over the past few decades, Sankoff (1979) and Romaine (1988b: 68, 304) argue that the effects of nativization upon the language have been relatively minor, and in the meantime, even before its adoption as a native language, Tok Pisin displayed structure as elaborated as any creole, including grammaticalized markers of tense, mood, and aspect, embedding structures, and extensive development in the lexicon. This has led Tok Pisin to be often described as an expanded pidgin, a designation also applied to the only recently nativized English-based pidgins of West Africa such as Nigerian Pidgin English. What is significant is that these expanded pidgins are essentially indistinguishable from creoles in their level of structural complexity, and that manipulation by adults has effected that complexity.

It has been more specifically argued that it is high usage among speakers of mutually unintelligible substrate languages, rather than between superstrate and substrate speakers, that sparks expansion, given that superstrate–substrate communication will often take place within contexts of a rather sociolinguistically narrow variety. For example, the expanded character of Naga Pidgin can be ascribed more to its use among speakers of various Naga languages than to its relatively constrained use between Nagas and the Assamese. Similarly, Chinese Pidgin English only acquired a degree of fluency when used between speakers of unintelligible dialects of Chinese, rather than between the Chinese and the British (Whinnom, 1971: 104). Whinnom's related suggestion that contact only results in the creation of stable pidgins when speakers of two or more languages use another language for communication (so-called "tertiary hybridization") has, however, been disputed (see Thomason and Kaufman, 1988: 196–7).

Pidgins also frequently pass through various geographical and sociolinguistic contexts in the process of expansion. For example, Hiri Motu began as a register of Motu used in trade with subordinate groups along the Gulf of Papua, became the general lingua franca of the Port Moresby area with the arrival of Europeans, and went on to be spread by the native police force into the interior, where it spread because of its association with high status, economic development and integration, despite the fact that Motu itself was not natively spoken there (Dutton, 1985). Similarly, Lingala emerged as a trade pidgin used between speakers of a few closely related Bantu languages along the Congo River in Central Africa, but has long since been established in urban centers as a lingua franca used in business, education, and the military (Knappert, 1979). We have also seen how Melanesian Pidgin English began as a shipboard lingua franca, was adopted as a plantation language, and has finally become the reigning language of the inter-ethnic city context, associated with education and achievement. Thus we see that the pidgin–creole–de-creolization life cycle formulation, while useful, tends to obscure the rich variety of interactions which a pidgin language can have with its sociological setting.

While many pidgins undergo the types of expansion discussed above, just as many persist in pidgin form over long periods of time. Russenorsk, for example, showed no signs of expanding significantly: Trade was consistently vigorous, but nevertheless there was no need for the adoption of a trade language as a primary one, although it was sometimes acquired at an early age (Broch and Jahr, 1984: 55). Similarly, pidgins such as Chinook Jargon and pidginized Eleman and Koriki in Papua New Guinea experienced little significant expansion during their long lifetimes. The Hall formulation perhaps unwittingly gives an impression of inevitability; however, cases such as the ones above demonstrate that a pidgin only expands in response to sociological motivations licensing such expansion. In the absence of such motivation, pidgins remain reduced but functional trade vehicles.

Finally, most pidgins which do not experience expansion eventually undergo language death when the sociological motivations for their existence cease to exist. For example, after 1850, Norwegian merchants began acquiring fuller competence in Russian because of longer stays in Russia than had obtained in the past. As a result, Russenorsk, previously spoken by all levels of the trade community, became associated with the fishermen in particular, and looked down upon as inferior to the actual Russian spoken by the merchants. The *coup de grâce* was delivered by the incursion of the large-scale cash trade in the first decades of the twentieth century, which eventually eliminated the need for the old barter trade, the last bastion of Russenorsk (Broch and Jahr, 1984: 55–8). Attitudinal factors can also spell the death of a pidgin. Because of its association with white racism, Fanakalo, a pidginized Zulu, is being eliminated in favor of pidginized Town Bemba or CiBemba in Zambia (Holm, 1989: 555).

2.5 Distribution

Pidginization tends to be treated as an "exotic" phenomenon in the literature, as an "extreme" example of language restructuring. However, this perspective may well be an artifact of the monolingual Western perspective, given that pidginization has been exceedingly common worldwide. While creole languages tend to cluster in tropical locations where the European powers established plantation colonies from the fifteenth through nineteenth centuries, pidgins have been documented on all natively inhabited continents in all possible climates. Pidgins appear to represent a universal and common human response to the need for constrained communication between groups speaking unintelligible languages – a need which can arise almost anywhere on earth.

The sheer ordinariness of pidginization becomes clearer when we note various pidgins which are only scantily documented in the literature, such as the wide variety of Indo-Aryan pidgins in India, or the innumerable pidgins as yet undocumented in Papua New Guinea, the most linguistically diverse area in the world.[5] This conception is further reinforced by an awareness that countless pidgins have been lost to history; for example, in the eighteenth century, Scandinavia was host to various trade pidgins such as Borgarmålet, a Swedish-Lappish hybrid (Broch and Jahr, 1984: 51).

3 Creole Languages

3.1 *Creole features and subtypes*

As mentioned above, creoles are usually more complex and structurally elaborated than pidgins. The differences between the "pidgin" and "creole" stages are not so evident if the pidgin has been in existence for a long time and has stabilized and become the primary language of its speakers before nativization takes place – as with New Guinea Tok Pisin – (Sankoff, 1979; Bickerton, 1981: 3–4; Romaine, 1988b: 68, 304). However, the differences are clearer in cases of *early creolized creoles*, that is, creoles which acquire native speakers and/or become the primary languages of their speech community fairly quickly after the initial contact situation (within a generation), so that the contact vernacular is at a rudimentary and variable pre-pidgin or jargon stage when creolization takes place. Thomason and Kaufman (1988) refer to the process which produces such creoles as *abrupt creolization*, and they see it as having applied to many of the world's known creoles, including "creoles that arose in the context of the European slave trade in Africa, the Caribbean area, and several islands in the Indian Ocean" (p. 148). Like Thomason and Kaufman (1988), Bickerton (1988: 272) believes that early creolized creoles are the norm rather than the exception; but unlike them, he believes that Hawaiian Creole English (HCE) belongs in this category.[6]

Some of the features shared by creoles but lacking in (rudimentary, early stage) pidgins like Hawaiian Pidgin English include:[7]

1 Movement rules. For instance, the Guyanese Creole [GC] sentence *Jan bin sii wan uman* "John saw a woman" can be realized as *a Jan bin sii wan uman* to focus the subject, *a **wan uman** Jan bin sii* to focus the object, and *a **sii** jan bin sii wan uman* to focus the verb (Bickerton, 1981: 52).

2 An article system (p. 56) which distinguishes between definite noun phrases (GC *di buk* "the book"), indefinites (GC *wan buk* "a particular book"), and nonspecifics (GC *buk* "books").

3 The encoding of such tense, modality, and aspect distinctions as anterior, irrealis, and punctual by invariant, preverbal markers, for in-

stance, *bin, go* and *a* respectively in GC, *te, ava* and *ape* respectively in Haitian Creole [HC] (p. 59).

4 Facilities for relativization and other complex sentence embeddings, with or without a relative pronoun [RP], e.g., GC *bo mi granfaada bin ga wan ool boot, [ø RP] bin ton dong batam wan big manggo chrii [ø RP] bin de rait a head a di biling* "But my grandfather had an old boat [which was] turned down underneath a big mango tree [that] was right in front of the building" (Irene, quoted in Rickford, 1987: 148).

Besides early and late creolized creoles, distinctions have also been drawn (Bickerton, 1988: 269–70, Arends, 1995: 16–17) between *fort* creoles, *plantation* creoles, and *maroon* creoles. *Fort* creoles refer to contact vernaculars which developed in and around the European outposts on the West African coast between the sixteenth and nineteenth centuries, primarily between Europeans and local Africans working in the forts or assisting in the slave trade.[8] The English, like the Portuguese, had several such forts, and Hancock (1986) has suggested that they spawned a Guinea Coast Creole English (GCCE) which in turn became the source of many of the Caribbean English-based creoles. By contrast, the Spanish did not have such West African settlements, and McWhorter (1995a) has surmised that the rarity of Spanish-based creoles in the New World might be attributable to this fact. The assumption that the crucial sociohistorical crucible for New World creoles was not the New World plantation but the West African forts from which most slaves came is a fascinating but not unproblematic one; there is reason to believe that most of the "sale slaves" who reached the New World did NOT know GCCE or any other fort creoles, while the West African hired hands (*grumettoes*) and "castle slaves" most familiar with such creoles were least likely to have gone to the New World (Goodman, 1987; Rickford, 1987: 46–51, 53–6). *Plantation* creoles, as their names imply, are those which are assumed to have been created or developed on (primarily sugar) plantations in the Atlantic, Pacific, and Indian Oceans to which ethnically diverse groups of slaves or indentured laborers were brought from other parts of the world. The relation between the demographics and social structure of such plantation communities and the processes of pidgin-creole creation or development which took place therein is not in itself a new topic (cf. Alleyne, 1971; Baker, 1982), but it has been the source of considerable new research in recent years (Singler, 1990a, 1993; Arends, 1995; Rickford and Handler, 1995). Finally, maroon creoles are those spoken among descendants of maroons or runaway slaves who escaped from slavery and set up their own communities, usually in inland and relatively inaccessible areas. Saramaccan in Suriname, South America, is the best-known maroon creole. Its distinctive non-European features may be due in part to the relative isolation which maroonage provides (Price, 1973; Alleyne, 1986; Arends, 1995: 16).

3.2 Theories of origin

One of the oldest and most hotly contested issues in pidgin-creole studies is how these languages arose, or more specifically, how their similarities (and to a lesser extent their relatively simplified and mixed characters; cf. Muysken, 1988: 285–6) are to be explained. Originally, the competition was between *polygenetic* theories, which assume that most varieties arose independently at different times and in different places, and *monogenetic* theories, which assume that most varieties are derived from one or a small number of ancestors which subsequently diffused or spread to other locations. But for the past two decades, discussions of the bioprogram theory – which is neither polygenetic nor monogenetic – have dominated the literature.

Polygenetic theories have the potential attraction of being universally applicable and not requiring the implausible assumption that every one of the world's pidgins and creoles is historically related. But they face this recurrent challenge – if these varieties are independent creations, how are their similarities to be explained? The basic strategy which polygeneticists adopt is to point to one or more factors in the contact situations that create pidgins and creoles which might cause them to develop in parallel ways.[9]

One such factor – and one of tremendous interest to sociolinguists – is the parallel social contexts in which pidgins and creoles arise and the parallel functions they are required to serve. This is indeed a component of the so-called *Independent Parallel Development* theory attributed to Hall (1966) by Todd (1974: 31) and Romaine (1988b: 92–102) and the *Common Social Context* theory attributed to Sankoff (1980) by Muysken (1988: 286–7) and Muysken and Veenstra (1995: 128). But one searches in vain in Hall and Sankoff for any well developed functionalist theory of this type. Hall (1966) is essentially an exposition of the baby talk theory, one which recognizes both superstrate and (some) substrate influence in the context of imperfect second language acquisition (see below). Sankoff (1980) is a multifaceted collection of articles, including pioneering discussions of grammaticalization in relation to discourse; but none of them articulates the "strictly functionalist perspective: the slave plantations imposed similar communicative requirements" attributed to them by Muysken (1988: 287). Foley (1988: 164) comes closer to providing the functionalist perspective which the names of these theories seem to suggest, but primarily in recognizing the possible contributions of foreigner talk (see below). While one might hope, from a sociolinguist's perspective, that research will eventually yield more fully developed functionalist theories of pidgin-creole genesis, we should be wary of overstating the contextual similarities among trade and plantation situations whose details are on reflection quite diverse and as yet not sufficiently well known.

For Bloomfield (1933: 472–3), as for Hall (1966: 5), the parallel factor in polygenesis is the process by which speakers of the superstrate might have deliberately simplified their language to facilitate its understanding and acquisition by substrate speakers. In its initial formulations, this *baby talk* theory (so called because adults produce similar simplifications to facilitate comprehension by children) was both simplistic and racist.[10] But an even bigger problem for it was to explain how separate acts of simplification by speakers of different superstrate languages (English, French, Portuguese, Chinook) could result in pidgins and creoles with so many striking structural similarities. The *nautical jargon* theory – that pidgins and creoles are outgrowths of an international jargon developed and spread by ship's crews – could explain some of the lexical items (e.g., *kapsaiz* "turn over", *hais* "lift") found in many (European-based) pidgins and creoles, but not their structural similarity. The notion that there are widespread if not universal patterns of *foreigner talk* (Ferguson, 1971; Ferguson and DeBose, 1977) – and that these involve conventional reduction processes similar to those found in pidgins and creoles[11] – has served to legitimize and rescue the baby talk theory somewhat. But the baby talk theory has other weaknesses, including the fact that it is often substrate rather than superstrate speakers who are the main creators and users of pidgin-creole varieties (Whinnom, 1971), the fact that pidgins and creoles are usually unintelligible to uninitiated speakers of the superstrate, and the unlikelihood that central pidgin-creole features resulted from deliberate simplification. As Taylor (1963: 810) has noted:

> the predicative systems of these three creole languages [Martinique Creole, Haitian Creole, and Sranan] cannot be explained as reduced or corrupt versions of those found in French or English . . . these characteristics, though shared by many West African and other non-creole languages, would hardly suggest themselves to a Western European seeking to simplify his own speech.

In these latter objections lie the kernels of alternative polygenetic theories of origin. If one focuses on the substrate speakers rather than the superstrate speakers, one might regard their creation of pidgins (at least) as the product of limited *second language acquisition* (Bickerton, 1977; Andersen, 1983), seeing the parallel factor as the set of linguistic, cognitive and other factors which produce similar kinds of interlanguage (or, to use Ferguson and DeBose's less felicitous term, "broken language"). Considerable doubt has been expressed recently, however, about whether pidginization really involves attempts to acquire a target language, rather than attempts to create a medium for interethnic communication (Baker, 1990: 111). Thomason and Kaufman (1988: 174–94) argue, in fact, that only a perspective which assumes that both superstrate and substrate speakers were involved in *mutual linguistic accommodation* can account for *differences* among pidgins with respect to their inclusion of universally marked features, like the presence of duals and trials in the pronouns of Bislama and Tok Pisin, a feature of the Austronesian substrate. Of course, no single substrate can account for all of the world's pidgins and creoles, but Alleyne (1980a), Boretzky (1983), Lefebvre (1986), Holm (1986), McWhorter (1992), and others have argued that Kwa and other West African languages are sufficiently similar with respect to serial verb constructions and other features found in Saramaccan, Haitian, and other Caribbean creoles spoken by African-derived populations for substrate influence to be the most plausible explanation.[12] This theory, referred to as *Afro-genesis* by Muysken (1988), has been attacked by Bickerton (1984, 1994) and by Muysken and Smith (1995) for failing to account adequately for differences between possible West African source languages with respect to putative substrate features, for failing to provide a scenario for the transmission of substrate features into the emerging creole, and for failing to explain why some features of the substrate but not others were incorporated in the derived creoles. However, the debate on these issues is far from closed, as articles in the *Journal of Pidgin Creole Linguistics* will attest. Afro-genesis is itself a subvariety of *substratist* theories, and such theories have received a big boost from the work of Keesing (1988) on the Oceanic substrate in Melanesian Pidgin English.

Monogenetic theories, unlike their polygenetic counterparts, come in only two varieties. The first is a *broad scope* variety which suggests that many of the world's pidgins and creoles are derived from a Portuguese contact language developed in the course of fifteenth- and sixteenth-century contacts between Portuguese and West Africans, perhaps itself related to Sabir, the medieval lingua franca of the Mediterranean. This theory, and its associated relexification hypothesis (required to explain how French, English, and other varieties evolved from a Portuguese–West African base) produced a great deal of excitement in the 1960s and 1970s for several reasons, including its historical linking of widely separated Atlantic and Pacific varieties.[13] However, it has since fallen into disfavor, partly because it is patently inapplicable to many pidgins and creoles (those that had no direct or indirect contact with the Portuguese) and because it makes an assumption which den Besten and others (1995: 88) consider "irrational" – that pidginization and creolization, alone of all human conceptual and cultural activities, happened only once, rather than again and again. The other monogenetic theory is *restricted in scope* to the English-based pidgins and creoles, which Hancock (1986) sees as descendants of a putative Guinea Coast Creole English (GCCE) which developed on the West African coast in the sixteenth and seventeenth centuries. As noted above, one key question is whether GCCE or any similar entity was in fact spoken by significant numbers of "sale slaves" and transported by sufficient numbers of them to influence the development of English in various parts of the Caribbean. Rickford (1987) is skeptical, but McWhorter (1995b) is not.

The theory which has in fact dominated discussions of creole genesis since the 1980s is Bickerton's (1981, 1984, 1986) *Language Bioprogram Hypothesis* (LBH), which views creoles as inventions of the first generations of children who acquire them natively. According to Bickerton, children who were born into contact situations where rudimentary pidgins or jargons were spoken drew on a species-specific bioprogram to transform them into the early creolized creoles evident in Hawaii, Jamaica, Haiti, and the Sudan. On the face of it this is a polygenetic theory, since it posits independent creation in the

separate places in which creole languages developed (note that this hypothesis is strictly limited to creole rather than pidgin origins). But in a sense it
is simultaneously a monogenetic theory, insofar as it sees the development of
these creoles as guided by a single linguistic bioprogram which is common to
all human beings. In any event, the LBH is so different from traditional polygenetic and monogenetic theories that it defies categorization in their terms.

Evidence in favor of the bioprogram includes the contrasts between the
rudimentary HPE spoken by Japanese and Filipino immigrants who arrived
between 1900 and 1920 and the expanded HCE spoken by people born and
raised in Hawaii thereafter, and the fact that the very features in which HPE
and HCE differ – movement rules, TMA markers, and so on (see above) – are
those found in creoles from a variety of different lexical bases elsewhere. The
fact that the lexical source languages (English, French, Dutch) of these creoles
do not contain the features indicates that they did not provide them, and the
fact that the HPE-speaking immigrants do not use the features rules out
monogenesis and most varieties of polygenesis as likely explanations for their
presence in the creoles. A third bit of evidence is the fact that the language of
children in non-creole-speaking communities – supposedly representing the
early effects of the bioprogram – often includes features found in creoles.
According to the LBH, the first creole-speaking children would have been
quite unusual in terms of first language acquisition worldwide, insofar as the
children would have had more expertise in the language than their parents.
But their exceptional nature would have been due to the fact that they were
born into a situation in which the language they had to acquire was a rudimentary rather than a full-fledged one, and the fact that as children – unlike
adults who have passed the relevant development stage – they had access to
the bioprogram to expand it.

Arguments against the bioprogram have been varied.[14] One of the earliest
was the fact that the LBH is not a comprehensive theory of creole genesis
insofar as it does not account for non-European-based varieties like Lingala
(Mufwene, 1984), nor for late creolized varieties like Tok Pisin. A quite different argument is that the HPE documented by Bickerton was not the real
progenitor of HCE, but that the latter had its roots in an older and more fully
developed English-based pidgin which replaced the earlier pidginized Hawaiian as a lingua franca in the late nineteenth century (Goodman, 1985;
McWhorter, 1993, 1994; see note 6). Bickerton's analysis of the TMA system in
a number of creoles has also been challenged (cf. papers in Singler, 1990b),
with the creoles looking somewhat less uniform than he had suggested and
perhaps less likely to have been the product of a single bioprogram. Another
criticism is that Bickerton's LBH scenario posits a smaller role for the parents
of the first creolizing children and less influence of the substrate languages
than seems likely (Alleyne, 1980b, 1986; Goodman, 1985; Holm, 1986; Thomason and Kaufman, 1988: 163–5). Singler (1986, 1992) was also the first to
suggest that nativization might have taken a long time to be accomplished
because of the low birth and survival rates and the high death rates in many

plantation communities, with the implication that locally born children might have had a much smaller role in the creation of plantation creoles than in Bickerton's LBH scenario. Both demographic and linguistic evidence have been introduced in recent years in support of the gradualism hypothesis – the view that many creoles developed over a long period of time rather than in the short time-span LBH requires, and that stabilization rather than nativization was the crucial milestone in their genesis (Carden and Stewart, 1988; McWhorter, 1992; Arends, 1995; Arends and Bruyn, 1995).

In the face of these criticisms of and questions about the LBH, Bickerton has been far from silent, airing his rebuttals and clarifications principally in the pages of the *Journal of Pidgin and Creole Studies* (e.g., 1987, 1991, 1992, 1994). Bickerton's critics have invariably responded with rejoinders of their own (Thomason, 1992; Singler, 1992; McWhorter, 1994; Arends 1995), contributing to the "fractious energy" of the field to which we alluded earlier. Overall, it is probably fair to say that most creolists see some role both for universals and for substrate influence in creole genesis (cf. Mufwene, 1986, and other contributions in Muysken and Smith, 1986). But whether they regard the former as evidence for an innate "bioprogram," and how much of a role they attribute to one or the other of these key elements are issues on which they remain sharply divided.

3.3 *The creole continuum and decreolization*

In some communities (e.g., Guyana, Hawaii, Jamaica) in which a creole (or "basilect") coexists with a lexically related standard language (or "acrolect"), there exists a continuum of intermediate varieties (or "mesolects") between them, as illustrated by Allsopp's (1958) list of alternative ways of saying "I told him" in Guyana (cf. Bickerton, 1975: 9–14 for discussion):

$$
\begin{array}{ll}
\text{ai tould hɪm} & \text{(acrolect)} \\[1em]
\left.\begin{array}{l}
\text{ai toːld hɪm} \\
\text{ai toːl ɪm} \\
\text{ai tɛl ɪm} \\
\text{a tɛl ɪm} \\
\text{ai tɛl i} \\
\text{mi tɛl i}
\end{array}\right\} & \text{(mesolects)} \\[1em]
\text{mi tɛl am} & \text{(basilect)}
\end{array}
$$

The traditional account of such continua (DeCamp, 1971a) is that they are later developments from an earlier situation in which only the creole and the standard existed. Over time, on this account, creole speakers gained greater opportunity and motivation to decreolize or modify their speech in the direction of the standard, producing the intermediate mesolects in the process.

Challenging this view, Alleyne (1971) suggested that differences in the social experiences and attitudes of different groups of slaves in the colonies (for instance, house slaves vs field slaves, old hands vs new arrivals, locally born vs African-born) might have led to continuum-like variability right from the start. And Bickerton (1986: 226), noting that the earliest Africans in the colonies were initially outnumbered by Europeans and would have had more exposure to the superstrate, suggested that the creole continuum "must have formed 'backwards' . . . acrolect first, then mesolect, then basilect, as the pyramid of slave society slowly formed itself." (On this point, see also Baker, 1991a: 267, 277.) Mufwene (1988, 1989) is also strongly skeptical about the notion of decreolization, particularly insofar as it assumes a monolithic and relatively invariant creole as starting point, and insofar as its existence is inferred from synchronic rather than diachronic evidence.

However, one can agree that present-day continuum situations must have been variable almost from their inception (in the sixteenth and seventeenth centuries for the Caribbean, in the nineteenth century for Hawaii) while still assuming that they were produced by processes of language learning and shift which we might regard as "decreolization." For one thing, even house slaves who acquired acrolectal varieties of English are likely to have done so gradually and via a series of interlanguage stages – basilang, mesolang, acrolang – that are structurally reminiscent of the points along a decreolizing creole continuum (Schumann and Stauble, 1983; Rickford, 1987: 34). Second, while the current basilects, mesolect(s), and acrolects might have come into being one, two, or three hundred years ago,[15] there is little doubt that quantitative decreolization has occurred in the interim, in the sense that the proportion of basilectal speakers has been declining and the proportion of speakers who control mesolectal (if not acrolectal) varieties has been increasing (Alleyne, 1980a: 192–4; Rickford, 1983: 300ff.). Third, decreolization in the qualitative sense – in which basilectal features and varieties historically attested are no longer evident – has clearly occurred in some communities (cf. Winer, 1993: 6, for Trinidad and Tobago, Rickford and Handler, 1994, for Barbados). Finally, if we adopt what I have elsewhere (Rickford, 1979: 411–13, 1987: 34–5) referred to as a polygenetic rather than a monogenetic model of decreolization, its current applicability to continuum situations would remain very strong. In a monogenetic model, the creation of the continuum would have occurred only once – whether in the seventeenth century or the nineteenth – and subsequent decreolizing speakers would be seen as *adopting* or acquiring existing intermediate varieties. In a polygenetic model, however, decreolizing speakers would be seen as actively *creating* intermediate varieties as they attempt to shift from basilect to acrolect, retracing paths similar to those who have done so before them because they are moving between similar starting points and end-points and are motivated by similar sociolinguistic considerations.

A related issue is whether it is possible to regard African-American Vernacular English (AAVE) as a decreolized form of an earlier American plantation creole. Recent debate has moved beyond the polarized positions of creolists like Stewart (1967, 1968) and Dillard (1972) who favored the decreolization position and dialectologists like Davis (1970) and McDavid and McDavid (1971) who opposed it. Scholars who have considered the issue more recently tend to use quantitative and other variationist evidence and to draw on data from the African-American diaspora in places like Samaná in the Dominican Republic, or Liberia. Some of them are ardent opponents of the (de)creolization hypothesis (Poplack and Sankoff, 1987; Tagliamonte and Poplack, 1988, 1994) and some of them ardent proponents (Baugh, 1980; Holm, 1984; Singler, 1991; Winford, 1992a; Rickford, forthcoming). But there is an interesting inter- mediate group of scholars who were stronger supporters of the creole hypo- thesis in earlier times but now have reservations, feeling that AAVE might have been a semi-creole or had some partial creole influence without having been a full-fledged creole (Holm, 1991; Mufwene, 1992; Winford 1992b).

Controversies about creole continua involve more than the diachronic issue of whether they can be viewed as the products of decreolization. There is also the issue of whether synchronic variation in so-called continuum com- munities is either as continuous or unidimensional as continuum models seem to suggest, the issue of whether continuum analysts have given adequ- ate consideration to the social, stylistic, and human dimensions of continuum variation, and whether the assumption that continuum change is always unilinear – towards the acrolect – is correct. For discussion of these issues, see Rickford (1987: 15–39), Carrington (1992), Alleyne (1994), Winford (1994), and De Rooij (1995).

4 Conclusion

Pidgins and creoles are fascinating examples of the extent to which and the ways in which languages can be generated and shaped through language contact. The study of these languages has been going on for over 200 years (Magens, 1770), and sociolinguists have been interested in them almost from the inception of modern sociolinguistics itself (Ferguson, 1959; Hymes, 1971). In this paper we have tried to sketch out the theoretical, methodological, and practical significance of these languages for sociolinguistics, and then to present, in somewhat greater detail, the synchronic and diachronic issues which occupy scholars of pidgins, creoles, and creole continua. We have not been able to describe in as much detail the human – expressive, sociopolitical, educational, and economic – advantages and challenges which these languages offer their language users. Devonish (1986), Romaine (1992), and Alleyne (1994) are good references to consult to pursue these issues further.

The field of pidgin-creole studies is, as noted in our introduction, a field full of excitement and "fractious energy," one in which new discoveries are con- stantly being made and old ideas are constantly being challenged and overturned. Sociolinguists should find in this field much from which they can learn, and much to which they can contribute.

NOTES

1 We wish to express our gratitude to Derek Bickerton and Angela Rickford for comments on an earlier version of this paper, while absolving them of responsibility for any errors it contains.

2 In the examples that follow, the following words are from Russian: *moja, snai, eta, samme, tvoja*; the other words are from Norwegian, but *på* is derivable from both languages.

3 Russian has no equative copula, but Norwegian does.

4 Compare Bickerton's (1984: 178) *pidginization index*, critiqued by Singler (1990a) and modified by Bickerton (1992).

5 See Foley (1988) for documentation of Pidgin Yimas, combining elements of Yimas and Arafundi and virtually unknown in pidgin-creole studies before Foley's work.

6 Thomason and Kaufman (1988: 352, n 1) believe, as Goodman (1985), Holm (1986), and McWhorter (1994: 87–9) do, that HCE developed from a pre-existing nineteenth-century Pacific English pidgin which was more structured than the "Hawaiian Pidgin English" (HPE) of Japanese and Filipino immigrants discussed in Bickerton (1981) and elsewhere. However, on this issue the co-authors of this article have different views, Rickford feeling that little evidence has been presented to confirm the prior widespread existence in Hawaii of a stable nineteenth-century Pacific English pidgin, and disagreeing with McWhorter that the HPE of Japanese and Filipino immigrants can be dismissed as a "halting . . . second language register of an English contact language which had taken root long before their arrival." Rickford is particularly impressed with the extensive demographic and textual evidence on the nature and development of Pidgin Hawaiian, Pidgin English, and Creole English in Hawaii compiled by Roberts (1995a, b) and Bickerton (1995).

7 See Bickerton (1981: 51–72) for 12 such features in various creoles.

8 Although they are generally referred to as creoles, these contact vernaculars must clearly have been non-native varieties to many if not most of their users, although the children of European/African unions may have learned them natively, and they might have become primary languages for some to whom they were not a native language.

9 It should be noted that the people whose work we will classify as polygeneticist do not necessarily or consciously classify themselves as such.

10 For instance, from Hall (1966: 5): "The European . . . would assume that the native's incomplete efforts at speaking the European's language were due, not to insufficient practice, but to inherent mental inferiority. So the European would conclude that it was useless to use 'good language' to the native, and

would reply to him in a replica of the latter's incomplete speech, adding also some of the patterns of baby-talk commonly used by mothers and nurses in his own country. The aboriginal, not knowing any better, would assume that this was the white man's real language and would delight in using it." Interestingly enough, the opposite was true in Papua New Guinea, where one European missionary appears to have "delighted" in learning Motu, but later realized that he was receiving a deliberately simplified version of it (Dutton, 1985).

11 See Foley, 1988: 165, table 1 for a convenient summary of simplifying processes and their results.

12 As Thomason and Kaufman (1988: 162) note: "the typological fit between numerous syntactic structures in Atlantic creoles and corresponding structures in most or all relevant Niger-Congo languages is surely too close to be accidental."

13 See Thompson, 1961, Whinnom, 1965, and other works cited in DeCamp, 1971b, and Todd, 1974.

14 It is striking that some of the best-known introductory texts on pidgins and creoles (e.g., Mühlhäusler, 1986) and even more recent introductory sociolinguistics texts (e.g., Wardhaugh, 1992, and Romaine, 1994b) do not include any arguments against the LBH.

15 This hypothesis assumes the existence of normal (i.e., non-decreolizing) language change in the interim – that is, that the acrolect or standard variety of the twentieth century would not be identical with that of the seventeenth century, because of drift and other factors. Even so, it should be pointed out that the textual evidence for the existence of *all* the currently available varieties in earlier periods (cf. Rickford, 1987; Lalla and D'Costa, 1990) is not as strong as some commentators (e.g., Gilman, 1993: 151; McWhorter, 1995b) have claimed.

15 Language Contact and Language Degeneration

COLETTE GRINEVALD CRAIG

1 Introduction

Although the phenomenon of language death is as old as the recorded history of the languages of the world, its systematic study is a relatively new field of linguistics and sociolinguistics. A series of important publications clustered around the mid-eighties has confirmed its having become a recognized concern and field of study (Dressler, 1972; Dorian, 1981, 1989; Schmidt, 1985; Hill and Hill, 1986; Taylor, 1992, from an SSILA conference in 1985).

For linguists, the scientific interest of the process of language death resides in the fact that many obsolescent languages undergo structural changes, thereby offering more data for the study of the general process of language attrition, which itself should turn out to be telling of the nature of human languages in general. For sociolinguists, the interest resides more in the study of the causes and circumstances of language death, a topic addressed in Brenzinger's contribution (see chapter 16).

The linguistic documentation of dying languages is sometimes labelled as "salvage linguistics." This type of research raises issues of fieldwork methodology, in that standard quantitative studies may be severely constrained by the very nature of the situation and qualitative studies require sensitivity to the particular relation of the last speakers towards their stigmatized obsolescent language. In addition, fieldwork on obsolescent languages raises all the questions of ethics inherent to research on marginalized and dominated populations, issues which are best addressed before and monitored during the time of fieldwork. Work on endangered languages also raises the issue of the position of academics towards efforts aimed at counteracting the process of language death, including their role in language preservation and language revitalization projects.

2 Labelling and Defining the Subject and the Field of Study

The phenomenon of language death has been considered under a number of labels; some studies address the issue under the specific label of "language death" or sometimes "language demise," but much of the relevant literature can be found under the labels of "language drift," "language shift," or "language replacement."

Language death refers to the complete disappearance of a language. Only in extreme cases will the death of a language be the result of the sudden death of a whole community of speakers. More often, death comes by in a situation of languages in contact and shifting bilingualism. Although the process of progressive language death often shares much with the process of historical linguistic change, it differs from it in the speed and the scope of the change, and ultimately in its final outcome. In this sense, Latin is not a dead language, because it did not disappear but rather changed enough to be considered to have given rise to new languages. But dead are the hundreds of languages that have vanished in the Americas since colonization, for instance, many of them without leaving more than a topographical trace, as well as the hundreds that had vanished before colonization, under the dominion of powerful indigenous invaders, such as the Aztecs in Middle America or the Incas in the Andes.

The metaphor of death brings with it the idea that death is a process. One talks of "dying" or obsolescing languages when death appears to be imminent, and of "endangered" and "threatened" languages when their fate seems sealed but their death less imminent. Languages, like people, may succumb to slow or sudden deaths, and how much impact the process of death has on the structure of the language is in part a matter of the conditions of the dying process.

The most extreme case of "sudden language death" occurs in the course of rapid and total annihilation of a population, an example of which is the case of Tasmanian. A particular case of sudden death is also when the last speaker of a language which had survived among a very small group of very isolated speakers dies, as was the extraordinary case of the death of the Yana language at the time of the death of Ishi, "the last wild Indian in North America" (Kroeber, 1961). In such cases of sudden death, linguists have relatively little to say, as the last speakers carry into death a fully functional language.

The case of "radical language death" is similar to that of sudden death in that it involves massive dying or killing of the speakers, but there are survivors, who opt to abandon their language for being too much of a liability for their survival. Such is the story of the deaths of Lenca and Cacaopera and the near death of Pipil in El Salvador in the thirties, as a result of the genocide of the indigenous populations at the hand of governmental forces recorded in history as "la matanza" (Campbell and Muntzell, 1989: 185).

The most common case of language death is that of a gradual one that spans various generations; it is the most likely type of language death to be accompanied by linguistic change. Various cases of this type of death have been documented, for instance, Eastern Sutherland Gaelic in Europe (Dorian, 1981), Mexicano (Nahuatl) in Latin America (Hill and Hill, 1986), Norwegian in the US (Haugen, 1989), and Dyirbal in Australia (Schmidt, 1985).

Language death may appear to be sudden but may in fact occur as the result of a long period of gestation, a situation discussed by Dorian (1981: 51; 1986: 74) under the label "language tip." It typically involves a case of sudden shift from a minority language to a dominant language after centuries of apparent strong survival. The loss of the ethnic language, Dorian argues, is the result of a long-standing assault on the language which has eroded its support from the inside. It can be traced through the evolution of the patterns of language use in specific families, ones in which parents and older siblings speak an ethnic language while younger siblings suddenly do not acquire it.

Sometimes the process of death affects first the lower registers of the language, leaving for last a few pieces of the most formal register. This type of bottom-to-top death has also been referred to as the "latinate" pattern. This is the case of the Yaqui of Arizona, for instance, which is surviving only in ritual contexts but which crucially marks membership in the ethnic community (Hill, 1983).

To the variety of language death patterns mentioned above corresponds a variety of types of speakers that can be plotted on the continuum of the process of language death, from native fluent speakers to nonspeakers (Schmidt, 1985; Dorian 1981, 1985, 1989; Campbell and Muntzel, 1989; Dressler, 1991). Among the native and fluent speakers, one distinguishes between older fluent and younger fluent speakers; the latter typically speak a somewhat changed form of the language which is still accepted by the whole community. This distinction between older and younger speakers is found, for instance, in the Dyirbal situation documented by Schmidt (1985).

A category of speakers most typical of the situation of language death is that of the "semi-speakers," defined by Dorian as imperfect speakers "with very partial command of the productive skills required to speak it, but almost perfect command of the receptive skills required to understand it" (1983: 32, also 1977, 1981). Although considered members of the linguistic community, their deviations from the linguistic norms of the community are considered as mistakes and they typically exhibit insecurity about their knowledge of the language. This category of speakers is broad enough to accommodate a range of people from relatively fluent speakers to very limited speakers sometimes referred to as "terminal" speakers.

Another category of speakers that needs to be included in the study of dying languages is that of "rememberers." These are speakers who may have been, at an early stage in life, native fluent speakers, or who may simply have learned only some elements of the language a long time ago, and who, in either case, have lost much of their earlier linguistic ability. Rememberers are typical of a situation of fairly advanced stage of language death, and are found in relative isolation. Sometimes the language memory of such speakers can be triggered enough for them actively to participate in salvage linguistic projects, but at times such speakers have been so traumatized about their speaking a stigmatized language that nothing can help them recall much of it.

3 Theoretical Approaches to the Study of Language Death

The process of language death itself has received numerous labels, such as language obsolescence, loss, decay, decline, attrition, contraction, or deacquisition. These labels reflect a general search for the similarities and the differences that relate it to other types of linguistic dynamism, such as first and second language acquisition, creolization and decreolization, aphasia, weakening of a first or second language, and historical change. Ultimately the goal is to discover what clues to organizational principles in language and in human cognition generally all these manifestations of language dynamism may provide. The assumption behind such concerted effort is that all cases of language change involve "the same functional and formal parameters of linguistic structure and [are] embedded in the same matrix of socio-cultural and neuropsychological determining factors irrespective of the direction of change" (Hyltenstam and Viberg, 1993: 25).

The putative relation between language death and language acquisition has been articulated in the "regression hypothesis" which claims that the process of language loss is a mirror image of that of language acquisition, i.e., that what is lost first is what is learned last. The original hypothesis was presented by Jakobson (1941) on the basis of phonological materials only. While this "regression hypothesis" has not been upheld in recent research on language acquisition and aphasia, it has not been adequately tested yet for the case of language loss, mostly for lack of sufficient research (de Bot and Weltens, 1991). The regression hypothesis presupposes that the processes of language acquisition and language loss are both gradual and patterned in identifiable sequenced steps, but research in the field of language death has not produced enough data yet to establish such patterns with any certainty (Dorian, 1989).

As for what could be learned from a comparison of language death with the other language in contact processes of pidginization, creolization and decreolization (see chapter 14), the assessment is the same, that there has not yet been enough systematic research on language contact phenomena to produce data comparable enough to, for instance, prove or disprove Bickerton's bioprogram hypothesis. Drawing a parallel between obsolescent language and pidgin language reveals common monostylism and reduced grammar, but the two differ in major ways, in the use of the languages and in the attitude of the speakers, as well as in the modes of acquisition.

Language death can also be studied as a special case of language attrition, a general term that includes different manifestations of language loss, such as aphasia and first or second language attrition, but productive hypotheses about the possible linguistic attributes of linguistic attrition are still in need of being generated (Andersen, 1982; Menn, 1989).

In sum, theorizing about language death has been largely articulated in the context of comparing it to other instances of language dynamism somewhat better known, as evidenced by several recent collections on the subject (Dorian, 1989; Seliger and Vago, 1991; Hyltenstam and Viberg, 1993). Ultimately, the goal of such research is to identify linguistic attributes of language progression and language regression in the hope that research on these dynamisms will have a bearing on the formulation of current linguistic theories, be they of a formal or a functional leaning.

4 Effects of Language Death on Language Structure

The process of language death affects all aspects of language use and language structure. Although the types and extent of language change depend on the sociopolitical and sociocultural context of the language death situation, it has not been possible so far to establish any more causal relations between context and linguistic changes in the case of language death than in the case of other situations of languages in contact. A good place to start an overview of the linguistic attributes of language attrition is Andersen (1982) and Campbell and Muntzel (1989), both of which are meant to be blueprints for research which promote cross-linguistic and cross-disciplinary perspectives.

4.1 Loss of registers and language forms associated with them

In a larger sociolinguistic and ethnolinguistic perspective, the first level of linguistic loss correlates with the loss of certain functions of the language. The most widespread case is that of the loss of higher functions, such as the use of the language in the public arena, including the sociopolitical and religious traditions which necessitate the handling of some formal style of language.

A case in point is the monostylism of terminal speakers of Breton who control only casual styles for intimate routine interactions (Dressler and Wodak-Leodolter, 1977; Dressler, 1991: 101). Another reported instance of reduction of language due to loss of register is the loss of frequency of use of subordinate clauses in Cupeno and Luiseno from southern California – languages for which subordinate clauses were a mark of the most highly valued style of language, the one used in public speeches.

Although the loss of some styles of language implies the loss of some specific discourse patterns characteristic of them, it is worth noting that such a loss in the obsolescent language may be partially compensated by the transfer of characteristic discourse patterns into the new dominant language of the speakers' community. Such a case of transfer is documented for Koyukon Athabaskan, which appears to be dying fairly suddenly but being replaced with a very specific community-wide variety of English which provides a strong sense of Koyukon identity for its speakers (Kwatcha, 1992).

Sometimes also, as mentioned in the discussion of the different types of language death, the pattern of loss is the reverse, with the more informal registers being lost and the more formal aspect of the language being the last one preserved, such as the formal language of prayers and incantations. This kind of latinate pattern is described for Southern Tzetal of southern Mexico, for which only four prayers were preserved that could be recited from memory by only four men, who could not give more than broad paraphrases of their meaning (Campbell and Muntzel, 1989: 185).

4.2 Lexical loss

The investigation of lexical attrition in cases of language death is not a straightforward matter of observation, as the general strategy of semi-speakers with limited linguistic resources is speech avoidance. Absolute lexical loss predictably involves words for objects that are not culturally relevant anymore. The case of body parts is interesting, because in some situations it is said to be an area of the lexicon resistant to loss, while it is specifically noted as one of loss in other situations. The loss of body-part lexicon is reported for a semi-speaker of Ontario Cayuga who, for instance, gave the word "foot" for "thigh," "buttocks" for "hip," and could not supply terms for "ankle" or "toe," "eyebrow" or "cheeks" (Mithun, 1989: 248).

In situations of long-term language contact and widespread bilingualism, one of the strategies to compensate for the widespread loss of native lexicon is one of replacement with vocabulary from the dominant language, referred to in the literature as the process of "relexification." Relexification has been much discussed in the context of creolization and decreolization, but it is also found in instances of language shift which lead to the death of a minority language, such as the situation of Tlazcalan Nahuatl documented by Hill and Hill (1977).

4.3 Loss in phonology

Three basic principles underlying observed phonological changes in cases of language attrition were proposed by Anderson (1982). The first one is that change results in fewer phonological distinctions, as amply demonstrated for

East Sutherland Gaelic (Dorian, 1981) or Breton (Dressler, 1972). An example from Pipil of El Salvador is the loss of contrastive vowel length which has no counterpart in Spanish. The second principle is that this simplification of the phonological system is counteracted by a pressure to preserve distinctions which are common to both languages in contact. The third principle is that distinctions with a high functional load will also be preserved, even if they do not exist in the other language.

Discussion about the weight of external factors (influence of dominant language) vs internal factors (principles of markedness) in changes observed remains inconclusive. In some cases, like the merger of the postvelar/q/ to velar/k/ in Tuxtla Chico Mam, the change could be attributed to either external or internal factors: Spanish does not have postvelars, and postvelars are more marked phonologically than velars (Campbell and Muntzel, 1989: 186). Such situations also point to the possibility of language change being the result of multiple causation, a principle found at all levels of language, not just in phonology.

Relaxation of phonological rules also creates new variations in the obsolescent language, when the application of rules becomes optional. Such is the relaxation of the final devoicing of l in Pipil which results in the free variation of l/l [devoiced] in final position (Campbell and Muntzel, 1989: 189). Another mark of dying language phonology is the occasional excessive use of some marked feature due to imperfect learning and probably also to the value given to the feature as a marker of identity. An example is the excessive glottalization reported in the speech of a speaker of Xinca (Campbell and Muntzel, 1989: 189).

4.4 Loss in morphology

Loss of morphology, in the form of reduction of allomorphy and levelling of paradigms is relatively well-documented and the object of reasonable hypothesizing by Andersen (1982: 97). Semi-speakers of Southern Sutherland Gaelic for instance were insecure about the gender and appropriate case of nominals, as well as the future and the conditional suffixes, while preserving the past tense better (Dorian, 1977). Obsolescing Dyirbal was also shown to have lost several of its morphological characteristics, including its original ergativity (replaced with an SVO nominative–accusative pattern) and set of case markers, and its very complex noun classification system (reduced to a simple gender system based on animacy and sex) as documented in Schmidt (1985, 1989). In Oklahoma Cayuga, a polysynthetic language at a stage of incipient obsolescence, language attrition takes the shape of a reduced productivity of the system of affixation which cumulates elements of background information on verbs. Even if the speakers still know all the suffixes, they may hesitate to combine several within a single verb form (Mithun, 1989: 248).

4.5 Loss in syntax

Losses in syntax are most often cases of attrition in the use of certain syntactic construction rather than the actual reduction of particular syntactic patterns. It is commonly reported that morphological tense/aspect or voice forms (such as future or passive) are dropped in favor of periphrastic ones, which become overused.

A classic example in this category of language loss is the demonstration of the loss of subordinate clauses in Cupeno and Luiseno already mentioned in section 4.1 (Hill, 1973). The same reduction in frequency of subordinate clauses is also documented for obsolescing Dyirbal. In Dyirbal, other syntactic signs of attrition include a breakdown in agreement rules operating in noun phrases and verb complex, a rigidification into SVO pattern of the tradition-ally extremely free word order, as well as a loss of the S-O pivot clause linking device that made Dyirbal a key language in the investigation of syntactic ergativity (Schmidt, 1985, 1991).

4.6 Articulating language structure and language use

To close the section on the impact of language death on language structure a reminder may be appropriate: Research on language shift and language death should always combine ethnographic and linguistic dimensions if it is to address the key problem of such situations, which is the articulation between the structure that dying languages may take and the use that is made of such languages. Such studies of the speech of the types of speakers associated with linguistic changes – younger fluent speakers and semi-speakers – should ideally include both language comprehension and language production, oral and written language where relevant, and all parts of grammar, including discourse structures.

5 On Fieldwork Methodology for Work on Endangered Languages

A traditional "field methods" course of the kind offered on many university campuses as part of graduate training programs in linguistics does little to prepare one for the realities of a field situation in general, and falls even shorter of preparing one for fieldwork on a dying language, an inherently more complex situation. Even if all fieldwork situations are essentially unique, it is still possible to outline some of the characteristics of fieldwork on obsolescing languages that make such experiences particularly challenging.

5.1 The responsibility of the field linguist

One of the burdens of fieldwork on endangered languages is to face the fact that in all likelihood one is and will be the only linguist ever to document this language, in view of the shortage of trained field linguists to attend to the documentation of the thousands of languages and dialects rapidly vanishing around the world today. Owning up to being "the" linguist for a dying language implies a particular approach to the work to be carried out in the field. For the sake of the field of general linguistics, the documentation must be both as reliable and as complete as possible in all areas of language structure, a task which necessitates adequate training in all subfields of general linguistics. For the sake of contributing to the advancement of the relatively new field of language death, the documentation of language structure must also be done in the context of a broader documentation of the language in use. This means paying particular attention to sociolinguistics while attending to grammar.

Working on a dying language also means being particularly careful not to filter out any information on the language and its use on the basis of theoretical prejudices, in view of the fact that the process of language death itself has not yet been documented adequately enough to be understood well in its specificity, and that one cannot anticipate the questions linguistics will ask in future of the data gathered. All this to say that the field linguist working on a dying language may feel competing pressures between the demands of an academic research career (focused and currently theoretically relevant work produced within time limits) and a responsibility to the field in the longer run for as complete and accurate a record as possible, to say nothing of the responsibility to the community of speakers, which will be addressed below.

5.2 Working with speakers of dying languages

It is one thing to talk academically about the different kinds of speakers found in a situation of language death, quite another to work with that reality. Field linguists usually seek out totally fluent speakers with some native linguistic talent and interest, but the more dire the situation of the language, the less choice the linguists have. A dying language means fewer speakers to choose from, and sometimes no choice at all. Working on the process of language obsolescence itself means by definition working with marginal speakers overlooked in the usual linguistic fieldwork, the semi- and terminal speakers mentioned above. And one characteristic of such speakers is their lack of linguistic confidence; this often translates into a heightened tension in the process of data gathering which is not to be underestimated and which has been widely reported in the literature on language death (Dorian, 1977, 1981, 1986; Schmidt, 1985; Dressler, 1991; Craig, 1992).

5.3   *Field methodology*

To talk about language obsolescence, one would ideally need to establish a linguistic norm or base from which to evaluate the type of change induced by the process of language death. However, the same reasons that hasten the demise of the language make establishing such a base often difficult if not downright impossible. Dying languages are usually the languages of very marginalized populations whose language has not received linguistic attention previously, hence it is common not to have materials that reflect the past "healthy" state of the language. An advanced stage of obsolescence also means that few speakers are left and the common impossibility of any standard quantitative research. The social marginality of the communities of speakers, and within them of the last speakers, also severely limits the possibilities of experimental methodologies.

   "Real time" studies in which older documentation of the language is compared to the present state of decay are rare in the literature, but a good example is Hill (1973) in which textual material on Cupeno and Luiseno from southern California was available over a span of 50 years. The data were abundant and varied enough to show that the reduction in the use of subordinate clauses was an attribute of the process of language death, independent of speaker, style, topic, or recording technique.

   More available is the possibility of a compensatory type of study referred to as "apparent time" study, in which the speech of older, and supposedly more traditional and "better" speakers, is compared to that of younger speakers who may be fluent and have acquired full communicative competence but who are also agents of language change. This is the major strategy of the two most comprehensive studies of the process of language death to date: that of Eastern Sutherland Gaelic (Dorian, 1981) and that of Dyirbal (Schmidt, 1985). Otherwise, information on language death comes from the kind of informal comparison made post facto with data collected not with a study of language death per se in mind, as in Mithun (1989).

   The main methodology in which students receive some training in the traditional university linguistic field methods courses, that of direct elicitation, is also about the most delicate to use in situations of language obsolescence. First conjure up the image of a work session somewhere in the tropics with an illiterate rain-forest dweller, a fluent speaker of his/her language with whom one shares a shaky knowledge of a working language, then imagine yourself asking this speaker to translate something like "If I had known that he was not going, I would have stayed" to check on conditionals in the language. Chances of the linguist getting anything close to an actual translation of this sentence are actually very very slim, as experienced fieldworkers know. And turning to asking about grammatical judgments is even less reliable, since the concept of grammaticality is a very elusive notion for speakers of unwritten, nonstandardized, and generally stigmatized languages. A safer route to the documentation of such languages is to collect samples of natural speech, narrative texts being a standard type of text collected, to work out with bilingual speakers a transcription and a translation for them, and then to tackle the morphemic and syntactic analysis through controlled direct elicitation from the texts themselves. There is another way around the problem, one few linguists have the genius, the inclination, or the time for, which is for the linguist to learn to speak the language to be able to conduct interviews in it (Ken Hale being one of the most famous for doing this). But obsolescent language means limited exposure to the language to be learned and even more limited opportunities for practice.

Now what happens when the language investigated is a dying language and the language is not spoken in the community anymore, and the older speakers can't or won't tell stories to a tape recorder, or some will but they can't help transcribe and translate them, and the semi- and terminal speakers available can't do it either or won't do it because it would look like disrespect toward the elder to give one's personal interpretation of someone else's account? What about "methodology" then? One hears about linguists in the US who participated in the survey of Californian languages sitting next to stricken older last speakers for hours waiting for them to provide some trickle of information, a few lexical words, a truncated verbal paradigm.

Methodologically one is better off studying the process of language death if one deals with a less terminal stage of it (but one cannot always choose), and studies a situation more likely to be referred to as one of language shift. In such a situation, there is enough of a population of fluent elder speakers, fluent younger speakers and semi-speakers to be able to turn to quantitative methodologies, based on the collection of data through surveys and questionnaires (Dorian, 1981; Schmidt, 1985). But rarely will it be possible to model research on dying minority/ethnic languages after the type of research done at present on the language shift of immigrant populations of Europe or the USA, such as the ones discussed by De Bot and Weltens (1991) or Silva-Corvalán (1991), for instance.

As for an experimental approach of the type used in the studies of language loss presented in Lambert and Freed (1982) or De Bot and Weltens (1991), which were based largely on grammatical judgments, it would seem unlikely that it would be even conceivable in many actual field situations of language death.

Salvage linguistics, as fieldwork on dying languages is sometimes called, is therefore characterized by field conditions which are not often amenable to the research methodologies taught in field methods and other methodological academic courses in linguistics departments.

6 Fieldwork Ethics for Work on Endangered Languages

As work on endangered languages is becoming an acknowledged priority of the linguistic profession, it also becomes necessary to develop a more consciously ethical model of field research in the face of increasingly more complex field situations.

6.1   *Response of the profession to the situation of endangered languages*

There are signs of an increasingly orchestrated response of the linguistic profession to the issue of the rapid decline of the vast majority of the languages of the world. Linguists are becoming engaged in the debate of whether and how to document, protect, and maintain endangered languages, much as biologists before them became engaged in the protection of endangered animal and plant species (Wurm, 1991; Krauss, 1992).

In the US, the debate has progressed through a chain of events in the Linguistic Society of America, starting with a special symposium on endangered languages in 1991, which was followed by the LSA resolution to respond to the situation by "encouraging the documentation, study, and measures in support of obsolescent and threatened languages" (LSA Bulletin no. 131), and by the creation of the LSA Committee on Endangered Languages, which established special sessions on endangered languages at the 1995 LSA meeting (Ken Hale, president). The debate on the position of field linguists working on endangered languages can be partly followed in a series of "Language" publications, starting with Hale and others (1992), debated by Ladefoged (1992), and refuted by Dorian (1993a).

Meanwhile the Permanent International Committee of Linguists sponsored the publication of a state of affairs study of endangered languages (Robins and Uhlenbeck, 1991) in time for the 1992 International Congress of Linguists in Quebec, which focused on the case of endangered languages.

The earliest and most intense scene of debate however was Australia, where field linguists were confronted in the 1980s with the issue of what constitutes responsible linguistics in the context of work on endangered aboriginal languages. In response to the statement of "Linguistic Rights of Aboriginal and Islander Communities" formulated by the Aboriginal Language Association in 1984, the Australian Linguistic Society endorsed in 1990 a statement of professional ethics which makes explicit the responsibility of the linguist toward the linguistic community studied (Wilkins, 1992: 174).

The issue of endangered languages is being raised in most parts of the world today by indigenous communities of speakers. In the US a move to protect Native American languages from the dangers of the English Only Movement led to the Native Language Act of 1990, which establishes the right of native communities to protect, maintain, and develop their ethnic languages. In Latin America it was a central theme of all the protests of indigenous peoples against the 1992 quincentenary celebrations of the supposed "discovery" of the Americas. A place to sense the new relation being established in much of the Americas between linguists and indigenous speakers is Guatemala, where

Mayan speakers have been articulating their expectations of linguists working on Mayan languages (Cojti, 1990; England, 1992).

An important point to make is that the responsibility toward endangered languages, as spelled out in the LSA 1992 resolution, encompasses "fostering the granting of degrees, positions, and promotion in academic institutions for such work," which is to say that the responsibility is not limited to linguistic fieldworkers. All faculty members, independent of their own sphere of specialization, can therefore contribute to minimizing the academic dissonance often noted between the demands of work on endangered languages and the demands of traditional academic careers, and make the work possible.

6.2 Fieldwork framework for fieldworkers: responsibility to the people studied

The complexity of research based on fieldwork resides in part in balancing multiple responsibilities toward various constituents, such as the people studied, the academic profession, and the sponsors. There is no tradition in the field of linguistics of discussing such issues of ethics, although a fairly ample literature on the matter exists in other fields that also rely on fieldwork, such as various branches of sociology or anthropology. Recent debates on the topic of fieldwork ethics are partly reflected in the updated versions of a number of professional codes of ethics in the social sciences, one particularly relevant for linguists being the 1990 revision of the American Anthropological Association code of ethics, for instance.

Doing fieldwork today is clearly not what it was at the turn of the century, or 50, or even 20 years ago. This evolution of a fieldwork framework is well captured in a recent work by Cameron and others (1993) which focuses on the issue of the power relationship between the researcher and the researched and outlines three frameworks. The "ethical framework" is the traditional academic framework of research ON the people, that of the time of the first codes of ethics of the profession; the "advocacy framework" which emerged in the seventies in the midst of social movements is about research ON and FOR the people, while the "empowerment framework" is a framework in the making that responds to the social conditions of present-day field situations and is about research ON, FOR, and WITH the people.

This last framework is characterized by a basic collaborative approach which establishes reciprocity between researcher and researched. Models of such collaborative relationships between academic linguists and indigenous communities are the Hualaapai project described by Watahomigie and Yamamoto (1987) and the Yipirinya Aboriginal project described by Wilkins (1992).

Working FOR and WITH the people means linguists getting involved in language maintenance and language revitalization projects. It also means building into the work the training of native and regional linguists whenever possible, as recommended in the LSA resolution too. Language revitalization of obsolescent languages is an issue of debate well articulated by Fishman (1991) who argues that it is a matter of ideology whether the attempt is even considered desirable (see also Dorian, 1987, for reasons for it). For those of the linguistic profession who believe it is, the question then turns to whether "reversing language shift" is possible, and if it is, what the responsibility of the linguists in the process might be.

An example of such a project which combines academic salvage linguistics and community language management is the Rama Language Project, a case of language revitalization of a very obsolescent language for ethnic identity purposes, led by a fluent semi-speaker language rescuer, and described by Craig (1992a, b).

7 Conclusion: Setting an Agenda

Priority should be given to the documentation of endangered languages, for the intrinsic scientific value of the knowledge encapsulated in those languages, for the human value of their role in cultural identity, for the scientific interest in the process of attribution of which language death is a case, for what aspects of human cognition are reflected in language structure.

There is a need for linguists to couple salvage linguistics and archiving efforts with their participation in efforts at revitalizing or maintaining threatened languages. The linguistic research must be as comprehensive as possible and address the issue of the articulation of language structure with language, as much remains to be understood about the actual process of language death. On the other hand, the demands of coupling academic research and language revitalization work is best handled by teams of academics in negotiated fieldwork and collaborative projects in which the participation of the affected population is effective and real.

Part III Linguistic Dimensions of Society

16 Language Contact and Language Displacement

MATTHIAS BRENZINGER

1 Introduction

The term "language displacement" will be employed in this chapter to refer to the processes preceding the extinction of languages. Whereas Craig investigates the effects of language shift on the structures of the disappearing languages (see chapter 15), contextual aspects of these processes will be dealt with here. Within this frame of reference declining and replacing languages, shifting speech communities, as well as settings of language displacement, will be discussed and illustrated. The process of language shift is the focus of the last part.

2 The Frame of Reference of Language Displacement

In all parts of the world, we observe an increasing tendency among members of ethnolinguistic minorities to bring up their children in a language other than their own mother tongue, thereby abandoning their former ethnic languages. These changes in language use by individuals might ultimately lead to the irreversible disappearance of the minority's original language. The new one, that is, the replacing language, is in many cases one of a few fast-spreading languages such as English, Mandarin (Chinese), Russian, Hindi-Urdu, Spanish, Portuguese, Arabic, French, Swahili, and Hausa.

No consensus has been reached among scholars on the extent of language displacement, although spectacular statements have been put forward in this regard. Hill (1978: 69) estimates that in the last 500 years at least half of the languages in the world have disappeared, and Krauss (1992) proposes that only 10 percent of the present languages of the world are "safe" and therefore not threatened by extinction in the future. Quite frequently scholars dispute the above statements, some in principle claiming that there is no such thing as language death at all, while others insist that language displacement never took place on a large scale and that only a few languages are threatened by extinction. The numerous language shifts and cases of language death addressed in this chapter should, however, suffice to demonstrate that language displacement is a matter of serious concern throughout the world.

2.1 The subject matter: Languages

In situations of language displacement, two opposing languages are typically involved, one which is replacing and one which is being replaced. The most common occurrence is that of a dominant, spreading language ousting a receding language.

The replacing language   As mentioned above, few languages play a major role as replacing languages within a global context. English is in a replacing position in relation, for example, to Australian Aboriginal languages, Indian languages in North America, and Celtic languages in Great Britain. Many languages have already become extinct in these language shifts through being replaced by English. The decline of the Celtic languages in Great Britain resulted in the extinction of Cornish and Manx with the deaths of the last speakers in 1777 and 1974; other Celtic languages, namely Gaelic in Scotland and Irish in Ireland, are entering a vulnerable stage, while only Welsh, with about half a million speakers, seems to be resisting the overwhelming pressures from English – at least for the time being. Considering its role as a replacing language, Görlach (forthcoming) demonstrates the impact of English in focusing on European contact situations.

"It is through our language that we exist in the world other than as just another country," stated Pompidou some 20 years ago (*The Economist*, July 9, 1994). For more than 350 years the Académie Française has tried to safeguard the French language by exercising attempts at linguistic purification to prevent it from becoming "bastardized." Whereas in 1539 King Francis I issued the Edict of Villers-Cotterets to establish French as challenging the then prestigious Latin among the educated elites, French developed into a suppressive language only in the final third of the nineteenth century. Then the French State started to discriminate against indigenous languages abroad and in France. (The British, in accordance with the policy of "divide and rule," supported the dominant languages in their colonies.) Language policy in francophone Africa was based on the use of French, since "les dialectes africains ne sont pas des langues de civilisation" (Davesne, 1933: 6). On the African continent, however, French didn't replace a single local language, but it had a strong impact on the minority languages in its own country. Until very recently, French language policy was explicitly aiming at replacing minority languages in France. President Pompidou stated in 1970: "Il n'y a pas de la place pour les langues minoritaires dans une France destinée à marquer l'Europe de son sceau" (Finkenstaedt and Schröder, 1992: 36).

Replacing languages on the African continent do not belong to the limited set of so-called world languages, but the vast majority are indigenous languages with a national, regional, or merely local distribution (cf. pp. 278–9). In some rare cases a language may be replaced by more than one other language. One example of this phenomenon is that of the Ligbi language in Ivory Coast. Whereas the majority of this ethnolinguistic group, numbering about 10,000, live in Ghana and still speak their own language, the 3,000 to 5,000 Ligbi in the Ivory Coast have abandoned their former ethnic tongue. According to their religious faith, the Islamic Ligbi shifted to Dyula as their new language, whereas the others adopted Kulang'o, a minor Gur language (Raimund Kastenholz, personal communication).

The replaced language The other role in language shifts is played by the language which is being replaced, either voluntarily or by force. So-called "dead languages," such as Latin, were never displaced but developed into daughter languages. Present-day French and Italian derived from Latin and "normal" language change processes affecting the language structure gave rise to these new languages. Complete language displacement, on the contrary, is characterized by the death of an ethnic tongue, which implies that the language is not transformed into a successive language.

Which languages are then, through the process of language displacement, in danger of becoming extinct? Whereas in most parts of the world it is quite obvious which languages are endangered, such as the American Indian languages in the US or Australian Aboriginal languages in Australia, this is not so clear in the many regions of Africa. In the following the term "minority language" will be used simply to indicate that a particular language is threatened by extinction. A seemingly obvious criterion for identifying minority languages is the size of the ethnolinguistic community.

In her studies of Australian languages, Schmidt regards languages spoken by more than 250 people as viable languages – the most widespread of the Aboriginal languages does not exceed 5,000 speakers anyway. In contrast to that, the Ogoni people in Nigeria regard themselves, though numbering 500,000, as a minority and state in their "Ogoni Bill of Rights" of December 1991, addressed to the international community, "that the Ogoni languages . . . are undeveloped and are about to disappear, whereas other Nigerian languages are being forced on us." Out of 400 languages spoken by the estimated 100 million Nigerians, over 380 are widely given the status of minority languages (Agheyisi, 1984).

These two examples demonstrate that the number of speakers is not an unambiguous indicator for detecting the actual risk of a language being replaced. Small speech communities, of course, are more susceptible to existential changes, which can result in a rapid decline of their ethnic tongue. The mere fact that only a few parents may decide not to use the minority language with their children already results in endangering the entire transmission from one generation to the next. Intermarriage and migration from rural to urban regions by just a few members can have a dramatic impact on the survival of a minority language. There are, however, many languages with small numbers of speakers but with strong loyalties which seem not to be threatened. Since these statistical facts do not suffice to identify minority languages, this concept has to be contextualized.

The most serious indicator of the vitality of a language, however, may be the ratio between the number of members of the ethnic group and the number of speakers of the ethnic tongue. That would mean an ethnic group with say 200,000 members, of whom only 50,000 were speakers of the ethnic tongue, would be regarded as being endangered, whereas a community with 3,000 members but 2,900 speaking the ethnic tongue would be seen as representing a healthy state. For example, the Zaramo and Bondei on the northern coast of Tanzania, both over 200,000 with regard to ethnic membership, are about to abandon their languages in favor of Swahili (Batibo, 1992: 88). The language of the Baiso of southern Ethiopia, even though the community numbers only 3,260 people, is not threatened by extinction in the near future since all Baiso speak the ethnic language.

Minority languages are languages which exist in environments hostile to them – the schools, media, administration, etc., being dominated by other languages. As they are limited to being used exclusively within the speech community, the external threat to minority languages derives from these other domains and the weight of pressure falls in line with the importance these domains hold within the community. Whereas many ethnolinguistic minorities on the African continent are not exposed to national education and media, this is not the case for most other minorities.

To reach a real insight into language shifts one has to study the speech community, as this is the scene in which language displacement takes place, as well as the social environment of the speech community.

2.2 The place of encounter: The speech community

Even though languages are spoken by individuals, it is in speech communities that languages survive or die. Members of ethnolinguistic communities shift from their old language to a new language and finally abandon the old ethnic tongue.

On account of individual shifts, for example, by urban elites or by speech communities in a diaspora, no languages die. And not all languages have died in shifting speech communities. Some have disappeared with the extinction of the entire monolingual community, as was the case with the Tasmanian people (Swadesh, 1948), the Yahi and Uto-Aztecan on San Nicolas Island (Hill, 1983), or the Yamana of Tierra del Fuego (Gusinde, 1933).

The extinction of ethnic languages in most cases results from a complete shift of an entire speech community. Some languages, however, "survive" the language shift in certain domains. Ge'ez, for example, is the liturgical language used by the Ethiopian Orthodox Christian Church, but to say it "survives" is somewhat misleading since, although all Orthodox Christians in Ethiopia study Ge'ez texts and songs, they are not able to communicate in this language.

Unwritten minority languages may also be employed in ritual contexts or as secret languages, but their use is rarely limited to such domains. Functional shifts in language use patterns reduce minority languages in most cases to being employed at least within the family and/or the old members of the community.

Language use patterns and language competence, as well as attitudes towards languages, differ within speech communities. Speech communities are not monolithic structures. Language loyalty, the most important language attitude with regard to the survival of minority languages, may be associated with old people, women, intellectuals, conservatives, leading figures, etc. It makes a big difference whether an isolated circle of intellectuals or politicians try to revive the language of an ethnolinguistic minority or a widely accepted group of, for example, religious leaders (Brenzinger, 1994). Variations of language use and attitudes have to be investigated, with the language's distribution within the speech communities. The distribution can be based on subsections with regard to generations, gender, levels of education, mobility, etc.

2.3 The setting: The social environment

The sociopolitical environment of ethnolinguistic minorities provides the components from which the package of reasons and motives for the actual language displacement is compiled. It also accounts for the mode of the language shift. Some shifts reflect a voluntary decision to abandon a language, whereas others are the result of coercion. However, in the vast majority of cases we find a mixture of these two scenarios, which means neither "language suicide" (Denison, 1977) nor "language murder" (Calvet, 1974). New value systems penetrate into communities, and social, economic, and ideological pressures have encroaching effects on the basis of language loyalty within the speech community itself.

Complete language shift, implying the disappearance of languages, is not a new phenomenon in the history of mankind. There must always have been speech communities which gave up their mother tongue, either by force from dominant groups or deliberately in the process of assimilating to dominant groups for reasons such as gaining prestige or materialistic benefits.

The environment of each language shift is specific and changes through the ongoing process. Depending on the sociohistorical horizon of a certain ethnolinguistic minority, as well as on the kind of approach from outside, the relevant social setting for a shift might be a modern state within the global setting, an imperial expansion, or a limited, regional context. Even with similar social environments, no two language contact situations are alike, and no two language shifts resemble each other. Within a certain category of setting, however, similar sets of factors prevail.

Three categories in which language displacement occurs can be distinguished: regional, imperial, and global settings. Even though imperial settings prevailed during the colonial period, settings of that kind had existed before and still exist today, though on a much smaller scale. The three categories should therefore not be understood as successive periods in a chronological sense (which would then mean procolonial, colonial, postcolonial), but as contexts which are characterized by common features in the environment of language contact.

Regional settings

Ethnolinguistic minorities in regional settings are characterized by a limited sociohistorical horizon. Since "Western" culture spreads throughout most parts of the world and reaches even remote places, regional settings are fast disappearing as environments of language displacement. Even for minorities in regional settings, one can suggest large-scale population movements for thousands of years causing language shifts and the extinction of languages. No specific information on language shifts in regional settings in the more distant past is available, and no written records of regional "traditional" shifts exist at all. (They do exist, of course, for shifts in imperial settings.). Therefore one has two means of illuminating language displacement events which have taken place in the past. First, one can try to reconstruct language history on the basis of modern language situations and, second, one can study the rare cases of "traditional" shifts which are taking place today.

Applying methods of historical linguistics, the language situation in East Africa, for instance, could be interpreted in the following manner: Dramatic changes in East African history have always been triggered by the arrival of waves of immigrants. They came from the central regions of present-day Sudan, from Ethiopia, but also from southern Africa. For the last 5,000 years, various Nilotic, Cushitic, and Bantu-speaking populations came to East Africa and spread, very often at the expense of indigenous populations, thereby causing language shifts and language death. Seldom were scholars able to detect the rare traces of displaced languages in surviving ones. An example of this kind is the language of the so-called Taita Cushites, remnants of which have been identified by Chrisopher Ehret and Derek Nurse (1981) in some Bantu languages, namely the Taita-Taveta, spoken in the southeastern part of Kenya.

Studies of present-day shifts in regional settings, i.e., those which are relatively unaffected by institutional pressures, suggest that long-term contacts among neighboring groups might have resulted in language displacements for quite different reasons and in various modes. Minorities which had been living in symbiotic relationships with dominant groups for a long time might have been forced to abandon the old language at some point.

This happened to the Aasáx, speakers of a Southern Cushitic language (Winter, 1979). Living in the Maasai plains in northern Tanzania, Aasáx-speaking hunter-gatherers were affiliated to the then dominant Maasai pastoralists. The effects of rinderpest from 1891 to 1896 changed this situation dramatically. Most Maasai lost their cattle, the base of social and economic life to them, and about 50 percent of the Maasai died during these years of hunger and of smallpox. The surviving cattleless pastoralists had to rely on the help of agricultural neighbors and the hunter-gatherer groups. Whereas the bigger agricultural communities managed to control the Maasai refugees, the weaker hunter-gatherer groups didn't succeed. The former Maasai lodgers in the course of time developed into occupation troops. In order to have total control of their new environment, the Maasai banned the use of the mother tongue of their hosts. At the time the Maasai started to leave the Aasáx settlements to build up new herds, many Aasáx had established close contacts with them. After a short period in which the language was still used by the men on their hunting parties, the final decline of the Aasáx language started about 1910. Assimilated to agricultural communities as well as pastoralists, the Aasáx ceased to exist within the following decade. After that, only a few individuals retained some knowledge of the Aasáx language. In 1973 and 1975 Winter was provided with the history of the Aasáx by the last speaker of the language, Kimíndet ole Kiyang'ú, who died in 1976, aged about 88 years.

Another traditional setting in which languages have been displaced is the spread of indigenous linguae francae replacing vernaculars. Autochthonous linguae francae were already growing in precolonial times. On the African continent, languages such as Swahili, Manding, Songhai, Hausa, and Amharic were widely spoken and many vernacular languages were replaced by them. Some of these expansions of indigenous languages share certain features with the following settings.

Imperial settings

Language displacement in imperial settings is characterized by the fact that the replacing language is the language of intruding powers which regard themselves as superior, and who expand with the ambition to extend their influence into other territories. The vast majority of known language displacements took place in such settings. At least for the last 2,000 years colonial expansion, as well as conquests motivated by religious conflicts, affected settings of language contact in most parts of the world.

Dominant extraneous powers violated the areas of others; brute force has been a feature commonly found, and in some cases the conquered people ended as the subject of genocide. Epidemic diseases often accompanied the killings, but it is not always clear whether the diseases actually took place or were just used as an excuse to hide genocide. In most cases, however, languages died before in the way that their speakers were forced to abandon the old mother tongue and to shift to the language of the conquerors. Brief examples from different parts of the world should demonstrate the extent of language displacement in these settings.

In *Southern Africa* the decline of autochthonous languages started with the arrival of the white settlers. Around 1650 the total population of South African Khoekhoe speakers must have been between 100,000 and 200,000. Within a few decades after the first European contact, the traditional economy and the social and political structure collapsed. Smallpox epidemics, as well as language shifts to Khoe-Dutch and Xhosa, led to the death of South African Khoekhoe, which was completed in the nineteenth century.

The San-speaking population spread over the total of modern South Africa, most probably for at least the last 8,000 years. They may have numbered around 10,000 to 20,000 people some 300 years ago. Only 10 speakers of a San language, that is, the /'Auo language in the Kalahari Gemsbok Park, have survived; all the others have been exterminated or absorbed into Afrikaans-speaking "Coloured" communities (Traill, forthcoming).

The history of language displacement in *Brazil* is one of the most cruel, and members of ethnolinguistic minorities are still physically threatened now. In 1500 A.D., only two years after Columbus explored the coasts of modern Venezuela, Pero Vaz de Caminha, in a letter to King Manuel of Portugal, described friendly exchanges of presents with the Indian population on their arrival in what is now Brazil. Nevertheless this was the start of the cruel suppression of the indigenous Indian population and reckless dominance by the invaders. The decline of the Indian population in Brazil since then has been dramatic. Slave expeditions, headhunters, as well as the regular military forces had their part in the reduction of the numbers of Indians from about 5 million to only about 200,000 today. Material interest was the leading motivation for many in the invasion of this continent, and still today ruthless fortune-hunters in search of gold kill Indians, tolerated by the government. The massacre in which illegal gold-hunters murdered at least 73 members of the Yanomami took place as recently as 1993, and no serious action has been taken by the Brazilian government of Itamar Franco.

Today's language situation in South America reflects the history of the indigenous Indian populations in that we do find large numbers of isolated languages. Many Indian languages have disappeared without leaving any linguistic trace, but of others at least ethnonyms or toponyms are known. Most of about 170 living Indian languages in Brazil survive in very small speech communities. In Brazil, Chile, and Argentina the indigenous popula-tion has been physically eliminated in large numbers, even entirely in Uru-guay, and many languages have disappeared with the death of their speakers. Apart from that, some indigenous linguae francae, such as Quechua, Tupi, and Guaraní, have spread with the support of the colonial power at the expense of minority languages (Adelaar, 1991).

When Captain James Cook annexed *Australia* for the British Empire on August 27, 1770, more than 250 languages were in use by different Aboriginal communities in Australia. After approximately 200 years of white contact, only 90 languages survived, 70 of which are threatened by extinction in the near future. Only about 10 percent of the Aboriginal people still speak in-digenous languages, that is, 30,000 people out of 300,000. Whereas in the past Aboriginal speech communities were made up of 4,000 to 5,000 speakers, today only about 8 languages have more than 1,000 speakers. Some 45 lan-guages, half of the remaining Aboriginal ones, rely on very limited numbers of speakers, that is, between 10 and 100. But even the "healthy" languages are threatened by extinction, since the pressure of "Western culture," responsible for the death of many Aboriginal languages in the past, is still increasing. Aboriginal languages not only disappeared through assimilation, but also as a result of massacres and diseases (Schmidt, 1990).

In the 1740s the Aleut people in *Siberia* and *Alaska* may have numbered between 12,000 and 15,000. Ruthless violence by intruding Russian fur-traders, as well as disease, were responsible for the dramatic weakening of the Aleut people, which numbered only about 2,000 to 3,000 in 1820. Japanese forces attacked the Aleutian islands in June 1942, taking the inhabitants as prisoners. Many of the Aleut people didn't survive the war.

After World War II, speech communities of some dialects of the Aleut lan-guage, *Unangam tunuu*, which is related to the Eskimo language, had disap-peared or declined. Others, for example, Attuan, still spoken in the 1950s, as well as the Aleut once spoken on the Shumagin Islands, have died since then.

In 1973 teaching of Aleut had been started, and teaching materials, grammars, and dictionaries have been written on the Aleut language. The future of these small speech communities is uncertain mainly because of their small numbers. Today active Aleut speakers in Alaska may be 500, the speakers of Eastern Aleut, mostly middle-aged or older people, up to about 450 (Bergsland, 1990).

Global settings

Today, most language displacements take place in a global setting, in that a modern state provides the environment of ethnolinguistic minorities. The worldwide domination of only a few languages and the speed of their spread is due to modern communication technologies. Physical pressure, dominant in colonial shifts, has been replaced by social and, more important, economic pressure in the global setting.

Many developing countries with a multilingual population regard this linguistic diversity as a threat to national unity and "nation-building." Supporting ethnic languages is very often seen as supporting separatism. In most developing countries institutional support in the media, schools, administration, etc. is restricted to a few dominant languages of national or international distribution, leaving the majority of indigeneous languages behind.

> Today the future of many languages is uncertain not only because their functional range is scaled down, but because they are never used for, and adapted to newly emerging functions which are from the start associated with another language . . . Lack of functional expansion and adaptation is thus a correlate and counterpart of scaled-down use. (Coulmas, 1992: 170)

The expansion of dominant languages is not achieved by physical violence, as described under the imperial category, but by means of spreading ideologies through the mass media and the education system. The "world economy" demands adjustment and reaches even remote rural areas in developing countries, as "world religions" do. Terms such as westernization, christianization, islamization, modernization, industrialization all point in the same direction, which is reduction of diversity. Assimilation by choice will be the main cause of the worldwide decline of minority languages in the future.

3 The Process: Language Shift

Language contact is a prerequisite for language shifts. Ethnolinguistic communities, usually those with minority status, become bilingual in that they still retain their own language and acquire the language of a dominant group in addition. Recessive use of the old language with intra-ethnic communication leads to the process of language displacement. The changing language behavior of members of an ethnolinguistic minority of this kind qualifies to disturb the fragility of a status quo. This unstable bilingualism may finally develop into monolingualism in the new language. The process of language replacement usually takes at least three generations. This is not a unidirectional development, but in the course of time successive phases with different characteristics modify the process before a language becomes extinct.

Complete language displacement can of course be studied through the rare cases in which the history of certain languages which no longer exist today has been documented. With the Arab conquest of Egypt in the seventh century the process began which finalized the displacement of Coptic. Before that, Coptic had been the spoken language of Egypt, written first in hieroglyphic script, then in the hieratic and later in the demotic form of writing. About 2,300 years ago the Egyptians adopted the Greek alphabet, elaborated by additional letters to represent the distinctive sounds of their language, which then was called "Coptic."

The decline of Coptic as a spoken language was caused by heavy discrimination from the new Arab rulers. Soon after the conquest Arabic became the only language used in administration and pressure to convert to Islam increased. One main factor responsible for accelerating the process of abandoning the Coptic language can be identified; that is the introduction of a progressively heavy capitation tax known as JIZYAH on non-Muslims. In 1672–3 the Dominican traveller J. M. Vansleb reported in his account of his journey to Upper Egypt of having met a certain Mu'allim Athanasius, who was regarded as the last Copt fluent in the Coptic language as a spoken medium. From the seventeenth century on Coptic "survived" only as the language of liturgy (Ishaq, 1991: 604–6).

For investigating the details of the processes leading to the extinction of languages, however, we rely heavily on shift situations which are obviously not completed yet. And in these cases we can never be sure whether changes in language behavior will eventually result in the extinction of the language or not.

Researchers in this field are regularly challenged at this point with the presumably central question of whether they can predict language death. In his review of *Investigating Obsolescence: Studies in Language Contraction and Death*, edited by Nancy Dorian in 1989, R. Hudson expressed his disappointment and concluded:

> The big question, though, is defined by Romaine: can we diagnose incipient language death? Obviously this is easy when no children are learning the language concerned, but are there any other more subtle symptoms, either in the social circumstances or in the language's structure? Knowing little about these things, I expected a positive, and simple, answer, but the book disabused me. The social circumstances under which languages die are surprisingly diverse, and, as we have seen, the language's structure tells us very little. (Hudson, 1990: 834)

As we have seen above, the setting influences language behavior. In the ongoing process of language shift there are often phases in which ethnolinguistic minorities react with maintenance strategies or at least increased overt language loyalty. They experience their language as being threatened by extinction and sometimes fractions of the speech community try to promote the fading language. In many cases attempts to maintain the language are started too late and are not serious enough; for example, language can be seen only as a symbol of identity, or there is no lobby to support and implement language maintenance.

Pressure on ethnolinguistic communities from outside may evoke language maintenance activities and resistance. But it also may undermine self-perception, which can then result in changes in language use patterns. This is when the "downward spiral of reduced language use and loss" may start its deadly circle. The interdependence of changing language use patterns and changes within the language structure has been demonstrated in this model by Schmidt (1990: 20–1). Limited use of the minority language leads to limited exposure to that language, which results in decreasing competence, lack of confidence in using the language, and increasing reliance on the dominant language. The circle then repeats itself on a lower level, by more limited use of the minority language.

4 Further Reading

In this chapter the discussion of language displacement is restricted to those cases in which the entire speech community of a certain language has been involved. In order to understand the processes of language shift, however, the study of many other related language-contact situations could provide valuable insights. Just to mention a few examples: Research on language maintenance and shift of immigrants in the United States (Fishman, 1966, 1978; Veltman, 1983) and Australia (Clyne, 1982), or the shift from Hungarian to German in the Austrian Oberwart (Gal, 1979) provide important case studies of the social contexts and processes of language shift, even though no languages die. Literature on language spread (Cooper, 1982; Lowenberg, 1988) and "language competition" (Wardhaugh, 1987) helps to identify the shift from the perspective of the replacing language.

Studies focusing on language death, that is, the displacement of minority languages which results in the extinction of languages, are not that numerous, but there has been a rapid increase during the last few years. In 1987 Fishman stated:

> There aren't many Nancy Dorians around who care to go back, time after time, to dying language communities, even for research purposes, although such communities contain the answers to many of the best, the most difficult and the most important questions: the questions of limits (of where and how to draw the line between dying and changing, between illness and health, between death and life). (Fishman, 1988: 3)

Working on Scottish Gaelic since the 1970s, Dorian is one of the pioneers in the field of investigating language death. Another piece of long-term research is that of R. M. W. Dixon (1991), who has been studying the decline of Dyirbal, an Australian Aboriginal language, for the last 30 years. And Dressler has published articles on the decline of Breton since 1972. Together with Wodak-Leodolter, he edited a topic issue on "language death" of the *International Journal of the Sociology of Language* in 1977. In "Spracherhalt – Sprachverfall – Sprachtod" Dressler (1988) summarizes relevant publications on the topic, by discussing them according to different perspectives and approaches. Several collections of articles on the subject have been published more recently, Dorian (1989), Beck (1989), Robins and Uhlenbeck (1991), and Brenzinger (1992), providing a more solid base for further studies.

17 Language Conflict

PETER HANS NELDE

Introduction

Throughout history, ever since the Tower of Babel was left unfinished, contacts between different languages have inevitably resulted in conflicts between speakers of those languages. These contacts between languages make up the domain of "contact linguistics." This paper discusses the principal issues in current research in language contact, and then addresses various conflicts among communities that are related to the phenomena of contact linguistics. We then outline a possible program of research based on an analysis of these conflicts, suggesting a pragmatic typology of language conflict. Any such discussion would be incomplete without also presenting some suggestions for the resolution of conflict, and we therefore conclude with some suggested strategies for the neutralization of language conflict.

1 History

During the past 20 years a marked change of emphasis has been noticeable in linguistics. The illusion of a completely homogeneous, Chomskyan linguistics community has given way to one which takes into account social, psychological, and individual components. The emphasis on purely formalistic, descriptive features has given way to a diachronic, sociocultural, political science of language, in short, one which incorporates nonlinguistic factors as well. Consequently, multidimensional strategies are replacing the (frequently) unidimensional "systemic linguistics." In place of the technical difficulties of describing the field of semantics, for example, new problems arose, namely those of variation and model diversification.

The inclusion of numerous related disciplines such as sociology and psychology, as well as discussion of speech act theories, areal linguistics, and the problems of language barriers pertaining to social-political issues, all led to a spectrum of methods whose potential for variation was both a strength and a weakness. Soon one of the central themes of variational linguistics included that of contact research or contact linguistics, whose historical tradition dates back to the nineteenth century. This area, depending on one's point of view, uses the methods of sociolinguistics or the sociology of language. It originated in the United States, where Weinreich's, Fishman's, and later Labov's work revived what had been frowned upon for a long time: field research of an empirical nature. At the same time completely new areas of socially dependent semi-, bi-, and multilingualism were (re-)discovered, including previously analyzed bilingual contacts in conflict zones (for example, French and English in Quebec). With the aid of the diglossia concept developed and expanded by Fishman, which replaced to a certain extent the idea of bilingualism as having pedagogical-historical significance, attention was now paid to the sociopolitically motivated difficulties of dialect speakers, socially underprivileged city dwellers, and mono- or multilinguals in language conflict zones who were handicapped in their chances for professional advancement.

In this context, creole and pidgin languages became the center of interest among linguists as full-fledged means of communication. In the United States, substratum and semi-languages of members of different classes were sociolinguistically described, and numerous forms of diglossia and/or triglossia were discovered in Europe: Not only are all European countries with the exception of Iceland multilingual, but they are also predominantly dialectal.

1.1 Contact linguistics

Contact linguistics in its narrow sense goes back to the early fifties (U. Weinreich, 1953). During the previous decades, cultural-linguistic contacts such as lexical borrowing had stood at the forefront of research. In Europe, the analysis of the linguistic contacts of classical languages and their effects had prevailed for a long time. Sociological and psychological aspects were first introduced by Weinreich, Fishman, and Haugen, who accorded special emphasis to external linguistic factors. In this way, the originally interlingual character of research shifted towards interethnic contacts, with interference and transference analyses, social and situational elements of language configurations, areas of language use (domains), attitudes, and stereotypes all brought forward.

1.2 Present topics in contact linguistics

Language planning and language politics have repeatedly called upon the research of contact linguists during the last few years, since the assumption has been made, for example, that multilingualism, as well as second and third language acquisition, may be of use to peace and cooperation between nations. Intensity, vitality (Haarmann, 1980, I), and the dynamics (Auburger, 1979; Breton, 1990; Labrie, 1990) of language contacts currently dominate discussion on the one hand, and phenomena such as multilingualism (see chapter 18) and language shift (see chapter 16) are being analyzed on the other.

In this way, the rapidly developing linguistics of the seventies and the eighties has opened up new dimensions. A renewed interest in diachronic aspects alongside predominantly synchronic features, its interdependence with numerous related disciplines, and its obvious relationship to political, historically motivated, and ideological situations and contexts create more opportunities for research in language contact and conflict. At the same time, they make the field of contact linguistics a challenging task which is worth dedication and effort. This has been, above all, to the advantage of linguistic minorities and threatened and endangered language communities.

1.3 Contact linguistics and multilingualism

Surprisingly enough, contact linguistic research in countries with linguistic minorities tends to be infrequent (in Europe: France, Russia; in Asia: China, Pakistan). However, linguistic investigations in multilingual countries are indispensable since political decisions are frequently based on regional linguistic situations. Above all, language must often remain the decisive criterion for judgment, since the population of multilingual areas cannot, in many cases, be differentiated from its neighbors by other means.

2 Defining Contact Linguistics

The term "contact linguistics" was introduced at the First World Congress on Language Contact and Conflict, held in Brussels in June 1979. An interdisciplinary branch of multilingual research, contact linguistics can be described as a triad of the following standpoints: language, language user, and language sphere.

Research in contact linguistics incorporates linguistic levels like phonology, syntax, and lexicon as well as discourse analysis, stylistics, and pragmatics. In addition, there are external factors such as nation, language community, language boundaries, migration, and many others. The type of language contact and multilingualism is also relevant, whether it manifests itself as individual, institutional, or state bilingualism or as social multilingualism; as diglossia or dialect; or as natural or artificial multilingualism, for which intermediate levels such as so-called semilingualism or interlingua also must be considered. In the process it is helpful to make a basic, simplifying distinction between autochthonous (indigenous) and allochthonous (migrant) groups, since language contact situations can rarely be isolated as single phenomena, but usually appear as a cluster of characteristics.

The structuring of social groups is of crucial importance to the language user. Besides the conventional differences of age, sex, and social relationship, minority status receives special attention from researchers in multilingualism.

Above and beyond these factors, all the sectors responsible for the social interplay of a language community play an essential role. In the last few decades sectors such as technology, industry, city, and administration, and most recently also media, advertising, and data processing, have been added to the traditional fields of religion, politics, culture, and science. In the educational/cultural sector the schools occupy a special place and are constantly exposed to new forms and models of multilingual instruction, for example, from North America and Canada. The question of whether bilingual and multilingual education can interfere with a child's right to use his or her mother (home, first, colloquial) tongue depends mainly on the integration intentions of language planners, with conformity and integration instead of language maintenance constituting the motivating forces behind multilingual instruction. To oversimplify the issue, the underprivileged have to submit to "bilingual" education and thus assimilation, while "foreign language" instruction is available to the sociological elite (see chapter 24). Contact processes that have concerned researchers in multilingualism since the beginning are partly diachronic, partly synchronic in nature. Besides language change, borrowing processes, interference, and language mixing, there are linguae francae, language shift, language maintenance and loss, code-switching (see chapter 13), and pidginization and creolization (see chapter 14).

The effects of such language contact processes can be registered by measuring language consciousness and attitudes. Language loyalty and prestige play a decisive role in the linguistic identity of any multilingual person, and extreme care must be taken in the interpretation of so-called language statistics (censuses and public opinion surveys).

Language spheres in which considerations of multilingualism have become indispensable extend over numerous areas of study. To name a few: language policy (see chapter 27), language planning, language ecology, language contact in multinational industries and organizations, language care and revitalization among minorities, as well as specific issues such as the strengthening of national languages.

A first synchronic overview of all areas of contact linguistics is given in the two volumes of the international handbook on *Contact Linguistics*; the first deals with theoretical and methodological issues, the second applies theoretical notions and prerequisites to all situations of language contact and conflict in Europe (Nelde et al., 1995).

3 Contact and Conflict

3.1 *Ethnic conflict and sociology*

Most contact between ethnic groups does not occur in peaceful, harmoniously coexisting communities. Instead, it exhibits varying degrees of the tension, resentment, and differences of opinion that are characteristic of every competitive social structure. Under certain conditions, such generally accepted competitive tensions can degenerate into intense conflicts, in the worst case ending in violence. However, given the fact that some ethnic groups do live peacefully together, the assumption of some sociologists that ethnic contact inevitably leads to conflict appears exaggerated. The possibility of conflict erupting is, however, always present, since differences between groups create feelings of uncertainty of status, which could give rise to conflict. Sociologists who have dealt with contact problems between ethnic groups define conflict as contentions involving real or apparent fears, interests, and values, in which the goals of the opposing group must be opposed, or at least neutralized, to protect one's own interests (prestige, employment, political power, etc.) (Williams, 1947). This type of conflict often appears as a conflict of values, in which differing behavioral norms collide, since usually only one norm is considered to be valid. Conflicts between ethnic groups, however, occur only very rarely as openly waged violent conflicts, and usually consist of a complex system of threats and sanctions in which the interests and values of one group are endangered. Conflicts can arise relatively easily if – as is usually the case – interests and values have an emotional basis.

The magnitude and the development of a conflict depend on a number of factors determined by the level of friction between two or more ethnic groups, the presence of equalizing or mitigating elements, and the degree of uncertainty of all the participants. Thus a one-sided explanation of the conflict, or one based on irrational prejudices, will fail. Very different factors influencing each other reinforce and "escalate" to cause group conflict. This group conflict is part of normal social behavior in which different groups compete with each other, and should therefore not be connoted only negatively, since in this way new – and possibly more peaceful – forms of coexistence can arise. On the other hand, tensions between ethnic groups brought about by feelings of intimidation can give rise to new conflicts at any time, conflicts which can be caused by a minority as well as by a majority group. As long as society continues to create new fears, because of its competitive orientation, the creation of new conflicts appears unavoidable.

3.2 *Political language conflict*

Along with sociologists, political scientists also assume that language contact can cause political conflict. Language conflicts can be brought about by changes in an expanding social system when there is contact between different language groups (Inglehart and Woodward, 1967). Belgium and French Canada are examples of this. The reasons for such a situation are the following: A dominant language group (French in Belgium, English in Canada) controls the crucial authority in the areas of administration, politics, and the economy, and gives preference in employment to those applicants who have command of the dominant language. The disadvantaged language group is then left with the choice of renouncing its social ambitions, assimilating, or resisting. While numerically weak or psychologically weakened language groups tend towards assimilation, in modern societies numerically stronger, more homogeneous language groups possessing traditional values, such as their own history and culture, prefer political resistance, the usual form of organized language conflict in this century. This type of conflict becomes especially salient when it occurs between population groups of differing socioeconomic structures (urban/rural, poor/wealthy, indigenous/immigrant) and the dominant group requires its own language as a condition for the integration of the rest of the population.

Although in the case of French-speaking Canada, English appeared to be the necessary means of communication in trade and business, nearly 80 percent of the Francophone population spoke only French, thus being excluded from social elevation in the political and economic sector. A small French-speaking elite, whose original goal was political opposition to the dominant English, ultimately precipitated the outbreak of the latent, socially motivated, language conflict.

Most current language conflicts are the result of the differing social status and preferential treatment of the dominant language on the part of the government. In these cases there are religious, social, economic or psychological fears and frustrations in the weaker group that may be responsible for the language conflict. However, a critical factor in the expansion and intensification of such conflict remains the impediment to social mobility, particularly of a disadvantaged or suppressed ethnic group (cf. the numerous language conflicts in multi-ethnic Austria–Hungary before 1918).

Language problems in very different areas (politics, economics, administration, education) appear under the heading of language conflict. In such cases, politicians and economic leaders seize upon the notion of language conflict, disregarding the actual underlying causes, and thus continue to inflame "from above" the conflict that has arisen "from below," with the result that language assumes much more importance than it may have had at the outset of the conflict. This language-oriented "surface structure" is used to obscure the more deeply rooted, suppressed "deep structure" (social and economic problems). Furthermore, multilingual conflicts in Europe, especially in urban societies, show quite clearly that language conflicts are caused primarily by attempts on the part of the dominant group to block social mobility.

3.3 *Language conflict and contact linguistics*

Even in contact linguistics the term *conflict* remains ambiguous, at least when it refers generally to social conflict which can arise in a multilingual situation (Hartig, 1980: 182). The notion appears to us essential here that neither contact nor conflict can occur between languages; they are conceivable only between speakers of languages. Oksaar (1980) correctly points out the ambiguity of the term *language conflict* as either conflict between languages within an individual or as conflict by means of language(s), including processes external to the individual. Similarly, Haarmann (1980: II, 191) distinguishes between interlingual and inter-ethnic language conflicts.

Among the founders of modern research in language contact – running parallel to the rapidly developing sociolinguistics and sociology of language – e.g., Weinreich and Fishman, the term conflict rarely appears. While Weinreich views multilingualism (bilingualism) and the accompanying interference phenomena as the most important form of language contact, without regard to conflict between language communities on the basis of ethnic, religious, or cultural incompatibilities, Fishman (1972: 14) grants language conflict greater importance in connection with language planning. Haugen (1966) was the first to make conflict presentable in language contact research with his detailed analysis of Norwegian language developments. Indeed, even linguists in multilingual countries (the former Yugoslavia, Switzerland, Belgium) resisted, until the end of the 1970s, treating conflict methodically as part of language contact research, since such an "ideologicalization" of language contact appeared to them as "too touchy" (Fishman, 1980: XI). Although conflict consequently has no systematic history, and is mentioned in Weinreich (1953: 151) only as a marginal phenomenon among bilinguals, the term *interference* led to an emphasis on the interlinguistic aspects (language and the individual) rather than dealing with more extralinguistic aspects (language and community). One reason for the late discovery of a term indispensable in today's contact research is to be found in the history of contact linguistics itself: In traditional language contact research (as well as in dialectology and research on linguistic change), the emphasis tended toward closed, geographically homogeneous and easily describable socioeconomic groups, rather than urban industrial societies, ripe for social and linguistic strife, whose demand for rapid integration laid the groundwork for conflict. However, it is precisely in modern urban society that conflicts result essentially from the normative sanctions of the more powerful group, usually the majority, which demands linguistic adaptation to the detriment of language contact, and thus preprograms conflict with those speakers who are unwilling to adapt.

Despite a less than ideal research situation essentially limited to empirical case studies of language conflict, the following statements can be made. Language conflict can occur anywhere there is language contact, chiefly in multilingual communities, although Mattheier (1984: 200) has also demonstrated language conflicts in so-called monolingual local communities. Language conflict arises from the confrontation of differing standards, values, and attitude structures, and strongly influences self-image, upbringing, education, and group consciousness. Thus conflict can be viewed as a form of contact or, in terms of a model, as a complementary model to the language contact model.

Contact linguists have either described conflict research as an integral part of language contact research (Nelde, 1983) or have dealt with special topics from the perspective of conflict. The methods used are heterogeneous and come from numerous neighboring disciplines (psycholinguistics and sociolinguistics, communication research, sociology, etc.). For lack of its own methods, this research still employs predominantly empirical procedures. Along with interview and polling techniques, privileged informants and representative sampling, prejudice research and stereotype and attitude observation, the past few years have seen combined investigation models such as socioprofiles and ethnoprofiles (Nelde, 1984a; Enninger and Haynes, 1984), community and polarity profiles (Wölck, 1985).

4 Essential Principles of Conflict Linguistics

These observations on language contact and conflict situations lead to some basic premises of contact linguistics, which, despite their occasional seeming triviality, merit consideration at this juncture:

1 Language contact – as we explained before – exists only between speakers and language communities, not between languages. Comparison of one and the same language in different contexts is therefore possible only in a quite limited way.
2 The statement that there can be no language contact without language conflict ("Nelde's Law") – K. de Bot in his GAL (Gesellschaft für angewandte Linguistik) presentation in Göttingen on January 10, 1989) – may appear exaggerated, but there is in the realm of the European languages at present no imaginable contact situation which cannot also be described as language conflict.
3 Contact linguistics usually sees language as a significant secondary sign of fundamental causes of conflict of a socioeconomic, political, religious, or historical sort. Thus, in a way, language conflict appears to be the lesser evil, since apparently it can be more easily corrected and neutralized than primary sociopolitical conflicts.
4 Contact linguistics, at the same time, makes it clear that conflicts should not be condemned as only negative, but rather, it proves that new structures which are more advantageous than earlier

ones, especially for minority speakers, can often result from conflicts.

5 Typology of Conflict

The current language conflicts in Europe, North and Central America, Southeast Asia, and parts of Africa can be viewed as situations of either *natural* or
artificial language conflict.

5.1 "Natural" language conflict

Natural language conflicts are those situations that have traditionally existed
between indigenous majorities and minorities. The extensive literature of
language conflict abounds with examples of this type, particularly those of
minorities pitted against official national or regional languages. Conflict has
frequently arisen in these situations of language contact because the linguistic
minority was not in a position to assimilate. This type of conflict can be found,
for example, in Europe along the Germanic–Romance and the Slavic–Germanic linguistic boundaries, and in Canada involving the French-speaking
minority and among a few indigenous peoples. Natural language conflicts can
become problematic when ideology on either side – not only the majority
but the minority as well – is used to intensify the differences that exist,
and peaceful coexistence between language communities can easily be threatened when the banner of language is hoisted as the defining symbol of a
people.

The conflict between Belfast and Connemara, for example, involves considerably more than just language: An urban, Protestant, working environment in fact has little if anything in common with a rural, Catholic region
of high unemployment. The issue of language only exacerbates these
differences.

A similar situation is reflected in the ideologically motivated opposition
between Afrikaans and English in Namibia and in South Africa. The vast
majority of the Namibian populace, regardless of race or social status, speaks
or at least understands Afrikaans. The country's official language, however, is
English, cast as the "language of freedom," though fewer than 3 percent of the
population speak it as their first language. Afrikaans, the former language of
instruction and administration, remains the "language of oppression."

More recently, the study of Russian has witnessed a rapid decline in the
former Eastern-bloc countries, and one can only speculate on the relationship
between the sudden lack of interest in Russian and the "de-ideologicalization"
of that language in the new republics. In the Croatian part of Bosnia–Herzego-
vina ("Herzeg"), all mentions of the term "Serbo-Croatian" have been

expunged from schoolbooks and replaced, not on linguistic but on ideological grounds, by the term "Croatian." Shakespeare was not the last to ask, "What's in a name?"

5.2 *"Artificial" language conflict*

Artificial, or self-imposed, conflict arises out of situations of compromise in which one or more language communities are disfavored. These situations have existed in every society from Babel to Brussels. Symmetric multilingualism, in which equal numbers of speakers are invested with equal rights and in which both language prestige and linguistic identities are congruent, is impossible, since one of the language groups will always be subject to stigmatization and/or discrimination, with conflict the inevitable result.

Artificial language conflict occurs especially when, motivated by the need for rapid international communication, politically influential economic powers export their languages (and their resulting socioeconomic influence) to their trading partners. Thus Russian (before 1990) and English have become languages of great economic expansion, despite a noteworthy lack of formal educational planning. Secondary schools in Strasbourg, for example, have abandoned study of the native German dialect for English (as the first "foreign language"), with the result that German is being lost as a local working language. It is offered as a second "foreign" language only to students over 12 years old, with the result that a passive knowledge of the mother tongue is now all that remains.

The European Union has provided interesting examples of artificial language conflict. In the debate over "Which language(s) for Europe?" the Danes years ago, in a spirit of genuine cooperation, opted to forgo the use of Danish. In retrospect, Denmark may appear to have resolved the issue in the early years of the European Union of reducing the number of official languages to at most two, with English and French destined to be the languages of international communication. The initial delight of London and Paris at this helpful suggestion was quickly dampened, however, since the Danes also suggested that the English should use French and the French should use English. After that suggestion, enthusiasm for the Danish solution quickly withered. The presence of several thousand translators and interpreters in Brussels suggests a return to the Tower of Babel. At the present time (1994), the 9 working languages of the 12 member states generate a total of ($9\times 8 =$) 72 language combinations. The enlargement of the EU by four members (1995) and by six or more additional member states in the coming years, with nine new languages, leads to so many mathematical combinations (incorporating 18 languages with theoretically equal status) that no assembly hall in the world would be able to accommodate meetings for all the interpreters.

These few examples amply demonstrate that the language conflicts that threaten the peaceful coexistence of peoples are not always the consequence of long-standing historical conflicts among language minorities. The new orders and restructuring of recent years have also led to sources of conflict that were not fully grasped just a few years ago. In any event, neither *natural* nor *artificial* conflict should be judged only negatively; rather, we should hope that out of conflict there may ensue new alliances and new solutions that will function better than any of the efforts of the past.

6 Two Language Conflict Situations

6.1 Belgium

Until the beginning of the 1960s, the principle in effect in Belgium, with rare exceptions, was the personality principle, which permitted French speakers to use their mother tongue freely in most daily situations. It was not until the linguistic legislation of the years 1962–3 that a precise demarcation of linguistic territories was effected by administratively establishing a linguistic border. By virtue of this fact the principle of territoriality was adopted. Nonetheless, more than ten years had to go by before the modes of corresponding application led to a new linguistic constellation in the country. Since then it has been possible to distinguish different linguistic territories as a function of linguistic planning:

1 Monolinguistic territories, made up of the two large unilingual regions of the country, Flanders and Wallonia, subjected to strict unilingualism, with Dutch to the north and French to the south.
2 The bilingual territory of the capital, Brussels, where Dutch and French each have their own linguistic infrastructure, which in principle prevents one language from being favored to the detriment of the other.
3 Monolinguistic territories provided with linguistic facilities for the minority (for example, Fouron-Voeren, Comines-Komen, Mouscron-Moeskroen). Because the establishment of a strict linguistic boundary cannot perfectly take into account the minorities located on one side or the other of this boundary, Belgian linguistic policy includes protective measures for the Dutch, French, and German border minorities (North Old Belgium, Malmédy). The territory officially recognized as German-speaking in eastern Belgium (Eupen, St Vith) is equally affected by this ruling, which means that French enjoys certain rights in this German-language sector.
4 Monolingual territories without particular rights for autochthons. Despite the fact that wide-ranging protection was assured even to very small minority groups, certain sectors still exist which are deprived of any kind of linguistic protection. This is notably the case for

German linguistic territories in Belgian Luxembourg like South Old Belgium (near the town of Arlon/Arel) and Central Old Belgium (near Bocholz-Beho north of the Grand Duchy). In these regions French was instituted as the sole administrative language.

This brief overview gives a picture of the modifications introduced by the territoriality principle in the Belgian organization of linguistic territories. At the same time it reveals the limitations of this principle, the systematic application of which could well be the source of new conflicts.

One of the main consequences of this rigorous partition of linguistic territories is that a new understanding of multilingualism has developed in Belgium, contrary to the rest of Europe. In fact, while the principle of territoriality applied in former Czechoslovakia and in Switzerland is mainly limited to two domains (those of administration and education), Belgium introduced the domain of the language of the workplace, that is, a regulation of official language use between employers and employees. These three domains have become organized, even in an officially bilingual region like Brussels, in unilingual networks of the two languages of the city. Thus, while individual multilingualism may be desirable, it is not prescribed by linguistic legislation. That is why, since the introduction of the principle of territoriality in bilingual regions, institutionalized (not individual) multilingualism has developed. With respect to linguistic practices, this means that in the whole country there are only unilingual educational institutions (schools, universities, training institutes), and in fact, an administration equally unilingual, even in the multilingual regions. Multilingualism can become extremely institutionalized, as evidenced by the case of the Belgian army, which has units for the three languages of the country, German, French, and Dutch.

Despite all the negative criticism the principle of territoriality has given rise to in the past, it can now be affirmed that Belgium – as was the case with Switzerland – owes a certain sociopolitical and economic stability to the principle of territoriality. The vehemence and emotion of linguistic conflicts have shown an inverse tendency the past few years since the implementation of the linguistic law.

6.2 *Canada and Quebec*[1]

Unlike Belgium, Canada's official language groups are far from equal in size. The French-speaking population of Canada, concentrated in Quebec, is clearly a minority, at 26 percent of the Canadian population. What is more, it only represents about 2 percent of the population of North America (Canada and the USA) and is thus subject to strong pressure to assimilate.

But more than the demographic relationship, it is the political system of Canada which determines how the linguistic question is to be tackled, and in particular the application of the principles of territoriality and personality.

Canada is a federation in which the governments, federal and provincial, have equal status. The member states, that is, the provinces, have conferred on the federal government limited power in certain areas of common interest, such as defense, foreign policy, and currency. The provinces, however, have retained complete autonomy in certain other areas, like health, employment, culture, and education.

Since language is not mentioned in the articles of the *Constitutional Law of 1867*, which established areas of jurisdiction, the federal and provincial governments are permitted to legislate jointly on language. First it must be determined whether the main object of the legislative measure touches a matter in the provincial or in the federal area of jurisdiction. This dual possibility of legislation on language has had the result that, as time goes by, different, if not opposing, concepts of the recognition of linguistic rights have developed between the federal and the provincial governments, especially in Quebec, but also in the other provinces.

Since 1963, the date of the establishment of the Commission of Inquiry on Bilingualism and Biculturalism, whose goal it is to improve relations between the two founding peoples of Canada, the evolution of concepts has progressed by different stages under the impulse of collectivities.

French-speaking Canadians demand services in their language. Facing the threat of secession by French speakers disadvantaged by Canadian institutions after a century of federalism, equal status was accorded to the French and English languages in federal institutions (the *Law Concerning the Status of Official Languages* of 1969 and the *Parliamentary Resolution on Language in the Public Service Workplace* of 1973). These two measures adopted by the federal parliament had the effect of establishing institutional bilingualism. They provide the French-speaking minority with more access to services in French and more proportional representation in public service.

French speakers in Quebec demanded increased protection of their language. The linguistic problem posed in the 1960s was in the area of provincial jurisdiction, since it concerned the language of education. The system of education in Canada, divided on the basis of confession (Catholic or Protestant), offered a choice of language of instruction at the time. In fact, the laws of supply and demand gradually brought about the substitution of English for French, as new immigrants and some of the French speakers wanted to benefit from the upward mobility to be had with bilingualism, and so chose English as the language of instruction for their children. The debate about free choice led to the progressive elaboration of an exhaustive linguistic policy, which took 8 years.

The *Law to Promote the French Language* of 1969 provided for several measures to promote French as language of the workplace, but the legislation for free choice provoked so much discontent among French speakers that the government was voted out of office.

The *Law Regarding the Official Language* of 1974, which replaced the 1969 law, made French the official language of the legislature and the provincial court, of the administration and public utilities companies, of the professions, of the workplace, and of business. It therefore extended into several fields in which the province exercised its jurisdiction. Although French was reinforced as the official language in these different areas, bilingualism generally continued in the background. As to the language of instruction, the law made French school obligatory, except for the children of the English minority and for French speakers and immigrants who had a certain level of knowledge of the English language, which was measured with the help of tests. The effect of this law was to territorialize the notion of the official status of French, but it maintained bilingualism as a collective right. Like the preceding law, this law aroused the discontent of French speakers, and it also contributed to the defeat of the government that introduced it.

In 1977 the *Charter of the French Language* was passed, and is still in effect. This charter reinforced the official status of French in the different domains of provincial jurisdiction, in certain cases suggesting French unilingualism, although English continued to be accepted in most areas. In the matter of education, a compromise in favor of immigrants (compared to the preceding law) abolished the tests and allowed children to attend English school if one of their parents or their older brothers and sisters had attended English school. This provision is known by the name of the Quebec Clause. Note that the language laws in Quebec evolved from the laws of supply and demand, at first codified as they were by recognizing individual rights, which provoked rejection by the majority of French speakers. Since that time the language laws have evolved progressively toward a territorial concept, while taking care to respect collective rights.

English speakers in Quebec, as a minority who spoke an official language, demanded protection by way of bilingualism. At the time of the 1982 repatriation of the Canadian constitution from London, which was done without the backing of Quebec, the federal government inscribed fundamental linguistic rights into the *Canadian Charter of Rights and Liberties*, part of the *Constitutional Law of 1982*. In addition to Articles 16 to 22, which covered rights concerning the status of official languages in federal institutions, Article 23 ruled on the right to education in official minority languages, a domain traditionally reserved for the provinces. No sooner was the question of the Quebec Clause submitted by the Protestant school commissions of Quebec, than the courts recognized that Article 23 had been drafted expressly to counter the *Charter of the French Language*, but they were obliged to declare the Quebec Clause unconstitutional. From that time on it was the Canada Clause of the Charter of Rights that would prevail. This clause provided that parents who had received their education in the language of the minority (or whose child had received his or her education in that language) anywhere in Canada have the right to send their children to schools of their choice. This clause reduced the range of the territorial concept that had been previously adopted by Quebec.

The Charter of Rights served to protect minorities who spoke an official language, French speakers outside of Quebec as well as English speakers in

Quebec. By their involvement, the English speakers of Quebec, recently made a minority in Quebec but still able to count on the fact that they belonged to the English-speaking majority of Canada, had succeeded in combating the territorial concept by the recognition of collective rights, where for about a century the French-speaking minorities of other provinces had been fighting a losing battle against the simple effects of the law of supply and demand.

These few examples culled from Canadian experience of recent years show the relationships of forces constantly involved in the process of normalization and substitution. For Quebec, the territorial concept represents the best way of favoring the normalization of French by way of institutionalized multilingualism. Since French speakers nevertheless wished to take collective rights into account, for traditional reasons particularly connected with their constitutional history, several adjustments have been made in favor of the collective rights of the English-speaking minority. But the position of the latter has been to call for integral bilingualism as a means of protection for themselves as an official Canadian language minority. From this point of view, the English-speaking minority of Quebec is defending the primacy of individual rights over collective rights. These opposing positions might appear to be irreconcilable.

These examples of linguistic legislation in Belgium and Quebec show that the concepts of territoriality and personality always represent important stakes in countries considered to have an enviable tradition of linguistic coexistence.

7 Five Principles for Neutralizing Conflict

The most recent surveys in Belgium, Canada, and Quebec point to the conclusion that measures of language planning like the principle of territoriality are not sufficient for avoiding conflicts, but they can soften the repercussions in the socioeconomic, cultural, and linguistic life of multilingual population groups. In this respect, the changes observed are less attributable to the principle of territoriality itself than to perspectives which are transformed when minority groups in the population are less stigmatized.

The Canadian and Belgian examples show that linguistic conflicts can be partially neutralized insofar as the following conditions are applied.

1 The introduction of the territoriality principle is limited to a few key areas like administration and education.
2 The institutional multilingualism that emerges leads to the creation of independent unilingual networks which grant equal opportunity of communication to minority and majority speakers and which exclude linguistic discrimination connected with the prestige language.
3 Measures of linguistic planning are not exclusively based on linguistic

censuses carried out by the respective governments; they should genuinely take into account the situational and contextual characteristics of the linguistic groups.

4 Linguistic groups in a multilingual country are not judged primarily quantitatively. Because they are in a minority situation, they should, on the contrary, be awarded more rights and opportunities for development ("positive discrimination") than would be due to them, based solely on their number and their proportion to the majority (for example, a lower number of pupils per class should be accepted for children of the minority).

5 The fact of according such quality to minorities by assuring them of more rights could, as suggested by the examples from Belgium and Quebec, result in fewer people adopting an ideological position or in a decrease in emotionalism at the moment of dealing with possible sources of linguistic conflict. Initial attempts permit at least a cautious measure of optimism.

NOTE

1 This section owes a great deal to Normand Labrie. I am extremely grateful for his expert assistance.

18 Multilingualism

MICHAEL CLYNE

1 What is Multilingualism?

The term "multilingualism" can refer to either the language use or the competence of an individual or to the language situation in an entire nation or society. However, at the individual level it is generally subsumed under "bilingualism." This may be because, while there are probably more bilinguals in the world than monolinguals, there are not perceived to be so many people who use more than two languages habitually. There are, of course, many rich multilingual situations in the world (see, e.g., Khubchandani, 1988, on India and Søndergaard, 1991, on the Dano-German border, to cite only two researched areas). For individuals, "normative" definitions (Van Overbeke, 1972) requiring those termed bi- or multilinguals to have equal competence in the languages, to have acquired them simultaneously, or to use them in the same contexts have proved unrealistic (cf. Haugen, 1973). Thus definitions now tend to be general ("methodological" in Van Overbeke's sense). A common definition of "multilingualism" would then be – "the use of more than one language" or "competence in more than one language." This allows for further refinement in the actual description to cover different levels of command or use of the various languages.

At the societal or national level, we have to distinguish between "official" and "de facto" multilingualism. For instance, Switzerland is an officially multilingual nation in that it has been declared such, but there, multilingualism is based on a territorial principle. While public documents for the entire nation are in French, German, and Italian, most people grow up monolingually in a canton which typically has one official language. Canada is officially a bilingual nation because English and French are enshrined in the Canadian Constitution as the official languages, but most Canadians still have regular (nonschool) contact with only one of these. Moreover, there are many other languages used in Canada today – over a hundred heritage languages brought to Canada by immigrant groups, some of them maintained for several generations and concentrated in particular areas, as well as the indigenous languages of the Indians and the Inuit (Eskimos). So Canada, while officially a bilingual nation, is a de facto multilingual one.

Societal multilingualism is created by contextual factors such as international migration (as in Argentina or the US), colonialism (e.g., in Wales or Kenya), international borders (e.g., the border between Austria and Slovenia), *Sprachinseln* (ethnolinguistic enclaves, e.g., Hungarian enclaves in Slovakia, Sorbian ones in Germany), and the spread of international languages.

In multilingual societies, in which the same languages are generally used by the same people, the various languages have differing functions. This situation is known, depending on the number of languages involved, as diglossia, triglossia, or polyglossia (see chapter 12). Almost the entire population of Paraguay employs Guaraní as the vernacular (L language) and Spanish as the language of the more formal or official domains (H language). The Luxembourgers have Letzebuergesch as their first language and the language of everyday interaction but they employ French and German more or less in complementary distributions as H languages with language functions, domains (contextualized spheres of communication, see section 5) and social class determining the choice. However, since 1984, Letzebuergesch has shared official status with French and German. It is therefore possible to use it in similar situations (Newton et al., forthcoming; Clyne, forthcoming). In Singapore, Standard English, Mandarin, Standard Malay, and Tamil are used as H languages in official domains, nonstandard English as the M(edium) language, and Hokkien, Cantonese, nonstandard Malay, or an Indian language other than Tamil as an L language for everyday purposes (Platt and Weber, 1980: 12).

The choice of language among multilinguals is determined according to social variables which will be discussed below (section 5). These social variables are also instrumental in code-switching between languages within the same stretch of discourse. Multilingualism, especially in more open settlement, has been characterized by dynamics which have been the focus of much research (see section 5).

2 Research Paradigms

As will be gathered from the above, the study of multilingualism embraces the study of the language systems in contact, the functions of the languages in society, the groups or communities in contact, and the speech of individuals using more than one language. These facets should not be seen in isolation from one another. They are part of a puzzle which can be disentangled only by seeing them as part of a whole. Thus the research methods for studies of multilingualism will be drawn from a range of disciplines and subdisciplines, including structural linguistics, sociolinguistics, sociology, psycholinguistics, social psychology, and demography. Accordingly, a number of distinct paradigms have been introduced into this field (cf. Clyne, 1991a: 159–60).

The *language contact* paradigm has focused on "language as a system" and has been extended to take account of sociolinguistic and psycholinguistic factors, embracing the processes of language contact and interactional patterns (e.g., Weinreich, 1953; Haugen, 1956; Gumperz, 1976; Giles et al., 1977; Neustupný, 1985).

The *language shift* paradigm is concerned with language use, the domains of use, and explanations of shifts from the use of one language to that of the other in certain situations or in general (e.g., Fishman, 1966, 1985, 1991; Veltman, 1983).

The *language death* paradigm overlaps with that of language shift but the object of the study is usually languages which are not represented elsewhere (e.g., Breton, American Indian, or Australian Aboriginal languages). Unlike language shift studies, language death research generally includes a consideration of the changing grammars of languages in the last stage of existence (e.g., Dorian, 1977, 1981; Dressler and Wodak-Leodolter, 1977).

The *language attrition* paradigm is concerned with measuring the loss of language skills in the individual's first language. This is frequently studied, however, by finding out about limitations in the *retention* of these languages (see, e.g., Weltens et al., 1986). As language attrition studies rarely have the benefit of longitudinal data, they have to rely on surrogate methods, such as comparing parents' and children's speech or immigrants' speech with that of people who remained in their native environment. *Retention* might be a more appropriate way than attrition of conceptualizing the problem. Among the issues challenging researchers are studies in all areas centering on the effects of using more than two languages, as well as on the activation of languages employed receptively and the reactivation of languages no longer used by the individual or the respective community.

3 Social Consequences of Multilingualism

Apart from particular national or regional tendencies, there is a constant tension between the forces of monolingualism and of multilingualism. This may be observed in the history of the US and Australia, both of which gradually replaced policies accepting multilingualism which were in existence for much of the nineteenth century, first by tolerant but restrictive ones (in the late nineteenth century) and then by ones rejecting multilingualism or any kind of cultural pluralism by the time of World War I. A shift to more accepting policies started in the 1960s in the US and in the early 1970s in Australia (see, e.g., Kloss, 1977; Fishman, 1985; Clyne, 1991a: chapter 1). Globally, there are corresponding waves of more positive and more negative policies towards multilingualism, with the period immediately before World

War I and between the wars essentially negative, reflecting xenophobia and monoculturalism, and the 1960s and 1970s positive, reflecting a quest for social equity, human rights, and a change from inhibiting structures. The tension between mono- and multilingualism may be observed in Europe today, where massification within the development of European integration is being counterbalanced by national revivals, especially in Eastern and Central European countries which have regained their political autonomy in recent years, and regional resurgence in Western Europe, e.g., in Italy and Germany. However, the inevitable economic and political interdependence may promote multilingualism and cultural autonomy at the regional as well as the wider international level. Population flow all over the world is another important factor promoting multilingualism. Attitudes towards immigrant languages, for instance, are determined to a large extent by immigration policy or an absence thereof. Western European countries who believe that the immigrants and their children are foreign "guest workers" and deny that theirs is a multicultural society will marginalize their "minority languages." They might make provision for "foreign" children, most of whom will have been born there, to learn their parents' language, but that language would not be offered to "majority" children. The Charter on Regional and Minority Languages, passed by the European Parliament in 1993, gives minorities rights to the use of their language in education, the media, public administration, care of the aged, and cross-border communication. However, this does not apply to immigrants.

4 Language Planning and Multilingualism

Language policies (see chapter 27) and/or community attitudes may enforce, support, accept, tolerate, or reject multilingualism or give special status to one or more than one language. Where language policies have been formulated to promote multilingualism, the motivation may be:

> Social – in the interests of equity for all groups;
> Cultural – to facilitate cultural maintenance;
> Political – to ensure the participation of all groups and/or gain their electoral support;
> Economic – to be able to harness language assets to the advantage of the country's balance of payments.

A few examples may be drawn from Namibia, Singapore, Australia, Canada, and Switzerland.

The language policy of the new *Namibia* gives official status to English only, although English is the native language of not more than 3 percent of the population and only 53 percent of the population have any competence in it. The adoption of English as the sole official language is due to the identification of the other two prior official languages, Afrikaans and German, with colonialism and/or oppression, and it was considered that there were too many African ethnic languages spoken for one of them to become an official language (Pütz, 1992). In contrast, *Singapore* has four official languages. Three of the languages – Mandarin, Malay, and Tamil – may be seen to represent the three major ethnic groups, the Chinese, Malays, and Indians. The other official language is English, the language of interethnic and international communication. Clearly the choice is on the basis of status. The majority of Singapore Chinese use a variety other than Mandarin at home, while a significant number of Singapore Indians are not native speakers of Tamil. By choosing English as an official language, Singapore has a vehicle of trade communication with the rest of the world. Mandarin opens doors to both Taiwan and the People's Republic of China. These language resources are also being developed by neighboring Malaysia, for example. The former Soviet Union had Russian as its overall official language but with each republic also being allowed a second official language for its own purposes (Lewis, 1972: 209). The disappearance of the overarching "imperial" language as an official language from the republics other than the Russian Federation, while giving full status to the language of the majority group, has diminished the position of many ethnic minorities (including the formerly privileged Russian minorities) in the newly independent republics.

Australia, while not declaring an official language, uses English as its national (i.e., de facto official) language. Both the National Policy on Languages (Lo Bianco, 1987) and the Australian Language and Literacy Policy (Dawkins, 1991) have followed the guiding principles:

> Competence in English for all;
> Maintenance and development of languages other than English;
> Provision of services in languages other than English;
> Opportunities to acquire second languages.

Most of the efforts have concentrated on education, with primary and secondary schools teaching children from all backgrounds a range of languages, including some of those of the immigrant groups, and about 38 languages examined in the end-of-secondary school examination. In addition, many public notices are published in a variety of languages of – especially – newly arrived immigrant groups, there are government and publically subsidized radio stations broadcasting in a total of over 60 languages, a state-run television service transmits films in community languages with English subtitles, local public libraries hold books, magazines, cassettes, and videos in the languages of the local community, and there is a telephone interpreter service available in about 90 languages (Clyne, 1991a). While the 1987 Lo Bianco Report was motivated by a combination of social, cultural and economic factors, more recent policies represented a change of emphasis to an economic rationale (Clyne, 1991b).

The declaration of an "official language," sometimes under the guise of "protecting a threatened" majority language or guaranteeing continuity of national cohesion, neither of which is usually under threat, will usually have the effect of undermining other languages. This is apparently behind the movement (Marshall, 1985) to make English the official language of the US. Such a declaration has already been promulgated with respect to over a quarter of the states of the US. The scapegoat is the largest minority language of the US, Spanish, and the casualties are bilingual ballots and many bilingual education programs.

In *Canada*, "official bilingualism" is intended to protect the "balance" between English and French, which had been tipped in the direction of English for most of Canada's history, for economic and political reasons. Following the Royal Commission on Bilingualism and Biculturalism (Royal Commission, 1965–70) and the declaration of the Official Languages Act (1969), while Canada had become increasingly bilingual as a whole, Quebec had become increasingly monolingual. In 1974 French was declared the sole official language of Quebec, though still conforming to constitutional prescriptions regarding parliamentary, legislative, and judiciary bilingualism (Fortier, 1994). Bill 101, the Charter of the French Language (1977), made French the language of work, business, and everyday life in Quebec, except for the education of children whose parents had received English-medium schooling in Canada. The revised Official Languages Act of 1988 represented an adaptation to the consequences of the Charter of the French Language. While Canada has declared itself a "multicultural" country, it is in fact also a multilingual one like Australia. There is the anomaly that, in the provinces of Alberta, Manitoba, and Saskatchewan, there are far fewer speakers of French than of a number of languages other than English which do not have any official status. Despite the sizable group of Franco-Ontarians, the same state of affairs exists in Toronto. The English component of the "imagined bilingual nation" of Canada is therefore giving a large proportion of its resources to French, especially in education (immersion and core programs) while disregarding some of its other assets. (However, facilities are being made available for the teaching of "heritage languages" *after* school hours.)

One can differentiate between *symmetrical* multilingualism, where all the languages have equal status, and *asymmetrical* multilingualism, where one at least of the languages has more status than the others.

In *Switzerland*, each of the national languages – French, German, and Italian – is equal despite substantial differences in the number of users – 73.5 percent of Swiss citizens have German as their first language, 20.1 percent have French, 4.5 per cent Italian, and 0.9 percent the regional official language, Rheto-Romansh (Albrecht and Mathis, 1990). The languages are distributed on a territorial principle, i.e., almost all cantons are German-language or French-language or Italian-language cantons rather than, say, bilingual. The same equality of status does not apply to *Singapore*. Malay is the national language but its special functions are limited to the national anthem and the national motto. Mandarin has been propagated in the majority Chinese community, and Tamil is the official language undergoing the greatest language shift, but in most respects the four languages – English, Mandarin, Malay, and Tamil – are officially equal. In fact, the originally "exotic" language, English, which is both the lingua franca between the ethnic groups and the medium of the link with most of the rest of the world, is often employed on its own (cf., e.g., Gupta, 1994). One is hard pressed to find a single notice in any other language at Changi International Airport in Singapore. In Australia and the US, it is clear that English is the dominant language, regardless of what other languages may at times be used in addition for particular purposes. Within the European Union, all official or national languages of member nations are equal, but the French version (and to a lesser extent, the English) is used as the basis of translations of documents into the other languages, which are not made available till later (Volz, 1993).

In his book, *Imagined Communities*, Anderson (1983) demonstrates the role of print languages (standard languages) when hitherto nonexistent nations were "invented." Print languages became the basis for national consciousness, especially in nineteenth-century Europe. The nineteenth-century German philosophers Herder and Humboldt saw language as the basis of a nation and a culture. Humboldt developed the twin theories of linguistic determinism and linguistic relativism (language plays a significant role in determining culture, and each language has a different way of "looking at the world"). Most of the nation-states of the nineteenth century were based on an entity comprising people of a single language background. (Belgium, with its French- and Dutch-speaking groups, was a notable exception.) There then existed side by side nations such as France, Germany, and Italy, which were conceived this way, and Austria–Hungary (and Russia) which were multilingual and multicultural entities. Since that time, there has been a myth that "national cohesion" is possible only through a single common language (see, e.g., Kedourie, 1961; Isajiw, 1980). This view is widespread in both Western and Eastern Europe, but it is challenged, for instance, by the Australian policy of unity within diversity. Of course English provides the communicative link, but Australia's multiculturalism has become part of its national identity and so multilingualism (English plus at least one other language) is contributing to national cohesion.

5 Functional Specialization of Languages in Multilinguals and in a Multilingual Society

Multilinguals are people who either belong to more than one language group or function within more than one language group. Fishman (1977) has made the point that the use of two or more languages in the long term depends on the need for these two languages (see also Bratt Paulston, 1994). The most clearcut examples are whole societies observing a functional distribution between two languages or distinct language varieties ("diglossia" whether in the sense of Ferguson, 1959, or of Fishman, 1967).

Multilinguals' choice of languages is determined according to:

Interlocutor Different people will be identified as, say, X, Y, or Z speakers. Such an identification will be made even by many who are themselves multilingual. Such people will be addressed in the appropriate language (Sankoff, 1971). Interlocutors who are monolingual will usually cause a code-switch even if they are passive participants in a conversation. The age of an interlocutor may influence the choice of the language. In both immigrant countries such as the US and Australia, and in stable bilingual situations such as parts of Burgenland (Gal, 1979), the minority language is frequently associated with the older generation and the majority language with the younger generation.

The interlocutor is the basis of one method of bringing up children bi- or multilingually, where both parents or different relatives consistently use their language to the child. It is difficult to break the nexus between interlocutor and language once a relationship has been established.

Role relationship Where the same interlocutors have multiple relationships (e.g., a family friend in a Hispanic context and a public-school teacher in an Anglo-American context), the language choice may be governed by the role relationship (Clyne, 1991a).

Domain The contextualized sphere of communication, e.g., home, work, school, religion, transactional, leisure or friendship, community group (Cooper, 1967). The home domain is often the last that survives in a minority language, but sometimes it is religion and/or a community group. Where there are several languages, their use may also be domain-bound, e.g., among some Mauritian immigrants in Australia, Mauritian Creole (the French creole of Mauritius) for home, Standard French for religion, English for the work and transactional domains.

A limitation of the use of a language to one domain can mean an impoverishment of the language; not using it in the home domain detracts from its liveliness and endangers its transmission into future generations, while using it solely in the home domain limits its ultimate usefulness, since speakers will be unable to cope with the interpenetration of domains such as talking about work or school at home.

Topic This overlaps slightly with the domain. Different types of experience associated with the two languages (e.g., in the homeland and the country of migration, or in the spheres associated with each language) will cause some people to switch languages to talk about their jobs, their present leisure activities, school, new technological developments, or particular forms of sport, to give a few examples (Haugen, 1953).

Venue Certain buildings or other venues (e.g., street, garden, home) are identified with a more public or a more private domain and therefore generate code-switching to the other language.

Channel of communication Some people who use one language for face-to-face communication will employ another for telephone communication. Some will speak one language to each other but write another (Clyne, 1991a).

Type of interaction Formal business communication tends to be in the language of the public domain (except in some cases when it is restricted to an ethnic group) while more informal interaction, including the telling of jokes and anecdotes, takes place in the language of the private domain (Clyne, 1991a).

Phatic function The use of a particular language can signal an attempt to create a specific effect, e.g., dramatic (Gumperz and Hernandez-Chavez, 1975; Appel and Muysken, 1987: 119; Heller, 1988).

The most important use of a "minority language" is boundary marking. The speakers of this language who may be perceived as an out-group by the dominant group are able, through their bilingualism, to exclude the latter. They become the in-group (Schermerhorn, 1970). The first generation of an immigrant group, for instance, may require their first language to communicate (especially with their families and friends) because of their limited competence in the national language. The second generation usually does not have this need. Where they use the "minority language" for anything but a language of communication with the older generation – especially if they employ it with their children – it is for reasons of symbolic identification or else because they are convinced by the value of bi- or multilingualism.

6 Language Maintenance or Shift

A number of attempts have been made to develop explanatory and predictive models relating to the dynamics of language maintenance (keeping up the use of a specific language entirely or in one or more domains) and language shift (shifting partly or wholly to the use of another language) (see chapter 20). Kloss (1966) argues that there are social variables, such as ethnolinguistic enclaves and religious insulation, that clearly promote language maintenance and others which, depending on their combination, may lead to either language maintenance or shift, e.g., the number of speakers and their educational attainment. Kloss suggests that a large community of speakers can afford more language maintenance institutions (e.g., ethnic schools, newspapers) but can also be "lost" easily in the mass of minority speakers. People with a high educational attainment can learn the majority language more easily and do not need the first language so much for communicative purposes but, because they do not have to devote so much time to acquiring the dominant language and culture, they have more opportunity to maintain the first language. Nevertheless, the relative size of a community of speakers (e.g., Spanish speakers in America, to cite one example) does appear to correlate significantly with language maintenance. The status and economic value of the language also tends to support language maintenance, while exogamy is usually a clear-cut factor promoting language shift.

A more controversial variable is the position of language as a core cultural value, which is the basis of a powerful explanatory model (Smolicz, 1980). Smolicz's argument is that each group has specific cultural values that are basic to their continued existence as a group, and language is such a value to some groups but not to others. Language attitudes do not always lead to language maintenance (cf. Fishman, 1985). There is evidence that the most successful language maintenance occurs in groups for whom language is intertwined as a core value with other core values, such as religion and historical consciousness or family cohesion, rather than those for whom language stands in isolation as an identity maker. This might explain the success of Greek but also why Hassidic Jews, who have no ideological commitment to Yiddish, maintain it much better in the US than do Yiddishist ideologues, because the former have specific domains in which they have to use it, owing to religious considerations (cf. Fishman, 1991: 195). While the Dutch practice multilingualism in the interests of communication, they attach relatively little importance to the Dutch language as a distinctive symbol of ethnicity; nor do they see the maintenance of other languages as an important issue for their own linguistic minorities (Extra and Verhoeven, 1993: 23). In addition, Dutch people are inclined to lose their language due to identity change in a predominantly Anglo-Celtic society such as the US, English-speaking Canada, or Australia. Some problems with the "core value" theory include defining the "group," for different sections of a large community may have different relationships to their language for political, social, or religious reasons, which sometimes motivate migration. Also, the same languages are maintained at different rates even in contact with similar languages and/or cultures. This applies, for instance, to Finnish and (American) English in Sweden, Denmark, and Norway (Boyd et al., 1992). The position of language within the cultural value system may alter in a dynamic situation between groups.

Another relevant model, that of Giles and others (1977), is intended to explain the role of language in intergroup relations. Their notion of ethnolinguistic vitality is based on the components: economic status, self-perceived social status, sociohistorical factors (e.g., experience of coping with minority status; cf. Kloss, 1966, and see above), and demographic ones (e.g., numbers, group distribution, and institutional support). Tajfel's model concerns the redefining of group attributes in relation to the majority group, while speech accommodation involves converging or diverging speech in relation to the majority. Aspects of the "core value" theory could be accommodated within the "ethnolinguistic vitality" framework. For instance, part of the ethnolinguistic vitality of Greek in immigrant situations is determined by a belief in the uniqueness of Greek culture and the authenticity of the language as the language of the New Testament, linking language, religion, historical consciousness, and identity.

Fishman (1985) proposes sets of measures for predicting relative survival rates of minority languages, while expressing caution as to their applicability. They are based on the number of speakers, adjusted for average age, institutional resources for language maintenance, and religious and racial distance from the "mainstream." (For a critique of this model, see Clyne, 1991a: 106–9.) The significance of insulation from the "mainstream" is stressed in Fishman's (1991) comprehensive study evaluating the success of attempts by groups in different parts of the world to reverse language shift (e.g., Maoris in New Zealand, some outback Aborigines in Australia).

7 Linguistic Consequences of Multilingualism

So far we have focused on the social and sociopolitical consequences of multilingualism. Perhaps the best developed field of study in this area is the effect of one language on the other. These effects are manifested at all levels of language – grammar, phonology, lexicon, pragmatics (the use of language in communication), and discourse (the level beyond the sentence).

7.1 Lexical transfers and their integration

Early research centered around the lexicon (vocabulary). What words were "borrowed" from one language to the other? The outcome was frequently "washing lists" of words which were sometimes rather repetitive. However, grammar and phonology were also dealt with and played a prominent part in the overall models proposed by Weinreich (1953) and Haugen (1956). In accordance with the normative definition of bilingualism current until fairly recently, bilinguals were expected to be "double monolinguals," which meant that they should not "mix their systems" and they should only switch between the languages deliberately. On the one hand, those areas of vocabulary where lexical transference took place were described; it occurred mainly where the L2 context of situation differed from that in which the L1 had been used. On the other, attempts were made to differentiate between those "borrowings" that were essential and therefore permissible, and those that were unnecessary and therefore unacceptable. However, it could be argued that lexical items are only transferred because they are needed by a speaker – because no exact equivalent is available to them or to create a particular stylistic effect. Far more significant than the actual lexical transfer itself is the type and degree of integration into the semantic, grammatical, phonological, and graphemic (writing or spelling) system of the recipient language. Phonological integration involves replacing some sounds (phonemes and phoneme realizations) and sound sequences that are nonexistent in or peripheral to the recipient language by more usual ones. There is a good deal of variation in phonological integration, depending on the speaker's command of the sounds of the recipient language, the desire to keep the two systems apart, and how much the item is accepted as a central part of the vocabulary of the recipient language. Where the recipient language has gender-marked articles and/or adjectival and noun inflections, transferred nouns are assigned a gender according to one or more of the following criteria – natural gender (il teacher or la teacher, Italian in Australia), gender of semantic equivalent in the recipient language (le job < le travail; la fence < la haie, la palissade, French in Australia), bilingual homophone (der roof < der Ruf, "reputation," despite *das* Dach, German in Australia), suffix (das Depart*ment*, i rul*er* (feminine, cf. roula, Greek in Australia). Noun plurals and past tenses of verbs are formed according to particular rules, often indicating how much the transfer is felt by the speaker or community to be part of the recipient language. (For instance, the past participle *geschrinkt* is more recognizable as "possibly foreign" than *geschrunken* (for "shrunk") in German in Australia.) In writing lexical transfers, the spelling system or script of the recipient language may be employed, e.g., Miß (Miss, German), or ΜΠΑDZET (budget, Greek). When a transfer is integrated semantically, the lexical field in the recipient language changes. In Australia, *fattoria* (Standard Italian, "small farm") has widely assumed the meaning of "factory" and English "farm" has been integrated as *farma* to denote a "farm" in the Australian sense. *Fattoria* is here a semantic transfer (where a meaning has been transferred from a word in the other language). Semantic transfers are due to interlingual identification where there is morphemic, phonological, or partial semantic correspondence and could be seen to constitute a very high degree of integration. They are used by people deliberately avoiding "language mixture" and are particularly prevalent in closed networks of speakers.

7.2 *Grammatical transference and grammatical change*

In contact situations, especially where the "minority language" is not maintained very well, and there is considerable isolation from the "heartland" of the language, grammatical change will occur quite rapidly. This may include a gradual typological change, say, from Subject-Object-Verb or a mixture of Verb-second and Subject-Object-Verb to Subject-Verb-Object (the general typology of the dominant language). There are tendencies in that direction as early as the first generation in Dutch–English bilinguals and in the second in

German–English bilinguals in Australia – the more advanced change in Dutch being attributable to both typological factors (drift towards a Dutch syntax determined by a fixed order of sentence elements due to the loss of case markings as in English) and sociolinguistic ones (greater language shift). Grammatical change may include the use of the masculine singular adjective as an unmarked adjective instead of an inflection (some second-generation Italian speakers in Australia and the US), or the overgeneralization of one gender and/or of one plural marker, and even the loss of verb inflections (in some second-generation bilinguals in Australia) (Clyne, 1991a: 176–86; Gonzo and Saltarelli, 1983; Bettoni, 1985).

7.3 Code-switching

Code-switching (see chapter 13) involves production in more than one language, within one sentence or between sentences within a stretch of discourse. It often occurs within structural constraints which may be language-specific or even universal (see Myers-Scotton, 1993b). It is often motivated by the social variables of code-choice (see section 5) and/or by a symbolic (us – them) function in conversation (see, e.g., Gumperz, 1982; Auer, 1984; Myers-Scotton, 1993a). Code-switching is frequently facilitated by grammatical convergence between the languages on the part of the speaker or community and by trigger-words of ambiguous affiliation (Clyne, 1991a: 193–6), for example,

> Sie war in New Guinea *when the Japanese came there and* dann haben's/ mußten sie 'raus von New Guinea *at the time of the war.* (Clyne, 1991a: 195)

(She was in . . . and then she had to leave New Guinea . . .) (To the speaker, who uses *New Guinea* in her German, it is part of both language systems.)

> Ja sprasivaju vas (Russian) *my dear friend* wos zol ig tun mit (Yiddish) *my daughter*? (Rót, 1985: 203)

(I tell you . . . what should i do with . . .)
(Trigger-words facilitate code-switching between three languages.)

8 Intercultural Communication in Multilingual Communities and Regions

Intercultural communication constitutes communication between people of different cultures, including the effects of different sets of communication patterns on one another. In regions of close cultural contact, such as the

Balkans or South Asia, groups of unrelated or only distantly related languages will form groups of languages known as *Sprachbünde*, which will influence one another in structure as well as in the lexicon (Becker, 1948). The influence will extend to the communication patterns of the language (*Sprechbünde*; Neustupný, 1978). In immigrant societies, the dominant language will tend to affect such patterns. For instance, the second and later generations in such countries as the US and Australia will tend to give up distinctions in pronouns or other forms of address, often overgeneralizing the informal (T) pronoun and first names.

While, in a multicultural society, there will be convergence towards the communication patterns of the dominant language, there will be people of vastly different cultural backgrounds communicating in that language as a lingua franca. Their discourse structures – length of turns in conversation, ways of maintaining and appropriating turns, tendencies towards overlapping speech, choice of complex interaction sequences (such as directive, apology and complaint sequences, all of which include other speech acts) – are all strongly influenced by their cultural value systems.

NOTE

1 I thank Florian Coulmas and Mark Newbrook for helpful comments on an earlier draft.

19 Language and Identity

ANDRÉE TABOURET-KELLER

[handwritten: linguistic culture.]

[handwritten: what is identity ??]

To Identify: Transitive vs Intransitive

The language spoken by somebody and his or her identity as a speaker of this language are inseparable: This is surely a piece of knowledge as old as human speech itself. Language acts are acts of identity (Le Page and Tabouret-Keller, 1985).

[handwritten right margin: Good quote]

The Greeks identified as non-Greek those whose speech sounded to them like *barbarbar* and called them *barbarians*; in 1978, in a field interview in Belize, an independent state since 1976 after a long period under British rule as British Honduras, the following dialogue took place:

> DR (the schoolboy interviewed): "Well, I would say I'm a Belizean, too. Co . . . Because erm, born in Belize, you know, I got to know about Belize a bit in history. An' originally, everybody called themselves Belizean, so I call myself a Belizean."
>
> LeP (the interviewer): "How do you recognize another Belizean?"
>
> DR: "Well, usually in Belize you find the language, the main language you know is this slang that I tell you about, the Creole. And you'd recognize them by that, you know. They usually have this, you know, very few of them speak the English or some of them usually speak Spanish." (Le Page and Tabouret-Keller, 1985: 216)

[handwritten right margin: belonging]

The two semantic fields of the verb *identify* are illustrated: In the first case, language is taken as an external behavior allowing the identification of a speaker as a member of some group, as in the case of non-Greeks identified by Greeks as foreigners by their way of speech. In the second case, language is taken as the means of identifying oneself, as when the Belizean schoolboy identified himself as Belizean, which meant for him, first, to be born in Belize, and, second but indirectly and certainly with some ambivalent feelings, to belong to a group also identified by its language, "this slang," "the Creole."

[handwritten right margin, Chinese: 群己 / 阶—下界安线近 / 语言有自己的, / Festure / shared norms / connotations]

Identifying *the others* as *the barbarians* is much more than nicknaming or naming them. It sets a frame within which the relationship will start and often develop. For it implies both that *they* are different from *us* and that *we* are different from *them*, and also, even if not explicitly, that they too are supposed to apply the same logic *vis-à-vis* ourselves. The Latin *alter* (or, at a later time, *alter alter*) expresses this complex process in a very condensed and apt way, stressing its mirror quality. Identifying *us* as *Creole* implies that at least some others exist who have a different identity. Identifying others or oneself is a means of differentiation and of opposition.

The Dynamics of Identities

An analogy may be of some help. The dynamics of ever-changing language in ever-changing human polylogues[1] takes place in a non-homogeneous, unlimited ocean containing mainlands, isles, and islets of relatively permanent usages based on a given linguistic stock, also only relatively permanent; these language pockets are located within larger sociolinguistic streamlets and streams. Personal identities although not parallel nor complementary to these variations, nevertheless show a similar kind of dynamic (Tabouret-Keller, 1989). At any given time a person's identity is a heterogeneous set made up of all the names or identities, given to and taken up by her. But in a lifelong process, identity is endlessly created anew, according to very various social constraints (historical, institutional, economic, etc.), social interactions, encounters, and wishes that may happen to be very subjective and unique.

We call identification processes those psychological processes by which identities are established. Although we are primarily concerned with language-embedded identities that rest on strictly symbolic means, such as family names, for example, we must not forget that identities may also exploit scopic materials, sensory elements among which visual features seem to occupy a pre-eminent place.[2] The global term *nonverbal*, commonly used to deal with them, calls for caution, because it suggests that these features are extralinguistic, which is not quite the same thing, as will become apparent further on. Every person exploits different layers of identities, forming more or less intricate and encased networks, some parts of which are loose and prone to frequent change and replacement, others being more or less permanent throughout the life span and across social and cultural space. We are identified, and identify ourselves, within the large space of the society of our time, within the different groups – institutional, professional, friends, etc. – we belong to, within the surroundings of our home, our office, our car, our out-of-door outfits, our in-door outfits, etc. A good deal of our overt and covert identities blend symbolic and nonverbal means, certain identifications seem to isolate scopic behavioral elements as if in a postural imitation. The problem of the possible independence in man of certain scopic or nonverbal behavioral elements from inclusion into language-steered symbolic systems remains open. It is central in cognitive theories and answers to it are still tentative, as in a postural imitation. In sociolinguistics we prefer to relate and include what may initially appear as purely nonverbal behavior in cultural constraints or trends that are never independent from symbolic mediation.

We must also stress that, as an oral behavior, language itself necessarily includes corporeal elements resulting from the physiological channels that our voice has to pass through and that give it its phonetic qualities, that is, the upper ends of the digestive and respiratory tracts. No wonder speech and language are so easily confused with life itself: Many organic associations are constantly at work between speech and breathing or eating.

Language and Identity: Complex Links

The link between language and identity is often so strong that a single feature of language use suffices to identify someone's membership in a given group. On the battle-field after their victory over the people of Ephraïm, the Gileads applied a language-identity test to sort out friend and foe. All of the soldiers were asked to pronounce the word *shibboleth*; those who pronounced the first consonant as [ʃ] were friends, those who pronounced it [s] were enemies and therefore killed at once (Judges: XII. 6). Hence a single phonemic feature may be sufficient to include or exclude somebody from any social group. But any other more complex symbolic language item, for example, a given name, may fulfil the same function. In the nineties, during a discussion in French about identity with other French-speaking adolescents of her age, a schoolgirl said: "It's my first name that spoils everything. Nobody pays attention, and as soon as the teacher calls my name at the beginning of the year, Bang! those who don't know me say, 'what name is this?' And I have to say my mother is German." This girl's first name was a Germanic name (Varro, 1995).

Language and Identity: Complex Binds

These examples show how individual identity and social identity are mediated by language: Language features are the link which binds individual and social identities together. Language offers both the means of creating this link and that of expressing it. Such features imply the whole range of language use, from phonetic features to lexical units, syntactic structures, and personal names.

Two main reasons can be used to explain the close link of language and identity. The first belongs to human psychology: Identification processes range all the way from the confluent identification of mother and new-born child by feeding at the breast or, more generally, nursing, to mere imitation of another, and to identification proper where someone adopts, consciously or unconsciously, a feature or a set of features of another's behavior. Language use offers the largest range of features and the most easily adoptable ones for identification, whatever such identification processes and the complementary identities may mean to their bearer and to those who observe them. The complexity of such behavior is best illustrated by the attempt to please someone by adopting, through identification, behavioral features of another person who one knows is appreciated by that person. Such an attempt may include, for example, such things as a kind of coughing to punctuate sentences as a style of expression. This would be an objective feature of conduct, but identification also involves all sorts of construed representations, such as types and stereotypes (Giles and Powesland, 1975; Le Page and Tabouret-Keller, 1985: chapter 6; Tabouret-Keller, 1991).

The second reason for the close identification of language and identity lies in their linkage by constitution and by law, as illustrated by the example of the Oath of Strasbourg. On February 14 in the year 842, Lewis the German and Charles the Bald, two grandsons of Charlemagne, took an oath of alliance against their older brother, who opposed the legitimate partition of their grandfather's kingdom (Balibar, 1993: 26). First each read the text of the oath in his own language. Then they switched languages: By speaking the Romance language to read out the text of the oath, the heir of Eastern France established it as the language for Western France. The heir of Western France did the same for the Germanic language for Eastern France by using it to read out the text of the oath. Each of the two languages was given legitimacy, but only as far as the dignity of the other was respected. All this took place under the authority of Latin, the language in which the history of the Oath of Strasbourg is recorded. Third, the spokesmen of the two princes swore fidelity to the alliance in their own languages, according to a text which was translated verbatim (*eadem verba*) from Latin into Germanic and Romance. This innovation came from the masters of grammar and literature who prompted the princes word for word. Not only did they not speak Romance, but it was important that the spoken text did not deviate from the written one, which was considered to be the authentic version.

Imposing on a language the dimensions of an institution, of legitimacy linked to power over a territory and over other institutions, especially law, has several consequences. The name of the language, corresponding to some kind of standardized form – in the case of the Strasbourg Oath, the two forms created by the grammarian advisors of the two kings, Germanic and Romance – achieves some degree of autonomy in people's thinking. According to Le Page (1980), naming a language makes it ready for reification and totemization, that is, it can be made into an object and given iconic status. Reification usually involves some body of doctrine (grammars, lexicon, a literature), totemization the adoption of a language as one of the defining social properties of a group. Members of a group who feel their cultural and political

Skate over 混过去

S/I (*threatened*)

identity threatened are likely to make particularly assertive claims about the social importance of maintaining or resurrecting *their language* (as, for example, in Wales, Quebec, Belgium, immigrant groups all over Europe, and numerous other communities throughout the world). We see here that identification is served by the name of a language that fulfills the symbolic function of representation, at both the social and individual levels, where it represents not only affiliation with a community or group, but all kinds of allegiance: to a religion, a political leader, an ideology. Fishman's chapter (20) in this book provides many examples of the expression of such collective identification processes.

Identification by a single feature of language use, as in the *shibboleth* example, or by a complex of features, as in the case of *the so-called Creole*, is only one side of the language binding function. The other is that a language's name serves as a label covering any kind of intuitive knowledge of what the "object" that it refers to may be – common use, a common standard, an idealized form of the language, etc. As such the name of a language serves as the basis of identification by means of a shared element. In such cases, identification with a partner is mediated, first of all, by the common label and, secondarily, but not necessarily, by direct behavioral identification with other participants in the same community, social group, faith, belief, ideology, etc. Other behavioral features may support the identification, for instance, dress, a flag (or any other symbol), shared by people one has never met before and will never meet afterwards. Language itself can function as such a symbol for which some are ready to die or kill.

Boundaries, but with Gaps   IMP.

Languages and the identities they carry with them generally imply a boundary marking function: The same identity prevails where and as long as the same language is spoken. Has this ever been true? It certainly is no longer true today, but it is true that the longer a territorial identity is perceived as embedded in the use of an idiom – more often than not, subsumed under a unique term that might designate the territory, the people, and their language – the stronger the representation of a highly focused unit of internal coherence. The strength of such a representation does not depend on permanent variation and change in language use: On the contrary, it helps to overlook these in favor of a unique identity supported by this unique term. This representation is even more focused when language as a named object – as an identification label, not as a linguistic behavioral feature – becomes by law the expression of power at the same time that it also becomes the main instrument by which this power is expressed and executed (Weinreich, 1968: 648). Modern nation-states, which today occupy almost all the world's territory, intervene in the idealized union of language and identity. They have many means of forcing a language upon their citizens, be it by the constitutional definition of a national, official, or state language, or by one of many other ways like control over the language(s) allowed for school education, for law and justice, etc. French is not only the name of a territory, of the people who live there, of the language that is supposed to be spoken by them, it is also by constitution the language of the citizen of the State of France, including overseas territories such as Martinique and Guadeloupe. As a matter of inherent paradox, though not openly expressed, the formation of states rests on discourse (and ultimately on law) justified by mother-tongue ideology, and calls on the territorial identity of a population at the same time that these states, in setting their frontiers, ignored the language people use and their identity (Tabouret-Keller and Le Page, 1986: 252). As a result, frontiers between states do not usually coincide with dialectal areas and thus most European states, if not all of them, include territories where languages other than the official ones are in use. In such cases, all sorts of distributions between citizenship identity, national identity, and language use identity, are found: *Spanish* by citizenship, *Catalan* by family origin, residence, and political choice, *Catalan* but also *Spanish* speaker. In a survey of language use in secondary schools in Alsace, in 1980, pupils between 12 and 14 were asked if they thought it possible to be *Alsatian* without being able to speak the Alsatian dialect; more than 50 percent answered *yes* (Ladin, 1982: 185).

Multilingual situations illustrate the two aspects of identification by language. A bilingual speaker may be identified by linguistic features deriving from language contact. In certain situations, this gives rise to feelings of inferiority, discrimination, or exclusion from the dominant group, or conversely, feelings of familiarity, recognition, complicity among those who share the language and/or the contact situation. The creativity of bilinguals, especially in oral language not controlled by the normative power of writing, will suffer repression through the totemization of the dominant language. Mastery of the latter is regarded as testimony to allegiance to the state that imposes it, and integration into a community mistakenly based on a single linguistic identity. Such sociolinguistic constraints point toward the subjective difficulties which often arise in contact situations.

Group Affiliation as a Matter of Relative Choice

Boundary functions of language imply the possibility for individuals to be both in their own group and out of the others' groups.[3] Such affiliations are of relative value, according to the strength of the identification with language, both as being used and being an identification label, or as only one of these functions. In a survey by Dabène in Grenoble among adolescents whose parents were immigrants from North Africa, one of them declared: "Arabic is my language, but I don't speak it" (Dabène and Billiez, 1987: 76). As well as language, groups themselves, via their leaders, their members, a common faith and holy oral or written bodies, their press and other media, may reify and totemize their existence with a name identical to that of what they consider to be their proper language. Membership in a group must satisfy some kind of need in its members, but groups are nothing without their members and it must be stressed that group leaders usually have an advantage in fostering and sustaining the group. One of the easiest means for this is to include the group's name and its attribute in discourse, to stress group affiliation by differentiating from others who don't possess the same advantages, who are easily recognized, by language use among other things.

Groups, whether formal or informal, are aware of and cannot ignore the boundary-marking function of language, if only by the name of the group. Names function in a double capacity of naming an organization and some kind of affiliation, as in *Cosa Nostra*, for example. Group affiliation is hardly something anyone can dispense with, but some groups one is part of willy-nilly, e.g., gender or age groups; some are imposed upon one, e.g., by social categorization; some one may choose whether or not to join, in which case one has more liberty to adhere to the constraints the affiliation implies.

The image of language, absorbed by the infant with its mother's milk, is one of the roots of the mother-tongue metaphor, the strength of which is due in part to the fact that the new-born child cannot escape dependence on adult's care for his survival (Tabouret-Keller and Le Page, 1986). In any case, the family group is certainly one one has to deal with, even by leaving it. Later on many want to join other groups by accommodating to their behavior, or by adopting what is perceived as their characteristic features, among which language behavior is often, although not always, the most overt. However, it is not necessarily the most important feature; virtually any product of the imagination can be employed for purposes of identification.

Joining a group is in itself a very complex process involving factors linked with the subjects' most subjective and intimate history, their situation and status in society, etc. Hence identity is rather a network of identities, reflecting the many commitments, allegiances, loyalties, passions, and hatreds everyone tries to handle in ever-varying compromise strategies. These imply language use to mark group affiliation, to reveal permitted or forbidden boundaries, to exclude or include, etc.

Theories about the Linguistic Aspects of Identity

To deal with language and identity, we must rely only on language itself. There are hence two possible avenues of approach: technical terms, as in linguistics, and metaphorical terms, as in all other disciplines, and in everyday language. This can be illustrated by every chapter of this book. Technical terms need to be defined and strictly contextualized; metaphors appeal to imagination, which is not only a great asset in identification processes but also in scientific research.

Both Giles and Le Page have developed theories addressing two questions that arise here: To what extent is group identity a matter of choice, and what are the conditions for admission to a linguistically defined group? What of people's feelings, motives, or loyalties?

Giles's accommodation theory is concerned with interactive behavioral events and rests on a definition of an ethnic group as "those individuals who perceive themselves to belong to the same ethnic category" (Giles, 1979: 253). In 1982, Giles gave the following definitions of his theory:

> A basic postulate of accommodation theory is that people are motivated to adjust their speech style, or accommodate, as means of expressing values, attitudes and intentions towards others. It is proposed that the extent to which individuals shift their speech styles toward or away from the speech styles of their interlocutors is a mechanism by which social approval or disapproval is communicated. A shift in speech style toward that of another is termed convergence and is considered often a reflection of social integration, whereas a shift away from the other's style of speech represents divergence and is considered often a tactic of social dissociation. (1982: 105)

An illustrative example of his theory is given by Giles, with Byrne (1982), in the case of two close but linguistically distinguished communities. According to this theory, the more chances of acquiring a quasi-native competence in the language of a group rise for an individual member of the other ethnic group when:

(a) his identification with his proper group is weak or the language of this group is not of central value to him;
(b) he is not inclined to believe that the intergroup relationship can develop in his group's favor;
(c) he perceives his own group as having a weak ethnolinguistic vitality;
(d) his perception of his own group is vague;
(e) he identifies with his community less in ethnic terms than in terms of membership in other groups, such as a profession.

In order to account for a series of complex behavioral data, Giles introduces an additional concept into accommodation theory, the concept of complementarity. Convergence and divergence may simultaneously operate on different linguistic dimensions. For example: "simultaneous shifts away from and towards the other in a dyad can occur in a way that can be regarded as totally integrative for both participants" (Giles, 1982: 122).

A good many theories applying to bilingual situations bear similarities to Giles's, for example, those of Wallace E. Lambert (1974, 1977), J. Cummins (1979), and J. Hamers and M. Blanc (1982). These are all based on the a priori existence of social, ethnic, regional, national, and professional groups, etc.

More generally, language contact situations are good cases to study language and identity fusion or disjunction. Some of them are dealt with in other parts of this book (see especially the chapters by Clyne (18) and Nelde (17)).

Although Giles regards Le Page's work on language behavior in multilingual communities as an important forerunner of accommodation theory (Giles, 1982: 105) the latter's theory differs fundamentally from Giles's by postulating that the speaker creates his linguistic system and speech acts as acts of projection (Le Page, 1968, 1978). Hence social groups need not be defined beforehand; it is the existence of the individual that is the basic postulate. For Le Page it is essential to stress that "the individual creates for himself the patterns of his linguistic behaviour so as to resemble those of the group or groups with which from time to time he wishes to be identified, or so as to be unlike those from whom he wishes to be distinguished" (Le Page and Tabouret-Keller, 1985: 181). Groups or communities and the linguistic attributes of such groups have no existential locus other than in the minds of individuals, and such groups or communities inhere only in the way individuals behave towards each other.

Speech acts are seen as acts of projection: "The speaker is projecting his inner universe, implicitly with the invitation to others to share it, at least insofar as they recognise his language as an accurate symbolisation of the world, and to share his attitudes towards it" (Le Page and Tabouret-Keller, 1985: 181).

> There is no system for the speaker to internalise other than that which he has himself created, which is already internal, and is already the idiosyncratic expression of this search for identity and role. To the extent that he is reinforced, his behaviour in a particular context may become more regular, more focused; to the extent that he modifies his behaviour to accommodate to others it may for a time become more variable, more diffuse, but in time the behaviour of the group – that is he and those with whom he is trying to identify – will become more focused. Thus linguistic systems, both in individuals and in groups, may be considered as focused or diffuse. (Le Page et al., 1974: 14)

An individual's ability to get into focus with those with whom he wishes to identify, however, is constrained. One can only behave according to the behavioral patterns of groups one finds it desirable to identify with to the extent that:

(a) one can identify the groups;
(b) one has both adequate access to the groups and ability to analyze their behavioral patterns;
(c) the motivation for joining the group is sufficiently powerful, and is either reinforced or lessened by feedback from the group;
(d) we have the ability to modify our behavior.

My own theory rests on the postulate that language, however defined, precedes any of us at birth, that the existential *locus* of *Homo sapiens*, be it individuals or groups, is in language itself. This postulate was developed in seminar work in 1987–8 (Tabouret-Keller, 1989: 15–17). Identification processes are not envisioned in the frame of a dual relationship between A and B, as if A identifies B, or A identifies with B. Rather, they take place in a three-part relationship: Identification between A and B is possible only insofar as these two have access to and are part of C.

A, B, and C are terms of different qualities. The former two represent individuals or groups, whereas C represents language in its symbolic function as the foundation of the human condition. According to this hypothesis, a three-part relationship is fundamental to human existence, while a dual relationship may suffice for all other living species. Except in the case of a strictly scopic identification, human beings are bound to language. We often adopt features of the manners and ways of behavior of others without being aware of, or having any explicit knowledge about, the process by which this happens. Yet such identifications make sense at some level of consciousness, and would still make sense were they to correspond to unconscious representations. Making sense means to depend on words.

Our various examples show two ways of how language creates people's identities. On one hand, the language someone speaks functions as a behavioral attribute by any of its elements; on the other hand, language supplies the terms by which identities are expressed. Both ways are subsumed under C. In the present two states deriving from the former Czechoslovakia, the Czech Republic and Slovakia, language politicians emphasize differences between the two varieties of the formerly common language spoken in the formerly united country. They hope this will enable the identification of anyone, by a sole behavioral speech feature, as citizens of one of the two countries. The armed commando that, on December 24, seized the French Airbus at Algiers airport, intending to blow it up, called itself *El-Mouakioune Bi Eddima* "those who sign with blood." This is alas no exception. E. J. Hobsbawm's latest book on the history of the present century provides many examples of this kind, from almost every country in the world.

We have to explain why people want to be identifiable by their language and ways of speech, and why they want to keep a name which reminds them of an allegiance that commands them to kill. A corollary of my thesis leads us to define identification as a process on which rests the operation of bringing together identities as social constructs and identities as subjective constructs. The distinctions we have introduced up to now were between the individual as a social unit and the person recognized in an institutionalized frame. We need here a third term to specify individuals as unique in that they alone have lived their own life, can speak their own words, and ultimately, must die their own death. The first two entities, individual and person, can be characterized by a series of objectifiable features, as studied and described in sociology, anthropology, and law, whereas the third, subject, can be characterized by the singular quality of mental processes, whatever this notion may refer to, from the Freudian concept of the three-layered mind to the sophisticated models of contemporary cognitive science. We claim that these elements which create a nexus between social objective and individual subjective modalities of identities are themselves identity terms. In that event, the same term functions on the social level, where it operates, for example, as an element of social integration, and on the individual level, where it serves, for example, as a catalyst of associative processes. The ways in which an identity term is invested in various social domains of discourse does not necessarily coincide with the subjective values associated with it. However, not every identity term has a subjective function, and not every subjectively invested identity is echoed in social dimensions and discourse.

Directions for Future Research

All research on language and identity starts from the assumption that identities make sense, that they are meaningful. Although some answers have been given in terms of symbolic functions of language and identities as language-embedded elements, the question remains open – for psychology more than for sociolinguistics – how exactly these symbolic functions operate. As yet, we do not know enough about the ways in which identities themselves mediate between the various symbolic resources of different groups and also how, under certain conditions, they function as a means of power in normative social systems.

Hobsbawm (1994: 3) discusses the fact that the historical memory of the beginning of World War I is no longer alive, and that "the destruction of the social mechanisms that link one's contemporary experience to that of earlier generations, is one of the most characteristic and eerie phenomena of the late twentieth century." To governments and especially all Foreign Ministries, he recommends a seminar on peace settlements. It is obvious from what he says about the peace settlements in 1918 and 1945, and from what we read in the press about attempts at bringing to an end the conflict in former Yugoslavia, that questions of identity are by and large ignored. It is true that war and peace involve more than lost and passionately desired identities, although these may suffice to justify an individual's or a group's actions. But war and peace cannot be understood if the powerful role of identities is ignored. Identities have a part to play in the continuation of war or peace, for example, when the identity as enemy is attributed to an entire population, as in the case of the Tutsi and Hutu in present-day Rwanda.

Finally, we do not know much about the ways in which identities function as cognitive means or modes of categorization (differentiation, unification, classification). As a cognitive means, identities serve to cope with social plurality. Further, they can soften, if not resolve subjective contradictions. We know almost nothing of the ways in which identities underlie exaltation or *sublimation*, but we suspect that they provide just a very fragile and uncertain bridge between a person and her society, for example, when it comes to dealing with serious social problems such as unemployment. How can people manage to share the ideals of discourse celebrating employment, work, and affluence when such ideals are out of reach for millions of people? The link between language and identity appears as one of the strongest social links, but also as one of the weakest, especially when the social future is as uncertain as it is at the end of the twentieth century.

NOTES

1 According to a widely accepted idea deriving from the work of Bakhtin, all speech, even inner speech, is dialogual. Speech includes the other, if not necessarily another partner. I suggest that the use of language, being fundamentally social, is polylogual rather than merely dialogual.

2 Scopic, although specific to vision, is used as a cover term for all identification processes resting on sensory data: visual, acoustic, tactile, gustatory.

3 A mathematical model for such an in and out running can be seen in the Möbius strip.

20 Language and Ethnicity: The View from Within

JOSHUA A. FISHMAN

Introduction

As the twentieth century draws to an end, anyone who keeps abreast of the news from the former Yugoslavia, the former USSR, Burundi and Rwanda, the West Bank and Gaza, Northern Ireland, Somalia, South Africa, and various other trouble-spots throughout the globe must be convinced of the importance of ethnicity in the relationships between individuals, on the one hand, and the relationships between collectivities, on the other. Nevertheless, important though it may be in human affairs, "ethnicity" is not an exact scientific term. Rather, like "race," "people," "nation," and "nationality," terms with which it is semantically associated, it pertains to one of those "perilous ideas" which the social sciences have initially borrowed from, then elaborated, and now share with popular discourse (Wolf, 1994–1).* Much of its importance in sociolinguistics stems from the fact that ethnic phenomena loom so large and resonate so tumultuously in the "outer (that is the non-academic) world." The word "ethnicity" per se is of rather recent prominence, however. Indeed, it is still not found in many languages in which more traditional terms such as "people," "nationality," "culture," and even "race" continue to be utilized. However the availability of all of the foregoing terms *as well as* "ethnicity" in modern English and in several other modern Western languages, means that both the semantic overlap between at least some of them, as well as the boundaries that divide them, need to be clarified.

---

* Works cited in this fashion are listed in the "external perspective" bibliography that comes immediately after the "Conclusions" section (p. 341). The *number after the date*, separated by a dash (e.g., 1950–1), indicates the *section* of that bibliography in which the cited work is listed. Additional suggested readings, above and beyond those cited in my discussion, are also listed in most sections of the bibliography.

The History of the Term in English (particularly American English)

The term itself has had an interesting but checkered history in English (Fishman, 1985a–1). Derived from the Greek *ethnos*, it initially shared the negative semantic load of the latter, denoting a human aggregate marked by heathenish, unsavory, unrefined, and undesirable qualities, in sum, by qualities that were "neither Christian nor Jewish." This negativity was initially intentionally conveyed by the earliest (third-century) Greek translation of the Hebrew Bible (or, most probably, only of the Pentateuch). This translation, known as the Septuagint, sought to parallel the Hebrew distinction between *goy* and *'am*, designations for god-obeying and instinct-sublimating peoples, on the one hand, and god-disobeying and self-gratifying peoples, on the other, be they Hebrews or others. *Ethnos* as the Greek counterpart to the Hebrew *goy*, implied all of the negativity of the latter (the counterpart to the positive term, *'am*, being *laos*), and this negativity, therefore, was part of the original semantic load of the English term *ethnicity* in its earliest (sixteenth-century) usage. Although the term has lost most of this "non-complimentary" penumbra in modern English, some of this still lingers in such popular designations as "ethnic hairdo," "ethnic food," or "ethnic music," to which an exotic rather than a refined quality is attributed.

However, in academic (as in most mainstream American) usage the semantic load of ethnicity has become substantially detached from its original implications and conditioned, primarily by influences stemming from the social sciences on the one hand, and, before that, from racist thought, on the other. The most common pre-World War II American (and European) designation for ethnonational origin was *race*. Not only did Blacks, Whites, and Indians belong to different races, but, as the United States immigration policy debate of the twenties and the early thirties clearly indicated, so did the Scandinavians, Germans, French, Irish, Italians, Poles, Russians, Eastern European Jews, etc., etc. *Ethnicity* came to the fore after World War II, when the term *race* was substantially discredited by its association with Nazism, and as *national origin*, its initial euphonious, replacement was recognized as being inapplicable for such nonimmigrant groups as Blacks and Amerindians, and, finally, as *culture* began to be recognized as having technical disciplinary ramifications associated with anthropology, not to mention its widely known connotations and denotations in quite different directions (e.g., "pop culture," "mass culture," "consumer culture," and "high culture"). The practically simultaneous loss of three such previously useful and widely used terms (race, national origin, and culture), by means of which to discuss a very visible and frequently stressed dimension of sociodemographic variability within the American population (more often than not "marked," i.e., non-mainstream origins), brought the term *ethnicity* to the fore. It was a term whose time had come. Its scientific associations (ethnographic, ethnography, ethnosciences, etc.) were generally unknown. As a relatively unencumbered term, it could fill the void caused by the unacceptability of other terms and it could mean, more or less, whatever one wanted it to mean within the penumbra of its predecessors. Its earliest use in this way among American sociologists was apparently in the work of Hollingshead (1950–1) and McGuire (1950–1). The uncontroversial "success" of the term in America also favored its subsequent adoption in Europe and elsewhere, wherever wartime and postwar boundary changes, deportations, and immigration led to far more (and more durable) cultural heterogeneity than had previously been the case.

What is Ethnicity?

In this chapter, we will use the term "ethnicity" as it has generally come to be used in educated, but not necessarily technical, American discourse, i.e., to signify the macro-group "belongingness" or *identificational dimension of culture*, whether that of individuals or of aggregates per se. Ethnicity is both *narrower* than culture and more *perspectival* than culture. There are many aspects of culture that are not (or are no longer) viewed as aggregatively identificational. The word processor on which I am writing this chapter and the book in which the reader is perusing it are both aspects of culture but – within modern cultures more generally – they are not indicative of ethnicity. However, if I take my word processor with me to Kirgyzia, it will be regarded as a Western European or American artifact, and if I take it elsewhere, to Niger or to Gaza, for example, it might even be looked upon as confirming or implying my being White or even Jewish.

The perspectival quality of ethnicity means that its specification or attribution is fundamentally subjective, variable and very possibly non-consensual. Some of the individuals who are defined as Xians by others (who consider themselves to be Yians) may actually not consider themselves to be Xians at all. And some of those who do *not* consider themselves Xians now, may come to consider themselves Xians five or ten years from now, or in the next generation. Finally, for some of those who *do* consider themselves Xians, their Xianship may be much more central or salient in consciousness and self-identity than it is for others. This variability in perceived and experienced ethnicity also leads to variability in its association with language.

The Link Between Language and Ethnicity

That there should be some link between language and ethnicity is obvious, since the major symbolic system of the human species must be associated with the perceived dimensions of human aggregation. If people group themselves

– or also group themselves – into differently speaking collectivities, as they naturally must at least as long as large numbers of monolinguals exist, then their languages become both symbolic of as well as a basis for that grouping. However, just as ethnicity itself is perspectival and situational, and therefore variable in saliency, so the link between language and ethnicity is also variable. For some (and in some historical and situational contexts) language is the prime indicator and expression of their own and another's ethnicity; for others, language is both merely marginal and optional (i.e., detachable) vis-à-vis their ethnicity (and that of "others" as well). Nevertheless, although the link between language and ethnicity is merely constructed or conditioned by social, contextual, and historical circumstances (rather than a constant given in the human condition), this "detached" scientific perspective on language and ethnicity does not keep the language and ethnicity link from being *experienced* as vital and as a basis for social organization and mobilization. To claim that this is a specious basis for social action is not only to be judgmental but (which is worse for social scientists) to miss much of the meaning in other people's lives, i.e., to miss the very meaning that it is the scientists' task to elucidate. It is precisely because external approaches so frequently lead to overlooking – rather than to studying, clarifying, and explicating – the very phenomenon under study, i.e., the perspectival and variable nature of the language and ethnicity linkage, that more internal or phenomenological approaches to such inquiry are particularly in order at this time.

In the daily rounds of intragroup life of ordinary folk, both language and ethnicity are often (perhaps even most often) implemented without much awareness. However, the process of modernization itself tends to render the language and ethnicity link more salient in consciousness. With increased intensities and frequencies of intergroup contacts and competition, on the one hand, and with the resulting weakening of traditional life in the face of cultural influences that are experienced as "supra-ethnically" modern (rather than as specifically "other-ethnic"), on the other hand, a protective and differentiating counteraction is often cultivated. Under these circumstances, the language and ethnicity link can not only become the basis of social action but it can also be transformative for those among whom it is salient. The transformation from an ethnic group to a nationality corresponds to (without being solely responsible for) this transformation of a quiescent feature of daily life into a mobilizing dimension for social action, a dimension which combines reason with commitment that is above or beyond reason, in the pursuit of solutions to the problems of that community that is defined by a particular language and ethnicity link. Although modernization is not a necessary factor in connection with such consciousness-raising, some cultures having ideologized the language and ethnicity link at various premodern stages of their histories, it has proved to be a virtually constant concomitant in that connection since the commercial, Industrial, and Romantic revolutions in late eighteenth-century Western Europe. Many of the claims and themes that initially arose in connection with the language and ethnicity linkages in Europe have now spread throughout the world and, indeed, as some degree of Westernization itself is a "time-released" phenomenon in the worldwide process of modernization and post-modernization, some of the initially Eurocentric language and ethnicity views and actions may now be as common or more common outside of Europe than within it. In addition, of course, there are everywhere also themes and subthemes that are either conditioned or colored by local, sui generis, historical experience. The exact cross-national distributional characteristics of the thematic content of positive ethnolinguistic consciousness still awaits further research based on much larger samples than those that have been studied thus far.

The Perceived Moral Basis of the Language and Ethnicity Link

The language and ethnicity link is often paralleled by a language and religion link. Religions are inevitably carried ("received") via languages and have long been adopted or "professed" by ethnolinguistic collectivities. The majority of the world's ethnocultures are predominantly of a particular traditionally associated religion to this very day, notwithstanding the demographic heterogenization and cultural secularization resulting from modernization or post-modernization. The resulting three-way link between language–religion–ethnicity provides a moral dimension to ethnolinguistic identity and ethnolinguistic consciousness (Mews, 1987–1). It is in this manner that language is frequently associated with the "soul" or the "spirit" of the nationality. Byelorussian [2]* is referred to as "the foundation of spiritual life" and Filipino [1] assures us that "a national soul cannot exist where there is not a common language." For Hebrew [1] the claim is made that it "emerges from the same fiery furnace from which the soul of the people emerges" and for Japanese [1] that it has "a close connection with the people's spirit." Since the metaphor of national "soul" and "spirit" may now be nothing more than that, i.e., picturesque turns of phrase (regardless of how much more it may have implied at the high-point of Romanticism), it should also be pointed out that there is no lack of conviction that the ethnic tongue is directly related to *materia santa* per se. Afrikaans [1] is described as "holy to us" and Irish [3] as "the bearer of an outlook on life that is deeply Christian." French in Quebec [1] is advocated as "intimately linked to our faith . . . to all that is dear to us, to all that is sacred." Maya Kaqchikel [1] is defended on the ground that "it is the

---

* Works cited in this fashion (i.e., language name followed by a [numeral]) are listed in this fashion in the "internal perspective" bibliography on pp. 342–3. The citations mentioned in the present paper, selected from 48 languages, constitute roughly 10 percent of those included in my forthcoming *The Beloved Language: The Content of Positive Ethnolinguistic Consciousness*, in which citations are analyzed from 76 languages.

language that God gave us" and Yiddish [3] as having been hallowed "by the truly righteous and the veritable saints of every generation, [having] absorbed so much sanctity of Torah and of the process of learning Talmud."

Morality per se is often directly linked to the preferred ethnonational tongue. Thus, advocates of Macedonian [1] castigate the adoption of any other language as acting "thanklessly toward our parents in return for their spiritual care and upbringing" and devotees of Manyjilyjarra [1] are convinced that the language and knowledge of the law, custom, and tradition are all one. Finally, in the most extreme stated moral claims, collective life and death per se are viewed as dependent on the language. Some Basque defenders are convinced that "the disappearance of Basque [1] would cause the ruin of the nation, beyond all hope of recovery" and Indonesian [1] is valued highly because "If you disappear or fade my people are doomed." Obviously, ethnolinguistic consciousness is not merely an instance of strongly held convictions but rather of convictions that often pertain to the ultimate realm of sanctity, morality, and ethnocultural and personal life and death. Given such views, it becomes obvious why, under circumstances of heightened ethnolinguistic saliency, actions are so frequently undertaken to foster and improve the ethnicity-suffused tongue. To act on behalf of the language is to act on behalf of the ultimate verities that are valued by some beyond life itself.

The Ethnic Suffusion of the Favored Language

The imagery of ethnicity commonly suffuses language consciousness. To begin with, the ethnically associated language is often perceived in kinship terms. Tamil [2] is depicted as a "mother . . . capable of feeding courage and exemplifying the authentic characteristics of the race" and Uzbek [1] is absorbed together with the "mother's lullaby." Nynorsk [2] is praised as "the language which enables us to sing so warmly about our mother and father" and Yaqui [1] as "the language of our parents and . . . tribal leaders." Swahili [2] is lauded as the unconscious creation of "countless generations of our Bantu forefathers" and Hausa [2] as "the language used by ancestors and bequeathed to [us], their descendants." But the ethnic link is not merely to kin, but, as a Navajo [1] formulation puts it, to "homes and communities throughout the Navajo nation." Indeed, the language is, in a sense, the primordial home, even as it is the ever-present home for those who may have no other that they can call their own. "Go back," a Bengali [1] advocate urges, "go back, you fool, go back to your home." The language is the people rendered audible. A Konkani [1] advocate is one of many to proclaim that "our language is a mirror of our society" and an Arabic [2] protagonist is one of many who are confident that it represents "the values and traditions that distinguish us from other human beings," just as a Black English [1] champion cites the language's "mighty achievement of having brought a people to its present place." Guaraní [1] is viewed as "the index of our nationality and the distinctive individuality of the Paraguayan people." "Abandon Slovene [1]," an advocate admonishes, "and we lose our people, for they will fall back into their previous state of national unconsciousness."

Actually, notions of directional causality between the language and ethnic consciousness vary. There are claims, such as the last one, from language to consciousness, and other claims that merely see the language as an exquisite reflection of its ethnoculture. In either case, the link between language and ethnicity is affirmed.

This is also clear when "history" is invoked as the metaphor for the experiences of the collectivity. A Chinese [1] spokesperson associates Potunghua with "our nation's long and illustrious history." Hindi [2] is viewed as reflecting "the history of our country." Finally, the language is believed to foster beneficial ethnocognitive and ethno-emotional characteristics in its associated ethnic collectivity. Norwegian Bokmal [1] is said to contain "the mighty breath of genius, sighing to awake and urge the masses onward" and Papiamentu [2] is "fiery, cheerful, spirited," so that "no sorrow nor joy can pass us by." Turkish [2] arouses "enthusiasm, exuberance, and dynamism" and Maori [1] is depicted as a reflection of "the inner life and feeling," much as German [2] is a "reflection of the world view and the essence of the German personality."

Clearly, the widely assumed relationship between the language and its people (or the people and its language) constitutes both a metaphysic and a cosmology. The assumed relationship provides a way not only of understanding one's own people and language and their place in creation, but of viewing all peoples, all languages, and all of creation. It is a partisan cosmology and a partisan metaphysic, of course, and both constitute points of departure for both much of the good and much of the evil in today's world. But it must also be kept in mind that there are no neutral and no harmless points of view with respect to intersocietal problem-solving. Furthermore, the language and ethnicity link is not always salient in human affairs. However, once it has been ideologized and widely raised to saliency it probably never disappears entirely from among its speech community and can be easily recalled to prominence when mobilization on that basis again seems advantageous. On the other hand, intragroup concerns, when they come to the fore, usually require quite different alignments from intergroup concerns and, under the former circumstances, language and ethnicity linkages are typically more quiescent, but even then they do not disappear.

The Imperative to Foster and Improve the Ethnically Favored Language

Dangers to the ethnically favored language are of two kinds: dangers to the language's status (i.e., as to its desired and implemented functions, intraculturally and even interculturally) and dangers to its corpus (i.e., as to the adequacy of its lexicon, writing system, or stylistic repertoire) vis-à-vis those statuses for which it is advocated. The organized pursuit of solutions to both of these sets of dangers constitutes the arena of language planning (see chapter 27). Our goal here will be to indicate how often both of these sets of dangers are commonly addressed within a language and ethnicity frame of reference, rather than as problems at the language level alone.

Status Planning

Efforts to improve the status of a language begin with the rejection of the insults and injuries – in terms of unjustifiably restricted or denigrated statuses – which have been visited upon it in the past. Such restrictions and denigrations are viewed as injurious to the survival not only of the language but of the community that it identifies and that identifies with it. Ainu [2] proclaims that "we will not ... go into the museum" and Byelorussian [2] rejects the "repression [that has] squeezed [it] out of almost all spheres of life." If English [2] can bemoan the fact that it "is not more generally studied" by its own speakers, then little wonder that Guaraní [1] castigates those of "its own children" who have ignored it "in pedagogical ... intellectual ... and scientific spheres." Irish [1] refuses to go along with the mistaken view that "this wailing over the language is all sentimentality (rather than anything of substance)" and Korean [1] bemoans the fact that it "is being attacked by foreign languages ... beaten up by Chinese ... stomped upon by Japanese and chased off the land by Western languages." Maori [2] refuses to continue to accede to the negative social conditions that have "led many Maori to devalue their language and their cultural heritage" and Navajo [1] undertakes to counteract the sad circumstances that have led to "less than half of the Dine' [the Navajo's name for themselves] children entering kindergarten this fall ... be[ing] speakers of the Dine' language." Norwegian Nynorsk [3] laments that its "written language has been suppressed, stigmatized as wrong or bad ... looked down upon ... [and] individuals not given the opportunity to use [it]" and Swahili [2] rejects its status as "a lowly language, below the prestige of the European ruler's English, a servant of the foreign rulers of our minds and of his language."

So much for the endless chorus of rejection of primarily functional insults, some coming from co-ethnic sources and others attributed to "other-ethnic" sources. One underlying feature of many complaints is the rejected implication that the beloved language is not (or cannot conceivably become) a fit instrument of modern pursuits and statuses. However, this is not an intellectually or emotionally uncomplicated issue, since many of the perceived virtues of the beloved language are associated with rural and traditional verities. Korean [1] recognizes that part of its problem is that "the whole country is changing to an urban industrial society," just as Norwegian Nynorsk [1] agrees that "to the farmer belongs the honor of being the deliverer of the language," and just as Swahili [2] admits that "the only sanctuary . . . which is still truly African is our mother tongue in its traditional use." Thus there is a tension between the uniqueness of the pre-modern past out of which the language has evolved and the power potentials of the modern arena to which its adherents aspire, even though the latter is accompanied by a rather more uniform "modern lifestyle" the world over. This tension between tradition and modernity is almost invariably resolved in the direction of modernity, but the claims of pre-modern ethnocultural authenticity are rarely fully set aside and they return to seek some of their due satisfaction in connection with corpus planning options, precisely because a "traditionally colored" modernity remains a viable and frequent compromise solution between the opposing goals of modernists and traditionalists.

The drive toward the statuses of modernity receives its dynamism from both general and specific sources. It is not only the anonymous and impersonal "world at large" which unjustifiably impinges upon the rightful perquisites of the beloved language and its community of devotees and defenders, but historic rivals and opponents do so even more aggravatingly. Just as Byelorussian considers itself particularly oppressed and maligned by Russian and Polish, English in the USA by British English, Dutch in Belgium by French, Frisian by Dutch, Irish (and Welsh) by English, and Norwegian Nynorsk by Dano-Norwegian (Bokmål), so Guaraní [1] complains about "the language of the [Spanish] conqueror," Hausa [1] rejects "the foreign language [English] which serves as our official language," Somali [1] objects to "foreign written languages of the colonizers and their lackeys," Sindhi [1] objects to the imposition of Urdu and Wolof [1] just as Haitian objects to that of French. Furthermore, various classical tongues are also referred to in advancing the beloved language's desired statuses (even though these statuses be thoroughly modern rather than classical). Amharic [1] bemoans those "scholars [who] like to write . . . only in . . . Ge'ez" and urges them to "abandon this old language of the church," just as the Europeans have done, with their respective religious classicals, in order to foster their individual vernaculars. Sixteenth-century English [1] (in Great Britain) opines that "Latin too was uncouth before it was used by savants for refined purposes" and sixteenth-century French [1] already compares its literary creations favorably with Greek and Latin classics, adding that the classic writers themselves wrote in their own vernaculars rather than in yet older languages of cultures other than their own. Similarly, Telugu [1] sweepingly declares itself to be "the best among vernaculars" insofar as fidelity to Sanskrit is concerned and Chinese [1] is proud of its link to classical Mandarin. Thus, the ethnoculturally beloved language's drive toward modern statuses (albeit modern statuses adequately clothed and colored by authentic local tradition) obtains reinforcement from all directions, from injured pride and trampled rights relative to languages of neighboring foreigners as well as from resentment against languages of colonizers from a distance, from comparisons with world history as well as from similarity to or competition with locally relevant classical traditions.

Another common feature of status aspirations for the beloved language is their postulation in terms of moral obligation and natural right. The language not only deserves to be protected and fostered, but it is one's duty to do so, i.e., a definite moral imperative is involved. The sanctity dimension that we have reviewed earlier enables language advocates to appeal in terms of absolute and irreducible values. It is precisely because the beloved language is so closely associated with other verities that the moral imperative to believe in and to defend them directly and obviously applies to it as well. Thus Irish [1] is considered to be "a sacred national trust" whose enhancement is "a national duty." "Refrancizing" Quebec [2] is viewed as "an act of love for our province, of piety toward our history." Hebrew [1] recognizes an obligation derived from the fact that the language "has served the Jewish people faithfully" and therefore it now, in due turn, deserves to be served. Similarly, Kaqchikel [1] invokes filial respect as the basis for its claims upon the current generation and Manyjilyjarra [1] calls upon respect for the ancestors in order to "make it multiply" and to keep "listening, interested, believing" in the language's importance. Uzbek [1] focuses on "the historical responsibility and duty which rests upon our shoulders" and Yiddish [2] proclaims that "we . . . must . . . exert ourselves to maintain it as long as we live," because "the [holocaust] martyrs so near and dear to us cried out in Yiddish in their last wailing screams, prior to their agonizing deaths." Clearly, for many the language is viewed as a moral entity that calls out for assistance from all who are righteous and responsible. In a moral universe, that which is just and true must not only be maintained and strengthened, but it must be clearly seen to be fostered, propagated, and defended against all who would detract from it or deny it its due.

The language status aspirations that are interpenetrated by ethnocultural devotion merit much more attention than we can possibly give them here. The struggle for a life with dignity for the beloved language is often a struggle not merely metaphorically and defensively put but quite literally and physically expressed as well. Serbian [1] speaks of using "language in a war for the liberation of intellectual and political consciousness" and French in Quebec [2] recalls that "our fathers fought for and . . . with their lives often paid for their choice . . . to remain Catholic and French . . . defend[ing] their language, written and spoken," regardless of the costs of doing so. Uzbek [1] calls for fidelity to the tradition of pre-Communist centuries past "to struggle boldly for our language's development," notwithstanding "invaders' flames," and Sindhi [1] resolves to "overcome all obstacles." Obviously, status change for the beloved language is usually a conflictual interethnic affair and is often part and parcel of the larger story of interethnic struggle. In the modern world, self-respecting languages are languages that are also implemented in the arenas of material statuses, reward, and pursuits – particularly in the workplace or marketplace, in government offices and operations, and in the institutions and processes of literacy. Our species is not notorious for freely and willingly sharing such accompaniments and expressions of power with less fortunate neighbors, and the latter cannot be entirely blamed, let alone be the only ones to be blamed, for refusing to passively accept subordination. When the late-modernizing or late-autonomy-gaining worm finally turns, it will necessarily disturb the peace and quiet of those who have attained privilege and recognition earlier. But in its own eyes, the worm's turning will not only be justified but long overdue, and indeed, merely following the examples well established in the surrounding world of nations and peoples, including of course, the examples of those very ones who object most loudly to the "incivility" of the late-turners, but who do not care to redress the injustices which the early modernizers themselves have perpetrated.

Corpus Planning

Just as one cannot make a silk purse out of a sow's ear, so one cannot discharge (or, at times, even pursue) modern power statuses for the beloved language without providing it with the outer vestments (the nomenclature, stand-ardized spellings, grammars, and stylistic conventions) that modern pursuits and modern institutions require. Although the perfection of the ethnically preferred language is roundly championed prior to corpus planning for mod-ernization, it inevitably transpires that the already perfect language requires human intervention in order to be more perfect yet, most particularly so for functions with which it has not hitherto been frequently associated. This is not a simple task, not only because many of those who have conserved the beloved language when its chances looked slim are also likely to be conserva-tives when it comes to language innovation, but also because such innova-tions must often be made while publications, formal schooling, and political (or even official) activities are already proceeding feverishly. Where does one begin, and how does one proceed, when it is necessary to build the new ship out of the old ship when the latter is already on the high seas and the crew is not all of one mind as to the advisability of the voyage? As with status planning, one begins corpus planning by rejecting the sneering assumptions of detractors and opponents that a sow's ear is a sow's ear and that nothing can be done to change or improve it.

Chinese [2] vows to ultimately set aside the "characters ... [that] are ... possessed of many inherent shortcomings [vis-à-vis Western languages]" and which penalize the development of the "country's socialist construction, econ-omy, and culture" and English in the USA [2] pleads that it not be considered "a vulgar dialect ... to be used only with deprecation," as is the "biased view" of partisans of British English. Finnish [1] realizes that it is "cumbersome and poor" because of its "delayed and hindered cultivation" by the pro-Swedish elite that has long ruled the country. Hausa [2] is certain that its limitations can be overcome, as were the former limitations of the earlier modernized Western tongues, namely, via "authoritative use." Berber [3] proclaims that its dialectal diversity is also "an opportunity and a richness [in connection with its future modernization], rather than a defect." Papiamentu [2] may only be "a dialect of Spain" but, even as such, it can "still have a place of honor" among other such dialects (Catalan, Gallego, Asturian, and even Castilian itself)! Furthermore, although corpus planning involves cultivation and stand- ardization in accord with professional linguistic expertise, the authenticity of the beloved language must not and need not be lost in the process. Rather than "twist it and turn it to make it look like the foreign languages we have learned," Tigrinya [1] counsels, "we must follow it along its own path." Traditional roots and forms can serve, both lexically and grammatically, to keep the ethnically preferred language from straying from its authentic na- ture, even as it loudly rejects the charge that it cannot be modernized.

The beauty and the richness of the beloved language are without peer and they fully merit the attention that it requires (as well as inspires) among those who attend to its modernization. Afrikaans [2] is the "sweetest sounding, the most gentle" tongue and Bengali [3] is likened to "a gracious beauty . . . a wondrous beauty . . . a resonant, profound and sublime symphony." Polish [2] is compared to "a harp hanging over the rivers of Babylon, expressing the poets' grief, reveille, and hope" and Telugu [3] "sounds harmonious even on the lips of the most illiterate. It has justly been called the Italian of the East." But aesthetics is merely the most obvious and superficial side of beauty. Purity is a matter of inner, spiritual beauty, a beauty which has been main- tained over ages past and should be fostered in the modernization process as well. Thus modern Turkish [1] "can come into being only when superfluous Perso-Arabic elements have been purged" and Swahili [2] warns against "foreign corruption" which can only convert it into "a bastard language." German [2] extols "the battle for the purity of the German language" as a "battle for the unity and the spirit of the German people."

Finally, elaboration too is a well recognized asset (perhaps the most widely claimed of all assets), the ethnically preferred language always having the most telling and necessary words, words strangely absent in contrasted ton- gues. Guaraní [1] is convinced that "no language in the world is comparable to ours . . . unsurpassable by the European languages . . . superior in natural wealth," and above all "superior to Spanish." Precisely because the beloved language is basically so excellent, it need not fear or feel crestfallen if corpus planning is required for the purposes of modernization. If properly con- ducted, its impact will merely be the intensification and demonstration of all that is outstandingly rich and subtle to begin with.

Corpus planning proceeds, often against great odds, to perfect the perfect and to systematize the sublime. While French [2] finds itself "capable of treating all the Arts and all the Sciences" (in 1635!) it nevertheless still pleads for the ultimate wealth that only writing can impart. By contrast the English [1] of roughly that time had to take comfort that "diligent labor" by "learned countrymen" was necessary to "enrich . . . [other] tongues," and therefore English too will benefit, "if our learned countrymen will . . . [devote] their labor" to it. So Hausa [1] points out today that English once needed "many years of writing and enrichment through borrowing of words" and Tok Pisin [2] is pleased at being "extremely adaptable" and "tolerant of change." The immediate focus of corpus planning is, of course, the written language (and therefore also the formal spoken language which is closest to and often merely the vocalization of a written or printed text). Putting a language to written use is itself another example, if indeed another example is still needed, of the fully interconnected nature of status planning and corpus planning. For a language to be used in school and by government (status planning) it requires a writing system, a spelling system, the nomenclatures and styles of academic and governmental communications, in short, the dictionaries, grammars, and style manuals (all corpus planning). All of the foregoing are also corpus planning goals and by-products that are simultaneously ethnoculturally infused and interpreted. Japanese [1] asserts that its script fully reflects the uniqueness and isolation motifs which are so prominent in Japanese consciousness. Uzbek [1] proclaims the need "to reclaim our age-old cultural legacy . . . the Arabic script." Scripts are not merely tools for written communication; they are treasured, deeply entrenched ethnocultural and ethno-religious symbols and enactments. However, traditional scripts too must often compromise, at least to some degree, with the demands of modernization, including even the demands put before somewhat "idiosyncratic" Latin-based scripts. In our very days, both German and Spanish have dropped a few of their remaining "esoteric" letters (esoteric from the perspective of English), because of the pressures of internationally standardized keyboards and computer systems. Similarly, the Basque font and Hibernian font (for Irish) have been largely discontinued, as has Fraktur (for German), because of the added encoding and decoding costs that they entailed, vis-à-vis ethnically unmarked fonts and, in some cases, because of unsavory political overtones that had become associated with them.

For *late*-modernizing languages the pressures to utilize the script and typeface associated with the mainstream of Western modernity are even greater, since these languages frequently still need to acquire written functions per se and, in addition, they often command too small a literacy-related clientele to be able to afford the added luxury of ethnically "authentic" non-Western scripts. When a Latin-based script was adopted (over its older Arabic competitor) for Somali, it was greeted by Somali [1] as "a day unforgettable in our history. Our language is to be written." With the passage of sufficient time and sufficiently unthreatened independence, a once "new" and "imported" writing system may also finally become indigenized and historically validated. There are few if any indications that Turkish will ever return to Perso-Arabic writing, and the special diacritics that it has introduced during the past 60 or so years into its Latin-based script adopted in the 1920s have served to render that script "obviously" Turkish, rather than foreign, to most of its speech community. It is impossible to predict whether there will be sufficient pressure upon Turkish to induce it to discard those diacritics in the future. On the other hand, it does seem that if the Soviets had permitted their captive nations to adopt the Turkish strategy in connection with their own Cyrillic scripts, instead of forcing a uniformly Russian-Cyrillic system upon most of them (e.g., not only on Moldavian, Tatar, Kalmik, Uigur, etc., but even upon Ukrainian and Byelorussian), there might be fewer efforts today to return to something more "authentically" pre-Communist (i.e., non-Russian in appearance). Barring substantial annihilation, it takes much longer for an elite to indigenize a writing system that has been forced upon it "against its will" than it does to adapt and indigenize one that is less identified with a historic rival, enemy, and oppressor.*

Summary and Conclusion

Almost every aspect of language is replete with ethnic significance and associations. Although this may be particularly true for the direct heirs of the successive nineteenth- and twentieth-century European romantic attachments to the vernaculars of every corner of that continent, that inheritance has by now been spread around the post-imperial globe and has excited similarly intense (although, at times, less functionally exclusive) passions almost everywhere and in apparently long-lasting fashion. Literacy movements, modernization processes, Christianization, democratization, State formation, cultural autonomy movements, all have utilized and fostered the language and ethnicity link for their own purposes. Although linguae francae also continue to spread (particularly English, but also several regionally more circumscribed linguae francae) and therefore the continued multiplication of locally valued, recognized, and protected ethno-vernaculars has not led to a general breakdown in interethnic or in international communication, the abiding nature of most of the conscious language and ethnicity linkages is such that the future of ever-growing segments of mankind will necessarily be a multilingual one. Even the native-born speakers of English in various prodominantly English mother-tongue countries may come to appreciate that in their case too there is a link between language and ethnicity. They too may have to struggle more in the future for many of the linguistic advantages that they have taken for

---

* In a full-blown treatment of ethnolinguistic consciousness, a word or two about *negative* ethnolinguistic consciousness would also be in order. Basically, negative imagery deals with the same substantive categories as does positive imagery. However, where functionally and demographically pervasive negative imagery is transmitted intergenerationally (it often is not), it tends to foster re-ethnification and/or relinguification of the speech community and therefore is ultimately self-liquidating.

granted before, such as giving papers in English all over the world. As even superpowers learn the necessity of winning friends and influencing people in an increasingly multipolar world, they may find out what mini-powers have long ago discovered, namely, that one can only get so far in any one language, English included. As a result, I would predict that in the future English mother-tongue speakers too will value English more as a marker of their own ethnicity and less as a worldwide litmus-paper test of intelligence and sophistication. Ethnization and de-ethnization are both constantly ongoing; what is ethnically unmarked to the "haves" (who constantly confuse their own characteristics with those of "general" [i.e., appreciably post-ethnic] modern civilization, which French and English are among their native speakers), is in part resisted and in part adopted by "have nots," for ethnically and nonethnically colored reasons of their own. At the moment (summer 1994), we seem to be in the midst of a recrudescence of language and ethnicity consciousness and the images and sentiments that such consciousness fosters. This currently heightened salience of language and ethnicity linkages may or may not continue far into the twenty-first century, but of one thing we may rest assured: In most cases the linkages themselves will continue indefinitely.

APPENDIX

A Brief "External Perspective" Bibliography

1 Culture, religion, and ethnicity/nationalism

Anon. 1985. *The Fairest Flower: The Emergence of Linguistic National Consciousness in Renaissance Europe.*
Breuilly, John. 1993.
Connor, Walker. 1994.
Eriksen, Thomas Hylland. 1994.
Fishman, David, et al. 1985.
Hollingshead, August E. 1950.
McGuire, Carson. 1950. (The term "ethnicity" occurs on p. 199.)
Mews, Stuart. 1987.
Suny, Ronald Grigor. 1993.
Williams, Colin H. 1993.
Wolf, Eric C. 1994.

2 Status planning

Cooper, Robert L. 1989.
Dua, Hans. 1992.
Fardon, Richard, and Furniss, Graham, eds. 1994.
Fishman, Joshua A. 1992.
Harshav, Benjamin. 1993.
Laitin, David D. 1992.
Tollefson, James W. 1991.

3 Corpus planning

Alisjahbana, S. Takdir. 1976.
Fellman, Jack. 1973.
Haugen, Einar. 1966b.

Jernudd, Björn, and Shapiro, Michael J., eds. 1989.
Rubin, Joan, et al. 1977.

Thomas, George. 1991.
Wexler, Paul. 1974.

"Internal perspective references cited (by language)"*

Afrikaans 1 = Anon. 1876. [*Our Afrikaans Nation and Language*]

Afrikaans 2 = Preller, G. Schoeman. 1905.

Ainu 2 = Kayano, Shigeru. 1987.

Amharic 1 = Gebreyesus, Afeworq. 1909.

Arabic 2 = Al-Fayad, Mohamed Jaber. 1984.

Basque 1 = Arana Goiri, Sabino. 1886.

Bengali 1 = Data, Madhusudan. 1866.

Bengali 3 = Azad, Humayan. 1984.

Berber 3 = Chakar, Salem. 1984.

Black English 1 = Baldwin, James. 1979. *Black English and the Education of Black Children and Youth.*

Byelorussian 2 = Anon. 1987. *Letters to Gorbachev: New Documents from Soviet Byelorussia.*

Chinese 1 = Yenbing, Shen. 1955.

Chinese 2 = En-lai, Chou. 1958.

English 1 = Mulcaster, R. 1582. (Spelling and punctuation modernized: JAF)

English 2 = Churchill, Winston S. 1908.

English in the USA 2 = Hughes, Rupert. 1920.

Filipino 1 = Rodriguez, Eulegio B., ed. 1940.

Finnish 1 = von Becker, Reinhold. 1820. Reprinted, 1929.

French 1 = Du Bellay, Joachim. 1549. Reprinted, 1939.

French 2 = Robertson, D. Maclaren. 1910.

French in Quebec 1 = Tardival, Jules-Paul. 1881.

French in Quebec 2 = Philippon, Horace. 1938.

German 2 = Bach, Adolf. 1961.

Guarani 1 = Statement (typewritten and unsigned), prepared for and passed along from hand to hand at the National Constitutional Convention of 1967.

Hausa 1 = Gusau, Sa'idu Muhamad. 1985.

Hausa 2 = Unsigned editorial. 1989. [National language].

Hebrew 1 = Nakht, Yaakov. 1908. [A time for action]. *Ha-olam*, 30, 501–2.

Hindi 2 = Das, Seth Govind. 1963, in Chand, Lakshmi, ed. [Hindi Language Movement]. Allahabad, Hindi Sahitya Sammelan, Prayag, 288–9.

Indonesian 1 = Yudho, S. 1933.

Irish 1 = O'Growney, Eugene. 1890.

Irish 3 = de Valera, Eamon. 1980.

Japanese 1 = Inoue, Tetsujiro. 1898.

Kaqchikel 1 = COCADI (Coordinadora Cakchiquel de Desarollo Integral). 1985.

Konkani 1 = Sardesai, Manohar. 1962.

Korean 1 = Lee, Oh-Tuk. 1992.

Macedonian 1 = Misirkov, Krste P. 1903.

---

* All originally non-English citations have been translated into English by colleagues who are specialists in the languages cited, rather than by JAF. Square brackets indicate English translations of originally non-English titles.

Manyjilyjarra 1 = Gibbs, Billy Milangka. 1988.

Maori 1 = Hauraki, Veronica. 1971

Maori 2 = Dewes, Koro. 1970.

Navajo 1 = Zah, Peterson. 1993.

Norwegian Bokmål 1 = Bugge, Sophus. 1899.

Norwegian Nynorsk 1 = Aasen, Ivar. 1909.

Norwegian Nynorsk 2 = Stoylen, Bernt. 1931.

Norwegian Nynorsk 3 = Noregs Maallag. 1976.

Papiamentu 2 = Daal, Luis. 1963.

Polish 2 = Rydel, Lucjan. 1908.

Serbian 1 = Skulic, Isidora. 1987.

Sindhi 1 = Syed, G. M. 1985.

Somali 1 = Adam, Hussein M. 1980.

Swahili 2 = Khalid, Abdallah. 1977.

Tamil 2 = Annadurai, C. N. 1960.

Telugu 1 = From the Vinukonda Vallabharaya, a mid-14th-century translation of a 13th-century Sanskrit original that deals with a flourishing Telugu empire.

Telugu 3 = Morris, Henry. 1890.

Tigrinya 1 = Ha., A. Ma. [= not a real name, but, rather, the initials of the author's name in the Ethiopic syllabary]. 1958.

Tok Pisin 2 = Lynch, John. 1976.

Turkish 1 = Gokalp, Ziya. 1923.

Turkish 2 = Press release. 1990.

Uzbek 1 = Daminov, Babamurad. 1989.

Yaqui 1 = Martinez, Maria. 1989.

Yiddish 2 = Shamir, Arye. 1992.

Yiddish 3 = Rubin, Shifre. 1992.

21 Global Scale Sociolinguistics

GRANT D. McCONNELL

1 Prologue

In this introductory section we will demarcate the area covered by the term "global scale sociolinguistics" by asking three questions relating to its historical underpinnings, its methodology, and methodological tools. If we consider sociolinguistics as a sort of generic label, one could then ask the question: What type of sociolinguistics? And to that query one could answer the sociology of language tradition, if sociolinguistics on a global scale is what we have in mind.

Next, we could ask the question: What specific methodology is applied to this tradition? The answer is, that both descriptive-comparative (historical/anecdotal/typological) and descriptive-analytical (questionnaire/statistical) approaches are available. The former is based on the language usage of human groups and the latter on a structured database resulting in numerous multivariate analyses, involving ascribed and acquired criteria of languages, their speakers and communities on the one hand, and the whole sociocultural universe with its countless variables on the other.

Finally, one could ask: What specific analytical constructs/tools are available to this tradition, which will allow it to better structure and subsequently analyze this sociocultural universe? First, there is the typologizing of both languages and social groups, which can give rise to numerous juxtapositions, comparisons, dichotomies, grids, and formulas, generally resulting in useful but gross types of measurements, and beyond that, comparisons with the all-encompassing sociocultural universe. How that universe impinges on human social groups and their languages can be tested and approximated at this stage by examining a number of "external" variables, in relation to "internal" variable "presence/usage" for languages or "representation/control" for groups. Through various types of multivariate analyses we can begin to monitor changes in both these internal and external variables, with the aim of arriving at valuable hypotheses regarding both causes and effects or even outcomes. Once more research has been done along these lines, we should be able to see beyond short-term, direct linear relationships to cyclical ones. Hence what is designated in any model as "internal/external" is only internal and external in a relatively restricted way, as in the case of a construct or a convention. The real nonmodular world is more systemic, layered, and cyclical in nature.

Apart from empirically recording, measuring, and mapping this presence/usage of languages and representation/control of groups, we also want to know more about specific criteria linked to maintenance and diffusion, so as to discover whether such criteria are universally so linked in time and space, or whether their action depends on types of contexts and more particularly types of language and community contact patterns. If these questions can be clarified by a process of continual testing (adding and discarding criteria) in context within the sociology of language research tradition, then much can be accomplished in the future toward understanding the play of social forces in general and the effectiveness of language planning in particular.

A structuring of the above analytical approach by the continuing preparation and application of new analytical tools and other frame-of-reference constructs is important and this we have done in particular for language (presence/usage) by developing (1) "an illustrated model of language development," which has allowed us to develop various types of vitality rates for languages and (2) "a general power model of contextual and vital forces and their resolution," which has allowed us to work on multivariate analyses (see details of these models in section 6).

If the sociology of language is preoccupied with language presence/usage in terms of social functions and roles, as well as the environmental forces of change that influence these roles, then it may be argued that some sort of program of control or planning should be applied to influence the course of events. Hence, language planning can be treated as a subdiscipline of sociolinguistics on a global scale and within it status planning, which refers specifically to the roles or purposes of languages in society and hence their relative importance. From a structured point of view the role of language in society is clearly a functional role (presence/usage) that perforce must be contextualized institutionally and geographically. Now it stands to reason that if this functional type role for language can be demarcated, it can also be recorded, measured, and even mapped. In doing so, we provide a fundamentally new, measurable, and internal type of variable, which designates "presence/usage" of a language in a society and against which many other external, sociocultural, and explanatory variables may be compared. This "internal" usage variable we have called language vitality, which reflects the "inner" force of a language's presence. As a concept, it can also be perceived in terms of development, as seen in the illustrated model of language development in section 6. Here it is structured and positive in outlook but it can also be seen as stable or even negative, when, for example, a language has a dropping vitality rate. Apart from its intrinsic interest and value as a quantified measurement of functional change, vitality rates are also a useful tool for specific comparisons and more global multivariate analyses. For this reason it constitutes a valuable tool for global scale sociolinguistics.

In considering the above three questions regarding (1) the type of sociolinguistics covered in this article, (2) the methodological approaches available, and (3) the supportive models and tools developed, we can more easily assess sociolinguistics on a global scale with regard to its present situation and future prospects. Then by adding the concepts of language planning and language vitality, we can better understand what is fully meant by sociolinguistics on a global scale. Let us now turn briefly to its relationship with other types of sociolinguistic studies, which also involve the study of language in society.

2   Sociolinguistics – Definitions and Orientations

This section gives two examples regarding the historical underpinnings of sociolinguistics on a global scale, namely, the sociology of language school of Fishman and the social linguistics school of Hymes.

The type of sociolinguistics most closely related to sociolinguistics on a global scale is that proposed by J. A. Fishman (1972) in *The Sociology of Language*. For him there are two parts to the sociology of language universe: (1) *"the descriptive sociology of languages"* and (2) *"the dynamic sociology of languages."* The descriptive part "is concerned with describing the generally accepted social organization of language usage within a speech community," and "tries to disclose the norms of language usage." The dynamic part seeks to answer the question, "What accounts for different rates of change in the social organization of language use and behavior toward language?" Fishman's definition is closely related to our global orientation, because its thrust basically concerns functional, institutional, and norm-oriented usage. Also, both orientations are heavily weighted in the macro sphere and language is clearly their main object of study.

Another type of sociolinguistics called social linguistics is that promulgated by Hymes (1974) in his *Foundations in Sociolinguistics: An Ethnographic Approach*. His is a cultural and communication rather than a primarily language-oriented approach. "It is rather that it is not linguistics, but ethnography, not language, but communication, which must provide the frame of reference within which the place of language in culture and society is to be assessed" (p. 4). Hymes sets out three goals of sociolinguistics, as follows:

> 1   *The social as well as the linguistic.* This covers social problems and language use, akin to Fishman's sociology of language approach.

2 *Socially realistic linguistics.* This is a Labovian approach involving "data from the speech community."
3 *Socially constituted linguistics.* This is specifically Hymes's approach and involves an infusion of linguistic form into social function. It is "social function that gives form to the ways in which linguistic features are encountered in actual life." But, according to Hymes, it is social function, through context, which not only gives form but also meaning to linguistic features, through the selection and grouping of linguistic elements. An additional modicum of meaning is added from the larger environment. "A 'socially constituted' linguistics is concerned with contextual as well as referential meaning, and with language as part of communicative conduct and social action" (pp. 195–7). Hymes's approach is vast, seeming to cover both the macro and micro spheres, and includes both contextual and referential meaning. Language for him is only a part of a larger universe of communication and both are embedded in an even broader social and cultural background from which ultimate meaning is to be sought.

Hymes's ethnography of communication approach was also adopted by others such as J. J. Gumperz (1972) in *Directions in Sociolinguistics* and later in M. Saville-Troike (1982) in *The Ethnography of Communication*. According to the latter author the ethnography of communication has two foci: "the description and understanding of communicative behavior in specific cultural settings" and the "formulation of concepts and theories upon which to build a global metatheory of human communication" (p. 2). Whether Hymes and his successors were successful in accomplishing these two aims remains a judgment of history. In the meantime communication theory has exploded well beyond the frontiers of language, which suggests that Hymes and others may well have been precursors of a broader sociocultural view of communication. From the viewpoint of sociolinguistics on a global scale, what is still lacking is a structured "language form–social function" model, supported by a global metatheory capable of hypothesizing language forms through social functions and the reverse. But even if this were accomplished, it would not nearly satisfy Hymes's ambitious plan for a larger general theory of communication and meaning well beyond the confines of language.

3 Global Scale Sociolinguistics and Language Planning

This section examines the definitions of language planning and shows how they vary in orientation depending on whether the focus is on language, society, or politics.

We have already mentioned above the link between global scale sociolinguistics and language planning. Language planning can be viewed or defined from several points of view even on a global scale, i.e., as being linguistically oriented, socially oriented, or politically oriented. These different orientations are interdependent; all are invariably linked to change and development, but the emphasis, from a definitional and objective point of view, can be distinct. If language planning represents change and development, it can also be seen as overcoming language, social, and political problems that impede desired change and development.

Below are examples of three definitions, each with its own orientation: (i) linguistic, (ii) social, and (iii) political:

(i) The linguistically oriented definition is that of Kloss (1967):
"The term Ausbausprache may be defined as 'language by development'. Languages belonging to this category are recognized as such because of having been shaped or reshaped, molded or remolded – as the case may be – in order to become a standard tool of literary expression (p. 29).

(ii) The socially oriented definition is that of Fishman (1987):
"For me, language planning remains the authoritative allocation of resources to the attainment of language status and language corpus goals, whether in connection with new functions that are aspired to, or in connection with old functions that need to be discharged more adequately" (p. 409).

(iii) The politically oriented definition is that of Abou (1987):
"The object of any planned linguistic change is to reduce competition between languages or language varieties and to rationally structure their coexistence within a society" (p. 11).[1]

The Kloss definition emphasizes language corpus goals and sees language in terms of its standardization, particularly as a written tool of modern society. Language planning is goal oriented in terms of language form (standard), which should also be a reflection of language function. In the Fishman definition there is mention of both status and corpus goals and these in relation to specific social functions. Abou's definition involves problem-solving on the political level and emphasizes a functional allocation of whole languages or varieties of languages within a sociopolitical order.

Language planning as a process has been widely described in the literature by Haugen (1966), Fishman (1974), Rubin and Jernudd (1971), and others. Haugen on a number of occasions (1966, 1983, 1987) proposed his "fourfold model" of language planning with its (1) selection, (2) codification, (3) elaboration, and (4) implementation. Figure 21.1 gives a modified cyclical version of LP, which is inspired by Haugen's earlier model. The cyclical model by its form intends to be dynamic in structure, distinguishing corpus (form) and status (function) phases of LP, including intermediary (form/function)

Figure 21.1 A cyclical model of language planning.

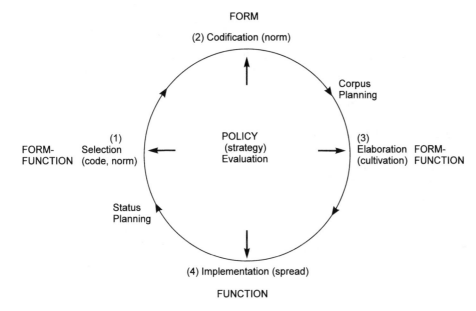

FORM

(2) Codification (norm)

Corpus
Planning

(1)
FORM-   Selection
FUNCTION   (code, norm)

POLICY
(strategy)
Evaluation

(3)
Elaboration FORM-
(cultivation) FUNCTION

Status
Planning

(4) Implementation (spread)

FUNCTION

phases. Central to the four peripheral steps is a fifth centrally situated policy step, which acts as a point of reference for the other steps. This contains a strategy and monitoring process, which amounts to a feed-back and evaluation operation for each step in the cyclical process.

4 Global Scale Sociolinguistics and the Descriptive Tradition

In trying to answer the question of what specific methodology or methodologies to apply to global scale sociolinguistics, we come up with the answer that both descriptive-comparative and descriptive-analytical approaches are available. It is the first or descriptive-comparative approach that will be discussed first in this section.

In the early development stages of the sociology of language much purely descriptive and historical case-study material became available. This was understandable and necessary, because there was much to cover and descriptive material of this nature was not widely known or was completely original in those first heady years of the 1960s, when sociolinguistics came into its own as a discipline. Few linguists had previously bothered to describe the functional roles of languages either within or between communities on a regional basis, or within or between states on a sociopolitical basis. In the meantime linguistics had moved from a structuralist and systemic to a social and functional stance, in which variation in language form was axiomatic of social function. Idiosyncratic forms were no longer seen as extraneous but as part of social function. A change in function or the grouping of functions could lead to change in linguistic form and also to subtle changes in meaning.

Two types of material are available in this descriptive tradition: (i) anecdotal, historical, case-study and portrait-type material that "tells a story" and reveals facts unknown before and (ii) more structured typological material, either nominal or statistical, that can lead to relationships of a comparative and contrastive nature with regard to languages and their social functions. Typological research was a part of the sociology of language from the beginning and includes such names as Kloss (1968), Ferguson (1966), Stewart (1962), and Rustow (1968). The earliest efforts concentrated on typologizing countries and languages, the latter usually from a functional perspective. These efforts were useful in categorizing descriptive data in the vast social sphere, but were also useful adjuncts to the quantitative tradition, as we will see in section 5.

This descriptive-comparative tradition covers the first part of the Sociology of language mentioned by Fishman, i.e., *the descriptive sociology of language*, which, to paraphrase him, aims at describing the *social norm of language usage* in a speech community. But the sociology of language goes beyond social norm to include individual behavior, for it also seeks to answer Fishman's now famous question: "Who speaks (or writes) what language (or what language variety) to *whom* and *when* and to *what end*?" Now the "who speaks to whom" part of the question is particularly interesting to analyze, because in singling out individual verbal exchanges between individuals, Fishman is in the micro sphere of face-to-face contacts. The "when" and "what end" parts of the question refer in the first instance to "frequency (how often)" or by inference "location," and in the second instance to "purpose," which can be linked to behavior and attitudes or to "locale or situation" by inference. Indeed, as worded, the question has an individual speaker micro-orientation rather than a functional social norm macro-orientation. The micro-orientation can be quite useful for a sample survey of smaller social networks and communities, which is probably what Fishman had in mind, but it is unlikely to be applicable to a full-blown macro survey.

Hence a question in the macro sphere would have to be worded quite differently, with specific reference not to the individual speaker but rather to the functional norm of a language in terms of its frequency of use in a specific context. The type of macro-oriented question could be as follows: "What language (or language variety) is used (spoken/written) *where* and with *what frequency*?" Here "frequency" refers to a scale of intensity of usage, e.g., all or most of the time, and "where" refers to some context, which in the first instance would be part of an institutional construct or domain and in the second instance a specific locale involving agents and an activity, e.g., someone on the telephone in the office. This question, which also implies a macro construct, is required for large-scale macro studies so that some order can be brought to such a vast universe as the social one. Fishman (1972) heavily emphasized domain not just for its own intrinsic value, but as a construct capable of both distinguishing and linking individual behavior with social norm behavior.

> Thus, domain is a sociocultural construct abstracted from topics of communication, relationships between communicators, and locales of communication, in accord with the institutions of a society and the spheres of activity of a speech community, in such a way that *individual behavior and social patterns can be distinguished from each other and yet related to each other.* (p. 442)

The sociology of language tradition is solidly anchored in both the macro and micro spheres and for that reason is a good basis on which to construct a global scale sociolinguistics. This sociolinguistics will require a firm descriptive foundation, and should be able to build on that already established, particularly with regard to typologies. It should also be capable of linking the macro and micro spheres, using appropriate models and questionnaire instruments. And it should, through the quantitative tradition, be able to capture better what Fishman termed the dynamic sociology of languages. Let us now examine the quantitative tradition.

5 Global Scale Sociolinguistics and the Quantitative Tradition

In this section we will discuss the second or descriptive-analytical approach, particularly with regard to the macro tradition.

In the 1960s, with the rapid evolution in language sciences, the quantitative tradition began to loom large in importance, so large that it cut across many linguistic schools and traditions. This tradition was particularly strong for what Hymes termed "socially realistic linguistics" (see above), i.e., the Labovian tradition, where social criteria were closely matched to purely linguistic characteristics, such as phonetic variations and their relationship to class structure. As a result of this tradition, certain kinds of linguistic variation became closely identified with class and other types of "vertical" social variables, particularly regarding urban areas. Historically this constituted a breakthrough, first in the link between linguistic and social variables per se, and secondly in the link between linguistic variation and vertical stratification. The link between linguistic variation and horizontal (spatial) variables had long been established in dialectology, but since the advent of sociolinguistics new demographic variables were being hypothesized almost daily. Once a conceptual and statistical link had been established between language and social variation, undoubtedly because of a strong influence from neighboring sciences such as sociology and psychology, the doors were open wide for incoming influences regarding the quantitative tradition. Hence new types of metalinguistics suddenly appeared, such as sociolinguistics, psycholinguistics, demolinguistics, and geolinguistics. The quantitative traditions of the parent disciplines were usually based on laboratory experimentation and small group testing for psychology, on social group and class sample surveys for sociology, and on appropriate data banks for demography and geography. Psycholinguistics continued this laboratory tradition through testing in the classroom and became focused on language learning, as well as measuring the influence of attitudes in language maintenance and spread. Sociolinguistics, which finally became a generic term for a number of traditions, continued the quantitative sociological tradition, through the use of social class criteria, particularly in the social linguistics tradition and a combination of the sociology and psychology traditions in the sociology of language tradition.

Both the social linguistics tradition of Hymes, Gumperz, Saville-Troike, and others and the sociology of language tradition of Fishman, Kloss, Ferguson, and others became heavily influenced by the quantitative-analytical tradition. The social linguistics school was always close to the face-to-face tradition of language discourse, conversation, code-switching and specifically addresses itself to Fishman's earlier question, "Who speaks what to whom?" The second or sociology of language school, as we noted, had the broadest outlook in that it attempted to deal both with face-to-face relationships and with language norms through the use of broader-based, more abstract constructs such as domain. Fishman should be credited with being one of the very few who attempted, through the use of the domain construct and the macro and micro spheres, to account for and explain language function and behavior in regard to language. Conceptually and methodologically, the key question was and is, how best to account for language and societal congruency, interdependency, and change?

Most micros have been testing specific locales only in a very few domains and most macros have not only shied away from detailed functional analyses but have simply ignored cognitive studies. Any progress that can be made toward dovetailing the two approaches, so that methodologically we become more effective and instrumentally more capable and powerful, will undoubtedly help sociolinguists to answer many more questions than they have hitherto been able to do. Unfortunately, very few seem concerned with developing and exploiting this macro–micro dichotomy either conceptually or pragmatically in terms of methodological integration or questionnaire preparation. The micros have involved themselves more and more in corpus/text analysis, particularly with regard to its interaction with computer technology involving automatic correction and translation. The macro thrust has either played itself out, or has remained at the descriptive and multivariate analysis levels, all the time using a very skimpy database as a basis of operation and analysis. Macro when compared to micro studies were, of course, always at a disadvantage regarding the database, due to its immensity, complexity, and to practical concerns such as data-gathering costs. This, together with the general paucity of national and international functional language data (other than in the school domain), has caused macro studies to become stuck in their own tracks.

Here we are beginning to operate within the second part of Fishman's sociology of language, which he called the "dynamic sociology of languages" (see above). But this stage cannot be realized in any definitive way without engaging in a full-scale data-gathering effort that is conceptually and methodologically structured. This, in turn, implies vast international surveys, which would require funding far beyond the present capacities of most international and national funding organizations. Unfortunately, the timing is poor as the present research focus is no longer on language studies. They are now considered developmentally irrelevant and not technically oriented enough to be worthy of scarce research and development funds. In terms of development issues both language and culture are now deemed to be either too explosive politically or too irrelevant developmentally to be worthy of more than the conventional lip service.

6 Global Scale Sociolinguistics: A New Conceptual Framework

In the earlier sections we presented a historical and analytical overview of the composition and directional thrust of what we have been calling sociolinguistics, that is, the study of language in a social milieu. We then briefly described its corollary, language planning, with particular focus on status planning, given its orientation to role and hence functional presence/usage. From there, we demonstrated empirically how functional presence/usage could be used as both a descriptive and a quantitative tool for both the descriptive and quantitative traditions.

In this section we will try to determine what kind of research thrust in global scale sociolinguistics can be mounted, so that the present stalemate in sociolinguistics and more particularly the sociology of language can be overcome, so that the macro–micro connection can be further developed, and so that disparate schools of thought in sociolinguistics can perhaps be brought closer together. In order that this should not be done in an ad hoc fashion, some kind of conceptual reference framework must be proposed, so that these various tendencies and concepts can find their legitimate places.

One such effort at structuring came from the psycholinguistic school, where an attempt was being made to evaluate group behavior in terms of perceived strength, i.e., how group members perceived their own strength and that of neighboring groups. It was argued that perceived in-group/out-group strength had an effect on group cohesion and, in extremis, long-term group survival. This perceived strength was called *ethnolinguistic vitality,*

which was a subjective vitality of own/other group cohesiveness, distinctiveness, and activity. The article in question, "Towards a theory of language in
ethnic group relations," co-authored by Giles, Bourhis, and Taylor, appeared
in *Language, Ethnicity and Intergroup Relations* (1977), edited by Giles. The
article enquires as to what structural variables would most likely influence
ethnolinguistic vitality and the answer is found in what is termed a "taxonomy of structural variables," which the authors place under three main
headings: (1) status, (2) demography, and (3) institutional support (see figure
21.2). What is of interest here is that Giles and others have proposed a
construct that includes both group and language, that the subjective or
cognitive evaluation of vitality is supported by three types of structural
variables, and that the third or institutional support variable is based on
representation in the case of a group and on functional usage in the case of a
language. Giles and others did not actually propose a quantified measurement of vitality but proposed nominal – high, low, medium – variables, or a
"vitality configuration" by ethnic group for each of the three variables. But
what was really innovative from a sociolinguistic point of view was this
juxtaposing of group and language in terms of presence and usage, as well as
the "three-factored view" of reality construct, which proposed an objective
set of situational and structural variables in what was basically a cognitive
approach. With these combinations of structured pieces of reality, some more
cognitive and micro-oriented and others more structural and macro-
oriented, a model of ethnolinguistic vitality was produced, which at least
pointed the way to further theoretical developments in the same direction. If

Figure 21.2 A taxonomy of structural variables affecting ethnolinguistic vitality.

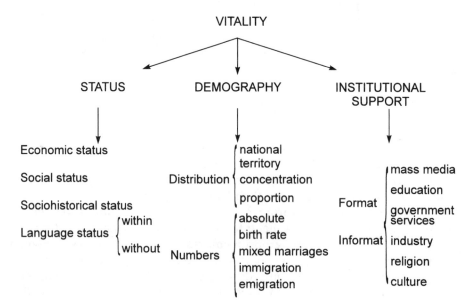

Fishman's phase of the "dynamic sociology of languages" is to be completely realized, or any metatheory of language and social structures created, such models are not only necessary but indispensable.

McConnell (1991), in *A Macro-Sociolinguistic Analysis of Language Vitality*, used the above taxonomy as an initial inspiration for two theoretical constructs, namely (1) "an illustrated model of language development" (see figure 21.3), where the macro structural analysis of language in society was proposed. This is conceived as three axes – according to degree of subtlety – with the outermost axis representing time and geographical space, the second axis that of social domain and its levels, and the innermost axis involving functions/products and their frequencies. The database lending support to this structure is to be found in the collection *The Written Languages of the World:*

Figure 21.3 An illustrated model of language development.

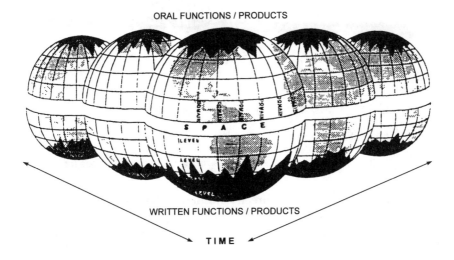

A *Survey of the Degree and Modes of Use*, edited by Kloss and McConnell. The combination of the above model and database has allowed us to quantitatively measure the vitality rate of any language in the world for which we have data, through the use of the standard questionnaire used in the written languages project. A detailed description of vitality rate calculations is available in McConnell and Gendron (1988), *Dimensions et mesure de la vitalité linguistique.*

The second theoretical construct is called (2) "a general power model of contextual and vital forces and their resolution" (see figure 21.4). This too is a macro structural model, but more specifically a contextual model of language contact, in which the institutional support structure in the Giles model, containing domains and functions, is resolved into an "internal" language vitality rate. This rate in turn can be mitigated by "external" pressures or sociocultural

Figure 21.4   A general power model of contextual and vital forces and their resolution.

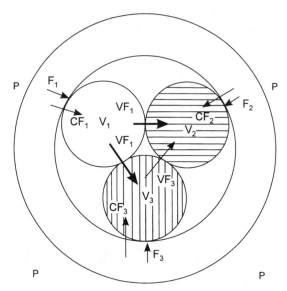

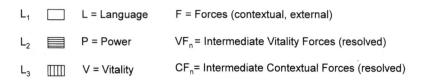

L_1 ☐	L = Language	F = Forces (contextual, external)
L_2 ▤	P = Power	VF_n = Intermediate Vitality Forces (resolved)
L_3 ▥	V = Vitality	CF_n = Intermediate Contextual Forces (resolved)

forces, which directly and indirectly influence the functional utility of any language, i.e., directly through the functional pressures of other languages and indirectly through various environmental influences. In the Giles model some of these environmental forces have already been included, namely demographic ones, but there are also status ones. These seem to refer to an evaluational status based on cognitive criteria. However, the point to be made here is that, in working on and developing contextual models for several regions and countries of the world, various external criteria can be tested regarding their influence on vitality to see if they are universally important, i.e., reoccurring in many heterogeneous contexts, or only incidentally important, i.e., relevant to certain types of contact configurations.

What can be further mentioned regarding the new research thrust in global scale sociolinguistics? First, in order to be successful it has to be hardnosed and applicable. Hence, there is the newly developed concept of vitality rates and their calculations. This can of course be further refined and other types of vitality rates prepared, such as those based on products alone, e.g., the number of books or the hours of broadcasting. Further, a cartography of language functions has now been developed that is quantified as vitality rates, most notably in the McConnell and Gendron *International Atlas of Language Vitality* (1993–95) series. A variation of this cartography based on the demographics of specific language functions (languages taught or used in the schools around the world) but geared to language spread in public and geographical space has also been published (see McConnell and Roberge, 1994).

Second, further research must be done on language contact situations around the world, testing various language contact scenarios with various configurations of variables. A cartography of contact configurations is also feasible as a result of this work but has not yet been developed. Finally, further modular work is required so that the conceptual frame of reference for global scale sociolinguistics can be expanded in order to include both macro and micro dimensions but also language and ethnic group orientations. Four questionnaires were recently developed by McConnell, Giles, and Harwood, which included a synthesis for (i) language in terms of functions, (ii) ethnic group in terms of representation/control, (iii) cognitive evaluations of language regarding functions, and (iv) cognitive evaluations of groups regarding representation/control. This inductive approach could be the first step leading to a metatheory of language and group regarding their sustenance and survival.

NOTE

1 Translated from: "L'objectif de tout changement linguistique planifié étant de réduire la concurrence entre les langues ou les variantes d'une langue et d'ordonner rationnellement leur coexistence au sein de la société."

22 Language and the Mediation of Experience: Linguistic Representation and Cognitive Orientation

MICHAEL STUBBS

It is obvious that there are relationships between language, thought, and culture, but saying exactly what these relationships are constitutes a puzzle of huge fascination and baffling complexity, and, despite a long history of debate, many points are unresolved. Often the question has been tackled by philosophers or psycholinguists. Here I will discuss the value of rethinking the question from a sociolinguistic point of view. I will emphasize its social significance, by giving examples from legal, scientific, and sexist and racist language. I will emphasize the need to look not (just) at language structure but at different uses of language. And after some initial conceptual discussion, I will emphasize an empirical approach based on text and corpus analysis.

1 The Structure of the Argument: Whorf and Others

Two essential concepts are *categorization* and *selection*. Every time we talk about anything, the words we use select some features of the world and ignore or play down others. This is simply unavoidable. Of course, the categories of language and of thought are not necessarily the same. This connection is what we have to discuss, and the everyday concept of the *stereotype* recognizes dangers. People are labelled and put into categories such as "immigrant," "working mother," or "teenager": It is then all too easy to jump to the conclusion that these individuals share group characteristics.

Many positions on the relation between language and thought have been formulated. These include (1) that cognition is dependent on language (Whorf, see below); (2) that language is dependent on prior cognitive development (Piaget); (3) that cognition simply *is* language, in the form of subvocal speech (a behaviorist position, as in Bloomfield); (4) that language and cognition are parallel; or (5) that they are initially separate in children's linguistic and cognitive development and later converge (Vygotsky). Nelson (1991: 278ff.) discusses these positions with reference to children's language acquisition.

Here I have space only to start from the well-known Whorfian position, and, on this basis, to develop some sociolinguistic approaches. Basic arguments and counter-arguments are well known:

Argument All languages refer to the same world, all people have much the same basic experiences and perceptions, and all languages have the same broad functions. Human reasoning relies on universal logical principles.

Counter-argument Different languages "cut up" the world in different ways, imply different worlds, and influence perception. Language and thought are therefore intimately related. Strong forms of this view have been succinctly formulated as: "The medium is the message"; "Our language does our thinking for us"; "If Aristotle had spoken Nootka (an American Indian language), then we would have a different logic."

Counter-counter-argument But languages are not incompatible. We can translate between them. And bilinguals speak different languages, but they do not perceive the world differently when they switch from one language to another.

And so the arguments continue. Translation is never perfect. Subtleties are always lost. Yes, agreed, but translators are aware of the challenge, and paraphrase is always possible.

In addition, such arguments have confusing characteristics. The arguments frequently slide between (exaggerated?) strong versions and (more plausible?) weak versions. Does language determine and mold thought, or merely facilitate and support it?

The arguments are often emotional, because they question common-sense world views, and because linguistic and cultural relativity is often felt to imply moral relativity.

Many different terms and metaphors are used. Does language "construct," "mediate," "code," or "represent" reality? To talk of the linguistic "construction" of reality implies a very active role for language. "Mediation" implies a weaker position. "Coding orientation" emphasizes that choice is possible among different codings, and that things are a question of frequency and habit. And metaphors can be misleading. A language is said to "cut up" nature, or to "reflect" or "mirror" reality. The mirror metaphor, in turn, implies that language passively expresses reality, rather than actively creating it (cf. section 2.4).

It is often difficult to tell the chicken from the egg. Do languages provide us with cultural categories? Or do they encode what is culturally important? But then, once the categories are established, they are imposed on speakers in following generations. A famous formulation of this puzzle was made by Marx (1852), who radically unified the individual and the social: "Human beings make their own history, but they do not make it of their own free will ... The tradition of all the dead generations weighs like a nightmare on the minds of the living."

Possibly the most fundamental problem with such arguments is the difficulty of breaking out of a vicious circle. It is *observed* that languages differ, and it is *concluded* that the thought of their speakers also differs. But what is the *evidence* that their thought differs? Well, the language that they use! We want to investigate the relation between language and thought. But in almost any situation we can imagine, the only access we have to thought is via language.

1.1 Some brief history: Linguistic relativism

Academic debates about language and thought are often traced back to 1757, when the Berlin Academy of Sciences asked: "What is the influence of people's opinions on the language, and of the language on the opinions of the people?" The prize-winning essay is thought to have influenced Herder (1744–1803) and in turn Humboldt (1767–1835), whose ideas underlie the concepts of *Sprachgeist* and *Volksseele* which became so important in nineteenth-century German Romanticism, that a language embodies the spirit of the people who speak it. Humboldt (1825) went on to develop a theory of "the genesis of grammatical forms and their influence on the development of ideas" (G. Williams, 1992: 30ff.).

Another major source is Saussurean structuralism, which leads almost inevitably to the view that the language system itself creates meaning. There are two opposed positions. The first is that meanings are external to language: They exist prior to their linguistic expression, which passively reflects external reality. Deriving from the work of Saussure, there is a contrary position. Meanings are internal to language: They depend on the oppositions and contrasts within a language, which actively construct a social reality.

The most explicit source is work by Sapir (1884–1939) and Whorf (1897–1941), who are usually (not entirely accurately) lumped together in this matter. The "Sapir–Whorf" hypothesis is usually quoted via statements in Whorf's papers, published from 1927 to 1941 collected posthumously (Whorf, 1956), and often taken as the classic source of the view that the grammatical categories of language construct implicit theories of the world. Famous passages in Whorf (1956) include:

> We cut nature up, organize it into concepts, and ascribe significances as we do, largely because we are parties to an agreement to organize it in this way – an agreement that holds throughout our speech community and is codified in the patterns of our language. (p. 213)

This is a claim about linguistic relativity. (Note the metaphor about "cutting nature up." Black (1959) criticizes Whorf's "vocabulary of the operating theatre.") But a view that languages embody conventions which "codify" thought slides easily into determinism:

> The agreement is, of course, an implicit and unstated one, *but its terms are absolutely obligatory*; we cannot talk at all except by subscribing to the organization and classification of data which the agreement decrees [pp. 213–14, emphasis in original] ... the forms of a person's thoughts are controlled by inexorable laws of pattern of which he is unconscious. (p. 252)

There were historical reasons for Sapir and Whorf being interested in such questions. Systematic investigation of Amerindian languages had shown them to be just as complex as classical European languages, but their categories seemed very different. The Sapir–Whorf version(s) of linguistic relativism were in fashion in the 1940s and fifties. They then went very much out of fashion, and seemed indeed to have the racist implication that different groups of people might have different cognitive capacities determined by their different languages. This turnaround was ironic, given the anti-racist stance which had motivated much of the study initially – that the native population of North America could not be dismissed as "primitive."

Fishman (1980, 1982) provides important summaries of various versions and criticisms of the Whorfian hypothesis. There are good accounts of Whorf within a critique of sociolinguistics (G. Williams, 1992) and within feminism (Cameron, 1992: 134ff.). And recently several more sympathetic interpretations of Whorf have appeared, e.g., Lakoff (1987: 304–37) and Lucy (1992a, b). Psychological and perceptual studies have often had extreme difficulty in deriving experiments to confirm or contradict specific Whorfian hypotheses. Progress has been made in some well defined areas, such as color vocabulary, where it is possible to design experiments to show possible behavioral effects of language. However, it is notoriously difficult in such areas to distinguish linguistic effects from social and cultural factors, such as the requirements of technological societies (for expanded color vocabularies) or of formal education. In addition, the semantic areas discussed are generally very narrow. Lucy (1992a, b) provides a substantial and very clear account of the history and logic of the argument from eighteenth-century Germany, via Boas and Sapir, to Whorf and his successors, plus his own case study of Yucatec Maya.

There are many other relevant lines of work, especially within phenomeno-logical traditions in philosophy (e.g., Husserl) which argue that society is always mediated by experience, and that meaning is constructed in human consciousness. Much in the later work of Wittgenstein is Whorfian in tone. Phenomenology has in turn influenced sociological views on the social con-struction of reality. And versions of discourse analysis have studied how discourse practices systematically form the objects whereof they speak: We don't speak a language, the language speaks us (Foucault, 1980; G. Williams, 1992: 248–58).

A famous contribution to the theory of codes is provided by Bernstein (e.g., 1973, 1990), who acknowledges Whorf (along with Marx and Vygotsky) as an important early influence. Bernstein (1990: 94) has characterized his work as tackling the classic sociological question: "How does the outside become the inside and how does the inside reveal itself and shape the outside?" His work, on how uses of language regulate both cognitive orientations and social identities, is a major theory of symbolic control and cultural reproduction, and a thorough discussion is well beyond the scope of this article. (See Atkinson, 1992, for an interpretation of Bernstein's work as a structuralist program which goes far beyond his work on language.) Halliday is the linguist who has consistently expressed sympathy with Bernstein's views, and who has de-veloped, with Bernstein, a theory of coding orientations. I will restrict myself to a discussion of Halliday's text-based version of coding theory below (sec-tion 2.3).

Historically, Whorfian views were also part of broader traditions of thought which debunk human freedom, and see humans condemned to the mercy of their evolutionary origins (Darwin), socioeconomic forces (Marx), the uncon-scious (Freud), or language (Whorf) (see Fishman, 1982). But the whole ques-tion remains unresolved. This is only to admit that we do not yet fully understand the relations between language, experience, reality, culture and the human mind.

1.2 *"The great Eskimo vocabulary hoax"*

One myth (for which Whorf (1956: 210) is partly responsible) should immedi-ately be disposed of. This is the view that "Eskimo has dozens of words for snow." Snow, so runs the argument, is important to Eskimos, so they have a fine-grained category system and lots of words for it. Well, they don't: They have a dozen or so (Pullum, 1991: 171). But then, so does English – snow, frost, ice, slush, sleet, blizzard, avalanche, cornice – not to mention compounds such as snowfall, snowfield, snowflake, snowdrift, snowstorm, snowball, snow-man, snowshoe, snowplow, etc. In fact, such compounds show how im-possible it is to count the words for snowy things in English. And the counting problem is much worse in dialects of Inuit and Yupik, since they are highly polysynthetic.

Even if these languages did have many words for snow, this would not be especially interesting. Groups usually have technical terms for things important to them. Cooks have terms for kitchen equipment and cooking methods; linguists have hundreds of linguistic terms (and specialist dictionaries); and skiers and mountaineers have even more words for different snow conditions.

What can be concluded from this? First, once such a myth is embedded, it is very hard to shift it. Like urban legends, it is "too good to be false." This is itself one effect of language on thought: Clichés take hold of people's imaginations, and are almost impossible to shift. Second, there is an implicit racism involved in the repetition of such stories. "We are prepared to believe almost anything about such an unfamiliar and peculiar group" (Martin, 1986, quoted by Pullum, 1991: 162). One should be especially wary of arguments about language and thought which are illustrated only from the language of some far-away "exotic" group about whose thought we have no independent evidence.

This myth shows the kind of argument we do not want. It is not sufficient to point to a loosely defined set of words, which are not fundamental to the conceptual system. Words for snow are as isolated as many words relating to cuisine in French, or to music in Italian. We need more interesting ways of looking for links between language and cognition.

1.3. Grammaticalization

The interesting arguments (as Whorf himself emphasized) concern not individual words, but lexical sets and syntactic constructions. There is particular interest in conceptual categories which are grammaticalized (Hopper and Traugott, 1993) in languages, since such categories are obligatory, and become automatic, habitual, effortless, unconscious, and therefore apparently "natural" (Lakoff, 1987: 319).

There are certainly areas of experience which are both abstract and differently grammaticalized in different languages, for example, in systems of tense, aspect, mood and modality, and evidentiality. It is common for such meanings to be marked in the grammar as obligatory categories, but languages differ considerably in what can and must be encoded. For example, in English, every finite verb must be marked for tense. But, like many other languages, standard modern Chinese has no tense system: Chinese is quite capable of specifying when an event takes place, but this is not obligatory. Other languages have tenses which distinguish between the remote past ("more than a few weeks ago"), the recent past ("but not today"), and earlier on the day of speaking, or employ aspect to encode events which have happened exactly once or repeatedly. Such distinctions may sound "exotic," but English has a tense form, sometimes known rather dramatically as the "hot news perfect." As opposed to English simple past forms (*he went*), perfect tense forms (*he has gone*) encode the present relevance of past events. So, when referring to single past events, a speaker has to choose between the two forms: The concept "current relevance" must be encoded in the morphology. (Although German has two similar forms, they do not encode this meaning distinction.)

In many languages it is obligatory to encode in the verb morphology the source of a speaker's evidence for what is said. The Papuan language Fasu encodes whether a statement is known or thought to be true because "I see it," "I hear it," "I infer it," "Somebody (I don't know who) says so," "Somebody (I know who) says so," or "I suppose so" (Trask, 1993: 95). And Lakoff (1987: 313ff.) similarly discusses the conceptual organization of space in Mixtec, an Otomanguean language.

However, it is difficult to know what to make of such examples. It is plausible that if speakers of a language have to encode time, space, or evidentiality every time they use a verb, then they will automatically think of the world in these categories. (And Nelson [1991: 292], for example, argues that coding of tense makes concepts of time salient for children.) But it is difficult to see what concrete, observable effects this could have on behavior.

Possibly the most convincing studies discuss not only such grammatical *potential* of different languages, but also the effect of systematic *selections* from this potential in actual language use in important social contexts. I will give such an example below, from work by Berk-Seligson (1990).

Whorf (1956: 88–9) pointed out that only some grammatical categories are overtly marked. Others, which he calls *cryptotypes*, are covert. Such covert categories must be internalized as semantic categories, otherwise they could not be manipulated automatically. Halliday (1990) gives the example that the idea "bigger is better" is "engraved into our consciousness" because of the way the grammar of English makes us ask questions. If we have no preconceptions about the size or length of a thing, we say *how big is it*? not *how small is it*? or *how long is it*? not *how short is it*? Again, perhaps it is when such concepts are not directly encoded that they reveal speakers' underlying assumptions. I will also give such examples below (cf. Halliday and Martin, 1993: 9, 113).

2 A Sociolinguistic Version of the Argument

I will now concentrate on a sociolinguistic formulation of the puzzle, and will assume that deterministic theory is untenable. I cannot believe that the limits of language are the limits of thought: Human intellectual history is full of examples of people finding new ideas and new ways to express them. However, language *mediates* our experience. There are many areas of human life of which we can have no direct experience at all, and where all our knowledge comes to us via language. It is therefore plausible that language *influences* thought, for most of us, at least some of the time. The question is: Can we pin down the linguistic mechanisms at work?

Nelson (1991) points out that a great deal of our knowledge of the world is acquired through language, and that many cultural concepts which children acquire early do not exist independently of the ways in which we talk about them: "home," "family," "work." Giddens (1991) provides a detailed socio-logical discussion of the consequences of virtually all human experience being mediated by other people's linguistic representations. Bell (1991) and Fowler (1991b) provide linguistic analyses of this mediation by the mass media.

Furthermore, the Sapir–Whorf hypothesis is untenable if it sees a language as homogeneous and static. Languages vary internally and change historically (and can *be* changed by some kinds of language engineering; see below), and they can be *used* in different ways. This is the point of most relevance to sociolinguistics. I will assume in fact that Whorf asked the right basic ques-tion, but formulated it wrongly. Rather than talking about the influence of language on thought, we can talk about the influence of uses of language on assumptions taken for granted. We can discuss

- not language structure, but language use in discourse;
- not grammar, but systematic selections from the grammar;
- not cognitive determinism, but coding orientations;
- not cognitive potential, but habits of thought;
- not causation, but mediation.

These are the fruitful emphases for sociolinguists, not individual psycho-logical versions of the Whorfian hypothesis, but versions which emphasize cognitive orientations. I will therefore concentrate on text- and corpus-based studies. There are many such studies within what is now often referred to as critical linguistics or critical discourse analysis: Fowler (1991a) is an authorita-tive definition of this field by one of its originators. And see Hodge and Kress (1993) on "language and ideology"; Fairclough (1989) on "language and power"; and Fowler (1991b: 1) on how newspaper language can "form ideas and beliefs."

So much, then, for the complex and sometimes highly abstract structure of the arguments. I will now discuss concrete examples from four socially im-portant areas.

2.1 Case 1: Racist discourse: Lexical sets

The choice of lexis often reveals different moral points of view: *George isn't stingy, he's thrifty.* Such lexical choices can be especially important in political debate: The same groups can be referred to as *terrorists* or *freedom fighters*. And depending on the point of view, one might talk of the settlement *or* invasion of Australia by Whites; the defence *or* invasion of Viet Nam by the Americans; the discovery of America *or* the genocide of Native Americans.

Sometimes sets of terms are involved. A recent student newsletter in my university in Germany criticized right-wing activities: One argument concerned fixed expressions which have become very frequent, such as *Fremden-hass* ("hatred of foreigners"), *Scheinasylanten* ("apparent/sham political asylum seekers"), and *kulturelle Überfremdung* ("cultural infiltration by foreigners"). It argued that such lexical creations crystallize thoughts, make them easy to refer to, presuppose the existence of such things, and therefore facilitate stereotyped reactions. For example, the coinage *Ausländerfeindlichkeit* (a second term for "hatred of foreigners") brings together the concepts of "foreigner" and "enemy" (*Feind*). Constantly used collocations lexicalize an area of experience, and give credence to the concept "foreigner-hatred." Wodak (1992, 1993) studied such racist discourse in Austria and concluded (1993: 226) that, although such discourse cannot be held responsible for causing racism, it "offers arguments and metaphors which can serve to legitimate prejudiced attitudes." It is plausible that constantly repeated formulations mediate and support ways of thought.

Notorious examples come from Nazi Germany, when a term from chess, *Endlösung* ("final solution"), was used to refer to the extermination of the Jews. Perhaps no one is fooled by such euphemistic newspeak? Yet such terms must have a function (dissimulation from self?) or they would not constantly be coined, in many different regimes, to avoid expressing the moral implications of actions. In the Gulf War, *collateral damage* meant "civilians killed." The perpetrators in the Balkan war seemed to find it easier to talk of *ethnic cleansing* than of populations being brutally tortured and murdered. The same types of examples keep recurring, as areas of meaning are relexicalized in ways which make genocide seem banal (Ehlich, 1989, provides analyses of language in Nazi Germany).

Phillipson (1992: 38ff.) analyzes terms (such as *nation, tribe, underdeveloped, developing, emergent nation, aid, culture, civilization*) which describe countries from a Western point of view and which characterize a racist, colonial, and postcolonial discourse (however benevolent its intentions might be).

2.2   Case 2: The construction of reality in courtrooms: Lexis and grammar

Consider more detailed cases where lexical choices create frames of reference with their own internal logic, and influence perception and memory. Courtroom examples are of crucial social importance.

Danet (1980) analyzes an American case where a doctor who had carried out a late abortion was convicted of manslaughter, and where vocabulary was an explicit topic in the trial itself. The same event can be talked about in different ways. For example, one might say: *the fetus was aborted* or *the baby was murdered*. Although each phrase can refer to the same external reality, very different moral points of view are encoded, and different assumptions about offence and guilt are implied. During the trial, the lawyers negotiated the different connotations of terms such as *products of conception, fetus, male human being, male child, baby boy* (and many others). When, as here, the meaning of an act is itself ambiguous (when does life begin? what do we mean by a "person"?), then it is impossible to separate what happened from the language used to talk about it. And such semantic choices are crucial to the outcome of the trial: If no "person" existed, then no manslaughter could have occurred.

There is always a category shift when one moves from *ways of talking* to *ways of thinking*. And it is impossible to discover what effect such lexical choices actually had on the jury. But one can analyze the points of view from which such lexical choices are made, the incommensurable frames of reference they assume, and the presuppositions they make. For example, *baby boy* connotes helplessness, within a caring frame of reference which presupposes that there is a life to be saved. Words such as *fetus, abortion*, and *termination* assume a medical frame of reference, rather than a criminal one. No terms are neutral.

In a famous experiment, Loftus and Palmer (1974) provided empirical evidence that lexical choices can influence perception and memory. They showed people a film of a traffic accident, and then asked questions such as *How fast were the cars going when they hit each other*? But they varied the question by using different verbs, and this influenced people's estimates of the speed. Higher estimates were given with verbs such as *smash* and *collide* than with *bump* and *contact*. Furthermore, when they were asked *Did you see any broken glass*? (there was none in the film), people who had been asked about the cars *smashing* into each other were more likely to say "yes." That is, using the word *smash* triggered preconceptions about both speed and likely consequences (broken glass). Individual words evoked a frame of reference in which various default assumptions were made. In this experimental case, subjects had direct access to the event itself, in the form of the film, yet language still influenced their perception and memory. In a real trial, of course, the jury has no such access: The members have nothing but the words used in the courtroom. It is therefore even more plausible that words will influence assumptions. It is a cliché to lawyers that the law "is a profession of words," and that a case is tried not on "facts," but on testimony, the representation of "facts" in language.

It is important to emphasize that the connotations of words do not arise from nowhere. They are constructed and maintained by frequent collocations across millions of words of language in use, and methods of text and corpus analysis can be used to identify the very different collocational profiles which words have. Consider again the Loftus and Palmer (1974) examples. From a corpus of 120 million words I extracted the most frequent collocates of words in the lexical field of "hit." (Clear, 1993, describes the methods in detail.) *Hit* itself has a wide range of uses, often metaphorical: This is shown by collocations with *earthquake, hard, jackpot, recession. Bump* connotes slow clumsy movements: Its collocates include *accidentally, lurch, stumble. Collide* co-occurs almost exclusively with large vehicles, including ships and aircraft. *Smash* connotes crime and violence: Its collocates include *bottles, glass, looted, window, windscreen. Strike* has metaphorical uses and is used with natural disasters: Its collocates include *blow, disaster, earthquake, lightning, suddenly, tragedy*.

These studies show that recurrent wordings can fix and transmit cultural meanings. Collocations, fixed phrases, idioms, catch phrases, clichés, and various prefabricated chunks of language can encode stereotypes and shared assumptions. They can be both linguistic and cultural units, and show that learning a language involves learning a culture, and not merely alternative labels for the same things.

These cases involve lexis. Berk-Seligson (1990) discusses legal cases where choices from the grammatical system may affect how meanings are represented. A central area of meaning in any courtroom concerns cause and effect, blame and responsibility: Who is guilty of doing what to whom? English has various constructions which can make agency more or less explicit. For example, a verb such as *break* allows several syntactic options, including:

- He broke the glass.   [transitive]
- The glass got broken.   [passive 1]
- The glass was broken.   [passive 2]
- The glass broke.   [intransitive]

The transitive expresses a chain of causation: The syntax NP-V-NP corresponds to the semantics of agent–action–effect. Passive 1 expresses action with no mention of agent. Passive 2 expresses either an action (cf. *The glass was broken by my brother*) or a state (*It was broken when I arrived*). The intransitive implies that something happened spontaneously through no one's fault. Every language has ways of talking about such things, but the syntactic means may differ. Berk-Seligson's research is on American courtrooms in which Spanish–English translation was being used. The key point is that Spanish also has several ways of encoding such meanings, but the distinctions do not correspond to those in English. The passive is very common in English courtroom discourse: It also exists in Spanish, but is much more formal and therefore tends to be avoided. But Spanish has two reflexive constructions:

- Se rompió el vaso.   "The glass broke."
- Se me rompió el vaso.   "The glass broke on me."

Whenever the interpreter translates, she or he is forced by the language to take (probably unconscious) decisions about exactly how blame is attributed.

In summary: The syntactic and semantic systems of different languages cannot always be mapped directly onto each other. Different distinctions are obligatory in different languages. And meanings may be skewed if certain selections are systematically made from the potential of the language.

O'Barr (1982) is an influential discussion of the relation between the language used in the courtroom and the outcome of legal decisions. Hodge and Kress (1993) discuss how causal processes are expressed directly or obliquely in choices from the transitivity system; Stubbs (1994) discusses how the frequency distribution of transitivity choices in two schoolbooks contributes to the "clause by clause synthesis of a world view."

2.3 Case 3: The construction of scientific reality: Lexis and grammar

Scientific language provides a case of an area where concepts and syntax seem to have developed together, and where this development is amenable to empirical text analysis. Halliday and Martin (1993) discuss the functions of lexis and grammar in scientific language. They start from two clear facts. (1) Scientific and everyday language are very different: e.g., it is well known that certain syntactic features, such as passive and nominalization, are common in scientific language. (2) Scientific and everyday world views are very different, indeed science often rejects common-sense understandings. They then look for the relation between these two facts.

In detailed textual studies, they analyze the scientific language used by Chaucer, Newton, and Darwin, and the language of contemporary school science books. They regard lexis and syntax as a "semiotic technology" (p. 221) which allows a "scientific reconstruction of the world" (p. 183). Classification is fundamental to science. Halliday and Martin give several examples of everyday and technical taxonomies from geography, biology, ornithology, and anatomy, and of the functions of technical names and classifications. Taxonomies organize the world as if all phenomena, including processes, were things: Technical verbs are rare. It is the job of science to construct different interpretations of the world, based on different organizing criteria. It is not possible to do science in everyday language. Technical terms are not just jargon: They organize the world differently.

Their argument is based mainly on analysis of different registers within a single language. Note that the case of science is itself a refutation of an extreme cross-linguistic Whorfian view, since the very different ideas of common sense, and of Newtonian and Einsteinian physics, represent radical shifts of world view *within* English and other West European language communities. (Their comparative analysis of English and Chinese scientific language, pp. 125–32, shows similarities, rather than differences.)

Their argument has other important characteristics. (1) It is evolutionary: "scientific language has evolved so that it can accumulate information" (p. 186). (2) It is functional: They are looking for a cognitive explanation of the heavily nominalized style of science. (3) It is probabilistic: It depends on the relation between language potential and language use. They argue that the cognitive effect comes from increased use of resources already present in the language. A new register is created by reconstructing the probabilities of use of, for example, passives and nominalizations. (4) And it is based on text analysis. Nominalizations have the discourse function of allowing information to be packaged: The grammar is used to encode things so that they can be referred to conveniently and used in arguments.

This discourse function relies heavily on grammatical metaphor. Metaphor is the substitution of one word for another. Grammatical metaphor is the substitution of one grammatical class or structure for another. Halliday and Martin (1993: 54–68) give an example of the progressive nominalization of a concept in the course of a scientific article on the fracturing of glass. Early expressions such as *a crack grows* give way to *the rate of crack growth* and finally to *the glass crack growth rate*. This nominal group can then act as subject or object of a verb: *we can decrease the glass crack growth rate 1,000 times*. Thus "the text itself creates its grammar, as it goes along" (p. 56). The "clausal variant precedes the nominal one" (p. 18), both in individual texts and also historically, in the development of scientific English. Note that this immediately disposes of Whorf's (1956: 215) idea that if our language classifies something as a verb then we will conceive of it as an event (or if as a noun then as an object). The language can encode the same phenomenon as a verb (*grows*) or as a noun (*growth*) for different discourse purposes.

Halliday's work on language as social semiotic is therefore a main contender for a radically revised Whorfian theory. Halliday takes the view – explicitly related to Whorf – that the lexico-grammar is "a theory of human experience" (p. 8), and that "the language of science has reshaped our whole world view" (p. 10). Grammar "construes reality," since every clause is a representation of the world, and clause by clause a world view is synthesized. But Halliday emphasizes language change and variation. We are not stuck with the grammatical categories of our language, since the potential of the grammar can be taken up in consistently different ways, and the development of science shows that the resources of the grammar can be used to interpret the world from different points of view.

The case of scientific language also emphasizes the cognitive effects of writing as a medium. There is a large literature which argues that writing is not merely spoken language written down, but that it facilitates certain kinds of (especially syllogistic) thinking which require chains of reasoning. Popper (1972) provides a famous discussion of this documentary world, which supports certain kinds of knowledge.

2.4. Case 4: Sexism: Patterns of frequency and distribution

Sexist language (see chapter 8) uses lexical and grammatical resources to represent the world from the point of view of the male. Feminist scholarship (e.g., Cameron, 1992) has rejected the mirror metaphor. Language does not "reflect" society: It is part of the social, it reproduces society, language change is social change. And feminist campaigns have attempted (often successfully) to change how language is used. However, this language engineering has been more successful at some linguistic levels than others, usually at the level of words and phrases. For example, the term *sexual harassment* is now widely used. It does not create the behavior referred to. This already exists, but naming something can bring it to consciousness, give it a social identity, and facilitate its identification (e.g., if necessary, for the law).

Features of surface morphology and grammar, such as the asymmetrical use of *he* and *she*, are also relatively easy to see, though often a matter of habit and less easy to control. However, there are more subtle aspects of their patterns which are more difficult to observe. It is easy to find examples of specific sexist usages, but more difficult to investigate the distribution of forms. Using computer assisted methods, I studied half a million words of spoken educated British English. I extracted all occurrences of *someone, somebody, anyone, anybody* (over 400) and looked for occurrences of pronouns referring to the same person in the immediate context:

(a) they, them, their, themselves   i.e., sex neutral;
(b) he or she, him or her, etc.   i.e., explicitly both;
(c) he, him, his, himself   i.e., male;
(d) she, her, hers, herself   i.e., female.

Examples of each type were:

(a) By the age of sixteen *anybody* who is going to be an academic should have done *their* general reading.
(b) *Someone* describing *himself or herself* as a middle-aged viewer.
(c) Why should *somebody* move here when *he* has to pay fifty thousand pounds . . . for a house?
(d) When *somebody* gets sufficiently . . . neglectful of *herself* – as my grandmother's now become.

Example (d) refers to a specific individual person that the speaker has in mind: I will call this a *definite* reference. Examples (a), (b), and (c) are references to hypothetical or unknown persons or to groups: I will call these *indefinite*.

The nonsexist *they* pattern was the most common. The forms *they* or *he or she* were much more common in indefinite sentences, though still used in four definite cases. However, *she* was used only in definite cases, whereas *he* was equally distributed between definite and indefinite. The overall distribution was still sexist.

Lakoff and Johnson (1980) write about metaphors and their effect on thought, and one might expect that they would be particularly sensitive to such aspects of language use. Yet in their example sentences, their own use of male and female pronouns is very asymmetrical. Males are mentioned over five times more often than females. There are about 40 examples of phrases such as *his argument, his ideas, his theory*; there are no such examples for *her*. But there are many examples such as *crazy about her, she cast her spell*. Lakoff and Johnson appear to have unthinkingly encoded a series of stereotypes: men are mentioned more often than (are more important than) women; men have ideas and theories, women evoke emotions.

Baker and Freebody (1989) analyze distributional patterns in books for children. In a corpus of initial reading primers, they find that words for individual children are always sex-specific: The singular sex-indefinite word *child* is entirely absent. The words *boy/boys* are more frequent than *girl/girls*. The word *boy* is more likely than *girl* to be singular: Boys appear more often as individuals, girls more often in groups. Some verbs occur only with *boy/s* as subject; no verbs occur only with *girl/s*: The implication is that boys engage in a wider range of activities than girls. Such a use of language itself constitutes and legitimates a concept of childhood. The language system provides resources which can be used in different ways, but the selections made are sexist.

These studies show that assumptions may be conveyed not only by individual words and phrases, but by the frequency and asymmetrical distribution of choices from the language system. Such features of language use are subject to habit, and are impossible to observe directly.

3 Conclusions: Agenda for Future Research

Much of the puzzle posed by Whorf and others remains unresolved: it is particularly difficult to escape the circularity of arguments where language is both cause and evidence. But I should attempt a conclusion, however cautious.

Few scholars these days argue that there is an ideal realm of thought which exists entirely independent of its expression in texts. There is widespread consensus that language is never neutral and texts are never innocent. Things can always be formulated differently, any linguistic expression of "the facts" selects some aspects of reality, and all selections are ideological. Such choices are not usually explicit, and are often denied (because they express group interests).

There are many variants of the view that language and thought are related. We know how Whorf's question can be reformulated to apply to the choices available within a language; and therefore apply not (only?) to language structure, but also to language use. It is plausible that if the world is repeatedly talked about in certain ways, then such "semantic habits" can influence thinking. These semantic habits are often not directly observable, because they are a matter, not of individual words, but of patterns of distribution and frequency.

There is no convincing evidence that language determines thought in any absolute way. On the contrary, all languages provide resources which are being constantly developed to express new ideas. However, there is evidence that linguistic choices can make people jump to unjustified conclusions. And it is highly plausible that, if these resources are constantly exploited in recurrent codings, then habits of language can lead to stereotyped thought. It is becoming clearer how such codings can be studied in texts and corpora. Also, the written medium can itself facilitate certain kinds of thinking: This is particularly relevant in the development of scientific thought.

As well as purely conceptual analysis, it is important to do empirical studies, which might concentrate on: (1) Socially important cases where language may influence assumptions, perceptions and stereotypes. (2) Corpus-based analyses of the frequency and distribution of fixed phrases and collocations. (3) Forms of language engineering which encourage speakers to change their language use. This has happened with success in scientific registers and in nonsexist language. (4) Forms of language education which teach students how to identify implicit points of view in texts, and how to express things in different ways.

Experience shows that educational approaches cannot make people avoid prejudiced and stereotyped thinking. But they can perhaps contribute "just that extra critical edge of consciousness" (R. Williams, 1976: 21).

NOTE

I am grateful to Gwyneth Fox, Director of Cobuild, Birmingham, UK, for permission to use the Bank of English corpus; to the Norwegian Computing Centre for the Humanities for permission to use the LOB corpus; and to Gabi Keck for detailed comments on an earlier draft.

23 Linguistic Etiquette

GABRIELE KASPER

The label *linguistic etiquette* refers to the practice in any speech community of organizing linguistic action so that it is seen as appropriate to the current communicative event. The scope of phenomena assembled under this label is thus much broader than what is suggested by the dictionary definition of *etiquette*, which restricts the term to denote "the formal rules of proper behaviour" (*Longman Dictionary of Contemporary English*, 1978: 373). Etiquette manuals from Erasmus of Rotterdam's *De civilitate morum puerilium* (1530) to the latest edition of *The Amy Vanderbilt Complete Book of Etiquette* (Vanderbilt and Baldridge, 1978) do not cover verbal routines such as the "rules for ritual insult" enacted among inner city African-American adolescents (Labov, 1972), yet they fall under the proposed definition. A related and more widely used term, *(linguistic) politeness*, is equally problematic because of its connotation of "deference" and "refined" behavior (e.g., Green, 1992a). For lack of preferable alternatives, both terms will be used interchangeably.

The "Phenomenon"

The somewhat nebulous definition proposed initially is indicative of much disagreement about the theoretical status and scope of linguistic etiquette. For most authors, politeness is a feature of language *use* (cf. the subtitle of Brown and Levinson's *Politeness: Some universals in language usage*). The action-theoretical view of politeness shared by Brown and Levinson (1978, 1987) and Leech (1983) firmly places linguistic etiquette in the arena of language use. Yet the same authors classify decontextualized speech acts as inherently polite or impolite. Fraser (1990: 233), commenting that the politeness of linguistic acts is determined by their occurrence in communicative contexts rather than by inherent properties, pushes the issue even further by noting that being "polite" is attributable only to speakers, not to language. But since social judgments are made on the basis of speakers' conduct, it is the conduct itself, whether in form of language use or other behaviors, that is routinely assessed as more or less polite relative to community values and norms. From a cross-linguistic perspective, Coulmas argues that language systems may be described as differentially polite, depending on the number of means specialized for politeness marking (1992: 321) and the level of delicacy encoded in polite forms. Watts, Ide, and Ehlich (1992) suggest that politeness operates at all three levels of analysis – in language systems, usage, and use, as implied by the title of their volume *Politeness in Language*.

A useful and fairly uncontroversial first distinction is between first-order and second-order politeness (Watts, Ide, and Ehlich, 1992: 3). *First-order politeness* refers to politeness as a folk notion: How do members of a community perceive and classify action in terms of politeness? Such assessments and classifications manifest themselves in etiquette manuals, the do's and dont's in socializing interaction, metapragmatic comments on what is and is not polite behavior, and so forth – what Fraser (1990) refers to as the "social norm view" of politeness. *Second-order politeness* is a theoretical construct, located within a theory of social behavior and language use. The distinction is thus methodological, because it specifies the relationship between statements about linguistic etiquette at different levels of analysis. The relationship is one of data to theory, as noted by Hobart from a social-anthropological perspective ("indigenous classifications in use are part of the empirical evidence," 1987: 36). First-order politeness phenomena, be they observable behavior or action-guiding cognitions crystallized as "core cultural concepts" (Wierzbicka, 1991), are the material on which researchers base their theorizing. In their unanalyzed form, core cultural concepts are like folk beliefs: They have no explanatory value in themselves, but need to be explained through second-order politeness theory – just as linguistic productions or grammaticality judgments need explanation through linguistic theory. Once analyzed in their historical and sociocultural context, such core concepts provide frameworks to explain practices of linguistic action in the community. Thus Mao (1994) demonstrated how Chinese interlocutors orient themselves towards the *face* notions *lian* and *mianzi* in giving and receiving invitations and offers (for further analysis of *mianzi* in conversational interaction, see Chen, 1990, 1991; in speech-act realization, Kasper, 1995). Observationally and descriptively adequate accounts of first-order politeness are needed in order for politeness theory to be firmly anchored in the communicative practices and conceptualizations of speech communities.

First-order politeness data come from a wide variety of sources, most of them observational or experimental studies of the current practices in communities or groups within larger communities (see below), carried out within the theoretical and methodological traditions of several disciplines: linguistic pragmatics, sociolinguistics, the social psychology of language, psycholinguistics, developmental psychology, communications, and anthropology. Studies adopting a historical perspective on linguistic etiquette in particular communities and in literature are likewise gaining ground; e.g., politeness in the Ancient Orient, Greece, Rome, the Middle Ages, and the German Early Modern period (see Ehlich, 1992; also Beetz, 1990, for the latter period, and Elias, 1977, for a social history of manners in Europe); in the Nibelungenlied (Rings, 1987); Chaucer (Eun, 1974; Sell, 1985a, b); Shakespeare's four major tragedies (Brown and Gilman, 1989) and Henry VIII (Magnusson, 1992); in the works of Lessing (Claus, 1983); Rabelais (Morrison, 1988); Stendhal (Crouzet, 1980); Hemingway (Hardy, 1991); seventeenth-century England and France (Klein, 1990) and the eighteenth-century philosophers, Berkeley and Shaftes-bury (Klein, 1986); Islamic culture (Ostrup, 1929); in languages such as Chinese (Yuan, Kuiper, and Shaogu, 1990; Song-Cen, 1991); French (Kremos, 1955; Krings, 1961; Held, 1988); Old Greek (Zilliacus, 1949); Japanese (Wenger, 1983); Korean (Soh, 1985); Old Polish (Wojtak, 1989); Russian (Popov, 1985); and classical Sanskrit (Van De Walle, 1991).

Politeness and the Cooperative Principle

A matter of controversy is the relationship of politeness to the Gricean *Cooperative Principle* (CP) (Grice, 1975). Views reach from entirely subsuming politeness under the CP to affording the CP and politeness equal status. According to Green (1992a, b), politeness, defined as "considerateness," is one of many maxims representing "instantiations in a context of the Cooperative Principle" (1992a: 6), on the same epistemological footing with the maxims of quality, quantity, relevance, and manner. Consequently, violating the politeness maxim gives rise to conversational inference, just as in the case of any other maxim – a point also made by Matsumoto (1989) with respect to inappropriate use of honorifics in Japanese.

In the best articulated politeness theory to date, Brown and Levinson postulate the Cooperative Principle and its four maxims as a "presumptive framework" assumed by conversationalists about the nature of talk (1987: 4). Quite unlike Green (1992b), they do not view politeness as yet another conversational maxim but rather as a motivating force for maxim violation. The reason for language users not to follow the most efficient course of action, as they would do by observing the Gricean maxims, is their concern for face (see below). While observance of the CP and concern for face are both underpinned by actors' rational orientations, these orientations are of quite different status. The CP represents participants' orientation to get on with the business of talk, or any other kind of linguistic (inter)action, in an optimally economical and efficient manner. Face, in its most general sense, encapsulates participants' mutual recognition as social members. Attending to face may be at odds with the CP, such as when a speaker violates the maxim of quantity or manner by being indirect. It is important that Brown and Levinson's view of politeness is *not* coextensive with attending to face concerns but considerably more narrow: Politeness operates only when face interests are at risk, and actors are therefore required to make strategic choices about how to handle imminent face threat. It is only these strategic options of handling face-threat that are called "politeness" in Brown and Levinson's theory. Their proposal is consequently referred to by Fraser (1990) as the "face-saving view" of politeness.

While politeness thus has a secondary status vis-à-vis the CP in Green's (1992a, b) and Brown and Levinson's (1987) theories, Lakoff (1973) and, in a much elaborated version, Leech (1983) see politeness as a coordinate construct to the CP. For Lakoff, pragmatic competence is constituted by two major "rules": "1. Be clear. 2. Be polite," where clarity amounts to a condensed version of the Gricean maxims, while politeness serves to avoid conflict between participants. In Leech's proposal of an "interpersonal rhetoric," the CP is complemented by a politeness principle (PP): "Minimize the expression of impolite beliefs" (1983: 79). Both CP and PP are "first-order principles," each elaborated by a set of "contributory maxims": the Gricean maxims in the case of the CP, and six maxims of politeness – the maxims of tact, generosity, approbation, modesty, agreement, and sympathy – in the case of the PP (pp. 131 ff.). The "conversational maxim view" (Fraser, 1990) of politeness thus comes in different versions, depending on how the relationship between the CP and politeness is conceptualized.

Yet another, perhaps the broadest view of politeness has been proposed by Fraser (1990) with his notion of the *conversational contract* (CC). On this view, politeness is seen neither as complementing the CP, nor as motivating deviation from it, but as the default setting in conversational encounters: "being polite constitutes operating within the then-current terms and conditions of the CC" (1990: 233). But since the same is true for the CP, *mutatis mutandis* ("being cooperative involves abiding by the CC," p. 233), and the difference between being cooperative and being polite is never explained, the conversational contract view appears to be predicated on an equation of "being cooperative = being polite = abiding by the CC," which does little to clarify, let alone present in empirically testable format, the interaction of communicative efficiency and relational concerns in linguistic exchange.

Universality and Relativity in Politeness Theory

The range of politeness theories – what are the phenomena they serve to explain, intra- and interculturally – has been yet another issue of contention among students of linguistic etiquette. Brown and Levinson (1987) and Leech (1983) explicitly assert universal status for their proposed theories. Reviewing their approaches and offering his own, Fraser (1990) provides no discussion of the purported universality and thus implicitly affirms the universality claim.

By contrast, Green (1992a, b) argues cogently for the universal applicability of the CP. Since, on her view, the conversational maxims are instantiations of the CP, demonstrated nonapplicability of some maxim or other in a particular cultural setting would not invalidate the CP itself. While thus conceding that conversational maxims may be culturally specialized, Green holds that cultural variation in maxim applicability is more likely to be an effect of different cultural values on the specific shape of a maxim than a question of whether a particular maxim is observed at all.

Politeness and the Notion of Face

Views opposing the universal availability of the proposed politeness constructs have mostly taken issue with the cornerstone of Brown and Levinson's theory, their notions of negative and positive face. *Negative face* is defined as "the basic claim to territories, personal preserves, rights to non-distraction – i.e. freedom of action and freedom from imposition." *Positive face* refers to "the positive consistent self-image or 'personality' (crucially including the desire that this self-image be appreciated and approved of) claimed by interactants" (1987: 61). The two complementary sides of face have been referred to by other authors as "distance vs. involvement" (Tannen, 1986), "deference vs. solidarity" (R. and S. B. K. Scollon, 1983), "autonomy vs. connection" (Green, 1992b), "self-determination vs. acceptance," or "personal vs. interpersonal face" (Janney and Arndt, 1992). Politeness is activity serving to enhance, maintain, or protect face: Addressing negative face results in *negative politeness* ("deference politeness," R. and S. B. K. Scollon, 1983), manifest in indirectness, formality, emphasis of social distance, and respect for the interlocutor's entitlements and resources. Positive face gives rise to *positive politeness* ("solidarity politeness," R. and S. B. K. Scollon, 1983), displayed in directness, informal language use, emphasis of common ground, appreciation of the interlocutor, her actions, possessions, etc. Positive or negative politeness *strategies* are redressive action, used to mitigate the *face-threat* which a linguistic act might pose for the interlocutor. In Brown and Levinson's theory, *face-threatening acts* are speech acts which clearly involve an interpersonal dimension – directives, commissives, and expressives, in Searle's (1976) classification. According to Green (1992a), all linguistic action involves face-threat of some kind; therefore politeness strategies are ubiquitously called for.

Different kinds of complaint have been voiced against the role of face in Brown and Levinson's theory. The common denominator of these objections is that the intended universality of the theory is untenable.

The first type of objection accepts the derivative role of politeness from face, but argues against the notion of face as "the public *self*-image that every member wants to claim for himself" (Brown and Levinson, 1987: 61, my emphasis). This social-psychological notion with its emphasis on individuals' self-generated projection of their favored persona has been contrasted, first, with the earlier formulation proposed by Goffman (1967). Goffman's (socio-logical) construct describes face as a *public* rather than personal property, "on loan" from society rather than an unalienable possession, and a negotiable outcome of social interaction (cf. Aston, 1988; Mao, 1994). The interpersonal orientation of Goffman's face concept is deemed more compatible with "nonwestern" face constructs (see Hu, 1944; Ho, 1975; Gu, 1990; Mao, 1994, for Chinese; Ervin-Tripp, Nakamura, and Guo, forthcoming, for a comparison of face concepts in English, French, Chinese, Japanese, Korean). Acknowledging the different premium placed on individuals' desires and social recognition by Anglo-American societies and Chinese and Japanese communities, Mao proposes a *relative face orientation:*

> an underlying direction of face that emulates, though never completely attaining, one of two interactional ideals that may be salient in a given speech community: the *ideal social identity,* or the *ideal individual autonomy.* The specific content of face in a given speech community is determined by one of these two interactional ideals sanctioned by the members of the community. (1994: 472, my emphasis)

Whereas Mao's face constructs thus embrace the relative placement of indi-viduals in social hierarchies, other authors view the notions of face and *place* as mutually exclusive. Both Matsumoto (1988, 1989) and Ide (1989) complain that Brown and Levinson's face constructs do not capture the principles of Japanese interaction because they do not include the acknowledgement of social relationships ("social relativism," "proper place occupancy," Lebra, 1976). Whereas Matsumoto rejects the notion of negative face as being inap-plicable to Japanese culture (a position also supported by Ervin-Tripp et al., forthcoming), Ide accepts the validity of positive and negative face, but sug-gests that this model be complemented by a component called discernment (*wakimae*), signalling social relationships. Politeness in any society comprises a "volitional" component (strategic politeness attending to face concerns) and discernment, or social marking. These two components of politeness are re-garded as universals; communities differ in the emphasis they put on each. Thus for Japanese interlocutors, "place" purportedly takes precedence before "face" (Ide, 1989).

Neither the strong place instead of face position (Matsumoto) nor the weak place before face variety (Ide) have yet received empirical support. While the comprehensive literature on honorifics in Japanese (Coulmas, 1992; Matsumo-to, 1993; see also references in Yoshinaga, Maeshiba, and Takahashi, 1992) attests the importance of social marking, it does not speak to the issue of (negative) face. At the same time, the literature on speech act realization in Japanese documents differential strategy use depending on context factors (e.g., Barnlund and Yoshioka, 1990, on apologies; Ikoma and Shimamura, 1993, on refusals; Ikoma, 1993, on expressions of gratitude; Kitao, 1990; Taka-hashi, 1992, on requests; Takahashi and Beebe, 1993, on corrections). Since a great number of the identified strategies are recognizably negative politeness strategies (e.g., *oisogashii tokoro* "you must be busy," *moshiwake arimasenga* "excuse me" to preface a request; apologetic expressions such as *sumimasen (deshita), gomeiwaku o okake si mashita* for conveying gratitude), the claim that negative face wants are absent in Japanese interaction is difficult to maintain. The assumption that social indexing may be more prevalent in some languages than others is well supported by the fact that in Asian languages such as Japanese, Korean, Thai, Javanese, and others, relationship marking is grammaticized in highly complex morphological systems, whereas such specialization is only rudimentary in European languages. A more problematic issue than the cross-linguistic comparison of obligatory social indexing is Ide's (1989) conjecture that Japanese linguistic etiquette emphasizes "discernment" more than strategic politeness. To date, no studies have been carried out to support this position, and indeed no measure has been proposed to test Ide's hypothesis. Furthermore, data-based studies on the use of honorifics reveal that, rather than being used invariably to index a specific social relationship, honorific use can alter in the same encounter, depending on the particular attitude the speaker wishes to convey (Cook, 1993, 1994). Empirical observation thus contradicts the claim that speakers "submit passively to the requirements of the system" (Hill et al., 1986: 348) once a particular status relationship has been identified. Rather than being entirely predetermined, social indexing remains a sociolinguistic choice, even when there is a strong statistical preference for particular usage. The forms actually chosen depend on the current state of the "conversational contract" (Fraser, 1990) and appear thus as more dynamic and "volitional" than static views of honorific language use suggest. From this perspective, unmarked use of honorifics simply reflects speakers' adherence to accepted politeness norms (cf. Green, 1992b).

Yet another line of criticism denies the role of face in politeness altogether. Watts (1989) asserts that, rather than being motivated by face concerns, politeness is located in the wider context of *politic* behavior, understood as (linguistic) activity serving to establish and maintain interpersonal relationships. With special reference to Chinese politeness, Gu (1990) argues that politeness is more appropriately seen as adherence to social norms than attending to individual's face wants. While these authors' proposals are thus at variance with Brown and Levinson's individualistic notion of face, they are quite compatible with the relative face concept proposed by Mao (1994).

Face and Self

Writers who recognize a role for face in linguistic etiquette have recently pointed out that face can be correctly understood only in the context of notions of self, emphasizing that such notions are necessarily informed by culturally varying perceptions of personhood and relationships between an individual and society. While a comprehensive review of studies on self concepts in different communities points to a consistent opposition between *interdependent* and *independent* notions of self (Markus and Kitayama, 1991), an alternative view questions the adequacy of categorizing cross-culturally varying self-orientations according to these categories, or even as ordered on a continuum between these. Thus Rosenberger (1989) argues against the popular belief of a consistent sociocentric self concept in the Japanese community, and for a dialectic model which captures the switches of the Japanese self (*jibun*) between opposing orientations: "group productivity, personal accomplishment, harmony or affection, and pure impulse or gratification" (1989: 89f.). Switching between these modes is brought about through the flow of a person's vital energy (*ki*) and actualization according to a social, spatial, and temporal context (see also Lebra, 1993). The key difference between "Western" and Japanese notions of self thus rests not so much in "independent"/"egocentric" vs "interdependent"/"sociocentric" orientations but in the diverging beliefs about the *unity* of self: The "Western" ideal of a consistent self that transcends conflicting contextual demands, and the Japanese ideal of an accommodative self that optimally responds to varying contexts and purposes. The ideological character of the "Western" construction of a consistent self has been illustrated in a lucid analysis of team sport in the US (Green, 1992b), demonstrating how athletes are required to switch from the individualistic orientation prevalent in the society at large to a strongly group-oriented, hierarchical subculture. The facility by which these adjustments are performed suggests that "Western" selves are more contextually sensitive than presumed by folk beliefs as well as some scientific models of self, e.g., in Freudian or Jungian psychodynamic theory. It is therefore important for research on linguistic etiquette to explore practices of social marking and strategic politeness in different groups and speech events within larger cultural communities in order to establish *intra*culturally varying orientations of self and face. Such research is not only indispensable for descriptively adequate accounts of politeness within and across cultures but also a necessary safeguard against unhelpful stereotyping along the received lines of "Eastern" and "Western" ways of perceiving personhood and social relations.

Variables in Linguistic Etiquette

Any theory of politeness has built into it the sociolinguistic axiom that politeness investment varies according to contextual factors. The two most elaborated theories, Brown and Levinson (1987) and Leech (1983), concur in this regard. First, they identify the same factors as independent variables in politeness marking: social distance (Brown and Levinson, Leech), social power (Brown and Levinson) or authority (Leech), and the degree of imposition associated with a given face-threatening act (Brown and Levinson) or the costs and benefits of an act (Leech). Second, both theories posit a linear relationship between these factors and politeness investment. Third, they both assume a positive correlation between politeness and indirectness.

Data-based studies lend strong support to the identified context variables, whereas the correlational issues are problematic. Each of the proposed factors represents a composite construct which is culturally and contextually elaborated and weighted. *Social power* includes factors such as:

- interlocutors' relative positions in social hierarchies (Becker, 1982; Becker and Smenner, 1986; Becker, Kimmel, and Bevill, 1989; Beebe and Takahashi, 1989a, b; Bryan and Gallois, 1992; Ervin-Tripp, O'Connor, and Rosenberg, 1984; Hill et al., 1986; Lampi, 1993; McMullen and Krahn, 1985; Morand, 1991; Pearson, 1988; Takahashi and Beebe, 1993);
- age; e.g., in communication by and with the elderly (Coupland, Coupland, and Giles, 1991; James, 1978; Milan, 1976) and children (Axia, McGurk, and Martin, 1987; Baroni and Axia, 1989; Bates, 1976; Bates and Silvern, 1977; Becker, 1990; Blum-Kulka, 1990; Clancy, 1986; Cook, 1990; Edelsky, 1977; Eisenberg, 1982; Ervin-Tripp and Gordon, 1986; Ervin-Tripp, Guo, and Lampert, 1990; Ervin-Tripp, O'Connor, and Rosenberg, 1984; Flavio, Perilli, and Ponterotto, 1984; Gleason, 1980; Gleason, Perlmann, and Greif, 1984; Kwarciak, 1993; Nippold, Leonard, and Anastopoulos, 1982; Ochs, 1988; Perlmann, 1984; Schieffelin, 1990; Schieffelin and Eisenberg, 1984; Smith-Hefner, 1988; Snow et al., 1990; Waller and Schoeler, 1985; Waller and Valtin, 1992; Watson-Gegeo and Gegeo, 1986; Wilhite, 1983; Zammuner, 1991);
- gender (Becker and Smenner, 1986; Bell, 1985; Bresnahan, 1993; Brouwer, 1982; Brouwer, Gerritsen, and De Haan, 1979; P. Brown, 1980, 1990; Burstein, 1989; Crosby and Nyquist, 1977; Dubois and Crouch, 1975; Eliasoph, 1986; Harris, 1992; Herbert, 1990; Hirokawa, 1991; Hoar, 1987; Holmes, 1984, 1989, 1990, 1993; Ide, 1982, 1983, 1992; Ide et al., 1986; Keenan, 1974; Lakoff, 1975; Loveday, 1981; Milan, 1976; Morgan, 1991; Preisler, 1986; Reynolds, 1985, 1989a,b, 1990; Shibamato, 1987; Smith-Hefner, 1981, 1988; Takahara, 1991; Watts, 1992; Yabar, 1975; Yamashita, 1983; Zimin, 1981);
- language impairment (Abbeduto, 1984; Bates and Wilson, 1981; Bliss, 1992; Rimac, 1986; Stemmer, 1994; Stemmer, Giroux, and Joannette, 1994).

Social distance (Boxer, 1993; Delisle, 1986; Garcia, 1992; J. H. and K. C. Hill, 1978; McMullen and Krahn, 1985; Miller, 1991; Morosawa, 1990) has been demonstrated to affect politeness in a more complex way than theoretically predicted. Reviewing a number of studies on speech act realization, Wolfson (e.g., 1989) concludes that rather than correlating in a linear fashion, social distance and politeness are related in a reverse bell-shaped curve ("bulge"):

Most politeness appears to be expended in negotiable relationships with familiars but nonintimates, such as coworkers and friends. In more fixed relationships at opposite ends of the social distance continuum, intimates and strangers, politeness is found to decrease. More recent evidence for the bulge hypothesis comes from studies on complaining (Olshtain and Weinbach, 1993) and expressions of gratitude (Eisenstein and Bodman, 1993).

While there is a comprehensive literature on the impact of social variables on politeness implementation, much less research exists on the influence of psychological factors. To some extent, this may simply reflect the fact that demographic variables are easy to identify whereas (social-)psychological factors are not. Ciliberti (1993) argues that interactional style is as much a product of participants' cultural background as of personality, and an analogous argument can be made for demographic profiles and personal variables. Slugoski (1985) demonstrates that familiarity (= social distance) has to be distinguished from affect (= psychological distance), a hypothesis supported by historical evidence from a study of politeness in Shakespearian tragedies (Brown and Gilman, 1989; on the impact of affect see also Boxer, 1993; Camras, Pristo, and Brown, 1985; Haviland, 1989; Sussman & Rosenfeld, 1982).

In addition to these participant variables, features of linguistic acts themselves – the *"imposition,"* or costs and benefits accruing from them – shape politeness enactment. For several speech acts, the elements of the composite construct "imposition" have been identified, for instance, in:

- requesting: urgency (Hermann, 1982; Morosawa, 1990), legitimacy (Hermann, 1982; Hoppe-Graff et al., 1985; House, 1989; Blum-Kulka and House, 1989; Hirokawa, Mickey, and Miura, 1991), the likelihood of the hearer's compliance and the speaker's psychological difficulty in carrying out the request (Blum-Kulka and House, 1989);
- apologizing: perceived severity of the offence, subsuming obligation to apologize and likelihood of apology being accepted (House, 1989; Olshtain, 1989; Vollmer and Olshtain, 1989; Bergman and Kasper, 1993);
- thanking: indebtedness, comprising the degree of received benefit and trouble undergone by the benefactor (Miyake, 1993; Ikoma, 1993);
- complaining: magnitude of social obligation violated by the offender (Olshtain, and Weinbach, 1993).

Participant factors and properties of contextualized linguistic action interact in complex ways and vary cross-culturally in their impact on linguistic politeness. For instance, in request performance, Israeli speakers varied their strategy selection according to requestive goal, age, and power (Blum-Kulka, Gerson and Danet, 1985); Japanese and German speakers modified their requests according to legitimacy and the likelihood of the hearer's compliance, but the German not the Japanese speakers made their strategy selection also contingent on urgency (Hermann, 1982; Morosawa, 1990); Israelis, Germans, and Argentinians differed in their perceptions of interlocutors' rights and obligations, the likelihood of the hearer's compliance, and the speaker's difficulty in performing the request (Blum-Kulka and House, 1989); requestees' obligation to comply was perceived as higher by American than by Japanese raters (Shimamura, 1993).

Just as the relationship between context variables and politeness varies intra- and interculturally, so does the relationship between patterns of linguistic action and their politeness value. Negative politeness strategies were perceived as more polite by Japanese residing in the US than by Japanese in Japan (Kitao, 1990). Japanese and Americans also gave different appropriateness judgments of requests with and without supportive moves (Shimamura, 1993). A particularly intriguing issue is the relationship between indirectness and politeness. Contrary to theory-derived predictions, it was conventional indirectness (e.g., preparatory strategies such as "can/could you") rather than nonconventional indirectness (hinting) that was rated most polite by Israeli, American (Blum-Kulka, 1987), and German (House, 1986) judges. The preference for conventional indirectness appears to be motivated by the balance struck between clarity and consideration, and low processing costs to the hearer. Consistent with this finding, Weizman (1985, 1989, 1993) has suggested that nonconventional indirectness is not motivated by politeness at all but by the "deniability potential" inherent in ambiguous language use.

Discourse Context

Rather than isolating specific context variables and examining their impact on politeness, a large body of literature explores the linguistic etiquette of different discourse contexts. Such contexts include:

- institutional discourse, e.g., courtrooms (Adelsward, 1989; Berk-Seligson, 1988; Cashion, 1985; Lakoff, 1989; Parkinson, 1981, Wright, 1987), medical discourse (Aronsson and Rundstroem, 1989; Aronsson and Saetterlund, 1987; Robin and Wolf, 1988), psychotherapy (Batten, 1990; Lakoff, 1989), academic advising (Bardovi-Harlig and Hartford, 1990, 1993), counselling (Erickson and Shultz, 1982; Fiksdal 1988, 1991), supervisory conferences (Roberts, 1992), special education conferences (DuFon, 1992, 1993), classroom discourse (Cazden, 1979; Chick, 1989; Ellis, 1992; Heath, 1983; Loerscher and Schulze, 1988; Sadow and Maxwell, 1983; White, 1989), consumer service agencies (Johnson and Fawcett, 1987), sermons (Dzameshie, 1992); citizen–bureaucracy interaction (Hero, 1986), opinion poll interviews (Johnstone, 1991; Johnstone, Ferrara, and Bean, 1992), church business meetings (Pearson, 1988);

- workplace communication (Bryan and Gallois, 1992; Chick, 1986, 1989; Clyne, Bell, and Neil, 1991; Holmqvist and Andersen, 1987; Myers, 1991; Nunes, 1981) and other professional interaction, e.g., aviation discourse (Linde 1988a, b), business negotiations (Ehlich and Wagner, forthcoming; Stalpers, forthcoming; Yamada, 1990), sales negotiations (Lampi, 1993), organizational interaction (Morand, 1991), sports teams (Green, 1992; Jones, 1992);
- interpersonal discourse, e.g., family dinners (Blum-Kulka, 1990; Blum-Kulka and Sheffer, 1993; Perlmann, 1984; Wilhite, 1983); dinner entertainment (Befu, 1986), phatic communion (Coupland, Coupland, and Robinson, 1992), intimate conversation (Frank, 1988), interpersonal decision-making (Scheerhorn, 1991/2);
- discourse in different media, e.g., telephone conversations (Clark and French, 1981; Plascencia, 1992; Schegloff, 1979; Sifanou, 1989), computer games (Covato, 1991), computer messages (Hama, 1991), translated discourse (DuFon, 1993; Knapp-Potthoff, 1992; Knapp-Potthoff and Knapp, 1987);
- written discourse, e.g., letters of request (Cherry, 1989; Pickett, 1989), business letters (Hagge, 1984; Hagge and Kostelnick, 1989; Larson, 1988; Limaye and Cherry, 1987; Marier, 1992), narratives (R. and S. B. K. Scollon, 1981), argumentative writing (Zammuner, 1991), scientific writing (Kreml, 1992; Myers, 1989), peer reviews (Johnson, 1992; Johnson and Yang, 1990).

The common message from these different studies is that linguistic etiquette is both a highly context-sensitive aspect of human communication and one that shapes context and participants' relationships. Politeness is thus not only determined by the current state of the conversational contract but a context-creating and modifying force in its own right.

Part IV Applied Issues

24 Sociolinguistics and Education

LUDO VERHOEVEN

During the past decades linguists, psychologists, and educationalists have been involved in a continuing debate on how language can be taught. Research on language education has sought answers to the question of how the development of spoken and written language can be fostered, from their origins in early infancy to their mastery as systems of representation for communication with others and for the inner control of thinking and feeling. Thanks to the input of sociolinguistics in educational research, the ways in which social equality can be enhanced through education have also received attention.

   In the present chapter a short review will be given of the study of language education. We begin with the processes involved in language learning and language teaching. In addition, we explore the ways in which language and literacy skills can be fostered through education. Then we go into the issue of equity in educational experience. Since language can be seen as a social marker of gender, class, and ethnicity, we will discuss ways in which classroom experiences may contribute to equality in school learning processes. We conclude with some generalizations derived from sociolinguistic theory and their implications for teacher training.

1 Language Learning and Language Teaching

1.1 Language, communication, and thought

The ability of individuals to communicate through language is both a unique and a universal human quality. The human capacity to think symbolically and to interpret and produce sounds makes it possible to create a language system. Human culture, social behavior and thinking would not exist without language. On the other hand, communication would be meaningless in the absence of thinking. Language and thinking are so closely connected that it is hard to discuss one without the other, for speech can serve thought and thought can be revealed in speech.

In both epistemology and cognitive psychology theoretical claims have been made in support of a dichotomous conception of language proficiency. In these claims linguistic knowledge is distinguished from language use. For instance, Chomsky (1965) made a distinction between grammatical competence, the knowledge possessed by the idealized native speaker, and performance, referring to the actual linguistic data. According to Chomsky, linguistic competence can be seen as an innate biological function of the mind that allows individuals to produce the indefinitely large set of sentences that constitutes their language.

The monolithic, idealized notion of linguistic competence was considered to be inadequate by a growing number of researchers. Taking a sociocultural approach to language as a starting point, a more elaborated concept of communicative competence was introduced by Hymes (1971). He argued that the concept of competence should be extended to include language use as well as sentence creation. Searle (1969) introduced the term "speech acts" as a counter claim to Chomsky's focus on cognitive processes. Austin (1962) speculated on the notion that using language may in certain circumstances be perceived as a kind of action rather than just cognition. In the context of language teaching Canale and Swain (1980) defined communicative competence as: "a synthesis of knowledge of basic grammatical principles, knowledge of how language is used in social settings to perform communicative functions, and knowledge of how utterances and communicative functions can be combined according to the principles of discourse." According to Canale and Swain, communicative competence is composed of four competencies: grammatical competence, discourse competence, strategic competence, and sociolinguistic competence. Grammatical competence covers the mastery of phonological rules, lexical items, morphosyntactic rules, and rules of sentence formation. Discourse competence refers to the knowledge of rules regarding the cohesion and coherence of various types of discourse. Strategic competence involves the mastery of verbal and nonverbal strategies to compensate for breakdowns and to enhance the effectiveness of communication. Sociolinguistic competence is related to the mastery of sociocultural conventions within varying social contexts. This type of competence involves rules that are sensitive to various factors, such as the context and topic of discourse, and the social status, sex, and age of participants. These factors account for stylistic differences or varying registers of speech.

With respect to the development of communicative competence in children, it is clear that children must not only acquire a repertoire of linguistic devices, but also a repertoire of sociolinguistic devices marking distinct registers.

Besides linguistic competence, the social roles associated with language use in varying contexts must be acquired (see Foster, 1990).

1.2 *Acquisition of communicative competence*

Grammatical competence

A fundamental problem of linguistics is to explain how a person can acquire knowledge of language. In the tradition of generative grammar an attempt has been made to solve the problem of language acquisition by studying the abstract principles in the complex syntax of adult grammar. In explaining language acquisition it is supposed that the language ability of human beings is constrained by universal grammar. This is defined as a set of language-specific principles, which contains some sort of language acquisition device: a neural mechanism tailored to the specific task of language acquisition. It is also assumed that language acquisition is a genetically transmitted process, and that the basic structures which make language acquisition possible are uniquely linguistic. A problem with the generative approach of language acquisition is that the factor of time is ignored. While explaining its apparent ease, rapidity, and uniformity, language acquisition is seen as an instantaneous phenomenon, idealizing it to a situation in which the child has at his disposal all of the principles and parameters of universal grammar and all linguistic data necessary to fix those parameters. As such, it is by no means clear how and in what order linguistic parameters are set, nor is it clear how apparent delays which characterize the developmental process can be explained.

Empirical studies give reason to believe that the process of language acquisition must represent an interaction between universal grammar and other cognitive functions. If it is true that there are no instantaneous linguistic principles underlying language acquisition, it can be questioned how in the course of time children acquire rules which relate syntactic forms and semantic functions. On the basis of an extensive series of cross-linguistic studies Slobin (1985) has proposed a set of universal operational principles for the construction of language. In their initial form these are believed to exist prior to the child's experience with language. In the course of applying such principles to perceived speech and the associated perception of objects and events, a basic child grammar will evolve, corresponding to the internal organization and storage of linguistic structures.

Discourse competence

There is good evidence that major points in development are associated with the appearance or transformation of new forms of mediation. A clear example is the transition from utterance to text. Later language development in child-

ren can be characterized by a growing command of discourse   ound ge 5,
developmental shifts take place from intra- to intersentential devices, from
basic structures to additional functions, from extra- to intralinguistic abilities,
and from contextual to decontextualized abilities.

A related marking point in children's development is the transition from
oral to written language. Learning to read and write involves much more than
the ability to decode print to speech and to encode speech in print. Registers
of written language require a different selection and organization of ideas
from those of oral language (see chapter 10). In written communication logical
and ideational functions are primary, whereas oral communication has more
informal characteristics. In oral communication the listener has access to a
wide range of contextual cues, while in written communication such cues are
almost completely absent. Accordingly, a distinction can be made between
context-embedded communication and context-reduced communication. For
children the transition from oral to written language can be thought of as a
critical event.

Strategic competence

Strategic competence refers to metacognitive abilities which are involved in
planning, executing, and evaluating language behavior. Strategies are goal-
directed cognitive operations used to facilitate performance. A distinction can
be made between strategies for planning, executing, and evaluating language
behavior. Strategies may be relatively conscious or relatively automatic. Successful strategy use enhances children's self-concept and attributional beliefs,
and these motivational states enhance the development of new strategies.

Monitoring plays an important role in oral language use. It involves concurrent control of ongoing speech, which may result in self-initiated repairs. By
matching strings of overt and covert speech with the intended message or
with standards of speech production, the speaker may become aware of a
difference between the intended message and speech, or of some sort of error,
and stop the flow of overt speech to make a repair. In developmental studies
it was found that children start monitoring their speech at a very young age.
In the course of primary school, the frequency of self-correction increases,
while the numbers of restarts and repeats decreases.

With respect to literacy tasks, there is good evidence that strategic competence improves academic performance. Examples of reading strategies are
skimming, recognizing text structure, activating background knowledge, contextual guessing, tolerating ambiguity, and rereading. Planning and revision
turn out to be the most crucial strategies in writing.

Sociolinguistic competence

Sociolinguistic competence enables the individual to cope with language situations in everyday life. Sociolinguistic competence refers to the knowledge of

stylistic differences, usually called register variation. Different types of situations may call for different types of language items, as well as different values and beliefs.

The development of sociolinguistic competence involves the elaboration of distinct sources of knowledge: person knowledge, referring to the moods, states, preferences, and intentions of people; knowledge of social categories, such as age, sex, and status in order to tune their linguistic behavior to the social context; and knowledge of how events are organized in the form of routines, as in telephone dialogues.

There is no agreement on the age level at which children learn to make some stylistic adjustments to varying contexts of language use. In line with Piaget's notion of egocentric speech, it was generally believed that children at kindergarten level are still incapable of applying rules of sociocultural appropriateness, and that the differentiation of speech registers is only learned in the course of primary school. However, more recently it has been shown that infants learn to take turns, to attract attention and direct it to objects of interest, and make demands without having control of grammatical structures. The extensive experience children have with social games helps them to acquire the ability to structure conversations at an early age.

1.3 The role of the environment

Based on the assumption of an innate component in language acquisition, it was generally believed that minimal linguistic input suffices to enable the child to learn a language. However, this view reduces language to a set of rules and principles which generate an infinite set of sentences. If we view language as a system of communicative social action, then what the child has to learn are rules and principles which relate forms and functions, and these functions may be semantic, pragmatic, or social. From research on linguistic input in young children, we know that the nature of the speech addressed to the child is characterized by modifications of the adult model, in particular at the level of paralinguistic features, syntactic features, and discourse features (see Snow, 1995). The most important facilitator of language development is the extent to which parents are sensitive to their children's communicative attempts, and their endeavors to extend the conversation while taking such attempts as a starting point. The semantic contingency of adult speech is a critical factor. Semantically contingent utterances include expansions limited to the content of previous utterances of the child, semantic extensions that add new information to the topic, questions demanding clarification of the child's utterances, and answers to the child's questions.

The role of social interaction in determining language form and function has been emphasized by Halliday (1975, 1985) in his systemic-functional linguistics. According to Halliday, the beginning stages of language development are related to limited functions. The child's meaning potential is said to increase as he or she learns to take on more social roles. Three situational variables are viewed as the constraining factors of the process of language development: the social activity generating the topic, the role relationships of the partici- pants in terms of contact, affect, and status, and the rhetorical modes they are adopting. As such, the theory provides insight into the social determining factors of variation in children's language development.

Another theoretical framework in which the role of social interaction in language learning has been emphasized is Soviet Activity Theory. In this theory it is assumed that individuals acquire knowledge and skills by partici- pating in activities with more experienced members of the culture. For learn- ing to be effective the child's intellectual growth must be contingent on mastering language as the social means of thought. The basic premise of activity theory is that development takes place on the social level within a historical-cultural context. In a dialogue with an adult the child has the opportunity to internalize the mental processes that occur on the social level. By means of social interaction mental processes move from interpsychological functioning to intrapsychological functioning. Vygotsky (1978) claimed that higher mental functions have a social origin and defines language as a sign system that can be used for symbolic activities permitting intellectual accom- plishments. Intellectual development demands the conscious realization of mental processes on the part of the child. The task of the adult can be seen as maximizing the growth of the intrapsychological functioning of the child. Vygotsky introduced the concept of a zone of proximal development as the distance between the actual developmental level of problem solving and the potential developmental level under guidance of an adult.

1.4 Teaching models

Any theory of language learning implies a theory of instruction. Adults can provide conditions that help children find linguistic patterns and regularities to solve communicative problems. During the past decades there has been a marked shift in the perspective of language pedagogy. Traditionally the focus was on direct teaching predetermined by a strict program that is controlled by the teacher. In such a transmission model of teaching, learning is seen as going from simple to complex knowledge and from smaller to larger skills. In principle, children are viewed as grammarians and lexicographers who have to extend their linguistic repertoires. Furthermore, there is a strong focus on the correctness of the learners' responses. The reproduction of predeter- mined responses is viewed as evidence of learning, whereas risk-taking is discouraged.

In recent years the focus moved toward children's competence to participate in communicative settings. The child was seen as a purposeful communicator, as a creator of meaning within social contexts. The focus shifted away from the form and the meaning of utterance toward the child's communicative intent. In addition to the elaboration of children's language system, the social context in which language behavior occurred was taken into account. Studies of conversations between children in the classroom and of teacher–child interaction formed the basis of new guidelines for language instruction (Weaver, 1990). In such a transactional model of teaching the emphasis is on learning being facilitated by the teacher, or by peer interaction. The ability to apply new knowledge and the ability to use strategies in a variety of contexts are seen as evidence of learning. Risk-taking on the part of the child is viewed as an essential part of learning.

The transactional model of teaching is based mainly on Vygotsky's theory of learning through social interaction. With reference to a Vygotskian approach to development, it is claimed that cultural tools, such as language and literacy, are optimally learned in social interaction with others. Through experience with language and literacy tasks in guided participation with skilled partners the child's repertoire can be gradually expanded. Two major conversational strategies have been described as ways to engage students in zones of proximal development: scaffolding and apprenticeship.

Scaffolding relates to a conversational strategy in which people build on and extend each other's statements and contributions. Through scaffolding the teacher is able to motivate the child to work on a task, to define the number of task steps related to the child's abilities, to diagnose discrepancies between the child's production and the ideal solution, and to control for frustration and risk in finding task solutions. Teachers may scaffold children's comprehension by introducing unfamiliar words before storytelling, so that their attention to the story line can be maintained. Tharp and Gallimore (1988) elaborated the metaphor of scaffolding toward a theory of teaching as assisted performance. According to this theory the child's performance can be assisted by the following means: modelling, contingency management, feedback, instruction, questioning, and cognitive structuring. Modelling refers to the imitation of the tutor's behavior by the child. Contingency management involves the use of rewards, such as praise and encouragement. By means of feedback the teacher is able to correct the child's performance. Instruction helps the child to regulate its own learning. By means of questioning the child can be invited to perform mental operations with assistance by the teacher. Cognitive structuring implies the provision of a structure for acting out a given task. In Vygotskian terms, these six ways of assisting children's performance constitute teaching within the children's zone of proximal development.

Apprenticeship refers to learning a cultural practice through collaborative actions with more skilled others (see Rogoff, 1990). This notion puts emphasis on an active role in children's development. The basic idea is that the child as a novice makes continuous attempts to make sense of new situations, while more skilled partners help the child to arrange tasks and activities in such a way that they are more easily accessible. Intersubjectivity, the shared understanding based on a common focus of attention, is seen as a crucial prerequisite for successful communication between the teacher and the child.

Cooperative group work can be viewed as a special case of apprenticeship. Small groups have proven to be quite effective in increasing language-learning opportunities for children. In small groups children have the opportunity to negotiate meaning, to transfer information, and to model their communicative strategies. Research on the ethnography of communication has emphasized the role of small groups in defining students as equal participants in spite of differences in abilities and sociocultural background. Working in small groups with minimal teacher assistance helps children with varying social backgrounds and intellectual skills to learn subject matter, solve problems, and develop social skills.

2 Teaching Language and Literacy

By definition, language education involves the learning of language skills – listening, speaking, reading, and writing. A basic assumption of language teaching is that all modes of language must be trained in all courses at varying school levels. Language learning should be viewed as inherently integrative. As children participate in classroom activities they are naturally able to connect the different modes of language use to learning. Besides the learning of language arts, children learn how to use language as an effective learning device. Given the close connection between language and thinking, language can be viewed as an instrument to develop higher-order cognitive skills. Because the roots of both language and thought are social, language learning will enhance children's social skills as well.

2.1 Fostering oral communication

Since language is not only used to describe the world but also to influence it, speech acts can be seen as basic units for the enhancement of children's discourse competence. By means of classroom discourse children have the opportunity to learn how to translate one's ideas into actions in the community. In order to be effective, classroom discourse must rely on the personal involvement of all participants (Cazden, 1988). Without involvement there will be no coordinated interaction, nor shared meaning. The more participants invest in supplying meaning, the deeper their understanding and the greater their sense of involvement will be. Research in interactional sociolinguistics has shown that coherence and personal involvement in spoken discourse is enhanced by the use of prosody, pauses, repetition, and overlap.

Major factors in classroom communication are mutual shared knowledge, situational characteristics, and personal perceptions. Shared knowledge refers to content, experience, and norm and value systems shared by the participants. Important situational characteristics are the participants and the context. The participation framework in the classroom determines the relation of all participants in the interaction to the utterance. Ethnographic studies have shown that the ratification of conversational contributions of children by other participants or by the teacher is crucial in maintaining their participation (cf. Phillips, 1983). Personal perceptions refer to individual differences in communicative intentions and the interpretations of ongoing events. Classroom discourse can go wrong if there is a mismatch in any of these factors. If the two participants are both native speakers corrections can be made very quickly. If, however, they don't share the same cultural background the situation gets much more complicated. There can be misinterpretations of idiomatic expressions, or inappropriate reactions to what a speaker said.

In order to help children to extend their communicative competence teachers must focus on both pragmatic and linguistic aspects of various speech acts. Pragmatic aspects include the cultural values and norms underlying speech acts in varying communicative contexts, e.g., the use of politeness expressions in varying contexts. Linguistic aspects include the repertoire of both direct and indirect speech. Two teaching devices seem to be important in helping children extend their communicative repertoire. One is instruction, including modelling, imitation training, and role playing. Instructions may provide the framework within which children's communicative activities are maintained, restructured, and elaborated. The second relevant teaching strategy is semantically contingent responding. By repeating or extending children's initiatives, responding to occasional questions and consistent queries by the child, and confirming children's assertions, the child's development of both language and communication can be supported.

2.2 Emerging literacy

The study of how young children growing up in a print-oriented environment succeed in understanding the functional and structural configurations of reading and writing has been a lively area of research for several years (see Sulzby and Teale, 1991). Many researchers focusing on emergent literacy attempted to show how children are making sense of how literacy works in their culture. Detailed analyses of literacy environments highlighted the importance of early encounters with print in the home. It was found that interactive activities, such as storybook reading, have a great impact on children's oral and written language development. Conditions which strengthen the relevance and purpose of literacy for learners are important for the development of literacy. A general conclusion of the research on emergent literacy was that the attainment of literacy can be stimulated by offering children a school environment where valid understanding about literacy can continue to emerge (Clay, 1991). In such an environment children have the opportunity to enhance the positive literacy experiences they have had prior to school. The development of a broad literacy curriculum in which language experiences are highly emphasized was therefore often promoted.

Though in many publications a language experience approach to literacy acquisition is promoted, it is generally accepted that a naturalistic model which relies exclusively on exposure and immersion does not fully justify the complex task of learning to read and write (Cazden, 1992). Accumulated research evidence indicates that, especially in a more advanced stage, children need sequentially structured activities that are mediated by a teacher or by skilled peers in order to acquire automatic (de)coding and appropriate strategies for reading and writing (see Adams, 1989). Through experience with literacy tasks in guided participation with skilled partners the child's repertoire of relevant strategies can be gradually expanded. However, in order to support children's motivations toward literacy it is important to focus on meaningful experiences, and to stimulate critical thinking in reading and creative expression in writing.

2.3 *Extending literacy*

Advanced reading and writing demands the development of vocabulary, insight into the structure of sentences and larger textual structures, such as episodes and paragraphs, and knowledge of rules for punctuation. Comparisons between expert and novice learners have also called attention to the importance of control processes, such as planning and monitoring reading and writing processes.

Literacy in advanced classes is fostered by teachers who plan lessons that have a clear conceptual focus. Students should be given time to reflect, to practice relevant strategies, and to achieve depth of meaning and understanding. Instruction should focus on principles and ideas that help children make connections between prior knowledge and the new information in the text. However, from observation studies we know that very little time is devoted to explicit or direct instruction in reading and writing strategies. Teachers spend more time on student assessment. They listen to students' reading of course-book texts or control their writing products for spelling or formulation errors. Traditional teachers tend to impart knowledge and strategies in a structured way, following a predefined sequence of reading and writing lessons in a fixed time schedule, forcing the student to assume a largely passive role.

In a learner-centered approach the teacher fulfills the role of a coach who shares control with her students (Langer, 1992). The teacher thus encourages discussion and provides detailed explanations about the scope and relevance of different strategies. Children are offered opportunities to build on their own strategies for acquiring and using knowledge independently. Learning is a result of interactions, such as experimentation, discussion, and elaboration in reading and writing conferences. In such groupings disagreement about textual inferences will provoke real questions which may turn into new ideas. In this way children learn to share ideas and to check the validity and appropriateness of these ideas. Strategies such as comprehension monitoring, using graphic organizers and activating prior knowledge must be taught not just as recipes for learning but as flexible learning devices. Students should come to realize that they can use language as a foundation for building new concepts and new structures of meaning. By doing so, they will gain more and more inner control and become less dependent on others and more confident in using their own strategies for reading and writing.

2.4 Teaching language to learn

Language education is not an end in itself. Language is at the center of the school curriculum because language is used to learn across the curriculum. Language, thinking, and learning cannot easily be separated. Learning should be seen as an active process in which children construct ideas about language as they engage in communicative settings. Learners are engaged in selecting activities, in attributing attention to specific parts of these activities, and in applying strategies for problem solving. Learning can be defined as a process in which new information is linked to prior knowledge. Learners integrate new information with what they already know. While being engaged in conversations, or while reading texts, learners continuously make predictions, monitor the outcome of these predictions, and seek a solution to problems they encounter. As such, language can be seen as an instrument to foster children's thinking and concept development (Collins and Mangieri, 1992). The cognitive processes involved in language learning can also be applied to other curriculum areas. Integrated language strategies can be used in curriculum domains, such as science, social studies, mathematics, and art.

Furthermore, schools should cultivate a climate that motivates children to explore the meaning of human experience through the language of literature. By using literature in the classroom, meaningful encounters with the most effective sources of human expression can be devised (see Cox and Zarrillo, 1993). Literature provides an in-depth study of universal values and needs, and it captures students' interests and challenges them to explore new avenues of meaning. Literature may involve the use of picture books, novels, folklore, poems, biographies, and nonfiction. By using trade books, print media, and electronic media across the curriculum children can be offered a broad variety of text structures and contexts to be explored. A literature-based program should not ignore children's ideas and interests. Relevant surveys have made clear that there are age-related differences. A literature-based program should also be based on the experiences children bring to school. It offers a good opportunity to attune the curriculum to the linguistic and cultural diversity in the school by allowing children to respond to literature in ways that are consistent with their gender, social class, and ethnicity.

3 Building on Language Variation

Languages and language varieties vary according to their status and social functions. The functions of language in the classroom are a special case of language in its social context. For many children there is a mismatch between the language spoken at home and the language used at school. At home they may speak a dialect or a language variety associated with gender, social class, or ethnicity (for an overview of research, see Andersen, 1990). The further development of such varieties and the learning of new varieties in school are highly dependent on teacher attitudes toward language diversity.

3.1 Dialect variation

Although dialect differences tend to become smaller as a result of geographical and social mobility and the influx of mass media, differences between language varieties spoken in varying regions remain. Thanks to the work of sociolinguists such as Hymes, Labov, and Trudgill, the belief that some language varieties are inherently inferior to others gradually lost some of its credibility. The postulate of equal opportunities for children requires that no varieties are discriminated against. To this end language variation among children must be recognized as valuable. All children, including monolinguals, have to learn a broad range of language varieties to facilitate effective communication in the social situations they will encounter.

Attitudes to dialect variation can have a great impact on the language curriculum. Children usually reflect the value system of their parents, varying from intolerance to strong personal allegiance toward the nonstandard dialect. Teachers not only vary in proficiency in using local dialects. They may also be prejudiced against using dialect in the classroom. Researchers such as Trudgill (1979) have made it clear that focusing on the standard language in education is almost certain to fail, and may lead to the loss of self-esteem and self-confidence by speakers of nonstandard varieties. Language awareness programs in culturally heterogeneous classrooms may help children to develop positive attitudes toward language diversity by sharing language experiences. By creating a supportive communicative environment, children are made aware of the social contexts in which different styles and varieties are appropriate. In this way children are helped to develop communicative skills in a functional repertoire of different language varieties.

3.2 Language and gender

There is reason to believe that the interactional achievement is not equally distributed between the sexes (see Coates, 1993; Wodak and Benke in chapter

8). Children learn to distinguish between gender-related differences in speech at an early age. Sex-related differences both in topic preference and in the use of linguistic forms are present in conversations among school-age children. Boys also tend to speak more than girls and to use more nonstandard forms. There is also evidence that language input models the sex-related differences in speech. Parents tend to provide different speech models for boys and girls, and mothers and fathers interact differently with them. Moreover, there is evidence that sex differentiation in speech styles is strengthened in single-sex peer groups.

An important question is how power relations reflected in conversations between men and women can be challenged and transformed in education. Teachers are able to influence the right to speak and the questions of when, where, and how much. By focusing on the distribution of speaking time and the allocation of turns, the teacher can discuss power relations among participants which contribute to defining their role in the interaction (Swann, 1992).

3.3 Language and social class

Families differ in social prestige, wealth, and education. Since language is learned in social interaction, there is variation in child language that correlates with social class. A classic example of this is the study of New York City speech by William Labov. He found that different pronunciations of speakers fall into a pattern reflecting social-class differences. The lower the position and status of people in the social-class hierarchy, the smaller the chance that they used standard language forms. In this context it was investigated to what extent the language of children revealed a similar pattern of social stratification. According to Labov, adolescents at about age 15 tend to move from the vernacular to standard-like forms. However, other studies suggest that shift toward adult norms takes place earlier, at about age 12, and that at an older age children use nonstandard forms in order to express group solidarity which implies the rejection of middle-class values.

Claims have been made that children from low socioeconomic backgrounds lag behind in language acquisition. According to Bernstein (1960), middle-class children develop an exploratory and explicit use of language ("elaborated code"), whereas lower-class children develop a more expressive and implicit language use ("restricted code"). Lower working-class children's speech was characterized by such features as short utterances of little syntactic complexity, frequent use of pronouns instead of nouns, and reliance on exophoric reference. Bernstein believed that the supposed limitations of a restricted code could result in cognitive deficits, as demonstrated by low IQ scores and poor school results.

Labov (1970) criticized this position by claiming that, although there are clear differences in the forms and values associated with language use in different social classes, the speech of middle-class children is not superior to that of lower-class children and children of different social classes are equally proficient in language skills. Research by Wells (1985) on the language development of children in Bristol demonstrated that the language used by children does not vary much with social class. Family experiences related to the value orientations of the parents turned out to be the relevant predictors of children's development, rather than parents' occupation and education.

From a sociolinguistic point of view, literacy is highly culture-specific. Heath (1983) showed how different kinds of literacy function in society. Analyzing the use of literacy in mill towns in the southern part of the United States, she uncovered seven dimensions of literacy use: instrumental, social-interactional, news-related, memory-supportive, communicative as substitute for oral messages, providing a permanent record, and confirmation. She found that the purposes of using literacy and the ways of using literacy were related to how people function in social networks.

For schoolteachers it is important to accept the variation in speech styles and registers as valid systems. Children should continuously be helped to bridge the transition from language and literacy practices at home to those at school. Language education should be seen as enrichment of children's home language. Within an atmosphere of tolerance and mutual respect, children must be made aware of the potential and validity of language variation in social context.

3.4 Language and ethnicity

From a sociocultural point of view, minority group members may feel the need to use two written codes serving two complementary sets of purposes. The primary function of the use of the majority language will be intergroup communication in the community as a whole; functions of the use of the minority language will be intragroup communication and expressing one's ethnicity. The motivation to learn seems to increase as societal institutions pay more attention to the native language and culture of the bilingual child. With respect to the acquisition of literacy, there is clear evidence that the motivation of children to learn to read increases as they become more familiar with the language and as they find themselves more competent to accomplish school tasks in that language (see Au, 1993).

For many ethnic minority children there is a mismatch between home language and school language (cf. Verhoeven, 1994). It can be assumed that children who receive literacy instruction in a second language are faced with a dual task: In addition to the characteristics of written language, they will have to learn an unfamiliar language. Failure to relate the instruction to the child's linguistic background may impede the acquisition of literacy. Due to contrary results in different settings, the benefits of the L2 submersion approach to literacy instruction are hard to assess. In experimental bilingual programs in Canada (immersion programs) it was found that children speaking English as a majority language reached a high level of L2 French literacy skills without their L1 literacy skills lagging behind. Quite contrary results were obtained in studies of direct literacy instruction in L2 in the United States and Europe when L1 was a minority language with low societal prestige. This paradox can be solved by assuming that in the latter context the learning of L2 reflects the loss of L1. Poor results in both languages will then be the consequence, because of feelings of ambivalence on the part of the minority group toward the majority group and the majority language, as created by the social milieu.

The actual educational programs for ethnic minority groups are not determined by psychological arguments or evaluation studies, but rather by political factors. Chances for education in a minority language are poor where the general policy is directed toward assimilation, but good where the development of ethnic identities is tolerated. Language policies in multilingual societies are determined by many factors, such as the number and importance of the minority languages in the society, their geographic concentration, their linguistic development, the social and religious structure of the population, the attitudes of the minority and majority groups, and the availability of teachers and learning materials.

4 Perspectives

The data reviewed in this chapter on language and education reveal at least three generalizations from sociolinguistic theory. The first is that language development at school involves not only the elaboration of a grammatical system, but also the ability to use language as an instrument for learning, and the ability to use language appropriately in varying contexts. This is important for defining the objectives of language education. The second generalization is the importance of social interaction in language teaching. The learning environments in which children are embedded form an essential part of what is going on when language is taught. Through guided interaction with other students and exposure to literary works students can be given the opportunity to develop as individuals within relevant cultural networks. The third generalization concerns the diversity of language behavior in the classroom. Sociolinguistic factors such as gender, class, and ethnicity play a significant role in the language-learning processes of children at school. Interactional sociolinguistics in modern educational settings provides a perspective which makes possible the exploration of the relationship of different discursive practices of language varieties.

The sociolinguistic study of language education should produce guidelines for teacher training. In the context of teacher-training programs, language should not be defined from an economic or technological point of view. Instead, the social context of language should be emphasized, taking into account sociocultural aspects of development and the concerns of different communities and individuals. Auerbach (1992) distinguished four pedagogical tendencies that can be derived from such an analysis: the notion of variability and context-specificity in language practices; the notion of language acquisition as a learner-centered process, developed primarily in opposition to mechanical pedagogy; the politicization of content in language instruction; and the integration of the voices and experiences of learners with critical social analysis. Taking an ideological view as a starting point, teachers should be trained to pay attention to the role of language practices in reproducing or changing structures of domination. The key to understanding language in context is to start not with language, but with context.

25 Bilingual Education

OFELIA GARCÍA

1 Introduction

Bilingual education involves using two languages in instruction. This article focuses on bilingual education within its sociolinguistic framework, looking especially at how language is used in educational settings to produce different linguistic outcomes. We start, however, by providing a historical overview of the development of bilingual education policy throughout the world, moving then to an analysis of the aims and types of bilingual education in the modern world.

2 History and Policies of Bilingual Education

Despite the great linguistic diversity in the world, educational systems have been largely monolingual, functioning in the language of the elite. In Europe, this educational tradition dates back to the Greeks and Romans who ignored local languages and insisted on Greek and Latin as languages of schooling (Lewis, 1976). In ancient Greece and the Roman Empire, those who spoke Greek and Latin, in addition to their local vernaculars, were held in high esteem. And so today, our Graeco-Roman traditions continue to uphold monolingual education in the language of the elite, as well as valuing those who speak the language of the elite over those who are sole speakers of local languages.

It has been this *monolingual educational practice* along with the higher prestige of *bilingual speakers of minority communities* that have been responsible for the *language death* (see chapter 15) of many speech communities, including the Scottish Gaelic one described by Dorian (1981), for the *language shift* (see chapter 16) of many ethnolinguistic groups (Fishman, 1991) and also for the *language spread* of many languages of high prestige, such as English (Fishman, Cooper, and Conrad, 1977).

The shaping of a new world, and the birth and growth of the United States throughout the eighteenth and nineteenth centuries, impacted on our monolingual educational tradition. In the United States, ethnolinguistic groups often valued their own non-English language as a symbol of culture over the English spoken in the new land, a commercial symbol of entrepreneurship and trade. And so bilingual education grew throughout the nineteenth century in the United States, organized by ethnolinguistic groups who ran their own schools (Pearlmann, 1990). Throughout the world, during this period, ethnolinguistic groups with sufficient resources organized schools that taught in their language, as well as in a majority language. However, the growth and development of universal public education in the late nineteenth and early twentieth centuries, coupled with an increase in nationalism, put a stop to this process. Monolingual education for ethnolinguistic minorities reigned supreme again throughout the world in the first half of the twentieth century.

During the 1960s ethnic identity became a concern of many groups throughout the world (Fishman, 1981). This greater interest in ethnicity was fueled in part by the independence of many African nations, the increased vitality of indigeneous groups throughout Europe, Asia, and the Americas, the growth of civil rights, especially in the United States, and the dynamic movement of immigrants and refugees throughout the world. Monolingual education was now openly blamed for the exclusion of language minorities from society. Thus, throughout the early 1960s, the use of the mother tongue, along with the majority language, especially in the initial years of schooling, became a much sought-after alternative.

Multilingual societies that had never publicly recognized their multilingualism started to acknowledge their diversity. European countries that had once insisted on monolingual instruction, such as Great Britain and Spain, adopted bilingual instruction for the education of regional minorities. For example, the Welsh Language Act of 1967 legalized the use of Welsh as a medium of instruction, and bilingual education spread throughout Wales (Baker, 1991). In Spain, the third article of the new Spanish Constitution of 1978 recognized Catalan, Basque (or Euskara), and Galician as official languages in their respective autonomous communities, and made those languages obligatory in schools in those regions (Siguán, 1988).

Beyond Europe, many countries had repressed the languages of powerless indigeneous groups. This was the case, for example, of the Maoris of New Zealand. Since the 1970s New Zealand has been involved in *reversing the language shift* (RLS) (Fishman, 1991) of Maoris. The *kohanga reo* or "language nest" movement consists of preschool centers where Maori is the only language used. Since 1984 *kaupapa Maori* schools, where Maori is used as the sole medium of instruction, except for an hour of English a day, have grown.

Other more linguistically heterogeneous societies also adopted bilingual and even multilingual education. For example, after many years of English-only education, the Philippines, after the 1973 Constitution made English and

Filipino official languages, adopted a bilingual education policy that used both Filipino and English as media of instruction in definite subject areas (Sibayan, 1991). Schools in India have followed a three-language formula since 1956, teaching English, Hindi, and the regional language, or another indigeneous language in Hindi-speaking areas (Sridhar, 1991). In Tanzania, where no single ethnolinguistic group predominates, schools now use the children's mother tongue in the first three years of elementary school. They then switch to Swahili as a medium of instruction, the present official and national language (Abdulaziz, 1991).

North America was also caught up in this greater recognition of the language of their ethnolinguistic minorities in education, and this greater flexibility in language of instruction was extended to include immigrant and refugee groups. In Canada, immersion programs in French for Anglophones have spread since the Official Languages Act of 1967 made English and French official. Especially since the 1970s, Canada has also supported *heritage language bilingual education programs* in which ethnic languages are the medium of instruction for about half the day (Cummins, 1992), as well as *heritage language lessons* in as many as 60 languages, held after school and weekends (see section 5).

In the United States, the genesis of publicly funded bilingual education had been the recognition of the possible value of using Spanish in the education of Puerto Ricans and Mexican-Americans, both groups of United States citizens who were failing in schools. Eventually, however, by the time the Bilingual Education Act was passed in 1968, non-English languages were only seen as useful to teach immigrants while they learned English. Under the Bilingual Education Act (Title VII of the Elementary and Secondary Education Act), federal funds became available to any school district that applied to implement instructional programs using the students' mother tongue. Although only for transitional purposes, that is, until the student became proficient in English, bilingual education for immigrants, and in particular for the numerous Spanish-speaking population, has spread throughout the United States. This growth has also been supported by the judicial decision known as *Lau v. Nichols* in 1974. Supporting the Chinese parents who had taken the San Francisco School Board to Court on the grounds that their non-English-speaking children were not getting equal educational opportunity, the US Supreme Court ruled that "something had to be done." Bilingual education, as well as English as a second language programs, have been the most popular ways of addressing the educational need of language minorities. The 1980 reauthorization of the Bilingual Education Act included funding for not only transitional programs, but also *structured immersion* and *dual-language programs* (for more extensive definitions of these types of bilingual education programs, see section 5 below). On the one hand, bilingual education federal funds became available for instructional programs that were monolingual and used only English (structured immersion). On the other hand, however, use of bilingual education federal funds, previously restricted to programs that used the non-

English language only transitionally, now became available for instructional programs where bilingualism and biliteracy were goals (dual-language programs).

Bilingual education programs abound today for the elite throughout the world, especially when a language of wider communication such as English is needed or when bilingualism in two prestigious languages is considered an intellectual distinction. And bilingual education programs for indigenous ethnolinguistic minorities have been successfully developed. But the use of two languages in instruction of immigrants, migrants, and refugees, even temporarily, has been controversial throughout the world. And in most places, despite the multicultural rhetoric, educational policies remain mostly monolingual for immigrants and refugees (see, for example, Stubbs, 1991, for Great Britain).

3 Aims of Bilingual Education

Some types of bilingual education promote *additive bilingualism*. In additive bilingualism students come into school speaking their mother tongue, and a second language is added. The result is clearly an individual who is bilingual. Other types of bilingual education, however, are involved in *subtractive bilingualism*. In situations of subtractive bilingualism, students are instructed in both their mother tongue and a second language. Eventually, however, instruction in the mother tongue ceases, with the second language becoming the sole medium of instruction and ultimately the only language of the student (Lambert, 1980). Educational programs that support additive bilingualism are also referred to as *strong*, whereas those which engage in subtractive bilingualism are referred to as *weak* (Baker, 1993).

Whether bilingual education promotes additive or subtractive forms of bilingualism is related to the reasons why the educational system uses the two languages. Often, bilingual education for the language majority promotes additive bilingualism, whereas that for the language minority develops subtractive bilingualism. Yet, as Fishman (1976) has argued, bilingual education with additive bilingualism as a goal can be beneficial for the minority, as well as the majority.

Ferguson, Houghton, and Wells (1977) have identified ten different aims of bilingual education, some having to do with the enrichment of the elite through bilingualism, others with the assimilation or the preservation of language minorities, yet others with societal integration, increased world communication, understanding, and pluralism.

Bilingual education is a complex phenomenon with multiple realities (Otheguy, 1982; Cazden and Snow, 1990). Beyond our original definition of bilingual education as the use of two languages in education, the term "bilingual education" has been extended to also encompass educational programs for students who are speakers of a minority language, even when instruction is *monolingual* (Hornberger, 1991). That is, for most lay people, bilingual education encompasses both the use of two languages in instruction, as well as the teaching of a second language to speakers of another language, even when the instruction takes place in the second language.

4 Advantages of Bilingualism

Bilingualism and multilingualism are important for both language majorities and minorities for *cognitive*, *social*, and *psychological* reasons.

Students who are bilingual and biliterate have been shown to have *increased cognitive advantages*, such as more divergent and creative thinking (Hudson, 1968), greater metalinguistic awareness and cognitive control of linguistic processes (Bialystok, 1987; Galambos and Hakuta, 1988), and increased communicative sensitivity (Genesee, Tucker, and Lambert, 1975). But in order to reap these cognitive advantages, bilinguals must have age-appropriate levels of competence in the two languages. Skutnabb-Kangas (1977) and Cummins (1981) have suggested that there are two *thresholds*. The first has to be reached so that children have no negative consequences from their bilingualism. But the second threshold has to be crossed in order for then to have positive cognitive advantages.

In addition to cognitive advantages, bilingualism and biliteracy can bring about *greater understanding among groups* and *increased knowledge of each other*. In fact, bilingual and multilingual education is true multicultural education, going beyond just expressing positive feelings to giving people an actual tool, bilingualism, to create greater knowledge and understanding. Bilingual education goes beyond multicultural education because it uses language to combat racism and inequality between different language groups. In that sense, bilingual education is also encompassed within the anti-racist education movement (Cummins, 1988).

To the cognitive and social advantages of bilingualism and biliteracy, one can add the *psychological benefits*, important especially to language minorities who lack self-esteem. It has been said, for example, that *bicultural ambivalence* is the greatest reason for the educational failure of language minorities (Cummins, 1981). Bilingual education in this sense is empowerment pedagogy, enabling the incorporation of the home language and culture in school, the participation of the community, the use of the home language in assessment, and the development of a reciprocal interactive curriculum (Cummins, 1986).

The next section will discuss the different types of instructional programs that bilingual education encompasses. The following two sections will then analyze the sociolinguistic and socio-educational principles that are responsible for the differing linguistic outcomes.

5 Types of Bilingual Education

Table 25.1 (adapted from Baker, 1993) lists the different types of bilingual education, grouped into three categories, with their differing characteristics. These types are discussed below.

Table 25.1   Types of bilingual education (adapted from Baker, 1993).

	Type of child	Language in classroom	Educational aim	Linguistic aim
I Monolingual education for language minority students leads to relative monolingualism				
1 Submersion	L minor	Major	Assimilate	Monolingualism
2 Submersion +withdrawal SL	L minor	Major	Assimilate	Monolingualism
3 Structured immersion (sheltered English)	L minor	Major	Assimilate	Monolingualism
4 Segregationist	L minor	Minor	Assimilate	Monolingualism
II Weak bilingual education leads to relative monolingualism and limited bilingualism				
1 Transitional	L minor	Minor to Major	Assimilate	Monolingualism
2 Mainstream + withdrawal F/SL	L major	Major and FL/SL	Enrichment	Limited bilingualism
3 Mainstream + supplementary F/SL	L major	Major and FL/SL	Enrichment	Limited bilingualism
III Strong bilingual education leads to relative bilingualism and biliteracy				
1 Separatist + withdrawal SL	L minor	Minor and major	Autonomy	Bilingualism
2 Two-way dual L	L minor and L major	Major and minor	Enrichment, pluralism	Bilingualism
3 Mainstream + supplementary heritage L	L minor	Major and minor	Enrichment, pluralism	Bilingualism
4 Maintenance	L minor	Minor and major	Enrichment, pluralism	Bilingualism
5 Immersion	L major	Minor and major	Enrichment, pluralism	Bilingualism
6 Mainstream bilingual	L major	2 major	Enrichment, pluralism	Bilingualism
7 Two/multi-way mainstream bilingual /multilingual	Many L major	Many major or major and minor	Enrichment, pluralism	Bilingualism

5.1 Monolingual education for language minority students leads to relative monolingualism

When language minority students are schooled solely in the language of a majority society, there is minority language loss. Unless the language minority community has other institutional or societal support for the maintenance and development of the minority language, children often become monolingual speakers of the majority language, either entirely so or relatively so, depending on societal and family circumstances.

Submersion

Popularly known as "sink or swim," this educational setting is simply mainstream education with no planning for the inclusion of students who do not speak the majority language. Linguistic differences are not overtly recognized in the curriculum. Language minority students are simply put into classes where instruction, materials, and assessment are solely in the majority language. Most language minority students fail to learn in these settings, although most become monolingual in the majority language in the process. This is the most common educational program for language minority students in societies that do not recognize their linguistic diversity.

Submersion + withdrawal second language classes

This type of program is the easiest to plan and requires the least resources, and thus may be the most popular in the world today. Language minority students attend mainstream classes where no provisions are made for them. In that sense, they are in submersion education in the majority language for all content. However, they are "withdrawn" or "pulled out" for second language instruction with a language teacher. The purpose of this type of program is then to facilitate the acquisition of the majority language, with little consideration paid to the education of the language minority student. As soon as students become bilingual, withdrawal for language instruction ceases.

Structured immersion

In this type of program, popular recently in the United States, language minority students are "immersed" in instruction which uses solely the majority language (Hornberger, 1991). Structured immersion differs from the submersion programs described above in that there has been educational planning. Instruction is solely for language minority students who are learning the majority language, with material in the majority language which has been designed for language learners, with a teacher who uses only the majority language. The purpose of the program is to accelerate the acquisition of the majority language, with little consideration as to the quality of the education students receive. As soon as children become bilingual they are transferred to mainstream monolingual classes. This further accelerates the shift to the majority language. In the United States, these programs are also known as "sheltered English."

Segregationist

Planned by a language majority which wants to exclude a language minority, this type of program uses solely the minority language in the education of the minority. This type of monolingual education aims to keep the language minority separate and excluded from participation in society. For example, South Africa under apartheid had a segregationist educational system for all Bantu speakers with instructions solely in their native language (Skutnabb-Kangas, 1981).

5.2   Weak bilingual education leads to relative monolingualism or limited bilingualism

When schools do not devote enough time and effort within their bilingual curriculum to the development of the nondominant language in the society, the student, at best, will have limited bilingual ability. This is the case not only for language majority students when the second language does not occupy an important place in the curriculum, but also for language minority students when instruction in the mother tongue ceases once the student has become proficient in the majority language.

Transitional

This type of educational program is most popular in the United States for the education of language minorities when some positive action has been taken. It requires planning and resources. Initially, the students' minority language is used, with the majority language being taught as a second language, most often by the same bilingual teacher. Progressively, both languages are used in instruction, with little compartmentalization between them. Eventually, students are transferred out of the bilingual classroom to a monolingual one. The transition from bilingualism in instruction when the student is monolingual to monolingual instruction when the student is bilingual is planned in order to accelerate the shift to the majority language (García, 1993).

Mainstream + withdrawal foreign/second language classes

This type of educational program is the most popular in order to teach a foreign or second language to students who speak a majority language. Students are in mainstream classes for all subjects and in addition are "pulled out" or "withdrawn" for foreign/second language instruction with a language teacher. This program also requires planning, although the degree of bilingualism attained by the students is often related to the importance granted to bilingualism in society. The length of study and curricular time devoted to the language, as well as the teaching strategies used, have linguistic consequences, with different programs producing students who have more or less bilingual ability.

Mainstream + supplementary foreign/second language classes

This type of education is popular among parents who want their children to become fluent in a second language not taught in the educational system. Students attend school in the majority language, but in addition go to supplementary classes or schools on weekends or after school where the foreign or second language is taught. For example, all over the world there are supplementary private English schools where students receive supplementary instruction in English. There are also schools which offer languages as an enrichment activity after school hours. Parents often pay additional tuition fees to send their children to these language lessons. As with the type above, differing results are produced, depending mostly on the parental and school commitment to bilingualism.

5.3 Strong bilingual education leads to relative bilingualism and biliteracy

When schools and communities spend considerable effort and resources to develop bilingualism, the students will have a greater possibility of becoming bilingual and biliterate. These strong forms of bilingual education involve considerable sacrifice on the part of parents and societies committed to bilingualism, with some degree of risk and hard, persistent work.

Separatist with withdrawal second language classes

The types of educational programs discussed thus far are usually organized by the majority. Separatist programs, however, are organized by the language minority itself when it has the power to do so. Instruction is through the medium of the minority language only, although the majority language is often taught as a subject in withdrawal classes. The purpose of this type of education is to prepare the language minority to pursue political autonomy. As an open educational alternative, this type of program is rare. A past example may be the *ikastolas* in the Spanish Basque region during the Franco regime. These underground Basque language schools were founded to promote Basque linguistic, cultural, and national identity.

Two-way/dual language

More popular as a means to achieve bilingualism, biliteracy, and biculturism through public funds are two-way programs, recently also called, in the United States, dual-language programs or two-way bilingual/immersion programs. These programs include both the majority and the minority, as both move toward bilingualism. Instruction most often involves linguistically heterogeneous groups. Both languages are used in instruction with compartmentalization, often having to do with time of day, and sometimes with a different teacher. The educational program is extended throughout the students' education. These programs have mixed results, often enabling language minority students to maintain and develop their ethnic language and thus become bilingual and biliterate, but not always being equally successful with language majority students.

Mainstream + supplementary heritage language classes

Often language minorities send their children to mainstream schools that function in the majority language, and also send their children to supplementary schools for heritage language classes. These classes are often after school or on weekends. Heritage language classes teach not only the ethnic or heritage language, but also the history and culture of the ethnolinguistic group. In some cases, most notably in Canada, heritage language classes are supported by the majority society. Most often, however, they are organized by the ethnolinguistic minority, and therefore require that the group be highly organized and have appropriate economic and educational resources. In the United States, for example, there are many supplementary ethnic language schools. Again, levels of bilingualism and biliteracy obtained through this type of education generally depend on family commitment. It is possible, however, to obtain high levels of bilingualism and biliteracy with this type of education, as long as the family and the immediate society provide the contextual support for the development of the ethnic language.

Maintenance

This type of educational program uses both a minority and a majority language throughout the education of the language minority. Both languages are compartmentalized, most often by using different teachers for instruction that takes place in different languages. Its aim is to promote the maintenance and development of the minority language and the increased knowledge of the minority history and culture, as well as the full development of the majority language and knowledge of its history and culture. Maintenance programs thus provide the enrichment that language minorities need and the pluralistic perspective needed by the majority society. Canada supports maintenance programs for language minorities under the name of heritage language bilingual education (Cummins, 1992). In the United States there are few maintenance educational programs supported through public funds, although private ethnic schools with maintenance goals abound (García, 1988; Fishman, 1988). Again, however, these schools most often require that the ethnolinguistic group be self-sufficient and economically viable. High levels of bilingualism and biliteracy are usually obtained.

Immersion

These programs have been designed for language majority students or speakers of high-status languages who wish to become bilingual. Initially, instruction is solely through the medium of the minority language with a bilingual teacher. Progressively, the majority language is also used in instruction. Instruction through the medium of both languages continues throughout the students' education. This type of program was originally designed and implemented in the French-speaking province of Québec, Canada, for Anglophone students who also wanted to become fluent in French. The program has been highly successful and has spread beyond the Canadian context. Lately, immersion programs for language majority children have extended to other societal contexts. For example, Catalonia and the Basque region of Spain have developed extensive immersion programs in Catalan and Basque (Artigal, 1991). Language majority students achieve high levels of bilingualism and biliteracy in these programs.

Mainstream bilingual

This type of program uses two languages throughout the students' education. It differs from maintenance programs in that all languages are here considered majority languages, and all students are of the majority. This is the case, for example, of *Dwibahasa* in Brunei, the educational system introduced in 1984 which requires instruction for all Malay-speaking children in both Malay and English (Jones, Martin, and Ozóg, 1993). The bilingualism and biliteracy of the entire population is guaranteed. This is also the case of trilingual education in the Grand Duchy of Luxembourg (Baetens-Beardsmore, Lebrun, 1991).

Two/multi-way mainstream bi/multilingual

This type of program also uses more than two languages throughout the students' education. There are students from different ethnolinguistic backgrounds, but all are considered majority students and all languages are granted equal value in the curriculum. The European Schools (Baetens-

Beardsmore, 1993) are the best examples of this type. Initially, all students in the European Schools are instructed through their mother tongue while receiving instruction in a second language. Instructional groups are also linguistically homogeneous in the beginning. Progressively, instruction is through both languages and groups are mixed. The aim of this education is clearly to have multilingual/multiliterate citizens. It differs from two-way dual language programs in that the languages involved are more equally valued and in that initial instruction is in linguistically homogeneous groups.

6 Some Sociolinguistic Principles

From extensive scholarly work on bilingual education in the last 30 years, as well as from the experience of many bilingual schools and programs that have been developed, the following sociolinguistic principles, related to the failure or success of developing bilingualism, can be derived:

6.1 *Monolingual instruction*

For most ethnolinguistic groups, exclusive use of one language in education generally leads to monolingualism. This is true for language majority groups, as well as language minority groups, unless, of course, the sociolinguistic vitality of the language minority is extremely strong in the ethnic community, as well as the home. Low-status languages most often need the support of an educational setting in their maintenance and development. Bilingualism, and especially biliteracy, are rarely obtained without the support of an educational setting.

6.2 *Bilingual instruction*

When two languages are used in instruction, bilingualism and biliteracy are obtained only by differentiating the roles of the languages in society. The language of lower status or lower use should initially be used extensively as a medium of instruction, regardless of whether students are of the language minority or majority (figure 25.1 displays this process). The language of higher status or higher use may be also used as a medium of instruction, provided the next sociolinguistic principle is present.

The use of two languages should be compartmentalized throughout the curriculum. *Compartmentalization* is easier when different teachers use different languages for instruction. In some cases, however, language compartmentalization can be achieved by allocating a specific language to a certain time of day, a certain day, certain subjects or specific physical locations, such as

Figure 25.1 The use of two languages in school should complement their use in society at the initial stage of developing bilingualism.

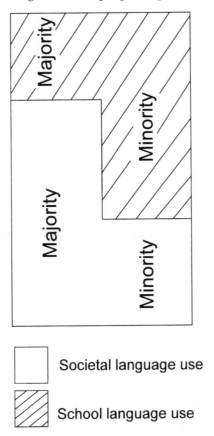

different classrooms and even schools. Prolonged use of the two languages without compartmentalization, whether subconscious or conscious, like that practiced in what is known as *concurrent translation*, usually leads to a shift to the high-prestige language, and thus is encouraged in transitional bilingual education. Concurrent use of two languages is useful then only in the *beginning* stages of bilingualism to contextualize second-language input in second-language instruction.

The students' *mother tongue* should always have a place in the school curriculum. Even if instruction through the medium of the mother tongue ceases eventually, the teaching of the mother tongue as a subject should be continued.

The teaching of a *second language* must go beyond second-language instruction methodology. That is, approaches such as the natural approach, the notional-functional approach, total physical response are only valuable in the very beginning stages of bilingualism. The second language must also be used as a medium of instruction, as well as taught as a subject in its own right.

The four sociolinguistic principles of bilingual instruction necessary for the development of bilingualism are present in *maintenance programs and mainstream with supplementary heritage language* for language minority students, as well as immersion programs, mainstream bilingual, and two/multi-way mainstream bi/multilingual programs for language majority students. They are less present in separatist and two-way dual-language programs.

These four principles are missing from transitional programs for minority students, and withdrawal foreign/second language classes and supplementary foreign/second language classes for the majority.

7 Some Socio-educational Principles

Even when we are fully cognizant of the sociolinguistic principles governing bilingualism, different agents must plan for full additive bilingualism through schooling. Parents, communities, school administrators and educators, and students themselves must actively commit themselves to bilingualism and biliteracy. To develop the bilingualism and biliteracy of all students, certain characteristics must be present in the educational agents and the educational culture of the school. These principles are adapted from Skutnabb-Kangas and García (1995):

7.1 Educational agents

A bilingual administration and staff

The administrators, teachers, paraprofessionals and clerical and custodial staff must be bilingual or be willing to work toward becoming bilingual. Whenever possible, they should be of different ethnicities and nationalities.

Highly qualified teachers of one language or the other who are bilingual

Teachers who are bilingual should, whenever possible, teach only in one language or teach only one language and they should have native or high levels of linguistic competence in the language in which they teach or that they teach.

Active parental participation and support

Parents must have made the choice of bilingual schooling for their children. They should be well informed, committed to bilingualism, and active participants in their children's education.

7.2 *Educational culture*

A completely bilingual educational context

The entire school system must be designed to promote bilingualism for all, multilingualism for some, monolingualism for none. It must encompass, whenever possible, both primary and secondary education and encourage a bilingual context where the two languages have a life of their own beyond the classrooms.

An educational language policy that aims to make students bilingual and biliterate

This is accomplished by giving the students' mother tongue an important function in the school curriculum and securing its role as a link to students' ethnolinguistic identity. The students' mother tongue should be used as a medium of instruction, as well as taught as subject matter in linguistically homogeneous groups. But its use should be clearly compartmentalized from that of the second language.

The students' second language should initially be taught in linguistically homogeneous groups using the students' mother tongue to make input comprehensible. Progressively the L2 should be increasingly used as a medium of instruction, first in context-embedded activities, that is, when the language is highly contextualized through visuals, gestures, and other paralinguistic cues, and progressively in more context-reduced activities. Once students can use both languages in context- embedded as well as context-reduced ways, linguistically heterogeneous groups are appropriate. Development of proficiency in context-embedded uses of the second language, or basic interpersonal communication skills (BICS), has been estimated to take approximately one to three years. Development of proficiency in context-reduced uses of the second language, or cognitive academic learning proficiency (CALPS), has been estimated to take approximately five to seven years (Cummins, 1981).

The educational policy must at all times also recognize the interdependence that exists between the two languages, and the fact that there is a common underlying bilingual proficiency, with both languages coming from the same central processor (Cummins, 1981).

Inclusive educational strategies that support bilingualism and biliteracy

An inquiry-based approach to learning uses the two languages as instruments for knowledge. In addition, a student-centered and interactive pedagogy, including the use of cooperative learning, whole language strategies, and the writing process should be followed.

Teaching material that is highly varied

Material should reflect language as used in different societal contexts, including a bilingual one.

Fair and authentic assessment

Assessment should not compare native speakers to second-language speakers. Assessment should be criterion-referenced or performance-based and conducted in the language of instruction or choice.

8 Conclusion

Bilingual education, both for minorities and majorities, has experienced tremendous growth all over the world in the last 30 years. This article has reviewed its historical development, looked at the different societal aims for bilingual education, analyzed the advantages of bilingualism, examined the different types of bilingual education, summarized the sociolinguistic principles responsible for the differing linguistic outcomes of bilingual education, and finally listed socio-educational principles associated with greater bilingualism and biliteracy.

26 Sociolinguistics and the Law

EDWARD FINEGAN

1 Introduction

The old chestnut that law is a profession of words captures the fact that codified law is expressed in words, from the Magna Carta to the Constitution of the United States, as well as in countless subsequent legislative codes and appellate court decisions in numerous jurisdictions. It likewise captures the fact that the resolution of civil disputes and the prosecution and defense of criminal cases also take place almost entirely through the instrumentality of language. Not only in its embodiment and execution is law a profession of words though, for the law also explicitly enshrines linguistic regulation of several kinds. Laws dictate what languages may be spoken or written and under what circumstances, which speech activities constitute language crimes, and even the exact wording of certain speech events and speech acts. The federal codes of the United States mandate court interpreters in some situations and the use of languages other than English in election ballots and school instruction under specified circumstances. If lying is not ordinarily a crime, doing so under oath is indictable perjury, and if a business intrigue to secure the best prices for raw materials is legal, conversation aimed at illegally securing those prices constitutes conspiracy to commit a crime – itself a crime even in the absence of further illegal activities. In the United States, incriminating oneself following arrest for suspected criminal activity can lead to a conviction, but if the police have failed to *read* one one's "Miranda rights," entitling one to consult an attorney before speaking to the police, a prosecution based on that self-incrimination may well be ruled vacuous. Similar provisions apply elsewhere in the English-speaking world.

Given that law is a profession of words, it is not surprising that linguists have played increasingly active roles as consultants and expert witnesses in legal arenas over the past couple of decades. Published reports of their involvement have also increased, with a recent bibliography (Levi, 1994) containing nearly 1,200 entries on linguistics and the law, twice the number in an earlier listing. A new journal called *Forensic Linguistics* began publication in 1994 and serves as an official organ of the International Association of Forensic Linguistics and the International Association for Forensic Phonetics, both formed since 1990. The contents of the new journal and the 1,200 citations in the bibliography range over specialties from acoustic phonetics and voice prints to semantics and speech-act theory. A substantial portion of the studies reflects the broad range of interests customarily subsumed under the umbrella of sociolinguistics, including dialectology, discourse analysis, and cross-cultural communication.[1] The present chapter identifies certain important issues at the interface of sociolinguistics and the law, and describes several studies that exemplify sociolinguistic applications in legal arenas.

As other chapters of this handbook illustrate, the core of sociolinguistics is the study of language use in social interaction. Sociolinguistics focuses on real language in everyday use, and not on idealized creations comparable to the physicist's laboratory vacuum or the biochemist's sanitized petri dish. Sociolinguistics examines language as it is spoken and written by women and men carrying out the ordinary and extraordinary activities of everyday life. Language shaped by social interaction within the law (or in violation of it), drafting contracts and legislation and resolving disputes as to their interpretation, arresting suspected lawbreakers and reading them their rights, and by direct and cross-examination of witnesses[2] all constitute examples of language use. Language use in legal settings is not essentially different in kind from dinner-table conversation, talk used in seeking diagnosis and treatment from a physician, or a department-store sales transaction. Although in perhaps the most dramatic ways, the use of language in legal settings can be crucial to the well-being of individuals and communities, it is amenable to the same kinds of sociolinguistic analysis as other language varieties. Like language use in any social situation, language in legal arenas indexes its setting and conforms to its situation functionally (with respect to its purposes, participants, and setting), as well as conventionally. In other words, language use in legal (and illegal) settings exhibits clusters of features that reflect its situational character, and in so doing shows itself exactly like all other language varieties.

There is still much that sociolinguists do not fully understand about the workings of language in the workplace and other arenas of daily life, but much that is already known gets overlooked in legal settings, despite its relevance. Unlike psychopathology, DNA testing, and other fields of scientific inquiry that are recognized as beyond the ken of courts, linguistic analysis is typically viewed as within the expertise of judges and juries alike. Judges pride themselves on their skills as producers and analysts of words and are not shy in making pronouncements about language whose equivalent with respect to psychology or biochemistry they readily acknowledge as beyond their ken (cf. Tiersma, 1993). Being a producer and consumer of words does not make one an informed language analyst any more than preparing a gourmet meal makes one a dietician or being psychologically sound makes one a clinical psychologist. As for juries, it is sometimes asked what they might be able to make judgments about, if not language. From a sociolinguistic perspective, that question is naive.

The present chapter focuses principally on the relationship between language use and the judicial system in the United States. The legislative and forensic issues raised here, however, are not unique to the United States, and parallels in the UK and Commonwealth countries are abundant, as well as in the European Union. In the sections to follow, we examine key sociolinguistic issues in three arenas of the law: in section 2 legislation concerning language in public life; in section 3 the involvement of sociolinguists as consultants or expert witnesses at trial; in section 4, ethical considerations and ethnographic perspectives.

2 Language and Public Life

Much of a society's smooth functioning depends on drafting effective legislation and on modifications to existing laws that affect the lives of communities and individual citizens in important ways. As a result, sociolinguists are playing an increasing role in educating a wider legal community beyond judges and juries about language use. Nowhere, perhaps, is this more true than in communities with a legal system using a dominant language that is not shared by many litigants and defendants. Given that so much in the social practice of citizens is impacted by statute and case law, sociolinguists can play a potentially significant role in helping to formulate, interpret, and apply laws that depend for their just application on an adequate understanding of human discourse within and across speech communities.

2.1 Bilingualism and the courts

In 1970 in the case of *U.S. ex rel. Negrón v. New York*, a federal Circuit Court of Appeals overturned the murder conviction of a 23-year-old Puerto Rican laborer working on Long Island, New York. The court ruled that Negrón, a monolingual speaker of Spanish with a monolingual English-speaking attorney representing him at trial, had his constitutional rights violated by the absence of a court interpreter. Noting that "To Negrón, most of the trial proceedings must have been a babble of voices," the court observed: "Considerations of fairness, the integrity of the fact-finding process, and the potency of our adversary system of justice forbid that the state should prosecute a defendant who is not present at his own trial," and it deemed the lack of a competent interpreter as absenting defendant Negrón. "The least we can require is that a court . . . make unmistakably clear to [a defendant] that he has a right to have a competent translator assist him, at state expense if need be, throughout his trial" (see Crawford, 1992: 238–40). The Negrón decision prompted the federal Court Interpreter's Act of 1978, which mandated provision of an interpreter for any criminal or civil action initiated by the federal government for litigants whose competence in English is deemed by the presiding judge to limit their ability to a fair trial. As Berk-Seligson (1990b: 35) points out, difficulties can arise in determining whether a speaker who knows some English needs an interpreter: "the judge must use his discretion in arriving at a linguistic evaluation that probably only a trained linguist could properly make." Implementation of the Court Interpreter's Act throughout the nation required the assistance of linguists in the training and testing of competent court interpreters, and procedures have been established for certifying court interpreters. Berk-Seligson (1990a) provides a detailed description of the many cross-cultural complications that can arise in the practice of court interpreting.[3]

In a very interesting case that did not warrant a court interpreter, Gumperz reports the story of a US Navy physician, a native speaker of Aklan who had been educated in Tagalog and English. Dr A was accused of perjury in connection with reports he made to an FBI investigator concerning medical treatment of a 16-month-old child. The child, suffering from second-degree burns, had been brought to a US Navy emergency room in which Dr A was on duty and, after suitable treatment for second-degree burns, was released to her parents. Several hours later, back in the hospital, she was diagnosed with third-degree burns and died en route to a burn center for treatment. The child's stepfather was subsequently tried for child abuse and convicted of manslaughter. At the trial, Dr A testified for the prosecution and was himself later indicted for perjury, the case hinging on whether or not Dr A had suspected abuse when the child was first brought to the emergency room. Dr A's testimony at the stepfather's trial appeared inconsistent with his replies to questions asked by the FBI investigator the morning after the child's death.

As Gumperz (1982: 168–9) assessed the case, it would have to be shown that "something in Dr. A's cultural and communicative background may at times create difficulties in interaction with English monolinguals. Yet the linguistic problem is too complex to be described simply as a matter of discovering evidence for what students of second language acquisition call interference: the transfer of grammatical features from the speaker's native language to the second language." Gumperz decided "to search for specific conversational exchanges or texts which exemplify relevant communicative difficulties and then to rely on interpretive analysis to discover differences in the actual processes of conversational inference through which interpretations are made." To this end he investigated Dr A's language use in different communicative situations, some of ordinary cognitive challenge, others of greater challenge. In addition, he analyzed grammatical features of Aklan that seemed relevant to the language of the alleged perjury. In his testimony at Dr A's perjury trial, Gumperz demonstrated that the contextualization cues characteristic of the physician's English differed from those of native speakers of English and that those differences had led to misinterpretation by the FBI investigator in an example of "crosstalk." His painstaking analysis helped persuade the court that Dr A had not in fact perjured himself and serves as a model of what a sociolinguist can offer the criminal justice system in reaching decisions founded on informed analysis rather than the sometimes blind beliefs of individuals in ethnically diverse communities in which members of one group may mistrust the motives and goodwill of those belonging to other groups. The case of Dr A is important in that he was a proficient speaker of English, whose bachelor's (though not his medical) degree was earned from a distinguished university in California. If such an educated and highly proficient speaker of English could mistakenly wind up as a defendant charged with perjury in what would seem a relatively straightforward speech event, it should not surprise us to learn of the extreme communicative difficulties faced by indigenous peoples of the West, whose native languages and customs differ radically from those of the dominant cultures in which they are now forced to operate.

Eades (1994) describes in fascinating detail the patterns of questions and answers that differentiate the Aborigines of Australia and Tasmania from the dominant Anglo-European culture surrounding them, differences that are magnified within the adversarial proceedings of the Australian criminal justice system, where Aborigines are greatly overrepresented among defendants. Of the significant cultural differences between Aborigines and Anglos there is so little understanding on either side that it is not uncommon for Aborigines whose command of English is relatively remote from the standard variety and whose familiarity with Anglo culture is proportionately little even to plead guilty to offenses which they have not committed rather than submit to alien forms of questioning or subject themselves to other culturally offensive consequences. Eades reports the story of four Aboriginal boys who had stolen a car and pleaded guilty to the offense. A fifth boy, who, unawares, joined his four friends after the theft, was arrested with them. When advised by his solicitor to plead innocent, the boy refused so as to avoid appearing in court without his mates. The picture of the clash between the cultural and linguistic practices impacting on language use in Australia is complex, and Eades's depiction is speckled with tales from solicitors that make a compelling case for urgent sociolinguistic study (and perhaps for overhauling the legal system).

Eades suggests, as have others, that there is need for court interpreters to serve as intermediaries between the Standard English-speaking courts and speakers of at least those varieties of Aboriginal English that are relatively remote from the standard varieties of the justice system. Such a policy decision would certainly require significant political and financial muscle, but the sociolinguistic and judicial issues entailed in implementing it are themselves considerable, and existing sociolinguistic knowledge would not immediately be sufficient to implement such a policy with great confidence. More research is definitely needed. What is true in Australia is also true among indigenous peoples in other parts of the Commonwealth and in the United States. By virtue of their limited English-language competence, many of the poorest and socially most marginalized citizens are deprived of the justice supposed to be guaranteed to all citizens. When, as with Native Americans and Australian Aborigines, the disadvantaged are the indigenous peoples whose lands have only recently fallen under Anglo-American traditions of law, the injustices appear grotesque. Unfortunately, adequate solutions remain elusive, as do the political and financial resources to implement them. Part of the challenge facing sociolinguists must be to help solve such challenges in ways that will be financially and politically realistic.

2.2 *Bilingualism and the schools*

Contrary to widespread belief among Americans, the United States has never had an official language. During the 1980s, there was considerable political action to designate English as the official language, even by constitutional amendment,[4] but no legislation potentially leading to an amendment has ever been voted on in Congress. What Congress has addressed, sometimes at the prompting of the courts, is legislation ensuring freedoms guaranteed by the Constitution but infringed by certain language practices. Over the past quarter-century several of those practices have fallen under the scrutiny and direction of federal law.

The United States has a long history of grappling with bilingualism, especially in the schools. Bilingualism in the schools was the concern of *Lau v. Nichols*, a landmark United States Supreme Court decision. In a suit brought by the parents of non-English-speaking Chinese students in San Francisco, the United States Supreme Court overturned an appellate court decision when it ruled that

> students who do not understand English are effectively foreclosed from any meaningful education. Basic English skills are at the very core of what these public schools teach. Imposition of a requirement that, before a child can effectively participate in the educational program, he must already have acquired those basic skills is to make a mockery of public education. We know that those who do not understand English are certain to find their classroom experiences wholly incomprehensible and in no way meaningful. (see Crawford, 1992: 251–5)

Basing its opinion on the Civil Rights Act of 1964, the Court cited the words of a prominent senator during the floor debate preceding the passage of the Act: "Simple justice requires that public funds, to which all taxpayers of all races contribute, not be spent in any fashion which encourages, entrenches, subsidizes, or results in racial discrimination" (see Crawford, 1992: 254). The participation of sociolinguists and other educators was required extensively in the implementation of the policy dictated by the *Lau* decision. Since that decision, official policy has been to provide bilingual education as an interim step on the path to education in English.

2.3 English only and the English Language Amendment

Also of concern to sociolinguists is the federal Voting Rights Act of 1965. As amended in 1975, the Act requires states under specified conditions to provide ballots and other voter information materials to members of certain language minority groups in their own language. Supporters of bilingual ballots point to the subsequent election of increasing numbers of minority group members to public office as a sign of the Act's success. Largely without the assistance of suitable professional guidance, however, the implementation of bilingual ballots led to numerous embarrassing glitches in various jurisdictions throughout the country. Of greater moment here is the backlash that bilingual ballots provoked from English-speaking majorities in some jurisdictions. For example, the implementation of bilingual ballots in San Francisco played a probably significant role in fueling a negative reaction whose force has not yet been spent. In 1983, in a move that launched an English-only movement nationwide, voters in San Francisco placed on the ballot and passed by a large majority a nonbinding resolution advising the United States Congress to repeal the bilingual provisions of the Voting Rights Act. While the US Congress paid no attention to the San Francisco resolution, California voters went on in 1986 to pass by a 73 percent majority a statewide "initiative" (Proposition 63) making English the official language of the state.

Despite opposition from sociolinguists and virtually all public officials, as well as in the print and broadcast media, English-only and official-English propositions and legislation have generally passed by large majorities. Arizona's Proposition 106, on the ballot in 1988, had been expected to pass by a large majority but, after the disclosure of what were interpreted as racist sentiments in certain internal documents of the private group fueling the official English movement, the proposition passed by only a single percentage point. Support for "US English," the group spearheading the drive nationwide, fell off dramatically, although voters in three other states passed similar propositions that same election month. Significantly, in 1990 a federal District Court judge struck down Arizona's Proposition 106, finding the law it enacted "so broad as to inhibit" constitutionally protected speech (Crawford, 1992: 288). By 1988, 48 of 50 states had considered official English legislation, and by 1990, 17 had enacted such legislation. A drive toward an official-English amendment to the United States Constitution, a major goal of "US English," appears to have been slowed by the decision concerning Proposition 106, and the prospects for a nationwide English language amendment are unclear. Sociolinguists have argued strongly against English language amendments on grounds ranging from their perceived racist overtones and potential negative consequences to the great intellectual and cultural resource bilingualism and multilingualism offer to a nation. But it is clear from various referendums and polls that the educational work of sociolinguists in regard to the values of bilingualism have not been as effective as they might be.

3 Sociolinguistic Applications in Forensic Settings

3.1 *Dialectology*

Dialectology, a traditional sociolinguistic focus, has proven pivotal in several cases, both civil and criminal. Certain criminal cases depend on identifying the speaker of a tape-recorded language crime, as with telephoned threats of violence or extortions or obscene calls. Given that a dialect represents the shared speech characteristics of a social group and not the unique characteristics of an individual, a demonstrable match between the dialect of a suspect's speech and that of a taped perpetrator is of course insufficient to prove guilt.[5] On the other hand, establishing that the dialect of a suspect *differs* from that of the perpetrator certainly raises at least reasonable doubts about the likelihood of guilt.

Ash (1988), a sociolinguist familiar with the Philadelphia speech community, carried out an analysis of the vowels of a man charged with making telephoned threats to the local police and fire departments. Her analysis demonstrated that the defendant's speech did not match the dialect of the taped threat, and she demonstrated how difficult it would be for speakers to change the vowel quality of their dialect in trying to disguise their voices. Commissioned by the defense, Ash's sociolinguistic analysis was made available to prosecutors and the court, and, though Ash did not get to present them at trial, the judge's directed acquittal of the suspect is believed to have been influenced by the sociolinguistic analyses. In a similar case, Labov (1988; cf. Labov and Harris, 1994) analyzed the dialect of a man arrested on suspicion of telephoning bomb threats to Pan American Airways in Los Angeles. The voice of a Pan Am employee, raised in New York City, working for Pan Am in Los Angeles, and known to be unhappy with his employer, was thought by some fellow employees to resemble that of the telephone threatener. Labov demonstrated to the court that the threatener did speak a dialect that, from the perspective of West Coast residents, may have resembled the employee's but that the threatener's dialect differed systematically and did not have the same geographical origin. Using acoustic analyses of the vowels in the words *bomb*, *there*, *off*, and *on* (taken from the telephoned threat, "There's gonna be a bomb going off on the flight to LA"), as well as others used by the caller, Labov demonstrated to the court's satisfaction that the defendant's New York City dialect did not match the caller's Boston dialect. Before ruling in the case, the judge asked the defendant to recite the pledge of allegiance to the flag (a familiar exercise for youngsters at school) and asked Labov to point out from that recitation any examples parallel to those that had been identified in the analysis of the threats. On the basis of all the testimony (involving more than sociolinguistic analysis), the judge found reasonable doubt of the employee's guilt and acquitted him. As in both the Philadelphia and Los Angeles cases, the intervention of a skilled language analyst can lead to a recognition that a defendant is not a likely perpetrator. In other instances, however, the intervention of an expert is too late to prevent or overturn what appears to be a mistaken conviction (see Milroy, 1983).

Involving the sociolinguistic analysis of dialect in a strikingly different way is a civil case brought by the parents of a group of students in an elementary school in Ann Arbor, Michigan. Known as the "Ann Arbor Decision," the case is reported in detail elsewhere (Center for Applied Linguistics, n.d.; Crawford, 1992: 255–7; Labov, 1982), and it is sufficient for our purposes to highlight the issues and indicate what role sociolinguists played in assisting the court. The parents of 11 African-American children attending Martin Luther King School sued the Ann Arbor district school board, invoking a section of the United States Code that provides as follows:

> No State shall deny equal educational opportunity to an individual on account of his or her race, color, sex or national origin, by . . . the failure by an education agency to take appropriate action to overcome language barriers that impede equal participation by its students in its instructional programs. (20 U.S.C. 1703 (f))

United States District Judge Charles W. Joiner wrote in his opinion (July 12, 1979):

> The case is not an effort on the part of the plaintiffs to require that they be taught "black English" or that their instruction throughout their schooling be in "black English," or that a dual language program be provided . . . It is a straightforward effort to require the court to intervene on the children's behalf to require the defendant School District Board to take appropriate action to teach them to read in the standard English of the school, the commercial world, the arts, science, and professions. The action is a cry for judicial help in opening the doors to the establishment.

In his analysis, Judge Joiner identified four issues in the case: whether the children have a language barrier; if so, whether it impedes their equal participation in the instructional program; whether, if there is an impeding barrier, the school board has taken appropriate action to overcome it; whether, if the school board has not taken appropriate action, its negligence denies equal educational opportunity on account of race.

About the existence of a language barrier, Judge Joiner noted:

> All of the distinguished researchers and professionals testified as to the existence of a language system, which is a part of the English language but different in significant respects from the standard English used in the school setting, the

commercial world, the world of the arts and science, among the professions, and in government. It is and has been used at some time by 80% of the black people of this country and has as its genesis the transactional or pidgin language of the slaves, which after a generation or two became a Creole language. Since then it has constantly been refined and brought closer to the standard English as blacks have been brought closer to the mainstream of society.

In his decision the judge lists a dozen significant features of Black English Vernacular, among them the deletion of word-final consonants, the use of the verb BE to mark recurring or continuous action, and the use of certain words with meanings that differ from those of standard varieties. He acknowledges "the thoughtful testimony" of "distinguished and renowned researchers and professionals" and cites published research from a dozen monographs written by sociolinguists including Geneva Smitherman, William Labov, J. L. Dillard, Ralph Fasold, Walt Wolfram, and others, some of whom had testified at trial on behalf of the plaintiffs. In a decision encouragingly reflecting the contributions of the experts, Judge Joiner found that the children's home language "is not itself a language barrier" but that it becomes one "when the teachers do not take it into account in teaching standard English." He ruled that "no matter how well intentioned the teachers are, they are not likely to be successful in overcoming the language barrier caused by their failure to take into account the home language system, unless they are helped by the [school board] to recognize the existence of the language system used by the children in their home community and to use that knowledge as a way of helping the children to learn to read standard English." He ordered the school board to offer such help.

3.2 Discourse

In other cases, sociolinguists have been called upon to assist courts in understanding the complicated nature of certain possibly criminal conversations in which dialect differences are not at issue. Shuy reports on several cases involving alleged bribery or conspiracy to commit a crime. Besides his scholarly reports (e.g., Shuy, 1990), he has written an accessible book called *Language Crimes*.[6] Before briefly discussing the methods of analyzing tape-recorded conversations that Shuy has pioneered, two preliminary matters need addressing.

The first is the challenge of making accurate transcriptions. As anyone who has transcribed tape-recorded conversation recognizes, it is often impossible to hear every word uttered, and uncertainty surrounds sometimes critical semantic information hidden in barely audible syllables, as with the subtle markers of negation in words like *didn't* and *can't*. Prince (1990) cites several cases where transcriptions made for the FBI differ significantly from those made by a professional linguist. In the two instances below, the (a) lines represent FBI transcriptions, the (b) lines transcriptions made by Prince herself; in her own transcriptions, Prince uses capital letters to mark heavy stress and indicates measured silences by noting their length in brackets; in each case, T represents the tape carrier, D the target and eventual defendant.

1 (a) T: . . . I don't know whether he said he followed him or they followed him when he left there. I don't know.

  (b) T: . . . I don't know whether he said HE followed THEM or THEY followed HIM when he left there. [4 sec]
       D: They can't HAVE anything.
       T: I don't know.

2 (a) D: Jesus Christ – that's a shame. I don't know what the hell to do.

  (b) D: Jesus Christ. [5 sec] That's a shame. [3 sec] I don't know what the hell to tell you.

   Such discrepancies make clear how significant is the potential for mishearing tape-recorded speech or not hearing parts of it at all (note that D's turn in 1(b) was missed altogether by the FBI transcriber). Even with goodwill and a commitment to seeking the truth, it is easy to mishear a taped conversation, all the more so when a listener may be inclined to presume that the target of a surreptitious recording is likely to be guilty (it is, after all, suspected wrongdoers who are the targets of surreptitious recordings). Given the crucial importance of context in interpreting language use of any kind, one listener's mindset may prompt one interpretation, another's a very different interpretation.

   Sociolinguists themselves, of course, are not immune from a mindset that steers transcription one way or another. Retained to make an "accurate" transcription of an allegedly inculpatory conversation, a sociolinguist may well have been provided at least a minimally exculpatory frame by defense counsel before hearing a taped conversation for the first time. To the extent that the language on the tape is explicit and unambiguous, different transcriptions may be uniform, but it is precisely with vague and potentially ambiguous expression that expertise is most needed, and professionals too must bring a context to bear when transcribing a conversation. All language use, productive and interpretive, is context-based – and to a greater extent than we typically realize. In an adversarial criminal justice system, it is perhaps inevitable that the competing goals of prosecutors and defense counsel will produce conflicting transcriptions of recorded conversations. Even were transcriptions to be made by the court (rather than the adversaries), the problem of bias would not be entirely solved because of the inherent difficulty of accurate transcription and the potential innocent bias of transcribers. Studies of court reporters hastily transcribing courtroom proceedings show certain biases, such as standardizing nonstandard dialect features of attorneys to a much greater extent than for witnesses and in writing *yes* for *uh-huh*, which of course does not always mean the same thing (Walker, 1990).

Given an agreed transcription, a second issue concerns interpretations of conversational exchanges. Shuy (1990) likens what a trained sociolinguist sees in a conversation to what a doctor sees in an X-ray. He emphasizes that linguists analyze *how* people talk and not just *what* they say. "The role of the linguist is to educate the jury on the structures and components of these oral communications, thereby enabling them to understand what is contained within these recordings in a manner otherwise not possible." Conversational exchanges, as customarily interpreted, reflect the "cooperative principle" (Grice, 1975), formulated to explain how ordinary condensed conversation gets reasonably well interpreted by interlocutors in the face of so much implicit reliance on context. Speakers cannot *express* all they intend to communicate and must rely on their interlocutor's understanding of *context* to supply much of the *content* they intend their interlocutors to grasp. Much – and arguably all – language expression is inexplicit and therefore vague or ambiguous, a proposition that can be simply illustrated with personal pronouns. The first-person pronoun *I* does not have a single unchanging referent but instead one that varies from speaker to speaker. Thus, only knowledge of who is uttering *I* permits identification of its referent. It is *context* and not *expression* alone that identifies the referent of the pronoun. With third-person pronouns like *he* and *them*, context alone cannot always furnish the referent. While interlocutors can be assumed to share some contextual information, as with the meaning of expressions like *here*, *today*, and *I*, as well as to identify the referents of relatively explicit expressions such as *Heathrow Airport* and *St Francis of Assisi*, the comparatively general content of pronouns and other reduced or elided expressions leaves considerable room for vagueness and ambiguity – and thus for misinterpretation. "That's Not What I Meant!" makes a good title for a book about misunderstanding because its ring is all too familiar to English speakers. Conversational interlocutors have no choice: We must use abbreviated expression and ellipsis and we must rely on context to fill in the blanks.

If interlocutors are operating on different wavelengths, as they must be when one of them is surreptitiously recording and guiding their conversation with a hostile intent, misinterpretation is almost inevitable – in the conversation itself and in subsequent hearings of the recording. Compounding the difficulty, when auditors (including jurors and judges) listen to such a taped conversation, their interpretive apparatus rests on their understanding of ordinary *cooperative* conversation in which interlocutors share an agenda or negotiate one. It is tough for jurors to stay mindful that a surreptitiously recorded conversation is not a cooperative one. Knowing that interlocutors may not behave the same linguistically when observed and not observed, sociolinguists face the observer's paradox (Labov, 1972: 61): "our goal is to observe how people use language when they are not being observed." Minimizing the effect of their intrusion into social settings is a methodological challenge for sociolinguists, a concern that has obvious application to the taping and analysis of surreptitious recordings. A tape carrier with a hostile

intent participating in a conversation cannot record what would have occurred without his purposeful intrusion.

The fact that a person carrying a recording device aims to get the target to
commit a language crime on record and steers the conversation in that direction has enabled sociolinguists to present evidence in court that the alleged
crime recorded in such a conversation may well have other, less sinister
interpretations, and several defendants have won acquittal on the basis of
such analyses. Shuy has been the most prominent sociolinguist in these cases
(but see also, e.g., Green, 1990; Prince, 1990), and one successful tool he uses
to help jurors keep track of what goes on in a conversation is topic analysis,
which demonstrates who raised which topics and how often. Response analysis, in turn, categorizes the responses to a given topic, such as postponing it,
changing it, or responding fully to an open-ended question. As Shuy (1990: 87)
notes, "The way a person selects from among these options gives clues to that
person's concerns, interests, and intentions." Finally, there is topic-flow analysis, which "maps the topics sequentially, noting the movement among substantive, corollary, and transitional topics, and marking the successes or
failures of the speakers in their efforts to achieve their goals." Shuy has
developed and refined these techniques, using them in numerous cases, including several that involve prominent politicians, to help juries see that what
seems obviously criminal in a cooperative conversation may have more be-
nign interpretations in a surreptitiously taped conversation, at least upon
more sophisticated inspection.

4 Conclusion: Ethics and Ethnography

4.1 Language experts and ethics

In the daily fare of dispute resolution and criminal prosecution that is the
staple of the judicial system, sociolinguists who serve as consultants and
expert witnesses inevitably face ethical challenges. As scholars accustomed
more to slow-paced and careful investigation with negligible pressure to come
down on any one side of an issue, language experts face exceptional challenges when participating in a vigorously adversarial system, all the more so
when the stakes for the principals can be so great and the rewards for the
consultant not insignificant. Several commentators have addressed the matter
of ethics in forensic linguistics (e.g., Chambers, 1990; Hollien, 1990b; Finegan,
1994), warning about the pitfalls of participating in such a system and offering guidelines to help ensure ethical behavior. Hollien (1990b) endorses the
notion that experts called by either side to a dispute should be seen as advocates and called consultants; the only "experts," as he sees it, are those called
by the court itself. Chambers (1990) suggests recommending other experts to
lawyers inquiring about cases for which the required expertise appears not to

be squarely in one's own research arena and not consenting to work on a case until after reviewing the law and inspecting the evidence. Finegan (1994) offers several guidelines, among them these: Don't allow yourself to assume that an attorney retaining your expertise has told you all that he or she could reveal about the case; distinguish between your roles as expert and consultant; and be aware that another expert may be providing opposing counsel with critiques of your analysis. The involvement of sociolinguists and other language scientists as experts and consultants is still in the early stages, and there is much yet to be learned substantively and much to be considered ethically.

4.2 Ethnography of law

In closing, it is worthwhile to note that anthropologists, no strangers to the study of law in remote and exotic cultures, have recently turned their analytical eyes and ears on the judicial systems of their own cultures. One particularly relevant and valuable project of this kind is that carried out by Conley and O'Barr (Conley and O'Barr, 1990; O'Barr and Conley, 1990). They examined the workings of small claims courts in Colorado, North Carolina, and Pennsylvania. Small claims courts handle relatively minor civil claims, and litigants ordinarily represent themselves before a judge or magistrate in informal proceedings without professional counsel. In their ethnographic inquiry, Conley and O'Barr sought to discover how litigants think about their cases and present them before a judge. In the 150 cases studied, the litigants displayed one of two "radically different orientations" toward the law, one relational, the other rule-governed.

> In conceptualizing a dispute, interpreting rights, and allocating responsibility for events, *relational* litigants focus heavily on status and social relationships. They believe that the law is empowered to assign rewards and punishments according to broad notions of social need and entitlement . . . Their accounts of their troubles emphasize the social networks in which they are situated, often to the exclusion of the contractual, financial, and property issues that are typically of greater interest to the court . . . Predictably, courts tend to treat such accounts as filled with irrelevancies and inappropriate information, and relational litigants are frequently evaluated as imprecise, rambling, and straying from the central issues.
>   By contrast, *rule-oriented* litigants interpret disputes in terms of rules and principles that apply irrespective of social status. They see the law as a system of precise rules for assessing responsibility, and reject as irrelevant everything not circumscribed within these rules . . . In presenting their cases in court, rule-oriented litigants structure their accounts as a deductive search for blame . . . Rule-oriented accounts thus mesh better than relational ones with the logic of the law and the agenda of the courts. (Conley and O'Barr, 1993: 58–9)

Such strikingly valuable and innovative ethnographic approaches to law and its language uses, stepping outside the inherited categories and boundaries of most social scientific research, are much needed and, one can hope, will substantially contribute to our understanding of the role of law in ordinary citizens' perceptions of the administration of justice. Sociolinguists, much involved in the implementation of social policy and the resolution of civil disputes, as well as in criminal trials, have in some ways acted as firefighters, addressing pressing problems as they occur. Such work is, of course, important. In looking at a larger picture, however, sociolinguists, like these ethnographers, may come to discern more clearly how complex is the interweaving between the institutions of law and the practices of social interaction, as well as the frequent and systematic conflict between them. A fresh ethnographic perspective may well show at a disadvantage not only those on the periphery of power and wealth but those who do not fathom the idiom of the law, whatever their native language and however well trained an interpreter they may be provided.

NOTES

1 Overviews of the study of linguistics and the law can be found in Danet, 1980, and Levi, 1990, 1994.
2 Valuable work has been carried out in the analysis of direct examination and cross examination; see, for example, Atkinson and Drew, 1979; Drew, 1990; Matoesian, 1993.
3 The challenges of translating in the courts of the United States are dwarfed by those facing the European Union. Discussion of the challenges facing the European Union lies beyond the scope of this chapter; interested readers should see Coulmas (1991) for a variety of perspectives.
4 S. I. Hayakawa, serving as senator from California in the United States Congress, introduced legislation to make English the official language of the United States in 1981; he later became one of the founders of US English, discussed below in section 2.3.
5 Voiceprints, sometimes viewed as comparable to fingerprints in their ability to identify an individual, are not regarded with unanimous trust by experts; see, e.g., Dumas, 1990; Hollien, 1990a.
6 Some language crimes have also been thoroughly studied from a speech acts point of view, as in Tiersma's treatments of perjury (1990) and defamation (1987).

27 Language Planning and Language Reform

DENISE DAOUST

1 Introduction

Language plays a crucial role in social interaction and is an all-important agent in the transmission of cultural and social values. It is shaped by the same political, social, and cultural forces which produce the world's diverse civilizations and cultures. For example, the spread of the Roman empire throughout Europe between around B.C. 750 and 200 A.D. resulted in the birth of the Romance languages. Could that have been prevented? Had the Romans devised a plan to create a monolingual empire? Surely not, and from today's point of view, the Romans cannot be said to have practiced a language planning policy.[1] Looking back at the situation, though, it stands out that the profound changes which took place resulted from choices, social and linguistic. Broadly speaking, language planning requires such a sociolinguistic context where choices between alternatives can be made. Clearly, though, since the word "planning" is used, these choices must be of a different nature from those which bring about natural change. In fact, as Fasold (1984: 246) has suggested, language planning is about "explicit" choices. As it turns out, the concepts of "choice," explicit or not, and "alternatives" are extremely complex. Yet, any attempt to define language planning without apprehending these concepts and addressing the question as to what role languages play in society, and how they can become objects of planning is sure to result in a narrowing of the scope of a phenomenon anchored deep within the dynamics of society.

1.1 The interrelation between language and society

How are linguistic choices made? As it turns out, even in so-called monolingual societies, linguistic choices are the rule. The fact that we say "gonna" instead of "going to" not only says much about our idiosyncratic way of using language, it also points to a number of social facts about the situation and domain of use, and reveals who we are from a sociodemographic and economic point of view. Language use reflects social stratification and is a form of social behavior (Labov, 1972a). Moreover, the study of these variant structures or sociolinguistic variables not only shows that there is social agreement in the use of language, but also that there is agreement as to the meaning of the differentiated use of language. This is why a speech community cannot be solely conceived as a group of speakers who all use the same linguistic forms, but rather "as a group who share the same norms in regard to language"[2] (Fishman, 1971; Labov, 1972a; Bright, Denison, in chapters 5 and 4 of this volume). The same holds true for different varieties of a language where choices run between subtle structural features of phonology, syntax, and lexicon to sometimes dramatically divergent local varieties or even between standard literary languages and altogether different oral varieties (Schiffman, chapter 12). Yet grammatical rules are but one set of the underlying rules speakers have to interiorize. Cultural and social rules are also needed to produce acceptable linguistic and sociolinguistic behavior. It is that competency which enables speakers to adjust to different speech situations and social expectations (Hymes, 1971 [1972]; Kasper, chapter 23).

Choice is further complicated in multilingual societies where speakers must also choose between different languages altogether and thus have to internalize complex linguistic and sociolinguistic rules to cover the entire scope of sociolinguistically acceptable behavior (Gumperz, 1968 [1972]; Clyne, chapter 18). How can a speech community be defined in such a context where different languages are in contact? The answer lies again in the social forces which dictate language use. In these societies, where social prestige and power are unevenly distributed, each variety of a language or each separate language is assigned a functionally differentiated social role, where the prestigious or "High" variety tends to monopolize the official and public functions while the "Low" or socially less valued variety is reserved for more private domains (Ferguson, 1959 [1972]; Fishman, 1967). Social forces reinforce this diglossic pattern, so that members of speech communities not only develop sociolinguistic competence in accordance with this pattern, they also develop shared norms about each linguistic variety and its usage. For example, a milestone study by Lambert (1967) showed that in the French-English bilingual Québec of the sixties, negative attitudes towards Québec French were not only quite uniformly shared by the English-speaking community but were almost as unanimously held by French-speaking Québecers.[3] These types of situations have brought scholars like Fishman (1971: 28) to define a speech community as "one all of whose members share at least a single speech variety and the norms for its appropriate use." Thus enlarged, the concept fits a wide variety of sociolinguistic situations worldwide.[4] Yet, to complicate things further, many linguistic choices are not made consciously. Shared norms are based on feelings, on judgments, and attitudes. And since complex speech communities are a composite gathering of subgroups who share different and sometimes divergent norms, language is both a unifying and a separating force which gives rise to such feelings as language loyalty (Garvin, 1973: 27) and nationalism (Fishman, 1972 [1989]). Moreover, it is these same social forces at work within society that set the direction for the future and account for language change, both linguistic and sociolinguistic. It is no wonder then, that language should be envisaged as a societal resource (Jernudd and Das Gupta, 1971) which, like other types of resources, could be shaped to achieve sociopolitical goals. In that sense, language planning is a future-oriented intervention in language which aims to influence language and language use (Rubin and Jernudd, 1971: xvi). By definition it must be a deliberate and conscious choice which might either support and accentuate the ongoing sociolinguistic direction of the speech community, or aim to curb it. However, the question of why language and language use would be planned remains. Who would undertake such a venture? And what exactly does it mean to plan language?

2 Evolution of the Concept

2.1 The standardization approach

Language planning, as a subject of study, has come a long way since 1959 when Haugen (1959 [1968]) gave his definition of the term[5] based on his analysis of the ongoing effort in Norway to modernize, promote, and implement a "national" language. Language planning was then seen as an activity concerned mainly with the internal aspects of language: It consisted in "preparing a normative orthography, grammar, and dictionary for the guidance of writers and speakers in a non-homogeneous speech community" (Haugen, 1959 [1968: 673]). It aimed to settle problems related to "the presence of conflicting norms whose relative status needs to be assigned" (Haugen, 1983: 270) or else it addressed the "language problems" of the developing nations through "graphization," "standardization," and "modernization" (Ferguson, 1968). The language planner's main task resided, within a social framework of conflicting languages, in the choice of the language or languages to be standardized, and in the choice of types of interventions, aiming at "regulating and improving existing languages or creating new common regional, national or international languages" (Tauli, 1968: 27). The comprehension of the whole process was akin to the "standardization" process as defined by Weinreich (1954 [1968: 314]) and Tauli (1968: 27).

2.2 The social components of the concept

At the time, language planning was seen as "a process of *more or less conscious,* planned, and centralized regulation of language" (Weinreich, 1954 [1968: 314], my emphasis). But, for Haugen, it consisted, even then, in "a deliberate" and thus conscious effort to intervene in the future of a language, this intervention being based on "knowledge concerning the past" (Haugen, 1959 [1968: 674]). Moreover, the whole process implied a decision, by the planners, as to the desired direction of language change. And although the end result was a "standard language," there was an awareness of the social components of such a linguistic product which was described by Haugen (1959 [1968: 674]) as aving "two mutually supporting aspects, on the one hand a generally accepted orthography, and on the other a prestige dialect imitated by the socially ambitious."

Since then, the concept of language planning has been refined to encompass both linguistic and sociolinguistic, economic and political aspects of the integration of language in society (as in Rubin and Jernudd, 1971; Weinstein, 1980; Weinstein, 1990).

2.3 *The management and social planning approach*

This broadening of the scope has led some scholars to approach language planning within a general social planning framework. Language is seen as a "societal resource," language planning a "decision-making" process seeking to solve "language problems" (Jernudd and Das Gupta, 1971: 211) or, in a more sociopolitical perspective, "communication problems" (Weinstein, 1980). This has led some to adopt a management point of view regarding language policies (Jernudd and Das Gupta, 1971) and to analyze it from a socioeconomic perspective (Thorburn, 1971; Jernudd, 1971; Grin, 1992).

Alongside these concerns, language planning studies taking into account societal multilingualism (Fishman, 1968; Fishman, Ferguson, and Das Gupta, 1968) helped develop an analytical framework. Such sociolinguistic concepts as language maintenance and shift, language dominance, linguistic minorities and diglossia, nationalism, nationism and ethnicity, became more and more of a concern to language planning scholars (Fishman, 1972). Emphasis was given to sociopsychological aspects of language behavior. Attitudes were seen as an all-important factor underlying language and sociolinguistic usage, language diffusion and change (Lambert, 1967; Cooper and Fishman, 1974; Giles, 1977; Cooper, 1982). Thus language planning is becoming a more integral part of sociolinguistics.

3 The Language Planning Components

If change in language and language use is the main target of the planning process, it is clear that, although linguistic variables are affected, language planning decisions and their implementation are motivated by nonlinguistic variables (Garvin, 1973: 24).

3.1 *Language planning problems and goals*

The devising of a language planning policy implies a vision of a future sociolinguistic situation that should be brought about. Yet surprisingly little effort has been made in trying to identify the objectives pursued. Language planning policies sometimes seem to develop as an afterthought following a period of sociopolitical turmoil such as when a country gains independence or when a political party is overthrown. Norway, for example, gained independence in 1814 and declared that the affairs of State would be carried on in the Norwegian language. Yet, until the 1880s, no indication was given as to which linguistic variety of Norwegian would be used.

Language policies are generally seen as a way of solving "language" or "communication problems" (Jernudd and Das Gupta, 1971; Weinstein, 1980). The different ways of dealing with these "problems" have led to the identification of three main types of objectives (Rabin, 1971; Rubin, 1984). Policies are said to pursue extralinguistic aims when they deal with changes in the social distribution of competing languages. For example, the spread of Swahili in Eastern and Central Africa (where it is an official language in Kenya and Tanzania, and a national language in Uganda) has important consequences, in that it deprives a number of native languages of political recognition. As for policies which seek to establish or change writing and orthographic systems, or to promote the spread of a specific pronunciation or linguistic variety, they are said to carry semilinguistic aims, since these types of interventions also have social and political consequences. For example, the fact that use of the Cyrillic script has been encouraged since the 1940s in the Republics of the former USSR, instead of the Latin script which had been previously imposed (in the 1920s), has important social repercussions in that it facilitates the acquisition of the Russian language, which uses Cyrillic, and thus makes cultural assimilation easier (Lewis, 1983: 322–3; Rubin, 1984: 8–9). Finally, when policies deal with vocabulary enrichment, standardization, and other types of intervention leading to the promotion of a linguistic norm, such as those of the French and Spanish language academies, they are classified as having linguistic objectives. Nahir (1984) lists 11 objectives ranging from language "purification," "standardization," and "modernization," through language "revival," "maintenance," and "spread" to "interlinguistic communication" at the national and international level.

Although these typologies are useful in sorting out specific aims, they do not encompass the full range of the underlying goals pursued by language planners and they do not yet constitute a comprehensive framework from which to classify and analyze the different types of language planning processes. As Rubin (1984: 9) has pointed out, the explication of goals is essential if any worthwhile evaluation of language planning is to be considered. Setting out the goals can help to minimize the distortion of the original goals as well as any backlash or boomerang effect which sometimes happen during the implementation phase. However, no clear-cut line can be drawn between the different types of objectives so that, in the long run, even linguistic aims serve sociopolitical goals. That is why language planning is more and more often seen as a way to resolve social, economic, and political problems through interventions in language (Weinstein, 1980: 56).

It is sociopolitical objectives which are pursued by language planning policies. This explains why the implementation of such goals-derived policies sometimes results in social turmoil. This aspect of language planning poses important ideological – and ethical – issues which must be dealt with in order to understand the whole process. In this frame of mind, Cobarrubias (1983: 63–6) has identified four language ideologies which motivate the undertaking of language reforms: "linguistic pluralism," "linguistic assimilation," "vernacularization," and "internationalism."

Linguistic pluralism

Linguistic pluralism promotes the "coexistence of different language groups and their right to maintain and cultivate their languages on an equitable basis" (Cobarrubias, 1983: 65). This can be achieved in a number of ways. For example, it might give rise to territorially based or individually based policies, or any combination of the two (Wardhaugh, 1992: 348). In Belgium, for example, French is officially recognized in the south, Flemish in the north, German in the east, while Brussels forms a bilingual French–Flemish district. The United States has also promoted some forms of pluralism at different times in its history, as when Louisiana was granted official bilingual status prior to its statehood (Cobarrubias, 1983: 65). Since 1968, Louisiana has adopted a law to promote the development of French. In Hawaii, the Hawaiian language was given official status alongside English in 1978. As for the rest of the States, although no federal law declares English the official language of the USA, and the State of New York officially tolerates the use of languages other than English, English had been given official status in at least 17 states by 1992 (Leclerc, 1992: 314–24). The US Bilingual Education Act of 1968 provides for bilingual programs designed to meet the needs of limited English-speaking students. This program, however, has many detractors, some of whom say that in reality, it does not pursue pedagogical improvement and cultural maintenance, but is actually a step towards acculturation of the minorities, since it is used as a transitory measure to the use of English as the sole language of education (Gray, 1987).

Although a policy based on a linguistic pluralism appears to be a democratic way of dealing with coexisting linguistic varieties, it nevertheless has its own weaknesses. Canada, for example, has a language policy based on both territorial and individual rights. Both French and English are recognized as official languages and speakers of both languages have access to public services in their own language (1969 and 1988 Official Languages Act, as well as the 1982 Constitution incorporating the Canadian Charter of Rights and Freedoms). Yet, this policy has failed to reduce the rate of assimilation of French-speaking minorities living in Western Canada where the overwhelming majority is English-speaking. In New Brunswick, the only officially bilingual province of Canada (since 1969), French speakers find it hard to assert their rights even though they make up 34.5 percent of the provincial population (1991 census). As far as the province of Québec is concerned, in spite of the fact that French speakers form the majority (82.5 percent in 1991) and that they have, since 1977, their own linguistic legislation declaring French the official language of Québec ("The Charter of the French Language"), it seeks political separation from Canada, partly because French-speaking Québecers, who represent 24.6 percent of the total 1991 Canadian population, nonetheless see themselves as a linguistic minority within Canada and fear for their language and culture.

Linguistic assimilation and nationalism

Nationalism often favors linguistic assimilation to make sure that every member of a speech community is able to use the dominant language (Cobarrubias, 1983: 63–4). This results in transferring prestige to and asserting the superiority of the dominant language. In extreme cases, linguistic minorities are given little or no rights. Revolutionary eighteenth-century France, which put forth one of the first modern language planning policies, pursued such a goal when the government planned to annihilate the French "patois" and other peripheral varieties spoken in France. Primary schooling was to be in standard French exclusively, and French was decreed the sole language of the law. In 1832, use of the orthographic rules approved by the French Academy became compulsory (Walter, 1988: 116). Russification of the former Soviet Union is another example of a linguistic assimilation. In 1938, a federal law stipulated that all non-Russian schools had to teach Russian as a second language. Although a subsequent 1958 law granted liberty of choice as to the language of education, the Russian language remained mandatory in all schools, alongside the national languages. In most Russian Republics, Russian remained in effect the language of education, so much so that students could study all through the primary and secondary levels in the Russian language. In Estonia, Moldavia, and Lithuania, the right to monolingual teaching in the national language was recognized, although some bilingual schools were permitted (Leclerc, 1992: 119–20).

Assimilation policies are sometimes repressive. For example, Indonesia practices a rather successful linguistic assimilation policy with Bahasa Indonesia. However, the inhabitants of Timor and Irian Jaya resent this policy. Yet, use of the indigenous languages is discouraged (Gauthier et al., 1993: 29).

The nation-state ideology, which, especially since the nineteenth century, greatly changed Europe's geopolitical map (Fishman, 1972 [1989: 97–175]), has gone hand in hand with the tendency to adopt a "national" or "official" language (Deutsch, 1968; Wardhaugh, 1992: 346), which endangered less socially powerful languages. Today, although there are some 185 recorded languages within Europe's 40 states, only 35 of these have official status (Grimes, 1988; Leclerc, 1992: 54). The situation is even more complex in other continents, where 155 states grant official status to 69 languages of a total of approximately 6,000 recorded languages.[6]

It is important to distinguish between *official* languages, which have the State's official recognition and are usually designated for use in official and public domains, and *national* languages, spoken by the majority of the people, and, in general, native to a country or State. National languages can be recognized officially as such and be used in public domains, usually in education. They nonetheless have an inferior status with regard to the official language. Whatever the official status granted to languages, it is clear that only a small number of the world's languages are thus recognized,[7] and that the majority of the world's languages have a minority status, politically speaking.

Minority status cannot be defined on the basis of a language's demographic strength alone. Some scholars therefore speak of "minorized" languages and linguistic communities (Daoust and Maurais, 1987: 16). In Madagascar, for example, only 1 percent of the population speaks French, yet French was the only official language until independence in 1960, when Malagasy was also given official status (Leclerc, 1992: 495–8). A sophisticated concept of linguistic minority takes into account not only geographic distribution, but also ethnic, sociocultural, and political factors, as well as the resulting sociolinguistic status. The historical status (indigenous or immigrant) of the community may also, in some situations, constitute an integral part of the definition.

Purism

Purism is closely akin to the ideology of linguistic assimilation, and brings about similar results. It can best be described in terms of feelings and attitudes towards an ideal form of a language, usually in a written state, and dissociated from everyday speech. This form of language is associated with specific aesthetic and sometimes moral values which represent the speech community's social ideal and is the norm (Labov, 1972a). Its mastery ensures social recognition and is therefore promoted by social institutions such as the educational system (Bourdieu, 1982), or official organizations such as language academies (L. and J. Milroy, 1991). As a result, deviant varieties have negative connotations, their use being discouraged in public domains. Purism developed in conjunction with Europe's drive towards the nation-state which is endowed with a national language, a separate language for each "nation" (Deutsch, 1968; Lodge, 1993: 2–3).

Internationalism

Internationalism, the ideology which consists in adopting a nonindigenous language of wider communication either as an official language or as language of instruction (Cobarrubias, 1983: 66) underlies the language planning policies of several postcolonial countries. In Gabon, for example, French is the sole official language; in Cameroon both French and English are official languages, while in Haiti Creole is recognized officially alongside French. Such a choice is motivated by the fact that international languages facilitate sociocultural, economic, and political communication with other countries and access to science and technology. In some countries where a large number of languages coexist, a language of wider communication is felt to be the answer to communication problems. It is also a way of avoiding the choice between two or more competing national languages.

Adoption of an international language is expected to promote modernization and participation in world trade and technology. However, on the negative side, it reinforces the minorization of indigenous languages. For example, in Madagascar, only 1 percent of the population is competent in French, one of its official languages, while the rest of the population speak only Malagasy. The fact that the official international language is usually spoken by a socially powerful elite not only reinforces the prestige of this language, but also invests the elite with ever more sociopolitical power. This situation is further complicated where the national language is not written or has only recently been provided with a system of writing and orthography. This ideology shows how nationalistic feelings can clash with socioeconomic and political realities. This exemplifies the distinction put forward by Fishman (1972 [1989: 109]) between "nationalism," characterized by feelings of uniqueness and the desire to develop culturally and otherwise, and "nationism" which pertains to the more pragmatic problems of fulfilling these expectations.[8]

Vernacularization

Vernacularization is an alternative to this kind of nationism. Indigenous or national languages are restored or modernized and officially recognized in lieu of or alongside an international language of wider communication (Cobarrubias, 1983: 66). Madagascar, where French and Malagasy both enjoy official status, is an example (Leclerc, 1992: 495–8). In 1978, as part of a general nationalization program, Malagasy was declared the language of education at the primary and part of the secondary levels, with French introduced as a second language in the second grade of the primary level. However, two kinds of problems have arisen. First, although Madagascar has a literacy rate of 44 percent (1986 statistics: Grimes, 1988: 254), standard Malagasy is spoken only by a small educated minority, which makes teaching in Malagasy difficult. Second, standard Malagasy has serious shortcomings as a language of education and, although it has undergone a standardization process since at least 1835 when it was used to translate the Bible, it is at present undergoing a process of destandardization (Bemananjara, 1987) and must be further modernized in order to become the language of education at the university level. Meanwhile, French continues to be used as the principal written language (Bemananjara, 1987: 311). By sending their children to French schools, the educated elites perpetuate the colonial diglossic model (Leclerc, 1992: 497).

Vernacularization sometimes involves the restoration of a literary language, as in Algeria and Tunisia, where Classical Arabic is now the official language in lieu of French (since 1976 in Tunisia and 1989 in Algeria). This poses special problems since Classical Arabic, a written language, is far removed from everyday "Dialectal Arabic" (Grandguillaume, 1990). Vernacularization policies can furthermore involve writing and orthography reforms, e.g., the adoption of the Roman alphabet for Turkish in the late 1920s. The writing of dictionaries and grammars, as for the Sami language of the northern parts of Scandinavia at the present time, is yet another aspect.

An extreme case of vernacularization is found in Israel, where a religious language, Hebrew, was revived and installed as a national language.

3.2 *Making choices and the fact-finding process*

Identifying problems and establishing goals is no small task, and the end results do not always match the original plan. Nonetheless, choices are made and they shape the future sociolinguistic reality. Ideally, these choices are based on comprehensive knowledge of the sociolinguistic context. Rubin (1971: 218) has suggested that the first stage in determining a language policy consists in "fact-finding" where the policy-maker investigates the "existing setting to ascertain what the problems are, as viewed both by persons who will execute the plan and by persons who will be the targets of the plan." All parameters of society should be scrutinized, social, cultural, political, and economic. The planner should be aware "of the social direction of each of these parameters"; otherwise, it will be impossible to carry out any plan. Goals should be established only after a thorough fact-finding program.

Such a program is time-consuming. It assumes a management-like approach within a decision-making model, as well as the participation of many specialists. Moreover, it implies the willpower to devise a blueprint for society and requires substantial financial resources. Few language-planning policies come close to this ideal. In some ways, Québec can be regarded as a model of language-planning policy and strategy. Its policy has taken the form of comprehensive linguistic legislation which clearly states the goals and objectives pursued, as well as the social philosophy underlying the law. The use of French is presented as a right and, in a way, this linguistic law has some of the characteristics of a constitution. By declaring French the "official language of Québec," the Charter of the French Language (Bill 101), in effect since 1977, states that it aims to make French the language of the State, as well as the "normal" language of work, teaching, communications, commerce, and business.

Target populations and domains are clearly identified and range from legislation and justice, the public sector and all intra- and intergovernmental communications, public signs and posters, commercial advertising, municipal and educational institutions, health and social services, as well as public utilities, professional corporations, and education from kindergarten to the secondary level. French is declared the language of work, commerce, and business. Firms of the private sector are required to offer their services in French and to ensure that French is the language of work at all levels.[9]

Québec's French language law was directly linked and in some way the actualization of recommendations issuing from a far-reaching sociolinguistic study carried out from 1968 to 1972 for the government of Québec, by the "Commission of Inquiry on the Situation of the French Language and on Linguistic Rights in Québec." In its final report, members of the Commission concluded that Québec Francophones formed a demographic and cultural majority, but a socioeconomic minority with respect to Anglophones, in Québec, Canada, and North America, and that French had to be preserved through different public means, including legislation, if necessary. Thus, even though Canada already had, since 1969, federal legislation declaring French an official language of Canada alongside English, the Québec government saw fit to legislate for language use in its territory.

3.3 *Who are the policy-makers and what type of plans do they devise?*

Who is responsible for establishing a language-planning policy, and what types of policies can be devised? In Canada, the (federal and provincial) governments assume the responsibility of setting up language-planning programs. This seems to be the trend nowadays, and although there are few pieces of legislation as comprehensive as the Canadian language laws, several governments have passed language legislation. Sometimes, provisions about language are incorporated in constitutions. This is the case in 297 sovereign and non-sovereign states (Gauthier et al., 1993). Such provisions range from the proclamation of official languages and national languages, as in the 1978 Sri Lanka constitution which declares Sinhalese the official language, and both Sinhalese and Tamil national languages, to articles guaranteeing the right of minorities to establish and administer their own schools, as in India's constitution of 1950. Public posting is also subjected to rules and regulations in some 180 states, sovereign and non-sovereign. For example, in Galicia, only the Galician form of toponyms or place names is official (Leclerc, 1989: 14, 182).

Language has been an object of legislation for a long time. For example, the English government passed the "Statute of Pleading" law in 1362, making English the language used orally in court, Latin being the official written language of court and justice. The present-day tendency to promote linguistic reform through legal and official means does not prevent individuals playing an important role in language reforms. Linguistic change is often brought about by individuals and organizations who exert pressure on governments, embodying the aspirations of their speech community. Pressure groups sometimes gain official recognition and become instrumental in language reform programs. In Israel, for example, a language committee was set up in 1890 by Ben-Yehuda to promote Hebrew as a vernacular language. In 1922 this committee achieved the recognition by the Palestine government of Hebrew as an official language, alongside English and Arabic. In 1953 this committee became the Hebrew Academy.

Two other individuals who played a central role in a language-planning endeavor were Ivar Aasen (1813–96) and Knud Knudsen (1812–95) who devised and promoted a "national" language for Norway when it gained independence from Denmark in 1814. Their course of action is instructive in more ways than one. Aasen's view of Norway's linguistic problems led him to search for the most authentic Norwegian linguistic structures, which he found in the oldest rural speech varieties. He went on to "create" a new language from composite parts of these different varieties, which he named the "Landsmål" (national language). It turned out, however, that his linguistic sources were less prestigious than the urban linguistic varieties used by the social elites, and thus proved hard to promote in the long run, although, at first, nationalistic feelings gave it a head start in spite of the fact that it had no native speakers (Haugen, 1959 [1968]; Gundersen, 1985). Knudsen, on the other hand, put forth a project aiming at adapting written Danish to an already existing Norwegian variety. The resulting Dano-Norwegian, later to be called the "Ryksmål" (State language), was based on two prestigious urban varieties. These two attempts to solve Norway's linguistic problems led into an impasse. In the 1880s both varieties were adopted officially and they have been in competition ever since. This example not only shows how profound an influence individuals can have, it demonstrates how risky language planning can be and how important it is to understand and evaluate the dynamics of society before embarking on such an endeavor.

The Norwegian situation poses another interesting problem in that the two competing varieties are in fact intercomprehensible (Haugen, 1959 [1968: 677]). In a sense, the present-day situation is not altogether different from the initial nineteenth-century situation. It has been argued (Jernudd, 1987: 499) that the local varieties or dialects of each of the national Scandinavian languages are more linguistically distant than the standard varieties of these languages. But, whatever the linguistic status of both languages, the wish to put an end to 400 years of Danish control was reason enough to promote a "purely Norwegian" language. And even though the use of the Danish written form of language may not have represented a real communication problem for at least part of the population, the Norwegians felt their language stood apart. This brings to the fore the fact that language cannot be solely defined by its linguistic specificities, nor by its communicative capacities. Judgment of its speakers as to its legitimacy and status has to be taken into account.[10]

3.4 *The specific objects of planning: The corpus–status distinction*

What is the object of language planning where it is seen as part of social planning? Although it is hard to draw a line between specific objects of planning, the corpus/status dichotomy introduced by Kloss provides useful heuristics. It emphasizes the dual nature of language planning, that is, its concern with both the linguistic and social aspects of language. "Corpus planning" refers to all actions aiming at modifying "the nature of the language itself" (Kloss, 1969: 81), while "status planning" is concerned with whether the social status of a language should be lowered or raised (Kloss 1969: 81). This dichotomy has set the trend in language planning studies for the past 25 years (as in Cobarrubias and Fishman, 1983; Laforge, 1987; Maurais, 1987; Weinstein, 1990; Marshall, 1991). However, corpus and status planning cannot be separated from each other. Care must be taken not to oversimplify the dichotomy. Language-planning policies can never be corpus-oriented or status-oriented exclusively. Another look at Québec's language-planning policy reveals that although the foremost aim was to promote the Francophones and build a new social image of French in order to improve its socioeconomic prestige, this was achieved in part by terminology planning using corpus-planning methods. In an evaluation study of terminological usage in commercial enterprises, I have shown that the social forces at work in speech communities at large are also at work in the micro-speech communities of enterprises. Norms develop about language and language use in much the same way in both types of speech communities, and these language norms are all about social prestige. As a result of terminology work in a firm, French technical terms may not be used with much higher frequency, but they gain legitimacy and workers at all levels develop favorable attitudes towards these terms (Daoust, 1991a, b; 1992, 1994). This example illustrates the effect of corpus planning on the status of a language.

3.5 *Implementation*

It is impossible to control all of the factors involved in language planning, social, political, and linguistic. Yet an overall implementation plan is the most promising precaution for avoiding haphazard results (Rubin, 1971; Cooper, 1989). The Norwegian case exemplifies the risks involved in the failure to design an implementation plan beforehand. Aasen's and Knudsen's proposed language norms gained recognition partly due to the nationalistic spirit of the time, and partly due to the fact that as schoolteachers they had access to the education system. When, by the end of the 1880s, the government took charge of language planning, it more or less adopted their diffusion method. As time went by, however, it developed a more formal implementation program, mainly through setting up language committees charged with the task of creating linguistic forms for each of the two official varieties of Norwegian. Having to deal with two competing varieties soon proved awkward and costly. In 1909 the government therefore undertook the risk of fusing the two into one. But this decision came too late, because the population was divided in its linguistic allegiance. In 1963 the government appointed a "language peace" committee which was to promote the dual linguistic heritage. This committee recommended the abandonment of the linguistic fusion policy (Haugen, 1983: 285). Thus the Norwegian government was forced to withdraw gradually from direct intervention. In a way, in spite of all the language reforms undertaken, Norway's implementation program was primarily focused on linguistic aspects, paying too little attention to the social side. The overall failure of the language reform policy exemplifies the fact that implementation of language planning decisions depends on nonlinguistic variables (Garvin, 1973: 24). As a result of his comprehensive investigation of this case, Haugen (1983: 275) proposed that the implementation phase be considered an educational process. This is what we see in his twofold descriptive model which accounts for both of the linguistic and the societal aspects of language planning.[11]

Table 27.1 Haugen's 1983 model of language planning.

	Form *(policy planning)*	*Function* *(language cultivation)*
Society (status planning)	1 Selection (of norm) (decision procedures) (a) identification of problem (b) allocation of norms	3 Implementation (educational spread) (a) correction procedures (b) evaluation
Language (corpus planning)	2 Codification (of norm) (standardization procedures) (a) graphization (b) grammaticalization (c) lexicalization	4 Elaboration[12] (functional development) (a) terminological modernization (b) stylistic development

The study of well-documented cases such as Norway's has helped to make implementation a built-in aspect of modern language planning policies. For example, the implementation process is specified in Québec's language law itself. The 1977 "Charter of the French Language" requires of large private enterprises that they obtain a "certificate of Francization" attesting that French is the language of work, or that the firm is implementing a "Francization program" aiming at satisfying the requirements of the law. The law stipulates the details of the administrative procedure involved in the Francization process of the firm from the moment it has to apply for the certificate, all the way to the content of the Francization program it must devise. Such a program requires: (1) knowledge of French by all personnel, including management; (2) use of French as a working language and in internal and external communication, whenever possible; (3) use of French in the firm's working documents, especially manuals and catalogues; (4) use of French in communication with clients, suppliers, and the public; (5) use of French terminology; (6) use of French in advertising; and (7) adoption of policies for hiring, promotion, and transfer which favor Francophones (article 141 of the law). In accordance with its exhaustive nature, the Charter specifies the mechanisms for the implementation of the policy. Three agencies were thus established to carry out the Francization mandate. One of these, the "Office de la langue française" (French Language Board), oversees the application of the law, and the design and dissemination of French terminology. All other domains covered by the law are dealt with in similar detail. As a result, although there were some complaints when the law was first enacted, the explicitness of the process helped its implementation and facilitated its acceptance (Bourhis, 1984; Daoust, 1984, 1990). Of course, the law made necessary the creation of a large administrative apparatus. Yet, in retrospect and in comparison with other language-planning projects, such as the Norwegian one, for example, the investment has paid off since there has been no social upheaval and the law has accomplished most of its objectives, at least from a socioeconomic point of view (Vaillancourt, 1993).

3.6 Evaluation

The last important component of language planning is evaluation. Remember that evaluation should be an integral part of the process, since language planning is a long-term future-oriented effort to change language and language use. Once a speech community has embarked on such an endeavor, there is no telling when it stops. Objectives must be periodically re-assessed, as well as implementation procedures. Since planned change usually interferes or at least intertwines with natural change, policies sometimes have to be adapted to new situations. For example, until recently no need was felt in France to protect the French language. However, under increased pressure from the spread of English, France in the early 1970s started to adopt measures for the defense of the French language. In 1972 Terminology Commissions were established, charged with the diffusion of French technical terms, and a law was enacted in 1975 to further prescribe the use of French in specific public domains. In 1994 the French government proposed yet another law regulating language use, requiring offenders to pay a fine. These measures come at a time when linguistic minorities all over the world seek to ascertain their linguistic rights. For example, in 1992 the majority of the members of the European Council adopted the European Charter of Regional and Minority Languages, thereby recognizing regional and minority languages as part of Europe's cultural heritage and committing themselves to adopt measures for the protection and promotion of these languages. At the same time the European Community faces the task of devising a language policy which must take into account the sociopolitical and economic needs of all its members. Minority protection is only one priority on its agenda (Coulmas, 1991a, b).

4 Conclusion

Language reforms rely on attitudes about language, on the shared norms of speech communities, both linguistic and sociolinguistic, and on nationalistic feelings and the resulting sociolinguistic dynamics relating to change. Change in linguistic behavior and in attitudes is what language planning is all about. However, in the long run, unguided sociolinguistic forces dictate the course of action. It is these forces that language planners must learn how to shape. Change is a time-related phenomenon, and in some ways, it is hard to evaluate its impact, and harder still to assess if it is to be attributed to language policies, which after all are only one of the factors shaping speech communities. In a sense, language-planning policies can best be evaluated through their symbolic impact. If it is true, as Cooper (1989: 184) claims, that language planning is more likely to succeed with respect to attitude than with respect to behavior, it must also be realized that, in the long run, it is attitudes which lead to change.

NOTES

1 See Lodge (1993) for a sociolinguistic type of analysis of the "birth" of French.

2 For an account of different studies whose results supports this assumption, see L. Milroy, 1987.

3 N.B. In a 1977 study, right after Québec had passed a linguistic legislation in favor of French, Bourhis has shown that English was still perceived as being prestigious by French-speaking Québecers (1984).

4 The 1988 edition of Grimes lists 6,170 different languages used throughout the world.

5 See Eastman (1983: 105–31) for an account of the evolution of language planning study.

6 As far as the other continents are concerned, the statistics are as follows: America has 6 official languages, 39 states, and 938 recorded languages; Asia has 37 official languages, 47 states, and 913 recorded languages; Africa has 16 official languages, 52 states, and 1,918 recorded languages; and

Oceania has 10 official languages, 17 states, and 1,216 recorded languages (Grimes, 1988; Leclerc, 1992: 56–9).

7   Actually, only a small number of the world's languages are used extensively. According to Leclerc (1992: 51–67), 9 percent of the world's population uses 3 percent of all languages, which means that some languages are used by very few people, so much so that more than 95 percent of all languages could be endangered.

8   See Fasold (1984: 292–315) for examples of nationalism–nationism conflicts.

9   For an analysis of Québec's legislation and language planning policy, see Daoust-Blais, 1983; Daoust, 1984, 1990; as well as Bourhis, 1984.

10 Wardhaugh (1992: 28–30) cites a few similar cases, among them the one about speakers of Cantonese and Mandarin, who say they share the same language although the two dialects are not mutually intelligible.

11 This is a revised model of his initial 1966 one which has served as an inspiration for most language planning scholars.

12 "Elaboration" corresponds more or less to what Neustupný (1970) calls "cultivation" although the latter seems to have a broader meaning in that it refers to the treatment of problems related to matters of correctness, efficiency, specialized functions, style, constraints on communicative competence, etc. (as seen in Rubin, 1973: 3–4). Haugen's notion refers more specifically to modernization of vocabulary and style.

Bibliography

Aasen, I. (1909) [On our language]. *Syn og Segn*, 12, 2–3. #20#

Abbeduto, L. (1984) Situational influences on mentally retarded and nonretarded children's production of directives. *Applied Psycholinguistics*, 5, 147–66. #23#

ABC (Australian Broadcasting Corporation) (1984) *Non-sexist Language Guidelines*. Sydney: ABC. #11#

ABC (Australian Broadcasting Corporation) (1989) *Thoughts that Glow and Words that Burn: An ABC Guide to Non-discriminatory Language*. Sydney: ABC. #11#

Abdulaziz, M. H. (1991) Language in education. A comparative study of the situation in Tanzania, Ethiopia and Somalia. In O. García (ed.), *Bilingual education. Focusschrift in honor of Joshua A. Fishman*, 75–86. Amsterdam: John Benjamins. #26#

Abou, S. (1987) Eléments pour une théorie générale de l'aménagement linguistique. In Lorne Laforge (ed.), *Proceedings of the International Colloquium on Language Planning*, May 25–29, Ottawa, 5–15. Québec: Presses de l'Université Laval. #21#

Abstracts (1986, 1988, 1990) *see* Le Page, R. B. (ed.) (1986 etc.) #1#

Abu-Haidar, F. (1989) Are Iraqi women more prestige conscious than men? Sex differentiation in Baghdadi Arabic. *Language in Society*, 18, 471–81. #8#

Achard, P. (1993) *La sociologie du langage*. Paris: Presses Universitaires de France. #Introd.#

Adam, H. M. (1980) *The Revolutionary Development of the Somali Language*. Los Angeles: African Studies Center, UCLA (Occasional Paper no. 20), 3–4. #20#

Adams, M. J. (1989) *Beginning to Read: Learning and thinking about print*. Cambridge, MA: MIT Press. #25#

Adamson, Lilian, and Rossem, Cefas van (1995) Creole literature. In J. Arends, P. Muysken, and N. Smith (eds), *Pidgins and Créoles*: An introduction, 75–84. Amsterdam and Philadelphia: John Benjamins. #14#

Adelaar, W. F. H. (1991) The Endangered Languages Problem: South America. In R. Robins and E. Uhlenbeck (eds), *Endangered Languages*, 45–91. Oxford and New York: Berg. #16#

Agheyisi, R. N. (1984) Minor languages in the Nigerian context: prospects and problems. *Word*, 35, 235–53. #16#

Agnihotri, R. K. (1979–82) *Processes of Assimilation: A sociolinguistic study of Sikh children in Leeds*. York: University of York D.Phil. diss. Ann Arbor, Michigan: U.M.I. #1#

Aitchison, J. (1991) *Language Change: Progress or decay*, 2nd edn. Cambridge: Cambridge University Press. #15#

Akinnaso, N. (1985) On the similarities between spoken and written language. *Language and Speech*, 28, 323–59. #10#

Al-Fayad, M. J. (1984) The importance of {the Arabic} language in human life. In S. Hamadi et al. (eds), *The Arabic Language and Arab Nationalism*. Beyrouth: Publications of the Center for Arabic Studies, 280–2. #20#

Alahdal, H. (1989) Standard and prestige: a sociolinguistic study of Makkan Arabic. PhD thesis, University of Reading. #3#

Albrecht, U. and Mathis, S. (1990) Die sprachlichen Verhältnisse in der Schweiz. In R. J. Watts und F. Andres (eds), *Zweisprachig durch die Schule / Le bilinguisme à travers l'école*, 71–81. Bern: Paul Haupt. #18#

Alexander, R. (1992) Fixed expressions, phraseology and language teaching. *Zeitschrift für Anglistik und Amerikanistik*, 40, 237–49. #22#

Alisjahbana, S. T. (1976) *Language Planning for Modernization*. The Hague: Mouton. #20#

Allen, C. (ed.) (1990) *Tales from the Dark Continent*. London: Futura. #6#

Alleyne, M. (1971) Acculturation and the cultural matrix of creolization. In D. Hymes (ed.), *Pidginization and Creolization of Languages*, 169–86. Cambridge: Cambridge University Press. #14#

—— (1980a) *Comparative Afro-American*. Ann Arbor: Karoma. #14#

—— (1980b) Introduction. In A. Valdman and A. Highfield (eds), *Theoretical Orientations in Creole Studies*, 1–17. New York: Academic Press. #14#

—— (1986) Substratum influences – guilty until proven innocent. In P. Muysken and N. Smith (eds), *Substrata versus Universals in Creole Genesis*, 301–15. Amsterdam: John Benjamins. #14#

—— (1994) Problems of standardization of creole languages. In M. Morgan (ed.), *The Social Construction of Identity in Creole Situations*, 7–18. Los Angeles: Center for Afro-American Studies, UCLA. #14#

Allsopp, R. (1958) The English language in British Guiana. *English Language Teaching*, 12, 59–66. #14#

Ammon, U., Dittmar, N., and Mattheier, K. J. (eds) (1988) *Sociolinguistics. Soziolinguistik. Ein internationales Handbuch zur Wissenschaft von Sprache und Gesellschaft*. Berlin and New York: Walter de Gruyter. #1#, #16#

Ammon, U., Mattheier, K. J., Nelde, P. H. (eds) (1990) *Sociolinguistica. International Yearbook of European Sociolinguistics 4: Minorities and Language Contact*. Tübingen: Niemeyer. #4#

Andersen, E. S. (1990) *Speaking with Style*. London: Routledge. #9#, #25#

Andersen, R. W. (1982) Determining the linguistic attributes of language attrition. In R. D. Lambert and B. Freed (eds), *The Loss of Language Skills*, 83–118. Rowley, MA: Newbury House. #15#

—— (1989) The "up" and "down" staircase in secondary language development. In N. C. Dorain (ed.), *Investigating Obsolescence: Studies in language contraction and death*, 385–94. Cambridge: Cambridge University Press. #15#

Andersen, R. W. (ed.) (1983) *Pidginization and Creolization as Language Acquisition*. Rowley, MA: Newbury House. #14#

Anderson, B. (1983) *Imagined Communities*. London: Verso. #18#

Andrzejewski, B. W. (1971) The role of broadcasting in the adaptation of the Somali language to modern needs In W. H. Whitley (ed.), *Language Use and Social Change*, 262–73. London. #11#

Ann Arbor decision: Memorandum, opinion, and order and the educational plan. (1979) Washington, DC: Center for Applied Linguistics. #7#

Annadurai, C. N. (1960) Open letter to party members, September 26, 1960. Subsequently [1981] published in his *Letters of an Older Brother to his Younger Brother*, 56–7. Madras: Paarinilayau. #20#

Annamalai, E. (1989) The language factor in code mixing. *International Journal of the Sociology of Language*, 75, 47–54. #13#

Anon. (1876) [Our Afrikaans nation and language], reprinted in G. S. Nienaber (ed.) (1974) *Die Afrikaans Patriot 1876: 'n Faksimilee-weergawe van die eerste Jaargang. 1876*, 35–7. Cape Town: Tafelberg. #20#

Anon. (1985) *The Fairest Flower: The emergence of linguistic national consciousness in Renaissance Europe*. Firenze: Accademia. #20#

Anon. (1987) *Letters to Gorbachev: New Documents from Soviet Byelorussia*, 2nd edn. London: Association of Byelorussians in Great Britain, 19–22. #20#

Appel, R. and Muysken, P. (1987) *Bilingualism and Language Contact*. London: Edward Arnold. #18#

Arana Goiri, S. (1886) El proyecto del Academia Bascongada. *Euskal-Erria*. n. 227/v. 14, 363. #20#

Ardener, E. (ed.) (1971) *Social Anthropology and Language*. London: Tavistock Publications. #1#, #4#

Arends, J. (1995) The sociohistorical background of creoles. In J. Arends, P. Muysken, and N. Smith (eds), *Pidgins and Creoles: An introduction*, 15–24. Amsterdam and Philadelphia: John Benjamins. #14#

Arends, J., Muysken, P., and Smith, N. (eds). (1995) *Pidgins and Creoles: An introduction*. Amsterdam and Philadelphia: John Benjamins. #14#

Arends, J. and Bruyn, A. (1995) Gradualist and developmental hypotheses. In J. Arends, P. Muyskens, and N. Smith (eds), *Pidgins and Creoles: An introduction*, 111–120. Amsterdam and Philadelphia: John Benjamins. #14#

Aronsson, K. and Rundstroem, B. (1989) Cats, dogs, and sweets in the clinical negotiation of reality: On politeness and coherence in pediatric discourse. *Language in Society*, 18, 483–501. #23#

Aronsson, K. and Saetterlund-Larsson, U. (1987) Politeness strategies and doctor-patient communication. On the social choreography of collaborative thinking. *Journal of Language and Social Psychology*, 6, 1–27. #23#

Artigal, J. M. (1991) Catalan and Basque immersion programs. In H. Baetens Beardsmore (ed.), *European Models of Bilingual Education*, 30–53. Clevedon: Multilingual Matters. #26#

Asad, T. (1980) Anthropology and the analysis of ideology. *Man*, ns 14, 604–27. #10#

Ash, Sh. (1988) Speaker identification in sociolinguistics and criminal law. In K. Ferrara et al., (eds), *Linguistic Change & Contact: Proceedings of the Sixteenth Annual Conference on New Ways of Analyzing Variation. Texas Linguistics Forum*, 30, 25–33. Austin: Department of Linguistics, University of Texas. #27#

Aston, G. (1988) *Learning Community: An approach to the description and pedagogy of interactional speech*. Bologna: Cooperativa Libraria Universitaria Editrice Bologna. #23#

Atiya, Aziz S. (ed.) (1991) *The Coptic Encyclopedia*. New York: Macmillan. #16#

Atkinson, J. M. and Drew, P. (1979) *Order in Court: The organisation of verbal interaction in judicial settings*. Atlantic Highlands, NJ: Humanities Press. #10#, #27#

Atkinson, M. and Heritage, J. (1984) *Structures of Social Action*. Cambridge: Cambridge University Press. #10#

Atkinson, P. (1992) *Understanding Ethnographic Texts*. London: Sage. #10#

Au, K. H. (1993) *Literacy Instruction in Multicultural Settings*. Orlando: Holt, Rinehart & Winston. #25#

Auburger, L. (1979) Zur Theorie der Sprachkontaktforschung: Ist die "Linguistique externe" keine "linguistique"? In L. Auburger and H. Kloss (eds), *Deutsche Sprachkontakte im Übersee*, 123–56. Tübingen: Narr. #17#

Auer, J. C. P. (1984). On the meaning of conversational code-switching. In J. C. Auer and A. DiLuzio (eds), *Interpretative Sociolinguistics: Migrants-children-migrant children*, 87–108. Tübingen: Niemeyer. #13#

—— (1995) The pragmatics of code-switching: A sequential approach. In L. Milroy and P. Muysken (eds), *One Speaker, Two Languages: Cross-disciplinary perspectives on code-switching*. Cambridge: Cambridge University Press. #13#

Auer, P. (1984) *Bilingual Conversation*. Amsterdam: Benjamins. #18#

—— (1991) Bilingualism in/as social action: a sequential approach to code-switching. In E.S.F. 1991b, II, 319–52. #1#

—— (1992) Introduction: John Gumperz's approach to contextualisation. In P. Auer and A. Di Luzio, *The Contextualisation of Language*. Amsterdam: John Benjamins. #10#

Auer, P. and Di Luzio, A. (1984) *Interpretive Sociolinguistics*. Tübingen: Narr. #1#

Auerbach, E. (1992) Literacy and ideology. *Annual Review of Applied Linguistics*, 12, 71–85. #25#

Austin, J. H. (1962) *How to do Things with Words*. Oxford: Oxford University Press. #25#

Axia, G., McGurk, H., and Martin, G. (1987) The development of social pragmatics: A cross-national study of the case of linguistic politeness. Paper presented at the Annual Conference of the Developmental Section, British Psychological Society, York, England (ERIC Document Reproduction Service no. ED287595). #23#

Azad, H. (1984) The Bangla language. Unpublished. #20#

Azuma, S. (1993) The frame-content hypothesis in speech production: Evidence from intrasentential code switching. *Linguistics*, 31, 1071–93. #13#

Bach, A. (1961) *Geschichte der deutschen Sprache*, 7th rev. edn [the first three of which appeared during the Nazi period]. Heidelberg: Quelle and Meyer. #20#

Backus, A. M. (1993) *Patterns of Language Mixing: A study of Turkish-Dutch bilingualism*. Weisbaden: Harrassowitz. #13#

—— (1996) Mixed discourse as a reflection of bilingual proficiency. In T. Hickey and J. Williams (eds), *Lanquage, Education and Society*. Clevedon and Dublin: Multilingual Matters and Irish Association of Applied Linguistics. #13#

Baetens-Beardsmore, H. (1993) The European school model. In H. Baetens-Beardsmore (ed.), *European Models of Bilingual Education*, 121–54. Clevedon: Multilingual Matters. #26#

Baetens-Beardsmore, H. and Lebrun, N. (1991) Trilingual education in the Grand Duchy of Luxembourg. In O. García (ed.), *Bilingual Education: Focusschrift in honor of Joshua A. Fishman*, 107–20. Amsterdam: John Benjamins. #26#

Baetens-Beardsmore, H. and Verdoodt, A. (1984) Les besoins en langues modernes/étrangères en Belgique et leur enseignement. *Courrier Hebdomadaire du Centre de Recherche et d'Information Socio-Politiques*, 1026–7, 1–39. #2#

Bailey, B. L. (1966) *Jamaican Creole Syntax: A transformational approach*. Cambridge: Cambridge University Press. #1#

Bailey, C.-J. N. (1973) *Variation and Linguistic Theory*. Washington, DC: Center for Applied Linguistics. #1#

Bailey, G., et al. (1991) The apparent time construct. *Language Variation and Change*, 3, 241–6. #5#, #9#

Bailey, R. W. and Görlach, M. (1983) *English as a World Language*. Ann Arbor, MI: University of Michigan Press. #7#

Baker, C. (1991) Bilingual Education in Wales. In H. Baetens Beardsmore (ed.), *European Models of Bilingual Education*, 7–29. Clevedon: Multilingual Matters. #26#

—— (1993) *Foundations of Bilingual Education and Bilingualism*. Clevedon: Multilingual Matters. #26#

Baker, C. and Freebody, P. (1989) *Children's First School Books*. Oxford: Blackwell. #22#

Baker, D. (1994) Democracy and Education. The cultural nature of numeracy. Proceedings of International Conference on Value in Education. Moscow. #10#

Baker, D. and Street, B. (1993) Literacy and numeracy; concepts and definitions. *International Encyclopedia of Education*, 3453–9. Oxford: Pergamon. #10#

Baker, P. (1982) On the origins of the first Mauritians and of the creole language of their descendants. In P. Baker and C. Corne (eds), *Isle de France Creole: Affinities and origins*, 131–259. Ann Arbor: Karoma. #14#

—— (1990) Column: Off target. *Journal of Pidgin and Creole Languages*, 5, 107–19. #14#

—— (1991a) Column: Causes and effects. *Journal of Pidgin and Creole Languages*, 6, 267–78. #14#

—— (1991b) Column: Writing the wronged. *Journal of Pidgin and Creole Languages*, 6, 107–22. #14#

Bakhtin, M. (1981) *The Dialogic Imagination*. Texas: Texas University Press. #10#

Bakhtine, M. (1977) *Le Marxisme et la philosophie du langage*. Paris: Editions de Minuit. #19#

Bakker, P. (1992) *"A language of our own," the genesis of Michif*. PhD dissertation, University of Amsterdam. #13#

Baldwin, J. (1979) If Black English isn't a language, then tell me what is? *New York Times*. July 29, section 4, p. E19. Reprinted in Geneva Smitherman (ed.) 1981. #20#

Balibar, R. (1993) *Histoire de la littérature française*. Paris: Presses Universitaires de France. #19#

Baltes, P. B., Reese, W. W., and Lipsitt, L. P. (1980) Life-span developmental psychology. *Annual Review of Psychology*, 31, 65–110. #9#

Bansal, R. and Harrison, J. (1983) *Spoken English for India*. Madras: Orient Longman. #11#

Baratz, J. (1968) Language and the economically deprived child: A perspective, *ASHA*, 10 (April), 143–5. #7#

Barbag-Stoll, A. (1983) *Social and Linguistic History of Nigerian Pidgin English*. Tübingen: Stauffenberg. #14#

Barbour, S. and Stevenson, P. (1990) *Variation in German: A critical approach to German sociolinguistics*. Cambridge: Cambridge University Press. #1#, #6#

Bardovi-Harlig, K. and Hartford, B. (1990) Congruence in native and nonnative conversations: Status balance in the academic advising session. *Language Learning*, 40, 467–501. #23#

—— (1993) Learning the rules of academic talk: A longitudinal study of pragmatic development. *Studies in Second Language Acquisition*, 15, 279–304. #23#

Barnlund, D. C. and Yoshioka, M. (1990) Apologies: Japanese and American styles. *International Journal of Intercultural Relations*, 14, 193–206. #23#

Baroni, M. R. and Axia, G. (1989) Children's meta-pragmatic abilities and the identification of polite and impolite requests. *First Language*, 9, 285–97. #23#

Barton, D. (1990) The Social Nature of Writing. In D. Barton and R. Ivanic (eds), *Writing in the Community*, 1–13. London: Sage. #10#

—— (1994) *Literacy: An introduction to the ecology of written language*. Oxford: Basil Blackwell. #6#

Barton, D. and Ivanic, R. (eds) (1991) *Writing in the Community*. London: Sage. #10#

Bates, E. (1976) Acquisition of polite forms: Experimental evidence. In E. Bates (ed.), *Language and Context: The acquisition of pragmatics*, 255–94. New York: Academic Press. #23#

Bates, E. and Silvern, L. (1977) Social adjustment and politeness in preschoolers. *Journal of Communication*, 27, 104–11. #23#

Bates, M. and Wilson, K. (1981) *Interactive Language Instruction Assistance for the Deaf*. Final report No. 4771. Cambridge, MA: Bolt, Beranek and Newman. #23#

Batibo, H. (1992) The fate of ethnic languages in Tanzania. In M. Brenzinger (ed.), *Language Death: Factual and theoretical explorations with special reference to East Africa*, 85–98. Berlin: Mouton de Gruyter. #16#

Batten, C. (1990) Dilemmas of "crosscultural psychotherapy supervision." *British Journal of Psychotherapy*, 7, 129–40. #23#

Baugh, J. (1980) A re-examination of the Black English copula. In W. Labov (ed.), *Locating Language in Time and Space*, 83–106. New York: Academic Press. #14#

Baumgardner, R. (1987) Utilizing Pakistani newspaper English to teach grammar. *World Englishes*, 6, 241–52. #11#

Baynham, M. (1993) Code-switching and mode-switching: community interpreters and mediators of literacy. In B. Street (ed.), *Cross-Cultural Approaches to Literacy*, 294–314. Cambridge: Cambridge University Press. #10#

BBC (British Broadcasting Corporation) (1979) *The Quality of spoken English. A report for the BBC by R. Burchfield, D. Donaghue, A. Timothy*. London: BBC. #11#

Beck, H. (ed.) (1989) *Germanische Rest-und Trümmersprachen*. Berlin: Walter de Gruyter. #16#

Becker, H. (1948) *Der Sprachbund*. Leipzig: Mindt. #18#

Becker, J. A. (1982) Children's strategic use of requests to mark and manipulate social status.

In S. Kuczaj (ed.), *Language Development: Language, thought and culture*, 1–35. Hillsdale, NJ: Erlbaum. #23#

—— (1990) Processes in the acquisition of pragmatic competence. In G. Conti-Ramsden and C. E. Snow (eds), *Children's Language*, 7–24. Hillsdale, NJ: Erlbaum. #23#

Becker, J. A. and Smenner, P. C. (1986) The spontaneous use of *thank you* by preschoolers as a function of sex, socioeconomic status, and listener status. *Language in Society*, 15, 537–46. #23#

Becker, J. A., Kimmel, H. D., and Bevill, M. J. (1989) The interactive effects of request form and speaker status on judgments of requests. *Journal of Psycholinguistic Research*, 18, 521–31. #23#

Beebe, L. M. and Takahashi, T. (1989a) Do you have a bag?: Social status and patterned variation in second language acquisition. In S. Gass, C. Madden, D. Preston, and L. Selinker (eds), *Variation in Second Language Acquisition: Discourse and pragmatics*, 103–125. Clevedon and Philadelphia: Multilingual Matters. #23#

—— (1989b) Sociolinguistic variation in face-threatening speech acts. In M. Eisenstein (ed.), *The Dynamic Interlanguage*, 199–218. New York: Plenum. #23#

Beetz, M. (1990) *Frühmoderne Höflichkeit. Komplimentierkunst und Gesellschaftsrituale im alt-deutschen Sprachraum* [Early modern politeness. The art of complimenting and social rituals in the old German area]. Stuttgart: Metzler. #23#

Befu, H. (1986) An ethnography of dinner entertainment in Japan. In T. S. Lebra and W. P. Lebra (eds), *Japanese Culture and Behavior*, 108–20. Honolulu, HI: University of Hawaii Press. #23#

Belazi, H. M., Rubin, E. J., and Toribio, A. J. (1994) Code switching and X-bar theory: The functional head constraint. *Linguistic Inquiry*, 25, 221–37. #13#

Bell, A. (1983) Broadcast news as language standard. *International Journal of the Sociology of Language*, 40, 29–42. #11#

—— (1984) Language style as audience design. *Language in Society*, 13, 145–204. #3#, #13#

—— (1991) *The Language of News Media*. Oxford: Blackwell. #11#, #22#

Bell, K. M. (1985) The relationship of gender and sex role identity to politeness in speech behavior. *Dissertation Abstracts International*, 45, 2678-B. #23#

Bemananjara, Z. (1987) Les langues et l'enseignement à Madagascar [Languages and education in Madagascar]. In L. Laforge (ed.), *Proceedings of the International Colloquium on Language Planning. Ottawa, May 25–29, 1986*, 307–14. Québec: Les Presses de l'Université Laval. #28#

Bentahila, A. (1992) Code-switching and language dominance. In R. J. Harris (ed.), *Cognitive Processing in Bilinguals*, 443–58. Amsterdam: Elsevier. #13#

Bentahila, A. and Davies, E. D. (1983) The syntax of Arabic-French code-switching. *Lingua*, 59, 301–30. #13#

Bentele, G. (1985) Die Analyse von Mediensprache am Beispiel der Fernsehnachrichten [The analysis of media language with special reference to TV news]. In Günter Bentele and Ernest Hess-Lüttich (eds), *Zeichengebrauch in Massenmedien* [Code usage in mass media], 95–127. Tübingen: Niemeyer. #11#

Bergman, M. L. and Kasper, G. (1993) Perception and performance in native and nonnative apology. In G. Kasper and S. Blum-Kulka (eds), *Interlanguage Pragmatics*, 82–107. New York: Oxford University Press. #23#

Bergsland, K. (1990) The Aleut Language of Alaska. In Dirmid R. F. Collis (ed.), *Arctic Languages: An awakening*, 177–84. Paris: UNESCO. #16#

Berk-Seligson, S. (1988) The impact of politeness in witness testimony: The influence of the court interpreter. *Multilingua*, 7, 411–39. #23#

—— (1990) *The Bilingual Courtroom: Court interpreters in the judicial process*. Chicago: University of Chicago Press. #10#, #22#, #27#

—— (1990a) Bilingual court proceedings: the role of the court interpreter. In J. N. Levi and A. G. Walker (eds), *Language in the Judicial Process*, 155–201. New York and London: Plenum Press. #27#

Bernstein, B. (1958) Some sociological determinants of perception: an inquiry in subcultural differences. *British Journal of Sociology*, 9, 159–74. #1#

—— (1960) Language and social class. *British Journal of Sociology*, 11, 271–6. #25#

—— (1971/1973) *Class, Codes, and Control. Towards a Theory of Educational Transmission.* London: Routledge and Kegan Paul. #Introd#, #22#

Berntsen, M. (1978) Social stratification in the Marathi speech of Phaltan. *Indian Linguistics*, 39, 233–51. #1#

Besnier, N. (1988) The linguistic relationship of spoken and written Nukulaelae registers. *Language*, 64, 707–36. #10#

—— (1994) The evidence from discourse. In P. Book (ed.), *Handbook of Psychological Anthropology*. Greenwood Press. #10#

Besnier, N. and Street, B. (1994) Aspects of literacy. In T. Ingold (ed.), *Companion Encyclopedia of Anthropology*. London: Routledge. #10#

Bettoni, C. (1985) Italian language attrition: a Sydney case-study. In M. Clyne (ed.), *Australia Meeting-Place of Languages*, 63–79. Canberra: Pacific Linguistics. #18#

Bhatia, T. K. and Ritchie, W. C. (1989) Special issue on code-mixing: English across languages. *World Englishes*, 8, 3. #13#

Bhattachariya, Divijen (1994) Naga Pidgin: Creole or creoloid? *California Linguistic Notes*, 24, 34–50. #14#

Bialystok, E. (1987) Influences on bilingual education on metalinguistic development. *Second Language Research*, 3, 154–66. #26#

Biber, D. (1988) *Variation Across Speech and Writing*. Cambridge: Cambridge University Press. #10#

Biber, D. and Finegan, E. (1993) *Sociolinguistic Perspectives on Register*. New York: Oxford University Press. #7#

Bickerton, D. (1971) Inherent variability and variable rules. *Foundations of Language*, 7, 457–92. #1#, #6#, #14#

—— (1975) *Dynamics of a Creole System*. Cambridge: Cambridge University Press. #1#, #14#

—— (1977) Pidginization and creolization: language acquisition and language universals. In A. Valdman (ed.), *Pidgin and Creole Linguistics*, 49–69. Bloomington: Indiana University Press. #14#

—— (1981) *Roots of Language*. Ann Arbor: Karoma. #14#

—— (1984) The language bioprogram hypothesis. *Behavioral and Brain Sciences*, 7, 173–88. #14#

—— (1984a) The language bioprogram hypothesis and second language acquisition. In W. E. Rutherford (ed.), *Language Universals and Second Language Acquisition*. Amsterdam: John Benjamins. #15#

—— (1986) Column: Beyond Roots: the five year test. *Journal of Pidgin and Creole Languages* 1, 225–32. #14#

—— (1987) Column: Beyond Roots: Knowing what's what. *Journal of Pidgin and Creole Language*, 2, 229–37. #14#

—— (1988) Creole languages and the bioprogram. In F. J. Newmeyer (ed.), *Linguistics: The Cambridge survey*. Vol. II. *Linguistic Theory: Extensions and implications*, 268–84. Cambridge: Cambridge University Press. #14#

—— (1991) On the supposed "gradualness" of creole development. *Journal of Pidgin and Creole Languages*, 6, 25–58. #14#

—— (1992) The sociohistorical matrix of creolization. *Journal of Pidgin and Creole Languages*, 7, 307–18. #14#

—— (1994) The origins of Saramaccan syntax: a reply to John McWhorter's "Substratal influence in Saramaccan serial verb constructions." *Journal of Pidgin and Creole Languages*, 9, 65–77. #14#

—— (1995) Development of pidgins and creoles: at last the facts! MS, presented to visiting Stanford Pidgin/Creole class at the University of Hawaii, Honolulu, May. #14#

Biondi, L. (1975) *The Italian-American Child: His sociolinguistic acculturation*. Washington, DC: Georgetown University Press. #9#

Black, M. (1959) Linguistic relativity: the views of B. L. Whorf. *Philosophical Review*, 68. Also in M. Black, *Models and Metaphors*. New York: Ithaca. #22#

Black English and the Education of Black Children and Youth. (1981) Center for Black Studies. Detroit: Wayne State University Press, 390–2. #20#

Bliss, L. S. (1992) A comparison of tactful messages by children with and without language impairment. *Language, Speech, and Hearing Services in Schools*, 23, 343–7. #23#

Blom, J.-P. and Gumperz, J. J. (1972) Social meaning in linguistic structures: Code-switching in Norway. In J. J. Gumperz and D. Hymes (eds), *Directions in Sociolinguistics*, 407–34. New York: Holt, Rinehart and Winston. #Introd.#, #1#, #5#, #13#

Bloome, D. (1993) Necessary indeterminacy and the micro-ethnographic study of reading as a social process. *Journal of Research in Reading*, Special issue: B. Street (ed.), *The New Literacy Studies*, 16, 98–111. #10#

Bloome, D., Pupo, P., and Theodorou, E. (1989) Procedural display and classroom lessons. *Curriculum Inquiry*, 19, 265–91. #10#

Bloomfield, L. (1933) *Language*. New York: Henry Holt. #14#

Blum-Kulka, S. (1987) Indirectness and politeness in requests: same or different? *Journal of Pragmatics*, 11, 131–46. #23#

—— (1990) You don't touch lettuce with your fingers: parental politeness in family discourse. *Journal of Pragmatics*, 14, 259–88. #23#

Blum-Kulka, S. Danet, B., and Gerson, R. (1985) The language of requesting in Israeli society. In J. Forgas (ed.), *Language and Social Situation*. New York: Springer. #23#

Blum-Kulka, S. and Sheffer, H. (1993) The metapragmatic discourse of American-Israeli families at dinner. In G. Kasper and S. Blum-Kulka (eds), *Interlanguage Pragmatics*, 196–223. New York: Oxford University Press. #23#

Boas, F. (1940) *Race, Language and Culture*. New York: Macmillan. #1#

Boeschoten, H. (1991) Asymmetrical code-switching in immigrant communities. In *Papers for the Workshop on Constraints, Conditions, and Models*, 85–100. Strasbourg: European Science Foundation. #13#

Bokamba, E. (1988) Code-mixing, language variation, and linguistic theory: evidence from Bantu languages. *Lingua*, 76, 21–62. #13#

Bolton, K. and Kwok, H. (1990) The dynamics of the Hong Kong accent: social identity and sociolinguistic description. *Journal of Asian Pacific Communication*, 1, 147–72. #6#

Bolton, K. and Kwok, H. (eds) (1992) *Sociolinguistics Today: International perspectives*. London: Routledge. #1#

Boretzky, N. (1983) *Kreolsprachen, Substrate und Sprachwandel*. Wiesbaden: Harrassowitz. #14#

Bortoni-Ricardo, S. M. (1985) *The Urbanisation of Rural Dialect Speakers: A sociolinguistic study in Brazil*. Cambridge: Cambridge University Press. #1#, #3#

Bott, E. (1957) *Family and Social Network*. London: Tavistock. #9#

Bouchard, P. (ed.) (1993) *Les actes du colloque sur la situation linguistique au Québec* [Proceedings of the Colloquium on the Linguistic Situation in Québec]. Québec: Government of Québec, Office de la langue française. #28#

Bourdieu, P. (1977) *Outline of a Theory of Practice*. Cambridge: Cambridge University Press. #Introd.#, #10#

—— (1982) *Ce que parler veut dire. L'économie des échanges linguistiques* [What Speaking Means. Linguistic Exchanges in a Socio-Economic Perspective]. Paris: Fayard. #28#

—— (1987) *Die feinen Unterschiede*. Frankfurt am Main: Suhrkamp. #8#

—— (1991) *Language and Symbolic Power*. London: Polity Press. #10#

Bourhis, R. Y. (1984) The Charter of the French Language and cross-cultural communication in Montreal. In R. Y. Bourhis (ed.), *Conflict and Language Planning in Quebec*, 174–204. Clevedon: Multilingual Matters. #28#

Bourhis, R. Y. (ed.) (1984) *Conflict and Language Planning in Quebec*. Clevedon: Multilingual Matters. #28#

Bouvier, J. C. (1973) Les paysans dromois devant les parlers locaux. *Ethnologie Française*, 3, 229–34. #6#

Boxer, D. (1993) Social distance and speech behavior: the case of indirect complaints. *Journal of Pragmatics*, 19, 103–25. #23#

Boyd, S., Berggren, H., Anderson, P., and Juntilla, J. H. (1992) Minority and majority language use among four immigrant groups in the Nordic region. Paper presented at the International Conference on Maintenance and Loss of Minority Languages, Noordwijkerhout. #18#

Boyer, R. (1993) Economies et finances internationales, le temps des nations n'est pas fini [International economies and finances: nation-states are not over]. In *L'état du monde 1994. Annuaire économique et géopolitique mondial* [The State of the World 1994. World's Economical and Geopolitical Yearbook], 573–6. Montreal: Editions La Découverte, Editions du Boréal. #28#

Braithwaite, E. K. (1984) *History of the Voice: The development of nation language in Anglophone Caribbean poetry*. London: New Beacon Books. #14#

Bratt Paulston, C. (1994) *Linguistic Minorities in Multilingual Settings*. Amsterdam: Benjamins. #18#

Bremer, K., Broeder, P. Roberts, Simonot, M., and Vasseur, M. (1996) *The Making of Understanding*. London: Longman. #10#

Brenzinger, M. (1992) Patterns of language shift in East Africa. In Robert Herbert (ed.) *Language and Society in Africa*, 287–303. Cape Town: Witwatersrand University Press. #16#

—— (1994) Language loyalty and social environment. In T. Geider and R. Kastenholz (eds), *Sprachen und Sprachzeugnisse in Afrika: Eine Sammlung philologischer Beiträge W. J. G. Möhlig zum 60. Geburtstag zugeeignet*, 107–15. Köln: Rüdiger Köppe. #16#

Brenzinger, M. (ed.) (1992) *Language Death: Factual and theoretical explorations with special reference to East Africa*. Berlin: Mouton de Gruyter. #16#

Brenzinger, M., Heine, B., and Sommer, G. (1991) Language death in Africa. In Robert H. Robins and Eugenius M. Uhlenbeck (eds), *Endangered Languages*, 19–44. Oxford and New York: Berg. #16#

Bresnahan, M. I. (1993) Gender difference in initiating requests for help. *Text*, 13, 7. #23#

Breton, R. (1990) Indices numériques et représentations graphiques de la dynamique des langues. In L. Laforge and G. D. McConnell (eds), *Diffusion des langues et changement social. Dynamique et mesure*, 211–20. Sainte-Foy: Les Presses de l'Université Laval. #17#

Breuilly, J. (1993) *Nationalism and the State*, 2nd edn. Chicago: University of Chicago Press. #20#

Bright, W. (ed.) (1966) *Sociolinguistics*. The Hague: Mouton. #1#

Bright, W. and Ramanujan, A. K. (1964) Sociolinguistic variation and language. In H. Lunt (ed.), *Proceedings of the 9th International Congress of Linguists, Cambridge, Massachusetts*, 1107–12. The Hague: Mouton.

Britto, F. (1986) *Diglossia: A study of the theory with application to Tamil*. Washington, DC: Georgetown University Press. #12#

Broch, I. and Jahr, E. H. (1984) Russenorsk: a new look at the Russo-Norwegian pidgin in Northern Norway. In P. S. Ureland and I. Clarkson (eds), *Scandinavian Language Contacts*, 21–65. Cambridge: Cambridge University Press. #14#

Brouwer, D. (1982) The influence of the addressee's sex on politeness in language use. *Linguistics*, 20, 697–711. #23#

Brouwer, D., Gerritsen, M., and De Haan, D. (1979) Speech differences between women and men: on the wrong track? *Language in Society*, 8, 33–50. #23#

Brown, P. (1980) How and why are women more polite: some evidence from a Mayan community. In S. McConnell-Ginet, R. Borker, and N. Furman (eds), *Women and Language in Literature and Society*, 111–36. New York: Praeger. #23#

Brown, P. and Levinson, S. D. (1978) Politeness: some universals in language usage. In E. N. Goody (ed.), *Questions and Politeness: Strategies in social interaction*, 56–289. Cambridge: Cambridge University Press. #23#

—— (1987) *Politeness: Some universals in language usage*. Cambridge: Cambridge University Press. #23#

Brown, R. (1973) *A First Language: The first stages*. Cambridge, MA: Harvard University Press. #7#

Brown, R. and Gilman, A. (1960) The pronouns of power and solidarity. In T. A. Sebeok (ed.), *Style and Language*, reprinted in R. Brown (1970). *Psycholinguistics*, 302–35. New York: Free Press. #1#, #12#

—— (1989) Politeness theory and Shakespeare's four major tragedies. *Language in Society*, 18, 159–212. #23#

Bruyn, A. and Veenstra, T. (1993). The creolization of Dutch. *Journal of Pidgin and Creole Languages*, 8, 29–80. #14#

Bryan, A. and Gallois, C. (1992) Rules about assertion in the workplace: effect of status and message type. *Australian Journal of Psychology*, 44, 51–9. #23#

Bucher, H.-J. and Strassner, E. (eds) (1991) *Mediensprachen, Medienkommunikation, Medienkritik* [Media languages, media communication, critiques of the media]. Tübingen: Narr. #11#

Bugge, S. (1899) [On the language conflict]. Subsequently published, 1907, in his [*Popular Scientific Talks*], 114. Kristiana [=Oslo]: Aschehoug. #20#

Burger, H. (1990) *Sprache der Massenmedien* [Language of mass media], 2nd edn. Berlin: de Gruyter. #11#

Burgoon, M. (1990) Language and Social Influence. In Howard Giles and Peter W. Robinson (eds), *Handbook of Language and Social Psychology*, 51–72. New York: John Wiley. #8#

Burstein, J. (1989) Politeness strategies and gender expectations. *CUNY Forum: Papers in Linguistics*, 14, 31–7. #23#

Calvet, L.-J. (1974) *Linguistique et colonialisme: petit traité de glottophagie*. Paris: Payot. #16#

Cameron, D. (1985) *Feminism and Linguistic Theory*. 2nd edn, 1992. London: Macmillan, #8#, #10#, #22#

—— (1990) Demythologizing sociolinguistics: why language does not reflect society. In J. E. Joseph and T. J. Taylor (eds), *Ideologies of Language*, 79–93. London: Routledge. #1#, #3#

—— (1990a) Introduction. In Jennifer Coates and Deborah Cameron (eds), *Women in their Speech Communities: New perspectives on language and sex*, 3–12. New York: Longman. #8#

—— (1992) *Feminism and linguistic theory*, 2nd edn. London: Macmillan. #22#

Cameron, D. and Coates, J. (1990) Some problems in the sociolinguistic explanation of sex differences. In Jennifer Coates and Deborah Cameron (eds), *Women in their Speech Communities: New perspectives on Language and Sex*, 13–26. New York: Longman. #8#

Cameron, D., Frazer E., Harvey, P., Rampton, B. and Richardson, K. (1992) *Researching Language: Issues of power and method*. London: Routledge. #10#

—— (1993) Ethics, advocacy and empowerment: issues of method in researching language. *Language and Communication*, 13, 81–94. #15#

Camitta, M. (1993) Vernacular writing: varieties of literacy among Philadelphia high school students. In B. Street (ed.), *Cross-Cultural Approaches to Literacy*. Cambridge: Cambridge University Press. #10#

Campbell, L. and Muntzel, M. C. (1989) The structural consequences of language death. In N. C. Dorian (ed.), *Investigating Obsolescence: Studies in language contraction and death*, 181–96. Cambridge: Cambridge University Press. #15#

Camras, L. A., Pristo, T. M., and Brown, M. J. K. (1985) Directive choice by children and adults: affect, situation, and linguistic politeness. *Merrill-Palmer Quarterly*, 31, 19–31. #23#

Canale, M., Mougeon, R., and Klokeid T. (1982) Forensic linguistics? *Canadian Journal of Linguistics*, 27, 150–5. #27#

Canale, M. and Swain, M. (1980) Theoretical bases of communicative approaches to second language testing and teaching. *Applied Linguistics*, 1, 1–47. #25#

Carden, G. and Stewart, W. A. (1988) Binding theory, bioprogram, and creolization: evidence from Haitian Creole. *Journal of Pidgin and Creole Languages*, 3, 1–67. #14#

Cardiff, D. (1980) The "serious" and the "popular": aspects of the evolution of style in radio talk 1928–1939. *Media, Culture and Society* 2, 29–47. #11#

Carrington, L. D. (1992) Column: images of creole space. *Journal of Pidgin and Creole Languages*, 7, 93–9. #14#

—— (1993) Column: Creoles and other tongues in Caribbean development. *Journal of Pidgin and Creole Languages*, 8, 125–33. #14#

Carrington, L. D. and Borely, C. (1977) The language arts syllabus, 1975: comment and counter-comment. St. Augustine, Trinidad: School of Education, University of the West Indies. #14#

Carver, C. M. (1987) *American Regional Dialects: A word geography*. Ann Arbor, MI: University of Michigan Press. #7#

Cashion, J. L. (1985) Politeness in courtroom language. Paper presented at the Annual Meeting of the Western Speech Communication Association. Fresno, CA (ERIC Document Reproduction Service No. ED254882). #23#

Cassidy, F. G. (1961) *Jamaica Talk: Three hundred years of the English language in Jamaica*. London: Macmillan, for Institute of Jamaica. #1#

—— (1970) Teaching Standard English to speakers of Creole in Jamaica, West Indies. In J. E. Alatis (ed.), *Twentieth Annual Round Table: Linguistics and the teaching of Standard English to speakers of other languages or dialects*, 203–14. Washington, DC: Georgetown University Press. #14#

Cassidy, F. G. and Le Page, R. B. (1967) *Dictionary of Jamaican English*. 2nd edn, 1980. Cambridge: Cambridge University Press. #1#

Cazden, C. B. (1979) Language in education: variation in the teacher-talk register. In J. E. Alatis and G. R. Tucker (eds), *Georgetown University Round Table on Languages and Linguistics 1979: Language in public life*, 144–60. Washington, DC: Georgetown University. #23#

—— (1988) *Classroom Discourse: The language of teaching and learning*. Portsmouth, NH: Heinemann. #10#, #25#

—— (1989) Contributions of the Bakhtin Circle to communicative competence. In *Applied Linguistics*, 10, 116–27. #10#

—— (1992) *Whole Language Plus: Essays on literacy in the United States and New Zealand*. New York: Teacher College Press. #25#

Cazden, C. B. and Snow, C. E. (eds) (1990) *English Plus: Issues in bilingual education*, 9–11. London: Sage. #26#

Cedergren, H. (1984) Panama revisited: sound change in real time. *Paper presented at Conference on New Ways of Analyzing Variation. Philadelphia: University of Pennsylvania.* #9#

Cedergren, H. and Sankoff, D. (1974) Variable rules: performance as a statistical reflection of competence. *Language*, 50, 333–55. #1#, #3#

Center for Applied Linguistics (n.d.) "The Ann Arbor Decision: Memorandum Opinion and Order & The Educational Plan." Arlington, VA: Center for Applied Linguistics. #27#

Chafe, W. (1982) Integration and involvement in speaking, writing and oral literature. In D. Tannen (ed.), *Spoken and Written Language: Exploring orality and literacy*. New Jersey: Ablex. #10#

Chaika, E. (1982) *Language: The Social Mirror*. New York: Harper and Collins. #Introd.#

Chakar, S. (1984) *Textes en linguistique berbere*, 35–7. Paris: CNRS. #20#

Chambers, J. (1993) Vernacular roots. Paper presented at NWAV 22, Ottawa, Canada. #7#

Chambers, J. K. (1990) Forensic dialectology and the Bear Island land claim. In R. W. Rieber and W. A. Stewart (eds), *The Language Scientist as Expert in the Legal Setting: Issues in Forensic Linguistics. [Annals of the New York Academy of Sciences*, 606], 19–31. New York: New York Academy of Sciences. #27#

—— (1992) Linguistic Correlates and Gender in Sex. *English World Wide*, 2, 173–218. #8#

—— (1992a) Dialect acquisition. *Language*, 68, 673–705. #9#

Chambers, J. K. (1994) *Sociolinguistic Theory*. Oxford: Blackwell. #Introd.#

Chambers, J. K. and Trudgill, P. (1980) *Dialectology*. Cambridge: Cambridge University Press. #1#, #3#, #6#

Charter of the French Language (1977). Ottawa: Queen's Printer. #18#

Chen, V. (1990/91) *Mien tze* at the Chinese dinner table: a study of the interactional accomplishment of face. *Research on Language and Social Interaction*, 24, 109–40. #23#

Cherry, R. D. (1988) Politeness in written persuasion. *Journal of Pragmatics*, 12, 63–81. #23#

Cheshire, J. (1982) *Variation in an English Dialect: A sociolinguistic study*. Cambridge: Cambridge University Press. #1#, #6#, #7#, #9#

—— (1983) The relationship between language and sex in English. In P. Trudgill (ed.), *Applied Sociolinguistics*, 33–49. London: Academic Press. #6#

Cheshire, J. (ed.) (1991) *English Around the World: Sociolinguistic perspectives*. Cambridge: Cambridge University Press. #8#

Cheshire, J. and Gardner-Chloros, P. (in press) Code switching and the sociolinguistic gender pattern. #8#

Chick, K. (1986) Interactional perspectives on the linguistic needs of Zulu work seekers. *Journal of Multilingual and Multicultural Development*, 7, 479–91. #23#

—— (1989) Intercultural miscommunication as a source of friction in the workplace and in educational settings in South Africa. In O. García and R. Otheguy (eds), *English across Cultures, Cultures across English: A reader in cross-cultural communication*, 139–60. Berlin: Mouton de Gruyter. #23#

Chomsky, N. (1957) *Syntactic Structures*. The Hague: Mouton. #1#

—— (1965) *Aspects of the Theory of Syntax*. Cambridge, MA: MIT Press. #25#

—— (1966) *Cartesian Linguistics*. New York: Harper and Row. #1#

—— (1992). On the nature, use and acquisition of language. In Martin Pütz (ed.), *Thirty Years of Linguistic Evolution*, 3–29. Amsterdam and Philadelphia: Benjamins. #17#

Chou En-lai (1958) Current tasks of reforming the written language. *Reform of the Chinese Written Language*. Peking: Foreign Language Press, 14–17. #20#

Churchill, W. S. (1908) The joys of writing. In Robert Rhodes James (ed.), *Winston S. Churchill: His Complete Speeches 1897–1963, vol. 1: 1897–1908*. New York and London: Bowker, 904. #20#

Cicourel, A. V. (1991) Theoretical and methodological suggestions for using discourse to recreate aspects of social structure. In A. Grimshaw et al., *What's Going on Here: Complementary studies of professional talk*. Norwood, NJ: Ablex. #Introd.#

Ciliberti, A. (1993) The personal and the cultural in interactive styles. *Journal of Pragmatics*, 20, 1–25. #23#

Claessen, J. F., van Galen, A. M., Oud-de Glas, M. M. (1978) De behoeften aan moderne vreemde talen. Een onderzoek onder bedrijven en overheidsdiensten. (Foreign language needs. A survey in industry and governmental departments). Nijmegen: Instituut voor toegepaste sociologie. #2#

—— (1978a) De behoeften aan moderne vreemde talen. Een onderzoek onder studenten en stafleden van universiteiten en hogescholen. (Foreign language needs. A survey of students and staff of universities and schools of higher education). Nijmegen: Instituut voor toegepaste sociologie. #2#

—— (1978b) De behoeften aan moderne vreemde talen. Een onderzoek onder leerlingen, oudleerlingen en scholen (Foreign language needs. A survey of pupils, ex-pupils and schools). Nijmegen: Instituut voor toegepaste sociologie. #2#

Clammer, J. (1976) *Literacy and Social Change: A case study of Fiji*. Leiden: E. J. Brill. #10#

Clanchy, M. (1979) *From Memory to Written Record: England 1066–1377*. London: Edward Arnold. #10#

Clancy, P. M. (1986) The acquisition of communicative style in Japanese. In B. B. Schieffelin and E. Ochs (eds), *Language Socialization across Cultures*, 213–49. New York: Cambridge University Press. #23#

Clark, H. and French, J. W. (1981) Telephone goodbyes. *Language in Society*, 10, 1–19. #23#

Claus, M. (1983) *Lessing und die Franzosen: Hoeflichkeit – Laster – Witz* [Lessing and the French: Politeness – vice – joke]. Rheinfelden: Schauble. #23#

Clay, M. M. (1991) *Becoming Literate: The construction of inner control*. Portsmouth, NH: Heinemann. #25#

Clayman, S. (1990) From talk to text: newspaper accounts of reporter-source interaction. *Media, Culture and Society*, 12, 79–103. #11#

Clear, J. (1993) From Firth principles: computational tools for the study of collocation. In M. Baker, G. Francis, and E. Tognini-Bonelli (eds), *Text and Technology*, 271–92. Amsterdam: Benjamins. #22#

Clermont, J. and Cedergren, H. (1979) Les "R" de ma mère sont perdus dans l'air. In P. Thibault (ed.), *Le français parlé: Etudes sociolinguistiques*, 13–28. Edmonton: Linguistic Research. #9#

Clifford, J. (1990) Notes on field notes. In R. Sanjek (ed.), *Fieldnotes: The making of anthropology*. Ithaca, NY: Cornell University Press. #10#

Clyne, M. (1982) *Multilingual Australia*. Melbourne: River Seine. #16#, #18#

—— (1984) *Language and Society in the German-speaking Countries*. Cambridge: Cambridge University Press. #1#

—— (1987) Constraints on code-switching: How universal are they? *Linguistics*, 25, 739–64. #13#

—— (1991a) *Community Languages: The Australian experience*. Cambridge: Cambridge University Press. #8#, #18#

—— (1991b) Australia's language policies: Are we going backwards? *Current Affairs Bulletin* 68 (6), November, 13–20. #18#

—— (forthcoming) *English as a Lingua Franca at Work*. Cambridge: Cambridge University Press. #18#

Clyne, M., Ball, M., and Neil, D. (1991) Intercultural communication at work in Australia: complaints and apologies in turns. *Multilingua*, 10, 251–73. #23#

Coates, J. (1990) Introduction. In Jennifer Coates and Deborah Cameron (eds), *Women in their Speech Communities: New perspectives on language and sex*, 63–73. New York: Longman. #8#

—— (1993) *Women, Men and Language*. London: Longman. #25#

Coates, J. and Cameron, D. (eds) (1990) *Women in their Speech Communities: New perspectives on language and sex*. New York: Longman. #8#

Cobarrubias, J. (1983) Ethical issues in status planning. In J. Cobarrubias and J. A. Fishman (eds), *Progress in Language Planning: International perspectives*, 41–85. Berlin, New York, Amsterdam: Mouton. #28#

Cobarrubias, J. and Fishman, J. A. (eds) (1983) *Progress in Language Planning. International Perspectives*. Berlin, New York, Amsterdam: Mouton. #28#

COCADI (Coordinadora Cakchiquel de Desarollo Integral) (1985) *El Idioma: Centro de Nuestra Cultura*. B'okob': Departamento de Investigaciones. #20#

Cojti, D. (1990) Linguistica e idiomas Mayas en Guatemala. In Nora England (ed.), *Lecturas Sobre La Linguística Maya*, 1–27. CIRMA La Antigua Guatemala.

Cole, M. (1985) The Zone of Proximal Development: where culture and cognition create each other. In J. Wertsch (ed.), *Culture, Communication and Cognition*. Cambridge: Cambridge University Press. #10#

Collins, C. and Mangieri, J. N. (1992) *Teaching Thinking: An agenda for the twenty-first century*. Hillsdale, NJ: Erlbaum. #25#

Collis, D. R. F. (ed.) (1990) *Arctic Languages: An awakening*. Paris: UNESCO. #16#

Conley, J. M. and O'Barr, W. M. (1990) *Rules versus Relationships: The ethnography of legal discourse*. Chicago: University of Chicago Press. #27#

—— (1993) Legal anthropology comes home: a brief history of the ethnographic study of law. *Loyola of Los Angeles Law Review*, 27, 41–64. #27#

Connell, R. W. (1993 [1987]) *Gender and Power: Society, the person and sexual politics*. Oxford: Polity Press. #8#

Connor, W. (1994) *Ethnonationalism: The quest for understanding*. Princeton: Princeton University Press. #20#

Contact Bulletin. (1994) Summer, 11, no. 2. #28#

Cook, H. M. (1990) The role of the Japanese sentence-final particle *no* in the socialization of children. *Multilingua*, 9, 377–95. #23#

—— (1993) Social meanings of Japanese humble verb forms as used by government officials. Paper presented at the Fourth International Pragmatics Conference, Kobe, July. #23#

—— (1994) The use of addressee honorifics in Japanese elementary school classrooms. Paper presented at the 17th L.A.U.D. Symposium on Language and Space, Duisburg, March. #23#

Cook-Gumperz, J. (1986) (ed.), *The Social Construction of Literacy*. Cambridge: Cambridge University Press. #10#

Cooper, R. L. (1967) How can we measure the roles which a person's language plays in his everyday behavior? In L. A. Kelly (ed.), *The Description and Measurement of Bilingualism*, 192–208. Toronto: Toronto University Press. #18#

—— (1989) *Language Planning and Social Change*. Cambridge: Cambridge University Press. #20#, #28#

Cooper, R. L. (ed.) (1982) *Language Spread; Studies in diffusion and social change*. Bloomington: Indiana University Press. #16#, #28#

Cooper, R. L. and Fishman, J. A. (1974) The study of language attitudes. *Linguistics: An International Review*, 15, 5–19. #28#

Coulmas, F. (1989) Language adaptation. In F. Coulmas (ed.), *Language Adaptation*. London: Cambridge University Press. #Introd.#

—— (1991) European integration and the idea of the national language. In F. Coulmas (ed.), *A Language Policy for the European Community. Prospects and Quandaries*, 1–43. Berlin and New York: Mouton de Gruyter. #28#

—— (1992a) *Language and Economy*. Oxford: Blackwell. #16#

—— (1992b) Linguistic etiquette in Japanese society. In R. J. Watts, S. Ide, and K. Ehlich (eds), *Politeness in Language: Studies in its history, theory and practice*, 299–323. Berlin and New York: Mouton de Gruyter. #23#

Coulmas, F. (ed.) (1991) *A Language Policy for the European Community: Prospects and quandaries*. Berlin: Mouton de Gruyter. #27#, #28#

Coulthard, M. (1994) Powerful Evidence for the Defence. In J. Gibbons (ed.), *Language and the Law*. London: Longman. #10#

Coupland, J., Coupland, N., and Robinson, J. D. (1992) "How are you?": Negotiating phatic communion. *Language in Society*, 21, 207–30. #23#

Coupland, N. (1980) Style-shifting in a Cardiff work-setting. *Language in Society*, 9, 1–12. #1#

—— (1984) Accommodation at work: some phonological data and their implications. *International Journal of the Sociology of Language*, 46, 49–70. #13#

Coupland, N., Coupland, J., and Giles, H. (1991) *Language, Society and the Elderly*. Oxford: Blackwell. #9#, #23#

Coupland, N., Giles, H., and Wiemann, J. M. (eds) (1991) *"Miscommunication" and Problematic Talk*. London: Sage. #8#

Covato, L. G. (1991) The design of an adventure game authoring tool for exploring polite requests in an English as Second Language context. *Dissertation Abstracts International*, 53, 430-A. #23#

Cox, C. and Zarrillo, J. (1993) *Teaching Reading with Children's Literature*. New York: Macmillan. #25#

Craig, C. (1992a) A constitutional response to language endangerment: the case of Nicaragua. *Language*, 68(1). #15#

Craig, C. G. (1992b) Miss Nora, rescuer of the Rama language: A story of power and empowerment. In K. Hall, M. Bucholtz, and B. Moonwomon (eds), *Locating Power: Proceedings of the Second Berkeley Women and Language Conference*, 80–9. Berkeley, CA: Berkeley Women and Language Group. #15#

Craig, D. (1971) Education and Creole English in the West Indies: some sociolinguistic factors. In D. Hymes (ed.), *Pidginization and creolization of languages*, 371–92. Cambridge: Cambridge University Press. #14#

—— (1980) Models for educational policy in creole-speaking communities. In A. Valdman and A. Highfield (eds), *Theoretical Orientations in Creole Studies*, 245–66. New York: Academic Press. #14#

Cravens, Th. and Gianelli, L. (1993) Gender, class and prestige in the spread of an allophonic rule. (in press) #8#

Crawford, J. (ed.) (1992) *Language Loyalties: A source book on the official English controversy.* Chicago: University of Chicago Press. #27#

Crosby, F. and Nyquist, L. (1977) The female register: an empirical study of Lakoff's hypotheses. *Language in Society*, 6, 313–22. #8#, #23#

Crouzet, M. (1980) Polémique et politesse ou Stendhal pamphletaire [Polemic and politeness, or Stendhal as pamphleteer]. *Stendhal Club: Revue Internationale d'Etudes Stendhaliennes*, 23 (89), 53–65. #23#

Cummins, J. (1979) Linguistic interdependence and the educational development in bilingual children. *Review of Educational Research*, 49, 222–51. #19#

—— (1981) The role of primary language development in promoting educational success for language minority students. In California State Department of Education (ed.), *Schooling and Language Minority Students: A theoretical framework*. Los Angeles: California State Department of Education. #26#

—— (1984) *Bilingualism and Special Education: Issues in assessment and pedagogy*. College-Hall: #10#

—— (1986) Empowering minority students: a framework for intervention. *Harvard Educational Review*, 56, 18–36. #26#

—— (1988) From multicultural to anti-racist education: an analysis of programmes and policies in Ontario. In T. Skutnabb-Kangas and J. Cummins (eds), *Minority Education: From shame to struggle*, 127–57. Clevedon: Multilingual Matters. #26#

Curran, J. and Seaton, J. (eds) (1991) *Power without Responsibility: The press and broadcasting in Britain*. London: Routledge and Kegan Paul. #11#

Currie, H. (1971) A projection of sociolinguistics: The relationship of speech to social status. In J. V. Williamson and V. M. Burke (eds), *A Various Language: Perspectives on American dialects*, 39–47. New York: Holt, Rinehart and Winston. #Introd.#

Cushing, S. (1994) *Fated Words: Communication clashes and aircraft crashes*. Chicago: University of Chicago Press. #Introd.#

Cuxtil, D. C. (1990) Lingüística e idiomas Mayas en Guatemala. In N. C. England and S. R. Elliot (eds), *Lecturas sobre la lingüística Maya*, 1–25. Guatemala City: Centro de Investigaciones Regionales de Mesoamérica. #15#

Daal, L. (1963) [Flowers of the mouth] in his [*Harvest of Scraps*], 96. Curacao: Boekhandel van Dorp. #20#

Dabène, L. and Billiez, J. (1987) Le parler des jeunes issus de l'immigration. In G. Vermès and J. Boutet (eds), *France, pays multilingue*, vol. I, 60–78. Paris: L'Harmattan. #19#

Daminov, B. (1989) [*Uzbekistan's Language and Literature*], May 26, 2.#20#

Danet, B. (1980a) "Baby" or "fetus": language and the construction of reality in a manslaughter trial. *Semiotica*, 32, 187–219. #22#

—— (1980b) Language in the legal process. *Law and Society*, 14, 445–564. #27#

Dante Alighieri (c. 1300) *De vulgari eloquentia*. #1#

Daoust, D. (1984) Francization and terminology change in Quebec business firms. In R. Y. Bourhis (ed.), *Conflict and Language Planning in Quebec*, 81–113. Clevedon: Multilingual Matters. #28#

—— (1990) *A Decade of Language Planning in Quebec: A Sociopolitical Overview*. In B. Weinstein (ed.), *Language Policy and Political Development*. 108–30. Norwood, NJ, : Ablex. #28#

—— (1991a) Terminological change within a language planning framework. In D. F. Marshall (ed.), *Language Planning. Focusschrift in Honor of Joshua A. Fishman*. 281–309. Amsterdam: John Benjamins. #28#

—— (1991b) The Evaluation of Sociolinguistic and Terminological Change in a Commercial Enterprise. *Terminology Science & Research*, 2, 44–60. #28#

—— (1992) Le rôle du poste comme facteur de changement des habitudes terminologiques dans une entreprise privée montréalaise [Occupation as a factor of change in terminological behavior within a private Montreal enterprise]. *Revue de l'ACLA, Actes du 23e Colloque annuel tenu à l'Université de Moncton à Moncton* [ACLA Bulletin. Proceedings of the 23rd, Annual Colloquium held at Moncton University, Moncton], 14, 71–93. #28#

—— (1994) L'importance de quelques opinions et attitudes sur le comportement terminologique dans un millieu de travail [The role of opinions and attitudes on terminological behavior in the workplace]. In Office de la Langue française and Université du Québec à Chicoutimi (eds), *Les actes du colloque sur la problématique de l'aménagement linguistique (enjeux théoriques et pratiques). Colloque tenu les 5, 6 et 7 mai 1993 à l'Université du Québec Chicoutimi* [Proceedings of the Colloquium on Language Planning (Theory and Applications). Held on May 5, 6 and 7, 1993 at the Université du Québec in Chicoutimi] vol. 1, 137–77. Québec: Government of Québec. #28#

Daoust, D. and Maurais, J. (1987) L'aménagement linguistique [Language Planning]. In J. Maurais (ed.), *Politique et aménagement linguistiques* [Language planning and language policies], 5–46. Government of Québec, Conseil de la Langue française and Paris, Le Robert. Québec: Publications du Québec. #28##

Daoust-Blais, D. (1983) Corpus and status language planning in Quebec: a look at linguistic education. In J. Cobarrubias and J. A. Fishman (eds), *Progress in Language Planning: International Perspectives*, 207–34. Berlin and New York: Mouton. #28#

Das, S. G. (1963) In Lakshmi Chand (ed.), [*Hindi Language Movement*]. Allahabad: Hindi Sahitya Sammelan, Prayag, 288–9. #20#

Data, M. (1866) The Bangla language. [*Fourteen-lined Poems*]: *The Sonnets*. Calcutta: Sree Iswar Chandra Basu, 2. #20#

Davesne, A. (1933) *La langue française, langue de civilisation en AOF*. Saint-Louis. #16#

Davis, H. and Walton, P. (1983) Death of a premier: consensus and closure in international news. In Howard Davis and Paul Walton (eds), *Language, Image, Media*, 8–49. Oxford: Blackwell. #11#

Davis, L. (1971). Dialect research: mythology and reality. In W. Wolfram and N. S. Clarke (eds), *Black-White speech relationships*, 90–8. Washington, DC: Center for Applied Linguistics.

Dawkins, J. (1991) *Australia's Language: The Australian Language and Literacy Policy*. Canberra: AGPS. #18#

de Bot, K. and Schreuder, R. (1993) Word production and the bilingual lexicon. In R. Schreuder and B. Weltens (eds), *The Bilingual Lexicon*, 191–214. Amsterdam: Benjamins. #13#

de Bot, K. and Weltens, B. (1991) Recapitulation, regression, and language loss. In H. W. Seliger and R. M. Vago (eds), *First Language Attrition*, 31–52. Cambridge: Cambridge University Press. #15#

De Rooij, V. (1995) Variation. In J. Arends, P. Muysken, and N. Smith (eds), *Pidgins and Creoles: An introduction*, 53–64. Amsterdam and Philadelphia: John Benjamins. #14#

de Valera, E. (1980) In Maurice Moynahan (ed.), *Speeches and Statements by Eamon de Valera, 1917–1973*. Dublin, Gill and Macmillan. #20#

de Vries, J. (1985) Some methodological aspects of self-report questions on language and ethnicity. *Journal of Multilingual and Multicultural Development*, 6, 347–68. #2#

—— (1988) Statistics on language. In U. Ammon, N. Dittmar and K. Mattheier (eds), *Sociolinguistics*, 2, 956–61. Berlin: de Gruyter. #2#

DeCamp, D. (1958–9) The pronunciation of English in San Francisco. Part I, *Orbis*, 7, 372–91; Part II, *Orbis*, 8, 54–77. #1#

—— (1960) Four Jamaican Creole texts. In R. B. Le Page (ed.), *Jamaican Creole*, 125–79. London: Macmillan. #1#

—— (1961) Social and geographical factors in Jamaican dialects. In R. B. Le Page (ed.), *Creole Language Studies II*, 61–84. London: Macmillan. #1#

—— (1971a) Toward a generative analysis of a post-creole speech continuum. In D. Hymes (ed.), *Pidginization and Creolization of Languages*, 349–70. Cambridge: Cambridge University Press. #1#, #14#

—— (1971b) Introduction: The study of pidgin and creole languages. In D. Hymes (ed.), *Pidginization and Creolization of Languages*, 13–39. Cambridge: Cambridge University Press. #14#

Delisle, H. H. (1986) Intimacy, solidarity and distance: the pronouns of address in German. *Die Unterrichtspraxis*, 19, 4–15. #23#

Den Besten, H., Muysken, P., and Smith, N. (1995). Theories focusing on the European input. In J. Arends, P. Muysken, and N. Smith (eds), *Pidgins and Creoles: An introduction*, 87–98. Amsterdam and Philadelphia: John Benjamins. #14#

Denison, N. (1968) Sauris: a trilingual community in diatypic perspective. *Man*, 3/4, 578–92. #4#

—— (1971) Some observations on language variety and plurilingualism. In E. Ardener (ed.), *ASA Monographs 10: Social Anthropology and Language*, 157–83. London. #4#

—— (1977) Language death or language suicide? In W. Dressler and R. Wodak-Leodolter (eds), Language death. *International Journal of the Sociology of Language*, 12, 13–22. #4#, #16#

—— (1980) Heterogenität und Kompetenz. In K. Lichem and H.-J. Simon (eds), *Hugo Schuchardt (Schuchardt-Symposium 1977 in Graz)*, 7–25. Wien: Österreichische Akademie der Wissenschaften. #4#

—— (1981) Conservation and adaptation in a plurilingual context. In W. Meid and K. Heller (eds), *Sprachkontakt als Ursache von Veränderungen der Sprach- und Bewußtseinsstruktur*. Innsbruck. #4#

—— (1986) Sociolinguistics, linguistic description, language change and language acquisition. In J. A. Fishman et al. (eds), *The Fergusonian Impact*. Vol. 1: *From Phonology to Society*. Berlin: Mouton de Gruyter. #4#

—— (1987) Romanisches im Zahrerdeutsch. In G. A. Plangg and M. Ileiscu (eds), *Akten der Theodor Gartner-Tagung (Rätoromanisch und Rumänisch) in Vill/Innsbruck 1985 (= Romanica Aenipontana XIV)*, 255–62. #4#

—— (1990) Spunti teorici e pratici dalle ricerche sul plurilinguismo con particolare riferimento a Sauris. In L. Spinozzi Monai (ed.), *Aspetti metodologici e teorici nello studio del plurilinguismo nei territori dell' Alpe Adria*. Tricesimo: Aviani Editore. #4#

—— (1992) Repertoire and norm in pluriglossia. *Grazer Linguistische Studien*, 38, 43–71. #4#

—— (1992a) Endstation Sprachtod? Etappen im Schicksal einer Sprachinsel. In A. Weiss (ed.), *Dialekte im Wandel*, 139–56. Göppingen: Kümmerle Verlag (= Göppinger Arbeiten zur Germanistik, Nr. 538). #4#

Denison, N. and Tragut, J. (1990) Language death and language maintenance. In U. Ammon, K. J. Mattheier, and P. H. Nelde (eds), *Sociolinguistica. International Yearbook of European Sociolinguistics 4: Minorities and Language Contact*. Tübingen: Niemeyer. #4#

Deuchar, M. (1990) A pragmatic account of women's use of standard speech. In Jennifer

Coates and Deborah Cameron (eds), *Women in their Speech Communities: New perspectives on language and sex*, 27–32. New York: Longman. #8#

Deutsch, K. W. (1968) The trend of European nationalism. In J. A. Fishman (ed.), *Readings in the Sociology of Language*, 598–606. The Hague and Paris: Mouton. #28#

Devonish, H. (1986) *Language and Liberation: Creole language politics in the Caribbean*. London: Karia Press. #14#

Dewes, K. (1970) The Pakeha veto. *Te Maori*, 2, n. 6, 5. #20#

Dijk, T. van (1988a) *News as Discourse*. Hillsdale, NJ: Lawrence Erlbaum. #11#

—— (1988b) *News Analysis: Case studies of international and national news in the press*. Hillsdale, NJ: Erlbaum. #11#

Dillard, J. L. (1972) *Black English: Its history and usage in the United States*. New York: Random House. #1#, #14#

DiSciullo, A. M., Muysken, P., and Singh, R. (1986) Government and code-mixing. *Journal of Linguistics*, 22, 1–24. #13#

Dittmar, N. (1976) *Sociolinguistics: A critical survey of theory and application*, trans. P. Sand, P. A. M. Seuren, and K. Whiteley. London: Arnold. #1#

—— (1977) *A Critical Survey of Social Sociologuistics*. New York: St Martin's Press. #2#

Dittmar, N. and Schlobinski, P. (eds) (1988) *The Sociolinguistics of Urban Vernaculars. Case Studies and their Evaluation*. Berlin: Walter de Gruyter. #8#

Dixon, R. M. W. (1991) A changing language situation: the decline of Dyirbal, 1963–1989. *Language in Society*, 20, 183–200. #16#

Dorian, N. C. (1973) Grammatical Change in a Dying Dialect, *Language*, 49, 413–38. #16#

—— (1977) The problem of the semi-speaker in language death. *International Journal of the Sociology of Language*, 12, 23–32. #Introd.#, #15#, #18#

—— (1981) *Language Death: The Life Cycle of a Scottish Gaelic Dialect*, Philadelphia: University of Pennsylvania Press. #4#, #15#, #18#, #26#

—— (1986a) Abrupt transmission failure in obsolescing languages: How sudden they "tip" to the dominant language communities and families. In V. Nikiforidu, M. V. Clay, M. Niepokuj, and D. Feder (eds), *Proceedings of the Twelfth Annual Meeting of the Berkeley Linguistics Society*. Berkeley: Berkeley Linguistics Society. #15#

—— (1986b) Gathering language data in terminal speech communities. In J. A. Fishman, A. Tabouret-Keller, M. Clyne, B. Krishnamurti, and M. Abdulaziz (eds), *The Fergusonian Impact*. Vol. 2 *Sociolinguistics and the Sociology of Language*. Berlin: Mouton de Gruyter. #15#

—— (1987) The value of language-maintenance efforts which are unlikely to succeed. *International Journal of the Sociology of Language*, 68, 57–67. #15#

—— (1993a) A response to Ladefoged's other view of endangered languages. *Language*, 69, 575–9. #15#

—— (1993b) Working with endangered languages: privileges and perils. In *Proceedings of the XVth International Congress of Linguistics*, 11–22. Les Presses de l'Université Laval. #15#

Dorian, N. C. (ed.) (1988) *Investigating Obsolescence: Studies in Language Contraction and Death*. Cambridge: Cambridge University Press. #4#, #15#, #16#

Douglas, M. (1986) *How Institutions Think*. Syracuse, NY: Syracuse University Press. #10#

Downes, W. (1984) *Language and Society*. London: Fontana. #3#

Dressler, W. U. (1972) On the phonology of language death: Papers from the Eighth Regional Meeting of the Chicago Linguistic Society, 448–57. Chicago: Chicago Linguistic Society. #15#, #16#

—— (1988) Spracherhalt – Sprachverfall – Sprachtod. In Ulrich N. Ammon, Norbert Dittmar, and Klaus J. Mattheier (eds) *Sociolinguistics. Soziolinguistik. Ein internationales Handbuch zur Wissenschaft von Sprache und Gesellschaft*, 1550–63. Berlin and New York: Walter de Gruyter. #16#

—— (1991) The sociolinguistic and patholinguistic attrition of Breton phonology, morphology, and morphonology. In H. W. Seliger and R. M. Vago (eds), *First Language Attrition*, 99–112. Cambridge: Cambridge University Press. #15#

Dressler, W. U. and Wodak-Leodolter, R. (1977) Language preservation and language death in Brittany. *International Journal of the Sociology of Language*, 12, 33–44. #15#, #18#

Dressler, W. U. and Wodak, R. (1982) Sociophonological methods in the study of sociolinguistic variation in Viennese German. *Language in Society*, 3, 339–70. #8#

Dressler, W. U. and Wodak-Leodolter, R. (eds) (1977) *Language Death (= International Journal of the Sociology of Language 12)*. The Hague: Mouton. #4#, #16#

Drew, P. (1990) Strategies in the contest between lawyer and witness in cross-examination. In J. N. Levi and A. G. Walker (eds), *Language in the Judicial Process*, 39–64. New York and London: Plenum Press. #27#

Du Bellay, J. ([1549] 1939). In *The Defence and Illustration of the French Language*, trans. by Gladys M. Turquet, 100–4. London: J. M. Dent. #20#

Dua, H. (1992) *Aspects of the Theory of Language Planning*. Mysore: Central Institute of Indian Languages. #20#

Dubin, F. (1989) Situating literacy within traditions of communicative competence. *Applied Linguistics*, 10, 171–81. #10#

Dubois, B. I. and Crouch, I. (1975) The question of tag questions in women's speech: They don't really use more of them, do they? *Language in Society*, 4, 289–324. #8#, #23#

DuFon, M. A. (1992) Politeness in interpreted and non-interpreted IEP (Individualized Education Program) conferences with Hispanic Americans. *Master's Abstracts International*, 30, 25. (University Microfilms No. 1345950), Master's thesis, University of Hawaii, 1991. #23#

—— (1993) Referential and relational meaning in interpreted discourse. *Journal of Pragmatics*, 20, 533–58. #23#

Dumas, B. (1990) Voice identification in a criminal law context. *American Speech*, 65, 341–8. #27#

Durand, J. (1993) Sociolinguistic variation and the linguist. In C. Sanders (ed.) (1993b), *French Today: Language in its social context*, 257–85. Cambridge: Cambridge University Press. #6#

Duranti, A. and Goodwin, Ch. (eds) (1992) *Rethinking Context: Language as an interactive phenomenon*. Cambridge: Cambridge University Press. #8#, #10#

Durkheim, E. (1938) *The rules of sociological method*. New York: Free Press. #1#

Dutton, T. (1983) Birds of a feather: a pair of rare pidgins from the Gulf of Papua. In E. Woolford and W. Washabaugh (eds), *The Social Context of Creolization*, 77–105. Ann Arbor: Karoma. #14#

—— (1985) Police Motu: Iena sivarai (its story). Port Moresby: University of Papua New Guinea Press. #14#

Dzameshie, A. K. (1992) Motivations for the use of politeness strategies in Christian sermonic discourse. *Dissertation Abstracts International*, 53, 1143-A. #23#

E.S.F.: European Science Foundation Network on Codeswitching and Language Contact, Strasbourg 1990–91:
  (1990a) *Papers for the Workshop on concepts, methodology and data, Basel 1990*. #1#
  (1990b) *Papers for the Workshop on constraints, conditions and models, London 1990*. #1#
  (1990c) *Papers for the Workshop on impact and consequences, Brussels 1990*. #1#
  (1991a) *Papers for the Symposium on code-switching in bilingual studies, Barcelona*. #1#
  (1991b) *Theory, significance and perspectives*. 2 vols. #1#

Eades, D. (1994) A case of communicative clash: Aboriginal English and the legal system. In J. Gibbons (ed.), *Language and the Law*, 234–64. London: Longman. #27#

Eagleton, T. (1990) *Ideology: An introduction*. London: Verso. #10#

Eastman, C. (1983) *Language Planning: An introduction*. Chandler & Sharp Publishers. #28#

Eastman, C. M. (ed.) (1992) *Codeswitching. Journal of Multilingual and Multicultural Development*. Special issue, 13, 1–2. #13#

Eckert, P. (1980) The structure of a long-term phonological process: the back vowel chain shift in Soulatan Gascon. In W. Labov (ed.), *Locating Language in Time and Space*, 179–220. New York: Academic Press. #9#

—— (1988) Sound change and adolescent social structure. *Language in Society*, 17, 183–207. #9#

—— (1989) The whole woman: sex and gender differences in variation. *Language Variation and Change*, 1, 245–68. #7#, #8#

—— (1989a) *Jocks and Burnouts: Social categories and identity in the high school.* New York: Teachers College Press. #9#

—— (1994) *Identities of Subordination as a Developmental Imperative.* Palo Alto: Institute for Research on Learning. #9#

Eckert, P. (ed.) (1991) *New Ways of Analyzing Sound Change.* San Diego: Academic Press.

Eckert, P. and McConnell-Ginet, S. (1992) Communities of practice: where language, gender, and power all live. In Kira Hall, Mary Bucholtz, and Birch Moonwomon (eds), *Locating Power. Proceedings of the Second Berkeley Women and Language Conference*, 89–99. Berkeley, CA: Berkeley University. #8#

Economist (1994) Comédie française, July 9th, 32. #16#

Edelsky, C. (1977) Acquisition of an aspect of communicative competence: learning what it means to talk like a lady. In S. Ervin-Tripp and C. Mitchell-Kernan (eds), *Child Discourse*, 225–43. New York: Academic Press. #9#, #23#

Edmondson, J. A., Feagin, C., and Mühlhäusler, P. (eds) (1990) *Development and Diversity. Language variation across time and space. A Festschrift for Charles-James N. Bailey.* Arlington: The Summer Institute of Linguistics and the University of Texas. #4#

Edwards, V. (1986) *Language in a Black Community.* Clevedon: Multilingual Matters. #1#, #3#

—— (1990) The speech of British Black women in Dudley, West Midlands. In Jennifer Coates and Deborah Cameron (eds), *Women in their Speech Communities: New perspectives on language and sex*, 33–50. New York: Longman. #8#

Edwards, W. (1990) Social network theory and language variation in Detroit. Paper presented at the Eighth Sociolinguistic Symposium, Roehampton, London. #3#

—— (1992) Sociolinguistic behavior in a Detroit inner city black neighborhood. *Language and Society*, 93–115. #1#, #8#, #9#

Edwards, W. F. (1983) Code selection and shifting in Guyana. *Language in Society*, 12, 295–311. #14#

Ehlich, K. (1992) On the historicity of politeness. In R. J. Watts, S. Ide, and K. Ehlich (eds), *Politeness in Language: Studies in its history, theory and practice*, 71–107. Berlin: Mouton de Gruyter. #23#

Ehlich, K. (ed.) (1989) *Sprache im Faschismus.* Frankfurt: Suhrkamp. #22#

Ehret, Ch. and Nurse, D. (1981) The Taita Cushites. *SUGIA – Sprache und Geschichte in Afrika*, 3, 125–68. #16#

Eisenberg, A. R. (1982) Understanding components of a spontaneous use of politeness routines by Mexicano 2-year-olds. Papers and reports on Child Language Development, Stanford University Department of Linguistics, 21, 46–54. #23#

Eklundh, K. (1986) Dialogue processes in computer-mediated communication. *Linköping Studies in Arts and Sciences*. #10#

Elias, N. (1977) *Über den Prozess der Zivilisation.* Vol. 1. Frankfurt a.M.: Suhrkamp. [English translation: The History of Manners, Vol. 1: The civilizing process. New York: Random House, 1978]. #23#

Eliasoph, N. (1986) Politeness, power and women's language: rethinking study in language and gender. *Berkeley Journal of Sociology*, 32, 79–103. #23#

Ellis, R. (1992) Learning to communicate in the classroom. *Studies in Second Language Acquisition*, 14, 1–23. #23#

Emeneau, M. B. (1956) India as a linguistic area. *Language*, 32, 3–16. [Reprinted in D. Hymes (ed.) (1964), *Language in Culture and Society*, 642–53. New-York: Harper and Row. #12#

—— (1964) Oral Poets of South India – the Todas. In D. Hymes (ed.), *Language in Culture and Society*, 330–43. New York: Harper and Row. #12#

—— (1974) *Ritual Structure and Language Structure of the Todas.* Transactions of the American Philosophical Society, ns 64(b). #12#

Engel-Wodak, R. and Rindler-Schjerve, R. (1985) Funktionen der Mutter beim Sprachwechsel. Konsequenzen für die Primärsozialisation und Identitätsentwicklung. *Linguistische Berichte, Sonderheft.* #8#

England, N. (1992) Doing Mayan linguistics in Guatemala. *Language*, 68, 29–42. #15#

Enninger, W. and Haynes, L. (eds) (1984) *Studies in Language Ecology.* Wiesbaden: Steiner. #17#

Equipe Euromosaik (forthcoming). *Survey of Minority Speakers.* Brussels: Task Force Ressources Humaines of the European Union. #2#

Erchak, G. (1992) *The Anthropology of Self and Behavior.* New Brunswick, NJ: Rutgers University Press. #10#

Erickson, F. (1975) Gatekeeping and the melting pot. *Harvard Educational Review*, 45, 44–70. #10#

Erickson, F. and Shultz, J. (1982) *The Counsellor as Gatekeeper.* London: Academic Press. #10#, #23#

Eriksen, T. H. (1994) *Ethnicity and Nationalism: Anthropological perspectives.* Boulder, CO: Pluto. #20#

Eroms, H.-W., Gajek, B., and Kolb, H. (eds) (1984) *Studia linguistica et philologica. Festschrift für Klaus Matzel zum sechzigsten Geburtstag.* Heidelberg: Carl Winter. #4#

Errington, J. (1989) A muddle for the model: diglossia and the case of the Javanese. Unpublished MS. #10#

Ervin-Tripp, S. (1969) Sociolinguistics. In L. Berkowitz (ed.), *Advances in Experimental Social Policy*, 4, 91–165. New York: Academic Press. #1#

Ervin-Tripp, S. and Gordon, D. P. (1986) The development of children's requests. In R. E. Schiefelbusch (ed.), *Communicative Competence: Assessment and intervention*, 61–96. San Diego, CA: College Hill Press. #23#

Ervin-Tripp, S., Guo, J., and Lampert, M. (1990) Politeness and persuasion in children's control acts. *Journal of Pragmatics*, 14, 307–31. #23#

Ervin-Tripp, S., Nakamura, K., and Guo, J. (forthcoming) Shifting face from Asia to Europe. In M. Shibatani and S. Thompson (eds), *Essays in Semantics.* #23#

Ervin-Tripp, S., O'Connor, M., and Rosenberg, J. (1984) Language and power in the family. In C. Kramarae, M. Schultz, and W. M. O'Barr (eds), *Language and Power*, 116–35. Belmont, CA: Sage Press. #23#

Escure, G. (1992) Gender and linguistic change in the Belizian Creole community. In Kira Hall, Mary Bucholtz, and Birch Moonwomon (eds), *Locating Power. Proceedings of the Second Berkeley Women and Language Conference*, 118–31. Berkeley, CA: Berkeley University, #8#

Eun, H. L. (1987) Polite speech: a sociolinguistic analysis of Chaucer and the Gawain poet. *Dissertation Abstracts International*, 49, 493–A. #23#

Ewing, A. (1984) Polish-English code-switching: a clue to constituent structure and processing mechanisms. In J. Drogo et al. (eds), *Papers from the Regional Meeting of the Chicago Linguistic Society*, 52–64. Chicago: CLS. #13#

Extra, G. and Verhoeven, L. (1993) Community languages in cross-cultural perspective. In G. Extra and L. Verhoeven (eds), *Community Languages in the Netherlands*, 1–28. Lisse: Swets and Zeitlinger. #18#

Fairclough, N. (1985) Critical and descriptive goals in discourse analysis. *Journal of Pragmatics*, 9, 739–63. #10#

—— (1989) *Language and Power.* London: Longman. #10#, #22#

—— (1992) *Discourse and Social Change.* London: Polity Press. #10#

Fairclough, N. (ed.) (1992) *Critical Language Awareness.* London: Longman. #10#

Fardon, R. and Furniss, G. (eds) (1994) *African Languages, Development and the State.* London: Routledge. #20#

Fasold, R. (1970) Two models of socially significant linguistic variation. *Language*, 46, 551–63. #1#

—— (1984) *The Sociolinguistics of Society.* Oxford: Blackwell. #3#, #28#

—— (1990) *The Sociolinguistics of Language*. Oxford: Blackwell. #Introd.#, #3#

Fasold, R. and Shuy, R. W. (eds) (1970) *Teaching Standard English in the Inner City*. Washington, DC: Center for Applied Linguistics. #1#

Fausto-Sterling, A. (1985) *Myths of Gender: Biological Theories about Women and Men*. New York: Basic Books. #8#

Fellman, J. (1973) *The Revival of a Classical Tongue*. The Hague: Mouton. #20#

Fenstermaker, S., West, C., and Zimmerman, D. (1991) Gender inequality. In *Gender, Family, and Economy: The Triple Overlap*. London: Sage. #8#

Ferguson, C. A. (1959) Diglossia. *Word*, 15, 325–40. Reprinted in Dell Hymes, *Language in Culture and Society*, 429–39. New York: Harper and Row. #Introd.#, #1#, #12#, #14#, #28#

—— (1965) *Directions in Sociolinguistics: Report on an interdisciplinary seminar*. U.S. S.S.R.C., *Items*, 19, 1–4. #1#

—— (1966) National Sociolinguistic Profile Formulas. In W. Bright (ed.), *Sociolinguistics*, Proceedings of the UCLA Sociolinguistics Conference, 1964, 309–24. The Hague: Mouton. #21#

—— (1968) Language development. In J. A. Fishman, C. A. Ferguson, and J. Das Gupta (eds), *Language Problems of Developing Nations*, 27–35. New York: John Wiley. #28#

—— (1971) Absence of copula and the notion of simplicity: a study of normal speech, baby talk, foreigner talk and pidgins. In D. Hymes (ed.), *Pidginization and Creolization of Languages*, 141–50. Cambridge: Cambridge University Press. #14#

—— (1977) Baby talk as a simplified register. In C. E. Snow and C. A. Ferguson (eds), *Talking to Children*, 209–35. Cambridge: Cambridge University Press. #9#

—— (1983) Sports announcer talk: syntactic aspects of register variation. *Language in Society*, 12, 153–72. #11#

—— (1991) Diglossia revisited. In A. Hudson (ed.) (1991) Studies in diglossia. *Southwest Journal of Linguistics*, 10. #12#

Ferguson, C. A. and DeBose, C. (1977) Simplified registers, broken language and pidginization. In A. Valdman and A. Highfield (eds), *Pidgin and Creole Linguistics*, 99–125. Bloomington: Indiana University Press. #14#

Ferguson, C. A. and Gumperz, J. J. (1960) *Linguistic Diversity in South Asia. International Journal of American Linguistics* (Special Issue), 23, 3. #1#

Ferguson, C.A., Houghton, C., and Wells, M. H. (1977) Bilingual education: an international perspective. In B. Spolsky and R. Cooper (eds), *Frontiers of Bilingual Education*, 159–74. Rowley, MA: Newbury House. #26#

Fernandez, M. (1993) *Diglossia: A comprehensive bibliography, 1960–1990, and supplements*. Philadelphia: John Benjamins. #12#

Ferrara, K., Brown B., Walters K., and Baugh J. (eds) (1988) *Linguistic Change & Contact: Proceedings of the Sixteenth Annual Conference on New Ways of Analyzing Variation*. Texas Linguistics Forum, 30. Austin: Department of Linguistics, University of Texas. #27#

Figueroa, E. (1994) *Sociolinguistic Metatheory*. Oxford: Pergamon. #Introd.#

Fiksdal, S. (1988) Verbal and non-verbal strategies of rapport in cross-cultural interviews. *Linguistics and Education*, 1, 3–17. #23#

—— (1991) *The Right Time and Pace: A microanalysis of cross-cultural gatekeeping interviews*. Norwood, NJ: Ablex. #23#

Finegan, E. (1994) Ethical considerations for expert witnesses in forensic linguistics. *Issues in Applied Linguistics*, 4, 179–87. #27#

Finkenstaedt, Th. and Schröder, K. (1992) *Sprachen im Europa von Morgen*. Berlin: Langenscheidt. #16#

Finnegan, R. (1988) *Literacy and Orality: Studies in the technology of communication*. Oxford: Basil Blackwell. #10#

Firth, J. R. (1951) *Papers in Linguistics, 1934–1951*. London: Oxford University Press. #1#

—— (1957a) A synopsis of linguistic theory, 1930–1955. In *Studies in Linguistic Analysis*. Special vol., *Philological Society*, 1–32. #22#

—— (1957b) Ethnographic analysis and language. In R. Firth (ed.), *Man and Society in Culture*, 93–118. London: Routledge. #1#

—— (1965) *The Tongues of Men*. London: Watts. #1#

Fischer, J. L. (1958) Social influences on the choice of a linguistic variant. *Word*, 14, 47–56. #9#

Fisher, S. and Todd, A. (eds) (1983) *The Social Organisation of Doctor Patient Communication*. Washington: Washington Centre for Applied Linguistics. #10#

Fishman, D. et al. (1985) Am and goy as designations for ethnicity in selected books of the Old Testament. In A. Joshua D. Fishman et al., *The Rise and Fall of the Ethnic Revival: Perspectives on language and ethnicity*, 15–38. Berlin: Mouton de Gruyter. #20#

Fishman, J. A. (1965) Who speaks what language, to whom and when? *La Linguistique*, 2, 67–88. #17#

—— (1967) Bilingualism with and without diglossia; diglossia with and without bilingualism. *Journal of Social Issues*, 23, 2, 29–38. Revised and reprinted as "Societal bilingualism: stable and transitional." In *Sociolinguistics: A brief introduction* (1970), 78–89. Rowley, MA: Newbury House. #12#, #18#, #28#

—— (1971) *Sociolinguistics*. Rowley, MA: Newbury House. #28#

—— (1971) The sociology of language. In J. Fishman (ed.), *Advances in the Sociology of Language*, Vol. 1, 217–404. The Hague: Mouton. #1#, #26#

—— (1972) [1978] Language and Nationalism: Two Integrative Essays. Part I: The Nature of Nationalism. *Language and Nationalism*. Rowley, MA: Newbury House. Reproduced in J. A. Fishman (1989), *Language & Ethnicity in Minority Sociolinguistic Perspective*, 97–175. Clevedon and Philadelphia: Multilingual Matters. #Introd#., #28#

—— (1972) The sociology of language. An interdisciplinary social science approach to language in society. Rowley, MA: Newbury House. [Reprinted in Th. Sebeok (ed.) (1974), *Current Trends in Linguistics*, 12, 1629–1784. The Hague: Mouton.] #2#, #11#, #17#, #21#

—— (1976) *Bilingual Education: An international sociological perspective*. Rowley, MA.: Newbury House. #26#

—— (1977) The social science perspective: keynote. In J. A. Fishman (ed.), *Bilingual Education: Current perspectives*, 1–49. Washington, DC: Georgetown University. #18#

—— (1980) Minority language maintenance and the ethnic mother-tongue school. *Modern Language Journal*, 64, 167–72. #26#

—— (1980). Prefatory notes. In P. H. Nelde (ed.), *Languages in Contact and in Conflict*, XI. Wiesbaden: Steiner. #17#

—— (1985) *The Rise and Fall of the Ethnic Revival*. Berlin: Mouton de Gruyter. #18#, #26#

—— (1986) Nationality-nationalism and nation-nationism. In J. Fishman, C. Ferguson, and J. DasGupta (eds), *Language Problems of Developing Nations*. New York: John Wiley. #10#

—— (1987) Conference comments: reflections on the current state of language planning. In Lorne Laforge (ed.), *Proceedings of the International Colloquium on Language Planning*, May 25–29 / Ottawa, 405–28. Québec: Presses de l'Université Laval. #21#

—— (1988) Language spread and language policy for endangered languages. In Peter H. Lowenberg (ed.) *Language Spread and Language Policy: Issues, implications, and case studies*, 1–15. Washington, DC: Georgetown University Press. (Georgetown University Round Table on Languages and Linguistics 1987). #16#

—— (1989) *Language & Ethnicity in Minority Sociolinguistic Perspective*. Clevedon and Philadelphia: Multilingual Matters. #28#

—— (1992) *Reversing Language Shift: Theory and Practice of Assistance to Threatened Languages*. Clevedon: Multilingual Matters. #Introd.#, #15#, #18#, #20#, #26#

Fishman, J. A. (ed.) (1966) *Language Loyalty in the United States*. The Hague: Mouton. #12#

—— (1968, repr. 1972) *Readings in the Sociology of Language*. The Hague: Mouton. #1#, #12#, #17#, #28#

—— (1972) *Advances in the Sociology of Language*. 2 vols. The Hague and Paris: Mouton. #12#, #28#

—— (1974) *Advances in Language Planning*. The Hague: Mouton. #21#

—— (1978) *Advances in the Study of Societal Multilingualism*. The Hague: Mouton. #16#

Fishman, J. et al. (1966) *Language Loyalty in the United States*. The Hague: Mouton. #16#, #18#

Fishman, J. A. et al. (eds) (1986) *The Fergusonian Impact*. Vol. 1: *From Phonology to Society*. #4# Vol. 2: *Sociolinguistics and the Sociology of Language*. #12#. Berlin: Mouton de Gruyter.

Fishman, J. A., Cooper, R. L., and Conrad, A. W. (1977) *The Spread of English*. Rowley, MA: Newbury House. #26#

Fishman, J. A., Cooper, R. L., and Ma, R. (1971) *Bilingualism in the Barrio*. The Hague: Mouton. #2#

Fishman, J. A., Ferguson, C. A., and Das Gupta, J. (eds) (1968) *Language Problems of Developing Nations*. New York: John Wiley. #28#

Flett, H. (1979) Notions of eligibility to public housing. In S. Wallman (ed.), *Ethnicity at Work*. London: Macmillan. #10#

Foley, W. A. (1988) Language birth: the processes of pidginization and creolization. In F. J. Newmeyer (ed.), *Linguistics: The Cambridge survey*, Vol. 4, 162–83. Cambridge: Cambridge University Press. #14#

Forson, B. (1979) Code-switching in Akan-English bilingualism. PhD dissertation, UCLA. #13#

Fortes, M. (1984) Age, generation, and social structure. In D. I. Kertzer and J. Keith (eds), *Age and Anthropological Theory*, 99–122. Ithaca: Cornell University Press. #9#

Fortier, D'I. (1994) Official language policies in Canada: a quiet revolution. *International Journal of the Sociology of Language*, 105/106, 69–97. #18#

Foster, S. (1990) *The Communicative Competence of Young Children*. London: Longman. #25#

Foucault, M. (1980) *Power/knowledge*. Ed. C. Gordon. London: Harvester. #22#

—— (1982) The order of discourse. In M. Shapiro (ed.), *Language and Politics*. Oxford: Blackwell. #10#

—— (1984) Disciplines and Sciences of the Individual. In P. Rabinow (ed.), *The Foucault Reader*. London: Penguin. #10#

Fouché, P. (1959) *Traité de prononciation française*, 2nd edn. Paris: Klincksieck. #6#

Fowler, J. (1986) *The Social Stratification of (r) in New York City Department Stores, 24 Years after Labov*. New York University: MS. #9#

Fowler, R. (1991a) Critical linguistics. In K. Malmkjaer (ed.), *The Linguistics Encyclopedia*, 89–93. London: Routledge. #22#

—— (1991b) *Language in the News: Discourse and ideology in the press*. London and New York: Routledge and Kegan Paul. #11#, #22#

Fowler, R., Hodge, R., Kress, G., and Trew, T. (1979) *Language and Control*. London: Routledge and Kegan Paul. #10#, #11#

Fox, J. A. (1973) Russenorsk: a study in language adaptivity. MA paper, University of Chicago. #14#

Fox, T. (ed.) (1991) *The Challenge of Information Technology and Mass Media for Small Linguistic Societies*. *Education Media International* [special issue], 28 (3). #11#

Frank, J. (1988) A comparison of intimate conversations: pragmatic theory applied to examples of invented and actual dialog. *SECOL Review*, 12, 186–208. #23#

Fraser, B. (1990) Perspectives on politeness. *Journal of Pragmatics*, 14, 219–36. #23#

Freebody, P. and Welsh, A. (eds) (1993) *Knowledge, Culture and Power: International perspectives on literacy as policy and practice*. Brighton: Falmer Press. #10#

Freire, P. (1985) *The Politics of Education; Culture, power and liberation*. London: Macmillan. #10#

Freire, P. and Macedo, D. (1987) *The Politics of Education: Culture, power and liberation*. New York: Bergin and Garvey. #10#

Furnham, A. (1990) Language and personality. In Howard Giles and Peter W. Robinson (eds), *Handbook of Language and Social Psychology*, 51–72. New York: John Wiley. #8#

Gal, S. (1978) Peasant men can't get wives: Language change and sex roles in a bilingual community. *Language in Society*, 7, 1–16. #9#

—— (1979) *Language Shift: Social determinants of linguistic change in bilingual Austria*. New York: Academic Press. #Introd.#, #1#, #3#, #13#, #16#, #18#

—— (1989) Between speech and silence: the problematics of research on language and gender. In Micaela Di Leonardo (ed.), *Gender at the Crossroads of Knowledge: Feminist anthropology in the postmodern era*. Los Angeles: University of California Press. #8#

—— (1989) Language and Political Economy. *Annual Review of Anthropology*, 18, 345–67. #10#

—— (1992a) Concepts of power in the research on code-switching. In European Science Foundation (ed.), *Summer School on Code-switching*, 135–52. #13#

—— (1992b) Language, gender, and power: an anthropological view. In Kira Hall, Mary Bucholtz, and Birch Moonwomon (eds), *Locating Power. Proceedings of the Second Berkeley Women and Language Conference*, 153–61. Berkeley CA: Berkeley University. #8#

Galambos, S. J. and Hakuta, K. (1988) Subject-specific and task-specific characteristics of metalinguistic awareness in bilingual children. *Applied Psycholinguistics*, 9, 141–62. #26#

Galindo, L. and Gonzales Velasquez, M. D. (1992) A sociolinguistic description of linguistic self-expression, innovation and power among Chicanas in Texas and New Mexico. In Kira Hall, Mary Bucholtz, and Birch Moonwomon (eds), *Locating Power. Proceedings of the Second Berkeley Women and Language Conference*, 162–70. Berkeley, CA: Berkeley University. #8#

García, O. (1988) The education of biliterate and bicultural children in ethnic schools in the United States. *Essays by the Spencer Fellows of the National Academy of Education*, IV, 19–78. #26#

—— (1992) Societal multilingualism in a multicultural world in transition. In H. Byrne (ed.), *Languages for a Multicultural World in Transition*, 1–27. Illinois: National Textbook Company. #26#

—— (1993) Understanding the societal role of the teacher in transitional bilingual education classrooms: lessons from sociology of language. In K. Zondag (ed.), *Bilingual Education in Friesland: Facts and prospects*, 25–37. Leeuwarden, The Netherlands: Gemeenschappelijk Centrum voor Onderwijsbegeleiding in Friesland. #26#

García, O. and Otheguy, R. (1988) The bilingual education of Cuban American children in Dade County's ethnic schools. *Language and Education*, 1, 83–95. #26#

Gardner-Chloros, P. (1987) Code-switching in relation to language contact and convergence. In G. Lüdi (ed.), *Devenir bilingue-parler bilingue*, 99–115. Tübingen: Niemeyer. #13#

—— (1991). *Language selection and switching in Strasbourg*. Oxford: Oxford University Press. #1#, #4#, #13#

—— (forthcoming) Code-switching in community, regional and national repertoires: the myth of the discreteness of linguistic systems. #1#

Garvin, P. (1973) Some comments on language planning. In J. Rubin and R. Shuy (eds), *Language Planning: Current issues and research*, 24–33. Washington, DC: Georgetown University Press. #28#

Gauchat, L. (1905) L'Unité phonétique dans le patois d'une commune. In *Aus romanischen Sprachen und Literaturen: Festschrift Heinrich Morf*, 175–232. Halle. #9#

Gauthier, F., Leclerc, J., and Maurais, J. (1993) *Langues & Constitutions. Recueil des clauses linguistiques des constitutions du monde* [Languages and Constitutions. Compendium of the World's Linguistic Constitutions]. Québec: Les publications du Québec and Paris: Le Conseil international de la langue française. #28#

Gebreyesus, A. (1909) [*Menelik II, King of Kings of Ethiopia*] Original Rome edition reprinted 1967. Asmara: Il Poligrafico. #20#

Gee, J. (1990) *Social Linguistics and Literacies: Ideology in discourses*. Brighton: Falmer Press. #10#

—— (1992) *The Social Mind: Language, ideology and social practice*. New York: Bergin & Garvey. #10#

Geider, Th. and Kastenholz, R. (eds) (1994) *Sprachen und Sprachzeugnisse in Afrika: Eine Sammlung philologischer Beiträge W. J. G. Möhlig zum 60. Geburtstag zugeeignet.* Köln: Rüdiger Köppe. #16#

Gellner, E. (1983) *Nations and Nationalism.* Oxford: Blackwell. #10#

Genesee, F., Tucker, G. R., and Lambert, W. E. (1975) Communication skills in bilingual children. *Child Development*, 46, 1010–14. #26#

Gibbons, J. (1987) Code-mixing and code choice: A Hong Kong case study. Clevedon: Multilingual Matters. #13#

Gibbons, J. (ed.) (1994) *Language and the Law.* Longman: London. #10#, #27#

Gibbs, B. M. (1988) In S. Davenport (ed.), [*Waterholes Belong to Us*], 2. Port Hedland: Western Desert Puntukurnuparna and Pilbara Aboriginal Language Centre. #20#

Giddens, A. (1976) *New Rules of Sociological Method.* London: Hutchinson. #10#

—— (1989) *Sociology.* Cambridge: Polity. #3#, #8#

—— (1991) *Modernity and Self-identity.* Oxford: Polity. #22#

Giere, U. and Hautcoeur, P. (1990) *A Selective Bibliography on Literacy in Industrialised Countries.* Hamburg: Unesco Institute for Education. #10#

Giglioli, P. P. (ed.) (1972) *Language and Social Context.* Harmondsworth, Middlesex: Penguin Education. #28#

Giles, H. (1973) Accent mobility: a model and some data. *Anthropological Linguistics*, 15, 87–105. #19#

—— (1977) Social psychology and applied linguistics: Towards an integrative approach. *ITL: A Review of Applied Linguistics*, 33, 27–42. #19#

—— (1979) Ethnicity markers in speech. In K. R. Scherer and H. Giles (eds), *Social Markers in Speech*, 251–89. London: Cambridge University Press. #19#

—— (1980) Accommodation theory: some new directions. *York Papers in Linguistics*, 9, 105–36. #19#

Giles, H. (ed.) (1977) *Language, Ethnicity and Intergroup Relations.* London and New York: Academic Press. #28#

—— (1984) *The Dynamics of Speech Accommodation. International Journal of the Sociology of Language*, 46. #1#

Giles, H., Bourhis, R., and Davies, A. (1975) Prestige styles: the imposed norm and inherent value hypothesis. In W. McCormack and S. Wurm (eds), *Language in Many Ways.* The Hague: Mouton. #10#

Giles, H., Bourhis, R. Y., and Taylor, D. M. (1977) Towards a theory of language in ethnic group relations. In H. Giles (ed.), *Language, Ethnicity and Intergroup Relations*, 307–48. London: Academic Press. #Introd.#, #18#, #21#

Giles, H. and Byrne, J. L. (1982) An intergroup approach to second language acquisition. *Journal of Multilingual and Multicultural Development*, 3, 17–40. #19#

Giles, H. and Coupland, J. (eds) (1991) *The Contexts of Accommodation: Dimensions of applied sociolinguistics.* Cambridge: Cambridge University Press. #1#

Giles, H., Coupland, N., Henwood, K., Harriman, J., and Coupland J. (1990) The social meaning of RP: an intergenerational perspective. In S. Ramsaran (ed.), *Studies in the Pronunciation of English in Honour of A. C. Gimson*, 191–211. London: Routledge. #6#

Giles, H. and Powesland, P. (1975) *Speech Style and Social Evaluation.* London: Academic Press. #6#

Giles, H. and Robinson, P. W. (eds) (1990) *Handbook of Language and Social Psychology.* New York: John Wiley. #8#

Giles, H. and Scherer, K. R. (eds) (1979) *Social Markers in Speech.* Cambridge: Cambridge University Press. #6#

Giles, H. and Smith, P. (1979) Accommodation theory: optimal levels of convergence. In H. Giles and R. St Clair (eds), *Language and Social Psychology*, 45–65. Oxford: Basil Blackwell. #6#

Giles, H. and St Clair R. (eds) (1979) *Language and Social Psychology.* Oxford: Basil Blackwell. #6#, #10#

Gill, R. (ed.) (1986) *Artificial Intelligence for Society*. London: John Wiley. #10#

Gilliéron, J. (1902–10) *Atlas linguistique de la France*, 13 vols. Paris: Champion. #1#, #7#

Gilman, C. (1993). Review of *Language in exile: Three hundred years of Jamaican Creole*, by Barbara Lalla and Jean D'Costa. *Journal of Pidgin and Creole Languages*, 8, 150–5. #14#

Gleason, J. B. (1973) Code switching in children's language. In T. Moore (ed.), *Cognitive Development and the Acquisition of Language*, New York: Academic Press. #9#

—— (1980) The acquisition of social speech routines and politeness formulas. In H. Giles, W. P. Robinson, and P. M. Smith (eds), *Language: Social Psychological Perspectives*, 21–7. Oxford: Pergamon Press. #23#

Gleason, J. B., Perlmann, R. Y., and Greif, E. B. (1984) What's the magic word: learning language through politeness routines. *Discourse Processes*, 7, 493–502. #23#

Goffman, E. (1967) *Interaction Ritual: Essays on face-to-face behavior*. New York: Anchor Books. #10#, #23#

—— (1974) *Frame Analysis: An essay on the organisation of experience*. New York: Harper and Row. #10#

Gokalp, Z. (1923) *The Principles of Turkism*. Leiden: E. J. Brill. #20#

Gonzo, S. and Satarelli, M. (1983) Pidginization and linguistic change in emigrant languages. In R. Andersen (ed.), *Pidginization and creolization as language acquisition*, 181–97. Rowley, MA: Newbury House. #18#

Goodman, M. (1971) The strange case of Mbugu (Tanzania). In D. Hymes (ed.), *Pidginization and Creolization of languages*, 243–54. Cambridge: Cambridge University Press. #1#

Goodman, M. (1985) Review of Derek Bickerton, 1981, Roots of Language. *International Journal of American Linguistics*, 51, 109–37. #14#

—— (1987) The Portuguese element in the American creoles. In G. G. Gilbert (ed.), *Pidgin and Creole Languages: Essays in memory of John E. Reinecke*, 361–405. Honolulu: University of Hawaii Press. #14#

Goody, J. (1977) *The Domestication of the Savage Mind*. Cambridge: Cambridge University Press. #10#

—— (1986) *The Logic of Writing and the Organisation of Society*. Cambridge: Cambridge University Press. #10#

—— (1987) *The Interface between the Written and the Oral*. Cambridge: Cambridge University Press. #10#

Goody, J. (ed.) (1968) *Literacy in Traditional Societies*. Cambridge: Cambridge University Press. #10#

Görlach, M. (1995) *New Studies in the History of English*. Heidelberg: Winter. #16#

Goyvaerts, D. L. and Zembele, T. (1992) Codeswitching in Bukavu. *Journal of Multilingual and Multicultural Development*, 13, 71–82. #13#

Grace, G. (1990) The "aberrant" (vs. "exemplary") Melanesian languages. In P. Baldi (ed.), *Linguistic Change and Reconstruction Methodology*, 155–73. Berlin: Mouton de Gruyter. #3#

—— (1992) How do languages change? (More on "aberrant" languages). *Oceanic Linguistics*, 31, 115–30. #3#

Graff, H. (1987) *The Legacies of Literacy: Continuities and contradictions in western culture and society*. Bloomington: Indiana University Press. #10#

Grandguillaume, G. (1990) Language and legitimacy in the Maghreb. In B. Weinstein (ed.), *Language Policy and Political Development*, 150–66. Norwood, NJ: Ablex. #28#

Gräszel, U. (1991) *Sprachverhalten und Geschlecht*. Pfaffenweiler: Centaurus Verlag. #8#

Graustein, G. and Thiele, W. (1987) *Properties of English Texts*. Leipzig: Verlag Enzyklopädie. #11#

Gray, T. (1987) Language policy and educational strategies for language minority and majority students in the United States. In L. Laforge (ed.), *Proceedings of the International Colloquium on Language Planning. Ottawa, May 25–29, 1986*, 255–87. Québec: Les Presses de l'Université Laval. #28#

Green, G. (1992a) *Implicature, Rationality, and the Nature of Politeness.* Unpublished manuscript, University of Illinois. #23#

—— (1992b) *The Universality of Gricean Accounts of Politeness; You gotta have wa.* Unpublished manuscript, University of Illinois. #23#

Grice, H. P. (1975) Logic and conversation. In P. Cole and J. L. Morgan (eds), *Syntax and Semantics*, Vol. 3: *Speech Acts*, 41–58. New York: Academic Press. #23#, #27#

Grillo, R. (1989a) *Dominant Languages.* Cambridge: Cambridge University Press. #10#

—— (1989b) Anthropology, Language, Politics. Introduction to R. Grillo (ed.), *Social Anthropology and the Politics of Language.* Cambridge: Cambridge University Press. #10#

Grimes, B. F. (ed.) (1988) *Ethnologue. Languages of the World.* Dallas, Texas: Summer Institute of Linguistics. #28#

Grimshaw, A. D. (1971) Sociolinguistics. In W. Schramm, I. Pool, et al. (eds) *Handbook of Communication.* New York: Rand McNally. Reprinted in J. A. Fishman (ed.), *Advances in the Sociology of Language*, 92–151. The Hague: Mouton. #1#

—— (1980) Social interactional and sociolinguistic rules. *Social Forces*, 58, 789–810. #Introd.#

Grin, F. (1992) Towards a threshold theory of minority language survival. *Kyklos*, 54, 69–97. #28#

Grosjean, F. (1988) Exploring the recognition of guest words in bilingual speech. *Language and Cognitive Processes*, 3, 233–74. #13#

Grosjean, F. and Miller, J. L. (1994) Going in and out of languages: an example of bilingual flexibility. *Psychological Science*, 5, 201–6. #13#

Gu, Y. (1990) Politeness phenomena in modern Chinese. *Journal of Pragmatics*, 14, 237–57. #23#

Gubrium, J. and Buckholdt, D. (1982) *Describing Care: Image and practice in rehabilitation.* Cambridge, MA: Oelschlager, Gunn & Hain. #10#

GUMG (Glasgow University Media Group) (1980) *More Bad News.* London: Routledge and Kegan Paul. #11#

Gumperz, J. (1968) The speech community. *International Enclyclopedia of the Social Sciences*, 381–6. Macmillan. Reproduced in P. P. Giglioli (ed.) (1972), *Language and Social Context*, 219–31. Harmondsworth, Middlesex: Penguin Education. #28#

—— (1971) *Language in Social Groups*, ed. A. S. Dil. Stanford: Stanford University Press. #1#

—— (1976) *The Sociolinguistic Significance of Code-switching* (University of California Working Papers). Berkeley: University of California. #18#

—— (1982) *Discourse Strategies.* Cambridge: Cambridge University Press. #1#, #10#, #13#, #18#

—— (ed.) (1982b) *Language and Social Identity.* Cambridge: Cambridge University Press. #10#

—— (1990) Theory and method in pluriglossia: the interpretive analysis of language usage. In L. Spinozzi Monai (ed.), *Aspetti metodologici e teorici nello studio del plurilinguismo nei territori dell' Alpe Adria.* Tricesimo: Aviani Editore. #4#

—— (1992) Contextualization and understanding. In A. Duranti and C. Goodwin (eds), *Rethinking Context*, 230–52. Cambridge: Cambridge University Press. #1#

Gumperz, J. J. and Hernandez-Chavez, E. (1975) Cognitive aspects of bilingual communication. In E. Hernandez-Chavez, A. Cohen, and A. Bergamo (eds), *El lenguaje de los chicanos.* Arlington, VA: Center for Applied Linguistics. #18#

Gumperz, J. J. and Hymes D. (eds) (1972) *Directions in Sociolinguistics: The ethnography of Communication.* New York: Holt, Rinehart and Winston. #1#, #21#

Gumperz, J. J. and Roberts, C. (1991) Understanding in intercultural encounters. In J. Blommaert and J. Verschueren (eds), *The Pragmatics of Intercultural and International Communication.* Philadelphia: John Benjamins. #10#

Gumperz, J. J. and Wilson, R. (1971) Convergence and creolization: a case from the Indo-Aryan/Dravidian border. In D. Hymes (ed.), *Pidginization and Creolization of Languages*, 151–68. Cambridge: Cambridge University Press. #1#

Gundersen, D. (1985) Le norvégien: des problèmes mais pas de crise véritable [Norwegian: Problems, But No Real Crisis]. In J. Maurais (ed.), *La crise des langues* [Language Crisis], 281–93. Government of Québec, Conseil de la langue française and Paris, Le Robert. Québec, Les publications du Québec. #28#

Günthner, S. and Kotthoff, H. (1991) *Von fremden Stimmen. Weibliches und männliches Sprechen im Kulturvergleich.* Frankfurt: Suhrkamp. #8#

Gupta, A. Fraser (1994) *The Step-tongue.* Clevedon: Multilingual Matters #18#

Gusau, Sa'idu M. (1985) [Your language, your pride; The importance of a mother tongue over a borrowed tongue]. *Gaskiya Ta Fi Kwabo.* January 26, 2. #20#

Gusinde, M. (1933) Zur Geschichte des Yamana-English Dictionary by Th. Bridges. *Anthropos,* 28, 159–77. #16#

Guttman, D. (1975) Parenthood: A key to the comparative study of the life cycle. In N. Datan and L. H. Ginsberg (eds), *Life-Span Developmental Psychology: Normative Life Crises.* New York: Academic Press. #9#

Guttman, L. (1944) A basis for scaling qualitative data. *American Sociological Review,* 9, 139–50. #1#

Guy, G. (1991) Explanation in variable phonology: an exponential model of morphological constraints. *Language Variation and Change,* 3, 1–22. #8#

—— (1993) The quantitative analysis of linguistic variation. In D. R. Preston (ed.), *American Dialect Research,* 223–49. Philadelphia: John Benjamins. #7#

Ha, A. Ma. [= not a real name, but rather the initials of the author's name in the Ethiopic syllabary]. 1958. [*Tigrinya Grammar Book*]. Asmara: Francescana. #20#

Haarmann, H. (1980) *Multilingualism,* 2 vols. Tübingen: Narr. #17#

Habermas, J. (1985) *The Theory of Communicative Action.* New York: Beacon Press. #Introd.#

Habick, T. (1991) Burnouts versus Rednecks: effects of group membership on the phonemic system. In P. Eckert (ed.), *New Ways of Analyzing Sound Change,* 185–212. San Diego: Academic Press. #9#

Hagge, J. (1984) Strategies for verbal interaction in business writing. Paper presented at the 35th Annual Meeting of the Conference on College Composition and Communication. New York City, NY (ERIC Document Reproduction Service No. ED246473). #23#

Hagge, J. and Kostelnick, C. (1989) Linguistic politeness in professional prose: a discourse analysis of auditors' suggestion letters with implications for business communication pedagogy. *Written Communication,* 6, 312–39. #23#

Hale, K., Krauss, M., Watahomigie, L., Yamamoto, A., Craig, C., Jeanne, L. M., and England, N. (1992) Endangered languages. *Language,* 68, 1–42. #15#

Hall, J. Kelly (1993) The role of oral practices in the accomplishment of our everyday lives. *Applied Linguistics,* 14, 145–66. #10#

Hall, K., Bucholtz, M., and Moonwomon, B. (eds) (1992) *Locating Power: Proceedings of the Second Berkeley Women and Language Conference.* Berkeley: Berkeley Women and Language Group. #8#, #15#

Hall, R. A. (1966) *Pidgin and Creole Languages.* Ithaca: Cornell University Press. #14#

Hall, S. (1978) The social production of news. In Stuart Hall et al. (eds), *Policing the Crisis: Mugging, the state, and law and order.* London: Macmillan. #11#

Halliday, M. A. K. (1975) *Learning how to Mean: Explorations in the development of language.* London: Edward Arnold. #25#

—— (1985) *Introduction to Functional Grammar.* London: Edward Arnold. #25#

—— (1985) *Spoken and Written Language.* Oxford: Oxford University Press. #10#

—— (1990) New ways of analysing meaning. *Journal of Applied Linguistics,* 6, 7–36. #22#

Halliday, M. A. K. and Martin, J. (1993) *Writing Science: Literacy and discursive power.* London: Falmer Press. #10#, #22#

Halmari, H. (1993) Structural relations and Finish-English code switching. *Linguistics,* 31, 1043–68. #13#

Hama, Y. (1991) The effects of impolite computer messages on workers. *Japanese Journal of Psychology,* 61, 40–6. #23#

Hamers, J. and Blanc, M. (1982) Towards a social psychological model of bilingual development. In H. G. Nelde (ed.), *Theorie, Methoden und Modelle der Kontaktlinguistik*, 131–44. Bonn: Dummlers Verlag. #19#

Hamilton, M., Barton, D., and Ivanic, R. (1994) (eds) *Worlds of Literacy*. Clevedon: Multilingual Matters. #10#

Hammond, J. (1990) Is learning to read and write the same as learning to speak? In F. Christie (ed.), *Literacy for a Changing World*. London: Falmer Press. #10#

Hancock, I. F. (1986) The domestic hypothesis, diffusion, and componentiality: an account of Atlantic Anglophone Creole origins. In P. Muysken and N. Smith (eds), *Substrata versus Universals in Creole Genesis*, 71–102. Amsterdam: John Benjamins. #14#

Hardy, D. E. (1991) Strategic politeness in Hemingway's "The short happy life of Francis Macomber." *Poetics*, 20, 343–62. #23#

Hargreaves, J. (1982) Sport, culture and ideology. In Jennifer Hargreaves (ed.), *Sport, Culture and Ideology*, 30–62. London: Routledge and Kegan Paul. #11#

Hargreaves, M. (1980) *Adult Literacy and Broadcasting: The BBC's experience*. London: Frances Pinter. #10#

Harris, M. B. (1992) When courtesy fails: gender roles and polite behaviors. *Journal of Applied Social Psychology*, 22, 1399–416. #23#

Harris, R. (1980) *The Language Makers*. London: Duckworth. #1#

Harris, S. (1991) Evasive action: how politicians respond to questions in political interviews. In Paddy Scannel (ed.), *Broadcast Talk*, 76–99. London: Sage. #11#

—— (1994) Ideological exchanges in British magistrates courts. In J. Gibbons (ed.), *Language and the Law*, 265–305. London: Longman. #10#

Harshav, B. (1993) *Language in Time of Revolution*. Berkeley: University of California Press. #20#

Hartig, M. (1980) *Soziolinguistik für Anfänger*. Hamburg: Hoffmann und Campe. #17#

Hartley, J. (1982) *Understanding News*. London: Methuen. #11#

Hartley, S. (1992) A study of the effects of sex and age on glottalisation patterns in the speech of Tyneside schoolchildren. Undergraduate dissertation, University of Newcastle upon Tyne. #3#

Hasan, R. (1992) Meaning in sociolinguistic theory. In K. Bolton and H. Kwok (eds), *Sociolinguistics Today*, 80–119. London: Routledge. #1#

Hatch, E. (1992) *Discourse and Language Education*. Cambridge: Cambridge University Press. #10#

Haugen, E. (1956) *Bilingualism in the Americas*. Alabama: American Dialect Society. #18#

—— (1959) Language planning in modern Norway. *Anthropological Linguistics*, 1, 8–21. Reproduced in J. A. Fishman (ed.) (1968), *Readings in the Sociology of Language*, 673–87. The Hague: Mouton. #28#

—— (1966a) Dialect, language, nation. *American Anthropologist*, 68, 922–35. [Reprinted in J. Pride and J. Holmes (eds) (1972), *Sociolinguistics*. London: Penguin.] #10#, #21#

—— (1966b) *Language Conflict and Language Planning: The case of modern Norwegian*. Cambridge, MA: Harvard University Press. #17#, #20#

—— (1973) Bilingualism, language contact and immigrant languages in the United States. In T. Sebeok (eds), *Current Trends in Linguistics*, 10, 505–91. The Hague: Mouton. #18#

—— (1983) The implementation of corpus planning: theory and practice. In J. Cobarrubias and J. A. Fishman (eds), *Progress in Language Planning*, 269–89. Berlin: Mouton. #21#, #28#

—— (1987) Comments on Selim Abou's Paper. In Lorne Laforge (ed.), *Proceedings of the International Colloquium on Language Planning, May 25–29, Ottawa*, 25–31. Québec: Presses de l'Université Laval. #21#

—— (1989) The rise and fall of an immigrant language: Norwegian in America. In N. C. Dorian (ed.), *Investigating Obsolescence: Studies in language contraction and death*, 61–74. Cambridge: Cambridge University Press. #15#

Hauraki, V. (1971) Language key to cultural survival. *Te Maori*, 2, n. 4, 3. #20#

Haviland, J. B. (1989) "Sure, sure": Evidence and affect. *Text*, 9, 27–68. #23#

Hawkins, R. (1993) Regional variation in France. In C. Sanders (ed.), *French Today: Language in its social context*, 55–84. Cambridge: Cambridge University Press. #6#

Heath, S. B. (1982) What no bedtime story means: Narrative skills at home and at school. *Language in Society*, 11, 49–76. #10#

—— (1983) *Ways with Words: Language, life, work in communities and classrooms*. Cambridge: Cambridge University Press. #10#, #23#, #25#

Held, G. (1988) Danken – semantische, pragmatische und soziokulturelle Aspekte eines höflichen Sprechakts (gezeigt am Beispiel des Französischen) [Thanking – semantic, pragmatic, and sociocultural aspects of a polite speech act (demonstrated by reference to French)]. *Klagenfurter Beiträge zur Sprachwissenschaft*, 13–14 203–27. #23#

Heller, M. (ed.) (1988a) *Codeswitching, anthropological and sociolinguistic perspectives*. Berlin: Mouton de Gruyter. #13#, #18#

Heller, M. (1988b) Strategic ambiguity: Codeswitching in the management of conflict. In M. Heller (ed.), *Codeswitching, Anthropology and Sociolinguistic Perspectives*, 77–96. Berlin: Mouton de Gruyter. #13#

—— (1992a) Code-switching, social institutions and symbolic domination. In European Science Foundation (ed.), *Summer School on Code-switching*, 69–92. #13#

—— (1992b) The politics of code-switching and language choice. *Journal of Multilingual and Multicultural Development*, 13, 123–42. #10#

Henley, N. M. and Kramerae, Ch. (1991) Gender, power and miscommunication. In Nikolas Coupland, Howard Giles, and John M. Wiemann (eds), *"Miscommunication" and Problematic Talk*, 18–43. London: Sage. #8#

Herbert, R. (ed.) (1992) *Language and Society in Africa*. Cape Town: Witwatersrand University Press. #16#

Herbert, R. K. (1990) Sex-based differences in compliment behavior. *Language in Society*, 19, 201–24. #23#

Heritage, J. (1985) Analysing news interviews: aspects of the production of talk for an overhearing audience. In Teun van Dijk (ed.), *Discourse and Dialogue*, 95–119. London: Academic Press. #11#

Hero, R. (1986) Citizen contacting and bureaucratic treatment-response in urban government: some further evidence. *Social Science Journal*, 23, 181–7. #23#

Hermann, E. (1929) Lautveränderungen in der Individualsprache einer Mundart. *Nachrichten der Gesellschaft der Wissenschaften zu Göttingen. Phl-his. Kl.*, 11, 195–214. #9#

Herrmann, T. (1982) Language and situation: the "pars pro toto" principle. In C. Fraser and K. R. Scherer (eds), *Advances in the Social Psychology of Language*, 123–58. Cambridge: Cambridge University Press. #23#

Hess-Lüttich, E. (1983) Jugendpresse und Sprachwandel [Print media for adolescents and language change]. *International Journal of the Sociology of Language*, 40, 93–105. #11#

Hewitt, R. (1986) *White Talk Black Talk: Inter-racial friendship and communication amongst adolescents*. Cambridge: Cambridge University Press. #1#, #10#

HFP [= Heidelberger Forschungsprojekt "Pidgin-Deutsch"]. (1975) Sprache und Kommunikation ausländischer Arbeiter. Kronberg: Scriptor Verlag. #14#

Hill, B., Ide, S., Ikuta, S., Kawasaki, A., and Ogino, T. (1986) Universals of linguistic politeness. Quantitative evidence from Japanese and American English. *Journal of Pragmatics*, 10, 347–71. #23#

Hill, C. and Parry, K. (eds) (1994) *From Testing to Assessment: English as an international language*. London: Longman. #10#

Hill, J. and Hill, K. (1977) Language death and relexification in Tlaxcalan Nahuatl. *International Journal of the Sociology of Language*, 12, 55–69. #15#

Hill, J. H. (1973) Subordinate clause density and language function. In C. Corum, T. C. Smith-Stark, and A. Weiser (eds), *You take the High Node and I'll take the Low Node: Papers from the Comparative Syntax Festival*, 33–52. Chicago: Chicago Linguistic Society. #15#

—— (1978) Language death, language contact and language evolution. In W. C. McCormack and Stephen A. Wurm (eds), *Approaches to Language: Anthropological Issues*, 45–78. The Hague: Mouton. #16#

—— (1983) Language death in Uto-Aztecan. *International Journal of American Linguistics*, 49, 258–76. #15#, #16#

—— (1990) Women's speech in modern Mexicano. In Susan Philips, Susan Steele, and Christine Tanz (eds), *Language, Gender, and Sex in Comparative Perspective*, 121–60. London: Cambridge University Press. #8#

—— (1993) Structure and practice in language shift. In K. Hyltenstam and A. Viberg (eds), *Progression and Regression in Language: Sociocultural, neuropsychological and linguistic perspectives*, 68–93. Cambridge: Cambridge University Press. #15#

Hill, J. H. and Hill, K. C. (1986) *Speaking Mexicano*. Tucson: University of Arizona Press. #15#

—— (1978) Honorific usage in modern Nahuatl: the expression of social distance and respect in the Nahuatl of the Malinche Volcano area. *Language*, 54, 123–55. #23#

Hinnenkamp, V. (1989) *Interaktional Soziolinguistik und interkulturelle Kommunikation*. Tübingen: Niemeyer. #10#

Hirokawa, R. Y., Mickey, J., and Miura, S. (1991) Effects of request legitimacy on the compliance-gaining tactics of male and female managers. *Communication Monographs*, 58, 421–36. #23#

Ho, D. Y. (1975) On the concept of face. *American Journal of Sociology*, 81, 867–84. #23#

Hoar, N. (1987) Genderlect, powerlect, and politeness. In C. A. Valentine and N. Hoar (eds), *Women and Communicative Power: Theory, research, and practice* (ERIC Document Reproduction Service No. ED294263). #23#

Hobart, M. (1987) Summer's days and salad days: the coming of age of anthropology? In L. Holy (ed.), *Comparative Anthropology*, 22–51. Oxford: Blackwell. #23#

Hobsbawm, E. J. (1994) *Age of Extremes: The short twentieth century, 1914–1991*. London: Michael Joseph. #19#

Hock, H. H. (1991) Principles of historical linguistics, 2nd edn. Berlin: Mouton de Gruyter. (Chap. 20, Linguistic change: its nature and causes.) #5#

Hockett, C. F. (1950) Age-grading and linguistic continuity. *Language*, 41, 184–204. #9#

—— (1958) *A Course in Modern Linguistics*. London: Macmillan. #6#

Hodge, R. and Kress, G. (1993) *Language as Ideology*, 2nd edn. London: Routledge. #22#

Hoenigswald, H. M. (1989) Language obsolescence and language history: matters of linearity, leveling, loss, and the like. In N. C. Dorian (ed.), *Investigating Obsolescence: Studies in language contraction and death*, 347–54. Cambridge: Cambridge University Press. #15#

Hoffman, L. (1984) *Vom Fachwort zum Fachtext: Beiträge zur angewandten Linguistik* [From Technical Vocabulary to Technical Texts]. Tübingen: Narr. #11#

Højrup, T. (1983) The concept of life-mode: a form-specifying mode of analysis applied to contemporary western Europe. *Ethnologia Scandinavica*, 1–50. #1#

Hollien, H. (1990a) *The Acoustics of Crime: The new science of Forensic Phonetics*. New York: Plenum. #27#

—— (1990b) The phonetician as an expert witness: ethics and responsibility. In R. W. Rieber and W. A. Stewart (eds), *The Language Scientist as Expert in the Legal Setting: Issues in forensic linguistics. Annals of the New York Academy of Sciences*, 606, 33–45. #27#

Hollingshead, A. E. (1950) Cultural factors in the selection of marriage mates. *American Sociological Review*, 15, 619–27. #20#

Holm, J. (1984) Variability of the copula in Black English and its creole kin. *American Speech*, 59, 291–309. #14#

—— (1986) Substrate diffusion. In P. Muysken and N. Smith (eds), *Substrata versus Universals in Creole Genesis*, 259–78. Amsterdam: John Benjamins. #14#

—— (1988) *Pidgins and Creoles*. Vol. I: *Theory and structure*. Cambridge: Cambridge University Press. #14#

—— (1989) *Pidgins and creoles*, Vol. II: *Reference survey*. Cambridge: Cambridge University Press. #14#

—— (1991) The Atlantic creoles and the language of the ex-slave recordings. In G. Bailey, N. Maynor, and P. Cukor-Avila (eds), *The Emergence of Black English: Text and commentary*, 231–47. Amsterdam: John Benjamins. #14#

Holmes, J. (1984) Women's language: a functional approach. *General Linguistics*, 24, 149–78. #23#

—— (1988) Paying compliments: a sex-preferential positive politeness strategy. *Journal of Pragmatics*, 12, 445–65. #23#

—— (1989) Sex differences and apologies: One aspect of communicative competence. *Applied Linguistics*, 10, 194–213. #23#

—— (1990) Politeness strategies in New Zealand women's speech. In A. Bell and J. Holmes (eds), *New Zealand ways of speaking English*, 252–76. Clevedon: Multilingual Matters. #23#

—— (1992) *An Introduction to Sociolinguistics*. London: Longman. #8#

—— (1993) New Zealand women are good to talk to: an analysis of politeness strategies in interaction. *Journal of Pragmatics*, 20, 91–116. #23#

Holmqvist, B. and Boegh Andersen, P. (1987) Work language and information technology. *Journal of Pragmatics*, 11, 327–58. #23#

Honey, J. (1985) Acrolect and hyperlect: the redefinition of English RP. In *English Studies* 66, 241–57. #6#

—— (1988a) First language didactics. Art. n° 183 in U. Ammon, N. Dittmar, and K. J. Mattheier (eds), *Sociolinguistics: An international handbook*, Vol. II, 1703–14. Berlin and New York: Walter de Gruyter. #6#

—— (1988b) "Talking proper": schooling and the establishment of English RP. In G. Nixon and J. Honey (eds), *An Historic Tongue*, 209–27. London: Routledge. #6#

—— (1989) *Does Accent Matter?* London and Boston: Faber. #6#

—— (forthcoming) *Standard English and its enemies*. #6#

Honey, J. R. de S. (1977) *Tom Brown's Universe*. London: Millington. #6#

Honikman, B. (1964) Articulatory settings. In D. Abercrombie et al. (eds), *In Honour of Daniel Jones*, 73–84. London: Longman. #6#

Hoppe-Graff, S., Hermann, T., Winterhoff-Spurk, P., and Mangold, R. (1985) Speech and situation: a general model for the process of speech production. In J. P. Forgas (ed.), *Language and Social Situation*, 81–97. New York: Springer. #23#

Hopper, P. J. and Traugott, E. C. (1993) *Grammaticalization*. Cambridge: Cambridge University Press. #22#

Hornberger, N. H. (1991) Extending enrichment bilingual education: Revisiting typologies and redirecting policy. In O. García (ed.), *Bilingual Education: Focusschrift in honor of Joshua A. Fishman*. Vol. 1, 215–34. Amsterdam: John Benjamins. #26#

Hornung, M. (1960) Die Osttiroler Bauernsprachinseln Pladen und Zahre in Oberkarnien. *Osttiroler Heimatkunde. Heimatkundliche Beilage des "Osttiroler Bote"*, Lienz, 28, Nr. 2–8. #4#

—— (1964) *Mundartkunde Osttirols. Studien zur Österr.-bair. Dialektkunde 3*. Graz-Wien-Köln: Böhlaus Nachf. #4#

—— (1972) *Wörterbuch der deutschen Sprachinselmundart von Pladen/Sappada in Karnien (Italien)*. Vienna: Österreichische Akademie der Wissenschaften. #4#

—— (1984) Alte Gemeinsamkeiten im speziellen Wortschatz südbairischer Sprachinseln. In H.-W. Eroms, B. Gajek, and H. Kolb (eds), *Studia linguistica et philologica. Festschrift für Klaus Matzel zum sechzigsten Geburtstag*. Heidelberg: Carl Winter. #4#

Horvath, B. M. (1985) *Variation in Australian English: The sociolects of Sydney*. Cambridge: Cambridge University Press. #1#, #3#, #8#, #9#

Hosali, P. and Tongue, R. (1989) *A Dictionary of Collocations for Indian Users of English*. Hyderabad: Central Institute of English and Foreign Languages. #11#

House, J. (1986) Cross-cultural pragmatics and foreign language teaching. In K. R. Bausch,

F. G. Koenigs, and R. Kogelheide (eds), *Probleme und Perspektiven der Sprachlehrforschung*, 281–95. Frankfurt: Scriptor. #23#

—— (1989) Politeness in English and German: the functions of "please" and "bitte." In S. Blum-Kulka, J. House, and G. Kasper (eds), *Cross-cultural Pragmatics*, 96–119. Norwood, NJ: Ablex. #23#

Houston, S. (1969) A sociolinguistic consideration of the Black English of children in Northern Florida. *Language*, 48, 599–607. #9#

Hu, H. C. (1944) The Chinese concept of "face." *American Anthropologist*, 46, 45–64. #23#

Hudson, A. (1991a) Studies in diglossia. *Southwest Journal of Linguistics*, 10. #12#

—— (1991b) Toward the systematic study of diglossia. *Southwest Journal of Linguistics*, 10, 1–22. #12#

—— (1992) Diglossia: a bibliographic review. *Language in Society*, 21, 611–74. #12#

Hudson, L. (1968) *Frames of Mind*. Harmondsworth: Penguin. #26#

Hudson, R. (1990) Review: *Investigating Obsolescence*, edited by Nancy Dorian, 1989. *Language*, 66, 831–4. #16#

Hudson, R. A. (1980) *Sociolinguistics*. Cambridge: Cambridge University Press. (2nd edn, 1990.) #1#, #6#, #8#.

Huffines, M. L. (1991) Pennsylvania German: convergence and change as strategies of discourse. In H. W. Seliger and R. M. Vago (eds), *The Study of First Language Attrition: An overview*, 125–37. Amsterdam: Benjamins. #13#

Hughes, R. (1920) Our Statish language. *Harper's Magazine*, May, 846–9. #20#

Hughes, S. E. (1992) Expletives of lower working-class women. *Language in Society*, 291–303. #8#

Humboldt, W. von (1825) Über das Entstehen der grammatikalischen Formen auf ihren Einfluss auf die Ideenentwicklung. *Abhandlungen der Königlichen Akademie der Wissenschaften zu Berlin*, 401–30. #22#

Hussein, R. F. and Zughoul, M. R. (1993) Lexical interference in journalistic Arabic in Jordan. *Language Sciences* 15, 239–54. #11#

Hyltenstam, K. and Viberg, A. (eds) (1993) *Progression and Regression in Language: Sociocultural, neuropsychological and linguistic perspective*. Cambridge: Cambridge University Press. #15#

Hymes, D. (1962) The ethnography of speaking. In T. Gladwin and W. C. Sturtevant (eds), *Anthropology and Human Behaviour*, 13–53. Washington, DC: Anthropology Society of Washington. #1#

—— (1964) Introduction: Toward ethnographies of communication. In J. Gumperz and D. Hymes (eds), *American Anthropologist*, 66/2, 12–25. #10#

—— (1964) *Language in Culture and Society*. New York: Harper and Row. #12#

—— (1971) *On Communicative Competence*. Philadelphia: University of Pennsylvania Press. Reproduced in J. B. Pride and J. Holmes (eds) (1972), *Sociolinguistics*, 269–93. Harmondsworth, Middlesex: Penguin Education. #25#, #28#

—— (1974) *Foundations in Sociolinguistics: An ethnographic approach*. Philadelphia: University of Pennsylvania Press. #10#, #21#

—— (1980) Commentary. In A. Valdman and A. Highfield (eds), *Theoretical Orientations in Creole Studies*, 389–423. New York: Academic Press. #14#

Hymes, D. (ed.) (1971) *Pidginization and Creolization of Languages*. Cambridge: Cambridge University Press. #1#, #14#

Ide, S. (1982) Japanese sociolinguistics: politeness and women's language. *Lingua*, 57, 357–85. #23#

—— (1983) Two functional aspects of politeness in women's language. In S. Hattori, K. Inoue, T. Shimomiya, and Y. Nagashima (eds), *Proceedings of the XIIIth International Congress of Linguists*, 805–8. Tokyo: Tokyo Press. #23#

—— (1989) Formal forms and discernment: two neglected aspects of linguistic politeness. *Multilingua*, 8, 223–48. #23#

—— (1992) Gender and function of language use: quantitative and qualitative evidence from Japanese. In L. F. Bouton and Y. Kachru (eds), *Pragmatics and Language Learning*, Vol. 3. Urbana: Division of English as an International Language, University of Illinois at Urbana-Champaign. #23#

Ide, S., Hill, B., Carnes, Y. M., Ogino, T., and Kawasaki, A. (1992). The concept of politeness: an empirical study of American English and Japanese. In R. J. Watts, S. Ide, and K. Ehlich (eds), *Politeness in Language: Studies in its history, theory and practice*, 281–97. Berlin: Mouton de Gruyter. #23#

Ide, S., Hori, M., Kawasaki, A., Ikuta, S., and Haga, H. (1986) Sex differences and politeness in Japanese. *International Journal of the Sociology of Language*, 58, 25–36. #23#

Ikoma, T. (1993) "Sorry for giving me a ride": the use of apologetic expressions to show gratitude in Japanese. Unpublished master's thesis, University of Hawaii at Manoa, Honolulu. #23#

Ikoma, T. and Shimura, A. (1993) Eigo kara nihongo e no puragumatikku toransufaa: "Kotowari" toiu hatsuwa kooi ni tsuite [Pragmatic transfer from English to Japanese: the speech act of refusal]. *Nihongo Kyoiku* [Journal of Japanese Language Teaching], 79. #23#

Indicateurs de la situation linguistique au Québec. (1992) Québec: Gouvernement de Quebéc, Conseil de la langue française. #2#

Inglehart, R. F. and Woodward M. (1967) Language conflicts and political community. In P. Giglioli (ed), *Language and Social Context*. New York: Penguin. #17#

Inoue, T. (1898) [Time for a decision regarding a new script]. In Nanette Twine (ed.) (1991) *Language and the Modern State: The reform of written Japanese*. London: Routledge. #20#

Isajiw, W. W. (1970) Definitions of ethnicity. *Ethnicity*, 1, 1. [Reprinted in J. Goldstein and R. Bienvenue (eds), *Ethnicity and Ethnic Relations in Canada*. Toronto: Butterworth.] #2#, #18#

Ishaq, E. M. (1991) "Coptic Language, Spoken." In Aziz S. Atiya (ed.), *The Coptic Encyclopedia*, Vol. 2, 604–7. New York: Macmillan. #16#

Ivanic, R. (forthcoming) *Writing and Identity: Studies in Written Language and Literacy*. Amsterdam: John Benjamins. #10#

Jabeur, M. (1987) A sociolinguistic study in Tunisia, Rades. Unpublished PhD dissertation, University of Reading. #3#

Jacobson, R. (1990) Socioeconomic status as a factor in the selection of encoding strategies in mixed discourse. In R. Jacobson (ed.), *Codeswitching as a Worldwide Phenomenon*, 85–110. New York: Peter Lang. #13#

Jacobson, R. (ed.) (1990) *Codeswitching as a Worldwide Phenomenon*. New York: Peter Lang. #13#

Jake, J. L. (1994 and forthcoming) Effects of the matrix language in second language acquisition. Manuscript submitted for publication. #13#

—— (1994) Intrasentential codeswitching and pronouns: On the categorial status of functional elements. *Linguistics*, 32, 271–98. #13#

Jake, J. L. and Myers-Scotton, C. M. (1994) German/French and Swiss German/Italian data set. #13#

—— (1996) Verbs in Arabic and English and lexical structure: paper presented at symposium on code-switching, Linguistic Society of America, annual meeting, 1/96. #13#

Jakobson, R. (1953) Results of the conference of anthropologists and linguists. *International Journal of American Linguistics*, Supplement, Memoir No. 8, 19–22. #1#

—— (1968) *Child Language, Aphasia, and Phonological Universals*, trans. A. R. Keiler from *Kindersprache, Aphasie, und allgemeine Lautgesetze*, (1968). The Hague: Mouton. #15#

Jakobson, R., Fant, C. G. M. and Halle, M. (1952) *Preliminaries to Speech Analysis*. Cambridge, MA: Massachusetts Institute of Technology Acoustics Laboratory, Technical Report 13. #1#

James, S. L. (1978) Effect of listener age and situation on the politeness of children's directives. *Journal of Psycholinguistic Research*, 7, 307–17. #23#

Janney, R. W. and Arndt, H. (1992) Intracultural tact versus intercultural tact. In R. J. Watts, S. Ide, and K. Ehlich (eds), *Politeness in Language: Studies in its history, theory and practice*, 21–41. Berlin: Mouton de Gruyter. #23#

Jawad, Abdel (1987) Cross-dialectal variation in Arabic: competing prestige forms. *Language in Society*, 16, 359–68. #3#

Jeanne, L. M. (1992) An institutional response to language endangerment: a proposal for a Native American Language Center. *Language*, 68, 24–6. #15#

Jernudd, B. and Shapiro M. J. (eds) (1989) *The Politics of Language Purism*. Berlin: Mouton de Gruyter. #20#

Jernudd, B. H. (1971) Notes on economic analysis for solving language problems. In J. Rubin & B. H. Jernudd (eds.). *Can Language Be Planned? Sociolinguistic theory and practice for developing nations*, 263–76. Honolulu: University Press of Hawaii. #28#

—— (1987) Essais sur les problèmes linguistiques [Essays on language problems]. In J. Maurais (ed.), *Politique et aménagement linguistiques* [Language Planning and Language Policies], 493–552. Government of Québec, Conseil de la langue française and Paris, Le Robert. Québec: Les Publications du Québec. #28#

Jernudd, B. H. and Das Gupta, J. (1971) Towards a theory of language planning. In J. Rubin and B. H. Jernudd (eds), *Can Language Be Planned? Sociolinguistic theory and practice for developing nations*, 195–215. Honolulu: University Press of Hawaii. #28#

Johnson, D. M. (1992) Compliments and politeness in peer-review texts. *Applied Linguistics*, 13, 51–71. #23#

Johnson, D. M. and Yang, A. W. (1990) Politeness strategies in peer review texts. In L. F. Bouton and Y. Kachru (eds), *Pragmatics and Language Learning*, 99–114. Urbana-Champaign: Division of English as an International Language, University of Illinois at Urbana-Champaign. #23#

Johnson, M. D. and Fawcett, S. B. (1987) Consumer-defined standards for courteous treatment by service agencies. *Journal of Rehabilitation*, 53, 23–6. #23#

Johnson, S. (1755) *A Dictionary of the English Language*. London. #1#

Johnstone, B. (1991) Individual style in an American public opinion survey: personal performance and the ideology of referentiality. *Language in Society*, 20, 557–76. #23#

Johnstone, B., Ferrara, K., and Bean, J. M. (1992) Gender, politeness, and discourse management in same-sex and cross-sex opinion-poll interviews. *Journal of Pragmatics*, 18, 405–30. #23#

Jones, G., Martin, P., and Ozóg, A. C. K. (1993) Multilingualism and bilingual education in Brunei Darussalam. In G. Jones and A. C. K. Ozóg (eds), *Bilingualism and National Development*, 39–58. Clevedon: Multilingual Matters. #26#

Jones, K. (1992) A question of context: directive use at a Morris team meeting. *Language in Society*, 21, 427–45. #23#

Joseph, B. D. and Janda, R. (1989) The how and why of diachronic morphologization and demorphologization. In *Theoretical Morphology*, 193–210. New York: Academic Press. #7#

Joseph, J. E. (1987) *Eloquence and Power: The rise of language standards and standard languages*. London: Frances Pinter. #6#

Joshi, A. (1985) Processing of sentences with intrasentential codeswitching. In D. R. Dowty, L. Karttunen, and A. Zwicky (eds), *Natural Language Parsing*, 190–205. Cambridge: Cambridge University Press. #13#

Jucker, A. (1992) *Social Stylistics: Syntactic variation in British newspapers*. Berlin: Mouton- de Gruyter. #11#

Kamwangamalu, N. (1989) Some morphosyntactic aspects of French/English-Bantu code-mixing. In B. Music et al. (eds), *Parasession on language Contact: Regional meeting of the Chicago Linguistic Society*, 157–70. Chicago: Chicago Linguistic Society. #13#

Kasper, G. (ed.) (1995) *Pragmatics of Chinese as Native and Target Language* (Technical Report #5). Honolulu: University of Hawaii, Second Language Teaching & Curriculum Center. #23#

Kaufman, D. and Aronoff, M. (1991) Morphological disintegration and reconstruction in first language attrition. In H. W. Seliger and R. M. Vago (eds), *First Language Attrition*, 175–88. Amsterdam: Benjamins. #13#

Kayano, Sh. (1987) [*Easy Ainu*]. Hokkaido, Shiratori, Nibutani Ainu-go Kyoshitsu, 5. #20#

Kedourie, E. (1961) *Nationalism*. London: Hutchinson. #18#

Keenan, E. (1974) Norm-makers, norm-breakers: uses of speech by men and women in a Malagasy community. In R. Bauman and J. Sherzer (eds), *Explorations in the Ethnography of Speaking*. Cambridge: Cambridge University Press. #23#

Keesing, R. (1988) *Melanesian Pidgin and the Oceanic Substrate*. Palo Alto: Stanford University Press. #14#

Keith, J. (1980) Old age and community creation. In C. L. Fry (ed.), *Aging, Culture and Society*. New York: Praeger. #9#

Kemp, W. (1979) L'histoire récente de *ce que, qu'est-ce que et qu'osque* à Montréal. In P. Thibault (ed.), *Le français parlé*, 53–74. Edmonton: Linguistic Research. #9#

Kemp, W. and Yaeger-Dror, M. (1991) Changing realizations of A in (a)tion in relation to the front a – back a opposition in Quebec French. In P. Eckert (ed.), *New Ways of Analyzing Sound Change*, 127–84. San Diego: Academic Press. #9#

Kennedy, C. (ed.) (1984) *Language Planning and Language Education*. London, Boston & Sidney: George Allen & Unwin. #28#

Khalid, A. (1977) *The Liberation of Swahili from European Appropriation*. Nairobi: East African Literature Bureau, 193–5. #20#

Khati, T. (1992) Intra-lexical switching or nonce borrowing? Evidence from SeSotho-English performance. In R. K. Herbert (ed.), *Language and Society in Africa*, 181–96. Johannesburg: University of the Witwatersrand Press. #13#

Khubchandani, L. M. (1974) Fluidity in mother tongue identity. In A. Verdoodt (ed.), *Applied Sociolinguistics*, 81–102. Heidelberg: J. Groos. #2#

—— (1983) *Plural Languages, Plural Cultures: Communication, identity, and sociopolitical change in contemporary India*. Honolulu: University of Hawaii Press. #1#

—— (1995) Linguistic census around the world. In *Actes de Simposi de demolingüística*, 109–18. Barcelona: Generalitat de Catalaña. #2#

Khubchandani, L. M. (ed.) (1988) *Language in a Plural Society*. Delhi: Banarasidass and Shimla: Indian Institute of Advanced Study. #18#

King, L. (1995) *Roots of Identity: Literacy in Mexico*. Stanford, CA: Stanford University Press. #10#

Kingsmore, R. (forthcoming) *Variation in an Ulster Scots Dialect: A sociolinguistic study*. Birmingham: University of Alabama Press. #3#

Kiparsky, P. (1989) Phonological change. In F. J. Newmeyer (ed.), *Linguistics: The Cambridge survey*, 363–415. Cambridge: Cambridge University Press. #7#

Kipp, S. J. (1980) German language maintenance and language shift in some rural settlements. *ITL Review of Applied Linguistics*, 28, 69–80. #18#

Kitao, K. (1990) A study of Japanese and American perceptions of politeness in requests. *Doshisha Studies in English*, 50, 178–210. #23#

Klann-Delius, G. (1987) Sex and language. In Ulrich Ammon, Norbert Dittmar, Klaus Mattheier (eds), *Sociolinguistics: An international handbook*, 767–80. Berlin: Walter de Gruyter. #8#

Klassen, (1991) Bilingual written language use by low-education Latin American newcomers. In D. Barton and R. Ivanic (eds), *Writing in the Community*, 38–57. London: Sage. #10#

Klein, L. E. (1986) Berkeley, Shaftesbury, and the meaning of politeness. *Studies in Eighteenth-Century Culture*, 16, 57–68. #23#

—— (1990) Politeness in seventeenth-century England and France. *Cahiers du Dix-septième*, 4, 91–106. #23#

Klein, W. and Dietrich, R. (1994) Conclusions. In R. Dietrich, W. Klein, and C. Noyau (eds), *Temporality in Second Language Acquisition*. Amsterdam: Benjamins. #13#

Klein, W. and Dittmar, N. (1979) *Developing Grammars: The acquisition of German syntax by foreign workers*. Berlin: Springer-Verlag. #13#

Kloss, H. (1966a) German-American language maintenance efforts. In J. A. Fishman (ed.), *Language Loyalty in the United States*, 206–52. The Hague: Mouton. #18#

—— (1966b) Types of multilingual communities. *Sociological Inquiry*, 36(2). #12#

—— (1967) "Abstand Languages" and "Ausbau Languages." *Anthropological Linguistics*, 9, 7, 29–41. #21#

—— (1968) Notes Concerning a language-nation typology. In J. A. Fishman, C. A. Ferguson and J. Das Gupta (eds), *Language Problems of Developing Nations*, 69–86. New York: John Wiley and Sons, #21#

—— (1969) *Research Possibilities on Group Bilingualism: A report*. Québec: Université Laval, C.I.R.B. #28#

—— (1977) *The American Bilingual Tradition*. Rowley, MA: Newbury House. #18#

Kloss H. and McConnell, G. D. (1978–94) *The Written Languages of the World: A survey of the degree and modes of use*. 4 vols. Québec: Presses de l'Université Laval. #21#

Kluge, F. (1967) *Etymologisches Wörterbuch der deutschen Sprache*, 20. Aufl. bearbeitet von Walter Mitzka. Berlin: de Gruyter. #4#

Knapp-Potthoff, A. (1992) Secondhand politeness. In R. J. Watts, S. Ide, and K. Ehlich (eds), *Politeness in Language: Studies in its history, theory and practice*, 203–18. Berlin: Mouton de Gruyter. #23#

Knapp-Patthoff, A. and Knapp, K. (1987) The man (or woman) in the middle: discoursal aspects of non-professional interpreting. In K. Knapp, W. Enninger, and A. Knapp-Potthoff (eds), *Analyzing Intercultural Communication*, 181–211. New York: Mouton de Gruyter. #23#

Knappert, Jan. 1979. The origin and development of Lingala. In I. F. Hancock, E. Polomé, M. Goodman, and B. Heine (eds), *Readings in Creole Studies*. Ghent: E. Story-Scientia. #14#

Knowles, G. O. (1978) The nature of phonological variables in Scouse. In P. Trudgill (ed.), *Sociolinguistic Patterns in British English*, 80–90. London: Edward Arnold. #6#

Kotthoff, H. (1992) Unruhe im Tabellenbild? Zur Interpretation weiblichen Sprechens in der Soziolinguistik. In Susanne Günthner und Helga Kotthoff (eds), *Die Geschlechter im Gespräch: Kommunikation in Institutionen*, 126–46. Stuttgart: Metzler. #8#

Kotthoff, H. and Wodak, R. (eds) (in press) *Communicating Gender*. #8#

Kramerae, Ch. (1990) Changing the complexion of gender in language research. In Howard Giles and Peter W. Robinson (eds), *Handbook of Language and Social Psychology*, 345–62. New York: John Wiley. #8#

Kranzmayer, E. (1956) *Historische Lautgeographie des gesamtbairischen Dialektraumes*. Graz-Köln: Böhlaus Nachf. #4#

—— (1960) *Die bairischen Kennwörter und ihre Geschichte. Studien zur österr.-bair. Dialektkunde* 2. Wien. #4#

—— (1981) *Laut- und Flexionslehre der deutschen zimbrischen Mundart*. Wien: VWGÖ. #4#

Kranzmayer, E. and Lessiak, P. (1983) *Wörterbuch der deutschen Sprachinselmundart von Zarz/Sorica und Deutsch Rut in Jugoslawien*. Klagenfurt. #4#

Krapp, G. P. (1919) *The Pronunciation of Standard English in America*. New York: Oxford University Press. #6#

Krashen, S. (1982) *Principles and Practices in Second Language Acquisition*. Oxford: Pergamon Press. #10#

Krauss, M. (1992) *A Broad Outline to the Language Endangerment Problem*. CIPSH/UNESCO. #16#

—— (1992a) The world's languages in crisis. *Language*, 68, 4–10. #15#

Kreml, N. M. P. (1992) Relevance, textual unity, and politeness in writing about science. *Dissertation Abstracts International*, 53, 2794-A. #23#

Kremos, H. (1955) *Höflichkeitsformeln in der französischen Sprache. Aufforderungs- und Bittformeln. Dankesbezeugungen*. (Mit historischem Rückblick bis ins 16. Jahrhundert). [Politeness formulae in the French language: Request and petition formulae. Expressions of gratitude. (With a historical review from the 16th century)]. Unpublished doctoral dissertation, University of Zurich, Switzerland. #23#

Kress, G. (1983) Linguistic processes and the mediation of "reality": the politics of newspaper language. *International Journal of the Sociology of Language*, 40, 40–57. #11#

—— (1985) *Linguistic Processes in Socio-cultural Practice.* Oxford: Oxford University Press. #10#

Kress, G. (ed.), (1976) *Halliday: System and function in language.* Oxford: Oxford University Press. #11#

Krings, H. (1961) *Die Geschichte des Wortschatzes der Höflichkeit im Französischen* [The History of the Vocabulary of Politeness in French]. Unpublished doctoral dissertation, University of Bonn. #23#

Krishnamurti, Bh. and Mukherjee, A. (eds) (1984) *Modernization of Indian Languages in News Media.* Osmania University, Hyderabad, India. #11#

Kroch, A. (1978) Towards a theory of social dialect variation. *Language in Society*, 7, 17–36. #7#

—— (1989) Reflexes of grammar in patterns of language change. *Language Variation and Change*, 1, 199–244. #5#, #7#

Kroeber, T. (1961) *Ishi in Two Worlds: A biography of the last wild Indian in North America.* Berkeley: University of California Press. #15#

Krzeminski, M. (1985) Präsentationsformen und Zuschauerbeteiligung [Presentational techniques and viewer participation]. In Günter Bentele and Ernest Hess-Lüttich (eds), *Zeichengebrauch in Massenmedien*, 265–73. Tübingen: Niemeyer. #11#

Kuhberg, H. (1992) Longitudinal L2-attrition versus L2- acquisition, in three Turkish children. *Second Language Research*, 8, 138–54. #13#

Kurath, H. (1949) *Word Geography of the Eastern United States.* Ann Arbor: University of Michigan Press. #1#

Kurath, H. and Bloch, B. (1939) *Handbook of the Linguistic Geography of New England.* Providence, RI: Brown University Press. #1#, #7#

Kurath, H. and McDavid, R. I. Jr. (1961) *The Pronunciation of English in the Atlantic States.* Ann Arbor, MI: University of Michigan Press. #7#

Kwatcha, P. (1992) Discourse structures, cultural stability and language shift. In A. R. Taylor (ed.), Language obsolescence, shift, and death. *International Journal of the Sociology of Language*, 67–74. Berlin, New York: Mouton de Gruyter. #15#

Labov, W. (1963) The social motivation of a sound change. *Word*, 19, 273–309. [Reprinted in W. Labov, *Sociolinguistic Patterns*, 1–42. Philadelphia: University of Pennsylvania Press.] #1#, #5#, #7#, #8#

—— (1964) Stages in the acquisition of standard English. In R. Shuy (ed.), *Social Dialects and Language Learning*, 77–103. Champaign, IL: National Council of Teachers of English. #9#

—— (1966a) The linguistic variable as a structural unit. *Washington Linguistic Review*, 3, 4–22. #1#

—— (1966b) Hypercorrection by the lower middle class as a factor in sound change. In W. Bright (ed.), *Sociolinguistics*, 88–101. The Hague: Mouton. [Revised version in W. Labov (1972), 122–43.) #5#, #8#

—— (1966c) *The Social Stratification of English in New York City.* Washington, DC: Center for Applied Linguistics. #2#, #3#, #4#, #5#, #7#, #9#

—— (1969a) Contraction, deletion and inherent variability of the English copula. *Language*, 45, 715–62. #1#

—— (1969b) The logic of nonstandard English. In J. Alatis (ed.), *Georgetown Monographs on Languages and Linguistics*, 22, 1–44. Washington, DC: Georgetown University Press. #7#

—— (1970a) The study of language in its social context. *Studium Generale*, 23, 30–87. [Reprinted in P. Giglioli (ed.), *Language and Social Context*, 283–307. New York: Penguin.] #1#, #17#

—— (1970b) *The Study of Non-standard English*. Urbana, IL: National Council of Teachers of English. #25#

—— (1971a) Methodology. In W. O. Dingwall (ed.), *A Survey of Linguistic Science*, 412–97. College Park, MD: Linguistics Program, University of Maryland. #27#

—— (1971b) The notion of system in creole languages. In D. Hymes (ed.), *Pidginization and Creolization of Languages*, 447–72. Cambridge: Cambridge University Press. #1#, #14#

—— (1972) Rules for ritual insults. In D. Sudnow (eds), *Studies in Social Interaction*. New York: Free Press. #23#

—— (1972a) *Sociolinguistic Patterns*. Philadelphia: University of Pennsylvania Press. #1#, #3#, #5#, #6#, #7#, #8#, #27#, #28#

—— (1972b) *Language in the Inner City: Studies in the Black English Vernacular*. Philadelphia: University of Pennsylvania Press. #1#, #6#, #7#, #9#

—— (1972c) Some principles of linguistic methodology. *Language in Society*, 1, 97–120. #7#

—— (1972d) The Social Motivation of a Sound Change. In W. Labov (ed.), *Sociolinguistic Patterns*, 1–42. Philadelphia: University of Pennsylvania Press. #9#

—— (1973a) The linguistic consequences of being a lame. *Language in Society*, 2, 81–115. #1#

—— (1973b) Where do grammars stop? *23rd Annual Round Table Meeting on Linguistics and Language Studies*, 43–88. Washington, DC: Georgetown University Press. #1#

—— (1980a) The social origins of sound change. In W. Labov, (ed.), *Locating Language in Time and Space*, 251–65. New York: Academic Press. #5#

—— (1981) *Field Methods used by the Project on Linguistic Change and Variation. Sociolinguistic Working Paper 81*. Austin, Texas: South Western Educational Development Laboratory. #1#

—— (1982) Objectivity and commitment in linguistic science: the case of the Black English trial in Ann Arbor. *Language in Society*, 11, 165–201. #7#, #27#

—— (1988) The judicial testing of linguistic theory. In D. Tannen (ed.), *Linguistics in Context: Connecting observation and understanding*, 159–82, Norwood, NJ: Ablex. #27#

—— (1989) The child as linguistic historian. *Language Variation and Change*, 1, 85–98. #9#

—— (1990) The intersection of sex and social class in the course of linguistic change. *Language Variation and Change*, 2, 205–54. #3#, #5#, #8#, #9#

—— (1991a) The three dialects of English. In P. Eckert (ed.), *New Ways of Analyzing Sound Change*, 1–44. New York: Academic Press. #7#

—— (1991b) *Sociolinguistic Patterns*. Philadelphia: University of Pennsylvania Press. #8#

—— (1994) *Principles of Linguistic Change, I: Internal Factors*. Oxford: Blackwell. #Introd.#, #3#, #5#, #7#, #9#

—— (forthcoming) *Principles of Linguistic Change, II: External Factors*. Oxford: Blackwell. #5#

Labov, W. (ed.) (1980b) *Locating Language in Time and Space*. New York: Academic Press. #5#

Labov, W., Cohen, P. and Robins, C. (1965) *A Preliminary Study of the Structure of English used by Negro and Puerto Rican Speakers in New York City*. Washington, DC: U.S. Office of Education and Welfare, Final Cooperative Research Report 3091. #1#

Labov, W. and Harris W. A. (1984) Addressing social issues through linguistic evidence. In J. Gibbons (ed.), *Language and the Law*, 265–305. London: Longman. #27#

—— (1986) De facto segregation of black and white vernaculars. In D. Sankoff (ed.), *Diversity and Diachrony*, 1–24. Amsterdam: John Benjamins. #1#, #3#

Labov, W., Yaeger, M., and Steiner, R. (1972) *A Quantitative Study of Sound Change in Progress*. Philadelphia: US Regional Survey. #7#

Labrie, N. (1990) Commentaires. In L. Laforge and G. D. McConnell (eds), *Diffusion des langues et changement social. Dynamique et mesure*, 297–302. Sainte-Foy: Les Presses de l'Université Laval. #17#

Ladefoged, P. (1992) Another view of endangered languages. *Language*, 68, 809–11. #15#

Ladin, W. (1982) *Der elsässische Dialekt – museumsreif? Analyse einer Umfrage*. Strasbourg: SALDE. #19#

Laferriere, M. (1979) Ethnicity in Phonological Variation and Change. *Language*, 55, 603–17. #9#

Laforge, L. (ed.) (1987) *Proceedings of the International Colloquium on Language Planning. Ottawa, May 25–29, 1986*. Québec: Les Presses de l'Université Laval. #28#

Laitin, D. D. (1992) *Language Repertoires and State Construction in Africa*. Cambridge: Cambridge University Press. #20#

Lakoff, G. (1987) *Women, Fire and Dangerous Things*. Chicago: University of Chicago Press. #10#, #22#

Lakoff, G. and Johnson, M. (1980) *Metaphors we live by*. Chicago: Chicago University Press. #22#, #23#

Lakoff, R. (1975) *Language and Women's Place*. New York: Harper and Row. #8#, #23#

Lakoff, R. T. (1973) The logic of politeness, or, minding your p's and q's. In C. Corum, T. C. Smith-Stark, and A. Weiser (eds), *Papers from the Ninth Regional Meeting of the Chicago Linguistic Society*, 292–305. Chicago: Chicago Linguistic Society. #23#

—— (1989) The limits of politeness: therapeutic and courtroom discourse. *Multilingua*, 8, 101–30. #23#

Lalla, B. and D'Costa, J. (1990) *Language in Exile: Three hundred years of Jamaican Creole*. Tuscaloosa, Alabama: University of Alabama Press. #14#

Lambert, R. D. and Freed, B. (eds) (1982) *The Loss of Language Skills*. Rowley, MA: Newbury House. #15#

Lambert, W. (1972) A social psychology of bilingualism. In J. Pride and J. Holmes (eds), *Sociolinguistics*. London: Penguin. #10#

Lambert, W. E. (1967) A social study of bilingualism. *Journal of Social Issues*, XXIII, 91–109. #28#

—— (1974) Culture and language as factors in learning and education. In F. Aboud and R. D. Mead (eds), *Cultural Factors in Learning*, 105–19. Bellingham: Western Washington State College. #19#

—— (1974) Effects of bilingualism in the individual. In P. A. Hornby (ed.), *Bilingualism: psychological, social and educational implications*, 15–27. New York, San Francisco, London: Academic Press. #19#

—— (1980) The social psychology of language. In G. Giles, W. P. Robinson, and P. M. Smith (eds), *Language: Social Psychological Perspectives*. Oxford: Pergamon. #26#

Lampi, M. (1993) Discourse organization and power: Towards a pragmatics of sales negotiations. In L. F. Bouton and Y. Kachru (eds), *Pragmatics and Language Learning*, Vol. 4, 195–208. Urbana: Division of English as an International Language, University of Illinois at Urbana-Champaign. #23#

Landry, R. and Allard, R. (eds.) (1994) *Ethnolinguistic Vitality. International Journal of the Sociology of Language*, 108. #Introd.#

Langer, J. (1992) *Literature Instruction: A focus on student response*. Urbana, IL: National Council of Teachers of English. #25#

Lanham, L. W. and MacDonald, C. A. (1979) *The Standard in South African English and its Social History*. Heidelberg: Julius Groos Verlag. #6#

Lankshear, C. (with M. Lawler) (1987) *Literacy, Schooling and Revolution*. London: Falmer Press. #10#

Larson, B. E. (1988) An investigation of grammatical differences in writing as found in Japanese and American professional letters. *Dissertation Abstracts International*, 48 (10), 2616-A. #23#

Lavandera, B. (1978) Where does the sociolinguistic variable stop? *Language in Society*, 7, 171–82. #1#, #3#

Lave, J. (1988) *Cognition in Practice: Mind, Mathematics and Culture in Everyday Life*. Cambridge: Cambridge University Press. #10#

Laver, J. (1950) *The Phonetic Description of Voice Quality*. Cambridge: Cambridge University Press. #6#

Le Page, R. B. (1952) A survey of dialects in the British Caribbean. *Caribbean Quarterly* (University College of the West Indies), 2, 4–11. #1#

—— (1957-8) General outlines of Creole English dialects in the British Caribbean. *Orbis* (Louvain) VI 373–91 and VII 54–64. #1#

——(ed.) (1960–1) *Creole Language Studies*: I. R. B. Le Page and D. DeCamp, *Jamaican Creole*; II. *Proceedings of the Conference on Creole Language Studies, Mona 1959*. London: Macmillan. #1#

—— (1968) Problems of description in multilingual communities. *Transactions of the Philological Society for 1968*, 189–212. #1#, #19#

—— (1972) Preliminary report on the sociolinguistic survey of Cayo District, British Honduras. *Language in Society*, 1, 1, 155–72. #1#

—— (1978) *"Projection, focussing, diffusion" or, steps towards a sociolinguistic theory of language, illustrated from the sociolinguistic survey of multilingual communities, Stage I: Cayo District, Belize (formerly British Honduras) and II. St. Lucia.* Society for Caribbean Linguistics Occasional Paper no. 9, School of Education, St. Augustine, Trinidad. [Reprinted in *York Papers in Linguistics*, 1980, no. 9, 9–31.] #1#, #19#

—— (1986–90) *Abstracts and Transcriptions of the York Workshops of the International Group for the Study of Language Standardization and the Vernacularization of Literacy* (IGLSVL). University of York, England: Department of Language and Linguistic Science. #1#

—— (1989) What is a language? *York Papers in Linguistics*, 13, 9–24. #1#

—— (1994) The notion of "linguistic system" revisited. *International Journal of the Sociology of Language*, 109, 109–20.

Le Page, R. B., Christie, P., Jurdant, B., Weeks, A. J., and Tabouret-Keller, A. (1974) Further report on the sociolinguistic survey of multilingual communities. *Language in Society*, 3, 1–32. #1#, #19#

Le Page, R. B. and Tabouret-Keller, A. (1985) *Acts of Identity: Creole-based approaches to ethnicity and language*. Cambridge: Cambridge University Press. #Introd.#, #1#, #4#, #6#, #7#, #14#, #19#

Le Robert (1992) *Dictionnaire québécois d'aujourd'hui* [Dictionary of Present-Day Québec French]. Montréal: Dicorobert. #28#

Lea, M. (1994) I Thought I could Write Until I Came Here: Student Writing in Higher Education. In G. Gibbs (ed.), *Improving Student Learning: Theory and Practice*. Oxford: OSCD. #10#

Lebra, T. S. (1976) *Japanese Patterns of Behavior*. Honolulu: University of Hawaii Press. #23#

—— (1993) Culture, self, and communication in Japan and the United States. In W. B. Gudykunst (ed.), *Communication in Japan and the United States*, 51–87. Albany: State University of New York Press. #23#

Leclerc, J. (1989) *La guerre des langues dans l'affichage* [Language War in Public Posting]. Montréal: Vlb éditeur. #28#

—— (1992) *Langue et société* [Language and Society]. Laval: Mondia. #28#

Lee, Oh-Tuk. (1992) [*Using Our Language Properly*]. Seoul, Hankil, 212–13. #20#

Leech, G. (1983) *Principles of Pragmatics*. London: Longman. #23#

Lefebvre, C. (1986) Relexification in creole genesis revisited: the case of Haitian Creole. In P. Muysken and N. Smith (eds), *Substrata versus Universals in Creole Genesis*, 279–300. Amsterdam: John Benjamins. #14#

Leinster-Mackay, D. (1984) *The Rise of the English Prep School*. Lewes: Falmer Press. #6#

Leith, D. (1983) *A Social History of English*. London: Routledge and Kegan Paul. #10#

Leitner, G. (1980) BBC English and *Deutsche Rundfunksprache*. *International Journal of the Sociology of Language*, 26, 75–100. #11#

—— (1983) *Gesprächsanalyse und Rundfunkkommunikation. Die Struktur englischer phone-ins* [Discourse analysis and radio communication: The structure of British phone-ins]. Hildesheim: Olms. #11#

—— (1984) Australian English or English in Australia. *English Worldwide* 5, 55–85. #11#

—— (1989) *BBC English und Englisch lernen mit der BBC* [*BBC English* and the learning of English with the BBC]. München: Langenscheidt. #11#

—— (1992) International Corpus of English. Corpus design – problems and suggested solutions. In Gerhard Leitner (ed.), *New Directions in English Language Corpora*, 33–64. Berlin: Mouton- de Gruyter. #11#

Leodolter (=Wodak), R. (1975) *Das Sprachverhalten von Angeklagten bei Gericht.* Kronberg: Scriptor. #8#

Lessiak, P. (1959) *Die deutsche Mundart von Zarz in Oberkrain, A. Grammatik mit Ergänzungen von E. Kranzmayer und A. Richter* (= Deutsche Dialektgeographie 50). Marburg. #4#

Levi, J. N. (1994) *Language and Law: A bibliographic guide to social science research in the U.S.A.* Chicago: American Bar Association. #27#

Levi, J. N. and Walker A. G. (eds) (1990) *Language in the Judicial Process.* New York and London: Plenum Press. #27#

Lévi-Strauss, C. (1963) *Structural Anthropology.* New York: Basic Books. #Introd.#

Levy, P. M. G. (1960) *La querelle du recensement.* Bruxelles: Institut Belge de Science Politique. #2#

—— (1974) *The Feed-back of the Legal Use of Statistical Data or the End of a Language Census.* Louvain: mimeographed. #2#

Lewis, E. G. (1972) *Multilingualism in the Soviet Union.* The Hague: Mouton. #18#

Lewis, G. (1976) Bilingualism and bilingual education: The ancient world to the Renaissance. In J. A. Fishman, *Bilingual Education: An international sociological perspective*, 150–200. Rowley, MA: Newbury House. #26#

—— (1983) Implementation of language planning in the Soviet Union. In J. Cobarrubias and J. A. Fishman (eds.), *Progress in Language Planning: International perspectives*, 309–26. Berlin, New York, Amsterdam: Mouton. #28#

Lewontin, R. (1982) *Human Diversity.* London: W. H. Freeman. #8#

Li Wei, Milroy, L., and Pong Sin Ching (1992) A two-step sociolinguistic analysis of code-switching and language choice: the example of a bilingual Chinese community in Britain. *International Journal of Applied Linguistics*, 2, 63–86. #3#

Li Wei (1994) *Three Generations, Two Languages, One Family.* Clevedon: Multilingual Matters. #3#

Lichem, K. and Simon, H.-J. (eds) (1980) *Hugo Schuchardt (Schuchardt-Symposium 1977 in Graz).* Wien: Österreichische Akademie der Wissenschaften. #4#

Limaye, M. and Cherry, R. (1987) Pragmatics, "situated" language, and business communication. *Iowa State Journal of Business and Technical Communication*, 1, 68–88. #23#

Linde, C. (1988a) The quantitative study of communicative success: politeness and accidents in aviation discourse. *Language in Society*, 17, 375–99. #23#

—— (1988b) Who's in charge here? Cooperative work and authority negotiation in police helicopter missions. Paper presented at the 2nd Annual ACM Conference on Computer Supported Collaborative Work (ERIC Document Reproduction Service No. ED301038). #23#

Lippi-Green, R. L. (1989) Social network integration and language change in progress in a rural alpine village. *Language in Society*, 18, 213–34. #1#, #3#, #8#

Lo Bianco, J. (1987) *National Policy on Languages.* Canberra: AGPS. #18#

Lodge, R. A. (1993) *French: From dialect to standard.* London: Routledge. #6#, #28#

Loftus, E. F. and Palmer, J. C. (1974) Reconstruction of automobile destruction. *Journal of Verbal Learning and Verbal Behaviour*, 13, 585–9. #22#

Lorber, J. and Farrell, S. A. (1991) Preface. In Judith Lorber and Susan A. Farrell (eds), *The Social Construction of Gender*, 1–6. London: Sage. #8#

Lorber, J. and Farrell, S. A. (eds) (1991) *The Social Construction of Gender.* London: Sage. #8#

Lorenzoni, G. (1938) *La toponomastica di Sauris, oasi tedesca in Friuli.* Udine: Istituto delle Edizioni Accademiche. #4#

Lörscher, W. and Schulze, R. (1988) On polite speaking and foreign language classroom discourse. *International Review of Applied Linguistics in Language Teaching*, 26, 183–99. #23#

Lotz, J. (1950) Speech and language. *Journal of the Acoustical Society of America*, 22, 712–17. #1#

Loveday, L. (1981) Pitch, politeness and sexual role: an exploratory investigation into the pitch correlates of English and Japanese politeness formulae. *Language and Speech*, 24, 71–89. #23#

Lowenberg, P. H. (ed.) (1988) *Language Spread and Language Policy: Issues, Implications, and Case Studies*. Washington, DC: Georgetown University Press. (Georgetown University Round Table on Languages and Linguistics, 1987). #16#

Lucy, J. A. (1992a) *Language Diversity and Thought: A reformulation of the linguistic relativity hypothesis*. Cambridge: Cambridge University Press. #Introd.#, #22#

—— (1992b) *Grammatical Categories and Cognition: A case study of the linguistic relativity hypothesis*. Cambridge: Cambridge University Press. #22#

Lüdi, G. (1992) Internal migrants in a multilingual country. *Multilingua*, 11, 45–74. #13#

Luke, A. (1988) *Literacy, Textbooks and Ideology*. Brighton: Falmer Press. #10#

Lynch, J. (1976) Letter to the editor. *Papua New Guinea Post Courier*. June 1, 2. #20#

Macaulay, M. (1990) *Processing Varieties in English: An examination of oral and written speech across genres*. Vancouver: University of British Columbia Press. #10#

Macaulay, R. (1977) *Language, Social Class and Education: A Glasgow Study*. Edinburgh: University of Edinburgh Press. #9#

McChesney, R. A. (1989) Media made sport: a history of sports coverage in the United States. In Lawrence Wenner (ed.), *Media, Sports and Society*. Newbury Park: Sage. #11#

Maccoby, E. and Jacklin, C. (1975) *The Psychology of Sex Differences*. Stanford, CA: Stanford University Press. #8#

McConnell, G. D. (1988) *Dimensions et mesure de la vitalité linguistique* [Language Vitality: Its dimensions and measurement]. Québec: International Center for Research on Bilingualism. #21#

—— (1991) *A Macro-Sociolinguistic Analysis of Language Vitality*, Geolinguistic Profiles and Scenarios of Language Contact in India. Sainte-Foy: Presses de l'Université Laval. #21#

McConnell, G. D. and Gendron, J.-D. (1993) *Atlas international de la vitalité linguistique/International Atlas of Language Vitality*. Vol. 1. *India*; Vol. 2. *Western Europe*. Québec: International Center for Research on Language Planning. #2#, #21#

McConnell, G. D., Roberge, B., et al. (1994) *Atlas international de la diffusion de l'anglais et du français: L'Enseignement*. A-24. Sainte-Foy: Presses de l'Université Laval. #21#

McConnell-Ginet, S. (1978) Intonation in a man's world. *Signs*, 3, 541–59. [Reprinted in B. Thorne, C. Kramarae, and N. Henley (eds) (1983), *Language, Gender and Society*, 69–88. Cambridge: Newbury House.] #8#

—— (1988) Language and gender. In Frederick J. Newmeyer (ed.), *Linguistics: The Cambridge survey*. Vol. IV. *Language: The socio-cultural context*, 75–99. Cambridge: Cambridge University Press. #7#, #8#

McConvell, P. (1988) "Mix-im-up": Aboriginal codeswitching, old and new. In M. Heller (ed.), *Codeswitching*, 97–149. Berlin: Mouton de Gruyter. #13#

McCormack, W. C. and Wurm, S. A. (eds) (1978) *Approaches to Language: Anthropological issues*. The Hague: Mouton. #16#

McCrum, R., Cran, W., and MacNeil, R. (1986) *The Story of English*. London: Faber and BBC. #6#

McDavid, R. I. and McDavid, V. G. (1971) [1951] The relationship of the speech of Negroes to the speech of Whites. In W. Wolfram and N. H. Clarke (eds), *Black-White Speech Relationships*, 16–40. Washington, DC: Center for Applied Linguistics. #14#

Mace, J. (1979) *Working with Words*. London: Chameleon Books. #10#

McEntegart, D. and Le Page, R. B. (1982) An appraisal of the statistical techniques used in the Sociolinguistic Survey of Multilingual Communities. In S. Romaine (ed.), *Social Variation in Speech Communities*, 105–24. London: Arnold. #1#

McGuire, C. (1950) Social stratification and mobility patterns. *American Sociological Review*, 15, 195–204. #20#

McIntosh, A. (1952) *An Introduction to a Survey of Scottish Dialects*. Edinburgh: Nelson.

MacKinnon, K. (1995) Report on Compass (Colloquium on Minority-language Population

Censuses), 1–4 Sept. 1993, University of Hertfordshire (UK). In *Actes de Simposi de Demolingüística*, 101–5. Barcelona: Generalitat de Cataláña. #2#

McLaren, P. (1988) Culture or Canon? Critical pedagogy and the politics of literacy. *Harvard Educational Review*, 58, 213–34. #10#

McMullen, L. M. and Krahn, E. E. (1985) Effects of status and solidarity on familiality in written communication. *Language and Speech*, 28, 391–401. #23#

McWhorter, J. (1992) Substratal influences on Saramaccan serial verb constructions. *Journal of Pidgin and Creole Languages*, 7, 1–53. #14#

—— (1993) Towards a new model of genesis: competing processes in the birth of Saramaccan Creole. PhD thesis, Stanford University. #14#

—— (1994) Rejoinder to Derek Bickerton. *Journal of Pidgin and Creole Languages*, 9, 79–93. #14#

—— (1995a) The scarcity of Spanish-based creoles explained. *Language in Society*, 24, 213–44. #14#

—— (1995b) Renewing our vows: Creole studies and historical linguistics. *Paper Presented at the Twenty-first Annual Meeting of the Berkeley Linguistics Society*, University of California, Berkeley, February. #14#

Magee, B. (1973) *Popper*. London: Fontana. #6#

Magens, J. M. (1770) Grammatica over det creolske sprog, som bruges paa de trende Danske Eilande, St. Croix, St. Thomas, og St. Jans i America. Copenhagen: Gerhard Giese Salikath. #14#

Magnusson, A. L. (1992) The rhetoric of politeness and Henry VIII. *Shakespeare Quarterly*, 43, 319–409. #23#

Mahootian, S. (1993) A null theory of codeswitching. PhD dissertation. Evanston, IL: Northwestern University. #13#

Malinowski, B. (1923) The problem of meaning in primitive languages. In C. Ogden and I A. Richards (eds), *The Meaning of Meaning*. New York: Harcourt Brace Jovanovich. #10#

—— (1935) *Coral Gardens and their Magic*. London: Routledge and Kegan Paul. #10#

Maltz, D. and Borker, R. (1982) A cultural approach to male-female miscommunication. In John Gumperz (ed.), *Language and Social Identity*. Cambridge: Cambridge University Press. #8#

Mao, L. R. (1994) Beyond politeness theory: "Face" revisited and renewed. *Journal of Pragmatics*, 21, 451–86. #23#

Marcais, W. (1930). La diglossie arabe. *L'Enseignement public*, 97, 20–39. #12#

Marier, P. (1992) Politeness strategies in business letters by native and non-native English speakers. *English for Specific Purposes*, 11, 189–205. #23#

Markus, H. R. and Kitayama, S. (1991) Culture and the self: implications for cognition, emotion, and motivation. *Psychological Review*, 98, 224–53. #23#

Marshall, D. F. (1986) The question of an official language. *International Journal of the Sociology of Language*, 60, 7–75. #18#

Marshall, D. F. (ed.) (1991) *Language Planning. Focusschrift in Honor of Joshua A. Fishman*. Amsterdam and Philadelphia: John Benjamins. #28#

Martin, L. (1986) Eskimo words for snow. *American Anthropologist*, 88, 418–23. #22#

Martinet, A. (1953/1963) Preface to U. Weinreich *Languages in Contact*, pp. vii–ix. New York: Linguistic Circle of New York/The Hague: Mouton. #1#

—— (1955) *Economie des changements phonétiques* [Economy of Phonetic Changes]. Bern: Franke. #5#

Martinet, A. and Walter, H. (1973) *Dictionnaire de la prononciation française dans son usage réel*. Paris: France Expansion. #6#

Martinez, M. (1989) The implementation of the Pascua Yaqui tribe language policy and the impact on the development of bilingual/bicultural education programs for Yaqui and O'odham students in a public school district. *Proceedings of the Eighth Annual International Native American Languages Institute. Tempe, INALII*, 182–208. #20#

Marx, K. (1852) Der 18te Brumaire des Louis Napoleon. Die Revolution. In K. Marx and F. Engels, *Werke*. Vol. 8, 1960. Berlin: Dietz. #22#

Matoesian, G. M. (1993) *Reproducing Rape: Domination through talk in the courtroom*. Chicago: University of Chicago Press. #27#

Matsumoto, Y. (1988) Reexamination of the universality of face: politeness phenomena in Japanese. *Journal of Pragmatics*, 12, 403–26. #23#

—— (1989) Politeness and conversational universals – observations from Japanese. *Multilingua*, 8, 207–22. #23#

—— (1993) The pragmatic functions of object honorification in Japanese. Paper presented at the Fourth International Pragmatics Conference, Kobe, July. #23#

Mattheier, K. (1984) Sprachkonflikte in einsprachigen Ortsgemeinschaften. In Els Oksaar (ed.), *Spracherwerb – Sprachkontakt – Sprachkonflikt*, 197–204. Berlin and New York: W. de Gruyter. #17#

Mattheier, K. J. (1980) *Pragmatik und Soziologie der Dialekte*. Translated citations in S. Barbour and P. Stevenson, *Variation in German: A critical approach to German sociolinguistics*. Cambridge: Cambridge University Press. #6#

Maurais, J. (ed.) (1985) *La crise des langues* [Language Crisis]. Government of Québec, Conseil de la langue française and Paris, Le Robert. Québec: Les Publications du Québec. #28#

—— (1987) *Politique et aménagement linguistiques* [Language Planning and Language Policies]. Government of Québec, Conseil de la langue française and Paris, Le Robert. Québec, Les Publications du Québec. #28#

Maybin, J. (1993) Dialogic relationships and the construction of knowledge in children's informal talk. In D. Graddol (ed.), *Language and Culture*, 142–52. Clevedon: BAAL/Multilingual Matters. #10#

Maybin, J. and Moss, G. (1993) Talk about texts: reading as a social event. *Journal of Research in Reading*, Special Issue: B. Street (ed.), *The New Literacy Studies* 16, 138–47. #10#

Mayerthaler, E. and W. (1990) Aspects of Bavarian syntax or "Every language has at least two parents." In J. A. Edmondson, C. Feagin, and P. Muhlhäusler (eds), *Development and Diversity: Language variation across time and space. A Festschrift for Charles-James N. Bailey*, 371–429. Arlington, VA: The Summer Institute of Linguistics and the University of Texas. #4#

Medicine, B. (1987) The role of American Indian women in cultural continuity and transition. In Joyce Penfield (ed.), *Women and Language in Transition*, 159–66. New York: NY Press. #8#

Mees, I. (1987) Glottal stop as a prestigious feature in Cardiff English. *English World-Wide*, 8, 25–39. #3#

Meid, W. and Heller, K. (eds) (1981) *Sprachkontakt als Ursache von Veränderungen der Sprach- und Bewußtseinsstruktur*. Innsbruck. #4#

Menn, L. (1989) Some people who don't talk right: universal and particular in child language, aphasia, and language obsolescence. In N. C. Dorian (ed.), *Investigating Obsolescence: Studies in language contraction and death*, 335–46. Cambridge: Cambridge University Press. #15#

Mens en ruimte (Man and Space) (1962). *Taalgrensonderzoek in België* (Language border inquiry in Belgium). Brussels: Mens en ruimte. #2#

Mesthrie, R. (1992) *English in Language Shift: The history, structure and sociolinguistics of South African Indian English*. Cambridge: Cambridge University Press. #3#

Mews, S. (1987) *Religion and National Identity*. Oxford: Blackwell. #20#

Milan, W. G. (1976) The influence of the sex and age factors in the selection of politeness expressions: a sample from Puerto Rican Spanish. *Bilingual Review*, 3, 99–121. #23#

Miller, R. S. (1991) On decorum in close relationships: why aren't we polite to those who we love? *Contemporary Social Psychology*, 15, 63–5. #23#

Milroy, J. (1981) *Regional Accents of English: Belfast*. Belfast: Blackstaff. #8#

—— (1983) Sociolinguistic methodology and the identification of speakers' voices in legal proceedings. In P. Trudgill (ed.), *Applied Sociolinguistics*, 51–72. London: Academic Press. #6#, #27#

—— (1992a) *Linguistic Variation and Change*. Oxford: Blackwell. #Introd.#, #1#, #3#, #8#

—— (1992b) Social network and prestige arguments in sociolinguistics. In K. Bolton and H. Kwok (eds), *Sociolinguistics Today*, 146–62. Cambridge: Cambridge University Press. #1#

Milroy, J. and Harris, J. (1980) When is a merger not a merger? The MEAT/MATE problem in a present-day English vernacular. *English World Wide*, 1, 199–210. #3#

Milroy, J. and Milroy, L. (1978) Belfast: change and variation in an urban vernacular. In P. Trudgill (ed.), *Sociolinguistic Patterns in British English*, 19–36. London: Edward Arnold. #3#, #8#

—— (1991) *Authority in Language: Investigating language prescriptivism and standardization*, 2nd edn. London: Routledge and Kegan Paul. #6#, #7#, #11#, #10#, #28#

—— (1993) Mechanisms of change in urban dialects: the role of class, social network and gender. *International Journal of Applied Linguistics*, 3, 57–78. #3#

Milroy, J., Milroy, L., and Docherty G. (1994) Glottalling and glottalisation: phonological and sociolinguistic perspectives. Paper presented at Second Phonology Workshop: From Cognition to Romance. University of Manchester. #3#

Milroy, J., Milroy, L., and Hartley, S. (1994) Local and supra-local change in British English: the case of glottalisation. *English World Wide*, 15, 1–32. #3#

Milroy, L. (1987a) *Language and Social Networks*, 2nd edn. Oxford: Blackwell. #1#, #3#, #6#, #7#, #8#, #9#

—— (1987b) *Observing and Analyzing Natural Language: A critical account of sociolinguistic method*. Oxford: Blackwell. #1#, #3#, #28#

—— (1992) New perspectives in the analysis of sex differentiation in language. In K. Bolton and H. Kwok (eds), *Sociolinguistics Today: International perspectives*, 163–79. London: Routledge. #1#, #3#

Milroy, L. and Milroy, J. (1992) Social network and social class: toward an integrated sociolinguistic model. *Language in Society*, 21, 1–26. #1#, #3#, #5#, #6#, #8#

Mishler, E. (1984) *The Discourse of Medicine*: Norwood, NJ: Ablex. #Introd.#

Misirkov, K. P. (1903) A few words about the Macedonian literary language. In Todor Dimitrovski et al. (eds), *About the Macedonian Language*, 49–57. Skopje: Macedonian Language Institute "Kriste Misirkov." #20#

Mitford, N. (1949) *Love in a Cold Climate*. New York: Random House. #1#

Mitford, N. (ed.) (1956) *Noblesse Oblige*. London: Hamish Hamilton. #1#

Mithun, M. (1989) The incipient obsolescence of polysynthesis: Cayuga in Ontario and Oklahoma. In N. C. Dorian (ed.), *Investigating Obsolescence: Studies in language contraction and death*, 243–58. Cambridge: Cambridge University Press. #15#

Moosmüller, S. (1987–88) Soziale Perzeption der Grundfrequenz und des Tonhöhenverlaufs bei Frauen und Männern. *Klagenfurter Beiträge zur Sprachwissenschaft*, 13–14, 411–32. #8#

Moosmüller, S. (1989) Phonological variation in parliamentary discussions. In Ruth Wodak (ed.), *Language, Power and Ideology*, 165–80. Amsterdam: Benjamins. #8#

—— (1994) Evaluation of language use in public discourse: Language attitudes in Austria. In Patrick Stevenson (ed.), *Sociolinguistics in the German-speaking Countries*. Oxford: Blackwell. #8#

Morand, D. A. (1991) Power and politeness: a sociolinguistic analysis of dominance, deference, and egalitarianism in organizational interaction. *Dissertation Abstracts International*, 52, 2207–A. #23#

Morgan, M. (ed.) (1994). *The Social Construction of Identity in Creole Situations*. Los Angeles: Center for Afro-American Studies, UCLA. #14#

Morgan, M. H. (1991) Indirectness and interpretation in African-American women's discourse. *Pragmatics*, 1, 421–51. #23#

Morin, Y.-C. (1987) French data and phonological theory. In B. Wenk, J. Durand and C. Slater (eds), *French Phonetics and Phonology*, 25 (291), 815–43. #6#

Morosawa, A. (1990) Intimacy and urgency in request forms of Japanese: a psycholinguistic study. *Sophia Linguistica*, 28, 129–43. #23#

Morris, H. (1890) *Simplified Grammar of the Telugu Language*. London: Kegan Paul, Trench and Trubner. #20#

Morrison, I. R. (1988) Remarques sur les pronoms allucutifs chez Rabelais [Remarks on the allocative pronouns in Rabelais]. *Zeitschrift für Romanische Philologie*, 104, 1–11. #23#

Mougeon, R. and Beniak, E. (1991) *Linguistic Consequences of Language Contact and Restriction*. Oxford: Oxford University Press. #13#

Mous, M. (1994) Unpublished data set on Ma'a/Mbugu. #13#

Mufwene, S. S. (1986) Universalist and substrate theories complement one another. In P. Muysken and N. Smith (eds), *Substrata versus Universals in Creole Genesis*, 129–62. Amsterdam: John Benjamins. #14#

—— (1992) Ideology and facts on African American Vernacular English. *Pragmatics*, 2, 141–66.

Mühlhäusler, P. (1986a) The standardization of Tok Pisin. *Abstracts 1986*, 105–7. #1#

Mühlhäusler, P. (1986b) *Pidgin and Creole Linguistics*. Oxford: Blackwell. #1#, #14#

Mühlhäusler, P. (1993) The role of pidgin and creole languages in language progression and regression. In K. Hyltenstam and A. Viberg (eds), *Progression and Regression in Language: Sociocultural, neuropsychological and linguistic perspectives*, 39–67. Cambridge: Cambridge University Press. #15#

Mulcaster, R. (1582) *The First Part of the Elementarie*. Reprinted in Manfred Görlach (ed.) (1991) *Introduction to Early Modern English*, 227–31. Cambridge: Cambridge University Press. (Spelling and puctuation modernized.) #20#

Müller, M. (1861–2) *Lectures on the Science of Language*, London: Longman, Green (cited from second edition 1862). #1#

Murray, S. O. (1983) *Group Formation in Social Science*, Carbondale and Edmonton: Linguistic Research. #1#

Muysken, P. (1988) Are creoles a special type of language? Creole languages and the bioprogram. In F. J. Newmeyer (ed.), *Linguistics: The Cambridge survey*, Vol. II, *Linguistic Theory: Extensions and implications*, 285–301. Cambridge: Cambridge University Press. #14#

—— (1991) Needed: a comparative approach. In European Science Foundation (ed.), *Papers for the Symposium on Code-switching in Bilingual Studies: Theory, significance and perspectives*, Vol. I, 253–72. #13#

Muysken, P. and Smith, N. (eds) (1986) *Substrata versus Universals in Creole Genesis*. Amsterdam: John Benjamins. #14#

Muysken, P. and Veenstra, T. (1995). Universalist Approaches. In *Pidgins and creoles: An introduction*, ed. by Jacques Arends, Pieter Muysken and Norval Smith, 121–34. Amsterdam and Philadelphia: John Benjamins. #14#

Myers, G. (1989) The pragmatics of politeness in scientific articles. *Applied Linguistics*, 10, 1–35. #23#

—— (1991) Politeness and certainty: the language of collaboration in an Al project. *Social Studies of Science*, 21, 37–73. #23#

Myers-Scotton, C. (1990) Intersections between social motivations and structural processing in code-switching. In *E.S.F. 1990b*, 57–82. #1#

—— (1991a). "Whither code-switching?" – Prospects for cross-field collaboration: a sequential approach to code-switching. In *E.S.F. 1991 II*, 319–352. #1#

—— (1991b) *Motivations and Structures in Code-switching; evidence from Africa*. Oxford: Oxford University Press. #1#

Myers-Scotton, C. M. (1993a) *Duelling Languages: Grammatical Structure in Codeswitching*. Oxford: Oxford University Press. #Introd.#, #13#

—— (1993b) *Social motivations for codeswitching: Evidence from Africa*. Oxford: Oxford University Press. #Introd.#, #13#, #18#.

—— (1993c) Common and uncommon ground: Social and structural factors in codeswitching. *Language in Society*, 22, 475–504. #13#

—— (1995a) Language processing and the mental lexicon in bilinguals. In R. Dirven and J. Vanparys (eds), *New Approaches to the Lexicon*, 73–100. Frankfurt: Peter Lang. #13#

—— (1995b) A lexically-based production model of codeswitching. In L. Milroy and P. Muysken (eds), *One Speaker, Two Languages: Cross-disciplinary perspectives*. Cambridge: Cambridge University Press. #13#

—— (1996) "Matrix language choice" and "morpheme sorting" as possible structural strategies in pidgin/creole formation. In A. Spears and D. Winford (eds), *Pidgins and Creoles: Structure and status*. Amsterdam: Benjamins. #13#

—— (forthcoming) A way to dusty death: The matrix Language turnover hypothesis. In L. Grenoble and L. Whaley (eds), *Endangered Languages*.

Myers-Scotton, C. M. and Jake, J. L. (1995) Matching lemmas in a bilingual language competence and production model: evidence from intrasentential code switching. *Linguistics*, 33, 981–1024.

Nahir, M. (1984) Language planning goals: a classification. *Language Problems & Language Planning*, 8, 294–327. #28#

Nakht, Y. (1908) [A time for action]. *Ha-olam*. 30, 501–2. #20#

Nartey, J. (1982) Code-switching, interference or faddism? Language use among educated Ghanaians. *Anthropological Linguistics*, 24, 183–92. #13#

Nelde, P. H. (1979) *Volkssprache und Kultursprache*. Wiesbaden: Steiner. #2#

—— (1984) Sprachkontakt als Kulturkonflikt. In H. Kühlwein (ed.), *Sprache, Kultur, Gesellschaft*, 31–40. Tübingen: Narr. #17#

—— (1992) Multilingualism and contact linguistics. In H. Pütz (ed.), *Thirty Years of Linguistic Evolution*, 379–97. Philadelphia and Amsterdam: John Benjamins. #2#

Nelde, P. H. (ed.) (1983) *Current trends in contact linguistics (Plurilingua I)*. Bonn: Dümmler. #17#

Nelde, P. H. et al. (1995) *Contact Linguistics: An international handbook of contemporary research*. Berlin and New York: De Gruyter. #17#

Nelson, K. (1991) A matter of time. In S. A. Gelman and J. P. Byrne (eds), *Perspectives on Language and Thought*, 278–318. Cambridge: Cambridge University Press. #22#

Neustupný, J. V. (1970) Basic types of treatment of language problems. *Linguistic Communications*, 1, 77–98. #28#

—— (1978) *Post-structural Approaches to Linguistics*. Tokyo: University of Tokyo Press. #18#

—— (1985) Language norms in Australian-Japanese contact situations. In M. Clyne (ed.), *Australia Meeting Place of Languages*, 161–70. Canberra: Pacific Linguistics. #18#

Newman, L. (1989) Writing in the legal community: constraints upon the writing processes of lawyers. PhD dissertation, University of Pennsylvania. #10#

Newton, G., Hoffmann, F., Hoffmann., J.-P., Russ, C., and Klees, P. (forthcoming) *Languages of Europe at the Crossroads – The Luxembourg Example*. Oxford. #18#

Nichols, P. C. (1983 [=1976]) Linguistic options and choices for black women in the rural South. In B. Thorne, C. Kramarae, N. Henley (eds), *Language, Gender and Society*, 54–68. Cambridge, MA: Newbury House. #8#, #9#

Nihalani P., Tongue, R., and Hosali, P. (1979) *Indian and British English: A handbook of usage and pronunciation*. New Delhi: Oxford University Press. #11#

Nippold, M. A., Leonard, L. B., and Anastopoulos, A. (1982) Development in the use and understanding of polite forms in children. *Journal of Speech and Hearing Research*, 25, 193–202. #23#

Nishimura, M. (1989) The topic-comment construction in Japanese-English code-switching. *World Englishes*, 8, 365–78. #13#

Noelle-Neumann, E., Schulz, W., and Wilke, J. (eds) (1994) *Fischer Lexikon Publizistik – Massenkommunikation*, 4th edn. [Fischer's Dictionary of Journalism – Mass Communications.] Frankfurt am Main: Fischer. #11#

Noregs, M. (1976) [The fundamental principles of Noregs Maallag]. Resolution adopted and first published in 1976 and reprinted in *The Principles and Accomplishments of Noregs Maallag, 1968–1989*, 1–2. Oslo: Noregs Maallag. #20#

Nortier, J. M. (1990) *Dutch and Moroccan Arabic in Contact: Code switching among Moroccans in the Netherlands*. Dordrecht: Foris. #13#

Nunes, S. A. (1981) Ordering and serving: an analysis of the social interactions of bartenders and waiters at a Waikiki drink call station. Unpublished master's thesis, University of Hawaii at Manoa, Honolulu. #23#

O'Barr, W. M. (1982) *Linguistic Evidence*. London: Academic Press. #22#

O'Barr, W. M. and Conley, J. M. (1990) Litigant satisfaction versus legal adequacy in small claims court narratives. In J. N. Levi and A. G. Walker (eds), *Language in the Judicial Process*, 97–131. New York and London: Plenum Press. #27#

Ochs, E. (1988) *Culture and Language Development: Language acquisition and language socialization in a Samoan village*. Cambridge: Cambridge University Press. #9#, #23#

—— (1992) Indexing gender. In Alessandro Duranti and Charles Goodwin (eds), *Rethinking Context: Language as an interactive phenomenon*, 335–58. Cambridge: Cambridge University Press. #8#

O'Donnell, W. R. and Todd, L. (1980) *Variety in Contemporary English*. London: Allen and Unwin. #6#

Office de la langue française and Université du Québec à Chicoutimi (eds) (1994) *Les actes du colloque sur la problématique de l'aménagement linguistique (enjeux théoriques et pratiques). Colloque tenu les 5, 6 et 7 mai 1993 à l'Université du Québec à Chicoutimi* [Proceedings of the Colloquium on Language Planning (Theory and Applications). Held on May 5, 6, and 7, 1993 at the Université du Québec in Chicoutimi] 2 vols. Québec: Government of Québec. #28#

Official Languages Act (1969) Statutes of Canada. #18#

Offord, M. (1990) *Varieties of Contemporary French*. London: Macmillan. #6#

O'Growney, E. (1890) The national language. *Irish Ecclesiastic Record*. 11, 982–92. #20#

Ohara, Y. (1992) Gender-dependent pitch levels: a comparative study in Japanese and English. In K. Hall, M. Bucholtz, and B. Moonwomon (eds), *Locating Power. Proceedings of the Second Berkeley Women and Language Conference*, 469–77. Berkeley, CA: Berkeley University. #8#

Oksaar, E. (1980) Mehrsprachigkeit, Sprachkontakt, Sprachkonflikt. In P. Nelde (ed.), *Languages in Contact and in Conflict*, 43–52. Wiesbaden: Steiner. #17#

Olshtain, E. (1989) Apologies across languages. In S. Blum-Kulka, J. House, and G. Kasper (eds), *Cross-cultural Pragmatics*, 155–73. Norwood, NJ: Ablex. #23#

Olshtain, E. and Weinbach, L. (1993) Interlanguage features of the speech act of complaining. In G. Kasper and S. Blum-Kulka (eds), *Interlanguage Pragmatics*, 108–22. New York: Oxford University Press. #23#

Olson, D. (1977) From utterance to text: the bias of language in speech and writing. *Harvard Educational Review*, 47, 257–81. #10#

—— (1988) Mind and media: the epistemic functions of literacy. *Journal of Communications*, 38, 3. #10#

—— (1994) *The World on Paper: The conceptual and cognitive implications of writing and reading*. London: Cambridge University Press. #10#

Olson, D. et al. (ed.) (1985) *Literacy, Language and Learning*. Cambridge: Cambridge University Press. #10#

Ong, W. J. (1982) *Orality and Literacy: The technologizing of the word*. London: Methuen. #6#, #10#

Orton, H. (1962) *Survey of English Dialects: Introduction*. Leeds: E. J. Arnold. #1#

Orton, H., Barry, M., Halliday, W. J., Tilling, P., and Wakelin, M. F. (1963–9) *Survey of English Dialects*. Leeds: E. J. Arnold. #3#

Orton, H., Sanderson, S., and Widdowson, J. (eds) (1978) *The Linguistic Atlas of England*. London: Croom Helm. #1#, #7#

Ostrup, J. (1929) *Orientalische Hoeflichkeit. Formen und Formeln im Islam. Eine kulturgeschichtliche Studie* [Oriental politeness. Forms and fomulas in Islam. A study in cultural history]. Leipzig: Harrassowitz. #23#

Otheguy, R. (1982) Thinking about bilingual education: a critical appraisal. *Harvard Educational Review*, 52, 301–14. #26#

Oud-de Glas, M. (1983) Foreign language needs: a survey of research. In T. van Els and M. Oud-de Glas (eds), *Research in Foreign Language Needs*, 19–34. Augsburg: Universität Augburg. #2#

Oxenham, J. (1980) *Literacy: Writing, reading and social organisation*. London: Routledge and Kegan Paul. #10#

Pakir, A. (1989) Language alternates and code selection in Baba Malay. *World Englishes*, 8, 379–88. #13#

Paltridge, J. and Giles, H. (1984) "Attitudes towards regional speakers of French." *Linguistische Berichte*, 90, 71–85. #6#

Pandharipande, R. (1990) Formal and functional constraints on code-mixing. In R. Jacobson (ed.), *Codeswitching as a Worldwide Phenomenon*, 15–32. New York: Peter Lang. #13#

—— (1992) Language shift in India, issues and implications. In W. Fase, K. Jaspaert, and S. Kroon (eds), *Maintenance and Loss of Minority Languages*, 253–75. Amsterdam: Benjamins. #13#

Pandit, I. (1990) Grammaticality in code switching. In R. Jacobson (ed.), *Codeswitching as a Worldwide Phenomenon*, 33–69. New York: Peter Lang. #13#

Parkinson, M. G. (1981) Verbal behavior and courtroom success. *Communication Education*, 30, 22–32. #23#

Parsons, J. T. (1952) *The Social System*. London: Tavistock Press. #1#, #3#

Paunonen, H. (1994) Language change in apparent time and in real time. *Paper presented at 23rd Annual Conference on New Ways of Analyzing Variation*. Stanford, CA. #9#

Payne, A. (1980) Factors controlling the acquisition of the Philadelphia dialect by out-of-state children. In W. Labov (ed.), *Locating Language in Time and Space*, 143–78. New York: Academic Press. #9#

Pearlmann, J. (1990) Historical legacies: 1840–1920. *Annals of the American Academy of Political and Social Science*, 508, 27–37. #26#

Pearson, B. (1988) Power and politeness in conversation: encoding of face-threatening acts at church business meetings. *Anthropological Linguistics*, 30, 68–93. #23#

Pederson, L., Leas, S., Bailey, G., and Bassett, M. (1986) *Linguistic Atlas of the Gulf States*. Athens: University of Georgia Press. #9#

Pennycook, A. (1994) Incommensurable discourses? *Applied Linguistics*, 15, 115–38. #10#

Perlmann, R. (1984) Variations in socialization styles: family talk at the dinner table. *Journal of Child Language*, 12, 271–96. #23#

Petersen, J. (1988) Word-internal code-switching constraints in a child's grammar. *Linguistics*, 26, 479–93. #13#

Petyt, K. M. (1980) *The Study of Dialect*. London: André Deutsch. #6#

Pfaff, C. (1979) Constraints on language mixing: intrasentential code-switching and borrowing in Spanish/English. *Language*, 55, 291–318. #13#

Philippon, H. (1938) *Mémoires du deuxième Congrès de la langue française au Canada*. Vol. 2, 108–13. Québec: Imprimerie du Soleil. #20#

Phillips, J. S. (1975) Vietnamese contact French: acquisitional variation in a language contact situation. PhD dissertation, Indiana University. #14#

Phillips, S. (1983) *The Invisible Culture: Communication in classroom and community on Warm Springs Indian reservation*. New York: Longman. #10#, #25#

—— (1992) The Routinization of Repair in Courtroom Discourse. In A. Duranti and C. Goodwin (eds), *Rethinking Context: Language as an Interactive Phenomenon*. London: Cambridge University Press. #10#

Phillipson, R. (1992) *Linguistic Imperialism*. Oxford: Oxford University Press. #10#, #22#

Pickett, A. M. (1989) ESL business letters of request: a discourse analysis of written text. Unpublished master's thesis, University of Hawaii at Manoa, Honolulu. #23#

Plangg, G. A. and Ileiscu, M. (1987) *Akten der Theodor Gartner-Tagung (Rätoromanisch und Rumänisch) in Vill/Innsbruck 1985* (= Romanica Aenipontana XIV). #4#

Plascencia, M. (1992) Politeness in mediated telephone conversations in Ecuadorian Spanish and British English. *Language Learning Journal*, 6, 80–2. #23#

Platt, J. and Weber, H. (1980) *English in Malaysia and Singapore*. Kuala Lumpur: Oxford University Press. #18#

Pool, J. (1991) The world language problem. *Rationality and Society*, 3, 78–105. #12#

Poplack, S. (1980) "Sometimes I'll start a sentence in Spanish y terminol Espanol": Toward a typology of code-switching. *Linguistics*, 18, 581–618. #13#

—— (1981) Syntactic structure and social function of code-switching. In R. Duran (ed.), *Latino language and communicative behavior*, 169–84. Norwood, NJ: Ablex. #13#

—— (1988a) Contrasting patterns in code-switching in two communities. In M. Heller (ed.), *Codeswitching: Anthropological and sociolinguistic perspectives*, 215–44. Berlin: Mouton de Gruyter. #13#

—— (1988b) Language status and language accommodation along a linguistic border. In P. Lowenberg (ed.), *Language Spread and Language Policy*, 90–118. Washington, DC: Georgetown University Press. #13#

Poplack, S. and Sankoff, D. (1987) The Philadelphia story in the Spanish Caribbean. *American Speech*, 62, 291–314. #14#

Poplack, S., Sankoff, D., and Miller, C. (1988) The social correlates and linguistic processes of lexical borrowing and assimilation. *Linguistics*, 26, 47–104. #13#

Popov, P. (1985) On the origin of Russian "vy" as a form of polite address. *Slavic and East European Journal*, 29, 330–7. #23#

Popper, K. (1972) *Objective Knowledge*. Oxford: Clarendon Press. #22#

Poulisse, N. and Bongaerts, T. (1994) First language use in second language production. *Applied Linguistics*, 15, 36–56. #13#

Preisler, B. (1986) *Linguistic Sex Roles in Conversation: Social variation in the expression of tentativeness in English*. Berlin: Mouton de Gruyter. #23#

Preller, G. Schoeman (1905) [Let us be serious about it], reprinted in D. J. C. Geldenhuys. 1967. *Uit die wieg van ons taal: Pannevis en Preller*, 57–89. Johannesburg: Voortrekkerpers. #20#

Preston, D. (1987) Domain-, Role- or Network Specific Use of Language. In U. Ammon, N. Dittmar, K. Mattheier (eds), *Sociolinguistics: An international handbook*, 690–9. Berlin: Walter de Gruyter. #8#

Preston, D. R. (1986a) Fifty some – odd categories of language variation. *International Journal of the Sociology of Language*, 57, 9–48. #7#

—— (1986b) Five visions of America. *Language in Society*, 15, 221–40. #7#

Price, R. (ed.) (1973) *Maroon Societies: Rebel slave communities in the Americas*. Garden City, NY: Doubleday Anchor Press. #14#

Pride, J. and Holmes, J. (eds) (1972) *Sociolinguistics*. London: Penguin. #10#, #28#

Prince, E. F. (1990) On the use of social conversation as evidence in a court of law. In J. N. Levi and A. G. Walker (eds), *Language in the Judicial Process*, 279–89. New York and London: Plenum Press. #27#

Pullum, G. (1991) *The Great Eskimo Vocabulary Hoax*. Chicago: Chicago University Press. #22#

Putnam, G. N. and O'Hern, E. M. (1955) *The Status Significance of an Isolated Urban Dialect*. *Language* Supplement, Language Dissertation 33. #1#

Pütz, M. (1992) The present and future maintenance of German in the context of Namibia's official language policy. *Multilingua*, 11, 293–324. #18#

Pye, C. (1992) Language loss among the Chilcotin. In A. R. Taylor (ed.), Language obsolescence, shift, and death. *International Journal of the Sociology of Language*, 75–86. #15#

Québec (1972) La situation de la langue française au Québec. Rappont de la commission d'enquête sur la situation de la langue française et sur les droits linguistiques au Québec. 3 vols. Québec: Editeur officiel du Québec. #27#

Quirk, R. (1982) Speaking into the air. In R. Hoggart and J. Morgan (eds), *The Future of Broadcasting*, 81–99. London: Arnold. #11#

Rabin, C. (1971) A tentative classification of language-planning aims. In J. Rubin and B. H. Jernudd (eds), *Can Language Be Planned? Sociolinguistic theory and practice for developing nations*, 277–9. Honolulu: University Press of Hawaïi. #28#

Rampton, B. (1992) Scope for empowerment in sociolinguistics? In D. Cameron, E. Frazer, P. Harvey, B. Rampton and K. Richardson, *Researching Language: Issues of power and method*, 29–64. London: Routledge. #10#

—— (in press) *Crossing*. London: Longman. #10#

Ramsaran, S. (ed.) (1990) *Studies in the Pronunciation of English in honour of A. C. Gimson*. London: Routledge. #6#

Rapport de la Commission du recensement linguistique (1960) Bruxelles: Ministère de l'Intérieur et Ministère des Affaires économiques. #2#

Reeve, J. (1989) Community attitudes to Australian English. In Peter Collins and David Blair (eds), *Australian English: The language of a new society*, 111–26. St. Lucia: University of Queensland Press. #11#

Reichstein, R. (1960) Etude des variations sociales et géographique des faits linguistiques. *Word*, 16, 55–99. #1#, #2#

Reid, E. (1978) Social and stylistic variation in the speech of children: some evidence from Edinburgh. In P. Trudgill (ed.), *Sociolinguistic Patterns in British English*, 158–73. London: Edward Arnold. #9#

Reynolds, K. A. (1985) Female speakers of Japanese. *Feminist Issues*, Fall, 13–46. #23#

—— (1989a) Gengo to sei yakuwari [Language and sex roles]. In N. W. E. Center (eds), *Joseigaku koza* [Women's Studies Lectures], 61–5. Tokyo: Daiichi Hoki. #23#

—— (1989b) Josei zasshi no kotoba [Language in women's magazines]. In T. Inoue (ed.), *Josei zasshi wo kaidoku-suru* [Decoding women's magazines], 209–27. Tokyo: Kakiuchi Shuppan. #23#

—— (1990) Female speakers of Japanese in transition. In S. Ide and N. McGloin (eds), *Aspects of Japanese Women's Language*, 1–17. Tokyo: Kuroshio Shuppan. #23#

Rickford, John. Linguistic Variation and the Social Order: a Creole Community Case Study. Unpublished manuscript. #9#

Rickford, J. R. (1979) Variation in a creole continuum: Quantitative and implicational approaches. PhD dissertation, University of Pennsylvania. #14#

—— (1983) What happens in decreolization. In R. Andersen (ed.), *Pidginization and Creolization of Languages*, 298–319. Rowley, MA: Newbury House. #14#

—— (1986) The need for new approaches to social class analysis in sociolinguistics. *Language and Communication* 6, 215–21. #14#

—— (1987) *Dimensions of a Creole Continuum*. Stanford: Stanford University Press.

—— (1991) Sociolinguistic variation in Cane Walk: a quantitative case study. In Jenny Cheshire (ed.), *English Around the World: Sociolinguistic perspectives*, 609–16. Cambridge: Cambridge University Press. #8#

—— (1992) Pidgins and creoles. In W. Bright (ed.), *International Encyclopedia of Linguistics*, Vol. III, 224–32. Oxford: Oxford University Press. #14#

—— (in press) The development of African American Vernacular English. In S. Mufwene, J. Rickford, G. Bailey, and J. Baugh (eds), *African American English*. London: Routledge. #14#

Rickford, J. R. and Handler, J. S. (1994) Textual evidence on the nature of early Barbadian speech, 1676–1835. *Journal of Pidgin and Creole Languages*, 9, 221–55.

Rickford, J. R. and Traugott, E. C. (1985). Symbol of powerlessness and degeneracy, or symbol of solidarity and truth? Paradoxical attitudes toward pidgins and creoles. In S. Greenbaum (ed.), *The English Language Today*, 252–61. Oxford: Pergamon Press. #14#

Rieber, R. W. and Stewart W. A. (eds) (1990) *The Language Scientist as Expert in the Legal Setting: Issues in forensic linguistics. [Annals of the New York Academy of Sciences, 606]* New York: New York Academy of Sciences. #27#

Rigg, L. (1987) A Quantitative Study of Sociolinguistic Patterns of Variation in Adult

Tyneside Speakers. Unpublished dissertation, Department of Speech, University of Newcastle upon Tyne. #3#

Rimac, R. T. (1986) Comprehension and production of indirect requests by language disordered and normal children: an examination of politeness and pragmatic development. *Dissertation Abstracts International*, 46, 3811–B. #23#

Rings, L. (1987) Kriemhilt's face work: a sociolinguistic analysis of social behavior in the Nibelungenlied. *Semiotica*, 65, 317–25. #23#

Rissel, D. R. (1990) Sex, attitudes, and the assimilation of /r/ among young people in San Luis Potosi, Mexico. *Language Variation and Change*, 1, 269–83. #8#

Roberts, C., Davies, E., and Jupp, T. (1992) *Language and Discrimination*. London: Longman. #10#

Roberts, J. (1992) Face-threatening acts and politeness theory: contrasting speeches from supervisory conferences. *Journal of Curriculum and Supervision*, 7, 287–301. #23#

Roberts, J. (1993) The acquisition of new and vigorous sound changes by Philadelphia children. Paper presented at the Twenty-Second Conference on New Ways of Analyzing Variation. Ottawa. #9#

Roberts, J. (1995a) A structural sketch of pidgin Hawaiian. *Amsterdam Creole Studies* (forthcoming). #14#

—— (1995b) Sociohistorical data on pidgin-creole development in nineteenth century Hawai'i MS. presented to visiting Stanford Pidgin/Creole class at the University of Hawaii, Honolulu, May. #14#

Roberts, P. A. (1988) *West Indians and their Language*. Cambridge: Cambridge University Press. #14#

Roberts, J. and Labov, W. (1992) Acquisition of a dialect. Paper presented at the Twenty-First Conference on New Ways of Analyzing Variation. Ann Arbor. #9#

Robertson, D. M. (1910) *A History of the French Academy, 1935[4]–1910 [sic]* 20–2. New York: Dillingham. #20#

Robins, L. S. and Wolf, F. M. (1988) Confrontation and politeness strategies in physician-patient interactions. *Social Science and Medicine*, 27, 217–21. #23#

Robins, R. H. and Uhlenbeck, E. M. (eds) (1991) *Endangered Languages*. Oxford and New York: Berg. #15#, #16#

Robinson, W. P. (1979) Speech markers and social class. In K. R. Scherer and H. Giles (eds), *Social Markers in Speech*, 211–49. Cambridge: Cambridge University Press. #6#

Rockhill, (1987) Gender, language and the politics of literacy. *British Journal of the Sociology of Education*, 8, 153–67. #10#

Rodriguez, E. B. (ed.) (1940) *President Quezon: His biographical sketch, messages and speeches*, 149–52. Manila. #20#

Rogoff, B. (1990) *Apprenticeship in Thinking*. New York: Oxford University Press. #25#

Romaine, S. (1982a) *Sociohistorical Linguistics: Its status and methodology*. Cambridge: Cambridge University Press. #1#, #5#

—— (1982b) What is a speech community? In S. Romaine (ed.), *Social variation in speech communities*, 1–24. London: Arnold. #1#

—— (1984) The sociolinguistic history of t/d deletion. *Folia Historica Linguistica*, 5, 221–55. #3#

—— (1984) The status of sociological models and categories in explaining linguistic variation. *Linguistische Berichte*, 90, 25–80. #1#, #5#

—— (1984) *The Language of Children and Adolescents*. Oxford: Basil Blackwell. #9#

—— (1985) Variable rules, O.K? or can there be sociolinguistic grammars? *Language and Communication*, 5, 53–67. #1#

—— (1988) *Pidgin and Creole Languages*. London: Longman. #1#, #14#

—— (1988a) Contributions from pidgin and creole studies to a sociolinguistic theory of language change. *International Journal of the Sociology of Language*, 71, 59–66.

—— (1989) *Bilingualism*. Oxford: Blackwell. #1#, #13#

—— (1989) Pidgins, creoles, immigrant and dying languages. In N. C. Dorain (ed.), *Investi-*

gating Obsolescence: Studies in language contraction and death, 369–84. Cambridge: Cambridge University Press. #15#

—— (1992) *Language, Education and Development: Urban and rural Tok Pisin in Papua-New Guinea.* Oxford: Oxford University Press. #1#, #14#

—— (1994) *Language in Society: An introduction to sociolinguistics.* Oxford: Oxford University Press. #Introd.#, #8#, #14#

—— (1994). Language standardization and linguistic fragmentation in Tok Pisin. In M. Morgan (ed.), *The Social Construction of Identity in Creole Situations*, 19–42. Los Angeles: Center for Afro-American Studies, UCLA. #14#

Romaine, S. (ed.) (1982) *Social Variation in Speech Communities.* London: Arnold. #1#

Rosenberger, N. R. (1989) Dialectic balance in the polar model of self: the Japan case. *Ethos*, 17, 88–113. #23#

Rosewarne, D. (1994) Estuary English – tomorrow's RP? *English Today*, 10, 1, Jan. #6#

Rosier, P. and Holm, W. (1980) *The Rock Point Experience: A longitudinal study of a Navajo school program.* Washington, DC: Center for Applied Linguistics. #26#

Ross, A. S. C. (1950) Philological probability problems. *Journal of the Royal Statistical Society* (London) Series B, XII, 31–45. #1#

—— (1954) Linguistic class-indicators in present-day English. *Neuphilologische Mitteilungen*, 55, 20–56. #1#

Rót, S. (1985) On the national variety of Australian English. *Annales Universitates Budapensiensis Ling.*, 16, 189–204. #18#

Royal Commission (1965–70) *Report of the Royal Commission on Bilingualism and Biculturalism.* 6 vols. Ottawa: Queen's Printer. #18#

Rubin, J. (1971) Evaluation and language planning. In J. Rubin and B. H. Jernudd (eds), *Can Language Be Planned? Sociolinguistic theory and practice for Developing Nations*, 217–52. Honolulu: University Press of Hawaï. #28#

—— (1972) Bilingual usage in Paraguay. In J. A. Fishman (ed.), *Advances in the Sociology of Language*, vol. 2, 512–30. The Hague: Mouton. #12#

—— (1973) Language planning: discussion of some current issues. In J. Rubin and R. Shuy (eds.), *Language Planning: Current issues and research*, 1–10. Washington, DC: Georgetown University Press. #28#

—— (1984) Bilingual education and language planning. In C. Kennedy (ed.), *Language Planning and Language Education*, 4–16. London, Boston, and Sidney: George Allen & Unwin. #28#

Rubin, J. and Jernudd B. H. (1971) *Can Language be Planned? Sociolinguistic theory and practice for developing nations.* Honolulu: University Press of Hawaii. #21#, #28#

—— (1971) Preface and Introduction: Language planning as an element in modernization. In J. Rubin and B. H. Jernudd (eds.), *Can Language Be Planned? Sociolinguistic Theory and Practice for Developing Nations*, pp. ix–xi and xiii–xxiv. Honolulu: University of Hawaii Press. #28#

Rubin, J. and Shuy, R. (eds.) (1973) *Language Planning: Current Issues and Research.* Washington, DC: Georgetown University Press. #28#

Rubin, J. et al. (1977) *Language Planning Processes.* The Hague: Mouton. #20#

Rubin, Sh. (1992) [Ascend higher (in virtue) – speak Yiddish!] *Dos yidishe vort.* March/April, 52. #20#

Ruble, D. N. and Ruble, Th. L. (1982) Sex stereotypes. In Arthur Miller (ed.), *In the Eye of the Beholder: Contemporary issues on stereotyping*, 188–254. New York: Praeger. #8#

Russell, J. (1981) *Communicative Competence in a Minority Group: A sociolinguistic study of the Swahili-speaking community in the Old Town, Mombasa.* Leiden: J. Brill. #1#

Rustow, D. A. (1968) Language, modernization, and nationhood – an attempt at typology. In J. A. Fishman, C. A. Ferguson, and J. Das Gupta (eds), *Language Problems of Developing Nations*, 87–105. New York: John Wiley. #21#

Ryan, E. B. and Giles, H. (eds) (1982) *Attitudes towards Language Variation.* London: Edward Arnold. #6#, #8#

Rydel, L. (1908) [Mother tongue speech]. *Straz Polska*, 1, 5–6. #20#

Sachdev, I. and Bourhis, R. (1990) Bilinguality and multilinguality. In Howard Giles and Peter W. Robinson (eds), *Handbook of Language and Social Psychology*, 293–308. New York: John Wiley. #8#

Sacks, H. (1972) An initial investigation of the usability of conversational data for doing sociology. In D. Sudnow (ed.), *Studies in Social Interaction*. New York: Free Press. #10#

Sacks, H., Schegloff, E., and Jefferson, G. (1974) A simplest systematics for the organisation of turn-taking in conversation. *Language*, 50, 696–735. #10#

Sadow, S. A. and Maxwell, M. A. (1983) The foreign teaching assistant and the culture of the American university class. Paper presented at the 16th Annual TESOL Convention, Honolulu, HI (ERIC Document Reproduction Service No. ED228897). #23#

St Clair, R. N. (1982) From social history to language attitudes. In E. B. Ryan and H. Giles (eds), *Attitudes towards Language Variation*, 164–74. London: Methuen. #6#

Salami, L. O. (1991) Diffusion and focusing: phonological variation and social networks in Ile-Ife, Nigeria. *Language in Society*, 20, 217–45. #1#, #8#

Samarin, W. J. (1971) Salient and substantive pidginization. In D. Hymes (ed.), *Pidginization and Creolization of languages*, 117–40. Cambridge: Cambridge University Press. #1#

—— (1995) The limitations of nativization in language change. Paper presented at the annual meeting of the Society for Pidgin and Creole Linguistics, held in conjunction with the annual meeting of the Linguistic Society of America, New Orleans, Louisiana, January. #14#

Sanders, C. (1993a) Sociosituational variation. In C. Sanders (ed.), *French Today: Language in its social context*, 27–53. Cambridge: Cambridge University Press. #6#

Sanders, C. (ed.) (1993b) *French Today: Language in its social context*. Cambridge: Cambridge University Press. #6#

Sankoff, D. and Laberge, S. (1978) The linguistic market and the statistical explanation of variability. In D. Sankoff (ed.), *Linguistic Variation: Models and Methods*, 239–50. New York: Academic Press. #9#

Sankoff, D., Poplack, S., and Vanniarajan, S. (1990) The case of the nonce loan in Tamil. *Language Variation and Change*, 2, 71–101. #13#

—— (1991) The empirical study of code-switching. In *E.S.F.* 1991, vol. I, 181–206. #1#

Sankoff, G. (1979) The genesis of a language. In K. C. Hill (ed.), *The Genesis of Language*, 23–47. Ann Arbor: Karoma. #14#

—— (1980) *The Social Life of Language*. Philadelphia: University of Pennsylvania Press. #14#

Santa Ana, O. A. (1992) Chicano English evidence for the exponential hypothesis: a variable rule pervades lexical phonology. *Language Variation and Change*, 4, 275–88. #8#

Santorini, B. and Mahootian, S. (1995) Code-switching and the syntactic status of adnominal adjectives. *Lingua*, 96, 1–27. #13#

Santos, T. (1992) Ideology in composition: L1 and ESL. *Journal of Second Language Writing*, 1, 1–15. #10#

Sapir, E. (1921) *Language: An introduction to the study of speech*. New York: Harcourt, Brace. #1#, #3#

Sardesai, M. (1962) [*We Want Our language*]. Margao, Goa, Konkani Bhasha Mandal, 2–3. #20#

Sato, C. J. (1985), Linguistic inequality in Hawaii: the post-creole dilemma. In N. Wolfson and J. Manes (eds), *Language of Inequality*, 255–72. Berlin: Mouton. #14#

Saville-Troike, M. (1982) *The Ethnography of Communication: An introduction*. Oxford: Basil Blackwell. #21#

Scannel, P. (ed.) (1991) *Broadcast Talk*. London: Sage. #11#

Schaff, A. (1984) The pragmatic function of stereotypes. *International Journal of the Sociology of Language*, 45, 89–100. #1#

Scheerhorn, D. R. (1991) Politeness in decision-making. *Research on Language and Social Interaction*, 25, 253. #23#

Schegloff, E. (1979) Identification and recognition in telephone conversation openings. In

G. Psathas (ed.), *Everyday Language. Studies in ethnomethodology*, 23–78. New York: Irvington. #23#

Scherer, K. R. and Giles, H. (eds) (1979) *Social markers in speech*. Cambridge: Cambridge University Press. #6#

Schermerhorn, R. A. (1970) *Comparative Ethnic Relations*. New York: Random House. #18#

Schieffelin, B. B. (1990) *The Give and Take of Everyday Life: Language socialization of Kaluli children*. Cambridge: Cambridge University Press. #23#

Schieffelin, B. B. and Eisenberg, A. R. (1984) Cultural variation in children's conversations. In R. L. Schiefelbusch and J. Pickar (eds), *The Acquisition of Communicative Competence*, 377–420. Baltimore, MD: University Park Press. #23#

Schieffelin, B. B. and Ochs, E. (1986) Language socialization. In *Annual Review of Anthropology*, 163–91. #9#

Schiffman, H. F. (1974) Language, linguistics and politics in Tamilnad. In Edwin Gerow and Margery Lang (eds), *Studies in the Language and Culture of South Asia*, 125–34. University of Washington Press, and Publications on Asia, No. 23, of the Institute for Comparative and Foreign Area Studies. #12#

—— (1991) Swiss-German diglossia. In A. Hudson (ed.), Studies in diglossia. *Southwest Journal of Linguistics*, 10, 173–88. #12#

Schilling-Estes, N. and Wolfram, W. (1994). Convergent explanation and alternative regularization patterns: *Were/weren't* leveling in a vernacular English variety. *Language Variation and Change*, 6, 273–302. #7#

Schlesinger, P. (1978) *Putting "reality" together: BBC news*. London: Constable. #11#

Schmidt, A. (1985) *Young People's Dyirbal: An example of language death from Australia*. Cambridge and New York: Cambridge University Press. #1#, #3#, #15#

—— (1990) *The Loss of Australia's Aboriginal Language Heritage*. Canberra: Aboriginal Studies Press. #16#

—— (1991) Language attrition in Boumaa Fijian and Dyirbal. In H. W. Seliger and R. M. Vago (eds), *First Language Attrition*, 113–24. Cambridge and New York: Cambridge University Press. #15#

Schramm, W. (ed.) (1975) *Mass Communications*. Urbana: University of Illinois Press. #11#

Schuchardt, H. (1884) *Dem Herrn Franz von Miklosich zum 20. Nov., 1883. Slawodeutsches und Slawo-italienisches*. Graz: Leuschner & Lubensky. #4#

Schumann, J. H. (1978) *The Pidginization Process: A model for second language acquisition*. Rowley, MA: Newbury House. #7#

Schumann, J. H. and Stauble, A.-M. (1983) A discussion of second language acquisition. In R. Andersen (ed.), *Pidginization and Creolization as Language Acquisition*, 260–74. Rowley, MA: Newbury House. #14#

Schütz, A. (1965) *Phenomenology of the Social World*. Evanston, IL: Northwestern University Press. #Introd.#

Scollon, R. and Scollon, S. (1981) *Narrative, Literacy and Face in Interethnic Communication*. Norwood, NJ: Ablex. #10#, #23#

Scollon, R. and Scollon, S. B. K. (1983) Face in interethnic communication. In J. C. Richards and R. W. Schmidt (eds), *Language and Communication*. London: Longman. #23#

Scotton, C. M. (1976) Strategies of neutrality: language choice in uncertain situations. *Language*, 52, 919–41. #13#

—— (1983) The negotiation of identities in conversation: a theory of markedness and code choice. *International Journal of the Sociology of Language*, 44, 115–36. #13#

—— (1986) Diglossia and code-switching. In J. A. Fishman (ed.) *The Fergusonian Impact*, Vol. 2: *Sociolinguistics and the Sociology of Language*, 403–15. Berlin: Mouton de Gruyter. #12#

—— (1988a) Codeswitching as indexical of social negotiation. In M. Heller (ed.), *Codeswitching: Anthropological and sociolinguistic perspectives*, 151–86. Berlin: Mouton de Gruyter. #13#

—— (1988b) Codeswitching and types of multilingual communities. In P. Lowenberg (ed.),

Language Spread and Language Policy, 61–82. Washington, DC: Georgetown University Press. #13#

—— (1988c) Self-enhancing codeswitching as interactional power. *Language & Communication*, 8, 333–46. #13#

Scotton, C. M. and Okeju, J. (1973) Neighbors and lexical borrowings. *Language*, 49, 871–89. #13#

Scotton, C. M. and Ury, W. (1977) Bilingual strategies: the social function of code switching. *International Journal of the Sociology of Language*, 13, 5–20. #13#

Scribner, S. and Cole, M. (1981) *The Psychology of Literacy*. Cambridge, MA: Harvard University Press. #10#

Searle, C. (1984) *Words Unchained: Language and revolution in Grenada*. London: Zed Books Distribution Centre. #14#

Searle, J. (1969) *Speech Acts: An essay in the philosophy of language*. Cambridge: Cambridge University Press. #25#

Searle, J. R. (1976) A classification of illocutionary acts. *Language in Society*, 5, 1–23. #23#

Sebba, M. (1993) *London Jamaican: Language systems in interaction*. London: Longman. #1#, #6#

Seliger, H. W. and Vago, R. M. (eds). (1991) *First Language Attrition*. Cambridge and New York: Cambridge University Press. #15#

Sell, R. D. (1985a) Tellability and politeness in the Miller's tale: first steps in literary pragmatics. *English Studies*, 66, 496–512. #23#

—— (1985b) Politeness in Chaucer: suggestions towards a methodology for pragmatic stylistics. *Studia Neophilologica*, 57, 175–85. #23#

Seminario de Sociolingüística da Real Academia Galega (1995). Datas sobre mapa sociolingüístico de Galicia. In *Actes de Simposi de demolingüística*, 126–34. Barcelona: Generalitat de Cataláña. #2#

Shamir, A. (1992) [About Yiddish and Jewish children in Byalistok]. *Yerushelayemer almenakh*, 22, 197–8. #20#

Shastri, N. S. (forthcoming). Code-mixing in the process of Indianization of English: a corpus-based study. *Indian Linguistics* (Pune, India). #11#

Shibamoto, J. S. (1987) The womanly woman: manipulation of stereotypical and nonstereotypical features of Japanese female speech. In S. U. Phillips, S. Steel, and C. Tanz (eds), *Language, Gender, and Sex in Comparative Perspective*, 26–49. Cambridge: Cambridge University Press. #23#

Shimamura, K. (1993) Judgement of request strategies and contextual factors by Americans and Japanese EFL learners. Unpublished master's thesis, University of Hawaii at Manoa. #23#

Shryock, H. S. and Siegel, J. S. and Associates (1973) *The Methods and Materials of Demography*. Washington, DC: US Bureau of the Census. #2#

Shuman, A. (1986) *Storytelling Rights: The uses of oral and written texts by urban adolescents*. Cambridge: Cambridge University Press. #10#

Shuy, R. (1986) Language and the Law. *Annual Review of Applied Linguistics*, 7, 50–63. #10#

Shuy, R. W. (1990) Evidence of cooperation in conversation: topic-type in a solicitation to murder case. In R. W. Rieber and W. A. Stewart (eds), *The Language Scientist as Expert in the Legal Setting: Issues in forensic linguistics*. [*Annals of the New York Academy of Sciences*, 606], 85–105. New York: New York Academy of Sciences. #27#

—— (1993) *Language Crimes: The use and abuse of language evidence in the courtroom*. Oxford: Blackwell. #27#

Shuy, R., Wolfram, W., and Riley, W. K. (1966) *A Study of the Social Dialects of Detroit*. Final Report Project 6–1347. Washington, DC: Office of Education. #7#

—— (1967) *Linguistic Correlates of Social Stratification in Detroit Speech*. Michigan State University: Final report, Cooperative research project, 6–1347. #1#

Sibayan, B. P. (1991) Becoming bilingual in English in a non-English environment. In O. García (ed.), *Bilingual Education: Focusschrift in honor of Joshua A. Fishman*, 283–96. Amsterdam: John Benjamins. #26#

Siegel, J. (1987) *Language Contact in a Plantation Environment: A sociolinguistic history of Fiji*. Cambridge: Cambridge University Press. #14#

Siehr, K.-H. (1993) *Abwickeln: brisantes Wort – brisanter Diskurs* [*Abwickeln*: a controversial word, a controversial discourse]. *Sprache und Literatur*, 72, 31–42. #11#

Sifianou, M. (1989) On the telephone again! Differences in telephone behaviour: England versus Greece. *Language in Society*, 18, 527–44. #23#

Siguán, M. (1988) Bilingual education in Spain. In C. B. Paulston (ed.), *International Handbook of Bilingualism and Bilingual Education*, 449–73. New York: Greenwood Press. #26#

Silva-Corvalán, C. (1991). Spanish language attrition in a contact situation with English. In H. W. Seliger and R. M. Vago (eds), *First Language Attrition*, 151–71. Cambridge and New York: Cambridge University Press. #15#

Silverman, D. and Jones, J. (1976) *Organisational Work: The language of grading/the grading of language*. London: Collier Macmillan. #10#

Silverstein, M. (1992) The Interdeterminacy of Contextualisation: When is enough enough? In Auer and di Luzio (eds), *The Contextualization of Language*. Amsterdam: John Benjamins. #10#

Simmler, F. (1991) Die Textsorte "Regelwerk"? und "Lehrbuch" aus dem Kommunikationsbereich des Sports bei Mannschaftsspielen und ihre Funktionen [The text type "rule book" and "teaching manual" in the communicational sphere of team sports and its functions]. *Sprachwissenschaft*, 16, 251–301. #11#

—— (1993) Zeitungssprachliche Textsorten und ihre Varianten. Untersuchungen anhand von regionalen und überregionalen Tageszeitungen zum Kommunikationsbereich des Sports [Print media types of text and their variants. A study of the communicational sphere of sports in regional and national newspapers]. In F. Simmler (ed.), *Probleme der funktionalen Grammatik* [Problems of functional grammar], 133–282. Frankfurt am Main: Peter Lang. #11#

Simpson, E. (1985) Translating in the Nigerian mass media: a sociolinguistic study. In F. O. Ugboajah (ed.), *Mass Communication, Culture and Society in West Africa*, 133–51. München: Saur. #11#

Sinclair, J. and Coulthard, M. (1975) *Towards an Analysis of Discourse*. Oxford: Oxford University Press. #10#

Singler, J. (1986) Short note. *Journal of Pidgin and Creole Languages*, 1, 141–5. #14#

—— (1990a) On the use of sociohistorical criteria in the comparison of creoles. *Linguistics*, 28, 645–59. #14#

—— (ed.) (1990b) *Pidgin and Creole Tense-mood-aspect Systems*. Amsterdam: John Benjamins. #14#

—— (1991) Copula variation in Liberian Settler English and American Black English. In *Verb Phrase Patterns in Black English and Creoles*, ed. by Walter F. Edwards and Donald Winford, 129–64. Detroit: Wayne State University Press. #14#

—— (1992) Rejoinder: Nativization and pidgin/creole genesis. *Journal of Pidgin and Creole Languages*, 7, 319–33. #14#

—— (1993) African influence upon Afro-American language varieties: a consideration of sociohistorical factors. In S. S. Mufwene (ed.), *Africanisms in Afro-American Language Varieties*, 235–53. Athens: University of Georgia Press. #14#

Skulic, I. (1987) Vuk Karadzic. *Zavicaj/Homeland*, 34, n. 319–26, 7. #20#

Skutnabb-Kangas, T. (1977) Language in the process of cultural assimilation and structural incorporation of linguistic minorities. In C. C. Elert et al. (eds), *Dialectology and Sociolinguistics*. UMEA: UMEA Studies in the Humanities. #26#

—— (1988) Multilingualism and the education of minority students. In T. Skutnabb-Kangas and J. Cummins (eds), *Minority Education: From shame to struggle*, 9–44. Clevedon: Multilingual Matters. #26#

Skutnabb-Kangas, T. and García, O. (1995) Multilingualism for all? General principles. In T. Skutnabb-Kangas (ed.), *Multilingualism for All*, 221–56. Lisse: Swets and Zeitlinger. #26#

Slobin, D. I. (1985) *The Cross-linguistic Study of Language Acquisition*. Hillsdale, NJ: LEA. #25#

Slugoski, B. R. (1985) *Grice's Theory of Conversation as a Social Psychological Model*. PhD dissertation, Oxford. #23#

Smith, A. (1986) *The Ethnic Origins of Nations*. Oxford: Oxford University Press: #10#

Smith, N. (1989) *The Twitter Machine*. Oxford: Blackwell. #Introd.#

Smith, P. M. (1979) Sex markers in speech. In Klaus R. Scherer and Howard Giles, *Social Markers in Speech*, 110–46. Cambridge: Cambridge University Press. #8#

—— (1985) *Language, the Sexes and Society*. New York: Basil Blackwell. #7#, #8#

Smith-Hefner, N. J. (1981) To level or not to level: Codes of politeness and prestige in rural Java. In C. S. Masek, R. A. Hendrick, and M. F. Miller (eds), *Papers from the Parasession on Language and Behavior: Chicago Linguistic Society*, 211–17. Chicago: Chicago Linguistic Society. #23#

—— (1988) Women and politeness: the Javanese example. *Language in Society*, 17, 535–54. #23#

Smolics, J. J. (1980) Core values and cultural identity. *Ethnic and Racial Studies*, 4, 75–90. #18#

Snow, C. E. (1995) Issues in the study of input: finetuning, universality, individual and developmental differences, and necessary causes. In P. Fletcher and B. MacWhinney (eds), *The Handbook of Child Language*. Oxford: Basil Blackwell. #25#

Snow, C. E., Perlmann, R. Y., Gleason, J. B., and Hooshyar, N. (1990) Developmental perspectives on politeness: sources of children's knowledge. *Journal of Pragmatics*, 14, 289–305. #23#

Soh, J.-C. (1985) Social changes and their impact on speech level in Korean. In J. D. Woods and R. R. K. Hartmann (eds), *Language Standards and their Codification: Process and application*, 29–41. Exeter: University of Exeter Press. #23#

Solan, L. (1994) *The Language of Judges*. Chicago: University of Chicago Press. #27#

Søndergaard, B. (1991) Switching between seven codes within one family. *Journal of Multilingual and Multicultural Development*, 12, 85–92. #18#

Song-Cen, C. (1991) Social distribution and development of greeting expressions in China. *International Journal of the Sociology of Language*, 92, 55–60. #23#

Spinozzi Monai, L. (ed.) (1990) *Aspetti metodologici e teorici nello studio del plurilinguismo nei territori dell' Alpe Adria*. Tricesimo: Aviani Editore. #4#

Sridhar, K. K. (1991) Bilingual education in India. In O. García (ed.), *Bilingual Education: Focusschrift in honor of Joshua A. Fishman*, 89–101. Amsterdam: John Benjamins. #26#

Sridhar, S. N. and Sridhar, K. (1980) The syntax and psycholinguistics of bilingual codemixing. *Canadian Journal of Psychology*, 34, 7–16. #13#

Staczek, J. (1993) The English language and the Gulf war: corpus linguistics, variation, and word-formation. *World Englishes*, 12, 15–24, #11#

Staley, C. M. (1982) Sex-related differences in the style of children's language. *Journal of Psycholinguistic Research*, 11, 141–58. #9#

Stalpers, J. (1995) The expression of disagreement. In K. Ehlich and J. Wagner (eds), *Discourse of Business Negotiation*. Berlin: Mouton de Gruyter. #23#

Stampe, D. (1969) The acquisition of phonetic representations. *CLS*, 5, 443–54. #8#

Stemmer, B. (1994) A pragmatic approach to neurolinguistics: requests (re)considered. *Brain and Language*, 46, 565–91. #23#

Stemmer, B., Giroux, F., and Joanett, Y. (1994) Production and evaluation of requests by right hemisphere brain-damaged individuals. *Brain and Language*, 47, 1–31. #23#

Stenson, N. (1990) Phrase structure congruence, government, and Irish-English codeswitching. In R. Hendrick (ed.), *Syntax and Semantics 23: The syntax of the modern Celtic languages*, 167–97. San Diego and New York: Academic Press. #13#

Stevenson, P. (ed.) (1994) *Sociolinguistics in the German-speaking Countries*. Oxford: Blackwell. #8#

Stewart, W. A. (1962) An Outline of Linguistic Typology for describing Multilingualism. In F. Rice (ed.), *Study of the Role of Second Languages in Asia, Africa and Latin America*, 15–25. Washington, Center for Applied Linguistics of the Modern Language Association of America. #21#

—— (1964) Urban negro speech. In R. W. Shuy et al. (eds), *Social Dialects and Language Learning*, 10–18. Champaign, IL: National Council of Teachers of English. #6#

—— (1967) Sociolinguistic factors in the history of American Negro dialects. *Florida Foreign Language Reporter*, 5 (2). #1#, #14#

—— (1968) Continuity and change in American Negro dialects. *Florida Foreign Language Reporter*, 6 (1). #1#, #14#

Stolcke, V. (1993) Is sex to gender as race to ethnicity? In Teresa De Valle (ed.), *Gendered Anthropology*, 16–36. London and New York: Sage. #8#

Stoylen, B. (1931) [The Norwegian language strengthens what is best in the life of our people]. *Norsk Aarbok*, 12, 5–7. #20#

Strassner, E. (1975) Produktions- und Rezeptionsprobleme bei Nachrichtentexten [Aspects of production and reception of news texts]. In Egon Strassner (ed.), *Nachrichten* [News]. München: Fink. #11#

Street, B. (1984) *Literacy in Theory and Practice*. Cambridge: Cambridge University Press. #10#

—— (1988) Literacy practices and literacy myths. In R. Saljo (ed.), *The Written World: Studies in literate thought and action*, 59–72. Berlin and New York: Springer-Verlag. #10#

—— (1993) Culture is a verb: anthropological aspects of language and cultural process. In D. Graddol (ed.), *Language and Culture*, 23–43. Clevedon: BAAL/Multilingual Matters. #10#

Street, B. and Street, J. (1991) The Schooling of Literacy. In D. Barton and R. Ivanic (eds), *Writing in the Community*, 143–66. London: Sage. #10#

Stubbs, M. (1976) *Language, Schools and Classrooms*. London: Methuen. #6#

—— (1980) *Language and Literacy*. London, RKP. #10#

—— (1983) *Discourse Analysis*. Oxford: Basil Blackwell. #10#

—— (1986) *Educational Linguistics*. Oxford: Basil Blackwell. #10#

—— (1991) Educational language planning in England and Wales: multicultural rhetoric and assimilationist assumptions. In F. Coulmas (ed.), *A Language Policy for the European Community*, 215–39. Berlin: Mouton de Gruyter. #26#

—— (1994) Grammar, text and ideology. *Applied Linguistics*, 15, 201–23. #22#

Sulzby, E. and Teale, W. (1991) Emergent literacy. In R. Barr and D. Pearson (eds), *Handbook of Reading Research*, Vol. 2, 727–57. New York: Longman. #25#

Suny, R. G. (1993) *The Revenge of the Past: Nationalism, revolution and the collapse of the Soviet Union*. Stanford, CA: University Press. #20#

Sussman, N. M., and Rosenfeld, H. M. (1982) Influence of culture, language, and sex on conversational distance. *Journal of Personality and Social Psychology*, 42, 66–74. #23#

Sutcliffe, D. (1982) *British Black English*. Oxford: Basil Blackwell. #6#

Swadesh, M. (1948) Sociologic notes on obsolescent languages, *International Journal of American Linguistics*, 14, 226–35. #16#

Swales, J. (1990) *Genre Analysis*. Cambridge: Cambridge University Press. #8#

Swann, J. (1992) *Girls, Boys and Language*. Oxford: Basil Blackwell. #25#

Swigart, L. (1992) Two codes or one? The insiders' view and the description of codeswitching in Dakar. *Journal of Multilingual and Multicultural Development*, 13, 83–102. #13#

—— (1994) Cultural creolization and language use in post-colonial Africa: the case of Senegal. *Africa*, 64, 175–89. #13#

Syed, G. M. (1985) *A Case for Sindhi Desh*. Bombay: Babani. #20#

Tabouret-Keller, A. (1989) Séminar d'antropologie du langage. *MSH Informations. Bulletin de la Fondation des Sciences de l'Homme*, no. 59, 15–17. #19#

—— (1991) Langue, miroir, discours, les lieux du même et du semblable. *Cahiers de Praxématique*, no. 18, *Le même et l'autre en discours* (sous la direction de J. Bres), 11–25. #19#

—— (1994) Langues et identités: en quels termes les dire? *Les cahiers de la francophonie, septembre*, no. 2, *Langues et identités*, 9–14.

Tabouret-Keller, A. and Le Page, R. B. (1986) The mother-tongue metaphor, *Grazer Linguistische Studien*, 27, 249–59. #19#

Tabouret-Keller, A. and Luckel, F. (1981) La dynamique sociale du changement linguistique: quelques aspects de la situation rurale en Alsace. *International Journal of the Sociology of Language*, 29, 51–70. #1#

Tagliamonte, S. and Poplack, S. (1988) How Black English *Past* got to the present. *Language in Society*, 17, 513–33. #14#

—— (1993) The zero-marked verb: testing the creole hypothesis. *Journal of Pidgin and Creole Languages*, 8, 171–206. #14#

Takahara, K. (1991) Female speech patterns in Japanese. *International Journal of the Sociology of Language*, 92, 61–85. #23#

Takahashi, S. (1992) *Transferability of indirect request strategies*. University of Hawaii Working Papers in ESL, 11, 69–124. #23#

Takahashi, T. and Beebe, L. M. (1993) Cross-linguistic influence in the speech act of correction. In G. Kasper and S. Blum-Kulka (eds), *Interlanguage Pragmatics*, 138–57. New York: Oxford University Press. #23#

Tannen, D. (1982) The myth of orality and literacy. In W. Frawley (ed.), *Linguistics and Literacy*. New York: Plenum. #10#

—— (1984) *Conversational Style*. Norwood, NJ: Ablex. #10#

—— (1986) *That's not what I meant*. New York: Ballantine Books. #23#

—— (1991) *You just don't understand*. New York: William Morrow. #8#

Tannen, D. (ed.) (1993a) *Framing in Discourse*. Oxford: Oxford University Press. #8#

—— (1993b) *Gender and Conversational Interaction*. Oxford: Oxford University Press. #8#

Tardival, J.-P. (1881) La Langue française au Canada. *Revue canadienne*, 17 (new series, 1), 259–67. #20#

Tauli, W. (1968) *Introduction to a Theory of Language Planning. Acta Universitatis Upsaliensis, Studia Philologiae Scandinavicae Upsaliensia 6*. Upsala: Almquist & Wiksell. #28#

Taylor, A. R. (ed.) (1992) *Language Obsolescence*. Berlin and New York: Mouton de Gruyter. #15#

Taylor, D. (1963) The origin of West Indian creole languages: Evidence from grammatical categories. *American Anthropologist*, 65, #14#

Taylor, G. (ed.) (1988) *Literacy by Degrees*. Oxford: Oxford University Press/SRHE. #10#

TESOL Quarterly (1993) Special Topic Issue: *Adult Literacies*, 27 (3). #10#

Tharp, R. and R. Gallimore (1988) *Rousing Minds to Life: Teaching, learning and schooling in social context*. Cambridge, MA: Newbury House. #25#

Thoburn, T. (1971) Cost-benefit analysis in language planning. In J. Rubin and B. H. Jernudd (eds), *Can Language Be Planned? Sociolinguistic Theory and Practice for Developing Nations*, 253–62. Honolulu: University of Hawaii Press. #28#

Thomas, B. (1990) Differences of sex and sects: linguistic variation and social networks in a Welsh mining village. In Jennifer Coates and Deborah Cameron (eds), *Women in their Speech Communities: New perspectives on language and sex*, 51–60. New York: Longman. #8#

Thomas, G. (1991) *Language Purism*. London: Longman. #20#

Thomason, S. G. (1983) Chinook Jargon in areal and historical context. *Language*, 59, 820–70. #14#

—— (1992) Response to Bickerton. *Journal of Pidgin and Creole Languages*, 7, 106–11. #14#

Thomason, S. G. (ed.) (1992) *Language, Journal of the Linguistic Society of America*. Baltimore: Linguistic Society of America. #15#

Thomason, S. G. and Kaufman, T. (1988) *Language Contact, Creolization, and Genetic Linguistics*. Berkeley: University of California Press. #1#, #13#, #14#

Thompson, J. B. (1985) *Studies in the Theory of Ideology*, London: Polity Press. #10#

Thompson, R. W. (1961) A note on some possible affinities between the creole dialects of the Old World and those of the New. In R. B. Le Page (ed.), *Creole Language Studies* 2, 107–13. London: Macmillan. #14#

Tiersma, P. M. (1990) The language of perjury: "Literal truth", ambiguity, and the false statement requirement. *Southern California Law Review*, 63, 373–431. #27#

—— (1993) The judge as linguist. *Loyola of Los Angeles Law Review*, 27, 269–83. #27#

Timm, L. (1975) Spanish-English code-switching: El Porque y how-not-to. *Romance Philology*, 28, 473–82. #13#

Todd, L. (1974) *Pidgins and Creoles*. London: Routledge and Kegan Paul. #14#

Tollefson, J. W. (1991) *Planning Language, Planning Inequality*. London: Longmans. #20#

Toon, Th. E. (1991) The sociopolitics of literacy: new methods in Old English dialectology. In P. Eckert (ed.), *New Ways of Analyzing Sound Change*. San Diego: Academic Press. #5#

Torres, L. (1989) Code-mixing and borrowing in a New York Puerto Rican community. *World Englishes*, 8, 419–32. #13#

Trail, A. (forthcoming) The Khoesan languages of South Africa. In Rajend Mesthrie (ed.) #16#

Trask, R. L. (1993) *A Dictionary of Grammatical Terms*. London: Routledge. #22#

Treffers-Daller, J. (1992) French-Dutch codeswitching in Brussels: social factors explaining its disappearance. In C. M. Eastman (ed.), *Special issue: Codeswitching. Journal of Multilingual and Multicultural Development*, 143–56. #13#

—— (1994) *Mixing Two Languages: French-Dutch contact in a comparative perspective*. Berlin: Mouton de Gruyter. #13#

Trömel-Plötz, S. (1984) *Gewalt durch Sprache*. Frankfurt am Main: Fischer. #8#

Trösser, Michael. (1983) Rundfunkmoderation bei Beteiligungssendungen – im Spannungsfeld zwischen Offenheit und Kontrolle [Anchoring on radio with special application to access programmes. The tension between media access and control]. *International Journal of the Sociology of Language*, 40, 77–91. #11#

Trudgill, P. (1972) Sex, covert prestige and linguistic change in the urban British English of Norwich. *Language in Society*, 1, 179–95. #1#, #8#

—— (1974a) *The Social Differentiation of English in Norwich*. Cambridge: Cambridge University Press. #1#, #3#, #5#, #6#, #9#

—— (1974b) *Sociolinguistics: An introduction*. London: Penguin. #1#

—— (1975a) *Accent, Dialect and the School*. London: Edward Arnold. #6#

—— (1975b) Linguistic change and diffusion: description and explanation in sociolinguistic dialect geography. *Language in Society*, 3, 215–46. #1#

—— (1979) Standard and non-standard dialects of English in the UK. *International Journal of the Sociology of Language*, 21, 9–24. #25#

—— (1983a) *Sociolinguistics: An introduction to language and society*. London: Penguin. #10#

—— (1983b) *On Dialect: Social and geographical perspectives*. Oxford: Basil Blackwell. #6#, #8#

—— (1988) Norwich revisited: recent linguistic change sin an English urban dialect. *English World-Wide*, 9, 33–49. #9#

—— (1990) *The Dialects of England*. Oxford: Basil Blackwell. #7#

—— (1992) Dialect contact, dialectology and sociolinguistics. In K. Bolton and H. Kwok (eds), *Sociolinguistics Today*, 71–9. London: Routledge. #1#

—— (1994) *Dialects*. London: Routledge. #6#

Trudgill, P. (ed.) (1978) *Sociolinguistic Patterns in British English*. London: Arnold. #1#, #6#

—— (ed.) (1983) *Applied Sociolinguistics*. London: Academic Press. #6#

Tsuzaki, S. (1971) Co-existent systems in language variation: the case of Hawaiian English. In D. Hymes (ed.), *Pidginization and Creolization of Languages*, 327–40. Cambridge: Cambridge University Press. #1#

Uchida, A. (1992) When "difference" is "dominance": a critique of the "anti-power-based" cultural approach to sex differences. *Language in Society*, 547–68. #8#

Ufumata, T. (1990) Acceptable models for EFL (with special reference to Nigeria). In S. Ramsaran (ed.), *Studies in the Pronunciation of English in Honour of A. C. Gimson*. London: Routledge. #6#

United Nations (1963) *Demographic Yearbook*. New York: United Nations. #2#

United Nations Department of Economic and Social Affairs (1959) *Handbook of Population Census Methods*. Vol. 3: *Demographic and social characteristics of the population*. New York: United Nations. #2#

Unsigned editorial. (1989) [National language]. *Gaskiya Ta Fi Kwabo.* August 26, 2. #20#

Vaillancourt, F. (1993) Le statut socio-économique du français et des francophones du Québec, 1977–1992: le rôle et l'avenir des politiques linguistiques [The socio-economic Status of French and Francophones in Québec, 1977–1992: the Role and Future of Language Policies], 67–89. In P. Bouchard (ed.), *Les actes du colloque sur la situation linguistique au Québec* [Proceedings of the Colloquium on the Linguistic Situation in Québec]. Québec: Government of Québec, Office de la langue française. #28#

Valdman, Albert (1988) Diglossia and language conflict in Haiti. *International Journal of the Sociology of Language,* 71, 67–80. #14#

Van De Walle, L. C. (1991) Pragmatics and classical Sanskrit: a pilot study in linguistic politeness. *Dissertation Abstracts International,* 53, 1503-A. #23#

Van der Wurff, W. (1990) Diffusion and reanalysis in syntax. PhD dissertation, University of Amsterdam. #3#

Van Overbeke, M. (1972) *Introduction à l'étude du bilinguisme.* Brussels: AIMAV. #18#

Varro G. (1984) *La femme transplantée: une étude du mariage franco-américain en France et le bilinguisme des enfants.* Lille: Presses Universitaires de Lille. #19#

—— (1995) *Les familles "mixtes" et leurs enfants dans l'Europe des Etats-Unies.* Paris: Armand Collin. #19#

Veltman, C. (1983) *Language Shift in the United States.* The Hague: Mouton. #Introd.#, #16#, #18#

Verdoodt, A. (1988) Organisation of the discipline of sociolinguistics. In U. Ammon, N. Dittmar, K. J. Mattheier (eds), *Sociolinguistics,* Vol. II Section 191. Berlin: Walter de Gruyter. #1#

Verhoeven, L. (1994) *Functional Literacy: Studies in Written Language and Literacy.* Amsterdam: John Benjamins. #10#

—— (1994) Linguistic diversity and literacy development. In L. Verhoeven (ed.), *Functional Literacy: Theoretical issues and educational implications,* 199–220. Amsterdam and Philadelphia: John Benjamins. #25#

Villegas, J. (1991) *Culturally Responsive Teaching.* Princeton; New Jersey: ETS. #10#

Vinukonda Vallabharaya, a mid-14th century translation of a 13th century Sanskrit original that deals with a flourishing Telugu empire. #20#

Virtanen, Tuija. (1992) Temporal adverbials in text structuring: on temporal text strategy. In A.-C. Lindeberg, N. E. Enkvist and K. Wikberg (eds), *Nordic Research on Text and Discourse,* 187–97. Abo: Abo Academic Press. #11#

Vollmer, H. and Olshtain, E. (1989) The language of apologies in German. In S. Blum-Kulka, J. House, and G. Kasper (eds), *Cross-cultural Pragmatics,* 197–218. Norwood, NJ: Ablex. #23#

Volosinov, V. (1973) *Marxism and the Philosophy of Language.* New York: Seminar Press. #10#

Volz, W. (1993) Deutsch im Übersetzungsalltag der EG-Kommission. In J. Born and G. Stickel (eds), *Deutsch als Verkehrssprache in Europa,* 64–76. Berlin: De Gruyter. #18#

von Becker, R. (1820) Reprinted in *Arwidssonista Snellmanlin. Kansallisia kirjoitelmia vuosilta 1817–1844,* 1929. Helsinki: Publications of the Finnish Literature Society, 105, 158–9. #20#

Voorhoeve, J. and Lichtveld, U. M. (eds.) (1975) *Creole Drum: An anthology of creole literature in Suriname.* New Haven: Yale University Press. #14#

Vygotsky, L. S. (1934) *Thought and Language.* Cambridge: University Press. #10#, #25#

Walker, A. G. (1990) Language at work in the law: the customs, conventions, and appellate consequences of court reporting. In J. N. Levi and A. G. Walker (eds), *Language in the Judicial Process,* 203–44. New York and London: Plenum Press. #27#

Waller, M. and Schoeler, J. (1985) Die Entwicklung des Verständnisses der situativen Variationsbreite unterschiedlich höflicher Fragen [The development of the comprehension of the situational variety of differentially polite questions]. *Zeitschrift für Entwicklungspsychologie und Pädagogische Psychologie,* 17, 27–40. #23#

Waller, S. and Valtin, R. (1992) Children's understanding of white lies. In R. J. Watts, S. Ide, and K. Ehlich (eds), *Politeness in Language: Studies in its history, theory and practice*, 231–51. Berlin: Mouton de Gruyter. #23#

Walter, H. (1988) *Le français dans tous les sens* [French in All Its Meanings]. Paris: Robert Lafont. #28#

Walters, K. (1994 and forthcoming) Diglossia, linguistic variation, and language change in Arabic. In M. Eid (ed.), *Perspectives on Arabic Linguistics VIII*. Amsterdam: Benjamins. #13#

Wang, W. S. Y. (ed.) (1977) *The Lexicon in Phonological Change*. The Hague: Mouton. #5#

Wardhaugh, R. (1987) *Languages in Competition: Dominance, Diversity, and Decline*. Oxford: Basil Blackwell. #16#

Wardhaugh, R. (1992 [1986]) *An Introduction to Sociolinguistics*, 2nd edn. Oxford: Blackwells. #8#, #14#, #28#

Watahomigie, L. and Yamamoto, A. (1987) Linguistics in action: the Hualapai bilingual/bi-cultural education program. In D. Stull and J. Schensul (eds), *Collaborative Research and Social Change: Applied anthropology in action*, 77–98. Boulder, CO: Westview Press. #15#

Watson-Gegeo, K. A. (1994) Language and education in Hawai'i: sociopolitical and educational implications of Hawai'i Creole English. In M. Morgan (ed.), *The Social Construction of Identity in Creole Situations*, 101–20. Los Angeles: Center for Afro-American Studies, UCLA. #14#

Watts, R. J. (1989) Relevance and relational work: linguistic politeness as politic behavior. *Multilingua*, 8, 131–66. #23#

—— (1992) Linguistic politeness and politic verbal behaviour: reconsidering claims for universality. In R. J. Watts, S. Ide, and K. Ehlich (eds), *Politeness in Language: Studies in its history, theory and practice*, 43–69. Berlin: Mouton de Gruyter. #23#

Watts, R. J., Ide, S., and Ehlich, K. (1992) Introduction. In R. J. Watts, S. Ide, and K. Ehlich (eds), *Politeness in Language: Studies in its history, theory and practice*, 1–17. Berlin: Mouton de Gruyter. #23#

Weaver, C. (1990) *Understanding the Whole Language*. Portsmouth, NH: Heinemann. #25#

Wei, L. (1994) *Three Generations, Two Languages, One Family*. Clevedon: Multilingual Matters. #13#

Weinreich, U. (1954) Is a structural dialectology possible? *Word*, 14, 388–400. Reproduced in J. A. Fishman (ed.) (1968), *Readings in the Sociology of Language*, 305–19. The Hague: Mouton. #28#

—— (1968a) *Languages in Contact: Findings and problems*. The Hague: Mouton. [First published 1953 [1963] as Publications of the Linguistic Circle of New York, no. 1, 1953.] #introd.#, #1#, #17#, #18#

—— (1968b) Unilinguisme et multilinguisme. In A. Martinet (ed.), *Le langage. Encyclopédie de la Pléiade XXV*, 647–84, Paris: Gallimard. #19#

Weinreich, U., Labov, W., and Herzog, M. (1968) Empirical foundations for a theory of language change. In W. P. Lehmann and Y. Malkiel (eds), *Directions for Historical Linguistics*, 95–189. Austin: University of Texas Press. #3#, #5#

Weinstein, B. (1980) Language planning in Francophone Africa. *Language Problems & Language Planning*, 55–77. #28#

Weinstein, B. (ed.) (1990) *Language Policy and Political Development*. Norwood, NJ: Ablex.

Weinstein-Shr, G. (1993) Literacy and social process: a community in transition. In B. Street, (ed.), *Cross-Cultural Approaches to Literacy*, 272–93. Cambridge: Cambridge University Press. #10#

Weiss, A. (ed.) (1992) *Dialekte im Wandel*. Göppingen: Kümmerle Verlag (= Göppinger Arbeiten zur Germanistik, Nr. 538). #4#

Weizman, E. (1985) Towards analysis of opaque utterances: hints as a request strategy. *Theoretical Linguistics*, 12, 153–63. #23#

—— (1989) Requestive hints. In S. Blum-Kulka, J. House, and G. Kasper (eds), *Cross-cultural Pragmatics*, 71–96. Norwood, NJ: Ablex. #23#

—— (1993) Interlanguage requestive hints. In G. Kasper and S. Blum-Kulka (eds), *Interlanguage Pragmatics*, 123–37. New York: Oxford University Press. #23#

Wells, G. (1985) *Language Development in the Preschool Years*. Cambridge: Cambridge University Press. #25#

Wells, J. C. (1982) *Accents of English*. 3 vols. Cambridge: Cambridge University Press. #3#

—— (1990) *Pronunciation Dictionary*. Harlow: Longman.

Weltens, B., De Bot, K., and Van Els, T. (eds) (1986), *Language Attrition in Progress*. Dordrecht: Foris. #18#

Wenger, J. R. (1983) Variation and change in Japanese honorific forms. *Papers in Linguistics*, 16, 267–301. #23#

Wenker, G. (1877) *Das rheinische Platt*. Düsseldorf: n.p. #7#

Wenker, G. (1895 ff.) *Der Sprachatlas des deutschen Reichs*. Marburg: Elwert. See also F. Wrede, (1926 ff.) *Deutscher Sprachatlas, auf Grund des von G. Wenker begründeten . . .* Marburg: Elwert. #1#

Werlich, Egon (1976) *A Text Grammar of English*. Heidelberg: Quelle und Meyer. #11#

Wertsch, J. (ed.) (1985) *Culture, Communication and Cognition: Vygotskian Perspectives*. Cambridge: Cambridge University Press. #10#

West, C. and Zimmerman, D. H. (1991) Doing gender. In Judith Lorber and Susan A. Farrell (eds), *The Social Construction of Gender*, 13–37. London: Sage. #8#

Wexler, P. (1974) *Purism and Language*. Bloomington: Indiana University Press. #20#

Whinnom, K. (1965) The origin of the European-based creoles and pidgins. *Orbis*, 14, 509–27. #14#

—— (1971) Linguistic hybridization and the "special case" of pidgins and creoles. In D. Hymes (ed.), *Pidginization and Creolization of Languages*, 91–115. Cambridge: Cambridge University Press. #14#

Whorf, B. L. (1956) *Language, Thought and Reality*, ed. J. B. Carroll. Cambridge, MA: MIT Press. #22#

Widdowson, H. (1978) *Teaching Language as Communication*. Oxford: Oxford University Press. #10#

Wierzbicka, A. (1991) Japanese key words and core cultural values. *Language in Society*, 20, 333–85. #23#

Wilhite, M. (1983) Children's acquisition of language routines: the end-of-meal routine in Cakohiquel language. *Language in Society*, 12, 47–61. #23#

Wilkins, D. (1992) Linguistic research under aboriginal control: a personal account of fieldwork in Central Australia. *Australian Journal of Linguistics*, 12, 171–200. #15#

Williams, C. H. (1993) *Called Unto Liberty: On language and nationalism*. Clevedon: Multilingual Matters. #20#

Williams, G. (1992) *Sociolinguistics: A sociological critique*. London: Routledge. #Introd.#, #1#, #10#, #22#

Williams, R. (1976) *Keywords*. London: Fontana. #22#

Williams, R. M. (1947) The reduction of intergroup tensions. *Social Science Research Council Bulletin*, 57, 40–3, #17#

Williamson, S. G. (1982) Appendix A. Summary chart of findings from previous research on language loss. In R. D. Lambert and B. Freed (eds), *The Loss of Language Skills*, 207–24. Rowley, MA: Newbury House. #15#

Winer, L. (1993) *Trinidad and Tobago* (Varieties of English around the World text series, vol. 6). Amsterdam and Philadelphia: John Benjamins. #14#

Winford, D. (1980) The creole continuum in the context of sociolinguistic studies. In R. Day (ed.), *Issues in English Creoles: Papers from the 1975 Hawaii Conference*, 51–76. Heidelberg: Julius Groos. #14#

—— (1985) The concept of "diglossia" in Caribbean creole situations. *Language in Society*, 14, 345–55. #14#

—— (1992a) Another look at the copula in Black English and Caribbean creoles. *American Speech*, 67, 21–60. #14#

—— (1992b) Back to the past: the BEV/creole connection revisited. *Language Variation and Change*, 4, 311–57. #14#

—— (1994) Sociolinguistic approaches to language use in the Anglophone Caribbean. In M. Morgan (ed.), *The Social Construction of Identity in Creole Situations*, 43–62. Los Angeles: Center for Afro-American Studies, UCLA. #14#

Winter, J. Ch. (1976) Language shift among the Aasáx, a hunter-gatherer tribe in Tanzania, *Sprache und Geschichte in Afrika* 1, 175–204. #16#

Wodak, R. (1981) Women relate; men report: sex differences in language behaviour in a therapeutic group. *Journal of Pragmatics*, 5, 261–85. #8#

—— (1983) Die Beziehung zwischen Mutter und Tochten bei schwierigen Kindern: Erstellung einer Typologie aus sozio- und psycholinguistischer Sicht. *Wiener Linguistische Gazette*, Beiheft 2. #8#

—— (1984) *Hilflose Nähe*. Wien: Deuticke. #8#

—— (1985) Aspekte des schicht-, geschlechts- und generationsspezifischen Lautwandels in Wien. Eine Untersuchung zum Sprachverhalten von Müttern und Töchtern. In Marlies Hellinger (ed.), *Sprachwandel und feministische Sprachpolitik: Internationale Perspektiven*. Opladen: Westdeutscher Verlag. #8#

—— (1986) *Language Behavior in Therapy Groups*. London: Academic Press. #8#

—— (1992) Antisemitismen im österreichischen Alltag. *Germanistische Linguistik*, 112/13, 215–53. #22#

—— (1993) Critical discourse analysis and the study of neo-racism in contemporary Austria. *Discourse and Society*, 4, 225–48. #22#

—— (1994) Critical linguistics and the study of institutional communication. In Patrick Stevenson (ed.), *Sociolinguistics in the German-speaking Countries*. Oxford: Blackwells. #8#

Wodak, R. and Andraschko, E. (1994) Frauen führen anders? *Erziehung heute*, 1, 41–7, and 2, 34–8. #8#

Wodak, R. and Schulz, M. (1986) *The Language of Love and Guilt*. Amsterdam: Benjamins. #8#

—— (1991) Meine Mutter ist meine beste Freundin. In Susanne Günthner and Helga Kotthoff, *Von fremden Stimmen. Weibliches und männliches Sprechen im Kulturvergleich*, 333–60. Frankfurt: Suhrkamp. #8#

Wodak, R. et al. (1987) *Sprachliche Gleichbehandlung von Mann und Frau*. Wien: Bundesministerium für Arbeit und Soziales. #8#

Wodak-Leodolter, R. and Dressler, W. (1978) Phonologische Variation in Colloquial Viennese. *Michigan Germanic Studies*, 6, 33–66. #8#

Wojtak, M. (1989) Grzecznosc postaropolsku w swietle pamietnikow Jana Chryzostoma Paska [Politeness in old Polish in the light of the diaries of Jan Chryzostom]. *Poradnik Jezykowy*, 8, 528–33. #23#

Wölck, W. (1985) Beyond community profiles: a three-level approach to sociolinguistic sampling. In P. Nelde (ed), *Methods in Contact Linguistic Research (Plurilingua V)*, 31–43. Bonn: Dümmler. #17#

Wolf, E. C. (1994) Perilous ideas: race, culture, people. *Current Anthropology*, 35, 1–12. #20#

Wolfram, W. (1969) *A Sociolinguistic Description of Detroit Negro Speech*. Washington, DC: Center for Applied Linguistics. #1#, #7#, #9#

—— (1991) *Dialects and American English*. Englewood Cliffs, NJ: Prentice Hall. #7#

—— (1993) Ethical considerations in dialect awareness programs. *Issues in Applied Linguistics*, 4, 225–55. #7#

Wolfram, W. and Adger, C. A. (1993) *Handbook on dialect differences and speech and language pathology*. Washington, DC: Center for Applied Linguistics. #7#

Wolfram, W. and Fasold, R. W. (1974) *The Study of Social Dialects in the United States*. Englewood Cliffs, NJ: Prentice Hall. #7#

Wolfram, W. and Schilling-Estes, N. (1993) *Dialects and the Ocracoke Brogue*. Raleigh, NC: The North Carolina Language and Life Project. #7#

—— (1995) Moribund dialect and the endangerment canon. *Language*, 71, 696–722. #7#

Wolfson, N. (1989) *Perspectives: Sociolinguistics and TESOL*. Cambridge, MA: Newbury House. #23#

Woolard, K. (1991) Linkages of language and ethnic identity: Changes in Barcelona, 1980–1987. In J. R. Dow (ed.), *Language and Ethnicity*, 61–81. Amsterdam: Benjamins. #13#

Woolford, E. (1983) Bilingual code-switching and syntactic theory. *Linguistic Inquiry*, 14, 520–36. #13#

Wright, J. (1898–1905) *The English Dialect Dictionary* (6 vols) and *English Dialect Grammar* (published by himself; reprinted 1961 by Oxford University Press). #1#

Wright, J. D. (1987) The effects of hedges and hesitations on impression formation in a simulated courtroom context. *Western Journal of Speech Communication*, 51, 173–88. #23#

Wurm, S. (1991) Language death and disappearance. In R. Robins and E. Uhlenbeck (eds), *Endangered Languages*, 1–17. New York: St. Martin's Press. #15#

Yabar, P. (1975) Sobre la particula japonesal *wa* en el habla femenina [The Japanese particle *wa* in women's speech]. *Lenguaje y Ciencias*, 15, 89–96. #23#

Yamada, H. (1990) Topic management and turn distribution in business meetings: American versus Japanese strategies. *Text*, 10, 271–95. #23#

Yamashita, M. Y. (1983) An empirical study of variation in the use of honorific forms in Japanese: an analysis of forms produced by a group of women in an urban setting. *Dissertation Abstracts International*, 44, 1780A. #23#

Yenbing, Sh. (1955) [*Kwanming Daily*]. November 23. Republished, 1957, in [*Collected Documents of the First National Writing Reform Conference*]. Peking: Wenzi gaige chubanshe, 8–10. #20#

Yoshinaga, N., Maeshiba, N., and Takahashi, S. (1992) Bibliography on Japanese pragmatics. In G. Kasper (ed.), *Pragmatics of Japanese as Native and Target Language* (Technical report #3), 1–26. Honolulu: University of Hawaii, Second Language Teaching & Curriculum Center. #23#

Yuan, J. F., Kuiper, K., and Shaogu, S. (1990) Language and revolution: formulae of the cultural revolution. *Language in Society*, 19, 61–79. #23#

Yudho, S. (1933) [My Language]. [*The New Post*]. 1, 261. #20#

Zah, P. (1993) *Proclamation; Proclaiming the Week of September 13–16, 1993, Dine' [=Navajo] Language Week*. Tuba City: Navajo Tribal Council. #20#

Zammuner, V. L. (1991) Children's writing of argumentative texts: effects of indirect instruction. *European Journal of Psychology of Education*, 6, 243–56. #23#

Zentella, A. C. (1987) Language and female identity in the Puerto Rican community. In Jocye Penfield (ed.), *Women and Language in Transition*, 167–79. New York: NY Press. #8#

Zilliacus, H. (1949) *Untersuchungen zu den abstrakten Anredeformen und Höflichkeitstiteln im Griechischen* [Investigation of abstract terms of address and politeness titles in Greek]. Helsingfors: Centraltrykkeriet. #23#

Zimin, S. (1981) Sex and politeness: factors in first- and second-language use. *International Journal of the Sociology of Language*, 27, 35–58. #23#

Index